ANCIENT AND MEDIEVAL JEWISH HISTORY

OTHER BOOKS BY SALO WITTMAYER BARON

A Social and Religious History of the Jews
Bibliography of Jewish Social Studies
The Jewish Community: Its History and Structure to the American
  Revolution
Modern Nationalism and Religion
The Jews of the United States, 1790–1840: A Documentary History
  (with Joseph L. Blau)
The Russian Jews under Tsars and Soviets
History and Jewish Historians: Essays and Addresses
Essays on Maimonides (editor)
Freedom and Reason (editor)
Judaism, Postbiblical and Talmudic Periods (with Joseph L. Blau)
Jerusalem: City Holy and Eternal
Steeled by Adversity: Essays and Addresses on American Jewish Life

ANCIENT AND MEDIEVAL JEWISH HISTORY

Essays by

SALO WITTMAYER BARON

Edited with a Foreword by

LEON A. FELDMAN

RUTGERS UNIVERSITY PRESS
NEW BRUNSWICK, NEW JERSEY

Library of Congress Cataloging in Publication Data

Baron, Salo Wittmayer, 1895–
  Ancient and medieval Jewish history.

  "In honor of the seventy-fifth birthday of [the
author]"
  Includes bibliographical references.
  CONTENTS: Moses and monotheism: a review of Freud.—
Reflections on ancient and medieval Jewish historical
demography.—The Israelitic population under the kings.
[etc.]
  1. Jews—History—Addresses, essays, lectures.
I. Title.
DS102.5.B3   910′.039′24   70–75674
ISBN 0–8135–0674–3

This volume was planned and its preparation commenced in honor of the seventy-fifth birthday of Salo Wittmayer Baron.

Contents

Foreword

THE FOLLOWING ESSAYS, written by Professor Salo Wittmayer Baron over a period of more than forty years, are now gathered in one volume honoring his seventy-fifth birthday. They do not present a continuous story; nevertheless, a uniform thread runs through them all. The main focus is on specific aspects of the social and religious history of the Jews, both terms used in their wider meaning. Social history includes also the main political and economic trends, while in the case of the Jews religious history covers much of the general cultural and intellectual history of the people as well. From the very beginning of his writings, Professor Baron set for himself the task of applying the methodology and latest findings of the social sciences to Jewish history. In this connection, therefore, while interpreting Jewish history, some of his major contributions deal with the important role of historiography and the concomitant exhaustive review of new bibliographical data.

A more comprehensive treatment of ancient and medieval Jewish history is available in Professor Baron's monumental *A Social and Religious History of the Jews* (2d edition, revised and enlarged, Philadelphia–New York, 1952–), of which to date fourteen volumes and one index volume have appeared. Thus far the history from the beginning until the end of the twelfth century is covered in full, as well as a large segment of the period from 1200 to 1650. There the reader will find much additional documentation, especially of a bibliographical nature, for many of the subjects treated in the present collection of essays.

In the present studies Professor Baron endeavors, first of all, to place his discussion of a topic in the broadest possible frame of reference, and then, on the basis of his analysis of the facts, to find the explanation for the principles he has established. He applies to his research his deeply rooted knowledge of all aspects of Jewish scholarship, both ancient and modern, together with his mastery of human knowledge. Whoever consults his bibliographical notes or the index volumes of his numerous works will find that they frequently contain elaborations of certain discussions and outlines of topics which constitute books in themselves.

The reader may also like to examine Professor Baron's earlier collection *History and Jewish Historians* (edited by Arthur Hertzberg and Leon A. Feldman, Jewish Publication Society, Philadelphia, 1964). The underlying theme of those essays, while not a "structured" discussion of Jewish history, constitutes a history of Jewish historical writing as interpreted by the foremost historian of the Jewish people of the present day.

In his essays here before us, Professor Baron has set as his goal not only giving an exposition of historical facts, an account of events, but also providing us with the principles which shaped the events. It is true, as the great polyhistor that he is, that he has for the most part succeeded in separating these two tasks. His historical vision of specific aspects of Jewish history is enshrined in his central outlook that the Jewish experience through the ages is not a series of isolated events but the result of the Jews' confrontation with the cultures of the world of which they have been a part.

To Professor Baron, Jewish history is the history of emancipation —the self-liberation of the Jewish people in its never completed journey of self-discovery. We must go back to our origins if we are to understand the historical development that brought the Jews to this very day. The movement of Jewish history cannot be divorced from its changing historical context, and to regard the nature of the Jews as an unchanging essence does violence both to their origins and to their goals. If we ask Dr. Baron in which way the Jews are different from all other nations, then he must answer this question "We are slaves unto Pharaoh in Egypt"—an Egypt which includes for the Jews virtually every people among whom they have lived.

This has been the experience of Jewish history since its very beginning, from ancient times, through the medieval period, till the present generation. During these centuries the Jews have suffered from a collective nostalgia longer, more persistent, more penetrating than any other people. As a result of this profound feeling of nostalgia, some of the most original ideas and revolutionary ideologies, both religious and secular, are indebted to them. Professor

Baron's answer stands in the line of classic Jewish thought: the Jews are a peculiar people because they have been the bearers of messianic religion of universal import!

Professor Baron had to confront the ever recurring question of why the Jews in their long history did not attempt to return to their homeland and have remained exile-oriented—in the past obviously. To be sure, the liturgical expressions of the yearnings for a return to the Promised Land remained purely religious, indeed messianic in character. To summarize his analysis of the factors which have shaped and are shaping the history of the Jewish people; when the Jews had more of a sense of history than of geography, the change began to occur. However, Dr. Baron has himself repeatedly stated that the struggle for emancipation is still going on, that the results of political and economic freedom are of too short an experience to prove this explanation and warrant a deeper and broader understanding of Jewish history.

In the course of years some reviews have appeared critically evaluating one or another detail presented by Professor Baron in these studies. After carefully weighing the evidence, the author felt that, on the whole, his observations required no alteration. This is true, for example, in the case of Professor Baron's critical review of Sigmund Freud's *Moses and Monotheism* (Essay 1), which became the target of some polemical remarks by Ernest Jones, M.D., author of the standard biography of the founder of psychoanalysis. In this case, as in all other instances, the ultimate judgment as to who is right must be left to whatever scholarly consensus may ultimately emerge after such debate.

It is our fervent wish that, by collecting these essays on historiography, we will be making a contribution to furthering the understanding of Salo W. Baron's methodology and of his conception of Jewish history.

The editor wishes to acknowledge his indebtedness to Jeannette M. (Mrs. Salo W.) Baron for her unreserved cooperation in the preparation of this volume. He is also grateful to his wife Caroline for her collaboration and technical assistance, to his former secretary Mrs. Mildred Handel for carefully typing and retyping the manuscript, to Michelle Kamhi for copy editing it, and to Lisa McGaw for preparing the index.

Special thanks are due to Mrs. Philip J. Levin and her late husband for their generous support of the Department of Hebraic Studies in Rutgers University which enabled Dr. Baron to occupy the Levin Visiting Professorship for several years until his retirement.

LEON A. FELDMAN

Acknowledgments

THE EDITOR acknowledges his great indebtedness to the following learned journals and publishers for their kind permission to reprint the essays written by Professor Salo W. Baron:

American Academy for Jewish Research:
  Abhandlungen zur Erinnerung an Hirsch Perez Chajes [Alexander H. Kohut Foundation, VII] (Vienna, 1933), pp. 76–136.
  Proceedings of the AAJR 12 (1952), 1–48.
  Rashi Anniversary Volume [Texts and Studies, I] (New York, 1941), pp. 47–71.
  Saadia Anniversary Volume [Texts and Studies, II] (New York, 1943), pp. 9–74.
  Harry Austryn Wolfson Jubilee Volume (Jerusalem, 1965), pp. 141–63.
Brit Ivrit Olamit [World Association for Hebrew Language and Culture, Jerusalem]:
  Essays on Jewish Thought and Culture in Honor of Aryeh Tartakower (Jerusalem, 1969), pp. 31–45.
Columbia University:
  Essays on Maimonides (New York, 1941), pp. 127–264.
Conference on Jewish Social Studies, Inc.:
  Jewish Social Studies 3 (1941), 243–72.
The Dropsie University:
  Studies and Essays in Honor of Abraham A. Neuman (E. J. Brill, Leiden, 1962), pp. 17–48.
The Historical Society of Israel, Jerusalem:
  Yitzhak F. Baer Jubilee Volume (Jerusalem, 1960), pp. 102–24.
International Council for Philosophy and Humanistic Studies, Paris:
  Diogenes, no. 61 (January–March, 1968), pp. 32–51.
Jews' College, London:
  Volume in Memory of Rabbi Isidore Epstein (in preparation)

Ohio State University, Department of History:
Lecture delivered at a colloquium on the Middle East, May 16, 1968.

The University of Chicago Press:
American Journal of Sociology 45, no. 3 (1939), 471–77.

Introduction

"UNITY WITHIN DIVERSITY" has become an important watchword in sociopolitical and religious debates. It also has long been accepted as an important ingredient in intellectual activity. A volume of collected essays understandably raises the question as to whether there are any links connecting the various aspects of the respective studies. The question of an underlying unity is doubly pertinent if the essays, as is the case here, were written over some four decades, were addressed to different audiences, and pursued a variety of specific aims, such as paying tribute in jubilee or memorial volumes to specialists in diverse fields, participating in scholarly conferences, delivering presidential addresses at learned societies, or commemorating some distinguished historic figures.

Even the unity of a single authorship may turn out to be fragile if that individual has undergone changes in methodology, basic approaches, or world outlook. In my case such changes were stimulated by my transfer at the age of thirty from the revolutionary Central-European environment of the First World War period to the "roaring twenties" of the United States, its Great Depression, the Second World War, the European Holocaust, and the rise of the State of Israel. These tremendous historic transformations exerted their influence on any interested observer; they had a double impact on one sensitized by his professional concern for a historical interpretation of current events against the background of the millennial evolution of his people.

Yet the following essays do reveal a certain fundamental line in the questions raised and the answers, however tentative, proposed for some important issues in the history of the Jewish people. They stress aspects hitherto largely neglected in historical research. Sometimes by merely stating a problem and turning the attention of the scholarly world to the need for its careful investigation, one may hope to stimulate further intensive research in this field.

ANCIENT DILEMMAS

Even the history of ancient Israel, which has been the center of attention by many first-rate minds over centuries and is the subject of instruction in thousands of universities, colleges, and seminaries throughout the world, still requires elucidation from new angles. One of these is the psychoanalytical approach to Old Testament religion and particularly to ancient Israelitic prophecy. The only example here presented relates to the highly suggestive study of *Moses and Monotheism* by the founder of modern psychoanalysis, Sigmund Freud. Despite my reverence for the master, I had to be severely critical of his use of dubious biblical data with their often reckless interpretations by certain biblical scholars early in this century. My critique (in Essay 1) was intended to be more a warning against philologically and historically unsupported evidence than against the method itself. One may still debate the issue about the adequacy of the results attained by mass psychology in any field and express particular doubts about the extent to which psychoanalysis may serve as a useful tool in interpreting contemporary mass phenomena, not to speak of such which occurred in the past for which the documentation is much too meager. However, a detailed psychoanalytical examination of such leading individuals as the Israelitic prophets by scholars well trained in both psychoanalysis and biblical research may still open up new vistas on the intriguing problems of how and why that great array of Israel's seers was able to make its immortal contributions to Jewish and human civilization. Regrettably, such a monographic study as Adolf All-wohn's *Die Ehe des Propheten Hosea in psychoanalytischer Beleuchtung* (Giessen, 1926) has had few followers in the forty-five years since its publication. However, the promise is still there.

Equally important for the understanding of the whole historical development of ancient Israel is the problem of its population growth and decline. Here the mystery consists not so much in penetrating the deep recesses of the human psyche as in the paucity of reliable source materials. In antiquity and the Middle Ages few societies and governments evinced deep interest in population statistics and trends. If they conducted censuses at all—some in fact did so not infrequently—they, as a rule, pursued such practical purposes as the ascertainment of the number of prospective taxpayers or soldiers. Thereby they directly invited evasion. The methods employed in counting human beings, too, were extremely crude. Nor were attempts made to repeat these performances in stated periods so as to assure the availability of comparative data revealing the existing upward or downward tendencies. Nor did the ancient rulers ever evince interest in gathering such vital demographic data as the age and sex distribution of the population under review, its natality and mortality rates, marriages and divorces (formal or informal), the effects of wars and pestilences on all these factors, and the like. Moreover, no real effort was made to preserve such compilations for the future. On the other hand, most contemporaries, even when they alluded to numbers of inhabitants, the size of armed forces, or the yields of certain taxes from which figures of taxpayers might be deduced, were often prone to overstate, sometimes quite recklessly, the numbers involved.

Nevertheless, the subject is of such vital importance that, at least according to a growing consensus among scholars today, it is worth pursuing by searching out every shred of evidence still available to us in the hope of reaching certain conclusions, however approximate and hypothetical these may necessarily remain. More than forty years ago I attempted to come to grips with this problem, as far as it related to ancient Israel under the Kings (Essay 3). Less certain about the actual statistical findings, I attempted to delineate, at least, the best methods which might be employed and to submit certain reasoned arguments for the acceptance or rejection of the data presented by the Bible and a few extrabiblical sources. Although my hope, then expressed, that my researches would be followed up by further detailed investigations has not yet materialized, I have nevertheless clung to the expectation that this work would be continued and offered some additional "Reflections" on demographic Jewish problems in ancient and medieval times (Essay 2). Scattered data and observations on this score are also included in a number of my other historical works.

Not that I consider research in historical demography a panacea. While a good case can be made for the nexus between population growth and decline and a people's cultural evolution, one always has to bear in mind the simultaneous operation of numerous other factors. As is shown in Essay 9, the tiny Jewish community of eleventh-century Troyes in the Champagne, which probably embraced no more than one hundred persons, could nevertheless be the seat of a major Jewish academy and serve as an intellectual focus for a large segment of European Jewry.

JEWS AND ARABS

Turning to the Middle Ages, we must bear in mind that between the seventh and the twelfth centuries a large majority of the Jewish people lived in Muslim lands. They developed a remarkable symbiosis with the various Arabic-speaking peoples amidst whom they dwelled and, together with their neighbors, reached a high degree of civilization, especially in the Golden Age of Spanish Jewry (A.D. 900–1200).

The story of the Jews under the rule of Islam has been told frequently from many angles, including that of the treatment of the Jewish minority by the medieval Muslim states. However, it was intriguing to find out how the Jews, or at least some of their intellectual leaders, viewed that domination by religiously and linguistically related, and yet often hostile, nations (Essay 4). This problem was doubly significant as the Jews, as well as Christians, enjoyed a vast measure of communal autonomy; so much, indeed, that the life of an average Jew was much more deeply affected by his own religious traditions, laws, and customs, and his self-governing institutions than by the enactments of a friendly or inimical government. I have endeavored, therefore, to illustrate the great interrelations between the inner history of the Jews and the simultaneous historical developments among the surrounding Muslim nations by the careers and thought processes of such outstanding Jewish leaders as Saadia, Halevi, and Maimonides.

In the case of Saadia (Essay 5) I have tried to show the impact of these environmental forces on the rise to power and the subsequent abrupt decline of this genuine Renaissance type of "universal man" and on his dream of the unification of world Jewry under an effective centralized Jewish regime. On the other hand, although Jews had long lived in a divided world, the sharp clashes between Christendom and Islam in the age of the Crusades forced some

Jewish minds to rethink their position in that world and to find new rationales for the perseverance of the Jewish people as a perennial "third force." The brilliant nationalistic answer to this perplexing problem, given by the great poet and thinker, Yehudah Halevi (Essay 6), has ever since exerted considerable influence on the thinking of medieval and modern Jews.

One of the major functions of the Jewish people in that divided world consisted in its great mediating role in both the international trade and the cultural exchanges. Remarkably, while the intellectual contribution of Jewry through helping to spread the heritage of Graeco-Roman science and philosophy among the Arabs and from them among the Western nations has been the subject of numerous investigations, our knowledge of the economic activities of medieval Jewry, especially in the Eastern lands, is still very limited. Most astonishingly, although medieval Jewry produced a number of philosophers and thinkers on various domains of life, it paid little attention to any kind of economic theory. A people which embraced leading international traders and bankers successfully conducted its business with all its complexities and ramifications without paying much attention to the conceptual underpinnings.

In trying to understand some of the approaches of the ancient and medieval Jews to economic pursuits, I had no recourse but to look at them through juristic spectacles, since law was the governing intellectual concern of the entire Jewish community. Choosing Maimonides as the most representative medieval Jewish jurist and philosopher, I tried to reconstruct his economic views by analyzing the numerous scattered references in his legal and philosophic works to such economically relevant issues as private ownership, price regulation, labor, and banking. These views are treated here as typical rather than personal. From the outset it was clear that Maimonides tried not to be a legal innovator but rather a codifier, summarizing the long-accepted legal teachings of the Talmud and geonim. Yet, keenly aware as he always was of contemporary practices and observances, he could not help modifying certain talmudic regulations, choosing between conflicting opinions, and paying considerable attention to contemporary business practices and other aspects of customary law. Great thinker that he was, he also resorted to occasional generalizations so that, despite his own denial of the importance of economic doctrines to his outlook on life, he may be considered a most representative spokesman of whatever rudimentary economic theories existed among the medieval rabbis. Here, too, the analysis (in Essay 7) was intended to serve as an incentive for further research—which, alas, has not yet materialized in a sufficient degree.

CHRISTIAN VARIATIONS

Much of that heritage of the Eastern lands was transferred by Jewish immigrants to Christian Europe. In many of these countries, the new arrivals encountered communities which had independent traditions reaching back to the ancient Roman Empire. With the new dynamism characteristic of their late Middle Ages the European nations forged ahead in developing a new material and intellectual civilization. They were aided thereby by the small but growing Jewish settlements described in Essay 8. At the same time, the Western Jewries built up a new branch of Judaism, the "Ashkenazim," whose most distinguished early protagonist was Rabbi Solomon Iṣhaki of Troyes, generally known in the abbreviated form of Rashi. His career and intellectual achievements were typical of the small pioneering Jewish communities in France and other Western lands which laid the foundation for the later remarkable expansion of European Jewry (Essay 9).

That expansion was both facilitated and hampered by the peculiar situation of European Jewry. On the one hand, Jews were treated by medieval Latin Christianity as aliens allowed to sojourn in Christian lands only because of the religious tradition that they would be preserved until the end of days. At the same time, as the descendants of the alleged Palestinian "Christ killers," they were always in danger of hostile attacks, unless they were protected by the powers that were. Thus developed the institution of medieval "Jewish serfdom," the origin of which has remained rather obscure. In my opinion, the great struggle between the Papacy and the Empire from the eleventh century on had a direct impact on the final formulation of that concept, with the Holy See and the imperial Crown contesting each other's claims to the supremacy over all Jews in Christian lands, indeed in the entire world (Essay 10). As a variant of the papal theory there appeared the doctrine of royal supremacy, which insisted that the Jews were "serfs" of any monarch under whose reign they lived. However, the term *serfdom* did not conjure in the minds of most medieval men the picture of true bondage that it connotes in our age. A further complication, however, set in when the medieval nations began consolidating their areas into national states. The incipient national consciousness, and the ensuing nationalist intolerance, became a major factor in the expulsion of Jews from the Western countries, particularly from England (1290), royal France (1306 and 1394), Spain (1492), Portugal (1497), and so forth. This much-neglected factor is briefly surveyed in Essay 11.

If some Jews hoped that the late medieval Renaissance and Humanism, stressing the dignity of individual man, would help them to overcome the extreme forms of medieval intolerance, these expectations were frustrated by the ensuing Reformation and Counter-Reformation, which led to sanguinary Wars of Religion and an actual intensification of the demands for religious conformity. As a result Protestantism, which started with the recognition that the existing Catholic regimes had been too oppressive toward their Jewish subjects, wound up in Luther and, to a lesser extent, Calvin preaching even greater intolerance toward the Jewish minority. Yet, unknown to these founders, the Reformation, particularly in its radical wings, combined with the rising tide of capitalism and modern science, in the end broke up the monolithic religious structure of the European societies and led to the mutual toleration of the diverse denominations. Ultimately, as a result of the deadlock of the Thirty Years' War, liberty of conscience began to shape up as a cardinal principle of public policy in many countries. This transformation, in the long run, benefitted the Jews, too, and, in many ways, helped to usher in the era of Jewish emancipation (Essays 12 and 13).

This process was but slightly impeded by the Catholic Reformation, which basically tried to refine the medieval doctrines of Catholicism, to reorganize its ecclesiastical structure, and to recapture some of its lost ground. But it affected far less the societal make-up of the Catholic nations and, in particular, introduced relatively few innovations in Judeo-Christian relations. That is why the

Council of Trent which, in its three sessions extending over two decades, reformulated the vast doctrinal realm of the Church, had rather little to say about the Jewish question. Only one aspect was discussed at some length in a committee: the problem of censorship of Hebrew books. But even here the conciliar labors were not completed when the Council adjourned in December 1563, its debates merely serving as a basis for a papal decree which proclaimed a new Index of Prohibited Books. It included far more moderate regulations concerning rabbinic literature than had been promulgated a decade earlier by the extremely intolerant Pope Paul IV (Essay 14).

ANALYTICAL UNDERPINNINGS

All these studies have only served to highlight my lifetime insistence on the deep interrelations between the social and religious history of the Jews as well as the fact that Jewish history can properly be understood only as part of the general history of the Western world. In rejecting what I called the "isolationist" approach to Jewish history I have tried in these essays, as in my other historical work, to analyze both the external and internal forces which alone can make us understand the vagaries, apparent and real, as well as the basic continuity of Jewish history.

In some respects these essays (and others yet to be collected) may serve as supplements to my comprehensive works, especially *A Social and Religious History of the Jews* (abbreviated *SRH*), the second edition of which (in fourteen volumes thus far with several more to come) covers the period from the beginning of Jewish history to the period of A.D. 1650; and my *Jewish Community: Its History and Structure to the American Revolution* (abbreviated *JC*).* Without subscribing to the one-sided approach of a

---

* The *terminus ad quem* of the latter work is evident. With the American Revolution and its separation of state and Church was ushered in the era of emancipated Jewish communities which radically differed in their authority and make-up from their predecessor communities in Europe. See, for instance, *Jews in the United States; 1790–1840: A Documentary History*, ed. by Joseph L. Blau and me, 3 vols. (New York, 1963); and my *Steeled by Adversity: Essays and Addresses on American Jewish Life*, ed. by Jeannette M. Baron (Philadelphia, 1971). The reasons, on the other hand, why I chose to consider

Fustel de Coulanges, who once exclaimed with abandon that he preferred one hour of synthesis to a lifetime of analysis, I have dedicated my most concentrated labors to major syntheses of the Jewish historic evolution. At the same time I have always realized that no structure is stronger than its component parts and that any work of synthesis presupposes careful analytical spadework in specialized areas. Because of this consideration I have found it necessary to explore, in particular, some of the more neglected or insufficiently comprehended areas of Jewish historiography. In this respect the fourteen essays gathered in this volume may serve as both a commentary on and a partial elaboration of the aforementioned comprehensive reviews.

1650, rather than 1492 or 1789, as the more appropriate turning point in the general "medieval" history of the Jews, are explained in my Preface to Volume IX of my SRH.

Abbreviations

Bab.	Babylonian Talmud
C.M.	(Maimonides) *Commentary on the Mishnah*
H.M.	(Maimonides) *Haggahot Maimuniot*
HUCA	*Hebrew Union College Annual*
HJH	*History and Jewish Historians: Essays and Addresses*, compiled with a Foreword by Arthur Hertzberg and Leon A. Feldman (Philadelphia, 1964)
H.M.	*Hoshen Mishpat*
j.	Jerusalem Talmud
JC	*The Jewish Community: Its History and Structure to the American Revolution*, 3 vols. (Philadelphia, 1942)
JQR	*Jewish Quarterly Review*
JSS	*Jewish Social Studies*
MT	Masoretic Text
M.	Mishnah
M.T.	(Maimonides) *Mishneh Torah*
MGWJ	*Monatschrift für Geschichte und Wissenschaft des Judentums*
MGH	*Monumenta Germaniae Historica*
M.N.	(Maimonides) *Moreh Nebukhim*
O.H.	*Orah Hayyim*
PAAJR	*Proceedings of the American Academy for Jewish Research*
PL	*Patrologiae cursus completus, series Latina*
Resp.	Responsum, Responsa
REJ	*Revue des études juives*
S.M.	(Maimonides) *Sefer Miṣvot*
Tos.	Tosafot
LXX	Septuagint (A = Alexandrinus, B = Vaticanus, L = Lucianus)
SRH	*A Social and Religious History of the Jews*, 3 vols. (New York, 1937); 2d ed. rev., vols. I–XIV (New York, 1952–69). Usually the second edition is quoted.
Y.D.	*Yoreh Deah*

ZAW   *Zeitschrift für alttestamentliche Wissenschaft*
ZDMG *Zeitschrift der Deutschen Morgenländischen Gesellschaft*
ZGJD *Zeitschrift für Geschichte der Juden in Deutschland*
ZHB   *Zeitschrift für hebräische Bibliographie*

All references to the Bible, New Testament, and Talmudim are given in their standard abbreviations.

ANCIENT AND MEDIEVAL
JEWISH HISTORY

PART I

Antiquity

I

Moses and Monotheism:
A Review of Freud*

IF A THINKER of Sigmund Freud's stature takes a stand on a problem of vital interest to him, the world is bound to listen. If the work so produced is also a remarkable human and historical document, if unwittingly it is a reflection of the profound changes in the entire mental atmosphere of Central Europe during the last decades, the reader's intellectual curiosity will receive stimuli in fields transcending the vast and ramified subject treated therein. The first two—smaller—sections of the work, which merely adumbrate the major theme, were published in 1937 in the German journal *Imago*. But the main Part III, which in the author's words "reduces religion to the status of a neurosis of mankind and explains its grandiose powers in the same way as we should a neurotic obsession in our individual patients," appeared too full of dynamite for an author living under the Catholic regime of Dollfuss and Schuschnigg. Its final composition had to await the conquest of Austria by Hitler, the subsequent persecution of Freud on ideological as well as racial grounds, and his escape to England, a nation which, although far more Christian in spirit than either Austria or Germany, bore with much greater composure a psychoanalytical critique of the Christian dogma. To be sure, this unusual genesis of the work has resulted in considerable technical shortcomings and endless repetitions. Freud himself, hitherto a master of literary presentation, which but a few years before had rightly earned for him the major Goethe prize in contemporary German literature, deeply deplores these shortcomings for making his discussion "as ineffectual as it is inartistic." Inartistic, yes, but far from ineffectual. If anything, the constant hammering of a few *leitmotifs* helps to impress upon the reader's mind those views of the author which at first appear to him farfetched or even repugnant, and to evoke the impression of certainty and logical cogency where,

* Reprinted from *American Journal of Sociology* 45, no. 3 (1939), 471–77.

by the very nature of the subject, everything is so profoundly uncertain and hypothetical.

The subject of Moses and the origins of monotheism lends itself, like few other topics in the history of religion, to extensive analytical treatment. The availability of a fairly large body of biographic and ethnological material, principally in the Bible, is enhanced by the great chronological gap between the events narrated therein and their record in its present form—which leaves it open to an endless variety of interpretations. A great deal of further folkloristic material, some of it doubtless also containing a kernel of historical truth, has been preserved in the more articulate, but still younger rabbinic and patristic literatures, of which Freud—perhaps to his credit—has made but little use. The well-known lack of agreement among modern biblical scholars and anthropologists on some of the most fundamental issues of biblical history likewise equips the analytical investigator with a mass of alternative suggestions from which he may choose those that best fit into the pattern of his theory. "The more shadowy tradition has become," says Freud, "the more meet is it for the poet's use." Nevertheless, perhaps as a result of being too much earth-bound and source-bound, I feel that I cannot quite follow him into this rarefied atmosphere of pure speculation.

In this work Freud elaborates and illustrates, by the specific example of Moses, his main thesis on the development of religion, which he first advanced in 1912 in his striking volume on *Totem and Taboo*. In its bare essentials the theory assumes a parallelism between the evolution of mankind, from its prehistoric stages to contemporary civilization, and the individual growth of man, from childhood to adult life. Just as in individual life the first five years after birth leave permanent impressions which, carried through a period of sexual latency to the age of pubescence, definitely condition adult psychic life and lay the ground for all human neuroses, so mankind at large is carrying in its subconscious mind the heritage of its all-important formative stage. Although forgotten during the long subsequent period of latency, the impressions of this prehistoric stage time and again come to the fore in the consciousness of civilized man. Following suggestions made by Darwin and Atkinson, Freud has long advocated the hypothesis that mankind had begun its career as a father horde, in which one strong male was the master and father of the whole horde. Unlimited in his power, he appropriated all females, and banished all males from the horde. At last a group of such exiled brothers "clubbed together, overcame the father, and—according to the custom of those times—all partook of his body." Of course, each of these brothers deeply desired to inherit the mantle which had thus fallen from the revered father's shoulders, but unable to overcome the resistance of the others and realizing that internecine fights were as dangerous as they were futile, compromised upon a new form of social organization based upon the recognition of mutual obligations. These were the beginnings of morality and law. Instead of each appropriating the women of the horde to himself, the brothers renounced them altogether and established exogamy as their guiding principle. They also found a substitute for the father in a totem, usually an animal, revered as the father of the tribe. In memory of what had happened to the primeval father, no one was allowed to kill it; but on a stated occasion it was consumed in a sacrificial repast. The new leaders of the brother horde thus

undid their deed by declaring that the killing of the father substitute, the totem, was not allowed, and renounced the fruit of their deed by denying themselves the liberated women. Thus they created two fundamental taboos of totemism out of the *sense of guilt of the son*, and for this very reason these had to correspond with the two repressed wishes of the Oedipus complex. Whoever disobeyed became guilty of the two only crimes which troubled primitive society.

Animal worship was subsequently replaced by human deities, and socially the matriarchate gave way to a reestablished patriarchal organization. But after a period of latency the dim memories of that early eventful revolution came back to haunt man, who by that time had attained a high degree of material and intellectual civilization.

For reasons which cannot fully be explained, in the fourteenth century B.C., under the reign of the Egyptian king, Ikhnaton, these memories blossomed out into the first, and perhaps the purest, form of a monotheistic creed. The details of Ikhnaton's memorable reform; its antecedents in the doctrines of the priests of the Sun Temple at On; the influences emanating from Syria, perhaps through the king's Syrian wives; and the impact of Egyptian imperialism can no longer be ascertained, because the successful opposition after 1350 B.C. destroyed nearly all pertinent records. In any case, however, it apparently would have remained but an interesting historical episode were it not for the work of one of Ikhnaton's Egyptian disciples, named Moses. Freud, after repeating many older arguments in favor of Moses' Egyptian origin, adds an interesting psychoanalytic explanation of the Moses legend. As Otto Rank had shown some thirty years earlier, this legend closely corresponds to a very widespread type of hero myth, except in one essential point, viz., that in Freud's view the hero actually came from the noble, rather than from the humble, family in the story. Sometime after 1350 B.C. this Egyptian prince, perhaps also governor of the province of Goshen, where a large number of Israelites had been living under Egyptian domination, tried to salvage the suppressed teachings of Ikhnaton by creating a new following among the Semitic settlers, taking them out of Egypt, and leading them to Palestine. In southern Palestine the new arrivals, as yet unprepared for the high spirituality of the new religion, murdered their leader—Freud here takes a clue from a fantastic "discovery" of Ernst Sellin—and joined a number of closely related tribes which had settled there before. Together the two groups soon came under the sway of another leader, whom we may conveniently designate as the Midianite Moses. This dualism of two religions and two founders, like the other dualities of Jewish history—two peoples forming one nation, its breaking up into two kingdoms, and the two names of the Deity —is the necessary consequence of the fact that "one section of the people passed through what may properly be termed a traumatic experience which the other was spared." After the Egyptian Moses' death, the "childhood experience" of the Jewish people entered once more a period of relative latency, during which only a small minority of Levites, descendants of the original small circle of native Egyptians around Moses, carried on the tradition of the lawgiver. Several centuries later, under the stimulus of the Israelitic prophets, the original Mosaic religion was reestablished as the national religion of Israel. This monotheistic creed thus became the revived memory of the primeval father. "The great deed or misdeed of primeval times, the murder of the father, was brought home to the Jews, for fate decreed that they should repeat it on the person of Moses, an eminent father substitute." With their new belief in God, the Father, went the expectation of the return of the lawgiver, as the Messiah (Freud could have used here another hypothesis of Sellin, since abandoned, that the expected Messiah of early Israelitic prophecy was Moses redivivus—a belief held long after by Samaritan schismatics); the conviction of Israel's chosenness; and most of the teachings of ancient Judaism, including imageless worship, ritualism, growth of spirituality, and circumcision. This last custom, clearly of Egyptian origin, was unwittingly taken over by Moses because of its inherent connection with the castration complex originating from the relationship between the primeval father and his sons. This Mosaic restoration of the primeval father still left some parts of the prehistoric tragedy unrecognized, however. Operating underground for several more centuries, they gradually generated that widespread feeling of guilt which characterized both the Jewish people and the entire Mediterranean world at the beginning of the Christian era. This sense of guilt once more resulted in the murder of a leader, but this time it was the Son who died in expiation for the primeval murder of the Father. This is, according to Freud, the underlying motif for Paul's doctrine of original sin, just as the Christian communion is but a resurgence of both the bodily partaking of the primeval father and its derivative, the sacrificial repast of the totem cults. Through the Crucifixion, on the other hand, the Christian religion truly became but a Son religion, and hence its triumph "was a renewed victory of the Ammon priests over the God of Ikhnaton." The Jewish people, which "with its usual stiff-necked obduracy" continued to deny the murder of their "father," consequently suffered severe persecution. The accusation of Christ-killing really means "You won't admit that you murdered God" (the primeval father and his reincarnations), whereas "we did the same thing, but we admitted it, and since then we have been purified."

This bold and ingenious reconstruction of the history of religion, of which a bare, and in many respects incomplete, outline has been presented here, is supported by a great many detailed, no less bold and ingenious, observations, which make the book worthwhile reading even for one who will ultimately disagree with its main thesis. But the method of the work is open to crucial objections. The extreme liberties admittedly taken by Freud with available biblical material are also illustrative of his utilization of the findings of modern anthropological and historical research.

When I use Biblical tradition here in such an autocratic and arbitrary way, draw on it for confirmation whenever it is convenient, and dismiss its evidence without scruple when it contradicts my conclusions, I know full well that I am exposing myself to severe criticism concerning my method and that I weaken the force of my proofs. But this is the only way in which to treat material whose trustworthiness—as we know for certain—was seriously damaged by the influence of distorting tendencies.

Many of us, unfortunately, will have to disagree. No, this is not the only way; it is not even the way of an author like Adolf Allwohn, who, with the help of psychoanalysis, has tried to reconstruct the subconscious erotic motivations of the prophetic career of Hosea—a subject, it may readily be granted, much more promising than the austere figure of Moses. Freud's unlimited arbitrariness in the selection and use of the little existing evidence renders the entire factual basis of his reconstruction more than questionable. The primeval father horde and the murder of the primeval father are considered by almost all contemporary anthropologists as a figment of imagination. The explanation of the subsequent rise of totemism, based upon a suggestion once made by W. Robertson Smith, is here upheld by Freud even though he knows that "more recent ethnologists have without exception discarded" Smith's theories. For the career of the historical Moses, he quotes outstanding modern scholars—Meyer, Gressmann, Sellin, Breasted—of whom he speaks with greater awe than he does of the original biblical sources and ancient monuments. But he selects from these writers some of their most fantastic views (often timidly advanced and sometimes later revoked by the authors themselves), drags them out of their context, and combines them into a new, artificial entity. The factual evidence for the Egyptian origin of Moses reduces itself largely to the etymology of the name; but this proof is no more conclusive than would be a parallel attempt to deduce from the name of Zerubbabel, the leader of another exodus of Jewish exiles, that he was a native Babylonian. The Jews probably adopted then, as ever after, the names prevalent among the national majorities in the midst of whom they chanced to live. Wholly untenable is Freud's attempted identification of the divine name, *Adonai*, in Israel's credo with the Egyptian "Aton." The Deuteronomic source has, of course, *Yahwe*. The substitute, *Adonai*, and its Greek equivalent, *kyrios*, are first clearly indicated in the Hellenistic period, a millennium after Moses. Neither is the violent death of Moses more than a farfetched hypothesis, largely relinquished by its author and shared by no other biblical scholar. Similar objections could also easily be raised against many other essential links in the Freudian reconstruction. Even if the entire factual background were proved beyond peradventure, however, as it is not, the old question would still remain as to whether the Freudian parallelism between individual and mass psychology (assuming the correct interpretation of the former) can be scientifically upheld. The "period of latency," particularly, which in the case of the lapse of time between the alleged murder of the primeval father and the appearance of Ikhnaton would extend over countless generations, presupposes an extent of transmission of memories through some sort of heredity which, Freud himself admits, is unequivocally rejected "by the present attitude of biological science." In short, the cause of psychoanalytical interpretation of the history of religion, brilliantly initiated by Freud and his disciples several decades ago, seems to me to have received a setback rather than to have made further progress through its present application to the historical career of Moses.

These considerations will probably carry little weight with "that minority of readers familiar with analytical reasoning and able to appreciate its conclusions" to which Freud, notwithstanding his sincere efforts at popularization, primarily addresses himself. To many of these initiates, the work, despite its scientific argumentation, will appeal as the pronunciamento of a revered prophet and sectarian leader, entirely immune in their eyes from the so-called rational, but essentially "psychically conditioned," and hence "prejudiced," attacks by outsiders. To the outsiders, however, much as they may admire the author's erudition and dialectical prowess, his ingenious structure will appear to be but a magnificent castle in the air.

2

Reflections on Ancient and Medieval Jewish Historical Demography*

INTEREST in contemporary Jewish demography has been growing in recent years, but very little has as yet been done to ascertain the size and composition of the Jewish population in earlier historical periods, particularly in antiquity and the Middle Ages. I need not expatiate on the importance of the rise and fall of populations for the history of any people in any period. Our generation, which has witnessed a world-wide population explosion unprecedented in size and universality, does not have to be told about the important effects such a growth, or conversely a decline, has on the entire socioeconomic, political, and even cultural life of a country. The Spanish sociologist Javier Ruiz Almanza well summarized his view in the pithy epigram: "History without demography is an enigma, just as is demography without history." And yet, as has been pointed out by Marcel R. Reinhard, "the classic works of history and demography share the curious peculiarity of ignoring one another." [1]

The scholar's reluctance to deal with Jewish demography of past ages is fully understandable. The difficulties of ascertaining the mere number of Jews in any particular country or period before the modern era are indeed staggering. Even contemporary Jewish demography, as we all know, leaves much to be desired, especially in the two countries of largest Jewish settlement, the United States and the Soviet Union. Yet the importance of the subject is so vital that one must not give up. In the following, I wish merely to submit a few general remarks about methods and approaches, rather than to propose any definite conclusions.

I

Our best information on population is usually derived from governmental censuses. In recent decades, wherever governments were

* Reprinted from *Essays on Jewish Thought and Culture in Honor of Aryeh Tartakower* (Jerusalem, 1969), pp. 31–45.

interested in inquiring about Jews as members of either a religious group or a nationality, the resultant computations bear with them the mark of authenticity. While still leaving a small margin of error, the Jewish statistics for Israel, Germany, Austria-Hungary before and after the First World War, Canada, and so forth appear to be fairly satisfactory. It must also be remembered that censuses are not an invention of the modern era. An Egyptian census was recorded as early as 3000 B.C. on the so-called Palermo Stone. During the Middle Kingdom, censuses were quite regular; some of them are mentioned in the ancient Egyptian literature. [2] Hence the census attributed by biblical sources to King David is not to be lightly dismissed. While the Egyptian censuses seem to have recorded all family members by name, the ancient Israelitic censuses (we surmise that there were others than that conducted by Joab for King David) may have been less detailed. But they still might serve as a basis for modern computations. Unfortunately, we know no more about them than the brief totals given in II Samuel 24 and I Chronicles 21. These two accounts, moreover, greatly diverge from one another, and the manifold attempts at reconciliation, including one suggested by me, leave a considerable residuum of doubt. [3]

No comprehensive censuses of Jews in or outside Palestine were conducted by the Jewish leaders of the Second Commonwealth. Only one such canvass is mentioned, as allegedly ordered by Emperor Claudius in the middle of the first century; according to the twelfth-century Christian chronicler Gregory Abu'lfaraj Bar-Hebraeus, that census had shown that 6,944,000 Jews lived at that time within the confines of the Roman Empire. [4] Of course, there were Jews outside the Empire, too, especially in Babylonia and other parts of the Parthian Empire, and in such outlying areas as southern Arabia, Ethiopia, and the like. None of these areas had ever had detailed censuses of population, and all estimates of the numbers of their inhabitants are based upon literary references which are rarely precise or dependable.

The situation is not much better with respect to the Middle Eastern countries during the Middle Ages. To be sure, some scholars have evinced interest in early Muslim population figures, and a good deal of raw material is available in the scattered tax lists and other records. But hardly any consistent effort has thus far been made to analyze these data thoroughly and to reconstruct the size and structure of any population, even on important local levels. [5]

Somewhat better was the situation in the Western lands. Here and there city councils for a variety of reasons made an effort to collect dependable data about the population of their communities. For instance, the Council of Pisa resolved in 1162 that five delegates should annually visit every quarter in town and list all heads of households and their property. [6] This was but a pious wish, however; we have hardly any information from this source relating to Pisan Jews in that period. Some of our best sources for medieval Jewish communities come to us from southern France. By order of King Robert a house-to-house canvass was made by the city syndics of Aix-en-Provence on July 20, 1341. It showed that at that time 1,205 Jews occupied 203 houses. According to a recent investigator, they formed about 10 percent of the city's population. This census also revealed that a Jewish "hearth" averaged 5.9 members, with certain households actually numbering between 20 and 30 persons. A similar census in Carpentras, on the other hand, conducted in 1471, yielded an average population of 5.2 individuals per Christian hearth and of only 4.3 per Jewish hearth. This low ratio was probably exceptional; it doubtless reflected the various trials and tribulations which affected that Jewish community, as contrasted even with that of Avignon, both under papal domination. A very cautious approach was taken by Richard W. Emery in estimating the Jewish population of Perpignan. Assuming, on the basis of partially preserved notarial registers, that some 100 Jewish families lived in the city at the end of the thirteenth century, he estimated the total Jewish population at only 300–400 persons, because "a community made up so largely of new immigrants probably contained more adult men and fewer women and children than we would find in an older settlement." But this calculation fails to take account of the general characteristic of Jewish migrations, which always consisted more of the movement of entire families, either simultaneously or in quick succession, than was the case among non-Jewish migrants. This phenomenon was most clearly observed during the period of Jewish mass migration from Eastern and Central Europe to the United States in 1890–1914 and elsewhere. [7]

These illustrations may suffice to show how difficult it is to generalize from individual figures transmitted in sporadic records. Perhaps our most reliable information comes from the North-Italian cities of Verona and Venice. In Verona we have fairly continuous records beginning with the fifteenth century. Two censuses were conducted in the years 1472–1500; they were followed by six censuses in the sixteenth century, seven in the following century, and so on. Here the Jewish segment of the population seems to have been more or less adequately counted. Similarly in Venice we have fairly reliable Jewish records from the sixteenth century on, but really none from the Middle Ages, since the Jewish privileges were not renewed after 1396 and only a few individuals are sporadically mentioned in the city proper until after the war with the League of Cambrai in 1509. [8]

Needless to say, the completeness and reliability of all these accounts is subject to doubt. Even the refined censuses of our days leave many questions open because some enumerators fail to contact temporarily absent persons, accept dubious answers to their questions given by one or another individual, and because of other well-known deficiencies. One of the main virtues of modern censuses is their periodic repetition so that, whatever faults they may have in certain details, they generally reflect quite well the prevailing trends in the rise or decline of populations and in other demographic movements. No such periodicity existed in ancient or medieval times, except in a few localities toward the end of the Middle Ages; hence we totally lack the advantage of comparative data for those areas.

Moreover, even if certain figures are recorded they are open to varying interpretations and credibility gaps. In regard to ancient figures, both Graeco-Roman and biblical, we are especially dependent on our acceptance or rejection of the ancient sources. On the whole, the extreme gullibility in this respect of earlier generations sharply contrasts with the general skepticism of modern scholars, whose criticism has often overshot the mark. Until the early eighteenth century the prevailing opinion was not only that the classical sources were generally dependable but also that there had been a constant deterioration in human life since ancient times, and that hence the populations of early modern Europe were necessarily much smaller than those of classical antiquity. For example, the seventeenth-century Spanish writer Alvarez Osorio claimed that in antiquity Spain had had to feed a population of some 78,000,000, which had declined to but 14,000,000 in the days of King Charles II (1665–1700). A century later another Spaniard, Martin de Loynaz, asserted without fear of contradiction that the Iberian peninsula embraced a population of 50,000,000 in the days of Julius Caesar, but only 19,000,000 in the days of the Catholic monarchs. [9] No less

level-headed a thinker than Charles de Secondat, Baron de Montesquieu, after "as careful a computation as is possible in matters of
this kind," was convinced that the world population of his day did
not amount to more than one-tenth of what it had been in ancient
times. [10] The first scholar seriously to question these assumptions
was David Hume, who, with his usual skepticism, placed serious
question marks before many numbers quoted in ancient sources. [11]
However, he did not offer any constructive suggestions as to how
these erroneous data could be replaced by more reliable ones. Not
surprisingly, his findings were challenged by many contemporaries.
In fact, he himself did not object to the publication of their dissenting views.

Since the days of Hume, modern criticism in this and other fields
has increased by leaps and bounds. It reached a climax at the turn of
the twentieth century, when the credibility of almost every ancient
source was denied unless there was very strong supporting evidence
in other sources. In regard to population data such skepticism
seemed doubly justified, as general observation had persuaded many
scholars that the large twentieth-century populations were of but
recent vintage and had had no parallels whatsoever in the remote
past. To mention only examples from the literature on ancient
Jewish population, it may suffice to quote Adolf Harnack and Arthur
Ungnad. In his famous work on the early mission and expansion of
Christianity, Harnack had to deal with Jewish population figures at
the beginning of the common era because of his major contention
that the Christian expansion was most successful in those areas
where Jewish communities had flourished in the first century. To
prove this thesis he argued that no less than 3,500,000 to 4,000,000
Jews lived in the various countries of the dispersion before the
Second Fall of Jerusalem. But he assumed that Palestine's Jewish
population at that time had not exceeded 700,000; he did it for no
other reason than that this was the approximate number of the
country's inhabitants in 1902, when he wrote his book. On the other
hand, Arthur Ungnad denied the historicity of the widely accepted
figure in Sennacherib's inscription about the deportation of 200,150
Judaeans from Palestine upon his retreat after his unsuccessful siege
of Jerusalem in the days of King Hezekiah. Contending that such a
figure must be too high, this German scholar actually recommended
an emendation—to read: 2,150—always a perilous expedient, doubly

so in this case, since the lower figure would render the royal boast completely meaningless. [12]

We must, of course, beware of such prejudgments. We now know that populations, like other aspects of human life, often alternately rise and decline. A well-known example is that of France, which, from the days of Caesar's Gaul to the eighteenth century, saw its population rise time and again to about 8,000,000, and fall to a smaller or larger fraction of that number. Even the seventeenth and eighteenth centuries had witnessed how during the seventy-two-year-long "glorious" reign of Louis XIV (1643–1715), the French population actually diminished by some 30 percent. In the lifetime of many of us, France maintained a more or less stationary population for several decades, but has substantially increased its numbers in the past three decades.

Hence the evaluation of the few census data preserved from ancient and medieval times depends on a general examination of other socioeconomic and cultural factors which make certain figures more acceptable than others. In the case of the census conducted by Claudius, first brought to the attention of students of Jewish history by Jean Juster in 1914, there has been considerable debate as to the allocation of the total of 6,944,000 between Palestine and the Roman dispersion. Juster himself, followed by Joseph Klausner, assumed that a majority (or slightly less) of the Jews living under the Roman regime around A.D. 50 still dwelled in Palestine. Both scholars postulated that as many as 3,000,000 to 5,000,000 Jews resided in what was called the Roman province of Judaea. We have seen that, without knowing of the Bar-Hebraeus record, Harnack leaned to the other extreme of attributing to Palestine less than 20 percent of the total number of Jews. My own preference has been to assume that Palestine embraced a little over 30 percent of world Jewry, that is, more than a third of the Jews counted by Claudius within the Empire. But some scholars objected to the Bar-Hebraeus figures. The late Avigdor (Victor) Tcherikover suggested that perhaps the Syriac chronicler mistook a census of Roman citizens for one of Jews. This suggestion, rather hesitantly made by Tcherikover, was taken up by Judah Rosenthal with greater firmness. [13] I still believe that Bar-Hebraeus did not commit that obvious error, but that he quoted some source (other than Eusebius) which attributed this census to Jews. In any case, the figure of nearly seven million

Jews, largely consonant with a variety of other socioeconomic data, may indeed prove helpful to us in reconstructing the size of the ancient Jewish population shortly before the fall of Jerusalem.

II

One major defect of the ancient and medieval censuses was their pragmatism; they were not dispassionate enumerations, but rather always pursued specific aims, which often aroused considerable opposition and at times vitiated their validity. They were for the most part conducted for fiscal or military purposes, governments usually trying to ascertain how much property could be taxed or how many men of military age were available for the defense of the country. Only occasionally do we hear of populations being counted for other reasons. For instance, Strasbourg conducted some enumerations in order to ascertain the amount of grain it would need to feed the population. In Venice the changing objectives are illustrated by the different officials to whom this task was assigned. Until 1540 it was the Council of Ten which arranged for, and supervised, the censuses, clearly for fiscal and military reasons. From 1540 to 1760, however, these functions devolved on the *Provveditori* and *Sovra-provveditori alla Sanità,* with the main emphasis on health. [14]

Understandably, just as governments were interested in increasing through censuses the yield of their taxes or in drawing more men into military service, so the population was often reluctant to be counted. In a talmudic source we hear of a typical incident preliminary to the collection by Persian officials of the regular capitation tax from the Jews of Babylonia. Upon receiving advance notice that Persian inspectors were coming to count the prospective taxpayers, we are told, R. Ze'era warned many local Jews to go into hiding together with their families. As a result fewer "heads" were counted, and the total charge upon the community at large was substantially reduced. [15]

The popular resentment toward censuses of any kind was also reflected in the scriptural story of King David's census, on which the biblical writer observed: "And again the anger of the Lord was kindled against Israel, and He moved David against them saying: 'Go, number Israel and Judah.'" When the census was completed, we are told, "David's heart smote him. . . . And David said unto the Lord: 'I have sinned greatly in what I have done; but now,

O Lord, put away, I beseech Thee, the iniquity of Thy servant, for I have done very foolishly.'" Nonetheless, God was so aroused that he afflicted Israel with a pestilence which killed 70,000 persons (II Sam. 24:1, 10, and 15). These biblical passages may indeed have served to discourage certain medieval Christian regimes from "annoying" their subjects with enumerations, and encouraged the subjects themselves to sabotage all censuses as best they could. [16]

Another drawback of the stress on the fiscal purposes of such statistics was that many counts were made not of the total population but only of prospective taxpayers. Wherever a "hearth tax" prevailed, the understandable tendency was to count only taxpaying "hearths," which, in any case, were not quite identical with "households." Even if the authorities tried to collect capitation taxes—which, dependent on time and place, usually started at a specified age, say between ten and eighteen years—the enumeration consisted in asking the heads of families either to state the total number of family members over that age or, more precisely, to indicate the names and ages of those members who were subject to the tax. Very likely, quite a few households tried to understate the number of taxpaying members. Even today, without such a motivation, enumerators find people (not only women) giving wrong answers regarding age, either out of vanity or because they do not know the precise birth years of their relatives. For a modern demographer it is extremely important to know the ratio of children below the age specified for the poll tax to the total population.

In the case of medieval Jews this factor is doubly significant, since most of the extant data concerning their numerical strength come from tax rolls. As is well known, in almost all countries medieval Jewry constituted a class of taxpayers of its own kind. In Muslim lands, the non-Muslims were from the beginning subject to a capitation tax, often graduated according to the taxpayers' wealth. According to our most important source of information, Ya'qub Abu-Yusuf's *Kitab al-Kharaj* (Book of the Land-Tax), Jews and Christians were divided into three classes: the majority of less well-to-do was to pay one gold dinar; the middle class, two gold dinars; and the wealthy, four dinars per family member. In practice, however, neither here nor in those Western countries which likewise had some form of Jewish capitation tax (for instance, the "Golden Penny" introduced by Louis the Bavarian in 1342 for the Holy Roman Empire) were the figures thus obtained used for the collec-

tion of actual payments from the individuals. As a rule they merely
served as a basis for the computation of a total amount to be
delivered by the local Jewish community—or, sometimes, as in Spain,
by a regional group of communities forming a *Colecta*. [17]

Obviously in all such cases the communities were interested in
securing a smaller tax base, whereas the governmental authorities
sought to increase the estimated total of Jews subject to the tax. As a
result, the tax finally paid was determined through protracted negotiations; the compromises arrived at were but remotely related to the
underlying population figures. In many areas, moreover, particularly
under Islam, certain categories of Jews and Christians were from
the outset exempted by law (among them women and children,
aged, infirm, and indigent persons). It is therefore up to the student
of demography to figure out on the basis of other sources what
proportion of the population consisted of these large tax-exempt
groups—a very arduous task indeed. In other countries, particularly
Spain, the historian also has to take account of specific tax privileges
granted by rulers to favored individuals. For the most part it was
the wealthiest and best-connected man in the community who
secured from the government a tax exemption for himself and his
family, an exemption which often persisted for several generations.
On the other hand, the Jewish community, whose tax burden as a
rule remained undiminished, deeply resented the loss of a wealthy
contributor whose share had to be made up by the rest of the community. In many cases communal protests led to the revocation of
such privileges; in others the communities threatened the favored
members with excommunication. All these factors have to be taken
into consideration whenever we use tax records as a basis for
computing local or regional Jewish populations. [18]

III

Because of the unsatisfactory nature of the existing documentation, particularly for Jewish demographic history, we must try to
buttress whatever sketchy information we may garner, by additional
methods of investigation. More than forty years ago I tried, in my
article on the ancient Israelitic population (see below), to formulate
certain hypotheses by using city areas as a basis for population
figures. [19] Since the original publication of that article, measurements of inhabited areas have been increasingly used in general

demographic research of past ages. For the population of ancient
Israel and the Second Commonwealth one can learn a great deal
from the size of Palestinian towns and hamlets during the first
millennium B.C. as evidenced through archaeological discoveries. To
be sure, we must always pay special attention to changing population densities within each area. A town may occupy a fairly large
tract of land, and even surround it with a wall, although the
population is as yet small and sparsely settled. In time the number
of inhabitants may greatly increase, ultimately causing extremely
crowded conditions. The usual result is that the settled area spills
over beyond the city walls, creating a sort of suburban settlement,
which may or may not be politically included in the original
municipality. This is in many cases the meaning of the biblical
phrase of חצרים or בנות. On the other hand, after the ravages
of a great war or pestilence, the population may sharply decline;
this may also be the result of major economic transformations.
One or another city may even turn into a ghost town. True,
in only a few cases do we have detailed information about the
losses sustained by certain communities as a result of a major
pestilence such as the Black Death of 1348–49. By carefully studying
the death registers in the small Burgundian town of Givry, P. Gras
has shown that the number of persons buried in 1348 was twenty
times the number indicated by the average annual mortality during
the preceding decade. The author reached the conclusion that about
half the villages' population must have been victims of the pest.
Mortality was not quite uniform in all areas or all segments of the
population, however. It was shown that three neighboring villages
around Cambridge suffered diverse losses, ranging from 47 to 70
percent of the inhabitants. In the case of Jews, we know that they
suffered losses not only as victims of the plague but also because
of the fantastic accusation of well poisoning, and as the objects of
massacres, *Judenbrände,* and expulsions. However, severe losses of
life occurred in both antiquity and the Middle Ages as a result
of numerous lesser pestilences, earthquakes, and floods, as well as
wars and famines, some of which had marked effects on the size of
the population, permanently or temporarily. In other words, area
measurements can be useful only if they are interpreted in the
context of the history of that area during the respective periods. [20]
Another matter seriously to be considered is the changing character of ancient and medieval cities. I have often tried to make clear

that in ancient Palestine and many surrounding countries the township not only was a center of commerce and industry but also embraced most of the agricultural population. The prevailing system was for a townsman to leave his home in the morning and proceed to his field or vineyard, work there during the day, and return to town in the evening. He did so largely out of habits formed during the early, unsettled periods of the Canaanite city-states and Israel's tribal divisions. Because of the prevailing insecurity, the farmer preferred to live with his family in a town—where he felt better protected, by the town wall and the presence of close neighbors, against unexpected raids from enemies or nomads. Hence the sociological differences between urban and rural populations were often blurred. At the same time agricultural activities could not reasonably be pursued at too great a distance from one's home. That is why a large number of small towns, rather than a few major metropolitan concentrations, met the socioeconomic needs of the country. I was not surprised to find that the small area of ancient Israel and Judah embraced no less than 400 townships, with a modicum of municipal autonomy and "urban" life. But they were located at an average distance of only four miles from one another. The number of inhabitants for the most part did not exceed 1,000 souls, and often fell considerably below that figure. [21]

Regrettably, we know very little about the number of Jewish farmers in any medieval country. [22] But as far as Jewish urban settlements were concerned, we can derive a good deal of information from the size of Jewish quarters. Although the quarters were not always clearly outlined, diligent research has discovered the boundaries of the Jewish residential sections in many cities. A careful investigation of certain ghettos has also yielded important information concerning the size of buildings, public and private, erected there in the course of succeeding generations. Here, too, there were many changes in time. For example, the Jews in Rome numbered some 3,000 persons when they were forced into a ghetto by Pope Paul IV in 1555. Two centuries later their number rose to about 12,000 in the same area. Even more startlingly, when the Jews of Frankfort were forced to move into their newly established ghetto in 1462 they seem to have embraced no more than 200 inhabitants. In the eighteenth century their population had increased to nearly 3,000. And yet the ghetto area had not been enlarged. The result in both cities was a terrific congestion, the need to build multistory

"skyscrapers" (especially in the Frankfort ghetto), and the other
adverse phenomena of dark, overcrowded, and unsanitary streets
and dwellings. [23]

Elsewhere and at other times conditions were somewhat better.
In the Middle Ages proper, the Western Jewish communities were
for the most part very small. Yet the difficulties of relating areas to
population density have been well illustrated by Michael Adler's
observations with respect to some medieval English Jewish communities. He found that the Jewish street in Bristol measured only
205 feet in length. Such a strip could not have accommodated
much more than 20 residential houses, in addition to some public
buildings, and yet he was able to list by name 53 Jews who lived
there between 1250 and 1290. Since recorded names often are but
a minority of actual residents, it may well be that Bristol accommodated no less than 100 Jewish families. Canterbury, too, apparently included only 20 houses on the Jewish street. Yet Adler was
able to identify no less than 69 Jewish men and 5 Jewish women
residing there between 1240 and 1270. Nevertheless, further detailed
studies of the areas occupied by Jewish quarters, the facilities
offered by some novel architectural methods (Jews are supposed to
have pioneered in building stone houses in England), the availability of public services, especially in public welfare and sanitation,
and so forth, ought indeed to furnish us, in time, with some valuable
insights also in regard to the growth or decline of population in the
Jewish quarters. [24]

IV

The above brief observations relate, however, almost exclusively
to one facet of demographic research, namely, the size of the Jewish
population in a given town, country, or period. The same holds true
for some such novel approaches to demography as those predicated
on what some American economic geographers call "basic" and
"nonbasic" economic factors. The basic factors in a town relate
principally to those activities which bring in money from the outside—such as a local industry which sells its products to neighboring
farmers and to other towns; physicians attending out-of-town
patients; local fairs; and the like. Nonbasic factors consist principally
of services rendered to the population within the city limits. In this
miniature mercantilistic system, it is often assumed, the town can

sustain a larger population when the basic factors significantly contribute to the town's economy than when the reverse is true. In the Jewish case many activities of moneylenders, merchants, and even artisans or doctors, if allowed to sell their goods or services to the population living outside the Jewish quarter, contributed to the basic growth-sustaining factors, whereas the proliferation of a communal bureaucracy, students, and persons living on public welfare naturally restricted these quarters' economic base and, with it, the size of the Jewish community. Although the utilization of this method even for general population research is still in its infancy, students of Jewish historical demography ought to remain watchful of the possibilites of applying such criteria to Jewish ghetto life, at least in conjunction with the other lines of research. [25]

Only after ascertaining some reasonable totals for individual Jewish communities or regions—in the case of Diaspora communities also the ratio of Jews to the total population—will it be possible to proceed to the investigation of such further demographic aspects as birth rates; mortality by age groups; general sex and age distribution; marriage and divorce rates; migratory movements; the kinds and frequency of diseases, including pestilences; criminality; and so forth. All these lines of investigation have methodological approaches and problems of their own. Here, too, general research must be modified to take cognizance of the Jews' different socioeconomic and religious realities. For example, it is fairly well known that in the Middle Ages the Gentile population had very little of a welfare system. Hence, as a rule, townspeople got married only after they were able to earn a living. In Jewish life, however, not only were early marriages promoted by the biblical commandment to procreate —according to the rabbis, this was the first "commandment" mentioned in the Bible—but families and the community at large also made every effort to facilitate youthful unions. Availability of medical aid was also indubitably superior among Jews than among the majority of the Christian population, which inhabited vast stretches of farmlands at a great distance from any doctor or hospital. Each of these aspects requires special consideration, and only many such researches from various angles may furnish us with a sufficient number of convergent hypotheses to make population studies of the older periods truly fruitful. However difficult this may be, it is anything but a hopeless task.

3

The Israelitic Population under the Kings[*]

THE QUESTION of population in every nation and every period is of great importance for the understanding of all facets of public life, economic and political as well as cultural. According to David Hume, it is "the most curious and important of all questions of erudition." [1] It is worthwhile, therefore, to discuss this question with regard to the early period in Israel, especially the period of the kings.

The difficulties are numerous. It is well known that the figures transmitted in the early sources are quite unreliable and that the demographic knowledge of contemporaries was utterly deficient. Nevertheless, scientific curiosity has never accepted the principle of *ignoramus et ignorabimus* but has made every attempt to solve such riddles despite the limited possibilities.

In fact, there have been basic changes in the approaches to this problem during the last two centuries. Montesquieu, for example, believed that, according to the most exact computations, the population of his day did not amount to even a tenth of that in the ancient period. [2] This view of the famous French thinker was the regnant opinion among scholars of his and the preceding generations. The first to object to that assumption was David Hume, who with his usual skepticism raised questions concerning this accepted notion. But he was satisfied with mere criticism [3] and did not attempt to replace the prevailing view with a theory of his own. As is usually the case with radical ideas, Hume's critique did not enjoy immediate acceptance in scholarly circles. In the mid-eighteenth century some of Hume's own compatriots, particularly Robert Wallace, combated his approach (interestingly, Hume himself encouraged Wallace to publish his rebuttal). [4] In contrast, nineteenth-century scholarship sided with Hume, and even went much further than he. At the end of the century, when historical criticism reached a peak, students began to examine the traditional sources with greater exactitude and discrimination. Karl Julius Beloch's *Die Bevölkerung*

[*] Translated from the Hebrew essay in *Abhandlungen zur Erinnerung an Hirsch Perez Chajes* (Vienna, 1933), pp. 76–136.

der griechisch-römischen Welt, published in 1886, has remained the standard work on this subject. Other scholars, such as Eduard Meyer, contributed important details. [5] The scholarship of this period went to the other extreme of Hume's predecessors. If the earlier investigators believed that ancient culture was superior in every respect to medieval and early modern civilization, and that, there-fore, it must have embraced a larger population, the late nineteenth-century scholars deeply believed in the continual evolution and progress of humanity. This belief was so universally shared that it sufficed for a student to show that according to such and such a source ancient Palestine, for example, had a population density equal to that of Belgium (the most populous European nation today) to serve as allegedly incontrovertible evidence that the source's figures were vastly exaggerated. [6]

But is there any basis for these presuppositions? We see with our own eyes that Egypt's population and its density now exceed those of Belgium in both absolute and relative figures. True, Egypt is very large; but the settled areas—that is, the Nile Valley and its delta—together amount to less than 4 percent of the country's area; that is, not more than 30,000 square kilometers, or about 12,000 square miles. [7] And yet, according to the official census, this limited area accommodated 12,750,918 inhabitants in March, 1917; and 14,168,756 in February, 1927. [8] Accordingly, the settled area of Egypt had an average population of 455 persons per square kilometer (whereas Belgium's average in that very year did not exceed 267 persons per square kilometer). [9] And these inhabitants still increased "like the sand of the sea": according to the official figures of 1924, the Egyptian births during that year amounted to 604,410, as against 343,515 deaths; [10] that is, the population grew by more than a quarter mil-lion inhabitants, or approximately 1.9 percent. Similarly, another Eastern region, Bengal, exceeds Belgium twelve times over in abso-lute population, and about equals it in population density. [11]

Needless to say, one cannot compare ancient conditions with those of our time. But we shall see that ancient Egypt in various periods embraced more than 7,000,000 inhabitants. Since we cannot assume that the habitable area has changed much from that time until the twentieth century—the Nile flows in a narrow valley (in places, no more than 160 meters wide, and rarely exceeding 3 kilo-meters in width) between mountains and hills on both banks;[12] it appears that in ancient times Egypt had approximately 230 inhabitants per square kilometer, and perhaps even considerably more. There were, to be sure, periods in antiquity and afterward when the population greatly declined, but allegedly there was also a time when it supposedly rose to over 20,000,000; namely, at the height of prosperity under the Caliphate of Baghdad. [13] Such ups and downs in history are well illustrated by the data supplied through the centuries by the official Chinese records. [14]

In general, we now view traditional sources with greater respect than did the scholars of the generation at the turn of the century. In that period of extreme criticism of the Bible and other ancient sources, Julius Wellhausen, Eduard Meyer, and other scholars had excessive confidence in the power of human reason to pass judgment on all aspects of ancient history. At times they reached "definitive" conclusions on the basis of reasoning alone, even in the face of clearly contrary statements in the ancient sources. [15] Today we are far more restrained. We neither assume that all the ancient sources are inferior and dubious nor believe that our reason is faultless. While the extreme criticism of the late nineteenth century undoubtedly performed a great service by destroying many erroneous notions deeply rooted in the minds of earlier generations, our primary task today ought to be one of positive reconstruction.

SLIGHT TEXTUAL DIVERGENCES

What is the nature of the sources? As in all facets of Jewish history of that period, we must place our main reliance on the facts recorded in the Bible, with a few rather important additions from outside sources more or less contemporary with the biblical events. We must first examine, therefore, how reliable these sources are.

It is generally known that one cannot depend on ancient sources with respect to figures; not even to the extent that we may rely on them in regard to other kinds of data. On the whole, manuscript copyists are more likely to make mistakes with numbers than with other words. Skeptics rightly contend that if someone hearing another person recite a number is usually unable to repeat it correctly, how much more likely are errors to occur in the copying and recopying of figures over generations. Even if the copyist makes a mistake in a word, the reader can perceive from the context that there is a corruption, whereas figures, as a rule, do not markedly alter the gist of the sentence, and a mistake thus more readily escapes detection. [16]

It is astonishing, therefore, to see that the numbers of importance to our inquiry [17]—whether occurring in the former prophets or in the Book of Chronicles—reveal almost perfect unanimity in the manuscripts of the Hebrew original, as well as in those of the ancient versions. Only in relatively few cases do we find any significant variants. Since this is a fundamental question, we will deal with it in some detail.

In the Book of Joshua no significant variations have been found in the pertinent figures, except in those relating to the lists of cities in chapters 15, 18, 19, and 21. Even here, however, the numbers in the vast majority of the various manuscripts and versions agree. This is the more remarkable as the texts often reveal variants in the names of the recorded cities and as the sum total does not quite agree with the individual numbers. [18]

Moreover, each of the few variants in the numbers of the cities can be explained.

1) Joshua 15:21–32 actually lists thirty-eight or thirty-four cities (only some Greek MSS list fewer names), whereas the total is given as "twenty and nine." Nevertheless, all the MSS and translations are in agreement, except for the Syriac, which reads "thirty and six," obviously the translator's emendation.

2) In Joshua 15:44, the B (Vaticanus) MS of LXX reads "ten" instead of "nine." This is clearly an emendation, because ten names are mentioned in that MS. The A (Alexandrinus) and L (Lucianus) MSS read "nine" as in MT. [19] The difference is not surprising in view of the general lack of unity in LXX.

3) In Joshua 15:57, LXX reads, on the contrary, "nine" instead of "ten"—also an emendation.

4) LXX introduces an additional verse after Joshua 15:59. This and item 12 below are the only instances involving numbers pertinent to this study where MT omits entire verses.

5) In Joshua 15:62, LXX B and A read "seven" instead of "six," because they misconstrued *midbar* ("wilderness") in the previous verse as the name of a city and corrected the total accordingly. LXX L reads "six" in spite of the same misconstruction.

6) In Joshua 18:28, LXX reads "thirteen" instead of "fourteen" because of the contraction of "Zela" and "Eleph" into one city, "Zela-Wa-Eleph."

7–10) LXX B omits the numbers entirely in Joshua 19:15, 22, 30, and 38, whereas LXX A omits them in 19:15 and 22 but includes them in 19:30 and 38. There is no need to think that these numbers are a late addition. [20] Each verse presents certain difficulties, and LXX omitted the numbers because of incomprehension. [21]

11) In Joshua 21:35, LXX (B only) omits "Dimnah with the open land about it" and thus reads "three" instead of "four."

12) Only in Joshua 21:37 ff. are there variants in the MSS and the Hebrew editions. Here, too, there is no essential difference in counting; MT omits two verses entirely, for reasons which need not be elaborated here.

In Judges, I have found only some minor changes in LXX from MT.

13) In Judges 8:4, LXX A reads "two hundred."

14) In Judges 8:10, three Hebrew MSS read "a hundred and twenty" instead of "a hundred and twenty thousand."

15) In Judges 10:4, instead of "And he had *thirty* sons that rode on *thirty* ass colts, and they had *thirty* cities," LXX B in all cases reads "thirty-two." LXX A follows MT for the second "thirty." Cf. I Chronicles 2:22.

16) In Judges 16:27, LXX B reads "seven hundred"; LXX A "three thousand."

17) In Judges 20:15, LXX B reads "twenty and three hundred" instead of "twenty and six thousand." This uncertainty is apparent also in other MSS: LXX A, Syriac, Vulgate, and Aquila all read "twenty and five thousand." Undoubtedly this figure is the result of an emendation, because according to verses 44–47 Benjamin lost twenty-five thousand men, only six hundred remaining alive. In order to match the numbers, the versions wrote "twenty and five thousand"; Josephus, too, gives this total. [22] On the other hand, the MT reading is acceptable in accordance with Ḳimḥi's commentary. [23]

18) In Judges 20:15 and 16, LXX, Syriac, and Vulgate omit one reference to "seven hundred chosen men." This emendation was to eliminate repetition.

On the other hand, many important figures in Judges occur with no variants. [24]

There are more variants in I and II Samuel than in Judges, but as a rule they are due to deliberate emendations and not to scribal errors.

19) There is the famous verse in I Samuel 6:19 about the people

of Beth Shemesh: "He smote of the people seventy men, fifty thou-sand men." Despite the difficulty—rational as well as grammatical (it is unreasonable to assume that a small town like Beth Shemesh held anywhere near fifty thousand inhabitants)—all the Hebrew MSS except three, [25] the versions, and LXX are in agreement. Only Josephus reads "seventy men" (*Antiquities* 6. 1), while Midrash Tanḥuma (editio princeps) Vayaqhel, 7, and Exodus Rabbah (MS Epstein) V, 9, read "seventy thousand men." [26] This verse presented difficulties to the ancients. The Targum separates the numbers: "He killed seventy of the people's elders and fifty thousand men of the populace." Similarly, the Vulgate states: *septuaginta viros et quin-quaginta milia plebis*. The Talmud (Sotah 35b): "R. Abahu and R. Eliezer were of different opinions: one said that there were seventy men but that each was the equal of fifty thousand, and the other held that there were fifty thousand men each of whom was the equal of the seventy members of the Sanhedrin." In order to correct the grammar, Ḳimḥi and Gersonides comment that though the word for "fifty" lacks the connective *vav* the phrase should be understood as "*and* fifty thousand." Most of the recent commentators offer vari-ous explanations of their own [27] or take the easy way out by deleting "fifty thousand men" and leaving only "seventy men," in agreement with Josephus. [28] It is difficult to explain how the number "fifty thousand" found its way from the margin into the text. [29] The best explanation appears to be that of the eighteenth-century commenta-tor Hassencamp, [30] who suggested "seventy men, five per thousand"; namely, that out of every thousand men five were slain—apparently, according to the number of Philistine "tyrants," a man per "tyrant" (since the city contained fourteen thousand men, seventy were killed). If, as will be seen below, even fourteen thousand is too large a figure for a town like Beth Shemesh, perhaps *elef* may be explained to mean "family" instead of "thousand." [31] It is understandable why Josephus, reporting only the fact that seventy were killed, omits the reason of five per thousand. Whether or not this explanation is the correct one, one can see why the Josephus text differs from MT.

20) The variants for I Samuel 8:12 can also be explained. In place of to set over them "captains of thousands, and captains of fifties," LXX reads "captains of thousands, and captains of hun-dreds," while Syriac has all three numbers and adds "captains of tens." It is obvious that the versions compared their texts with the known division, and that they give all four or only the first two.

21) In I Samuel 9:22, LXX reads "about seventy" instead of "about thirty."

22) Similarly, in I Samuel 11:8, while all the Hebrew MSS as well as the versions agree with MT, LXX reads "six hundred thousand" instead of "three hundred thousand" and "seventy thousand" instead of "thirty thousand," and Josephus [32] has "seven hundred and seventy thousand." However, LXX, and following it Josephus, read "seventy" in place of "thirty." [33] At any rate, even if we do not agree with Schulz that LXX recognized that the numbers were not historically valid, and that therefore it indulged in exaggeration, [34] we must admit that this, too, is not a mere scribal error.

23) In I Samuel 13:5, LXX L and the Syriac version read "three thousand" instead of "thirty thousand" chariots. It is obvious that the emendation was made in order to have the number conform to the number of charioteers, two to a chariot.

24) In I Samuel 15:4, LXX B reads "four hundred thousand" instead of "two hundred thousand" (also Josephus *Antiquities* 6. 7. 3) and "thirty thousand" instead of "ten thousand," whereas the other versions agree with MT. LXX L omits the concluding phrase "and ten thousand men of Judah." LXX A reads only "ten thousand" instead of the first "two hundred thousand." These changes likewise appear to have been made intentionally rather than as scribal errors.

25) In I Samuel 18:27, LXX B and L read "one hundred" instead of "two hundred." It is obvious that this change stems from their effort to harmonize this verse with Saul's demand (18:25) and with David's statement (II Samuel 3:14). It is for this reason that LXX A omits the number altogether. There is no real difficulty, however. As Gersonides comments, "In place of a hundred Philistine foreskins he brought him two hundred in order to indicate his success." In this connection it should be mentioned that Josephus (*Antiquities* 6. 6. 10. 2–3, 198 ff.) always speaks of "six hundred heads" instead of "a hundred foreskins." Just as he omitted "foreskins" in order not to irritate his Greek readers, so he exaggerated the number in order to praise David's strength. [35]

26) In I Samuel 22:18, in the story about the priests of Nob who were slain by Doeg the Edomite, LXX gives the number of priests as "three hundred and five" and Josephus as "three hundred and fourscore and five" [36] in place of MT's "fourscore and five." Clearly the MT figure is the more plausible one; since the priests

were members of Ahimelech's family. [37] The number of eighty-five male adults in one family is unusual enough, as will be seen below; "three hundred" is preposterous. How did it come about? It has been suggested that one text read 'שמ for שמונים, which were taken to be an abbreviation of שלש מאות ("three hundred"); that another text had 'שמ twice; and that, as a result, Josephus read "three hundred and fourscore and five." This theory is untenable, because 'שמ could also be read as "six hundred" or "seven hundred"! Most modern commentators state simply that LXX exaggerated as usual. [38]

27–29) In I Samuel 23:13, LXX in all its versions has "four hundred" in place of MT's "six hundred." In 27:2 and 30:9, this change occurs only in LXX B. This is not a scribal error, but an emendation to have the number conform to I Samuel 22:2. Actually, however, there was not necessarily a contradiction; it is quite possible that David's men grew from a band of four hundred to a battalion of six hundred. [39]

30) In II Samuel 6:1, there is another example of a common phenomenon: LXX reads "seventy thousand" instead of "thirty thousand."

31) In II Samuel 8:4, there is a basic difference between MT and LXX. In place of "a thousand and seven hundred horsemen," LXX B has "a thousand chariots" and "seven thousand horsemen" (LXX A "seven thousand chariots"). Here, too, it is not a scribal error that is responsible for the difference, but an attempt to eliminate discrepancies: LXX B conforms here to I Chronicles 18:4. [40] One need not question why LXX retains MT's figures for 10:18 despite the obvious discrepancy; the Greek versions were not consistent.

32) In II Samuel 8:5, LXX A omits δύο ("two").

33) In II Samuel 17:1, all versions agree with MT. Only LXX L reads "ten thousand" for "twelve thousand." No great importance need be attached to this, however. [41]

34) Second Samuel 23:18 is perhaps the most interesting verse in the two books of Samuel from the point of view of textual changes. The ketib, many Hebrew MSS, and the Syriac version read "the chief of the captains [ha-sheloshim]"; this fits the context better than the reading in the ḳere, LXX, and the Vulgate: "the chief of the three." The latter reading, too, is not an instance of a scribe's "thoughtless" [42] error, but an effort to have this verse agree with I Chronicles 11:20. [43]

35) Three Hebrew MSS omit the second "thousand" in II Samuel 24:9.

Despite the large number of variants in the verses of the two books of Samuel, there are many more verses in which there is general agreement among all versions and MSS. [44]

36) For I Kings 5:25, LXX (5:11) reads "twenty thousand" instead of "twenty" measures of oil. Here, too, the reason for the discrepancy is apparently a desire to harmonize the verse with another, II Chronicles 2:9. Actually the number as given in Chronicles is more logical and is therefore quoted by Josephus and Theodotion.

37) In I Kings 5:30, MT and all versions except LXX read "three thousand and three hundred" who ruled the people; LXX B (5:16) has "three thousand and six hundred," LXX A reads "three thousand and five hundred," and LXX L "three thousand and seven hundred." Also in I Kings 9:23, instead of "five hundred and fifty" who ruled the people, LXX B reads "three thousand and six hundred" and LXX L "three thousand and seven hundred." (LXX A is like MT.) In both verses the change was an attempt to have the figures conform to II Chronicles 2:1 and to their conviction (shared by the author of Chronicles) that this figure is more likely if the one hundred eighty thousand workers mentioned in the preceding verses had three thousand six hundred supervisors; that is, fifty men per supervisor. In fact, however, there is a basic difference between the one hundred fifty thousand foreign workers and the thirty thousand Israelites.

38) Although LXX B omits MT's "a hundred and twenty thousand" from I Kings 8:63 (several MSS do include it, but apparently under the influence of Hexapla), [45] it must be realized that the entire section of the verse, including "and sheep," is missing in that version. It is difficult to believe that these words were missing in the original source, because, in similar contexts, sheep are generally mentioned together with the large cattle. In addition, it is hardly likely that LXX, which tended to increase such numbers *ad majorem dei gloriam,* would not have mentioned such a large number of sacrifices. We undoubtedly have here an example of a *homoioteleuton;* that is, the Greek translator or one of his copyists skipped from one *elef* to another, a type of mistake not infrequent among copyists. [46]

39) I Kings 9:23; see above, item 37.

40) In I Kings 9:28 all versions, including LXX A and L, follow MT. Only LXX B reads "a hundred and twenty" instead of "four hundred and twenty" talents. Here, too, we see an unnecessary attempt at harmonization, with verse 14.

41) In I Kings 10:26, LXX B reads "four thousand stalls for horses" and LXX L reads "forty thousand horses" for MT "a thousand and four hundred chariots." The reason for the emendation is obvious; MT itself has different reports on this number: I Kings 5:6 reads "forty thousand stalls of horses"; this is followed by all the versions. Only a single Hebrew MS reads "four thousand"; this reading was influenced by II Chronicles 9:25, which expressly mentions "four thousand stalls," whereas II Chronicles 1:14 has "a thousand and four hundred chariots," as does I Kings 10:26. Understandably, LXX likewise tried to emend the reading, but while the L text emends the noun to "horses" in accordance with I Kings 5:6, in order to minimize what was considered an obvious exaggeration, the B text, according to the usual method of LXX, prefers the number given in II Chronicles 9:25. (However, the writer overlooked the version in II Chronicles 1:14.) In any case, this was not a copyist's error; apparently the redactors of Kings and Chronicles were following the different sources they had before them. In attempts to reconcile the different reports, LXX recorded figures contradictory to one another. In fact four Hebrew MSS, too, read "a thousand and seven hundred" instead of "a thousand and four hundred."

42) In I Kings 12:21, LXX B alone substitutes "a hundred and twenty thousand" for "a hundred and fourscore thousand" chosen men, whereas all the other versions conform to MT—in II Chronicles 11:1, even LXX B keeps MT's number. Hence this change is of no particular importance.

43) In I Kings 20:15, LXX makes several important changes. Instead of "two hundred and thirty-two" it has "two hundred and thirty," and it replaces "seven thousand" with "sixty thousand" in B and L. Apparently LXX was not satisfied with the number "seven thousand" for the entire people of Israel and therefore increased it to "sixty thousand," possibly to "six hundred thousand," if the missing word was רבוא ("ten thousands"), rather than אלף ("thousands"). The word "two" was omitted, possibly because of its unusual position between "two hundred" and "thirty" (מאתים שנים ושלשים). At any rate, the two changes seem to have been made intentionally.

44) In I Kings 20:30, all the MSS and versions, except the Syriac, agree with MT. The Syriac has "twenty and five thousand" instead of "twenty and seven thousand," possibly in order to emphasize that only a fifth of the Syrian army remained after the defeat by Israel.

45) In II Kings 3:4, LXX A omits "a hundred thousand lambs."

46) In II Kings 6:25, LXX's change from "fourscore" pieces of silver to "fifty" was undoubtedly made because in their opinion the reported price of eighty pieces of silver (the equivalent of more than seventy dollars today) for an ass's head was exaggerated, even during a siege. For this reason they referred to fifty pieces of silver, which better harmonized with the five pieces mentioned at the end of the verse, though they probably considered both an overstatement.

47) In II Kings 7:1, LXX B omits "and two measures of barley for a shekel." This is not a conscious alteration from MT, but merely a copyist's *homoioteleuton* from the first "shekel" to the second.

48) In II Kings 23:33, LXX L and the Syriac version read "ten talents of gold" for MT's "a talent of gold." This change, too, seems to have been made purposely, while in II Chronicles 36:3 LXX leaves the number unchanged.

49) In II Kings 25:19, LXX A reads "seven men" for "threescore men."

Otherwise, however, many verses in I and II Kings are left unchanged,[47] in both the numerous extant MSS and versions.

In the two books of Chronicles, which contain numerous figures, there likewise are relatively few variants.

50) In I Chronicles 4:27, LXX renders "three" instead of MT "six."

51) In I Chronicles 5:21, LXX (and one Hebrew MS) has "five thousand" camels for "fifty thousand." This, too, is apparently not a scribal error but an emendation to eliminate the exaggeration evident to the ancients from experience as it also is to modern scholars (the higher figure seems especially exaggerated when compared with only "two thousand asses").

52) In I Chronicles 11:11, LXX L reads "nine hundred" for "three hundred"; Syriac (one MS): "eight hundred." The latter variant is undoubtedly an emendation in accordance with II Samuel 23:8. Both translators doubtless thought that the chief officer must have slain more than Abishai, who killed "three hundred" (cf. II Samuel 23:18 and I Chronicles 11:20).

53) In the long list of numbers in I Chronicles 12:25–38, there is only one minor change, in verse 36: while MT and all other versions cite "twenty and eight thousand and six hundred," LXX reads "twenty and eight thousand and eight hundred." This may

be an instance of a scribal error, a repetition of the preceding "eight."

54) In I Chronicles 15:7, six Hebrew MSS have "two hundred" for MT "a hundred," and four Hebrew MSS have "twenty" for "thirty." Here the copyist may have been influenced by the preceding verse. There are several variants in figures in one Greek MS [48] both here and in the two preceding verses. Since they do not occur in the important MSS, they need not be considered here.

55) In I Chronicles 21:5, LXX A changes MT's "four hundred threescore and ten thousand" to "four hundred fourscore thousand." Some Greek MSS omit the end of the verse about Judah. The omission is due either to the apparent contradiction to II Samuel 24:9 (although the compiler of Chronicles apparently did not see this passage in Samuel [49]) or—as seems more probable—to a copyist's *homoioteleuton* from the first *hereb* to the second. The reason for the variant in A is unclear.

56) In II Chronicles 7:5, the words "a hundred and twenty thousand sheep" are missing in four Hebrew MSS and in LXX B; see above, item 38.

57) In II Chronicles 11:21, LXX B and Josephus (*Antiquities* 8. 101) write "thirty concubines" for "threescore concubines" in MT. This may indeed be a minor scribal error.

58) In II Chronicles 14:7, all the MSS and versions agree with MT's "two hundred and fourscore thousand," except for LXX A, which has "two hundred and fifty thousand"—again a substitution of "fifty" for "fourscore."

59) In II Chronicles 17:11, LXX B and three Hebrew MSS omit the end of the verse from "rams" on. The omission is likewise explainable as due to a *homoioteleuton* from the first *me'ot* to the second.

60) In II Chronicles 28:8, LXX increases MT's "two hundred thousand" to "three hundred thousand." Perhaps the increase in the number of women and children was made in order to correspond better with the figure of "a hundred and twenty thousand" adult males mentioned in verse 6. For, as will be seen later, the ratio of adult males to the entire population was at most 1:4.

With respect to Chronicles, the instances in which the versions agree with MT are much more numerous than those which disagree. [50]

It will be observed later that many other biblical books contain numbers which are of great concern to us. The variants from MT with respect to these numbers are very few.

The variants described above are tabulated in Table 1.

As the table clearly shows, for the large majority of the 345 verses of the Former Prophets and Chronicles which contain demographically relevant numerical data—and some contain more than one number—there are no textual variants whatsoever. When changes do occur, they are mainly in LXX. In only seven cases do the Hebrew manuscripts contain numerical variants; even there only three or four (in one case six) manuscripts out of hundreds differ from MT. This is also true of the versions other than LXX. The so-called Targum of Jonathan does not differ from MT at all; the Syriac version has eight variants; and the Vulgate, four. With respect to LXX, we have seen that in 25 of the 52 verses here analyzed LXX B or A agrees with MT (see above, Nos. 2, 9, 10, 11, 13, 15, 17, 25, 28, 29, 32, 38–43, 45, 47, 49, and 55–59); and in four more cases (Nos. 23, 33, 48, and 52) only the most radical version, L, generally unreliable, differs from MT, while both of the main manuscripts agree with the accepted text.

These facts are, of course, inconclusive. It is worth noting, however, that the variants are neither numerous nor important, despite the fact that numbers are generally subject to error. In many places the variants can be explained as intentional emendations. Only in the changes from "thirty" to "seventy"—MT has the smaller figure and LXX the larger in the three instances mentioned (Nos. 21, 22, and 30)—and in the changes from MT "fourscore" to "fifty" in LXX, which are found twice (Nos. 46 and 58), can we speak of scribal errors. Similarly, when a section of a verse is missing, as in the six instances cited (Nos. 38, 45, 47, 55, 56, and 59), the copyists may indeed have erred, but merely because of a *homoioteleuton.*

It is also important to observe that the largest number of changes between MT and LXX is found in I Samuel and I Kings, while the smallest is in Judges and Chronicles. One may conclude from this (again disregarding older assumptions) that when the Greek translation of Chronicles was made, the book was regarded as a sacred scripture in which no changes were permitted, while Samuel and Kings were considered less inviolable. In view of the changing attitudes to the sacred character of the biblical books during the several decades of the second century B.C. between the translation of the Former Prophets and that of Chronicles, it is even more sur-

Table 1. Variants from MT
(numbers in parentheses refer to items analyzed above)

Book	Total number of verses reviewed	Hebrew MSS	LXX	Aquila	Peshitta	Vulgate	Josephus	Verses with no variants
Joshua	46	1 (12)	10 (2–11)	–	1 (1)	–	–	34
Judges	54	1 (14)	4 (13, 15–18)	1 (17)	2 (17, 18)	2 (17, 18)	–	48
I Samuel	25	1 (19)	10 (20–29)	–	2 (20, 23)	1 (19)	5 (19, 22, 24–26)	14
II Samuel	19	1 (35)	5 (30–34)	–	–	1 (34)	–	13
I Kings	21	–	8 (36–43)	–	1 (44)	–	1 (36)	12
II Kings	22	–	5 (45–49)	–	1 (48)	–	–	17
I Chronicles	107	1 (54)	5 (50–53; 55)	–	1 (52)	–	–	101
II Chronicles	51	2 (56, 59)	5 (56–60)	–	–	–	1 (57)	46
	345	7	52	1	8	4	7	285

prising to note that the Greek translators of the Former Prophets considered Chronicles to be the older and more reliable source. As we have seen, they emended a number of verses in Samuel and Kings to conform with Chronicles, rather than vice versa. [51] Some modern scholars, to be sure, claim that both Chronicles and LXX made use of a manuscript of Kings which was different from that employed by the Masorites. This conclusion is not supported by the evidence presented here, however. Moreover, in most instances, it is difficult to explain how such strange and important changes occurred in the manuscripts available to the Masorites in the period after the LXX, a period when definite *matres lectionis* and reverence for the traditional texts were firmly established. It is more logical to assume—if we apply historical criticism free of preconceived notions —that the editor of Chronicles possessed not only Kings but also earlier sources. This holds true even if, according to current opinion, he made use of a sort of "Midrash to Kings"—because the author of this "Midrash" undoubtedly also availed himself of earlier sources. Since, during his editing of Chronicles, Kings was not yet considered a canonical text, from which one must not deviate; the editor of Chronicles occasionally followed a source which differed from Kings. The Greek translators apparently considered Chronicles the more dependable source (with their characteristically uncritical approach they may have identified it with the "Book of Chronicles of the Kings of Judah" mentioned several times in Kings) and therefore emended Kings accordingly. [52] One must conclude that, if the current opinion that the LXX translation of the Former Prophets was made around 200 B.C. is true, Chronicles was composed at least several generations earlier.

As was indicated above, however, it is impossible to draw definite conclusions from a study of numbers alone. My aim here in reopening these problems and in reexamining certain matters that biblical criticism has neglected, was but incidental to my quest for demographic source material. What is most important for our purposes is the conclusion that at the beginning of the common era, at the very latest, the numbers mentioned in the Bible had already assumed the form they have today. Whatever changes in the sources had occurred in earlier centuries, and whatever emendations were made by redactors to eliminate inconsistencies, represent but a very small percentage of the accepted numbers, the majority of which have no variants at all. As will be seen later, in the case of those numbers which are most relevant for a study of the population of ancient Israel, all the texts remarkably agree—in an area which is both complex and recondite.

We are confronted with another problem, however: how much credence can be placed in these early sources themselves? A solution cannot be arrived at through critical examination of the texts alone, but must be based on a comprehensive investigation of the inherent probabilities in their broader context. We must examine the many-sided population problems and in ancient times consider the conditions in other countries during that period in order to obtain more reliable criteria, so as to corroborate or refute the data furnished by the ancient sources. [53]

SOCIOECONOMIC PROBABILITIES

Natural increase. Of prime importance to the entire question of population is natural increase, which clearly determines population size so long as it is not canceled by "destructive" (to use Malthus' term) factors. It is well known that natural increase is greatest in countries which practice polygamy. While economic conditions in most countries of this type, including ancient Israel, limit polygamy for the majority of the population, they also make every child an important addition to his father's assets. Malthus' "preventive" factors are therefore of little importance. It is quite probable that the commandment "Be fruitful and multiply" would not have been so acceptable to the masses were it not for these propitious economic conditions.

It is true that the Bible does not mention many instances of polygamy. Those which are recorded mainly concern influential persons who were possessed of considerable wealth and therefore were able to maintain many wives and raise more than the average number of children. Yet these examples can shed some light on the institution in general.

Clearly it was unusual even for kings to possess a harem as large as King Solomon's. [54] His many wives were primarily symbols of his great power and glory; his royal predecessors and successors did not have comparable harems. [55] Nevertheless, many instances of polygamy and multiple progeny outside royal circles are mentioned in the Bible. The following outstanding examples are mentioned in the historical portions of Prophets and Hagiographa: Among the

Judges, Gideon had seventy sons; [56] Jair the Gileadite, thirty sons; Ibzan, thirty sons and thirty daughters; and Abdon, forty sons and thirty grandsons. [57] David begot fifteen sons in Hebron and Jerusalem together "beside the sons of the concubines; and Tamar was their sister." [58] During his time Saul's servant Ziba had fifteen sons. [59] King Rehoboam fathered twenty-eight sons and sixty daughters. [60] After him King Abijah married fourteen wives and begot twenty-two sons and sixteen daughters. [61] Ahab had seventy sons. [62] In the list of Levite families in Chronicles we find that Obed-edom had sixty-two sons; Meshelemiah, eighteen sons and brothers; Hosah, thirteen sons; and the like. [63] It is not surprising, therefore, to read that Shimei the Simeonite, who had only sixteen sons and six daughters and whose "brethren had not many children," belonged to a family that did not multiply "like to the children of Judah." [64] As was mentioned earlier (see No. 26), in connection with the priests of Nob who were killed by Doeg the Edomite, it is reported that there were no less than eighty-five men in Ahimelech's immediate family.

If we add what is related about the Patriarchs, especially about Jacob, who went down to Egypt with seventy people, and about Abraham, who begot many children by his concubines, we realize that in these times families with many children were not infrequent. One can therefore assume that the natural increase alone could at least double the population from generation to generation.

Slaves. The question of slaves is also important in this context. It is obvious that where a country acquires a large number of slaves there is a corresponding population growth. On the other hand, such an increase may be only temporary. Even in countries like Greece and Rome, which at the height of their power maintained tens of thousands of slaves, the growth of the population was not materially affected by the slaves, because it was more economical at times to purchase slaves abroad than to raise them at home, a process which took many years. In addition, many of the male slaves were employed at tasks which kept them away from women. [65] In the Eastern countries, where the system of polygamy permitted slaveowners to treat their female slaves as wives or concubines, the natural increase of the slave population must have been that much lower. [66] Slaves were usually unable to obtain wives, except in rare cases when an owner presented them with female slaves or his own daughters. [67] Since such instances were few and far between, they were not an important factor in population growth.

Slavery was apparently not widespread in Palestine. (For that matter, even in Italy, center of the mighty Roman Empire, slaves never exceeded 30 percent of the population. [68]) It is quite certain that the number of slaves was greater at the beginning of the period of the kings than later. A distinction must be made, of course, between Canaanite and Hebrew slaves. This is not the occasion to determine whether the latter actually were Israelites or whether —as seems to me—they belonged to a special category. [69] In any case, they became slaves almost exclusively because of their inability to pay debts. [70] As early as the Code of Hammurabi we find a prohibition against keeping such people enslaved more than three consecutive years. [71] As is well known, Jewish law also required manumission, after six years. The legal status of the Hebrew female who was sold by her father into slavery was different; yet here, too, the law required that the owner either take her as wife, give her to his son in marriage, or free her. At any rate, she was not enslaved permanently; even if she remained a slave, she had to be manumitted at the end of six years like the male slave, at least according to Deuteronomy 15:17. While it is possible that not all the laws were obeyed to the letter, especially since in these matters the early laws in the "Book of the Covenant" were not spelled out in detail but were expanded by later formulations in Deuteronomy and Leviticus (which went so far as to demand liberal provisions for the manumitted slave), it is safe to assume that in controversial cases the slave demanded his due according to law and that public opinion was on his side. Therefore, the number of Hebrew slaves undoubtedly remained very small throughout the generations.

As for the Canaanite slaves, a distinction must be made between the two periods mentioned above. From the beginnings of the monarchy, including the reign of Solomon, the Jewish people were in an era of political expansion and were extending their might over their neighbors. At that time they took many captives, most of whom becames slaves. After the division of the kingdom and the resultant political decline, more captives were lost than gained in the wars. It can therefore be assumed that the number of Canaanite slaves was greater during the period of David and Solomon than later.

The economic decline influenced the growth of population generally and that of the slave population in particular. When the available food supply decreased, the possibility of supporting a large population was diminished. As a result of the general economic decline, the number of free workers increased; the daily wage became so low that it was more economical to hire workers as needed than to purchase slaves and maintain them throughout their lives. [72] Since money during that period was very costly, [73] a purchase price of thirty shekels per slave, for instance, involved an annual expense of six to eight shekels in interest alone—a sum that equaled the average annual wage of a free laborer. The Bible, in seeking to endear the Hebrew slave to his master, states: "For to the double of the hire of a hireling hath he served thee." [74]

In addition, there was always the danger that a slave would escape if his owner was overly oppressive. That incidents of runaway slaves were of frequent occurrence [75] is indicated by the prohibition in Deuteronomy 23:16 against returning an escaped slave to his master. Such incidents not only directly decreased the number of slaves but also served as a powerful deterrent to the purchase of any but absolutely necessary slaves. [76]

Mortality and natality. The population of Palestine consisted therefore in the main of free men (in the legal sense), [77] whose rate of reproduction generally depended on their own personalities and economic status. For that reason great importance attaches to the ratio of deaths to births. Unfortunately, dependable figures are lacking here, too. There is no doubt that the ancients possessed little information on this subject and could not give us what is called today "precise vital statistics." It is worthwhile, however, to examine several basic factors.

First of all, there is no mention of infanticide or of the slaying of slaves by their masters during the period of the kings of Israel and Judah. Palestine, unlike Greece and Rome, did not sanction exposing defective infants or aged slaves to the elements. On the contrary, the slaying of a free child or of a Canaanite slave was punished most severely. As a last resort, parents could legally bring about the death of a "disloyal and defiant son" only through a court sentence. The primitive Canaanite practice of sacrificing children to idols—a custom which persisted in Tyre and Sidon down to the period of the Israelitic monarchy—had practically disappeared in Israel. While rare examples are mentioned in the Bible, such sacrifices, if any, did not substantially affect the population size of any generation.

Population was more severely affected by *disease*, however, especially by the frequent pestilences, which were intensified by the warm climate and the lack of sanitation. One source describes the death of not less than seventy thousand people in three days because of an epidemic. [78]

Famine. There is less information about the effects of famine during the years of drought which were so common during both the Canaanite and Israelite eras. There is little doubt, however, that few deaths resulted from outright starvation. Not only is there no mention of death from famine (except during periods of siege) in the sources, but Palestine was so near countries rich in grain crops (especially Egypt and Babylonia) and there were such intensive economic relations among these advanced countries that it is almost impossible that crop failures in one area would not have been at least partially made up by surplus produce from another. Occasional famines nevertheless influenced population size in another way. In such times many inhabitants emigrated to other countries. These migrations continued even after the great migratory movements of Semitic peoples during the third and second millennia B.C. had stopped. The Aramaean and Nabataean migrations before and after 1000 B.C. are well known. An unsolved question is whether during this period Egypt no longer absorbed new waves of immigrants from neighboring Palestine as she had in the past. The settlement in Elephantine, which occurred much earlier than the destruction of the Temple, indicates that more was involved than the mere transfer of mercenaries by the kings of Palestine to Egypt [79]—a transfer which, in some respects, constituted a forced emigration.

War. Neither famine nor pestilence was responsible for the greatest number of deaths; the main killer was war. Whether a war was foreign or civil, the death toll in the area of combat was always very high, not only among the soldiers but even more among the general population, including women and children. The Bible speaks a number of times of the need to destroy the indigenous population of Canaan. Although the conquerors could not carry this out in many instances—and, therefore, according to the biblical tradition itself, [80] permitted the native population to continue living peacefully in many localities—there were occasions, both during the era of settlement and later on, when they indiscriminately destroyed the local inhabitants. Suffice it to mention the example of the Amalekites during the reign of Saul, whom Samuel ordered to "slay both man and woman, infant and suckling." [81] And the narrative about David after the capture of Rabbat-Ammon: "And he brought forth the people that were therein, and put them under saws, and under harrows of iron, and under axes of iron, and made them pass through the brick-kiln; and thus did he unto all the cities of the children of Ammon." [82] Although the sense of this verse is not entirely clear, and many commentators have found it difficult to explain, the simplest meaning is that it refers to the captives' unnatural death. Many incidents in which conquered peoples were exterminated can be cited. Nor was the phenomenon limited to Palestine; in all wars in ancient times, whether conducted by great empires or tiny city-states, much blood was spilled. On account of its small area, the whole of Palestine often was like a single battlefield, open to frequent raids by neighbors.

Even more cruel were the civil wars—as noted by Tacitus in another context [83]—because the victor could not easily sell his captives into slavery. The ancient tradition that an entire tribe was destroyed because of an incident concerning a concubine at Gibeah was undoubtedly based on some historical event. [84] Civil warfare was particularly frequent in the Northern kingdom. At the least, with every change of ruler, all the members of the previous reigning family were slain by the new king to prevent an uprising by the heirs of his predecessor. In some respects, even the wars between Israel and Judah were civil wars, and Tacitus' remark applies to them, too.

Since the period after Solomon was marked by almost ceaseless external and internal warfare, it can be assumed with certainty that the population decreased greatly. On the other hand, Solomon's long and peaceful reign must have seen a tremendous rise in population. Even under David, when the Jews fought constantly with their neighbors, almost all battles were waged outside the area inhabited by Israel. There is no comparison between the death toll in such wars and the heavy toll among both soldiers and civilians when a land was invaded by a cruel conqueror. The conclusion seems inescapable that the population of Israel grew until Solomon's death and declined thereafter.

Sex and age distribution. Another important question concerning population is the numerical ratio between the sexes and between various age groups. This question is particularly important in our discussion, because the Bible frequently mentions the number of males twenty years and older. It is known that in most European countries just prior to the First World War the ratio of males twenty and older to the general population was 27–29 percent. Only in France, in 1911, was the ratio somewhat higher, 34 percent. The obvious reason is that in a country whose natural increase is small, as was the case in France at that time, the proportion of adults in the population is always above average. If we apply the converse of this principle to Palestine in the period of the kings, when the birth rate was very high, we must assume that the ratio of males twenty years and over was not more than 25 percent. While infant mortality was undoubtedly high—as it is today in many Oriental countries—accounting for the survival of a relatively small number of children, there were more victims among adult males during the frequent wars than among other segments of the population. The ratio of males of military age to the general population in Palestine was therefore approximately 1:4 and not, as stated occasionally, 1:3. [85]

There were not many in the age group of sixty and over. Although it is impossible to learn the average life span in the various periods of antiquity, there is no doubt that in a country of high natality and mortality, the average life span was so short that but few attained the age of sixty.

We have no definite facts about the ratio of males to females. Some Middle-Eastern peoples have an even higher male birth ratio than is common in the West, but there is no firm basis for discerning fundamental racial differences in this pattern. (Suffice it to compare, for instance, the high birth rate of the French Canadians, with the low natality among the French in their native country during the decades preceding the First World War.) However, even if more males were born than females, the male death rate was much higher, too. Only a low ratio of adult males in the population permitted the practice of polygamy among some men without forcing others to remain bachelors all their lives. Apparently almost all adult Israelites obeyed the commandment to be fruitful and multiply; at least our sources make no mention of "old bachelors." Under prosperous political and economic circumstances—when not only was the death toll among adult males low but many could afford to marry more than one wife each—there may have been a shortage of marriageable females. This would explain why female virgins were often spared by conquerors, while all others were slain.

Urban and rural distribution. Also important to our discussion is the ratio of the urban to the rural population. Here lies, in my opinion, the basic difference in population distribution between the past and the present. It is generally thought today that only highly industrialized countries are thoroughly urbanized and that agricultural states are largely rural, possessing relatively few towns, for the most part of very small size. After the special development of the Middle Ages, our cities have grown largely out of rural settlements, developing slowly into centers of industry and commerce. This was not true in the past, however. In all Mediterranean countries, from western Asia and Egypt to Greece and Rome, there was less political distinction between *urbs* and *rus* than was common in the Middle Ages and is still apparent today. Every ancient regarded himself as the inhabitant of a town even if he did not actually reside within its walls. [86] Most residents of the ancient cities earned their livelihood by tilling the soil. This system explains, to some extent, the peculiar phenomenon pointed out by Max Weber [87]: the historical sources for ancient Israel, like those for other ancient lands, rarely record independent villages of free farmers. Obviously, most farmers were regarded as inhabitants of towns. It is not surprising, therefore, that the Bible—as well as other documents, such as the Tell el-Amarna letters and the Assyrian inscriptions—speaks only about a variety of towns, [88] and not about rural settlements.

Cities of varying sizes were thus quite numerous in ancient times. Scipio the Younger's amazed observation about the multitude of cities in Egypt, which he visited under the reign of Ptolemy VII Physcon, [89] is corroborated by all Egyptian traditions. To be sure, the figures in ancient Egyptian sacred writings which mention eighteen thousand towns, and those of other documents which list thirty thousand or more towns under Ptolemy I Soter, [90] are evidently exaggerated: were we to accept the latter estimate, we would have to assume one township per square kilometer of the inhabitable area, on the average. Yet the true number of towns must have been very large indeed. Diodorus, quoting Hecataeus of Abdera, speaks (according to many manuscripts) of three thousand cities in Egypt, which much more closely reflects historical reality. [91]

Crossing over to ancient Israel, one observes that all the sources mention many towns. The most interesting source probably is Thutmes III's early list (15th cent. B.C.), which enumerates 118 or 119 towns. Most of these towns were in the north between the Mediterranean Sea and the Jordan River. Even if, as some modern scholars maintain, [92] ten of these towns actually belonged to Judah,

and five to Transjordan, at least a hundred towns were located in
the small area between the borders of Judah and Lebanon and
between the Mediterranean and the Jordan. What is even more
surprising is that all, or nearly all, these towns were self-governing
(Taanach and Jibleam are by no means certain exceptions from this
rule [93]). It seems likely that the Egyptian ruler listed only those
towns that had entered into an alliance against him and were therefore each headed by a separate ruler. It is possible that many
smaller towns and, especially, the "habitations" were not even
mentioned in this list. These numbers are corroborated by other
lists of towns in Egyptian inscriptions. The inscription in the temple
at Karnak also lists other victories of this famous pharaoh and mentions 270 towns which he conquered in northern and central Syria.
The towns, which revolted against Rameses II, were all located in
a small area of central Palestine (apparently only in Ephraim and
several sections of Galilee). Nevertheless they were numerous
enough to form an alliance and to revolt against a mighty king.
The list of towns captured by Shishak I (ca. 930 B.C.) when he
attacked Palestine is incomplete; even the capital city of Jerusalem
is not mentioned. [94] The large numbers in all these lists should cause
little surprise, because Palestinian towns were crowded close together. On the outskirts of Jerusalem they were so dense that northward within a radius of but six to ten kilometers were Gibeah
(Gibeat Shaul), Gibeon, Michmosh, Mizpeh, etc., the distances between which were even smaller. Even in Transjordan, which was
always less densely populated, we find, for instance, that Jazer, [95] a
large town, was no farther from the capital Rabbat-Ammon than
twelve or fifteen kilometers, and from Heshbon about twenty-two
kilometers. [96] Between them were located many dependent hamlets.

Undoubtedly, most towns were quite small. There were also different categories: independent towns, and towns subordinate to a
larger town or city. This relationship is reflected in the frequent
biblical phrase "the town and its suburbs." The villages were in
the nature of "suburbs" of the larger towns. If one may compare
conditions mentioned in the Mishnah and the Talmud with those
of an earlier era, four types of settlement can be discerned: [97] the
large town, or kerakh ("fortified city"); the medium-sized town, or
'ir ("city, town"); the smaller town, or tir ("habitation"; during the
biblical period tirah meant "an encampment of tents"); and the
smallest settlement of all, the kefar ("village"). [98] Apparently every

kerakh [99] was surrounded by a wall; when an *'ir* was walled it was called *'ir beṣurah* ("fortified town").

Since the towns were mainly small, one cannot deduce the size of the population from their number; nor is an increase in their number proof of population growth. Towns tend to continue to exist even under conditions which would make the foundation of a new town impossible. Normally, there is a constant rise in the number of towns, because the older towns remain and new ones are added. Of course, there have been exceptions. For instance, the era of destruction in the wake of the Mongolian invasion of western Asia brought about a marked decrease in the number of towns. Aside from that crisis, unequaled in all history, the destruction of a given town has usually been of temporary duration. In Palestine only one town, Jericho, ceased to exist after its conquest; and tradition tells us that even Jericho was rebuilt despite the curse imposed upon it [100] (it may never have been entirely laid waste [101]). On the other hand, we read of the founding of new towns throughout the generations. It is sufficient to recall the best-known example, the building of Samaria on a spot that had formerly been an uninhabited hill. [102] It is, therefore, not surprising that Sennacherib reports that his conquests in Judah—aside from Jerusalem, which he unsuccessfully besieged—included forty-six fortified towns and numberless others. [103]

An examination of economic conditions in those times will help shed light on these matters. Just as the political distinction between city and village is essentially the result of the developments of the Middle Ages, so the economic differences between them are of comparatively recent origin. In ancient times the city was not exclusively a center of "urban" occupations; nor was cultivation of the soil limited to rural inhabitants. Actually town dwellers were mainly what we would call "farmers" today. While they had to go outside the town to till their fields and vineyards, their actual habitation was within its walls, as a protection against the raids by brigands or enemies which were so common then. A large number of small towns—in contrast to the relatively small number of large cities today—thus met the economic and social needs of the times. If a variety of small towns was necessary in all ancient countries, it was doubly so in ancient Israel with its great natural diversity. Its small area embraced so many different climates and topographic conditions—suffice it to note the differences between the seashore and Transjordan, between the mountains and plains, between North and South, and so forth—that no less than forty different natural regions have been counted. [104] For all these reasons, numerous small political areas clustered around tiny urban centers.

Another basic factor must be emphasized. According to Karl Julius Beloch, [105] it is axiomatic that a country which exports grains and wine is underpopulated, while a country which imports its staples has a comparatively large population. This principle applies, however, only to Western countries today. Generally, it is quite possible for a highly productive agricultural country to feed a larger population than its own. While a commercial people pays for imported food from the sale of its industrial output or from commercial profits, an agricultural land must export even some of its nonsurplus produce in payment for necessary imports. It sometimes is forced to do so by cutting down the food supplies of its own population.

Once again, Egypt serves as a good example. As was stated earlier, its population in 1925 was nearly 14 million, living in a limited area. (In 1970 it increased to 34 million in a slightly larger area.) In that year the excess of imports over exports of all food products was valued at only 2,306,000 Egyptian pounds. [106] If we judge by the then normal price of wheat—14 Egyptian pounds per 100 kilos (although in 1925 there was an unusual rise in price [107])—they imported little more than 16 million kilos, or less than 1.25 kilos per capita for the entire year. This amount supplied only a tiny portion of the population's requirements; the rest came from domestic production. In addition, it must be realized that in the preceding few decades Egypt had begun to increase its cotton production. In 1925 the area allotted for cotton consisted of 22.5 percent of all cultivated lands. [108] Even if we assume that a certain portion of this area was formerly wasteland [109] and that cultivation is more efficient today than in ancient times, it is still remarkable that what remained under grain cultivation in such a small area could feed so many millions. Since there was intensive cultivation in ancient times (including the digging of irrigation ditches for better use of the waters of the Nile), it is quite possible that during the Pharaonic period the annual productivity was not much smaller than today. We also know that during the period of the Roman occupation of Egypt, when the population amounted to at least 7–8 million, the country was constantly able to export a substantial portion of its agricultural output to the imperial capital of Rome.

For this reason, one must not draw the conclusion that, because Palestine exported agricultural products, it possessed a small population. [110] One must consider the entire economic structure, especially the country's foreign trade. Within the scope of this study, of course, I cannot analyze these complicated problems in detail, but can only refer to a few major aspects. It cannot be denied that over the centuries Palestine exported not only its excellent fruits, wine, and grapes but also grains. The figures for Solomon's payment to Hiram, king of Tyre, for wood and labor Hiram had supplied in the building of the Temple (according to one source, Solomon paid "twenty thousand measures of wheat, and twenty measures of beaten oil"; [111] according to another, "twenty thousand measures of beaten wheat, and twenty thousand measures of barley, and twenty thousand baths of wine, and twenty thousand baths of oil" [112]) are indicative of the state of Palestine's general economy during that period. On the other hand, it is known that there were large imports of manufactured articles: excavations have revealed that much pottery was imported from Mediterranean islands, whether directly or through the Phoenicians, although an important local ceramic industry was being developed at the same time. The importation of metals was very important for the economy; ancient Israel possessed some iron and copper mines, [113] but their output was not sufficient for the country's growing needs, especially the military. Equally well known are the expeditions sent by Solomon and Hiram to Ophir in order to obtain gold, ivory, and exotic beasts to adorn the king's palace and the Temple. It seems that even when the Red Sea was barred to Israel by the no longer subject Edomites, trade relations with southern Arabia did not cease entirely, and caravans continued to bring gold and spices from Arabia Felix. [114] Palestine paid for all these imports with the excess of its agricultural production.

This export did not prevent the population from expanding in normal times, however. To the extent that luxuries were imported for the king and the wealthy, the populace was made poorer, since its consumption was reduced in order to provide "excess" produce to pay for the imports. But so long as there remained enough produce to provide the very minimal level of subsistence prevalent in Eastern lands, the population did not decline. One must distinguish, of course, between periods of prosperity and depression. During the reigns of David and Solomon, and later in such exceptional times as the reign of Rehoboam II, subject nations paid tribute to Israel in gold and silver or in agricultural produce and livestock. [115] The cost of importing precious metals was thereby reduced, and a local excess of agricultural products was achieved. It was different when the enemy was victorious: then it was the Israelites' turn to pay tribute; whatever form this took, it was ultimately paid for in agricultural products, which meant a general tightening of the belt. Moreover, the enemy often laid waste many areas of the country, so that agricultural productivity was reduced. During such periods, we must assume, the poor often did not have even minimal sustenance. The direct results were greater infant mortality, emigration (to the extent that it was feasible, as stated earlier), and the other usual adverse manifestations of defeat and famine. It is therefore obvious that the population of Palestine must have declined after the Solomonic era.

POPULATION ESTIMATES

What, then, was the population of ancient Israel in the period of the kings?

It is clear from the above that the number was not stable throughout the period; the population was almost certainly greater under David and Solomon than later. An analysis of the available data will now follow.

Official censuses conducted by governments, as we recall, were sufficiently common even in ancient times. Precise lists are extant from the time of the Middle Kingdom in Egypt, in which the members of each family were listed by its head in a declaration under oath. Eduard Meyer is justified in his statement [116] that it is only by accident that still older lists have not come down to us. Actually, important statistical information is found on the Palermo Stone, dating from the Second Dynasty (about 3000 B.C.). [117] It is, therefore, not surprising that in ancient Israel, too, a number of censuses were made (albeit of a slightly different nature), especially during periods of orderly administration.

Our basic source is the biblical account of the census taken by Joab, David's chief of staff, of males of military age. There is a longer version in II Samuel 24 and a shorter one in I Chronicles 21;

the final figures vary in the two accounts. The first (II Sam. 24:9) reads: "And Joab gave up the sum of the numbering of the people unto the king; and there were in Israel eight hundred thousand valiant men that drew the sword; and the men of Judah were five hundred thousand men." The version in I Chronicles (21:5) is: "And all they of Israel were a thousand thousand and a hundred thousand men that drew sword; and Judah was four hundred three-score and ten thousand men that drew sword." Most significantly, there are no important variants in either the manuscripts or the versions of these verses. [118] It must be assumed, therefore, that these figures are as they appeared in the primary sources. But the question remains, how historically dependable are the facts recorded in the sources, such as the numbers of people counted by the enumerators? Modern critics place little credence in them, claiming that the figures are exaggerated. If, they state, we accept Samuel's figures totaling 1,300,000 men and we add at least twice that number for all the women and the men under twenty, the population of Palestine would approximate four million, an impossible figure for so small a country. [119]

Let us analyze all the possibilities dispassionately, however. According to the thesis I stated earlier, the number of soldiers should be multiplied by four, with the result that the population under David's reign would have amounted to about five million. With respect to the conflict between the figures in Samuel and Chronicles, almost all modern commentators accuse the Chronicler of his usual exaggeration. However, the Chronicler's figure of 470,000 Judeans is actually 30,000 less than Samuel's figure. It is reasonable to assume that his first figure of 1,100,000 also represents a decrease and that, therefore, it stands for the entire army—Israel and Judah together. [120] Since the Chronicler's figure of 470,000 Judeans is more exact than Samuel's round number of 500,000, it may be supposed that Samuel's figure for the Israelites—800,000—is also a round number and that actually there were tens of thousands fewer. It appears, then, that Samuel's actual sum total was not much greater than 1,200,000. The remaining difference of little more than 100,000 men between the totals in Samuel and Chronicles can be accounted for when we consider that Chronicles explicitly states: [121] "But Levi and Benjamin he did not number among them; for the king's word was abominable to Joab." We must bear in mind that Benjamin had undergone great sufferings during the Gibeah conflict and that the tribe's "mighty men of valour" numbered exactly 59,434, [122] while the number of adult male Levites was about 54,000, estimated from another account in Chronicles. [123] Thus there appears to be no basic disagreement between the two sources: Chronicles gives a more precise figure of 1,100,000, which excludes Levi and Benjamin, whereas Samuel adds these two tribes and gives a more approximate sum of 1,300,000.

We may perhaps assert, therefore, that the two texts are mutually corroborative. Yet one may still ask to what extent their figures are really acceptable. One fact must be kept in mind: the census was taken in a much larger area than ancient Israel proper. According to II Samuel 24:5–8, it began in Aroer (located at the Arnon Wadi), continued to the land of Tahtim-hodshi (which apparently should be emended—according to almost all modern commentators, who base their reading on the LXX L version—to the land of the Hittites at Kadesh, that is, on the Orontes River), and reached Sidon and the stronghold of Tyre "and all the cities of the Hittites and of the Canaanites." Although the text adds "they went out to the south of Judah, at Beersheba," it does not mean that they stopped there, since the country south-southwest of Beersheba was not desert land in that period. [124] In addition, the entire richly populated Edomite settlement stretched to the east.

Certainly, David's chief of staff had no reason to limit himself to the geographic confines of ancient Israel. David, the greatest conqueror in Israelite history, who had occupied most of the neighboring countries, is said to have extended his reign over an area stretching from the Red Sea to hundreds of kilometers north of the mountains of Lebanon, and from the Mediterranean to the Euphrates. Since the census was taken for two reasons—to find out how many men were eligible for military service and to establish the tax rolls—it was not necessary for David's commander to distinguish between the real Israelites and the subject peoples.

It is surprising only that the boundaries of Moab are not mentioned. Apparently David did not wish to commence with Moab, either because its population had suffered great losses in defeat; or, as seems more likely, because he was waiting for Joab's return from his census-taking of Judah. At any rate, it is almost certain that Joab reached Kadesh on the Orontes River in Syria and included in his census the conquered Aramaean tribes. This hypothesis is to some extent corroborated by the Aggadah. The fact that Joab and his men spent nine months and twenty days at this task—and yet, according to Chronicles, did not complete it—drew surprised comment from the talmudic sages. They readily perceived that a counting of the Jews in Palestine could have been accomplished in much less time, and they inferred that Joab had delayed the execution of his mission because he thoroughly disliked it. [125]

The inclusion of other peoples in the census also explains the strange ratio between Judah and Israel. On the basis of area and other factors, the ratio is usually assumed to be 1:3 (see below), whereas here it is given as less than 1:2. The reason is that the figure for Judah includes all the neighboring peoples (the Edomites, the Moabites and, possibly, some of the Philistines), while that for Israel includes only the Ammonites, the rest of the Philistines, and some of the Aramaean tribes.

The entire area of the census measured at least 50,000 square kilometers, [126] on which lived a population of high density. Contrary to Eduard Meyer's opinion, [127] Edom was thickly populated at that time, as were the Transjordan areas of Moab, Ammon, the two and a half tribes, and the Aramaeans. It is, therefore, not surprising to find throughout the area an average density of 100 persons per square kilometer. The population of Israel *per se* may have been even more concentrated; nevertheless, it constituted not much more than one-third of the total population covered in the census.

An examination of the figures for Egypt and Babylonia is enlightening. At their height these countries were richer and mightier than ancient Israel, even during David's reign; their populations were also larger. To be sure, the Egyptian statistics are obtained from somewhat later Greek sources. Yet, as quoted from Hecataeus of Abdera by Diodorus Siculus (who is generally precise in his figures), [128] it appears that during the period of the last Pharaohs— that is, shortly before Cambyses' conquest—Egypt embraced some 7,000,000 inhabitants. Accordingly, the density (for the populated area of about 30,000 square kilometers) was about 230 persons per square kilometer. These figures are corroborated by Herodotus, who lived only a short time later and made use of an Egyptian source contemporary with the census and undoubtedly based on accurate official lists. [129]

It is quite possible that during periods of growth in the Early and Middle Kingdoms, the population was greater than at the end of the period of independence after the Assyrian and Persian con-

quests. Especially during the Middle Kingdom, Egypt greatly
extended its sway over its neighbors and brought back countless
slaves, either captured in war or imported on Phoenician ships. [129a]
In addition to this increment and the natural increase by birth, a
constant stream of immigrants steadily augmented the Egyptian
population. Only rarely did an invading enemy destroy an appreci-
able segment of the population. Wars fought on foreign soil took
little toll, even over thousands of years, because the methods of warfare were very primitive.

What has been said here about the population of ancient Egypt
also applies to Babylonia in its heyday. This country, despite its
large size, was only partially inhabited, its population clustering
around the Euphrates River (rather than around the Tigris, contrary to present practice). [130] This limited area of habitation, while
slightly larger than that during the reign of Caliph Omar, when it
measured only 11,000 square kilometers, [131] was never greater than
30,000 square kilometers, even if we count all the area up to the
Thirty-fourth Parallel. [132] Yet the population numbered in the millions. As will be seen later, the capital city alone contained some
400,000 inhabitants. At the beginning of Persian rule, the Babylonians, together with some of their neighbors, paid the treasury
1,000 silver talents, while the Egyptians paid only 700 talents.
Babylonia's population was therefore at least as large as that of
Egypt. [133]

A comparable population distribution existed in Assyria, whose
plain is extremely narrow and whose habitable area was not greater
than 12,000 square kilometers. [134] Yet, this small country succeeded
in conquering the Babylonian Empire and in building the capital of
Nineveh, a beautiful walled city containing hundreds of thousands
of inhabitants.

Observing that Egypt, Babylonia, and Assyria often had a density
of at least 200 souls per square kilometer, and at times had one even
greater than that, one cannot regard an average number of 100 persons per square kilometer in ancient Israel and its neighboring countries in their prime as exaggerated. It is certain, moreover, that at
the end of the Second Commonwealth the population of Palestine
was at least 2.5 million, and possibly 3 million in an area larger than
Judah during David's reign but smaller than his kingdom as a
whole. [135] As mentioned above, we assume that there was not a continuous growth in the population, but rather periods of rise and

decline. What was possible in population size in Herod's time and later was not impossible during David's and Solomon's reigns.

The above figures are supported by most other sources referring to the period of the early kings, if we discount the occasional obvious exaggerations. There is one basic difference, however: unlike David's census, which enumerated one whole segment (the adult males) of the population, other sources list only smaller groups—for example, the number of warriors who participated in some battle, the number slain or captured, or the number of workers engaged in some task. The totals estimated from such partial figures are not trustworthy, since even contemporaries could only deduce them by guesswork. This basic difference must be kept in mind; and even some undoubtedly exaggerated figures do not, as some modern investigators have insisted, reflect on the reliability of David's census.

Nevertheless, these figures, too, have a certain value. If, as I have tried to show above, the numbers have been transmitted directly from early sources, and the question is only how well-informed and accurate were the authors of these sources who were contemporaneous or nearly so with the events described, then it is important for us to know what these recorders themselves regarded as possible. In the final analysis, they addressed themselves to their own generation and could therefore not afford to be too fanciful in their exaggerations. Obviously, texts of much later date than the narrated events inspire less confidence; that is why we rely least upon the latest source, in this case the Chronicler. While for David's census and several other reports, Chronicles draws on early sources and possibly even, directly or indirectly, on official lists extant from David's time, its sources for other numbers undoubtedly dated from a period much posterior to the events reviewed. Moreover, the Chronicler doubtless intentionally exaggerated at times in order to extol the Almighty.

While numbers generally tended to loom larger with the passage of time, one must not ascribe this penchant exclusively to a desire to glorify the past. The exaggeration in Chronicles, like that in the writers of the late Roman Empire, is readily understandable. Glorification of the past is characteristic of individuals and peoples in a period of decline. Just as old men are likely to extol their youthful years with extreme overstatements, because those years had, indeed, many advantages over old age, so in world history during periods of growth there is a belief in development and progress. On the other hand, periods of decline are marked by pessimism about the present and a belief in a golden age of the past. During the period when most of the Chronicler's sources, as well as his own work, was composed—namely, from the Babylonian Exile through the Return, down to the Hellenistic era—the status of the Jewish people was inferior to that under the reign of the Israelitic kings. Even the period of the divided monarchy did not compare in power and glory with the reigns of David and Solomon. However, one must refrain from drawing the false conclusion that all late writings are unreliable; they are, after all, sometimes based upon early sources, and they frequently view events in better perspective than their modern successors.

One of the important questions concerns the numbers given in Chronicles for the various tribes. In one passage it is expressly stated that the count occurred "in the days of David." [136] It seems possible that these numbers were preserved in special scrolls, according to tribes and perhaps also to the larger clans, and were actually used by the Chronicler, or at least by his sources. This hypothesis has some support in the fact that he has refrained from using any but transmitted data; for that reason we are given the clan lists of only three or four tribes. We have already cited the figures for the tribes of Levi and Benjamin; these figures are not rounded off and are to be considered factual if we accept as historically valid the total number of those counted by David's order.

The same may be said of the tribes of Issachar and, to a certain extent, Asher. The number of Issacharites is given as 87,000, which fits with the total number of persons counted; this number is also corroborated by the number of clans—fifteen, each containing an average of 5,800 persons. [137] The figures cited in Numbers [138] do not controvert these data. [139] According to I Chronicles 7:40, Asher numbered 26,000. This figure is surprising: both the number of clans (thirty-seven) mentioned in Chronicles and the numbers in the Pentateuch and in Chronicles itself [140] lead us to expect a much higher figure. Perhaps this tribe, living near the coast and possessing natural and commercial resources, attracted the attention of conquering armies and thus suffered great losses during the Philistine attacks. Located as the tribe was between the Sidonians and the Philistines, it would have lost both territory and population. At any rate these figures show that the compiler of Chronicles does not always exaggerate; even though they seem to contradict his own figures and those given in the Pentateuch, which he undoubtedly knew, he apparently attempted to transmit all of them as he found them.

With respect to the numbers given in the story about King David's coronation in Hebron (I Chron. 12:23–38), it cannot be assumed that an actual count was taken of all who came to that celebration. The figures were from the outset a mere guess, and in themselves are therefore of little importance to us. What interests us are, first, the relationship between the numbers and, second, the reliability of the original source. It is obvious that the compiler faithfully adhered to his sources. He must have been surprised by the fact that only 6,880 members of David's own tribe of Judah and 7,100 of the neighboring tribe of Simeon (which generally followed Judah) had attended, whereas no less than 50,000 had come from Zebulon, 37,000 from Naphtali, and as many as 120,000 from the two and a half Transjordanian tribes. Yet he did not alter the record on his own. [141]

Elsewhere, in the report (I Chron. 27:1–15) that David divided the people into twelve equal "courses," each of 24,000 men, the equality of division is suspect, though not entirely impossible. [142] If "courses" were organized in such a way that each served a month, it is reasonable to assume that they were of about equal size. There would then have been 288,000 men in all the Israelitic tribes. A comparison with the great census shows that this figure might well represent the total of all the Israelite males aged twenty and over. When we add the priests and the Levites as the remnants of the unintegrated original inhabitants, we arrive at the ratio that we have established for Israelitic Palestine as against the entire Davidic empire, 1:3. It is worth noting that if this tradition is valid, it seems that David had already divided the country into political entities based upon population (although he still maintained the tribal division, as indicated by I Chronicles 27:16–22, which tells of his appointing captains of the tribes).

On the other hand, the figures about Saul's and David's armies are unreliable. It is interesting, however, that they all fit into a definite pattern and are, therefore, not mutually exclusive. While the numbers themselves, given in thousands and tens of thousands, are undoubtedly exaggerated, the relationship between them is fairly consistent; moreover, they seem to have been taken without change from the original sources. If, for example, the figure in I Samuel 4:10 of 30,000 Israelite foot soldiers lost is an overstatement, the fact of a serious defeat is historically true. There is no mention of horsemen and chariots, which, indeed, had not yet been used in the days of Samuel. The other verses also appear to be more or less consistent. On occasion the writer himself seems to be aware of his exaggeration. [143] Generally he is less concerned with precise numbers than with the broad aspects of the events.

Thus one cannot expect complete objectivity. Since in each case acceptance, modification, or rejection of a particular figure must be left to each investigator's discretion, we cannot avoid arbitrary decisions. While many verses are undoubtedly close to the truth, [144] others are marked by overt exaggeration, although even some of these may not be wholly useless. [145]

We do have two reports of a census taken during Saul's reign, [146] but Saul's count cannot be compared with that of David. According to Scripture itself, it was not the entire population in its respective settlements that was counted, but only those who joined the army. Since such counts were taken as a matter of course by military commanders, who had to know the size of their forces, we cannot deny the historicity of the census *per se;* however, the accuracy of the numbers given in the two passages in the book of Samuel is highly questionable.

We have no definite figures about the population in the time of Solomon; but the tangential information we do possess largely corroborates his father's census. Thus when we read that Solomon's *corvée* force consisted of 180,000 men supervised by "three thousand and three hundred" (or "three thousand and six hundred") overseers, [147] we have no reason to regard these figures as an exaggeration. He really had need of the thirty thousand cutters of trees in Lebanon, "fourscore thousand that were hewers in the mountains" (stonecutters; perhaps also ironworkers), "threescore and ten thousand that bore burdens": the construction of the Temple, the royal palace, and other buildings lasted twenty years and required many workers, given the primitive technology of the period. In general, public works of this type were performed by tens of thousands of laborers (we have already mentioned Pliny's report about the number of people working on the Egyptian pyramids). An enormous work force was necessitated by the crude tools available and by the lack of good roads (despite the "royal highways" that were in existence as early as the megalithic age). If a report from a later period [148] is true, that Solomon constructed a large highway, similar to the Roman roads, this project, too, surely required a large labor force. It must be remembered that in those days wagons and chariots were employed only for military purposes or for pleasure and display, while heavy burdens were transported by camels and donkeys or, often, on the backs of porters. It is also a fact that people working under the lash are less productive than voluntary workers; thus more of them are required. The report that 150,000 of Solomon's laborers were foreigners residing in Palestine and only 30,000 were Israelites (according to Kings) is also credible, because at that time many inhabitants had not yet become integrated with the Israelites. In addition, the conquered (rather than merely tributary) areas readily supplied manpower for *corvée* labor.

The aforementioned numbers of Solomon's horses, chariots, and horsemen—notwithstanding the contradictions between the sources —seem plausible if we accept some median figures. [149]

About the later kings we have but scant information. The report in I Kings 12:21 that Rehoboam gathered "all the house of Judah, and the tribe of Benjamin, a hundred and fourscore thousand chosen men" is not improbable, despite the vast number, because in times of great crisis he tried to draft as many men as possible from among the two loyal tribes. This number actually conforms with what was said above about the result of his grandfather's census, if we take into account the natural increase during the prosperous Solomonic period. On the other hand, the number given in II Chronicles 12:3 for King Shishak's army, which attacked Palestine during Rehoboam's reign, is not based upon precise enumeration. The ratio between 1,200 chariots and 60,000 horsemen is unusual; and the addition of the remark "the people were without number" indicates that the author was not concerned with exact figures.

The size of Rehoboam's son Abijah's forces, mentioned in II Chronicles 13:3, may not refer to actual combatants, but rather to their potential strength. Even this was based not on a new census but on memories of the Davidic period. In any event, the population ratio between Israel and Judah is almost the same as in that census. However, the number cited in verse 17 is obviously exaggerated, as are those of the soldiers under Asa, king of Judah (II Chron. 14:7), and of the army of Zerah the Ethiopian (*ibid.*, v. 8). It is worth noting, however, that no mention of iron chariots is made in connection with Asa's army, and only three hundred chariots are attributed to Zerah.

Only once do we find a number which is surprisingly small; but it, too, is reasonable. It is reported that Ahab numbered the Israelites as only "seven thousand," [150] a figure which can be explained by the fact that after the unforeseen attack by Syria only a small number of Israelites escaped to Samaria. Actually we have an outside source relating to Ahab in the famous inscription of the Assyrian King Shalmaneser III about the battle of Karkar, in which Ahab participated as Aram's ally. According to the inscription, Ahab headed two thousand chariots and ten thousand foot soldiers. [151] It is worth noting that the author of Kings refrained from changing that small number, although it must have seemed questionable to him. Contrariwise, the alleged slaying of "a hundred thousand footmen in one day" [152] is undoubtedly exaggerated. It should be mentioned in this context that an official census of "all Israel" is said to have been taken by Jehoram son of Ahab (II Kings 3:6), but the results are not given.

As is well known, conditions in Judah improved briefly in the reigns of Amaziah and his son Uzziah. Nevertheless, the figure in II Chronicles 25:5 of "three hundred thousand" males twenty and over is undoubtedly a gross exaggeration, even if we add to the Judeans the Edomites who had been subjugated by Amaziah. Moreover, the word "gathered" implies that he had assembled all the men in one place, which is surely impossible. It is also difficult to believe that "a hundred thousand" Israelite "men of valour" were hired by Amaziah at a total cost of "a hundred talents of silver," which would indicate a price of 3 (or 3.6) shekels per man. [153] On the other hand, the report that "ten thousand" Edomites were defeated by Amaziah in the Valley of Salt is most probably accurate. [154] The number of captives (mentioned only in Chronicles) and the number of slain in the cities of Judah [155] are plausible; so are the figures in II Chronicles 26:12 and 13 relating to the "two thousand and six hundred" heads of families and the "three hundred thousand and seven thousand and five hundred" soldiers ready "to help the king [Uzziah] against the enemy." It is not stated that all the soldiers had assembled in one spot, but only that this was the number of males twenty and over. Moreover, this figure very likely included some of the subjugated Edomites and Philistines and perhaps also tribute-paying Ammonites.

We have now reached the period of the destruction of Samaria and the war against Sennacherib. Here we have much important information. It is stated in II Kings 15:19 and 20 that Menahem king of Israel imposed a tax of fifty shekels on each "man of valour" when he had to pay a tribute of "a thousand talents of silver" to Pul king of Assyria. Assuming that a talent at that time contained 3,000 shekels, the "men of valour" numbered 60,000. Since these men were undoubtedly the owners of large estates, whose income enabled them to purchase their own arms and to pay taxes, some idea can be formed of the size of the population. While some scholars believe that the reference is to all soldiers twenty and over, [156] the fact is that soldiers able to equip themselves were few in number. As mentioned earlier, one of the reasons for the small number of slaves in Palestine was the low wage scale for agricultural laborers, who were either landless or whose land was too small to support a family. It is therefore certain that many of the farmers were hired workers and not "men of valour." Likewise, few of the craftsmen and traders in the urban population were among the "men of valour." If we add these free residents and slaves to the "men of valour," the adult male population would be at least three or four times greater than 60,000. If the "men of valour" together with their families numbered approximately 240,000, it would not be an overstatement to say that in Menahem's time the northern kingdom possessed a population of 800,000 to 1,000,000. [157]

This estimate refers only to the period before 733 B.C. In that year Tiglath-pileser III occupied most of the land of Samaria and exiled most of its inhabitants, only the capital city and its surroundings (Mount Ephraim, etc.) remaining independent. [158] The environs fell into Shalmaneser's hands in 725. We are not told what happened to the inhabitants, but it seems that some of them went into distant exile. Finally, Sargon captured Samaria itself and, according to his inscription, [159] exiled 27,290 people—a large proportion of its inhabitants, although it is possible that their number was increased by refugees who had flocked to the city before the siege.

These numbers are corroborated by the information we possess about Sennacherib's subsequent war with Judah. Most scholars accept the claim in his famous inscription that he sent 200,150 men, women, and children into exile. [160] Sennacherib did not succeed in capturing Jerusalem. As will be seen below, the population of the capital may be estimated to have consisted then of 30,000 during normal times. Undoubtedly many refugees swelled the ranks of the inhabitants prior to the siege, and the city must have contained at least 50,000 to 60,000 persons who had sought refuge from the enemy. It is also probable that not all the inhabitants of the country had been exiled, even if that was Sennacherib's intention—a matter about which we have no information. Many thousands must have hidden in caves or escaped temporarily to neighboring countries hoping to return to their native land after the conflict. It can be estimated, therefore, that Judah possessed at the end of the eighth century B.C. at least 300,000 to 350,000 inhabitants. Taking the ratio of the population to the area of some 4,000 square kilometers, the density was 70–80 persons per square kilometer. Most of the country of the Ten Tribes was more densely populated, because its economic and political development was higher (Galilee was always the most productive area in Palestine); on the other hand, there were less populous areas as well, notably in Transjordan. It is also probable that after the defeat many northerners fled southward, augmenting the ranks of Judah in the following two decades. [161] At any rate, the population density of Israel was probably not too far removed from that of Judah, and its 12,000 square kilometers therefore embraced about 800,000 to 1,000,000 inhabitants. Both states jointly did not have more than approximately 1,100,000 to 1,300,000 people at that time. Considering the influence of political and economic decline upon population figures, the decrease from the period of David is not surprising. [162] The Bible contains no direct reference to the size of Israel's population or the army at that time. We are told twice that "a hundred and fourscore and five thousand" of the camp of the Assyrians were smitten by a pestilence. [163] While this number is not above suspicion, [164] it is in line with the number of captives who are said to have been exiled from the country.

This devastation of the countryside in the days of Hezekiah left its permanent impress upon the land. Even if we assume that most of the refugees returned after the danger was over, [165] they, together with the remnant, could not have numbered much more than a hundred thousand, or but a third of the prewar population. Notwithstanding the repatriation of a few of the distant exiles, the catastrophic effects of Sennacherib's occupation were felt until the destruction of Jerusalem itself. As a result, the Edomites were able to penetrate northward, settling as far as Hebron. While this penetration was prompted mainly by the pressure of their southern neighbors, the Nabataeans, the progress of the Edomites was made possible by the decline of the population of Judah. Until that time it was Judah which had thrice conquered Edom—in the reigns of David and Solomon, Jehoshaphat, and Amaziah-Uzziah—but Edom had never controlled Judah. [166] Despite the general opinion that the Edomite expansion took place after the destruction of the First Temple, it was actually a slow and gradual process, the best opportunity occurring after Judah's invasion by Sennacherib. Judah's decline also explains why Babylonia in 597 B.C. [167] annexed the southern portion, which was weakly held by the Judeans, rather than the north, which was nearer.

A similar situation may have occurred in 733, when Assyria annexed those northern Israelitic areas which for more than a hundred years (from Baasha to Jeroboam II) had been under Aramaean rule. [168] The Israelite character of the population had been weakened by that time, and the ensuing decades did not suffice to make it wholly Israelitic again. The Edomite infiltration may also explain the peculiar hatred which arose between Judah and Edom in the period just before the Destruction of the Temple, and not only after the Restoration, when the returning Jews found their country occupied by Edomites. [169] This must be kept in mind in considering the period of the Destruction of the First Temple—at least after 597 B.C. —when the area of Judah no longer extended to the Red Sea, nor even to Beersheba, but perhaps only to Hebron. On the other hand, the last kings of Judah, especially Josiah, exploited the weakness of Assyria at the end of the seventh century to penetrate northward, annexing Beth-el and Jericho and reaching, if only temporarily, Megiddo. [170] Nevertheless, the general area of Judean settlement had greatly decreased, apparently occupying only about 2,500 square kilometers in 586, instead of the former 4,000.

That is why the traditional figures relating to the population in the period of the Destruction of the Temple in 586 are relatively small. Even if Judah had interveningly recovered from its devastation by Sennacherib, the constant warfare from the period of Josiah onward caused a decline, or at least arrested the growth, in the population. During that period, therefore, Judah probably numbered no more than about 150,000 persons.

A large proportion of the population was exiled by Nebuchadnezzar to Babylonia, not in a single expulsion but over a period of years. The figures in the sources are not clear on this point. One source states that in the seventh year of Nebuchadnezzar's reign "three thousand Jews and three and twenty" were exiled; in the

eighteenth, "from Jerusalem, eight hundred thirty and two persons";
in the twenty-third, "seven hundred forty and five" Jews; and that
"all the persons were four thousand and six hundred." [171] Modern
commentators usually explain that the first group came from the
provinces; the second, from Jerusalem; and the third, some years
later (from both). [172] Another source presents entirely different figures: II Kings 24:14–16 states at first that the king of Babylon carried away "all Jerusalem, and all the princes, and all the mighty
men of valour, even ten thousand captives, and all the craftsmen
and the smiths"—and then, more precisely, "all the men of might,
even seven thousand, and the craftsmen and the smiths a thousand."
The difference cannot be settled by saying that Jeremiah refers only
to males, because he uses the general term "persons [nefesh]." The
discrepancy has foiled all the commentators. [173] It seems to me,
however, that the sources recording the number of exiles comple-
ment each other in the following fashion: In Nebuchadnezzar's

seventh year (598 B.C.) 3,023 [174]
eighth year (597 B.C.) 8,000 men [175]
eighteenth year (587 B.C.) 832 persons [176]
nineteenth year (586 B.C.) 10,000 persons ("the rest of the people") [177]
twenty-third year (582 B.C.) 745 persons [178]

were exiled. To review the historical development: In 598 the Babylonian king conquered all the lands up to the Brook of Egypt, [179]
including Judah (with the exception of Jerusalem). At that time he
exiled 3,023 "Jews" (or Judeans = Yehudim) from the south. The
figure in Jeremiah (52:28) refers specifically to "Jews," as distinct
from Edomites who had settled among them and may also have been
exiled (at any rate, there is no direct reference to Edomite aid to
Nebuchadnezzar against Jehoiakim, whereas hostile bands of Aramaeans, Moabites, and Ammonites [180] are mentioned). Upon Jehoiakim's death his son Jehoiachin ascended the throne while the war
was still going on. During Jehoiachin's brief reign Nebuchadnezzar
captured Jerusalem, in 597, and exiled the king's family, together
with 7,000 "men of might" and 1,000 craftsmen and smiths. [181] At the
same time Nebuchadnezzar placed Zedekiah on the throne and
annexed the southern area up to Hebron. At the end of the ninth
year of Zedekiah's rule (588–587 B.C.) the war broke out anew. In
587, the eighteenth year of Nebuchadnezzar's reign, the Babylonian
king exiled 832 men from Jerusalem. This small number comprised

those who had "fallen away" to the Chaldeans during the war, in accordance with Jeremiah 38:19. [182] It is explicitly stated that some of the captives were taken by Nebuzaradan to Babylon. [183] After approximately a year and a half Jerusalem fell (586 B.C.). The king and his men were captured in Jericho, and "the rest of the people" were exiled to Babylon by Nebuzaradan. How many exiles were there after "the poorest of the land" had been left to be "vine-dressers and husbandmen"? It is hard to determine, but surely fewer than the 27,290 who had been exiled from Samaria; after all, the smaller country of Judah had suffered destruction after destruction. Perhaps the passage in II Kings 24:13–14 does belong here, since almost all scholars agree that it is out of place in its present context. If so, there were 10,000 captives, including "all Jerusalem," and in fact also all the princes, men of valor, craftsmen, and smiths who had remained behind after the first deportation or had arisen during the intervening eleven years. Finally, in 582, perhaps as a penalty for participating in Gedaliah's assassination, 745 "Jews" were exiled from among the remnant, which in the meantime had been increased by returning refugees and reduced by those who escaped to Egypt. (The use of the term "Jews" once again denotes the ethnic Jewish group in contrast to the other settlers who had infiltrated into the depopulated country.)

What was the proportion of the 598–582 exiles to the total population? The answer depends upon our conclusions about the numbers for the two great deportations in 597 and 586. There is little doubt that in the first exile only adult males were counted, although they went into exile with their families. Multiplying by four, we obtain a figure of 28,000 persons for the families of the "men of valour" and 4,000 persons for the families of the craftsmen. Less than 20 percent of the entire population belonged to the soldier families and less than 3 percent to the craftsmen. Taking into account that not all were exiled at the same time, however, but that quite a number of both categories remained, it is not surprising that we obtained the aforementioned 24–30 percent ratio of soldiers to the rest of the population in Menahem's time. The 10,000 exiles in 586—if we are correct in assigning that number to that year—included more persons (female as well as male) of the "poorest of the land" than of the soldiers and craftsmen. The total of all the exiles during the 598–582 period numbered approximately 47,000, or about one-third of the population. If we allow for those

who were undoubtedly exiled from the provinces in 587, when
Nebuzaradan captured Judah before laying siege to the capital
(the number of these exiles is not mentioned in the Bible); those
who were slain or died of famine; and the numerous refugees both
during the war and after Gedaliah's assassination, we realize that
the population suffered a serious decline. The larger towns were
most affected, while the smaller settlements of the vinedressers and
husbandmen better managed to stay on. The extent of the country's depopulation is evident from the prophecy (perhaps slightly
exaggerated) made by Jeremiah (44:2) in Egypt about Jerusalem and the cities of Judah: "This day they are a desolation,
and no man dwelleth therein," a fact largely corroborated by
archaeological findings, especially for the city of Jericho. [184] While
a remnant continued to dwell in the country, even prior to the
Restoration, the number of those who returned (according to
Ezra-Nehemiah: "forty and two thousand three hundred and threescore, beside their men-servants and their maid-servants, of whom
there were seven thousand three hundred thirty and seven; and
they had two hundred singing men and singing women") [185] was
small compared to the Jewish community on the Tigris and
Euphrates, which probably was increased by remnants of the
ancient exiles from Samaria. As is well known, those exiles had
settled in Halah, Habor, at the Gozan River, and in the cities of
the Medes. [186] From the first three places it was easy to reach the
environs of the great "rivers" and particularly those areas around
the city of Nippur, where the exiled Jewish community was concentrated. This ramified problem is beyond the scope of the present
study, however.

CITIES

All these matters are partially corroborated by investigations into
the urban settlements in Palestine. It was mentioned earlier that
Oriental countries of the past cannot be compared to European
countries in the Middle Ages and in modern times. Even at the end
of the nineteenth century, before Zionist colonization brought some
industrialization into the country, Palestine's urban population was
relatively large. In the 1870s it was estimated at about 30 percent
of the total population. A more accurate census, held some years
later, indicated a growth of 115 percent in the urban population and

only 70 percent in that of the villages. [187] Generally, economic conditions in the 1870s and 1880s were less favorable than in the period of the kings. It is highly probable, therefore, that in ancient times the urban population constituted an even larger segment of the inhabitants of Palestine.

As I have earlier stated, the cities, while numerous, were small. If we take Thutmes III's list of cities as a basis for comparison, one finds that the north had more than one hundred towns in an area of 5,000 square kilometers. Accordingly, the ethnographically Israelitic area in the two kingdoms contained from three to four hundred towns. A large number of these were surrounded by walls. Hence it is not surprising to read in Sennacherib's well-known inscription that he had captured, in Judah alone, forty-six walled towns and others "without number." [188] There appear to have been at least a hundred to a hundred and fifty settlements that could be called towns or cities in the southern kingdom.

Further corroboration is derived from the description of the conquest in Joshua 13 ff., a source older than the period of the Destruction of the Temple. [189] The tribe of Judah (together with Simeon [190]) received 112 (or 123) [191] towns, mentioned by name—even if we do not include the Philistine towns which were under Israel's political control but cannot be considered Jewish settlements. Benjamin [192] had 26 towns. The southern kingdom thus contained 138 (149) towns in all.

As to the northern kingdom we have accurate figures for only four tribes [193]: Zebulun had 12 towns; Issachar, 16; Asher, 22; Naphtali, 19. In addition, 18 towns can be assigned to the territory of Dan. [194] In Transjordan Reuben appears to have received 13 or 14 towns (with or without Aroer), which are mentioned by name as within its boundaries, and "all the cities of the table-land, and all the kingdom of Sihon king of Amorites." Gad obtained "all the cities of Gilead and half the land of the children of Ammon." Only four towns in the "valley" are mentioned by name. The half tribe of Manasseh possessed, in part, "all the villages of Jair, which are in Bashan, threescore cities." Perhaps we ought to read "thirty cities"— as in Judges 10:4 (LXX "thirty-two"; I Chronicles 2:22 "three and twenty")— instead of "threescore." [195] The descriptions relating to Ephraim and the other half of the tribe of Manasseh are even less detailed. Considering, however, that Ephraim was the largest tribe and the most urbanized, and that it contained no fewer towns than

Judah, the towns of the northern kingdom numbered at least 250.

At this point one should mention the number of towns which, according to tradition, were allotted to the Levites among the southern and northern tribes. [196] The ratio is 13:35, although it may have been somewhat higher in the north to compensate for the smaller number that they received in Judah and Simeon (9 out of 112 or 123) for reasons which need not be entered into here. In Zebulun the ratio was 1:3 (this number is somewhat suspect); in Issachar, 4 out of 16, or 1:4; in Asher, 4 out of 22, or 1:5.5; in Naphtali, 3 out of 19, or 1:6.3. [197] Since even in Ephraim they received only 4 out of a possible 100 or more towns, we can assume that their average ratio in the north was 1:7. This gives us a total of 245 (7 × 35) towns in the north. Since the ratio of Levite towns in the south is only 1:11, the average ratio in all of Palestine is 1:8, and the total number of all the towns in Palestine is 384 (8 × 48). [198]

Dividing the area of ancient Israel by a round 400—the approximate number of towns—we note that, on the average, there was a town for each 40 square kilometers and the distance between urban settlements was about 6 kilometers. This is not surprising in view of what has been said about the role of cities in those times. Moreover, we know that there were even shorter distances between some cities. As was mentioned earlier, Diodorus' figure of 3,000 cities in Egypt gives a ratio to the settled area of one city per 10 square kilometers —a very densely populated region, indeed. The difference in development between Israel and Egypt accounts for the different ratios.

These urban settlements were for the most part so small that even the citizens of the walled cities did not always live within the walls. This was especially true of growing cities; the walls were not rebuilt from generation to generation to accommodate the population increase. Only in the case of ancient Babylon do we read that two sets of new walls were constructed in succession—in Nebuchadnezzar's days. [199] But this was related to the extraordinary development—unparalleled in the ancient Middle East—of a city which but one hundred years before (in 689) had been almost totally destroyed by Sennacherib. Nor did ancient Rome contain within its walls more than a fraction of its inhabitants. Growing cities were therefore always densely populated within their walls and embraced additional dwellers outside them.

How many persons may we then attribute to an average permanent urban settlement? Taking as a basis for comparison modern

Middle-Eastern cities, we note that in the 1880s Baghdad had one inhabitant per 33 square meters, Jerusalem one per 35, and Jaffa one per 30. [200] Once again the difference between East and West must be kept in mind. In the East, a warm climate and other factors permit very small dwellings, requiring a limited area. [201] Israel was more densely populated in its ancient heyday than in the early twentieth century; but, in my opinion, C. Schick goes to the other extreme in overestimating the density when he states that at the time of the second fall of Jerusalem there was one person per 8.78 square meters, or 10.5 square yards. At most, the population density of ancient Israel was comparable to that of mighty Tyre during its almost unbroken era of peace and prosperity before its conquest by Alexander the Great—when it contained what might be called the skyscrapers of antiquity. [202] When Alexander entered the city, he found about 70,000 inhabitants in an area of 90 hectares, [203] or one person per 13 square meters. Considering that the degree of development of each city varied, that at times a city wall may have enclosed some open spaces, and that occasionally the political entity of a city included the sparsely inhabited environs beyond the wall, we can conclude that ancient Israelitic towns required an area of some 15–50 square meters per inhabitant. It must be remembered that the role of the Palestinian city was to protect and shelter the surrounding farmers, who accepted the necessarily limited living quarters so long as they could have the protection of the walls during emergencies.

Regrettably, we know about the area of but a few ancient Israelitic cities. Our main reliance is on archaeology, since written records offer no clues (except in the case of Jerusalem at a later period). While archaeology cannot give us precise information about the total size of any city, it can furnish us reliable evidence concerning the circumference of the walls. For example, we know that in the Canaanite period Jericho included within its walls an area of 2.35 hectares; Taanach, 4.8 hectares; and Megiddo, 5 hectares. [204]

Assuming that at that time, when Canaan had attained a high degree of cultural development—although not the equal of that of the subsequent Israelitic population—the ratio was one person per 30–50 square meters, we derive the following estimates: Jericho, 500 to 700 inhabitants; Taanach, 1,000 to 1,400; Megiddo, 1,000 to 1,500. These numbers do not appear too small when we consider

that military forces in the El-Amarna period were also very minute—
for example, an expedition of twenty soldiers was deemed sufficient
to be sent to Egypt. [205] With the passage of time the situation
changed, of course, and cities grew either in area or in population
density. Jericho, for instance, had a wall 180 meters larger when it
was rebuilt during the period of the Israelitic kings; its area was
increased to approximately 4 hectares. [206] M. Lurie [207] is correct in
his conclusion that, based upon the size and number of its houses,
Jericho's population was 1,000 to 1,500 and at most 2,000, which
gives us a ratio of one inhabitant per 20–40 square meters.

A city of 1,000 to 2,000 in population was thus considered important in ancient Israel, because the great majority of the hundreds
of townships embraced a population of 1,000 or less. There were,
of course, much larger cities, particularly the two capitals, Samaria
and Jerusalem. About the first we have almost no information,
except through some comparison with the latter. As to the much-
debated population of the southern capital, most modern scholars
have arrived at the figure of 25,000 at the time of the Destruction. [208]
It is best to start with the information we possess about the city
from a later period and to work backward. Although space here
does not permit a detailed analysis, the following can be ascertained: At the end of the Second Commonwealth the circumference
of the wall surrounding Jerusalem measured, according to Hecataeus
of Abdera, 50 stadia; according to "The Letter of Aristeas," 40; and,
according to Josephus, only 33. The variation is perhaps due to
differences in defining the length of a stadium. I do not think I am
exaggerating if I estimate the area of the city at that time to have
been about 300 hectares. [209] Jerusalem at the time of Josephus was,
accordingly, about one-third the size of Babylon during Nebuchadnezzar's reign or of Alexandria during its prime in the reign of the
early Roman emperors, and one-fourth as large as Rome itself during its period of grandeur in time of the Aurelian emperors. Since
in those days Rome's population was about a million and Babylon's
about 400,000, it is not surprising that Jerusalem's had reached
almost 200,000. This means a ratio of one person per 15 square
meters, a plausible figure. [210] It had thus grown from the days of
Hecataeus, when it was estimated at only 120,000 inhabitants. [211]

What was the population of Jerusalem before the destruction of
the First Temple? We have only a slight record from the beginning
of Israel's domination over the city. While the source is undoubtedly

of late origin and is found only in I Chronicles 9, it appears to have been based upon early, authentic documents. [212] According to this information, the city contained 690 families of the tribe of Judah, 956 of the tribe of Benjamin, and 1,760 of the priests. The large number of priestly families should not cause us to view the statistics with suspicion, because, if we accept the existence at that time of a specialized group charged with the sacred cult, it undoubtedly was concentrated around the royal palace, in the area where the Temple was shortly to be erected. At any rate, it is to be assumed that the Levites were also included in the number of priests, although Levites are separately mentioned only later, when the "porters in the gates" are said to have totaled 212.

True, it is likely that the compiler of Chronicles confused here figures based upon conditions in his own time with those of the ancient period. Yet this relates only to the priests and does not invalidate his numbers pertaining to Judah and Benjamin. On the contrary, the numerical relationship of the families of the two tribes—the majority belonging to Benjamin, which inhabited the neighboring area—is proof that the figures were taken from an early source, and is corroborated by the names mentioned in the context. The two tribes numbered 1,646 families in all—or 2,000, if we add some of the members of Ephraim and Manasseh. Inasmuch as families were large and often had a number of slaves, there would have been well over 10,000—perhaps 20,000—inhabitants.

While Jerusalem may not have been so populous right after its conquest by David, it very probably reached this size during the years of his reign (which, according to tradition, lasted thirty-three years in Jerusalem). During Solomon's reign it undoubtedly gained in size. Since it gradually became the real center of Judah, we should not assume that its population decreased markedly during the period of economic decline. As mentioned above, cities possess a peculiar vitality which sustains them during periods of depression, so long as there is no severe and decisive crisis. Even in times of depression the population usually remains static, although, relatively speaking, this might be considered a sign of decline. Even after the defeat by Sennacherib, when the state was reduced to the environs of Jerusalem, the great religious revival under Josiah and the centralization of worship in the capital helped maintain the former size. (Centralization may indeed have been facilitated by the concentration of the Judean settlement in the vicinity of

Jerusalem after the gradual penetration of the Edomites into the country as far as Hebron.) But we must not assume that the city continued to grow much under Josiah or that it reached the heights which it was to attain during the Second Commonwealth. At that time it not only was the geographical center of Palestine but also the spiritual magnet for the many Jewish settlements in the Diaspora (a fact noted even by King Agrippa I [213]), whose members numbered in the millions.

To establish the population of Jerusalem on the basis of the city's territorial extent during the period of the First Commonwealth is far more difficult, because its exact size is unknown. I. Benzinger's assertion [214] that the area of the city before the Babylonian Exile was half of what it was at the end of the Second Commonwealth is undoubtedly exaggerated. In the period of Sennacherib, when the population of all Judah was slightly more than 300,000, Jerusalem could not have contained more than one-tenth of that number, or 30,000. [215] Even this number was possible only because the city had attained that size during the reigns of David and Solomon, when it served as the capital of a much larger country and retained it during the subsequent decline. Samaria's situation was different. Although the Northern state was three times as large as Judah, its capital was only slightly bigger than Jerusalem. While all the figures with respect to this city are purely speculative, [216] it would not be unreasonable to suppose that its population before 722 was 30,000 to 50,000.

To sum up, ancient Israel before the year 733 B.C. possessed from 300 to 400 cities, most of which contained only about 1,000 inhabitants, while the two capitals each had a population of about 30,000 or more. Between these two extremes there undoubtedly existed medium-sized cities. Just as there is good reason to believe that the five Philistine cities which existed for hundreds of years as independent city-states, capable of waging mighty wars, possessed populations of 5,000 or more, so must it be assumed that there were Israelitic and Judean cities of comparable size. The urban population in the two kingdoms amounted at that time to at least 400,000, or about a third, in a general population of 1,200,000. This conforms to what might have been expected on the basis of my earlier general reasoning.

Table 2 summarizes my conclusions. It is evident from the table that while the general population decreased in the period from 1000

Table 2.   Population of Ancient Israel *

	1000 B.C.	733–701 B.C.	586 B.C.
Judah	450,000	300,000–350,000	150,000
Israel	1,350,000	800,000–1,000,000	—
All of ancient Israel	1,800,000	1,100,000–1,300,000	150,000
Per square kilometer	100	70–80	60
Conquered peoples	3,000,000	—	—
Number of cities in ancient Israel	300–400	300–400	60–70
Urban population	400,000	400,000–500,000	70,000–80,000
Jerusalem	15,000–20,000	30,000	20,000
Samaria	—	30,000–50,000	—

* Figures are approximate

to 733, the urban segment remained constant, and actually rose in proportion to the rural population. The two capital cities, especially, expanded both in population and in area. During the decline of Judah, after 733, the urban population likewise suffered less than the rural.

The ratio of urban inhabitants to the entire population can be estimated as follows:

In 1000 .... 22.5 percent
In 733–701 .... 36–38 percent
In 586 .... 46–53 percent

The reason for the increasing percentage is obvious. Despite the size of the country during David's and Solomon's reigns, many cities were still inhabited largely by non-Israelites; little by little the Israelites became the majority, and finally all the inhabitants blended into one people. After the division of the two kingdoms new or rebuilt cities, such as Samaria and Jericho, were established, while Jerusalem continued to develop. In addition, defense requirements increased, because of the frequent attacks upon the country and the villagers' quest for shelter behind strong city walls. During the seventh and early sixth centuries almost all the population of Judah became concentrated in and about Jerusalem. Most of the time the cities suffered fewer population losses than the countryside. This situation was interrupted, however, by the catastrophic Assyro-Babylonian invasions, which were much more destructive of the cities than of the villages.

PART II

Medieval Islam

4

Some Medieval Jewish Attitudes
to the Muslim State[*]

WE POSSESS a rather considerable literature of both primary and
secondary sources relating to the treatment of the "protected subjects" (*dhimmis*) in the great Caliphate and its successor states in
medieval Islam. True, that information is often one-sided and
incomplete: the medieval Arabic sources, from which it is largely
derived, tend to stress certain dramatic events, for the most part
unfavorable to the religious minorities, rather than the daily rhythm
of life in calmer periods. Critics of A. S. Tritton's well-known study
of the status of the minorities in the Caliphate have rightly pointed
out that, because Tritton referred almost exclusively to these one-
sided sources, his book reads like a collection of records of unmitigated oppression. [1] We know much less about the attitudes of these
"minorities" (for a long time the Christians and the Zoroastrians
had actually constituted the majorities in their respective areas) to
the Islamic state, however. Understandably, spokesmen for these
groups refrained from defining their respective outlooks in comprehensive and detailed formulations. Even the relatively few casual
and often oblique references to existing conditions have thus far not
been subjected to that close and many-sided scrutiny on the part
of modern scholars which they deserve. Hence the following observations are intended more to raise questions than to supply definitive
answers.

The difficulties of ascertaining such attitudes are indeed staggering. To begin with, one can hardly consider that the same attitudes
characterized the three major non-Muslim religions: Christianity,
Judaism, and, for a time, Zoroastrianism. There certainly was a basic
difference between the outlook of Greek-Orthodox Christians and
Zoroastrians, who from dominant majorities quickly saw themselves
transformed into tolerated minorities, and that of Jews, who merely
exchanged one new set of masters for two earlier ones. Even those

[*] The substance of this essay was presented in a lecture delivered at a colloquium on the Middle East at Ohio State University at Columbus, Ohio, on
May 16, 1968.

Christian sects who welcomed the Arab conquerors as liberators from the severely oppressive Byzantine regime, after a few genera- tions, looked yearningly toward the independent Christian states in both the eastern and western Mediterranean. It is truly amazing how little solidarity existed among these embattled minorities, which often fought one another more sharply than their common adversary, Islam. [2]

A second, even more decisive, obstacle to a true comprehension of the prevailing Jewish attitudes—and I speak of attitudes in the plural because no single approach to the question was universally shared by the various Jewish communities—stems from the lack of adequate documentation. Obviously, we do not know to what extent the ideas formulated by the few outstanding leaders whose works have come down to us, such as Saadia, Halevi, or Maimonides, reflected the thinking of the Jewish masses. The man in the street, Jewish, Muslim, or Christian, was as a rule quite inarticulate. His feelings are generally reflected only in occasional, indirect references in chronicles, homilies, folkloristic tales, or responsa, references which, however, rarely shed light on basic political problems, including personal attitudes to the state and to society at large. Grievances about the alleged wrongdoings of certain officials, even if true, need not demonstrate a general hostility to the administra- tion of the country. On the other hand, a monarch's benefactions or friendly words might have been readily extolled beyond their merits by personal favorites, and been uncritically accepted in wider circles. If we hear, for example, of frequent accusations by Jews that the Muslim judiciary was deeply corrupt, these were not necessarily a reflection of prevailing hostility to the central government; still less did they reflect on the attitude to the state as such. Denuncia- tions of this type were frequently heard in Muslim circles as well, and they were indubitably justified in a great many instances. In addition, rabbis had a special motivation in exaggerating the short- comings of the Muslim tribunals, so as to enhance the willingness of their coreligionists to repair exclusively to Jewish courts. Yet at least in the case of the Baghdad courts we have the noteworthy recognition by R. Hai Gaon that they were careful in admitting only truthful witnesses and that the deeds arranged by them were fully acceptable to Jewish tribunals—though elsewhere Muslim courts were "full of lies and prevarications" and, hence, their documents had to be disqualified. Many provincial judges, especially in

Kairuwan and Spain, were roundly repudiated by the rabbis; Moses b. Ḥanokh of Cordova, for example, wrote: "Their sentences are unjust even when they deal with Muslims, how much more so in the case of Jewish parties. They rely on testimony borne almost exclusively by false witnesses." [3]

CHRONOLOGICAL DIVERSITIES

It may be taken for granted that attitudes changed with changing realities. There were, of course, basic transformations during the later Middle Ages and early modern times, when the dominant groups in the Muslim world were Mongols, Mamelukes, and Turks; alongside Persians, and Africans of predominantly Berber origin. Even during the first six centuries of Muslim rule, the age of Arab predominance, one may distinguish three major periods: (1) the expansion and consolidation of the Great Caliphate during the first three centuries; (2) its dissolution into component parts during the following century and a half; and (3) the era of the Christian Crusades and the Mongolian invasions, lasting another century and a half and beyond. Regrettably, our documentation concerning Jewish life and thought during much of that early, decisive period is extremely limited, since at that time very little was written by Jews on any subject, and still less has come down to us. It so happens that during the first two centuries after the *Hejirah* all the major decisions of Islam were made concerning political structure and theology; for it was at that time that the Qur'an, the sayings of Muḥammad, and other elements of tradition and law received their vital formulations, which affected the thinking of Muslim sages, jurists, and administrators for all following generations. With respect to the status of "unbelievers," the so-called Covenant of 'Umar (which may or may not have been proclaimed during the short reign of 'Umar II [717–20]) succinctly summarized the existing discriminatory regulations aimed at establishing the superiority of the Muslims over the large masses of the *ahl adh-dhimma*.

Echoes of Jewish reactions to these far-reaching decisions are very scarce. Whether in the liturgical output of *piyyuṭim* or in the homiletical lucubrations of the various *midrashim*, the continuity of the talmudic thinking of the Perso-Byzantine age is so obvious that only a few allusions to the Muslim period have been detected. Assembled with, or interpolated into, earlier sayings, these allu-

sions help us date the documents in question, but tell us little
about existing conditions or political attitudes. Nor are the juridically interesting compilations of the *Sefer ha-Ma'asim* and the
various *massekhtot qetanot* any more informative. Even from the
mid-eighth century on, when a trickle of more comprehensive
exegetical and halakhic works by Jews, both Rabbanite and Karaite,
began to appear, very little can be deduced from the sources concerning any kind of political theory which may have underlain the
juridical considerations. To some extent the various apocalyptic-
messianic writings of the period are more revealing. Despite their
general vagueness and frequent escapes from reality, they offer us a
few glimpses into the thought processes of their authors, who must
have reflected some of the deep yearnings of the masses. For one
example, the *Tefillah* (Prayer) of R. Simon b. Yohai has been
ingeniously reconstructed by Bernard Lewis as consisting of four
distinct layers, dating from the seventh century to the era of the
Crusades, and as significantly mirroring the changing views of some
Jewish leaders. In all deductions from such deliberately obscure
compositions, however, we must bear in mind the caveat recently
suggested by Paul J. Alexander with reference to medieval Christian
apocalypses: "It will not do to interpret every apocalyptic prophecy
as a *vaticinium ex eventu* and to base the date of apocalyptic documents on such an assumption. In interpreting an apocalypse the
historian should never lose sight of the possibility that the author
may have been an intelligent observer of current affairs and have
attempted genuine prophecies of future happenings based on his
appraisal of the direction in which events were moving." [4]

Only from the tenth century on do we possess an extensive Jewish
literature in Arabic, Hebrew, and Aramaic which furnishes us insights into the thinking of some of the outstanding leaders of those
generations. But this was the period of the so-called Renaissance of
Islam, a term which by no means typifies the state of affairs in most
Muslim countries even in that era. It was still less characteristic of the
permanent relationships between the ruling groups and their subjects throughout the Middle Ages. The tenth century coincided,
moreover, with. the progressive dissolution of the Caliphate. Even
medieval Arab historiography recognized that the years 920–21
were a dividing line between the still united empire, extending from
India to the Atlantic, and the rise of independent states which were
often locked in combat with one another. According to Hamzah

al-Isfahani, the prosperity of the Arabian Empire had lasted only 177 years and now gave way to growing anarchy. With reference to slightly later conditions, another Arab historian, Jalalu'ddin as-Suyuti, graphically described the great confusion in all affairs of the Caliphate in 936-37. [5]

Long before this political disintegration, and contributing to it, there arose within both the majority and the minorities great internal divisions. For the most part they assumed the form of sectarian movements and generated a great many divergent intellectual expressions. In certain circles, religious and philosophic debates dominated the thinking of various groups, which often cut across denominational lines. Even the caliphs of the ninth century, including the fairly orthodox Harun ar-Rashid as well as the more liberal Al-Ma'mun, greatly enjoyed listening to such debates between exponents of diverse religious and philosophic points of view. One might say that with the revival of Greek learning also came an appreciation of ancient rhetoric, and one can almost imagine that the ancient Sophists were once again arguing, under new guises, their varied approaches to the riddles of human existence. Among these disputants, as a rule, reason reigned supreme. Even Abu 'Umar Aḥmad ibn Sa'id, a visiting Muslim Spaniard of the tenth century, was shocked by the unwonted spectacle of mutual toleration which he witnessed in the philosophic conventicles of the imperial capital. He later recalled:

I twice attended their [the philosophers'] assemblies. . . . At the first session there were present not only Muslims of all sects, but also agnostics, Parsees, materialists, atheists, Jews, and Christians, in short, infidels of all kinds. Each of these sects had its spokesman, who had to defend its views. As soon as one of these spokesmen entered, the audience stood up reverently, and no one sat down until the spokesman took his seat. . . . "We are assembled to discuss matters," one of the unbelievers declared, "you all know the conditions. . . . Each one of us shall use exclusively arguments derived from human reason." These words were universally acclaimed. [6]

This spirit of mutual toleration soon gave away, however, in the sharp conflict between Islam and Christendom during the era of the Crusades. Suddenly the Jews found themselves placed between two violently warring civilizations, and suffered from the increased religious fanaticism on both sides. To be sure, the Jewish people had long since learned to live in a divided world. For a millennium one important segment of Jewry had resided in Parthia-Persia, while a larger mass had flourished and declined under the Graeco-Roman civilization. Now the majority dwelled under the rule of Islam, but a substantial, growing minority lived under Christendom, at that time torn asunder by the Great Schism between East and West. It took the extraordinarily keen perceptiveness of a Maimonides to realize that the future of Jewish culture rested with the small Western communities, filled with a pioneering spirit and a zest for learning, rather than with the languishing Middle-Eastern masses. [7]

Both ancient and medieval Jewish sages often saw a hidden blessing in that life between two worlds. Not only did some ancient rabbis coin the well-known religiously inspired epigram that God had bestowed his grace upon Israel by dispersing it among the nations to spread the religious and ethical teachings of Judaism, but an early medieval writer actually claimed that God had divided the world "in order to preserve Israel." [8] Yet there is no question that the major upheaval caused by the Crusades induced Jewish thinkers like Halevi and Maimonides to reassess the Jewish position in a divided and mutually antagonistic world.

RUDIMENTARY POLITICAL THEORY

We must bear in mind, however, that medieval Jewish thinkers in general devoted little time or effort to speculations on political problems. Even economic theory, which might have reflected the daily concerns of the Jewish masses as well as the leaders, found no spokesmen among Jewish intellectuals. When I tried to obtain some kind of understanding of the economic views held by an authoritative thinker like Maimonides, I had to derive most of my information indirectly, from the Fustat sage's statements relating to law or to general philosophy. [9] Even less directly relevant to their outlook on domestic policies or international relations are the casual observations scattered through the vast range of rabbinic letters. The philosophers themselves, in fact, paid but scant attention to the political doctrines espoused by Plato, Aristotle, or Alfarabi. [10]

Unlike the Christian scholastics, medieval Jewish thinkers, especially Maimonides, did not regard the state as the fruit of sin but a necessary evil. Nor were Muslim leaders, despite the greater political orientation of their faith, necessarily advocates of state power. According to S. D. Goitein, "religious people shunned government

service and regarded government in general as the very substance of
the forces which opposed God's rule on earth. A pious man would
not accept an invitation to dine from a government official . . . since
most of government's revenue was thought to emanate from extor-
tions, law-breaking, and oppression of the weak." [11]

Most Jewish thinkers, on the other hand, though far from
enthusiastic on the subject, considered the state and other social
aggregations essentially God-willed institutions. The individuals or
groups in power could behave sinfully and commit untold misdeeds
without reflecting upon the institution as such. This was particularly
true of the personal conduct of the ruler. Partly because of fear of
retribution for adverse criticism, and partly because of the widespread fashion of epistolary flattery, but most decisively because of
the age-old tradition, going back to Jeremiah, that Jews pray for
the welfare of the country (and its rulers) in which they reside,
Jewish subjects rarely cast aspersions even on evil monarchs. Summarizing the vast documentation available in the Genizah, written
largely under governments of bad repute among modern historians,
S. D. Goitein observes:

Nowhere . . . do we find the slightest allusion to this state of affairs,
nor any word of disapproval or criticism. Rulers are mentioned in
connection with impressive acts of justice or favors granted by them,
or when their armies were, or were expected to be, victorious in
battle. The opposite, states of oppression and lawlessness, defeats, as
well as economic disasters, are never attributed to them, but are
accepted as a decree of God. . . . The person of the ruler was
sacrosanct.

In a later period, Maimonides, echoing Aristotle, considered human
beings "social animals" and clearly implied that, without agreement
upon submission to a leader, "so that the natural variety be submerged in the great conventional harmony and the community be
well organized," there would be no well-ordered human life. At the
same time these thinkers did not totally reject voluntary separation
from the community, and the leading of a lonely existence, if the
society in which one lived happened to be dominated by evil forces.
Maimonides admits that

if all the cities a man knows, or has heard of, follow a bad course as
in our day, or if he is prevented through the insecurity of the roads,
or through illness, from emigrating to a city where good customs

prevail, he ought to live a lonely life. . . . But if evildoers and sinners make it impossible for him to stay in the city without mixing with them and adopting their wicked customs he ought to withdraw into a cave, an abandoned field, or a desert. [12]

Other, more mystically inclined authors, like Baḥya ibn Paquda, evinced greater appreciation for a solitary life devoted to contemplation and mystic union with the Deity. But these differences were of minor importance to the Jewish community at large, most members of which unhesitatingly recognized the state as an indisputable reality.

No Jewish life in the dispersion would have been possible without the recognition by Jews that their fate greatly depended on the behavior toward them of their non-Jewish monarch and his subordinates. Some compromise between the communities' desire to stave off external interference with their traditional way of life and the rulers' wishes to control the conduct and resources of their subjects had been effected long before the third century, when the Babylonian rabbi Mar Samuel formulated his famous maxim "The law of the kingdom is law." While leaving the implications of this principle and its wide ramifications undefined, the sage of Nehardea clearly conveyed the idea that Jewish law recognized the validity of state enactments affecting all citizens, including Jews. His medieval successors likewise refrained from formulating comprehensive political theories of their own, because, as Maimonides phrased it, "on all these matters philosophers have written many books which have been translated into Arabic, and perhaps those that have not been translated are even more numerous. But nowadays we no longer require all this, namely the statutes and laws, since men's conduct is determined by divine regulations." [13] Nonetheless, as a subject minority, Jews had to recognize that obedience to state enactments was a necessary condition for their survival.

Remarkably, we find little in the Jewish literature written under Islam of the argument, presented by many medieval rabbis living under Christian domination, that Jews were "aliens" to the soil, which belonged to the Christian rulers; and that the latter, having of their own will extended protection to these aliens, were also entitled to withdraw it. Perhaps this divergence may be explained by the fact that the Jews had lived in Palestine, Babylonia, and the surrounding Middle-Eastern countries without any real break for many centuries before the advent of the Arabs. Connected with the ancient origins of their communities was the relative absence of expulsions from, and readmissions to, individual Muslim lands, while such occurrences became increasingly frequent in the Western countries during the later Middle Ages. True, the somewhat abnormal Caliph Al-Ḥakim in early eleventh-century Egypt could, in a fit of intolerance, destroy Christian and Jewish houses of worship, without necessarily suppressing the two faiths. More radically, the Almohade sect, after seizing power first in Morocco and then in Spain, actually outlawed both Judaism and Christianity. However, even after this exceptional outburst of total intolerance, the rulers required mainly lip service on the part of the alleged new believers, a great many of whom in fact retained their loyalty to their ancestral faiths. In general, Jews felt that whatever local expulsions occurred were the result of temporary disorders, rather than of any long-range policy on the part of any major Muslim state seeking in this way to solve the minorities question. Undoubtedly, in the minds of most Jews as well as Christians, emigration from a Muslim country appeared as a matter of personal preference or as a result of economic pressures, and not as enforced by a formal decree or conscious governmental policy of exclusion. It must have sounded strange to an Eastern Jew to read the distinction, drawn by the fourteenth-century Barcelona rabbi Nissim b. Reuben Gerondi, between the obedience due by Jews to a non-Jewish king and that owing to a ruler of their own faith. He contended that the maxim " 'the law of the kingdom is law' applies only to a Gentile king, for the land is his and he may threaten them [the Jews] with expulsion if they refuse to keep his ordinances. Not so a Jewish king, since all of Israel are equal partners in the Land of Israel." [14]

Not that the rabbis were prepared to accept every royal enactment, however arbitrary. In the West they aimed their shafts at *new* regulations which basically diverged from existing customs or were intended to be sharply discriminatory against Jews. In the purportedly stable thirteenth-century society, even Thomas Aquinas advised the duchess of Brabant not to raise Jewish taxes beyond their customary level. In contrast, the Eastern rabbis, such as Maimonides, stressed the limitation of the royal prerogatives, which had to conform with the original understanding between the subjects and the monarchy. Discussing the specific case of the king's right to expropriate private houses in order to build bridges, open roads, or construct walls, Maimonides stressed that the monarch's measures were legitimate "if the inhabitants of that country had agreed that he was their lord and they his subjects ['abadim, literally "serfs"]; but if he had not thus been accepted, he merely was like a powerful robber and like [a member of] a gang of armed highwaymen whose law is not law. Such a king and all his officials are to be considered robbers in every respect." Here we have echoes of the Muslim idea of ijma' (catholic consent of the population) as a major source of law, and of the scholastic adumbration of the later, more fully developed doctrine of the "social contract." [15]

It was indeed in the realm of economic and, particularly, fiscal relations that Jews maintained their major contacts with their respective governments. From the outset the Muslim states recognized the autonomy of the dhimmi populations and their right to self-determination, not only in the religious sphere but in many fields of social and economic life as well. However, all Muslim rulers beginning with Muḥammad himself expected from their "protected subjects" the payment of considerable special taxes. From the original land and capitation taxes the fiscal structure grew into a ramified body of legal enactments and administrative practices which varied from country to country and period to period but which were, as a rule, quite burdensome. Only a few Jewish leaders fully perceived that there were some advantages for their people in this system. A story told by an ancient chronicler reports that, toward the end of the ninth century, Caliph Al-Mu'tadhid wished to express his appreciation for the loyalty of his Jewish subjects by forgiving them the payment of all taxes. To which the then-leading Baghdad Jewish banker, Netira, is said to have objected by arguing: "Through his taxes the Jew insures his position. By eliminating all imposts the caliph would give free rein to the Arabs to shed Jewish blood." He advised the monarch merely to reduce the taxes to their original low level. [16]

In daily practice, of course, many taxpayers tried to evade payment, under subterfuges of one kind or another. While generally insisting that the state's fiscal enactments were valid if they were not discriminatory or totally arbitrary, the rabbinic leaders made some exceptions where their people's conscience repudiated the justice of the impost. For one example, the Muslim authorities in a certain locality (probably in North-African Kairuwan) made a practice of collecting taxes or court-imposed fines due from absentee taxpayers by confiscating the latter's possessions. In some cases they seized the taxpayer's wife and submitted her to all sorts of torture to enforce her husband's return and his payment of all tax arrears. This practice was felt by the Jewish community to be illegal. One escaping taxpayer was advised by his neighbors to hand his wife a faulty writ of divorce and to entrust her with his property to the full value of the "settlement" guaranteed her by her original marriage contract. When approached by the tax collectors, she could claim that, as a divorcee, she was not responsible for her former husband's obligations. Later on, when all danger was past, the couple could be reunited in their old place of residence or elsewhere, by securing from a Jewish court an annulment of the irregular divorce. Inevitably some rabbinic leaders countenanced such evasions when, with the rest of their community, they felt that illegal acts on the part of the government could be combated only by some such extralegal evasions. [17]

Here we see the seeds of a serious legal conflict, at least in theory. The very formulation "The law of the kingdom is law," conveying the idea that Jewish law must respect royal enactments, presupposed that the validity of royal law in the ultimate sense depended on its recognition by Jewish jurists. Certainly, if a government demanded from Jews the violation of any of their religious fundamentals, Jews were not to obey, because their own laws relating to religious conformity were, in their firm belief, divinely ordained and hence superior to any enactments emanating from human beings. As far as the state was concerned, on the other hand, Jews enjoyed their religious self-determination only because, and to the extent to which, it had been granted them by the royal power of its own free will or, at best, because the king followed Muḥammad's injunction concerning the toleration of "the people of the book." Here lurked, indeed, the perilous possibility of a sharp clash of conflicting sovereignties between what the Jews considered their *ius divinum* and the positive laws enacted by the states. In practice, however, such a clash was avoided in the Middle Ages because both Muslim and Christian rulers had long since learned to respect their own *ius divinum*. Without being pressed to its extreme logical conclusion, therefore, Mar Samuel's maxim sufficed to smooth the relations between the Jews and their Gentile masters. [18]

REGIONAL AND ETHNIC VARIATIONS

Such expressions of separatism did not seriously impinge on Jewish patriotism, however. In general, religious differences loomed much larger than political divisions. In fact, whatever national feeling developed in the Middle-Eastern countries during medieval and early modern times was deeply intertwined with religious allegiance. Even in the early twentieth century, if two Balkan brothers professed Islam and Greek Orthodoxy, respectively, they would have been called a Turk and a Greek by their neighbors. It is a matter of record that the famous exchange of Turkish and Greek populations which was arranged by the League of Nations in the 1920s to establish peace between Turkey and Greece consisted in the removal of some 360,000 Muslims of whatever tongue or ethnic origin to Turkey and a similar evacuation, from Turkey to Greece, of about 190,000 Greek-Orthodox, whether or not they were of Greek ancestry and knew the Greek language. The fluidity of frontiers, moreover, and the constant divisions of areas through military conquests, contrasted, after the initial turbulent period, with the great stability of the religious denominations, even sects, as well as of the four leading schools of Muslim jurisprudence which remained in more or less permanent control over certain areas. [19]

Not surprisingly, like their neighbors, Jews developed a deeper love for the particular region they inhabited than for the state at large. The ancient conflicting claims for hegemony between Babylonian and Palestinian Jewry were, if anything, intensified now under the rule of early Islam. Saadia, himself a native of Egypt and but a recent arrival in Babylonia, even extolled the supremacy of that country with respect to certain liturgical formulations and objected to the use of the prayer *Ve-or ḥadash 'al Ṣiyyon ta-ir* for Palestine before the messianic era. [20]

More extreme was Pirqoi b. Baboi's attempt to force Palestinian Jewry to submit to the doctrines and practices prevailing in Babylonia. The Palestinians reacted in kind: in order to stress the exclusive jurisdiction of their country's leadership in proclaiming a new month, they did not hesitate to plunge the entire Jewish world into great confusion by declaring dates different from those accepted in Babylonia for the celebration of a new moon and the ensuing holidays. Possibly only Saadia's vigorous and persistent intervention checked this self-assertive effort of the Palestinians, who were led by the equally ambitious Aaron Ben Meir. It was with respect to this very issue that the homilist who compiled the so-called *Pirqe de-R. Eliezer* had exclaimed with abandon: "Even if righteous and wise men live in the dispersion, while Palestine has only herders of sheep and cattle, the intercalation of a month for a leap year may be proclaimed only by the herders of sheep and cattle." So jealous were the Jerusalemites of their exclusive controls that, when a Babylonian congregation in their city wished to elect a rabbinic leader of its own, they appealed directly to the caliph to stop that "outrageous" division of authority. "For when two authorities are permissible," they wrote, "there would be permissible three or even more [leaders], and this would lead to endless anarchy." [21]

Remarkably, the Jews of Spain, who had suffered severely under the Visigothic domination and enjoyed respite only after A.D. 711 under the Islamic rule which they had helped to bring about, often waxed rhetorical about the superiority of their country over all others. A tenth-century rabbi wrote: "From ancient times to the present, Spain has been the seat of learning. It is well known that when Alexander the Great wished to ascend to heaven he was advised by the Palestinian sages to proceed to Spain, where he would find wise men whose ancestors had been established there from the days of the First Exile. The sages of the Mishnah consulted them and in turn answered their inquiries." This claim reminds one of similar legends expounded by Spanish Jews under the later Christian domination, except that the motivation of the later Jewish homilists was even more obvious: if they could assure their Christian neighbors that Jews had settled in the country in the days of King Solomon as was allegedly attested by a tombstone inscription of Adoniram, King Solomon's general, buried in Spain, they could not be included by the Christians among the descendants of those ancient Palestinian Jews accused of participating in the crucifixion of Jesus. Another legend, in part accepted by the Christian world, contended that a Spanish archisynagogus, Eleazar, a contemporary of Jesus, had happened to be in Jerusalem during the great trial and had pleaded for clemency for the founder of Christianity. This inner conviction of the unmatched excellence of their Spanish heritage varied so little under the changing suzerainties over the country that, as late as the fifteenth century, Moses Arragel, who helped leading Christian churchmen to translate the so-called Alba Bible into Spanish, could boast that Spanish Jewry towered over all other Jewish communities by being "distinguished in four ways: in lineage, in wealth, in virtues, and in science." [22]

We can also readily understand the reluctance of governors to see local taxpayers leave their bailiwicks for other parts. This was particularly true with regard to Jews and other *dhimmis,* not only in Egypt with its heritage of state capitalism but also in Iraq and elsewhere. Egyptian taxpayers were not permitted to leave without passports, issued only after an attestation that all tax arrears had been paid. In an extreme case, an Alexandrian woman was severely punished, we are told, because she had lost her passport when her son, who was holding it for her, was devoured by a crocodile. [23]

Before long, regional rivalries also led to feelings of superiority on the part of various ethnic groups within Islam. The Arabs understandably glorified their ancestors of the days of Muḥammad. Some families traced, with particular pride, their descent from one or another of the Messenger's first followers in Mecca and Medina. Other Muslims, however, especially those residing in self-assertive countries like Persia and Spain, resented these vainglorious contentions of unexcelled parentage. Some of them must also have been aggrieved by the widespread prohibition forbidding non-Arab Muslim men to marry Arab women. As a result there appeared manifestations of opposing racism, such as that espoused by the school of the so-called Shu'ubiyyah and its chief spokesman, Ibn Garcia, in Spain. Typical of that controversy was Ibn Garcia's statement that the ancestors of many subjugated nations had produced Caesars and Khosroes at a time when the Arabs still were but "guardians of dirty camels." [24]

Jewish leaders may not have minded the Muslim prohibition of intermarriage between Jewish males and Muslim women, since they themselves were equally opposed to intermarriage unless the non-Jewish partner, male or female, converted. (Clearly, mixed marriages would have been a more serious menace to the Jewish minority than to the Muslim majority.) But they probably resented the indirect pressure for conversion exerted by the Muslim penalty of capital punishment for illicit sex relations between *dhimmis* and Muslim women. In several cases Christian bishops escaped the penalty only by speedy conversion to Islam. More important, the constant assertion of Arab superiority was particularly galling to Jews, who recalled the biblical tradition that Ishmael, the purported ancestor of the Arabs, was the son of the slave girl Hagar, whereas their own ancestry went back to Abraham's full-fledged wife, Sarah. References to Arab rule as that of *ben ha-amah* ("son of the slave girl") abounded in medieval Hebrew poetry and apologetics. If, on their part, non-Arab Muslims had to concede at least the exceptional greatness of Muḥammad the Arab, Jews were under no such constraint. Notwithstanding the Islamic law which placed blasphemy against the founder of the faith under capital punishment, many Jewish writers alluded to him as the "Madman." Whether or not we accept the opinion of some modern scholars that Muḥammad was an epileptic, his erratic behavior must have adversely impressed contemporaries, particularly those who repudiated his message. Understandably, Maimonides and others tried to disprove the frequent assertions of Arab apologists that the advent of the Messenger had been clearly predicted in the Hebrew Bible. Nor did the sage of Fusṭaṭ fail to mention the tradition that the Arab prophet had been personally responsible for the destruction of 24,000 (according to another version, 52,000) Jewish lives—an obvious exaggeration. [25]

Connected with these racist debates were claims of superiority based on geography and climate. Some of these boasts, combined with the denigration of others allegedly less fortunate, remind us of certain modern environmental (including climatological) interpretations of history, such as those of Henry Thomas Buckle, which attribute differences between national histories mainly to geographic factors. In our days of purported Nordic superiority one reads with interest the "biological" explanation (cited below, p. 134) offered by the distinguished Toledan judge Saʿīd ibn Ahmad al-Andalusi (1029–70), for the then-backward condition of Moorish Spain's Christian neighbors north of the Pyrenees.

With respect to Jews we find a somewhat different inversion. The renowned Muslim scholar Al-Jaḥiz (d. 859), himself of African descent, claimed that, because of their constant inbreeding and its impact on their native endowment, Jews were incapable of abstract thinking. In modern times, on the contrary, Werner Sombart has attributed the important Jewish share in the rise of modern capitalism precisely to the Jews' long-term talmudic training, which made them especially adept at thinking and calculating in abstract terms. [26]

Jewish thinkers could not remain unaffected. Like Saʿīd, his compatriot, Moses ibn Ezra, a resident of Granada, looked down not only upon the Christians but also on the Jews living in their midst, including those inhabiting the northern parts of Spain. When, because of warlike developments, he was forced to leave his beloved native city and settle in Toledo and other parts of Christian Spain, he became an ever-unhappy, maladjusted refugee, who felt like "a plucked rose among thorns and thistles." [27]

It was left to Moses' contemporary Yehudah Halevi to develop a comprehensive theory about the native superiority of the Jewish people over all other nations. Without being a racist in the modern sense—he recognized the general rabbinic rule that, by joining the Jewish faith a proselyte automatically becomes a descendant of Abraham, Isaac, and Jacob, and a member of the "chosen people"— he conceded to the anti-Jewish polemists, both Muslim and Christian, that the Jews' powerlessness was the result of divine wrath. But he insisted that even the Christians offer their deepest veneration to their great martyrs, to Jesus and the apostles, rather than to the kings, statesmen, or conquerors who appear to wield the greatest earthly power. In his opinion, this fact alone completely disproved the hasty judgment of some observers who "from our degradation, poverty, and dispersion infer the extinction of our light, and conclude from the greatness of others, their conquests on earth, and their power over us, that their light is still burning." On the contrary, Halevi argues, Israel is like a heart among the nations, "at the same time the most sick and the most healthy" among the organs of the body. The Jewish people alone has been natively endowed by God with the gift of prophecy to a degree unmatched by any other people. Any reader of Halevi's famous dialogue, the *Al-Khazari,* could readily deduce therefrom his complete denial of Muḥammad's prophetic mission and, with it, of the very justification for Islamic rule over Jews. It is small wonder, then, that many readers among both the Arabic-speaking and the Western Jews shared his opinion. The book's popularity, especially in its Hebrew translation, is attested by the fact that it appeared in no less than twenty editions between 1506 and 1887. [28]

With more piety than philosophy, Maimon b. Joseph, Maimonides' father, eloquently argued that Muslim power was in no way proof of Islam's religious superiority. Seeking to comfort his fellow sufferers under the intolerant Almohade regime, he wrote:

It is our duty to rely on the Lord, to believe in Him and not to cavil about His promises. Just as we do not doubt His existence and no apprehension enters our heart, since He has promised to bring us nigh unto Him, so we shall not be confused by the enormous power of the nations, their long duration, and vast multitudes, or by what they say or hope for. For we rely on the Lord and believe in His promises, despite their lording it over us, oppressing and vanquishing us. [29]

Apart from these changing relations to the government and society at large, there were enough intergroup tensions to contribute to considerable ill will between the denominations. The Muslims may have been less prone than the European Christians to stage large-scale massacres among their Jewish neighbors; but individual assaults on Jews, and even anti-Jewish riots, were by no means uncommon. There was an element of reality behind the perpetuation of the talmudic statement that a Jew who sells his house to a Gentile might be liable for damages accruing therefrom to his Jewish neighbor, who could argue: "You have placed a lion at my doorstep." More frequently Jews were exposed to contemptuous treatment not only by Arab officials but also by ordinary Arabs inferior to them in cultural and economic standing. Of course, there also was occasional friendly intercourse among members of the various groups: a gaon actually felt prompted to advise Jewish innkeepers to keep away Muslim guests, "lest they ogle" their wives. But, for the most part, the separation in denominational quarters helped prevent many clashes. [30]

MODUS VIVENDI

All these theoretical discussions should not obscure the fact that, at least in quiescent periods, the majority of Jews and other minorities evinced little concern about the state and general political developments. Residing predominantly in its own quarters, the Jewish group almost everywhere possessed its own powerful communal organization, which affected its daily life much more deeply than did the state authorities. In full control of its own educational, judicial, and welfare systems, the Jewish community jealously guarded its independence. While it could not prevent the state from occasionally passing laws which infringed upon its freedom of worship, for instance, by forbidding them to erect new synagogues, such laws were often evaded, as by giving the synagogues the external appearance of private houses. In addition, Jews sometimes benefited from the complacency and widespread corruption of the Muslim bureaucracy

As a matter of principle, moreover, the government generally refrained from enforcing laws requiring changes in ritual or belief. If, from 825 on, the Caliphate even refused to interfere in sectarian controversies within the community, and thus helped to extend the enjoyment of minority rights to heterodox sects such as the Karaites, this was a sign of its religious toleration, not an attempt to undermine the unity of the Jewish people. Nor, as a rule, did the government oppose efforts by Jewish communal leaders to safeguard the exclusive authority of Jewish courts in intramural litigations. Jewish leaders were, of course, unable to prevent Jews from repairing to Muslim courts in litigations with non-Jews. Occasionally, when powerful Jewish individuals successfully defied summonses or sentences issued by Jewish tribunals, the rabbis themselves allowed appeals to Gentile courts. But, under ordinary conditions, a Jew citing a coreligionist before non-Jewish authorities was denounced as an "informer," that is, as one of the most reprehensible of criminals in a community facing constant danger from malicious denunciations. On the whole, the Arab-Jewish symbiosis developed along the lines of mutual acceptance of existing differences and the recognition that direct cooperation between them was expected only on certain basic matters of general interest.

Nonetheless, a certain degree of assimilation and mutual adaptation proceeded apace. In the early centuries of Islam, the Arabs were on the receiving side with respect to cultural achievements and amenities. In time, however, the new culture established by the Renaissance of Islam exerted a pervasive influence on the outlook and behavior of the minorities as well. The Arabic language, especially, became a major unifying factor. No matter how much the Jewish leaders preached the priority in age and quality of the Hebrew language, which they and most of their neighbors regarded as the most ancient of all languages, they wrote most of their works in Arabic. Even if many of them knew Hebrew better than Arabic, they used the Arabic medium in their communications with other Jewish scholars, albeit they employed the Hebrew alphabet. Only Saadia's famous Bible translation seems to have been originally written in Arabic characters, apparently with the view of eliciting the interest of non-Jewish readers. Ultimately many Jews considered their Judeo-Arabic a semisacred language, but a step removed in holiness from the Hebrew tongue. In these ways there developed a *modus vivendi* which operated to the mutual advantage of both Arabs and Jews over the centuries.

5

Saadia's Communal Activities*

COMMUNAL LEADERSHIP was the great passion of Saadia's life. It permeated all his labors in public affairs and literature, to a degree unparalleled among the other geonim. One may not agree with the statement that all of Saadia's writings, "without exception, served the one purpose of defeating the Karaites." But one shall not deny that anti-Karaite and generally antisectarian controversy was focal in Saadia's whole attitude to life and that it found expression even in remote corners of his scholarly creativity. Not unjustly he became "that man" for many Karaites and some Rabbanites of the subsequent generations. [1] His literary struggles against the sectarians, and even against the radical Bible critic Ḥiwi al-Balkhi, were nevertheless tame and mellow as compared with his passionate conflicts with Aaron Ben Meir or David b. Zakkai.

Even his purely scientific work had many earmarks of communal action. His philological treatises were intended to facilitate and purify the use of Hebrew among the masses and thereby help retain the paramount link of Jewish unity, the informed observance of Jewish law. [2] His Bible translation ("combining all the virtues of the Aramàic Targum with the compactness of the Septuagint" [3]) and his more extensive commentary apparently were written, unlike other works by Jewish authors of the period, in Arabic rather than Hebrew characters, and had decidedly apologetic overtones. They seem to have been addressed just as much to the Arabs as to the Jews, and were written in such good Arabic as to forestall the sort of ridicule which some Arab authors had heaped on Saadia's predecessors among the Christian translators, including the famous Ḥunayn ibn Isḥāk. [4] His chief philosophic treatise was to serve a variety of communal purposes: the defense of Judaism against Christianity; the repudiation of heretical teachings; the reconciliation, for the intellectual minority, of traditional Judaism with contemporary philosophy; and so forth. [5] We shall see that his personal struggles, too, colored some of his teachings and affected the very arrangement of this oldest classic of medieval Jewish philosophy. Even with his

* Reprinted from *Saadia Anniversary Volume*, American Academy for Jewish Research [Texts and Studies, II](New York, 1943), pp. 9–74.

great liturgical work, printed in 1941, he intended, as perhaps no one had before, to unify world Jewry by placing in the hands of the various congregations a basic, uniform prayerbook. [6] It goes without saying that his juridical activity as gaon and as an author of halakhic treatises was of direct communal import.

Saadia regarded communal action as so important that he sweepingly allowed the interruption of the Sabbath rest "for the consideration of matters of public concern." While he could readily invoke pertinent talmudic discussions supporting his views, he may indeed have gone beyond the literal meaning of his sources. There may be a grain of truth in Aaron (Khalaf) ibn Sarjado's accusation that Saadia, during his conflict with David b. Zakkai, did not hesitate to carry gifts to state dignitaries on the day of Sabbath. [7] Anyone familiar with the moodiness of, and the constant shifts in power within, the caliph's administration, however, will understand how dangerous it often was to delay intervention for a single day.

In spreading his attention over many disciplines, moreover, Saadia defied the then-growing trend toward specialization. In the ninth and tenth centuries the amount of human knowledge had so vastly increased that even the great scholars of the generation felt constrained to devote all their energies to the cultivation of a single discipline. One who dabbled in various sciences was somewhat disparagingly dubbed "litterateur" (adib, akin to the connotation sometimes given today to the term "journalist"). [8] But Saadia felt that he could fulfill his mission of serving the Jewish community only if he did a great deal of pioneering in various fields, indeed in practically all the fields affecting communal unity. Though of a strictly rationalist bent, he wrote a commentary on the mystical Sefer Yeṣirah which, together with the considerable influence exercised by an old paraphrase of his philosophic work, made him appear, to later generations of Jewish mystics, as one of the founders of Kabbalah. [9] The fact that he achieved great mastery in every one of those disciplines and that he became, to cite Abraham ibn Ezra, the ראש המדברים בכל מקום (the chief spokesman in all areas), may in retrospect have been readily acknowledged by subsequent generations, but it took a man of his courage, tenacity, and devotion to communal responsibilities to undertake and carry through such a diversified task.

Little wonder that Saadia's communal activities have attracted the attention of some of the most brilliant and soundest Jewish scholars in recent generations. From Rappaport, Geiger, and Graetz to Harkavy, Bacher, Schechter, Abraham Epstein, Poznanski, Halevy, Eppenstein, Bornstein, Malter, and Mann—to mention only those who are no longer with us—many serious investigators have devoted years of untiring labor to amass the ever-growing source material and to analyze it with a precision and penetration which place their studies among the best examples of modern Jewish scholarship. [10] Nevertheless, there still are enormous lacunae in our knowledge, even of some of the simplest biographical sequences. While much will remain obscure until the discovery of new sources, a reexamination of the available material, especially in the light of the better-known history of the Caliphate during that period, may help clarify a few controversial or hitherto unsuspected elements in Saadia's life and activity. Many of these explanations, to be sure, will of necessity but add to the mass of hypotheses offered in the existing literature. But this very multiplication from new angles may not be devoid of value, inasmuch as it may increase the plausibility of converging hypotheses and help eliminate those which hopelessly diverge from one another.

THE IMPERIAL BACKGROUND

The dynamic transformations in Saadia's life can be fully understood only by taking cognizance of the great crisis of empire which occurred during his lifetime. In the first decades of his life, until about 920, the Caliphate succeeded not only in maintaining its essential unity but also, in some respects, in restoring the imperial power of the celebrated reigns of Harun ar-Rashid and Al-Ma'mun. In 904–5, the imperial generals reconquered Egypt and, by eliminating the semi-independent reign of the Tulunids, reestablished the caliph's sovereignty from the Nile to the borders of India. Upon his death in 908, Caliph Al-Muktafi left behind a fairly orderly administration, with a well-stocked treasury valued (together with jewelry and real estate) at 100,000,000 dinars [11]—the equivalent of some $400,000,000 at the present gold standard and many times that amount in purchasing power. Even then, manifold forces of disintegration were operating under the surface, but they did not destroy the illusion of growing imperial unity in the minds of most of Saadia's contemporaries.

The last two decades of Saadia's life, however, witnessed an unprecedentedly speedy imperial decomposition. The year 926, two years before Saadia's accession to the gaonate of Sura, marked the turning point in the centuries-old struggle between Byzantium and the Caliphate. The Christian Empire, theretofore on the defensive, now rapidly expanded eastward and southward, and before long threatened to engulf most of western Asia. Even farther reaching was the inner dismemberment of the Caliphate. Speaking of conditions in 944, Al-Mas'udi still described the Empire as extending from Fergana and Khorasan to Tangier and from the Caucasus to Jeddah near Mecca, and as covering an area of 3,700 parasangs from east to west and 600 parasangs from north to south. But he had to admit that it already was a house divided against itself, similar to the ancient empire of the Diadochs. [12] "In the year 325 [936–37]," says another Arab historian, "affairs fell into great confusion. The provinces became a prey either to a rebel that seized them or to a prefect who would not pay the state revenues, and they became separate independent princes and nothing remained in the possession of ar-Radhi but Bagdad and the Sawad [the district in its vicinity]." [13]

The three caliphs reigning in the period of Saadia's greatest activity well personified the forces of dissolution. Since their personalities greatly affected the central administration and, hence, indirectly influenced the supreme leadership of the Jewish communities, it may be worthwhile to recall their characterization by an Arab historian. Al-Muktadir, who reigned from 908 to 932, is described by As-Suyuti as follows: He "had good sense and sound judgment but was addicted to sensuality and drinking and profuse in his expenditures. His women had entire influence over him. . . ." Of his successor, Al-Kahir, who ruled only a year and a half (932–34), a commentator is quoted as saying that "he was violent and bloodthirsty, of a depraved disposition, volatile and inconstant and addicted to intemperance and had it not been for the munificence of his Chamberlain, Salamah, the whole country would have been ruined." [14] Ar-Radhi (934–40), styled "beneficent, liberal and accomplished, skillful in versifying, eloquent and a patron of men of learning," was often considered the "last of the real caliphs." [15] Both he and Al-Muktadir, moreover, died an unnatural death at the hands of rebels, while Al-Kahir was deposed and blinded, as were both of the following caliphs, Al-Muttaki (940–44) and Al-Mustakfi (944–46). After 946, a few years after Saadia's death, the population of the capital witnessed "the spectacle of three personages who had once held the highest office in Islam but were now deposed, blinded and objects of public charity." [16]

The next highest office, that of vizier, was also constantly changing hands. The three most distinguished viziers during Saadia's active years were ʿAli ibn al-Furat, ʿAli ibn ʿIsa, and Muhammad ibn Muḳlah. Apart from being arrested, fined, and tortured after almost each deposition, Ibn al-Furat actually lost his life, while Ibn Muḳlah died in prison after having been severely mutilated. Ibn ʿIsa survived various severe punishments and lived to a ripe old age, becoming the grand old man of the Empire. But his asceticism, profound learning, and piety did not save him from frequent exile, bodily injury, and threats of execution. [17] Compared with these chief dignitaries of the state, the exilarchs and geonim of the period led a rather secure and sheltered life. Only a few of them were deposed, and but two were banished. The civil administration of the Empire, moreover, was rapidly losing ground; and, from the days of Muʿnis "the Victorious," a eunuch in the imperial harem who rose to the rank of chief commander, the praetorian generals increasingly controlled all governmental affairs. Muʿnis himself, together with two of his chief associates, was executed by Al-Ḳahir; but he was followed by a succession of military chieftains who held undisputed sway over both the nominal caliphs and the viziers.

These imperial transformations could not fail to affect the capital, where, or in whose vicinity, Saadia spent most of the years of his active communal leadership. The once flourishing metropolis now witnessed recurrent famines and bread riots, invasions of hostile armies, the flight of well-to-do inhabitants, and a general state of unrest, which augured badly for any type of consistent Jewish leadership. By 940–42, after a "terrible inundation" and repeated occupations by warring armies there "was a famine the like of which had never been seen in Bagdad": people actually fed on corpses. Before long, "the principal men of Bagdad fled," and conditions became so deplorable that landlords began to let their houses free of charge or even paid tenants for keeping them in a state of repair. [18]

Baghdad's decline must have affected the control exercised by the central organs of Jewry over coreligionists in the far-flung provinces. It has long been recognized that the rise of the North-African and Spanish centers was, at least in part, due to the disintegration of the

Great Caliphate and to the imperial rivalries between Muslim rulers, who tried to stimulate the independence of their local Jewries. All these factors first became clearly discernible in Saadia's lifetime, and had a considerable impact on his communal leadership.

EARLY ACTIVITIES

Apart from the composition of the *Egron* at the age of twenty, the first datable public appearance of Saadia seems to have been his polemical treatise against 'Anan, the founder of Karaism. According to Abraham ibn Ezra, Saadia wrote this treatise at the age of twenty-three (i.e., in 905). Since only disjointed fragments of the work are preserved, [18a] it is difficult to ascertain its compass. We are diffident even about speaking of its real public appearance, inasmuch as a later Karaite author (Sahl b. Maṣliaḥ) contended that Saadia himself never published any of his anti-Karaite polemics. [19] If this contention is correct, as is likely, it means that Saadia wrote his pamphlets on this subject for private circulation only, and not for sale in any of the numerous book marts of the Islamic world. This likelihood is reinforced by the fact that none of the great Rabbanite leaders of his or former generations had deemed it wise to take up the cudgels against the Karaite sectarians in public writings. Only two of the earlier geonim are known to have taken any stand on the new schism. Naṭronai b. Hillai, though sharply condemning it, did not even care to secure a copy of 'Anan's *Sefer ha-Miṣvot*. Hai b. David, a short time before Saadia, allegedly translated that work into Hebrew so as to stress point by point its indebtedness to rabbinic sources, but evidently intended his rebuttal only for internal use. [20] Daring as may have been Saadia's departure from the traditional policy of ignoring sectarian trends, he, too, undoubtedly prepared his pamphlet for restricted circulation only.

The purpose of Saadia's treatise may perhaps be detected in its coincidence with the return of Egypt to the effective control of the Baghdad administration. There is some indication that the Tulunid rulers of Egypt had somewhat favored the Karaite sectarians. [21] Now, with the reestablishment of the caliph's control, Saadia may have envisioned some united communal action, under the direction of the Baghdad leaders, to check the further expansion of the heterodox movement. This aim could have been readily accomplished by placing an array of arguments against the Karaites' founder—whose memory was little cherished at the seat of the exilarchate, from which he had been ousted a century and a half before—in the hands of a few key men in Babylonia, Palestine, and Egypt.

To be sure, ever since 825 the imperial administration had professed indifference to sectarian divisions among the "unbelievers" and, in principle, had allowed every dissident group to organize its own community. [22] Nevertheless, in practical application, it undoubtedly allowed the central leadership of Jewry some leeway in controlling inner dissensions. Unfortunately, we do not possess the transcript of any decree of appointment addressed by a caliph to an exilarch. However, the fact that such a decree, concerning a Nestorian *catholicos*, extant from the twelfth century, distinctly empowered the head of the Nestorian Church to arbitrate in sectarian dissensions [23] and that, at that time, the Egyptian *nagid* formally served as the representative not only of the Rabbanites but also of the Karaites and Samaritans, [24] would tend to confirm the impression that some such authority had never been totally withdrawn from the Jewish prince of captivity as well. In short, it certainly is not impossible that a man of Saadia's daring and vision should have reacted to the prevailing trend of reunifying the Empire clearly visible under Al-Muktafi by cherishing the parallel notion of reunifying Eastern Jewry.

This vague possibility must remain in abeyance, however, pending further documentary evidence. For the time being we do not even know whether this anti-Karaite attack had any connection with Saadia's departure from Egypt. If we are to take the assertion of his opponent, Ben Meir, at face value, it was Saadia's father who was "forced out" of Egypt, settled in Palestine, and later died in Jaffa. [25] It is possible that Saadia went with him, but a motive for his doing so is unknown. If he did it under the stimulus of persecution, as Malter assumes, [26] we would have to postulate governmental rather than sectarian action. The fact that such "force" is indicated only in the case of his father, of whose anti-Karaite activities we know absolutely nothing, and that it is mentioned disparagingly by Ben Meir as reflecting on the father's character would indicate that Saadia had not suffered in the cause of Rabbanite Jewry. This circumstance also militates against the assumption that he had fled from Egypt in 913/14 during the occupation of his native Fayyum by the Fatimid invaders. [27] Neither is there any evidence, as Mann suggests, [28] that Saadia went abroad in search of a teaching position.

From his correspondence with Isaac Israeli in Kairuwan (however nonchalantly it was later mentioned by Dunash ibn Tamim), the three significant letters which he was to write during the Ben Meir controversy to his former disciples and associates in Egypt, and the tenor of the two letters he addressed to the Egyptian communities upon his elevation to the gaonate, [29] it clearly appears that before leaving Egypt he had served there as a teacher whose words were expected to carry weight many years thereafter. On the other hand, a long time was to pass before he secured a post at the Pumbedita academy in Baghdad. The only function we find him performing in Palestine seems to have been that of a student to the celebrated teacher Abu-Kathir of Tiberias. [30] One might with equal plausibility argue either that he joined his father—for whatever reasons the latter may have left—out of sheer filial piety or, what seems more likely, that he was driven by a spirit of adventure and scholarly curiosity to visit other countries, to stay at various academies of learning, and to contact large numbers of scholars and teachers. Such travels for the satisfaction of intellectual curiosity were quite frequent among the Arabs of the period. Saadia's younger contemporary Abu Hatim of Samarkand (d. 965) is recorded as having visited some one thousand different teachers, in cities from Tashkent to Alexandria. [31] Another contemporary and personal acquaintance, the famous historian Al-Mas'udi (d. 956), spent most of his life traveling, from China to Madagascar, and from Ceylon to the Caspian Sea. True, unlike their Muslim confreres, rabbinic scholars had little need of going far and wide in search of traditions, since at that time the Babylonian and Palestinian academies served as the accredited preservers of the ancient lore. But this may have been a double inducement for Saadia to visit at least these two countries. In any case, he himself seems to indicate, in one of his aforementioned letters to Egypt, that he journeyed from school to school. [32]

Whatever the motives, Saadia probably left the country abruptly and, very likely, without the necessary authorization. Egypt was the only province of the Caliphate which, because of both its ancient traditions and its peculiar economic structure which had all the earmarks of state capitalism, tried effectively to control the movement of its population. It was, in fact, the only province to insist on passports and emigration permits. (We recall the noteworthy illustration, recorded by Severus, of a *dhimmi* woman who was severely fined because she had lost her passport together with her son when

they were swallowed by a crocodile. [33]) An unauthorized departure
may have been the reason for Saadia's apparent inability to return
to his native land in later years. [34]

He may well have made an effort to return. The much-debated
"itinerary," originally published by Schechter, [35] seems to have this
particular connotation. The phrase ועתה אתה הוא אדני יי"י מעירי
הוצאתני, אל חפצי תובילני ולשלום . . . לבית אבי תשיבני appears to be a
prayer for a safe return to his native land, not necessarily to the house
of his father, who may then have lived in Palestine. The preceding
על כן שם . . . את פניו ללכת . . . [אר]צה כנען וארצה . . . is to be filled
in by מצרים—rather than בבל, as is usually done—for anyone
familiar with Near-Eastern geography knows that a traveler going
from Baghdad via Arbela and Mosul in the direction of Palestine
travels with a general orientation toward Egypt rather than away
from Egypt. As a matter of fact, the highway running from Baghdad
to Mosul, Aleppo, Damascus, and Ramleh was considered the chief
artery of communication between the capital and the Nile Valley. [36]
The prayer that God should shield him against the vicissitudes of the
journey and the attacks of his enemies, for he had done it all for the
glorification of the divine name and the holy Torah, would fit in
well with a fearful anticipation of the prospects of his return.
Unfortunately, just as the author sets out to describe the "news"
(כי שמע כי) which induced him to undertake the journey, our
fragment becomes illegible. As a matter of fact, however, we are
told that on this occasion he did not progress beyond Mosul, because
travelers arriving there from Syria told him that the severe winter
and huge snowfalls had already claimed many men on the road. He
therefore utilized his enforced leisure to write a biography of
R. Judah the Patriarch, which had been requested of him. Such a
request, incidentally, though not quite extraordinary at the time,
inasmuch as "the biographical literature of the Arabs was exceed-
ingly rich," probably had some bearing on the Karaite-Rabbanite
controversy relating to the composition of the Mishnah. [37] No date
is given in the itinerary, except for a rather obscure reference to
בן עשרים . . . , which, if referring to Saadia, would indicate that it
was written before 912, when Saadia was thirty years old. [38] If so,
his sojourn in Babylonia may well have preceded his prolonged stay
in Palestine. It seems that, after a few years in the Holy Land, he
resumed his residence in Baghdad, some time before the summer
of 921. [39]

EXILARCHIC CONFLICTS AND NATHAN THE BABYLONIAN

During the second decade of the tenth century much happened in the central administration of the Eastern Jewish communities which deeply affected Saadia's subsequent work, although at first he seems to have taken no direct part in the struggles. The events leading to the deposition of Mar 'Ukba and to the rise of David b. Zakkai to the position of exilarch and of Kohen Ṣedek to that of gaon of Pumbedita are still full of obscurities. In particular, there exists the rather obvious contradiction between the description of the events by their main historian, Nathan the Babylonian, and the exact chronological data supplied by Sherira Gaon. Graetz, Friedlaender, Ginzberg, and Malter have given more credence to Nathan, while Mann, following in the main Halevy, has repudiated Nathan's veracity, or at least reliability, as compared with that of Sherira. [40] The pilpulistic attempts at harmonization by Halevy need not be seriously considered. But even Mann's more earnest rejection of Nathan's account because of its anecdotal and supernatural adornments, which were quite customary among the Arabian historians of the day, is too facile, gliding over, rather than resolving, the existing difficulties. [41] Since Nathan's chronicle is one of our major sources of information concerning Saadia's later public activities, a few brief remarks on its nature and the date of its composition may not be amiss at this point.

It has been plausibly demonstrated [42] that Nathan's account originated in the period after 942 (the date of Saadia's death) and before 953 (the elevation of the new exilarch, Hezekiah, whom he does not mention; this date may be put back a few years, if we assume that Hezekiah had a predecessor in his father's cousin, Solomon b. Josiah, who became exilarch in 945).[43] However, the subsequently discovered relationship between Nathan and his teacher, Ḥushiel in Kairuwan, has tended to indicate that Nathan's chronicle was written in North Africa after Ḥushiel's arrival there in 960 or later. [44] The chronological difficulties have been increased by the fairly general agreement among modern scholars that Nathan's vivid description of the installation of an exilarch was based upon his own presence at the installation of David b. Zakkai, whose assumption of the exilarchic position may now be dated at about 916–17. Yet if Nathan was old enough to attend that ceremony, he

would have been too old to become anyone's pupil when he wrote
his account some five decades later at the academy of Ḥushiel. [45]

Some of these difficulties may be removed by closer examination
of Nathan's narrative. First of all there is absolutely no evidence that
he attended David b. Zakkai's installation. A careful reading of the
account indicates that David at first enjoyed the support of only the
academy of Sura, whereas that of Pumbedita, led by Kohen Ṣedek,
for three years thereafter repudiated his authority. [46] Therefore,
Nathan's description of an installation at which the Pumbedita gaon
occupied a seat of honor to the left of the newly elected exilarch
could not possibly refer to the much-embattled elevation of David.
To postulate Nathan's presence at the installation (about 890) of
David's predecessor, 'Uḳba, on the other hand—a possibility somewhat supported by his description of the electoral assembly meeting
in such a private house as Neṭira's—further increases the chronological difficulties. Unless we assume that his description of the exilarch's
installation is based entirely on hearsay, [47] we must conclude that he
attended the installation of David's son in 940–41. The fact that this
son did not survive his father by more than seven months would not
preclude the possibility of his having been installed sometime before
his death. Nathan's equivocal statement ובקשו להנהיג בנו במקומו may
perhaps be explained to mean that David's son, though installed,
failed to secure the caliph's confirmation and that, hence, he was not
yet the officially recognized exilarch. Possibly Ar-Radi's death on
December 18, 940, and the generally unsettled state of affairs, prevented the formal appearance of the exilarch-elect at Court and the
issuance of the regular imperial decree of appointment. These disturbances, incidentally, doubtless also accounted for the execution of
the only remaining candidate eligible for the exilarchic office, under
the flimsy accusation of an anti-Muslim blasphemy. [48] Should this
hypothesis prove correct, we might readily understand not only why
Nathan, two decades later, while living in Kairuwan, joined
Ḥushiel's academy, where he was asked to write a description of
the Jews of Baghdad during the recent period (probably in connection with some claims of 'Uḳba's family to recognition of its superior
status), but also why certain relatively minor inaccuracies crept into
his story of the conflict between 'Uḳba and the academy of Pumbedita, a conflict which probably ended before he was born. [49]

There is no doubt that Nathan's account of Kohen Ṣedek as head
of the Pumbedita academy and leading the opposition to 'Uḳba can-

not be strictly reconciled with Sherira's record that the academy was until 917 under the leadership of his grandfather Judah. Moreover, Neṭira, the Baghdad banker whose great influence was coresponsible for overthrowing 'Uḳba, is known to have died in 916, a year before R. Judah. On the other hand, it is quite possible that Kohen Ṣedeḳ was, even before 916, a most influential member of the academy, perhaps its *alluf* or even *ab bet din,* and as such appeared to be the main protagonist in the conflict with 'Uḳba. Possibly Judah Gaon was too old or unworldly to see through the fight with the exilarch over the contested revenue from Khorasan. [50] One need recall only the role played a few years later by Saadia, then a private citizen or at best *alluf* of Pumbedita, in the controversy with Ben Meir, a role which easily overshadowed that of the exilarch and the three geonim in the minds of contemporaries and later generations. Nathan's inaccuracy would then consist merely in his calling Kohen Ṣedeḳ *rosh yeshibat Pumbedita,* whereas at that time he was not yet formally its chief spokesman. But such an inaccuracy is easily excusable in a writer of the latter part of the tenth century, whose memory and whatever notes he may have had with him went back to the 930s, when Kohen Ṣedeḳ (d. 936) was the actual head of the academy. As a matter of fact, Nathan may not have intended to assert that Kohen Ṣedeḳ was gaon at the time of the controversy but may simply have given him a title under which he was generally known to Nathan's associates in Kairuwan. [51] Similarly, we find in the brief fragment of the anonymous description, written after Saadia's death (there is the usual ז״ל after his name), of the differences between Saadia and Ben Meir that Saadia's title is given four times as ראש אלמתיבה and twice as אלנאון. [52] Of course, during the Ben Meir controversy Saadia was not yet gaon.

Leaving aside his evident misunderstanding concerning the Sura geonim, [53] who play but a minor role in the narrative, Nathan's account may thus be taken as historical. We may try to understand the events somewhat better in the light of the contemporary developments in the administration of the Caliphate. The opposition to 'Uḳba was effectively supported by the leading Jewish bankers, Joseph b. Phineas and his son-in-law, Neṭira, probably acting in cooperation with Joseph's partner, Aaron b. Amram. Walter Fischel has collected considerable information from Arabic sources, which shed new light on these Jewish court bankers and their influence on the political and economic evolution of the Caliphate. [54] He has not made clear the specific stages in this evolution, however. From the evidence hitherto available, it appears that the influence of these court bankers reached its apex under the three vizierates of Ibn al-Furat. Almost all the important transactions recorded in connection with them refer to the years 908–12, 918, 923–24. To be sure, At-Tanukhi contends that, in order to preserve public credit and "to uphold the dignity of the office," these bankers were allowed to continue their services "until their death," despite changes in the administration. However, one cannot help feeling that 'Ali ibn 'Isa, whose general fiscal policy was one of retrenchment and of relieving the burdens of the taxpayers, made less use of the Jewish agents' ability to raise the imperial revenue than did his far more lavish colleague. In fact, in his two recorded transactions with them, one detects an undercurrent of hostility, the vizier using threats to force the bankers to extend him loans on the security of future revenue from Al-Ahwaz, which they administered, or of letters of credit which had not yet fallen due. [55] It appears likely, therefore, that the deposition of 'Ukba, culminating in his exile from the Empire under the threat of confiscation of all his property, was effected by the ruthless Ibn al-Furat rather than by the more humane, if sanctimonious, Ibn 'Isa. In that case it must have occurred during the three years and eight months of Ibn al-Furat's first vizierate, which ended abruptly in 912. [56]

For approximately four years the exilarchic office remained vacant, until, under the pressure of Jewish public opinion, which resented the prolonged absence of an official spokesman from the royal councils, it was filled again by the elevation of David b. Zakkai, 'Ukba's first cousin, who had probably been too young to succeed his father directly in about 890. The extended waiting period in filling 'Ukba's place may have been due principally to Netira's opposition and, possibly, to his ambition to act as the sole spokesman for the Jewish people. He is recorded as having at least once before intervened, to prevent the cancellation of all Jewish poll taxes—which was allegedly contemplated by Al-Mu'tadid (892–902). [57] It is not unlikely, therefore, that the promoters of David's election had to remain silent until after Netira's death in 916. Despite Kohen Sedek's continued opposition, the academy of Sura, supported by the Jewish public at large, proclaimed David exilarch, very likely in 916. The academy of Pumbedita, however, continued to ignore the new exilarch. This attitude of aloofness was main-

tained even after the death of Judah Gaon and the election of
Mubashshir, rather than Kohen Ṣedek, as his successor. Mubashshir
was evidently satisfied with election by his colleagues and did not
seek to obtain the customary exilarchic confirmation. Kohen Ṣedek,
too, while apparently remaining in Al-Anbar-Pumbedita, long refused to recognize the exilarch. His attitude may have been stiffened
by Ibn al-Furat's return to power in June, 917, and the expectation
of some effective intervention on the part of the Neṭira family.
However, the vizier's sudden disgrace, after but thirteen months in
office, must have shattered all these hopes. Kohen Ṣedek was now in
a more receptive mood to listen to the persuasive voice of the
revered blind teacher Nissi al-Nahrawani, and to make peace with
David in 919, three years after the latter's installation. In return,
David proclaimed Kohen Ṣedek the official head of the Pumbedita
academy, in lieu of Mubashshir. The officiating gaon refused to
surrender his authority, however, and for years the two factions
continued their activities side by side in the capital and its vicinity,
until their reconciliation in Elul, 922, which lasted only until
Mubashshir's death three months later (or, according to another
reading, in 925), when Kohen Ṣedek became the uncontested head
of the academy, in permanent cooperation with the exilarch. This
reconciliation was undoubtedly accelerated by both the growing
power of David b. Zakkai and the urgent need of unity to oppose
the ambitious schemes of Aaron Ben Meir, [58] as well as by the
persuasive powers of Saadia, who then joined the ranks of the
Pumbedita academy as one of its outstanding *allufim*.

THE BEN MEIR CONTROVERSY

There is no evidence that Saadia had any share in the struggles
between 'Uḳba and the academy of Pumbedita or in the subsequent conflict between the two Pumbedita factions. His first public
entry into the controversies affecting the central leadership of
Jewry was in 921–22, during the famous conflict over control of the
Jewish calendar. This conflict, of which Aaron Ben Meir, the head
of a Palestinian academy probably situated at the capital, Ramleh,
was the initiator, found Saadia as the protagonist of the opposing
side. Since this controversy has been fully discussed in the previous
literature, [59] a few brief remarks will suffice here.

The interrelated problems of the Jewish calendar and chronology had long before engaged Saadia's attention. From the few references concerning his early *Refutation of 'Anan*, we may deduce that on that occasion he had already gone to extremes in combating the Karaite attempt at reversion to the celebration of the New Moon by observation. [60] He may already then have expressed the view that the Jewish calendar had always been based upon astronomic computation, and that the latter actually was of Mosaic origin. [61] In this view, designed to buttress the rabbinic tradition and demonstrate its Mosaic foundations, against the Karaite contention that the entire system of Oral Law was an innovation of later generations, Saadia did violence even to the unequivocal statements in the Talmud, and found no followers among the less militant rabbinic authorities of subsequent generations. In the rage of controversy, he did not hesitate to reinterpret history in a way which, although it violated historical fact, served his major historic purpose of combating heresy. [62]

Little wonder that, while living in Palestine, he maintained his interest in the complex problems of the Hebrew calendar. On one occasion, some time before 917, he was puzzled by a certain legal aspect of the *Molad*, particularly the rule relating to the $642\frac{2}{1080}$ parts of an hour (the equivalent of some 35 minutes), which was to play such a great role in the subsequent controversy. It appears that he had already had some misgivings about the teachings of the local leaders, possibly Ben Meir himself, and had addressed an inquiry on this score to R. Judah Gaon, the head of the Pumbedita academy. [63]

The matter came to a head in 921 when a decision had to be made in regard to the application of this rule for the years 4682 and 4684. The decision seems to have been complicated by the natural difference of some 56 minutes in the moon's appearance on the horizons of Palestine and Babylonia. Although as late as 835 the Babylonian leaders had recognized the supremacy of the Palestinians in all matters pertaining to the calendar, and even now they disclaimed any wish to remove the basis of the computation from the Holy Land, [64] their control was by 921 so firmly established that most Jewish communities readily followed their computation. The intricacies of the Hebrew calendar were such that a shift of but a few minutes before or after noon of the New Year 4684 (923) would have necessitated an adjustment in the length of the months of Marḥeshvan and Kislev two years ahead of time;

that is, they would have to be proclaimed to be of twenty-nine or thirty days' duration each. Ben Meir, a vigorous personality, felt bold enough to reassert Palestinian hegemony in this field and to decide that both months be proclaimed deficient, thus defying the Babylonian leadership. One easily understands the repercussions the disagreement had on the subsequent observance of all holidays, which were celebrated on different dates in various countries or even communities, dependent on whether they followed the leadership of Palestine or of Babylonia. Saadia was quite emphatic in urging three Egyptian rabbis to intervene with their coreligionists in favor of the Babylonian standpoint: "Be energetic in this matter day and night, morning and evening, because it is more important than trade and daily bread and every urgent business." [65]

It is difficult to assume that Ben Meir failed to appreciate the consequences of his undertaking. He must have known that, unless the Babylonian leaders yielded without a fight and consented to his decree, the ensuing division among the Jewish communities would be extremely serious. He must also have realized that in the event of open controversy the Jewish leaders of Baghdad could invoke the assistance of the imperial government. We know that he was familiar, from personal experience, with the workings of the Baghdad administration, since, only a few years before, he had gone to the capital to enlist its assistance against his Karaite opponents in Palestine. In fact, the Karaites seem to have been so powerful in the Holy Land as to cause his imprisonment and threaten his life. Apparently only the intervention of the Muslim officials, prompted by the Baghdad Jewish leaders, saved him from further severe persecution. [66] That he nevertheless now ventured to defy the Babylonian authorities must have been due to some special patronage which he enjoyed in either Baghdad or Ramleh. In a subsequent letter, he mentions, indeed, the well-known court banker Aaron b. Amram as "a savior of the generation" and intimates that Aaron was somewhat helpful to him during the entire controversy. [67] We know from other sources that Aaron, now apparently acting alone after the decease of his partner, Joseph b. Phineas, still had considerable influence in the official circles of the capital. [68] There is no evidence, however, that he was at that time opposed to David b. Zakkai, though he may have resented David's original election. [69] It is more likely that, without directly supporting the Palestinian leader, he maintained some sort of benevolent neutrality, and that

Ben Meir relied primarily on his own ability to negotiate with the Muslim officials in Palestine. [70] He may have expected that the evident preoccupation of the imperial administration with the aftermath of the renewed assault on Egypt by the Fatimids in the year A.H. 307 (919–20), and the unrest created in Baghdad by famine and local disorders in 920–21, would prevent direct government intervention in an apparently domestic problem of Palestinian Jewry. (Hamzah of Isfahan, we recall, later declared the years 920–21 to have been the turning point in the entire history of the Abbasid Caliphate, whose prosperity had lasted for 177 years but now gave way to increasing anarchy. [71])

This scheme might possibly have worked and the Babylonian leaders might have accepted such a *fait accompli,* were it not for Saadia's intervention. Saadia was then residing in Aleppo. We do not know how long or for what purpose he was there. The community of Aleppo, of immemorial antiquity, became quite prosperous under early Islam and apparently was intellectually quite alert in the days of Saadia. Unfortunately, we do not have much information concerning its cultural life at that time; but inscriptions found in its old synagogue show that the building had been erected in 833. Running counter to repeated Muslim prohibitions against the erection of new synagogues, the possession of such a building appeared long precarious. That is undoubtedly why at an early date Aleppo Jewry had reinterpreted the date of the inscription as referring to A.D. 342, and thus as antedating Islam by some three centuries. [72] Whether or not Saadia came to Aleppo only as a transient on his journeys between Palestine and Babylonia it is difficult to say. His letters to his Egyptian disciples, though referring to a prolonged sojourn, seem to imply that it was as temporary as his previous stay in Mosul. [73] His official residence at that time must have been in Baghdad, since he expresses painful surprise that the Egyptian students, perturbed over the Ben Meir proclamation, had addressed their inquiries to the Babylonian leaders not through him but through one David b. Abraham, another Egyptian resident of the capital. He surmised that, having for six and a half years lost all contact with him, they doubtless did not know that he had transferred his residence to Baghdad. [74]

Upon hearing in the summer of 921 of Ben Meir's action, Saadia immediately realized its far-reaching implications. It touched him to the quick because it was bound to affect the great goal he had set for himself: to help in the reunification of Eastern Jewry. He evidently possessed no authority to intervene. As far as we can tell, he still was but a private citizen, whose early works may have gained him some reputation, but whose words need not have carried any weight in the community. He seems therefore to have written to Ben Meir (whom he undoubtedly knew from his stay in Palestine) a series of private letters, pointing out the seriousness of the matter and trying to persuade him to desist. After returning to Baghdad, he learned of Ben Meir's proclamation that both Marḥeshvan and Kislev were to be made deficient. No alternative remained but to urge a joint official action by the exilarch and the two (or three) geonim. [75]

The new exilarch, David b. Zakkai, had been in office long enough, and was sufficiently convinced of the necessity of upholding his authority, to be rather easily persuaded to undertake the required action. Undoubtedly more difficult was the task of enlisting the support of the two academies. That of Sura had been in eclipse for a number of years and was at the time headed by an apparently insignificant teacher, Jacob b. Naṭronai, while the academy of Pumbedita was then embroiled in the aforementioned controversy between Mubashshir and Kohen Ṣedeḳ. Mubashshir seems to have been indebted to Ben Meir for support extended to him in his conflict with the exilarch and the antigaon. [76] But it seemed imperative now to present a united front to the rebellious Palestinian leader. It must have required considerable tact and persuasiveness on the part of Saadia to bring the parties together and to induce them to issue letters and proclamations in behalf of all the central authorities of Eastern Jewry. [77] Saadia seems not only to have been the main factor in the negotiations but also to have drafted the communications which, under exilarchic and geonic signatures, were sent out to Ben Meir and his associates and to the various communities of the dispersion.

It is remarkable that, despite numerous threats included in the communications, which contrasted with the earlier conciliatory letters, the Babylonian leaders were satisfied with purely ecclesiastical censures. They even went out of their way to suggest arbitration. When this was refused and Ben Meir demanded the discontinuation of all further correspondence, they excommunicated him; appealed to all communities throughout the world; and published a documentary record of the transactions (a sort of blue book), for the benefit of contemporaries, who were urged to read it annually in the month of Elul, and of future generations. But, as Saadia himself makes clear, "they have not taken pains to obtain decrees from the royal administration." [78] Ben Meir was apparently prepared to face the consequences. [79] We can only guess at the reasons for the moderation displayed by Saadia and his associates. As mentioned above, Aaron b. Amram may have refused to cooperate with them. [80] They may also have hesitated to add fuel to the controversy, which had assumed the proportions of a public scandal, to the elation of Karaites and non-Jews. [81] The main reason, however, may have been the reluctance of 'Ali ibn 'Isa, then vizier in effect if not in name, to intervene in sectarian disputes, which at that time were disturbing the entire Muslim world with their noise and rioting. We know that, despite his great piety and learning, this "good vizier" himself had been the object of frequent attacks by fanatically orthodox Muslims, including the famous Al-Ash'ari. Moreover, notwithstanding his previous opposition to Ibn al-Furat's employment of Christian secretaries, 'Ali, too, had quite a few Christian counselors. Among them was a Christian banker, 'Isa, who seems to have had his ear as much as the Jewish bankers had had that of Ibn al-Furat. Very likely the Christians, surfeited with their own sectarian controversies, were none too prone to advise action in regard to internal Jewish disputes. Even if it was 'Ali whose order had saved Ben Meir from impending persecution by the Palestinian Karaites, he and his advisers may have been more inclined to use their imperial power to check sectarian persecutions than to abet them. [82]

The ecclesiastical censures may or may not have proved effective. Our sources fail to indicate any retreat on the part of Ben Meir. [83] Nor do we read that any of his successors gave up their claim to the Palestinian control of the calendar. With their independence promoted by the dissolution of the Caliphate and the incorporation of Palestine into the anti-Baghdadian Fāṭimid Empire, new opportunities arose for the reassertion of their claim. Indeed, more than a century later (1083), we learn from the *Scroll of Abiathar*, it was unequivocally reaffirmed in both theory and practice. [84]

AT PUMBEDITA AND SURA

Though the controversy with Ben Meir apparently ended without a decisive victory for his side, Saadia had demonstrated his

power and usefulness to the Babylonian leaders. Whether or not
this was his first direct cooperation with them, it seems that they
speedily decided to attach him permanently to the then-leading
academy of Pumbedita. In the letters written at the end of 921
and in 922, we find his signature followed by the titles *rosh kallah*
or *alluf*, which belonged to the highest ranks in the academy. [85]
He used the *alluf* designation in many letters and as an acrostic in
poems during the six subsequent years, until his elevation to the
gaonate of Sura.

During these years he was engaged in intensive literary work,
always bearing in mind its communal aspects. Outstanding among
his polemical writings of the period was his reply to Ḥiwi al-Balkhi,
apparently written in 926–27. The intriguing personality of Ḥiwi—
a Bible critic of a radical rationalist bent, who did not refrain from
making almost syncretistic use of Christian, Zoroastrian, and Muslim
doctrines, and of the teachings of such Muslim heretics as Al-
Rawandi, a communist sectarian allegedly of Jewish descent—
although frequently discussed, has not yet been fully explained. [86]
It will remain obscure until a lucky find furnishes us with at least
a fragment of his own work, which has thus far been known only
from citations by opponents, especially Saadia. Even more important than the literary figure of Ḥiwi is his communal influence. In
the sixty years which elapsed between the publication of his book
and Saadia's refutation, Eastern Jewry seems to have been permeated with so many contradictory trends—rationalism vs. mysticism,
orthodoxy vs. sectarianism, staunch adherence to the law vs. its
widespread neglect—that even such a critical work as Ḥiwi's had
found its way into the school system without immediately evoking
an articulate protest. [87] Like some of the orthodox Muslims in their
sphere, Saadia, despite Muʻtazilite leanings, feared the pernicious
influence the critical, or rather "smart-alecky," questions of Ḥiwi
might exercise upon young, immature minds. For this reason, he
found it necessary to publish a refutation answering Ḥiwi's two
hundred queries point by point. Written in a fairly complex rhymed
Hebrew, this refutation could not possibly have been addressed
to the school children who reputedly used Ḥiwi's textbook, but
rather was intended for their teachers and communal leaders.
Unfortunately, the fragment of Saadia's work recovered by the late
Professor Israel Davidson and the few other replies which can be
reconstructed from quotations in the later literature do not give

us satisfactory clues to the immediate incentives for Saadia's intervention, the intended distribution of his pamphlet, or the share, if any, of the exilarch and the two geonim in its promotion. The missing introduction, if it were recovered some day, might supply us with some such information. [88]

On May 22 (or 23), 928, Saadia was finally appointed to the leadership of the academy of Sura. The antecedents of his appointment are very interesting, from many angles. The academy of Sura had long been declining. Ever since the center of the Empire had shifted to Baghdad, Pumbedita—especially after its removal, complete or partial, to the capital—had received increasing attention. Sura, to be sure, remained an important Jewish community. In fact, two Arab historians have preserved the text of a letter addressed by 'Ali ibn 'Isa to the Sabian court-physician Sinan in A.H. 306 (918–19) in answer to the latter's inquiry concerning the treatment of *dhimmis* during a pestilence which had been ravaging the provincial communities. We learn from this letter that at that time the vast majority of Sura's population was Jewish. [89] However, the city's standing as a national center had greatly declined by the early tenth century, when appointments to the gaonate were made without due regard to the exalted traditions of the academy. By 926 the vigorous leader of Pumbedita, Kohen Ṣedeḳ, obtained frank recognition of Pumbedita's equality: it was decided that thenceforth all donations sent to the academies by outside communities without designation of one recipient should be divided equally between the two academies, discontinuing an immemorial practice of giving Sura two-thirds and Pumbedita only one-third of such revenue. [90] Sura's decline was so marked that thought was seriously given to discontinuing the academy there altogether and to transferring the few remaining officials and students to the sister academy of Pumbedita-Baghdad. [91]

When calmer counsels prevailed, David b. Zakkai made a determined effort to revitalize the Sura academy, by appointing Saadia to its gaonate. Nathan the Babylonian's picturesque description of his conversation with Nissi al-Nahrawani need not be fictitious. Similar consultations about appointments to important positions are frequently recorded for the upper reaches of the Muslim bureaucracy. [92] As we have seen, Al-Nahrawani himself had already been instrumental in bringing about a reconciliation between David b. Zakkai and Kohen Ṣedeḳ. David's refusal to listen to Nissi's warning

concerning Saadia's fearlessness and self-assertion is best explained
in the light of Sura's financial stringency, which evidently called for
vigorous leadership and immediate fund raising. David therefore
overcame not only whatever apprehensions he may have had as to
Saadia's pliability—he tried to safeguard himself by imposing on
the gaon an unusual solemn oath of fidelity—but also his own and
the academy's indubitable reluctance to appoint one who was not
of the ruling families, and who was, moreover, a "foreigner." [93] In
Sura's critical situation, however, Saadia's foreignness and contacts
with other Jewries may have been regarded as a blessing rather
than a shortcoming.

We learn on that occasion that Saadia entertained excellent relations with the Jewish court bankers of the period, "the children of
Neṭira and Amram"; that is, the descendants of Aaron b. Amram
and of Joseph b. Phineas's son-in-law, Neṭira. One of Neṭira's sons,
Sahl, is actually designated in the family chronicle as Saadia's
pupil and as one "who had in his possession the books written by
Saadia." [94] Twelve years had passed since Neṭira's death after a
quarter century of fruitful public activity. It stands to reason that
the master-pupil relationship between Saadia and Sahl had been
established when Saadia was teaching at the Pumbedita academy
in Baghdad, or earlier. Now, after his elevation to the gaonate of
Sura, he could be expected to utilize his connections with these
leading bankers to the best political, as well as economic, advantage
of his academy. It may have been more than a mere coincidence
that Saadia's appointment followed by only about a week the first
accession of Muḥammad ibn Muḳla to the chief vizierate of the
Empire. One could legitimately anticipate that under Ibn Muḳla
the influence of the Jewish bankers upon state affairs would the
more readily increase, as the new vizier had long been a member
of Ibn al-Furat's faction and during his early, humbler activities in
the capital must have been in touch with his former chief's main
fiscal agents. His recorded stay in the province of Al-Aḥwaz (after
his banishment from Baghdad in 923), where the bankers had for
many years served as the principal tax farmers, may have reinforced
the amicable relations, notwithstanding his personal disagreement
with Ibn Al-Furat's third vizierate. As clever and unscrupulous
as his predecessor, the new vizier—incidentally, "one of the most
celebrated calligraphists in the history of Islam"—must have realized
that he, too, could make very good use of the services of the Jewish

bankers in increasing both the state's and his own revenue. As a matter of record, the treasury of Al-Aḥwaz at that time, doubtless owing in part to the bankers' efforts, showed a sizable accumulation of funds, valued at 1,005,000 dirhems (some $280,000). [95]

In the growingly unstable conditions of the Caliphate, Saadia's extensive travels and far-flung personal relations could likewise be expected to prove useful in enlisting widespread voluntary support to make up for the losses sustained through the decrease in collections from the provinces under Sura's official jurisdiction. Letters of solicitation to various communities in the dispersion had often been sent out by both academies when in distress, and the exilarch was reasonably sure that Saadia would successfully follow this example. [96] His influential contacts with Egypt, in particular, would serve him in very good stead, for, despite numerous foreign invasions and the ravages of a corrupt bureaucracy, Egypt still was one of the wealthiest provinces of the Empire, and its Jewish communities had already laid the foundations for the marvelous cultural and economic expansion they would experience under the Faṭimids.

Almost immediately upon assuming office, Saadia addressed a letter to his former associates in Fusṭaṭ, clearly combining an appeal for support for the academy with an emphasis on his own political connections, which might prove useful to Egyptian Jewry. This letter of solicitation is, unfortunately, incompletely preserved, but one may deduce from the extant fragment that he asked them to address their legal inquiries—usually accompanied by generous donations—to the academy of Sura. He also intimated that, if the recipients should ever require assistance from the imperial administration, they should not hesitate to call upon him and he would be glad to ask his Baghdad friends to see to it that their wishes were favorably considered. He concluded with an announcement that he would follow up this letter with another, containing moral exhortations. [97]

This second letter of exhortations is extant almost complete. [98] While speaking with great elation of his new office and of the great obligations resting on his shoulders, and while keeping his homily on the high level of general ethics, Saadia nevertheless succeeded in reinforcing his previous solicitation. Of thirty-one exhortations, each beginning with the solemn בני ישראל, at least seven have a direct bearing upon the communal obligations of the recipients and on their duties (implied rather than expressed) toward a great academy of learning such as Sura. [99] But few of the exhortations deal with such basic problems of Judaism as the messianic hope, the immortality of the soul, and the basic unchangeableness of the Torah. Many others, though generally moralistic, may easily have conveyed to sensitive contemporaries appealing overtones hidden behind a maze of protective verbiage. [100] The main emphasis again was placed on the demand that the Egyptian Jews send regular inquiries to Sura—inquiries which, it did not require any specific explanation, would usually be accompanied by appropriate *douceurs.* [101]

Geonic letters of solicitation became much more frequent in the subsequent generations, when the regularity of collections from the provinces gave way under the disruptive forces in the Caliphate. Nehemiah and Sherira often stooped to rather undignified levels in asking Jews of Egypt, Kairuwan, and other countries to send money to Babylonia. Regular local committees had to be organized and entrusted with the task of fund raising. Their leaders were often addressed by the exalted heads of the academies in terms so flattering that even the profusion of titles which had crept into both Arabic and Hebrew correspondence during the tenth century does not quite explain them. [102] In comparison, Saadia spoke in an authoritative tone, intimating that he was bestowing rather than receiving benefits.

We are not informed as to how effective this and possibly many other such interventions by Saadia were. Neither do we know whether his far-flung correspondence, attested from many quarters, also had as one of its main objectives the enlisting of inquiries with accompanying donations. According to Ibn Daud, Saadia was in touch with even the distant Spanish communities of Cordova, Elvira, Lucena, Bajjana, Kalsana, Seville, and Merida. [103] Nonetheless, his main reliance was on the revenues from the district around Sura. With his militant temper and insistence upon geonic authority, he may have been a hard taskmaster. There is obvious exaggeration in the subsequent accusation of David b. Zakkai that he had oppressed the people under his jurisdiction and had severely chastised them for every infraction. [104] But his rigid insistence upon the letter of the law is reflected also in many of his legal decisions. For example, answering an inquiry concerning the validity of a particular marriage ceremony, he did not hesitate to order that all persons responsible for that legally inadequate ceremony be excom-

municated, "even if they be scholars like R. Shela." [105] He seems to
have been particularly implacable wherever he sensed heretical
leanings. That is doubtless why he so readily accepted R. Yehudai
Gaon's opinion—perhaps itself dictated by the first flush of anti-
Karaite feeling—that anyone who forgets to recite the *Sefirah* benediction on the first evening may never again recite it during that
entire season. [106] Such severity was evidently justified only in periods
of heated sectarian strife. [107] It was doubly justified, indeed imperative, to reassert the authority of the Babylonian leadership, tottering
under the overwhelming forces of dissolution which were then
undermining the entire established order.

Small wonder that some of Saadia's measures created ill will and,
it appears, fairly widespread resentment. Even his friends, the
bankers, may not have liked his strict reiteration of the talmudic
penalties for usurious transactions and the moralistic advice that
one ought not to charge interest even to Gentiles. [108] Interested
parties, on the other hand, undoubtedly resented such departures
from older law as Saadia's distinction between movables and
immovables in regard to neighbors' rights of preemption. [109] Many
other controversial decisions must have stemmed from Saadia's
judicial proceedings or literary writings, which antagonized one or
another vested interest or rooted ideology. But of his numerous
contributions to Jewish jurisprudence the few chance remnants can
give us only a very faint inkling.

There was one doctrine, however, gradually formulated by Saadia
in the years of his rise to power, which must have provoked the
sharpest, most widespread antagonism. His idea that in every generation there arises an outstanding sage whose supreme authority
should be acknowledged by all other leaders, since it is his great
merit and achievement alone which sustains the generation, doubtless aroused bitter resentment among the established leaders. Suspicion became ever more intense as Saadia made it increasingly
obvious that he considered *himself* the outstanding sage of his
generation. His doctrine reached its clearest formulation in the
Sefer ha-Galui, the fourth section of which was entirely devoted to
the demonstration that "God does not leave His people in any
generation without a scholar whom He inspires and enlightens so
that he in turn may so instruct and teach the people as to make it
prosper through him. And the occasion thereto has been what I
have personally experienced in what God, in His grace, has done

for me and for the people." [110] Though not encountered in such a bold formulation in any of Saadia's previous writings—unless it be in his *Commentary* on the Psalms—the doctrine is largely implied in the remarkable *haftarah* prescribed by him after the decease of a great scholar; [111] in his aforementioned exhortations to his Egyptian friends to support scholarship as the nation's lifeblood; and even in his teaching that the eternity of Israel is interrelated with that of the Torah, whose effectiveness is determined by the efficacy of its greatest expounders. [112] In his *Book in Support of the Traditional Laws,* which he later incorporated into his philosophic work, Saadia speaks of the specific distinctions conferred by law, rather than reason, on certain days, foods, etc. Among them, he says, there is also the significant "distinction of a certain person, as a prophet or leader" (more correctly, *imam,* כאלנבי ואלאמאם) who offers to humanity the following advantages: "to receive his instruction, to ask his intercession; for people to incline towards godliness that they may attain something like his own rank; or that he make it his care to improve mankind if possible, etc." In view of the long-established tradition that the ancient sages had succeeded the Israelitic prophets, it was easy to argue that the mantle of prophecy had descended upon the outstanding sages of each generation—a conception for which Saadia may have received powerful stimuli from the Arabian doctrine of the hereditary transmission of the prophetic soul, a doctrine which was later to play an enormous role in the world outlook of Halevy and, to a certain extent, also in that of Abraham b. Ḥiyya. [113]

These startling ideas, with direct application to his own great mission, had long been maturing in Saadia's mind and must have come to the fore in many of his acts and utterances during the early years of his administration. Some of his enemies may have been naïve enough to cling to such externals as his frequent use of vocalized and accentuated Hebrew texts resembling Scripture, a use which they considered as lowering the prestige of the Prophets to Saadia's level. Saadia could easily answer this reproach by referring to his unequivocal declaration that ancient prophecy had long been extinct, by pointing out that his work had none of the three earmarks of prophetic books (namely, the revealed character of their message; their attestation by miracles or by other, genuine prophets; and their acceptance by the people as sacred writ—another variation of the idea of *ijmaʿ*); and, finally, by stressing that there was no harm in the use of vowels and accents for greater popularization. [114] Of course, few of Saadia's vocalized texts were readily understandable to the unlearned masses, upon whom, on more than one occasion, Saadia heaped his scorn, in the manner of a typical "intellectual aristocrat" of the age. [115] Even the few border-line readers who might have been assisted by vocalization certainly had little use for the symbols of biblical cantillation. Much more serious, however, were Saadia's far-reaching public enactments—such as his promulgation of an official prayerbook, apparently without consultation with the exilarch or his colleague and former chief in Pumbedita; some measures, no longer identifiable, which he took to stem one of the recurrent pestilences; and the rumors, which must have been spreading, of his toying with the idea of computing the date of the coming of the Messiah. [116]

Apparently it was also in those years that Saadia's new genea-logical claims came to the fore, perhaps in answer to critics of his appointment to the gaonate. These claims, which bear the earmarks of an *ad hoc* fabrication, are obviously characteristic of Saadia's extremism; indeed, of his subversive attitude toward the established leadership. By tracing his descent back to Shela, the son of Judah, he clearly implied that his parentage was even purer than the Davidic ancestry of the exilarch, with its stigma of Judah's illicit relations with Tamar. His reputed descent from Ḥanina b. Dosa, reported by Ibn Daud but evidently stemming from his own asser-tions, must have evoked in the minds of contemporaries (if indeed the connection was not specifically brought to their attention by Saadia himself) such talmudic reminiscences as that relating to an alleged divine voice from Mt. Horeb calling daily "The entire world is being sustained on account of My son, Ḥanina." The contrast formulated in another utterance of Rab, "the universe was created only for the sake of Ahab b. Omri and Ḥanina b. Dosa; this world for Ahab b. Omri, the world to come for Ḥanina b. Dosa," could likewise be turned to good advantage in Saadia's struggle against the princely power of the exilarch. Ḥanina's father, moreover, whom Saadia directly quoted as an ancestor in his *Esa meshali* and whose name he chose for his own son, was also clearly a prototype to be followed during Saadia's stormy life. There is little doubt that Saadia identified Ḥanina's father with Dosa b. Horkinas, the famous and successful controversialist of the first (or second) century. [116a] All these claims must have appeared to numerous contemporaries to be more than mere genealogical playfulness or the satisfaction of some petty ambition. They rather seemed to buttress Saadia's bid for supreme, undisputed leadership.

Such doctrines and behavior must have appeared dangerous to many public-spirited citizens, including David b. Zakkai, Kohen Ṣedeḳ, and his vigorous lieutenant, Aaron ibn Sarjado. They were doubly dangerous in a man of Saadia's extraordinary gifts and attainments. They implied, above all, as was clearly stated two centuries later by another Baghdad gaon, Samuel b. 'Ali, that the Jews in the dispersion have "neither a king nor war, nor anything that would necessitate a king. They need, therefore, only one who would lead them, enlighten them, teach them the commandments of their religion, hand out justice and decide for them the law." [117] They certainly could at any time be turned against the exilarch in power; indeed, against the exilarchate as an institution. Sooner or later a break was unavoidable.

THE CONTROVERSY WITH DAVID B. ZAKKAI

The occasion for a conflict with the exilarch offered itself within two years after Saadia's elevation to the gaonate. From a garbled account by Al-Ḳasim b. Ibrahim, a ninth-century Arab jurist, it appears that the exilarch had special charge for the protection of Jewish minors. [118] This function must have been combined with some general administrative and judicial supervision over the inheritance of estates, although judicial decisions involving fine legal points may have been referred to the court of one or both geonim for final confirmation. [119] Jurisdiction in this field appeared doubly valuable to the exilarchs, as it was combined with considerable revenue from perfectly legitimate administrative and judicial fees. [120] Of course, the system lent itself to numerous abuses. Many Muslim judges are known to have enriched themselves from bribes and other spoils arising from controversies over hereditary rights. [121] Likewise, there must have been no end to rumors and suspicions in regard to the exilarch's role in the settlement of wealthy estates.

Soon a case arose in which Saadia and the exilarch failed to see eye to eye, and the long-smoldering conflict between them broke out. Unfortunately, modern historical literature treating of the controversy has largely followed the lead of the original sources, with their definite bias in favor of Saadia. [122] Nevertheless, it appears that Saadia had more than an even share in starting the conflict. Our main source of information, Nathan the Babylonian, in the typical style of literary historians, has reported the picturesque incidents and conversations—actual or fictitious [123]—which from the early request by David that Saadia sign a certain decision taken by the exilarchic court in a litigation over a large inheritance of some 7,000 dinars ($28,000) led to the ejection of David's son by Saadia's attendants when the young man, losing patience after several fruitless intercessions, threatened the gaon with physical violence. But Nathan fails to inform us of the legal substance of the issues involved; hence, we are in no position to form an opinion as to the justice of either party's contentions. Certainly the charge of 10 percent of the amount involved in what appears to have been a long and arduous proceeding, though high, does not seem to be excessive. Whether or not it was imposed on both parties in the litigation, it was a perfectly overt performance which smacked of no corruption. The subsequent mutual accusations of "bribery" need not be taken too seriously in an age when bureaucratic corruption was so widespread that Ibn al-Furat in 917 established a regular "Secret Profits' Bureau" to recapture some of the graft for the benefit of the state. [124] The exilarch may have had just as valid grounds for his decision as those which were commended by Saadia himself in a previous case. Their validity was, in fact, recognized by Kohen Ṣedek and Aaron ibn Sarjado, the future gaon of Pumbedita. Saadia, superior to them all in learning, and having special expertise in the laws of inheritance, on which he had long before written a halakhic monograph, [125] may have found some real flaws. But instead of privately informing the exilarch of his objections he played what appears in retrospect to have been a political game designed to discredit both the exilarch and his colleague of Pumbedita.

In any case, this immediate cause of the break was soon forgotten (it is hardly mentioned in the extant fragments of the controversial writings); and the basic issues, the incompatibility of the two vigorous personalities and the fundamental divergence in their conceptions of Jewish leadership, came clearly to the fore. It is also possible that the fall of Ibn Muḳla in June, 930, encouraged David b. Zakkai to take a firmer stand toward the recalcitrant gaon, whose protectors, the Jewish bankers, seemed to have lost, at least temporarily, some of their influence in court circles. The main power behind the throne now was the commander Muʻnis the Victorious, who may well have listened to the advice of his Christian clerk, Stephen, in all matters referring to protected subjects. Moreover, Muʿnis' friend ʿAli ibn ʿIsa, the former vizier, was recalled from exile and for a time held various influential positions. It seems that in his capacity as assistant to his cousin, the vizier Sulayman ibn al-Ḥasan, he dealt with the controversy between the exilarch and the gaon, as mentioned by Al-Masʿudi. [126] The Arabian historian, unfortunately, refers to the matter rather briefly, within an excursus on the Septuagint inserted into his story of the Ptolemaic kings of Egypt, and hence fails to indicate ʿAli's own predilection or the outcome of the proceedings before him. It is likely, however, that ʿAli, who at that time was so much perturbed over the sectarian controversies within Islam that he wrote a special treatise *Against Sectarianism*, tried merely to mediate between the opposing Jewish factions. He either deliberately refrained from deciding the issue in favor of one side or else had no time to make a decision before Sulayman's deposition (August 13, 931) and his own banishment from Baghdad (October 17, 931). [127]

During the first year of the controversy Saadia still felt strong enough to depose the exilarch and to proclaim an antiexilarch in the person of David's brother, Ḥasan-Josiah. He also wrote the first edition of his stinging pamphlet, the *Sefer ha-Galui*. David reciprocated by deposing Saadia and appointing Joseph b. Jacob bar Satia to the gaonate of Sura, regretfully contrasting Joseph's noble parentage with Saadia's ignoble foreignness. Together with Kohen Ṣedek he also proclaimed a ban on Saadia, while Ibn Sarjado carried on the literary feud, descending to very low levels of vilification. [128] Partisanship between the opposing factions reached a peak. There was street rioting of the kind frequently witnessed in Baghdad between the Shafiʿites and the Hanbalites. It was aggravated by the general state of unrest and by the constant rioting and looting, in all quarters of the capital, by an undisciplined soldiery and famished mobs. At times, Saadia's life was in danger. [129]

Before long, Saadia and his associates suffered complete defeat. Ḥasan-Josiah was exiled by the government to distant Khorasan, [130] while Saadia had to go into hiding in Baghdad. This seems to have occurred in 932–33, at the time of the great upheavals which cost Al-Muḵtadir his life and ended in the execution of his enemy Muʿnis. Since our main sources, Nathan and Sherira, are quite hazy about the chronology of these events, it is almost impossible to ascertain which vizier decided the issue against Josiah and Saadia. But it is evident that, in the prevailing disorder, the 60,000 dirhems (some $16,000)—a paltry sum in the days of Ibn al-Furat—offered by Ibn Sarjado at the right moment to the proper official, civil or military, outweighed the influence of those Jewish bankers who supported Saadia. Sahl b. Neṭira, his particular disciple and ardent admirer, seems to have altogether withdrawn to Al-Aḥwaz; however, by 936 the unsettled conditions spread to that district, and during a military mutiny there Sahl himself seems to have died an unnatural death—the frequent fate of those who dabbled in imperial politics at that time. [131]

Saadia used this period of enforced isolation to very good advantage. Although Abraham ibn Daud is undoubtedly wrong in saying that Saadia wrote all his books during that period, there is little doubt that many of his major contributions to Jewish literature date from then. The final revision of his *Siddur* may not have been issued by him at the time of his eclipse, since he speaks throughout with the authority of a gaon. Certain portions of the book, moreover, were clearly written earlier, at the time of his service as *alluf* of Pumbedita. Its official proclamation, too, very likely occurred during the first period of his gaonate in 928–30. [132] Nevertheless, some prayers seem to reflect Saadia's sufferings during the controversy, [133] and they may have been inserted into the text during a subsequent revision.

His major philosophic work, the *Kitab al-Amanat wa'l-I'tiḳadat*, was likewise written, or at least compiled from earlier essays, during those years. The date 933 is clearly indicated in Saadia's own passage. [134] It has long been recognized that the treatise was not written as a unit, but that most of its chapters, particularly the important tenth chapter, were issued as separate studies, often under individual titles. [135] It has also been noted that purely metaphysical problems were of secondary interest to Saadia and that the focus of his attention lay in apologetics and ethics, especially social ethics. [136] Moreover, the book seems to have been directed at his opponents, especially David b. Zakkai. One cannot help feeling that, despite the lofty, theoretical level maintained in the metaphysical and apologetical sections of the work, the final chapters on ethics bear the unmistakable imprint of controversy. Saadia's description of the disadvantages of ambition and the struggle for power, and his characterization of the autocratic ruler, not only recall the general abuses of government in his day but are almost cut to order to personify David b. Zakkai. [137] The practical advice given to readers culminates in the counsel to abhor, on a par with idleness, striving for power and vengeance; to pursue the golden mean of moderately yielding to the other ten major human motivations; and most important, to turn for guidance to wisdom and its bearers, the sages. [138]

However that may be, upon his resumption of office in 937 after a reconciliation with David under the impact of public opinion and the intervention of Bishr b. Aaron (probably Aaron b. Amram's son), Saadia seems to have become considerably mollified. Not only did he make peace with the exilarch, but, upon the latter's death and the decease of his son and heir, Saadia took his grandson, aged twelve, home for safety and more thorough education. [139] In public affairs, too, he seems to have steered a much more moderate course. To be sure, it may still have been due to his influence, or at least to the reluctance of his former colleagues to antagonize him, that after Kohen Ṣedeḳ's decease in 936 the academy of Pumbedita failed to elect Aaron ibn Sarjado, Saadia's sworn enemy, to the position of gaon. Ibn Sarjado, despite his vigor, wealth, and connections—he was Bishr b. Aaron's son-in-law and had served as *alluf* of Pumbedita for many years—failed to secure the appointment to the gaonate until 943, a year after Saadia's death. [140]

Nothing is known about the declining years of Saadia's life. The situation in Baghdad became, as mentioned before, increasingly unbearable. The same Al-Baridi who in A.H. 321 (933–34) had shamefully maltreated the Jews of Tustar and extorted 100,000 dinars from them now occupied Baghdad. He became one of the most ruthless collectors of the state's revenue, especially on the part of the protected subjects. Jews and Christians were publicly beaten and even executed for alleged tax defaults. Looting by soldiers, a catastrophic flood, the spread of the plague, and growing famine destroyed all forms of civilized life. "A *kur* of wheat fetched 316 dinars," and the corpses of the dead served as food for the survivors. [141] Little wonder that under these unspeakable conditions in the capital and its environs, become doubly harrowing after Al-Baridi's victory over Ibn Ra'id on March 7, 942, Saadia grew increasingly despondent. The dream of his life, the reunification of Jewry throughout the vast expanses of the Empire lay shattered under the ruins of the Empire itself. He died on Iyar 26 (May 16), 942, broken-hearted—Ibn Daud says *min ha-marah ha-sheḥorah* [142]—

leaving the academy of Sura in such bad straits that his successor (formerly his rival), Joseph b. Jacob, not long thereafter gave up his residence in Sura and moved to Baṣra. For at least four decades thereafter there was no academy in Sura, the few remaining scholars joining the ranks of the academy of Pumbedita. Ibn Sarjado was magnanimous enough to receive these associates of his former enemy with open arms and to assign them to positions of influence in those provinces which had previously belonged to the sphere of control of the Sura academy. [143]

6

Yehudah Halevi:
An Answer to a Historical Challenge *

IT IS an old Jewish custom to make use of anniversaries for a comprehensive "reckoning of the soul." The observance of the eighthundredth anniversary of Yehudah Halevi's death has not only served to remind the Jewish people of the greatness of their cultural heritage and the necessity of their carrying on in the midst of gravest dangers but has given them a better understanding of the way in which the repeated crises in their history have been effectively met under the guidance of Jewish leaders and thinkers. In the midst of confusion and suffering, and through the din of epochal changes as well as petty strife engendered by the Second World War, the celebrations have also given us a welcome pause to review the life and work of the greatest Hebrew poet after the conclusion of the Bible, a man whose contribution to medieval thinking has retained much of its original freshness and vigor.

It makes little difference that the chronological basis for these celebrations is somewhat dubious; that, by a historical irony, neither the exact date of Halevi's decease nor that of his birth was preserved by his otherwise highly appreciative contemporaries. If on this account the man who emphasized history above all his predecessors in medieval Jewish thought was a victim of the historical forgetfulness of medieval Jewry, his life and work have long since been fully vindicated by a grateful posterity. Some of his poems, which even in his lifetime were recited, collected, and read in many countries throughout the Mediterranean world, early found their way into the liturgical collections of the entire people, and thus stirred the emotions of untold generations. In recent years his poems, more fully recovered from the world's major libraries, have been assembled and published in critical editions and translated into

* This essay is based on an address delivered at the octocentennial Halevi celebration sponsored by the Canadian Jewish Congress in Toronto, February 23, 1941, and later printed, in expanded and annotated form, in *Jewish Social Studies* 3 (1941), 243–72.

various languages, and have once more become a treasure-trove for Hebraic Jewry. His philosophic *magnum opus* in its original Arabic may have gradually lost its hold upon the mind of his people, for only one Arabic manuscript of the fifteenth century and a few fragments were available to its scholarly editor a few decades ago. But in its Hebrew garb—two Hebrew translations were completed within seventy years after the author's death—it continued to inspire generations of thoughtful Jews. Frequently commented upon by prominent students of Jewish philosophy, extensively cited by leading authorities, translated into Latin and into several modern languages, the *Kitāb al-Khazari* (or *Kuzari*) often was the subject of both widespread and intensive reading by the Jewish public at large. [1] No less than twenty editions of the Hebrew text are known to have appeared in the years 1506–1887, several more having left the printing presses during the past, more articulate decades. [2] A review of the memorable experiences of this great poet and philosopher against the background of his stormy age, which unavoidably conditioned his great intellectual achievement, may still yield many a fruitful lesson for our own perplexed and intellectually groping generation.

GROWING TENSIONS

As Halevi probably was born in Tudela, [3] sometime before 1075, he began life in an era of comparative quiet on the Iberian Peninsula. This period may perhaps best be characterized as one of "appeasement." The wealthy and cultured Moors, though hopelessly divided under a great variety of "petty kings," would have been more than a match for their Christian neighbors had they felt their civilization threatened by the onslaught of the backward but youthful forces of the north. Eleventh-century Spain represented in this respect a curious inversion. Christianity, which had begun as a pacifist, altogether other-worldly religion, was now outwardly a creed of zealous, fighting young peoples who considered war both a religious and a civic duty. The Muslims, on the other hand, whose religion had begun as a religion of the sword, whose founder was as much an empire-builder as he was a prophet, [4] had now settled down to enjoy the fruits of an advanced civilization. Deeply satiated, they wished to be left alone to the enjoyment of their intellectual as well as material benefits. At the time when Halevi lived in Cordova, this former capital of the western Caliphate, although in gradual eclipse since 1013, was still "the pearl of the universe," as it was styled by a contemporary German nun. [5] Possessing a multifarious population, which at one time resided in some 113,000 houses, and equipped with beautiful mosques, schools, and a university which preceded in age and rivaled in splendor its sister institutions in Cairo and Baghdad, the city looked down on the "barbarians" of the north in scorn mixed with apprehension. Among Cordova's seventy libraries there was one assembled by a scholar-king which is said to have counted four hundred thousand works, listed in a catalogue of forty-four volumes. This at a time when a few score miles to the north a monastic scholar was proud of having two hundred volumes at his disposal. The petty rulers of the Moorish kingdoms of Seville, Granada, Valencia, Badajoz, Saragossa, and Toledo, among whom there was more than one esteemed poet, and one author of an encyclopedia in fifty volumes said to have been composed exclusively on the basis of works assembled in his own library, were more than ready to appease their Christian neighbors by paying regular annual tribute, rather than confront them at swords' points. [6]

Halevi, as a child, undoubtedly partook of that general feeling of security. His own native city of Tudela was the center of a fertile agricultural region, the cereals and fruits of which were widely famed. Although under early Muslim rule it often was the seat of Moorish rebels and was frequently retaken by Christians, it was thoroughly pacified by 'Abd-ar-Raḥmān III and was then and later, according to a recently recovered geographic work of Al-Ḥimyari, the only city in Spain which never shut its gates for the night. [7] Halevi's family and he undoubtedly enjoyed the fruits of that high Spanish-Muslim and Spanish-Jewish civilization which had flowered in the great achievements of Ibn Ḥazm, Ibn Gabirol, and many other scholars and writers, whose work often presupposed "a mental development" which "was not attained in Europe until the nineteenth century." [8] Among the eight or nine million Iberians of that age [9] there must have been hundreds of thousands of Jews, who, often living in close settlements, enjoyed extensive self-government and played a conspicuous role in the economic, political, and cultural life of the peninsula. Except for the heavy, and often arbitrary, taxation which afflicted them, even more severely than it did the rest of the much-exploited population, they had few grounds for complaint. Even in the areas reconquered by the Christians, we read of the metropolitan city of Barcelona as having "an equal number of Jews and Christians," and of nearby Tarragona as being "a city of Jews." Similarly, at the southern extremity, Granada, the shining citadel of Muslim culture to the end of the Middle Ages, which but a few decades before Halevi's prolonged sojourn there had replaced Elvira as the capital of one of the petty Muslim kingdoms (1113), was still called by the Arabs *Ighranāta al-yahūd,* "Jewish Granada." [10] This designation was due not only to the belief—mentioned by Al-Ḥimyari and perhaps based on fact—that the Jews had been its first settlers but also to the overpowering influence of such individuals as Samuel ha-Nagid, the renowned poet-diplomat, and of such families as the Ibn Ezras, and, in general, to the number, economic status, and cultural power of the Jewish community, which had long remained intact, notwithstanding the brutal bloodletting of 1066. [11] In neighboring Lucena, where Halevi apparently received instruction from the great jurist Isaac Alfasi, and served as secretary to Isaac's famous successor Joseph Ibn Megas, we learn from Idrisi (about 1150) that the Jews "occupied the center of the city and did not allow the Muslims to penetrate into their quarter. The population [i.e., the Jews] is wealthier there than in any country under Muslim domination. . . ." [12]

In Halevi's childhood, however, rumblings of a new age were distinctly audible to attentive ears. The era of appeasement was speedily drawing to its close. Already there had appeared in the north the Christian hero Rodrigo Díaz de Vivar, the famous Cid Campeador of legend and poetry. Whether or not he was consciously dreaming of a united *Hispania,* an ideal which had never been lost through the ages of Muslim domination, his exploits helped initiate the decisive phase of the Spanish *reconquista* in the two centuries from 1045 to 1250. In 1085, Toledo, the ancient capital of Visigothic Spain, was recaptured by Alphonso VI of Castile and permanently remained a Castilian possession. To counteract these expansionist trends, the Moorish kings called to their assistance Yusuf ibn Tashufīn, the Almoravid ruler of Morocco, who in 1086 speedily defeated the Castilian army in the renowned battle of Sagrajas (Zalaca). Before long, however, the ally turned out to be a rapacious conqueror: he returned in 1090 to overrun Granada and the rest of Muslim Spain, uniting it for a while under Almoravid rule. The conflict now assumed all the features of a war of religion, in which Christian Crusaders battled with fanatical Muslims seeking death on the battlefield as the greatest achievement for fighters in a "holy war." Simultaneously, the clash between Islam and Christendom assumed world-wide proportions, with the Christian Crusaders marching to reconquer the Holy Land, a task which they temporarily accomplished in 1099.

Little wonder that in the new clime of ruthless intolerance and mutual annihilation the old easygoing ways and the liberal cultivation of arts and letters gave way to increasing repression. The Muslim jurists of the Malikite school, victorious in Morocco since 1048, now spread their doctrines through the newly conquered province proclaiming the superiority of *taklid* (full acquiescence in tradition) over *ijtihad* (independent interpretation). The works of Al-Ghazali, whose defense of religion against rationalism seems to have left an indelible imprint upon the thinking of Halevi, were now being put to the flames throughout Morocco and Muslim Spain, because in his renowned *Revivification of the Sciences of Islam* he had ventured to expose the drive for power and personal gain which had motivated many of these famed expounders of the law. The jurists of Granada who, carrying on the tradition of the more liberal era of the "petty kings," vigorously protested against this suppression of the books of a much-revered author, were arrested and their leaders severely punished. [13] Before long, even the Almoravid rule proved ineffective, and a few years after Halevi's departure from Spain the country was overrun by the still more fanatical hordes of Almohades, who, in the name of their "unitarian" principle, proclaimed the exclusiveness of Islam and, thenceforth, the complete suppression of both Christianity and Judaism in the entire Almohade Empire.

Even before this outburst of utter intolerance, unique in Muslim annals, the Jews had begun to feel the impact of the new era. They may still have overlooked the signs of the age when three thousand of their coreligionists were massacred on the streets of Granada in 1066 by the Muslim populace, aroused by the anti-Jewish poem of a Muslim of Elvira. The assault, though greatly stimulated by popular slogans and invectives against Jewish "dominion," had evidently been cleverly engineered by the personal enemies of the Jewish vizier of Granada, Yehosef, the son of Samuel ha-Nagid. But the intense suffering of Jews throughout the peninsula after 1085, as a result of the holy wars between Islam and Christendom, could not be thus minimized. In the battle of Sagrajas, reports an exaggerating chronicler, 40,000 Jews, distinguished from other combatants by black and yellow turbans, fought in the Christian armies. [14] They were "re-warded" before long with a Christian pogrom in Toledo and other sections of Castile and Leon (1109), even though the Crusaders had been specifically enjoined by Pope Alexander II to leave the Jews unharmed. In the privileges given in 1118 by Alphonso VII of Castile to the Christian community of Toledo, a full amnesty was granted to the perpetrators of the 1109 massacre. Going beyond the tradi-tional objection of the Church to Jewish control over Christians, reechoed in the epistle of Gregory VII to Alphonso VI (1081), Alphonso VII was forced to promise in 1118 that "no Jew, not even a converted Jew, shall exercise any jurisdiction over any Christian in Toledo or its territory." [15] When, on the other hand, Muslim Spain was overrun in 1090 by the Almoravid hosts, the Jewish community also suffered greatly. With the advent of the intolerant Almohade rule in 1145–50, the glorious period of Arabian-Jewish collaboration on the peninsula was brought to a speedy end. Halevi, undoubtedly voicing a widespread feeling among his coreligionists, complained in one of his poems that the Jews had been victimized by "the hosts of Seir and Kedar," i.e., Christendom and Islam, and that "when these are locked in battle, we fall as they go down." [16]

To add to the confusion, Jewish refugees from Muslim parts drifted to the Christian regions, but found life there extremely difficult. Apart from the economic difficulties—even the daughters of King Al-Mu'tamid, deported to Morocco by the Almoravids, were fortunate to be able to earn their living by spinning [17]—there were serious problems of cultural adjustment. For example, Moses ibn Ezra, who held out longer than his brothers but was finally forced to leave Granada and flee to Castile, for the remainder of his life complained of the "desert of savages" to which he saw himself exiled. Sure of his superiority he constantly consoled himself that, after all, in the eyes of humanity the difference between him and his new neighbors was quite evident, and that he was but a "plucked rose among thorns and thistles." He was so evidently unable to earn a livelihood or to make the necessary mental adjustment among the "boorish" Castilians that Halevi addressed a poem to him, urging that, despite all risk of danger and unavoidable suffering, he return to his old haunts. [18]

Such maladjusted refugees, knocking at the gates of various Jewish communities, helped to spread the culture of Muslim Spain, but demonstrated to all the insecurity of Jewish life. Where else were they to go, however? Apparently, very few Jewish Spaniards thought of proceeding north of the Pyrenees, to France, England, or Germany. The economic opportunities in the tiny, for the most part newly arisen, urban centers in those areas were decidedly limited. At best a small number of traders and moneylenders could hope to eke out a meager (as measured by Muslim standards of the time) and precarious existence. The advanced arts of horticulture and truck-farming practiced by the Jews in Spain were practically unknown in the northern lands, and the opportunities for Jews to enter into agriculture in lands increasingly monopolized by feudal lords and their villein farmers were almost nil. Culturally, too, one could expect but little from these backward regions. This was a short time after the great Toledan judge Saʿīd al-Andalūsi (1029–70) had given to a credulous audience the following "biological" reasons for Nordic inferiority:

Because the sun does not shed its rays directly over their heads their climate is cold and atmosphere clouded. Consequently their temperaments have become cold and their humors rude, while their bodies have grown large, their complexion white and their hair long. They lack withal sharpness of wit and penetration of intellect, while stupidity and folly prevail among them. [19]

In short, the prospect of settling in northwestern Europe must have appeared as formidable to a Spanish-Jewish refugee then as that of migrating to Paraguay or New Caledonia appeared to a German refugee in the 1930s. The rumors, undoubtedly exaggerated, of the great anti-Jewish massacres from France to Central Europe in 1096 must have served as a final deterrent. It took many years of still more severe persecutions under Western Islam and of the relative stagnation of Jewish intellectual endeavor under Eastern Islam, coupled with the gradual progress in the civilization of Western Christendom, for the keen eyes of Maimonides to detect that the future of Judaism really rested with the relatively few Jews of France and of the Christian West in general. [20] In Moses ibn Ezra's and Halevi's day, however, eyes were turned eastward rather than to the West or North. But the East, too, was under attack. The Holy Land lay prostrate under the trampling phalanxes of Crusaders, who nearly exterminated the flourishing Palestinian-Jewish communities. In reaction to the Crusades, the Muslim East, too, witnessed a growth of religious fanaticism and intolerance, which must have brought back to the Jews the memory of their shattering experiences under the reign of the half-crazed Al-Ḥakim, the eleventh-century ruler of Egypt and Palestine. The future of world Jewry looked very bleak indeed.

The external difficulties of Spanish Jewry were increased by forces of internal disintegration. Close social and intellectual intercourse with their Moorish neighbors had produced assimilatory trends which threatened to submerge the identity of large portions of peninsular Jewry. Halevi himself had to admit the overwhelming environmental pressure, when he complained that "we, through our sins, incline daily more towards them." [21] Cases of conversion to the dominant creed were rare in neither the Muslim nor the Christian areas. Especially in Halevi's lifetime the combined pressure of pogroms and legal discrimination seems to have brought about so many conversions as to constitute a serious social problem. We have seen that the Christians of Toledo had successfully sought to obtain a royal privilege exempting them from the overlordship of even Jewish converts to Christianity. Soon after Halevi's time, a convert to Islam, Samuel ibn 'Abbas, hailing from neighboring Morocco, became one of the leading Muslim polemists against Judaism. There is some indication that Halevi himself was at some time or other subjected to the pressure of conversion, which he successfully resisted.[22] Among those who remained within the fold, a variety of heterodox currents introduced a constant element of dissension and weakness. While we have no evidence of a Spanish counterpart of Ḥiwi al-Balkhi, who, two centuries before Halevi, had subjected the Pentateuch to searching rational criticism of a kind unrivaled before the days of the European Enlightenment, we learn about numerous Jews who neglected to observe the traditional laws and even rationalized such neglect by accepting some extreme doctrines of Muslim thinkers. Even before Averroës, Halevi's younger contemporary, many Jews on the peninsula were ready to listen to the teachings of those who claimed that the Deity had no knowledge of particulars and hence was not interested in the actions of man. The forces of religious Jewry itself were divided by the unceasing onslaught of Karaism, which constituted a problem of sufficient gravity for Halevi to devote a substantial portion of his philosophic work to combating its doctrines.

NATIONALIST REORIENTATION

More than anyone else in his day, Halevi was sensitive to these internal and external forces of disintegration. In his early years, evidently spent in the Muslim environment of Tudela, he seems to have felt but slightly the growing friction between the Muslim and Jewish populations in his native city, which came to the fore immediately after Tudela's conquest by the Christians in 1115. [23] Before that date, relations were still outwardly amicable, and Halevi may well have come under the influence of his older Muslim compatriot, the "Blind Poet of Tudela." Halevi's sense of security was further enhanced when he reached Granada, where he was received with open arms by the four Ibn Ezra brothers. It was a period when the greatest of his predecessors, Solomon ibn Gabirol, could view the situation of Jewry so complacently as to write his major philosophic work in entirely nondenominational terms; so much so, indeed, that for centuries thereafter his *Fountain of Life* was ascribed by Christian scholastics to either a Christian or a Muslim author named "Avicebrol." Notwithstanding his impatience with dissenting friends and intellectual rivals, which was perhaps merely the expression of youthful rashness—he was but slightly over thirty when he died, in 1058—Ibn Gabirol could preach religious tolerance with a warmth rarely encountered in medieval letters. [24]

In this atmosphere of relative detachment, Halevi, too, could indulge in writing conventional love poems and wine ditties, poems of friendship, and other personal lyrics having little, if any, reference to the state of Jewry in his day. [25] Even in his religious poems of that period, as in those of Ibn Gabirol, we find a lofty restatement of the ancient ideals of religious Judaism, without direct reference to the events of the day or to the dangers threatening the people in exile. No doubt the problem of exile was there all the time. Especially the contrast between the powerful "son of the slave girl" (an allusion to the alleged Ishmaelite origin of the Arabs) and the distressed descendants of Isaac and Jacob was too obvious to escape attention. However, one could be satisfied with a mild, more or less stereotyped, protest and with an expression of hope that this situation would not last. [26] At most, if one were deeply religious, one could speculate with greater or lesser emotional intensity on the coming of the Redeemer and the glories of the messianic age. Undoubtedly stimulated by Christian chiliastic movements, a large part of European Jewry seems to have expected the arrival of the Messiah at the completion of the first millennium after the fall of Jerusalem (1070; or rather, according to the Jewish computation, 1068). Ibn Gabirol, too, seems to have set his heart upon this date, his premature death alone preventing him from seeing his dream come to naught. Before the Almoravid ravages, however, neither Halevi, still in his youth, nor his contemporaries show any signs of the keen disappointment which must have affected large circles of Spanish Jewry and added another element to their internal disintegration.

Poetry of the type written by the youthful Halevi was extremely fashionable in Moorish and Jewish circles. Kings and diplomats, soldiers and businessmen, all indulged in some sort of versification. This poetry was often stilted by the heavy chains of the difficult Arabic *ars poetica*, of which, for instance, Halevi's mentor, Moses ibn Ezra, was both a practical exponent in his own poems and a theoretical protagonist in his treatise on Hebrew poetry. But these technical difficulties seem to have deterred few; they rather whetted the appetite of many poets, talented and otherwise. The popularity of versification often reached ludicrous extremes: many official documents, such as passports, were sometimes issued in rhymed prose. Halevi, however, was not merely a follower of fashion when he became a poet. Though in the later years of his life, under the impact of the great crisis, he did begin to turn away from poetry as his main medium of expression, it is still very doubtful whether we ought to accept at face value the tradition recorded two decades later by his self-styled disciple Ibn Parḥon, that in old age Halevi vowed to quit versifying altogether. Even when he seems to be speaking disparagingly of poetry, as when he refers to it as the mere "foam" upon the sea as contrasted with wisdom, which is like the vast expanse of the sea itself, he (like Ovid in the *iam iam* of the well-known anecdote) was still writing great poetry. [27]

The increasing seriousness of the Jews' situation, however, induced him to turn, apparently in his sixties, to a systematic presentation of his ideas on Jews and Judaism. Though written in the form of a Platonic dialogue and often filled with poetic similes, the work nevertheless was characteristic of the scholarly philosophic prose of the period. Consciously apologetic, emphasizing in its subtitle that it was a "Book of Argumentation and Demonstration in Aid of the Despised Faith," the *Al-Khazari* undertook to redefine Judaism for both the outside world and its own adherents, with due cognizance of the contemporary crisis. This work gives us an insight not only into the author's versatile mind and thinking, matured under the strains and stresses of a busy, eventful, often dramatic, career, but also into the manifold factors which, positively and negatively, influenced the position of Jewry.

While this work was still in progress Halevi seems to have despaired of the effectiveness of his literary endeavors, as he did of the benefits of his medical ministrations. Animated by a deep sense of guilt, for the immediate causes of which we have not as yet any satisfactory explanation, he suddenly decided to abandon his busy medical practice in one of the largest cities of Spain (possibly Toledo); to leave behind his family, which included a beloved grandson and namesake, Yehudah (Spanish Jewry did not object to calling children by the names of their living grandparents [28]); and to give up nearly all of his fairly considerable earthly possessions in order to proceed to Palestine. Of course he knew that the country had been for years under the domination of the Jew-baiting Christian Crusaders, and that, especially from the Jewish point of view, it was in a desolate state, offering little in the way of physical or cultural amenities to pilgrims or settlers. Nevertheless, believing that Palestine, even at its worst, held out greater promise for the Jews than any other country in the East or West—"better is one day on God's soil," he declared, "than a thousand in foreign lands; the ruins of the Divine Mount are more friendly than a palace and castle elsewhere; for here I shall be redeemed, while there I must serve a cruel master"—he decided, as apparently did many others among his Spanish coreligionists, to spend the end of his days on the sacred soil. [29]

It is one of the consequences of the tragic neglect of historical data by Halevi's contemporaries and successors that we do not know how and when he reached the goal of his journey. For some reason his sojourn in Egypt and Syria, his final stations before the Holy Land, dragged on much longer than he had expected. Lavishly entertained by a great many friends and admirers, and apparently earning his own living through the customary commercial channels,[30] he spent some two years in Damietta alone, where, almost within reach of the Palestine frontier, he continued arguing with his friends about the imperative necessity of his settling in the Holy Land[31] but was apparently long unable to cross the border. The well-known legend of his death in Jerusalem at the hands of a Bedouin raider whose horse's hoof struck the poet while he sang his immortal *Ode to Zion* may contain a grain of historical truth; but the last historically attested events in his life lead us only to Egypt and, possibly, Tyre, at the northern fringe of Palestine. The place of his decease, like the exact day in July 1141, will remain shrouded in darkness until perhaps some day a lucky find will help clear up this historically and psychologically significant riddle.

ZIONIST IDEOLOGY

Halevi's entire life and work, but especially his decision to proceed to Palestine, his composition of the famous Zionide poems, and the novelty of his apologetic argumentation, were clearly answers to the historical challenge of his period and environment. Like most of his compatriots of the cultured classes, he was a student of Graeco-Arabian philosophy and ethics, but he increasingly realized the futility of some of its answers with respect to the hard and fast realities of his age. "And let not the wisdom of the Greeks beguile thee," he finally exclaimed, "it has flowers but no fruit." [32] This does not mean that he wished to abandon the rational approach to life. As a matter of fact, notwithstanding his sharp critique of the prevalent rationalist trends in Arabian thought—he was undoubtedly influenced by a similar critique in Al-Ghazali's *Tahafut alfalasifa* (The Incoherence of Philosophers)[33]—Halevi remained basically a rationalist to the end of his life. It was as a rationalist that he argued that human cognition is wholly inadequate for the task of penetrating the deep mysteries of existence. Out of this epistemological skepticism he argued that human reason unaided could never decide, for example, whether the universe was primordial or created. "The question of eternity and creation is obscure, whilst the arguments are evenly balanced. The theory of creation derives greater weight from the prophetic tradition of Adam, Noah and Moses, which is more deserving of credence than mere speculation. If, after all, a believer in the Torah finds himself compelled to admit an eternal matter and the existence of many worlds prior to this one, this would not impair his belief that *this* world was created at a certain epoch and that Adam and Eve were the first human beings." [34] In short, the only guidance man possesses to the perplexities of existence is given to him by tradition, by the continuing heritage of his ancestors, which alone may determine his choice among all the possible alternatives advanced by reason, as exemplified in the contradictory opinions of scholars and thinkers. [35]

The most important element in tradition is the original Sinaitic revelation, wherein God himself communicated a series of basic truths to the Jewish people and through it to mankind. The authenticity of this revelation cannot be doubted, since it was witnessed by an entire people of 600,000 adult males, in addition to women and children—who thereafter handed down the story of that theophany to their children and grandchildren, to the present day. This unique Sinaitic experience, in which God's voice was heard not by an individual prophet, as is claimed by the exponents of Christianity and Islam, but by an entire people of average men and women, is further confirmed by the admission of its veracity by the Christian and Muslim opponents of Judaism. At the very beginning of Halevi's dialogue, the Christian spokesman assures the king that the Torah and the records of the children of Israel "are undisputed because they are generally known as lasting and have been revealed before a vast multitude." When the Muslim representative, too, expresses his reliance upon the Biblical tradition, as to which "no suspicion of deceit and imagination is possible," the king promptly deduces that the Jews "constitute in themselves the evidence of the divine law on earth" for all believers in a revealed religion. [36] The weight of this argument, derived from the unwitting testimony of a religious opponent, can be fully appreciated only if one realizes how important its inverted application to the testimony of Jews and their Scriptures has been for the survival of Jewry, particularly in Christian Europe. The Sinaitic revelation was amplified in many details by direct divine communications to individual men from Adam to Moses before it and to the Israelitic prophets thereafter. It is this truth, attested by history and fortified by the testimony of a long historical evolution, which is superior to the ephemeral truths detectable by human reason unaided by tradition. These historical truths, to be sure, must not conflict with human reason. "Heaven forbid that I should assume what is against sense and reason" and "Heaven forbid that there should be anything in the Bible to contradict that which is manifest or proved. . . ." [37] But it is the task of a philosopher to square the findings of history with the findings of reason; if necessary, adjusting the latter, as the more elastic ones, to the former, which, based upon fact, are essentially immutable.

From this point of view, we may understand the basic assumptions of Halevi, and the logical conclusions which he felt justified in drawing from them. If history thus teaches us to abandon our reliance upon a more or less blind, uncontrolled succession of cause and effect in nature, if we have to assume that all is guided by a theistic principle, a divine will and providence, the history of man, and especially of Israel, assumes a new, cosmic significance in the divine scheme of existence. [38] Referring to the well-known talmudic saying concerning the seven things created prior to the world, Halevi declares:

It was the object of divine wisdom in the creation of the world to create the Torah, which was the essence of wisdom, and whose bearers are the just among whom stands the throne of glory and the truly righteous, who are the most select, viz., Israel, and the proper place for them was Jerusalem, and only the best of men, viz., the Messiah, son of David, could be associated with them, and they all entered Paradise. Figuratively speaking, one must assume that they were created prior to the world.

In this sense the exodus from Egypt rivals in significance the creation of the world, not only as equal motivations for the Sabbath rest commandment but because both are equally "the outcome of the absolute divine will, not the result of accident or natural phenomena." [39] The very knowledge of God is no longer a typically philosophic quest for objective truth, like the knowledge of any object in nature, but a deep concern with the source of all being, with its purposes and means. Therein lies the superiority of the prophet over the philosopher, which is similar to the superiority of the poet over the diligent student of poetic arts, or that of a traveler in foreign lands over the most assiduous reader of travelogues. [40] Historically, too, it is attested that God has never addressed himself directly to a philosopher, but always to philosophically untrained prophetic messengers. What really distinguishes prophets from other men is a superior native capacity, a mental predisposition which, bestowed upon them by grace divine, makes them as different from other human beings as are humans from animals.

It is here that Halevi found most of his answers for the difficulties of Jewish existence. If prophecy is the crowning human achievement, the Jewish people, from whom were recruited all the prophets recognized not only by the Jews but by the entire civilized world known to Halevi, must be a people of marked distinction. Distinguished by its holy tongue, the oldest and the most perfect [41] of all languages and the only medium of divine revelation, as well as by its Holy Land, which is placed by nature in the center of all climates and which (together with its immediate environs) has been the only scene of revelation, this people evidently occupies a unique position in the divinely ordained world. Its career, clearly the greatest product of human history, has not been created by the usual processes of historical evolution and human exertion, like that of many other peoples and religions, but by the sudden will of God. Answering the king's statement that religions usually arise in the minds of single men, who gradually gain an increasing following or—perhaps alluding to the actual events during the conversion of the Khazars—"a King arises and assists them, also compels his subjects to adopt the same creed," the rabbi replies: "In this way only rational religions, of human origin, can arise. . . . A religion of divine origin arises suddenly. It is bidden to arise, and it is there, like the creation of the world." [42] The Jewish people, moreover, which in its entirety listened to the revealed word of God at Mount Sinai, has remained unique because of its native predisposition to prophecy, which makes it a truly "chosen people," a people natively different from, and superior to, all other peoples.

Halevi pushes this conviction to extremes shared by neither the other medieval Jewish philosophers nor by the dominant rabbinic opinion of any period. His imaginary rabbi shocks his royal interlocutor by saying:

Any Gentile who joins us unconditionally shares our good fortune, without, however, being quite equal to us. If the law were binding on us only because God created us, the white and the black man would be equal, since He created them all. But the Law was given to us because He led us out of Egypt, and remained attached to us, because we are the cream of mankind.

Referring to the divorce of the Ammonite and Moabite wives enforced by Ezra, he triumphantly exclaimed: "I do not believe that any other people than the chosen would give a similar proof of their obedience to their Law." The superhuman gift of prophecy is so much restricted to born Jews that even full-fledged proselytes can never become direct media of divine communication. [43] This extreme racialism of Halevi, to be sure, is undoubtedly mitigated by his acceptance of the rabbinic doctrine that a proselyte, by divesting himself of all bonds with his former religious community, becomes a child, newborn into the creed of Abraham. In Halevi's day it was already customary for most proselytes to assume the symbolic name of Abraham or Sarah and to recite in their prayers the recurrent phrase "the God of *our* Fathers, Abraham and Isaac and Jacob," thus affirming their newly won racial descent from the patriarchs of Israel. Neither would Halevi have denied the prevalent rabbinic law which placed descendants of proselytes completely on a par with born Jews. [44] However, for him, being a Jew was not only a difference in degree but one of quality, the quality of a prophetic and, hence, superhuman, nation versus ordinary humankind.

This very quality also explains Israel's sufferings. "Israel amidst the nations is like the heart amidst the organs of the body; it is at one and the same time the most sick and the most healthy of them." [45] Just because of its exposed position the Jewish people is more sensitive than all others to the great changes in its environment; but at the same time it has that great quality of survival which has made it outlast many other nations and will carry it to the end of days. The Jews have no power. They are ruled by others and are often oppressed; they live in more or less permanent exile. Many an observer "infers the extinction of our light from our degradation, poverty and dispersion and concludes from the greatness of others, their conquests on earth and their power over us that their light is still burning." But this rash conclusion is disproved not only by the fact that the two prosperous religions of Christianity and Islam are sharply antagonistic to one another, though there evidently cannot be two opposing truths, but also by the fact that the same Christians and Muslims in extolling the merits of their greatest men invariably point to their saints, martyrs, and sufferers for their faith, rather than to their powerful rulers or valiant soldiers. Powerlessness as such is, from the standpoint of ultimate religious values, a virtue rather than a fault, in the life of any human group. To be sure, unlike the martyrs of the other faiths, the bulk of the Jewish people are involuntary sufferers and sustain their exilic fate without true benefit. But could they not immediately alter their status by the mere act of conversion to the dominant creeds? Could not, especially, the prominent Jews "escape this degradation by a word spoken lightly, become free men, and turn against their oppressors, but do not do so out of devotion to their faith?" [46] The greatest achievements of culture and civilization go hand in hand with inferiority in power and political dominion. That is why, Halevi asserts, following a venerable tradition first formulated in Hellenistic Jewish literature, all human culture may be traced back to Israel, which taught the Babylonians, Medes, and Greeks, by whom in turn were nurtured the contemporary Muslim and Christian civilizations. In the future, too, it matters little how many adherents Judaism shall count. "We are not even a body, only scattered limbs, like the 'dry bones' which Ezekiel saw." Nevertheless, the Jews are the real "living" people, contrasted with the "dead" nations which try to be their equals but whose fortunes vary "in accordance with the largeness or smallness of their number, with their strength or weakness, disunion or unity, following upon natural or accidental causes." On the contrary, should the Jewish people ever dwindle to but a single Jew it would still continue to exist and ultimately be regenerated for the final salvation in the messianic era. [47]

These extreme racialist contentions, which may sound quite strange to a contemporary student of religion, will be better understood against the background of the discussions in Halevi's time. Spain in that day, even though a most effective melting pot for persons of many races and tongues, was nevertheless rather race-conscious. The *sakaliba* (the term originally denoted the slave population, but then referred generally to people of European origin north of the Alps) and *muwalladūn* (native Spaniards of mixed racial origin), even after their adoption of Islam, were long distinguished from the dominant Moorish group, which in itself represented a mixture of Arab and Berber strains. The constant process of assimilation and intermarriage, which, according to a modern Spanish authority, [48] had reduced the Arab component in the blood of King Hishām II (976–1009), for instance, to less than one-thousandth, did not completely eliminate the mutual feelings of superiority which were harbored by the various groups. Halevi was undoubtedly familiar with the epistle (*risālā*) of Ibn Garcia, a Muslim of Basque origin who in Halevi's youth had sharply attacked the dominant Arab element for its racial conceit. Utilizing numerous arguments assembled by Persian and other Oriental opponents of the Arabs, belonging to a movement styled the *Shuʿubiya*, Ibn Garcia argued that the Arabs had been "guardians of dirty camels," herders of sheep and cattle, etc., at a time when the ancestors of the subjected nations had produced Caesars and Khosroes. He also harped on the oft-alleged descent of the Arabs from Hagar, Sarah's slave-girl, which reminds one of the *ben ha-amah* of Hebrew literature. While stressing the superiority of the fair-skinned, civilized, wine-drinking Western peoples over the brown consumers of coarse food from the East, he constantly reverted to a historical argument. [49] In the vein of a modern apologist, he emphasized the achievements of the non-Arab Persians, who had once saved the Arabs from the Ethiopians but were soon repaid by conquest and extermination. To be sure, as a Muslim he had to acknowledge the greatness of Muhammad, who, as he says, had purified the Arabs of their unclean religious rituals, and had taught the Christians to abandon their trinitarian doctrine and their reverence for the cross. However, such a singular phenomenon as Muhammad proves nothing for his race, just as gold is usually found in sand. Some Eastern writers went further and emphasized that, even according to the sacred history of Islam, only four of the numerous prophets addressed by God were of Arabian origin. Similar attacks upon the Arab race, coupled with exaltation of the cultural superiority of other peoples, were so common that one Muslim author was alleged to have been paid by a Byzantine emperor to write a book disparaging the dominant group of the Caliphate. The Jews, free of Muslim religious restraints, did not hesitate to speak in derogatory terms of Muhammad himself, whom they often styled "the madman," [50] although, according to the Muslim statutes, blasphemies against Muhammad by an infidel were punishable by death.

The chief concomitants of the doctrine of the Chosen People are, for Halevi, the requirement of strict observance of the commandments and the messianic ideal of Judaism. Unlike most of his rationalist confrères, Halevi did not inquire into the reasons for the main body of Jewish ceremonial law. Rather like patients implicitly obeying the orders of a trusted physician, the Jews must, in his opinion, unquestioningly accept the burden of the Law. In fact, Halevi considers the obligation a distinction rather than a burden, and declares it to be one of the great advantages of living in the Holy Land that the Jew is there given the opportunity of observing more rather than fewer commandments, such as the agricultural laws applicable to Palestinian soil alone. [51] Neither shall we find anywhere in Halevi's presentation any vestige of the ancient doctrine that the advent of the Messiah will terminate the validity of the ceremonial law. For him the messianic era is a sort of ceremonial super-Judaism, not some form of emaciated Judaism. At the same time, he refuses to surrender or in any way compromise the basic universalism of the messianic expectation. The preservation of the Jewish people through the untold sufferings of the exile, from which each and every individual could have been liberated by paying sheer lip service to another creed, can have meaning only if it contains the mystery of a seed sown in the soil of mankind to blossom out into a tree uniting all humanity in the messianic era.

God has a secret and wise design concerning us, which should be compared to the wisdom hidden which falls into the ground, where it undergoes an external transformation into earth, water and dirt, without leaving a trace for him who looks down upon it. In the same manner the law of Moses transforms each one who honestly follows it, though it may externally repel him. The nations merely serve to introduce and pave the way for the expected Messiah, who is the fruition, and they will all become His fruit. Then, if they acknowledge Him, they will become one tree. Then they will revere the origin which they formerly despised. [52]

However, being a realist by nature, Halevi seems not to have indulged in apocalyptic dreams or forebodings of an immediate deliverance. To be sure, under the impact of his people's great sufferings, which "made me forget all the sufferings of my forefathers," he sometimes became impatient with the slow and inscrutable ways of divine redemption, and in many poems he asked the anxious question: "How much longer?" [53] But unlike his Spanish compatriot Derei, who in the 1130s initiated a messianic movement among his coreligionists; and unlike the well-known mathematician Avendeath, who looked forward to the appearance of the supernatural Messiah about 1186, [54] Halevi considered the messianic future a religious dogma of unquestioned validity, yet waived all intentions of calculating the time of its realization. Neither did he follow the leadership of Abraham b. Ḥiyya, the well-known Savasorda of medieval and early modern European mathematics and astronomy, who in his *Megillat ha-megalleh* developed what we may style as a full-fledged astrological conception of history, positing on the basis of his astrological computations the speedy redemption of the Jewish people in 1129. Halevi was much more reticent. Even when in one of his liturgical compositions for the New Year's services he joyously exclaimed "Lo, the day of redemption is near," [55] he was merely voicing a generally accepted conviction. His solution, although much more modest, seemed at least personally more satisfactory to him.

Without awaiting the advent of the Messiah, he proceeded to Palestine, both in fulfillment of his life-long preachment and in expectation of personal expiation and deliverance. "Palestine is especially distinguished by the Lord of Israel," he declared, "and no function can be perfect except there. . . . Heart and soul are only perfectly pure in the place which is believed to be specially selected by God." His program is well summarized in a verse which he wrote to answer a friend who had in vain tried to dissuade him from exposing himself to the dangers of the journey, as well as in the peroration of the rabbinic spokesman in *Al-Khazari*. In the former, Halevi exclaimed, "Have we either in the East or in the West a place of hope wherein we may trust except the land that is full of gates toward which the gates of Heaven are opened?" The rabbi in the dialogue, referring to Psalms 102:14–15, clinches his entire exposition by saying: "this means that Jerusalem can only be rebuilt when Israel yearns for it to such an extent that they embrace her stones and dust." [56] It seems to have been the greatest tragedy of Halevi's life that, until the last two months of his life, Palestine's stones and dust escaped his eager embrace. [57]

What does Halevi mean to the present generation? Apart from the esthetic pleasure and profound joy given to readers of his immortal poems, Halevi's work and life contain more than one valid message for our own times. Much of his Platonic and Aristotelian verbiage may have lost its meaning for our contemporary thinkers, just as his physical and astronomical world outlook has long since been abandoned by modern science. This fate Halevi shares with all of his contemporaries, be they Jewish, Christian, or Muslim. We cannot even claim that his philosophy exercised any influence upon the progress of philosophic thought under Islam or Christendom, as did for instance the more renowned *Guide for the Perplexed* of Maimonides, which through the very fact of its interdenominational influence demonstrated the basic unity of the human mind in an age of extreme religious intolerance. But perhaps precisely because the metaphysical and logical ingredients of Halevi's philosophy were so much subordinated to his emotional appreciation of Jewish and world realities, his philosophy captured the imagination of later generations of Jews much more strongly than some of the more ambitious and more thoroughly disciplined works of his confreres.

His racism, too, may arouse considerable objections. Especially

his own coreligionists, who in this century have become the victims
of racist extremism, have learned through bitter experience what
excesses may be generated by the acceptance of such a concept of
the preordained racial superiority of one nation over another. Not
that Halevi is to be placed on a par with the Nazi exponents of
racism. By the very nature of the Jewish position in the world, the
racial superiority claimed by him for the Jews could not be combined with a theory of violence and forcible world domination. But
even the doctrine of the Chosen People will be rejected, on purely
rational grounds, by many Jews, as well as Christians, outside of the
camp of strict fundamentalists. Any student of modern anthropology
will realize the great diffusion of the notion of chosenness in the
consciousness of members of many ethnic and religious groups and
the fragility of the realistic background of all such assertions.
Halevi's brand of messianism, too, as well as his insistence upon the
strictest observance of the ceremonial law as a means of preserving
the Jewish people and as a mark of its great distinction have also
been repudiated by many modern Jews, especially among the
reformers and agnostics.

Nevertheless, we can still learn much from Yehudah Halevi. His
great perseverance in a period of world-wide crisis, his courage and
undaunted spirit, which taught him to stand upright in the midst of
persecution and danger and to derive therefrom greater clarity and
singleness of purpose rather than be thrown back into intellectual
confusion, are in themselves examples to be followed by any threatened people. Even more so is his serene faith in history and the long-
range forces of destiny high above the brute realities and implacable
forces of nature. His exposition of powerlessness as a superior
counterpart to the forces of state supremacy may also be fully
appreciated by contemporary Jewry. His firm belief, finally, in the
Palestinian ideal—not only as part of a dim and distant messianic
expectation but as an immediate goal, to be sought despite the great
obstacles erected by the power politics of every age—has long served,
and will continue to serve, as a source of inspiration and faith for
countless Jews on the verge of despair.

7

The Economic Views of Maimonides[*]

ECONOMIC SCIENCE AND JEWISH LAW

MAIMONIDES was not an economist. This is true not only in the sense of modern economic science, as it has developed since the days of the mercantilist theoreticians, but also as compared with the theories of some of the leading thinkers of medieval Islam and Christendom. We shall search in vain in his writings for a program such as that given by Ibn Khaldun to his "new science," which was to investigate, among other matters, "the occupations to which men devote their work and their effort, the lucrative professions, the crafts which supply a livelihood, the sciences and the arts." [1] Nor did he ever evince direct interest in economic problems, as did Thomas Aquinas, who devoted to them several special treatises as well as extensive passages in his major works. It is truly remarkable that the Jewish people, whose transformation into a predominantly mercantile group had made rapid progress during those very centuries in which Jewish scholasticism and jurisprudence reached their highest degree of fruition, never produced an economic thinker to lend theoretical formulation to the existing reality.

Maimonides himself, in his early treatise on *Logical Terms,* clearly suggests the reason for this failure. Partly following the Aristotelian classification, he places the sciences under the two main headings of "theoretical" and "practical" philosophy. The latter, also called "human science" or "political science," consists of four subdivisions, for the second of which he uses the term "domestic economy," or rather "the government of the household" (הנהגת הבית), which is a literal translation of the Greek οἰκονομία. This science of economics he defines rather narrowly as "the science by which [the head of the household] knows how the members are to help one another and how they are to be provided for in the best possible way in accordance with the requirements of a given time and place." [2] However, after also briefly discussing the two types of "politics," he concludes the discussion by stating:

[*] Reprinted from *Essays on Maimonides* (New York, 1941), pp. 127–264.

On all these matters philosophers have written many books which have been translated into Arabic, and perhaps those that have not been translated are even more numerous. But nowadays we no longer require all this, namely the statutes and laws, since man's conduct is [determined] by the divine regulations. [3]

Many years later Maimuni reiterated in his *Guide* that it is exclusively "the true law, which as we said is one, beside which there is no other law, viz. the Law of our teacher, Moses," which can direct the Jew toward the attainment of his physical as well as spiritual perfection. [4]

This belief in the exclusiveness of the Torah's guidance in social philosophy is shared not only by such an outspokenly "nationalist" thinker as Yehudah Halevi [5] but also by Abraham ibn Daud, Maimonides' immediate, and highly influential, Aristotelian predecessor. In the third chapter of his *Exalted Faith*, entitled "Mental Therapy," [6] Ibn Daud explains that

the goal towards which practical philosophy is striving is the attainment of happiness. This can be achieved first, by ethics; secondly, through domestic economy; thirdly, through political laws. But we shall show that this is found in our Law in the fullest possible way. [7]

The repudiation of an independent economic science thus conceived, of course, has nothing to do with an ascetic denial of the importance of economic endeavor. The realities of Jewish life, the constant process of the adjustment of the Jews to the changing economic trends, and their increasing dependence on the fiscal interests of the governments in their revenue-producing activities were too tangible and inescapable for even their most idealistical-minded leaders to ignore. The jurists, especially, were forced to acknowledge the vital importance of economic transactions in the life of their people. Enjoying a large measure of judicial self-government, the Jews had to regulate many phases of their industrial and commercial life by a process of continual legal adaptation. Maimonides himself devotes three entire books (XI–XIII) of his great legal code to matters predominantly economic, while numerous references of economic interest are included in the remaining eleven books. In his philosophical *magnum opus* he consciously avoids discussing problems other than metaphysical and physical ones, [8] but in his remarkable attempt to detect the rational basis of the biblical-talmudic commandments he emphasizes the fact that the aim of the Torah is twofold: "the well-being of the soul and the well-being of the body," the latter being established "by proper management of the relations in which we live one to another." He is even ready to concede that measures concerning the well-being of the body are "anterior in nature and time, although inferior in rank," to those aimed at the promotion of the well-being of the soul. In enumerating the fourteen classes of biblical legislation, he assigns the fourth to commandments relative to charities, loans, and gifts; the fifth, to responsibility for damages; the sixth, to crimes, particularly those committed against property; and the seventh, altogether to civil law (*dinei memonot*). [9] His son, Abraham Maimuni, otherwise far more otherworldly and mystical, comes quite close to economic determinism when he states that the extent of a person's reliance on God and the firmness of his faith is largely determined by the nature of his calling. Men entirely dependent on human beings for their sustenance will, in his opinion, be found generally weak in their faith, whereas tillers of the soil and hunters, whose livelihood so greatly depends on chance, will usually appear among the staunchest believers. Midway between these two extremes come merchants and traders. [10]

Thus it was not lack of recognition of the economic springs of human conduct, but the conscious attempt to prevent the Graeco-Arabic social philosophy from modeling the economic relations among Jews, which determined the relative aloofness of medieval Jewish thinkers. This attitude is doubly remarkable in the case of Maimonides, for whom the "theoretical philosophy" of the ancients was wholly on a par with the Jewish sources of divine revelation and for whom Aristotelian metaphysics became far more than a mere *ancilla theologiae*. [11] Nothing but a firm conviction of the inadequacy of Aristotelian economics, politics, and even ethics for the realities of Jewish life can explain this consistent negation. What benefit could a minority people in Exile, whose political and economic life was determined by a complex variety of external and internal forces, derive from a social philosophy reflecting conditions in a more or less normal, autochthonous society? While medieval Arabs and Christians could proceed to a profitable reinterpretation of Greek social teachings in terms of their religiously oriented, but still mainly political, realities, the Jews turned for enlightenment exclusively to their own largely nonpolitical literature. For more

than a millennium, prophets, priests, and scribes had striven hard
to build the new and unique structure of Judaism in Exile, and had
achieved in the talmudic law and doctrine a synthesis of the conflicting forces which was to remain essentially intact until the new
era of Emancipation. [12]

The all-powerful principle of talmudic social legislation, to
counteract the innate economic appetites and to subjugate them
to the dictates of morality, added force to Maimonides' and his
confreres' denial of autonomy to economic thinking as well as to
economic behavior. Saadia, while unable to repudiate the truth of
the assertions—which he presents with dramatic clarity—concerning
the all-pervading power of money, points out the psychological and
moral insecurity attached to its possession and concludes with the
advice that everybody should appreciate it to the extent of trying
to keep what God has bestowed upon him, but should not take
special pains in order to acquire it. Bahya, discussing three major
moral and psychological aspects of controlling a large fortune,
demands from its owner inner humility and recognition of the
divine grace which alone has given it to him. [13] Maimonides, too,
realizes that some of the strongest human fears are centered around
the loss of money and that men usually value their money on a
par with, or even above, their lives, but he emphasizes the insecurity
of its tenure and man's relative independence of earthly possessions.
Accepting the classification of "ancient and modern" philosophers,
he declares "the perfection as regards property," in the acquisition
of which people spend most of their days, to be the lowest of the
four degrees of human perfection, inferior not only to those of
intellectual achievement and ethical conduct but even to that of
physical beauty, because at best it means the attainment of "perfectly imaginary and transient things." [14]

Thus regarding excessive economic appetites not only as prejudicial to the higher morality but also as disturbing "the order of
the people of the city and the government of the household,"
Maimonides contends that it is "among the objectives of the perfect
Law to remove the desires, to disparage them and to reduce them
to the absolutely indispensable minimum." [15] The Torah (which
naturally includes for Maimuni the entire system of Oral Law)
alone can furnish both elucidation in fundamentals and regulation
in all detailed economic matters. That is why the juridical works of
Maimonides and his confreres reflect their economic teachings, as

well as the modifications forced upon them by changing economic realities, much better than do their strictly philosophic writings. To be sure, many legal adjustments were due to the inner workings of a juristic technique, which, in Judaism as in Islam, [16] frequently pursued its own independent course. The intensive study of legal minutiae in the great academies of learning followed its own peculiar logic and methodology and led to many new formulations which can be explained neither by the original tradition nor by the evident new social needs. Once established, moreover, such new formulations not only colored economic theory but also influenced, through the force of judicial precedent, economic practice in both application and evasion.

Bearing all this in mind, we may view the economic doctrines incorporated by Maimonides into his juristic as well as philosophic works as both a truly representative over-all summary of the general rabbinic attitude toward economic life and a reflection of the numerout adjustments made by the vast and prosperous Jewish community under medieval Islam. The compass of the present analysis need not be limited to subjects which Maimuni himself would have included in the field of domestic economy. Did not Alfarabi put agronomy and navigation in a class with "physical" sciences? Whether or not Maimuni accepted this classification, he certainly placed matters of national economy, apparently even the problems affecting slaves, largely in the field of political science in its narrower sense. Nevertheless, for our purpose a comprehensive discussion only of Maimonides' most significant economic teachings, in the contemporary meaning of the term, may yield a more or less satisfactory result.[17]

ECONOMICS AND SOCIAL JUSTICE

The cornerstone of all of Maimuni's socioeconomic views is the old Aristotelian doctrine of the innate social propensities of man. Like many Arab thinkers—whose prevalent deductive method was scorned by the social empiricist Ibn Khaldun—and like Thomas Aquinas, he invokes the well-known Aristotelian statements concerning the origin of organized society. "It has already been fully explained that man is naturally a social being and that, by virtue of his nature, he seeks to form communities." And it is "the domestic order which is the principal base of the polity." [18] Among the main psychological springs of social cooperation appears to be the force of imitation, since it is "the innate way of man to follow his friends and associates in his opinions as well as in his deeds" [19] and, more, the yearning for love by one's fellow men. With special reference to Aristotle's *Nicomachean Ethics*, Maimuni emphasizes that "it is well known that man throughout his life requires persons who love him"; and he sees a great advantage in the religious festivals and the consumption of the "second tithe" in Jerusalem, which fostered love among members of various social groups. Such love is naturally strongest among close relatives, and greatly cements the unity of the household. [20] But the ultimate motive for the creation and maintenance of political forms is man's realization of the great differences in character, as well as economics between individuals and groups. Although Maimuni nowhere mentions the alternative of *bellum omnium contra omnes*, as he does not recognize, even in theory, any discrepancy between a natural and a civilized state, he clearly implies that it is fear of the ensuing anarchy which leads men to agree to submission to a leader, "so that the natural variety be submerged in the great conventional harmony and the community be well organized." [21]

Such social coexistence imposes, of course, many obligations upon the individual. The ultimate goal of the chosen few may, and should, be lonely intellectual achievement, a life in the realm of other-worldly contemplation, where not only their own earthly desires and the demands of the flesh become meaningless but where, in their meditative aloofness, they need have no consideration for their fellow men. However, even these chosen few, Maimuni emphasizes, must not withdraw mentally into the realm of the superlunary world, which, as was claimed by some philosophers, is the sole domain of Providence. Taking his cue from Jeremiah 9:22–23, he insists

that the perfection in which man can truly glory is attained by him, when he acquires, to the extent of his ability, the knowledge of God and the recognition of His Providence over His creatures as it manifests itself in His creating and continually governing them. Having acquired such knowledge, he will be determined always to seek loving-kindness, judgment and righteousness and thus to imitate the ways of God, as has frequently been explained in this treatise.

The wisest of men thus must share with the common mass of humanity the responsibilities imposed upon all by the existing conditions of human society. [22]

In their economic endeavors, too, men must remain mindful of the ultimate social aim. "Men engaged in such transactions must not refrain from mutual assistance in order to promote their common interest; neither of the parties must strive to increase only his own profit, and that he alone should enjoy the whole benefit of the transaction." It is therefore the duty of every Jew not only to love his coreligionists as himself but "to have compassion over the other fellow's property as much as over that belonging to himself." Conversely, "most of the damage done to people in the various states arises from the lust for money and its accumulation and the excessive desire to increase possessions and honors." [23]

The prevention of social injustice and oppression is thus one of the major aims of political, as well as religious, legislation. To achieve the well-being of the body, one must first "remove violence from among men; that is to say, that everyone shall not be guided in his actions by his likes and dislikes or by his power to act, but that everyone shall constantly do what is good for the common welfare." [24] Following the rabbinic doctrine, Maimuni includes the prohibition of "robbery" among the universal laws common to all mankind and consequently obligatory for all "sons of Noah," too. These six or seven Noahidic commandments have all the attributes of "natural" laws in medieval scholasticism, although Maimonides and his Jewish confreres could not, of course, claim for them any superiority over the "positive" laws of Judaism, all of which were supposed to be derived from the same *ius divinum* and to have retained their binding force in the post-Mosaic age only through their inclusion in the divine revelation to Moses. "He who robs from his fellow-man," says Maimuni, "an object of the value of one *peruṭah* [the smallest coin] acts as if he took his life." The appropriation of money which came into one's temporary possession with the consent of the owner is equal to robbery, and both forms are strictly prohibited, even with respect to the property of pagans. Neither is the right of capturing booty in war wholly consonant with the idea that Israel's camp is like God's temple. [25]

The objective of both civil and criminal law is to regulate economic life and to prevent injustice, not so much for the sake of the individual as for that of society as a whole. Although "mercy" is undoubtedly one of the paramount principles of ethics and of Jewish law, failure to punish the criminal would but perpetuate a class of persons of evil design. "They are feeble-minded who contend that the abolition of all penalties would be an act of mercy towards men; on the contrary, it would be perfect cruelty to them and injury to the social order." [26] The same argument is advanced by Maimuni to justify the extreme measures to be taken against instigators to heresy, "because cruelty against those who mislead the people to seek vanity, is real clemency to the world." [27] That is also why one of the major prerequisites for a judge in Israel should be "a strong heart to save the oppressed from the oppressor." [28] Thus, in Maimuni's opinion the major purpose of the criminal law is the safeguarding of the interests of society; that is, primarily the prevention of crime. To be sure, he wholly deprecates neither the element of correcting the criminal through various psychological modifications of the prescribed penalties nor that of retaliation, the primitive expression of direct retribution. Although recognizing the talmudic sages' departure from the rigid biblical *ius talionis*, he nevertheless concedes it to be the basic, divine law of biblical revelation. His own preference, however, is decidedly for meting out only such punishment as would supply the most effective deterrent to the repetition of the crime by the original perpetrator or his would-be emulators. [29]

Social solidarity includes, in the Maimonidean theory, the extreme obligation for each individual actively to interfere whenever he is in a position to prevent a wrong. "He who can protest and does not do so, is himself guilty of the transgression for which he had failed to reprimand the transgressor." In the case of murder and incest, failure to prevent the crime is equivalent to breaking one positive and two negative commandments; in all other cases, to that of one prohibition. Although forced to admit that mere failure to act cannot be punished by the usual single or double flagellation, Maimonides insists that it is one of the gravest offenses, particularly, if the preventable crime consists in incitation to heresy. He who fails to participate in the suppression of any form of heresy by fearing the false prophet, failing to advance an accusation against him, or merely hesitating to assassinate him because of his high station in life, commits a grievous sin. While this requirement bears all the earmarks of sheer theory, it reveals the extent of the individual's responsibility toward society as visualized by the philosopher. [30]

This extreme social solidarity is for Maimuni also the guiding principle which ought to govern economic relationships. Economic enterprise is in itself neither an evil nor a good. Its value is measured by its effects upon both the individual and society. Although the idea is nowhere stated in so many words, the tenor of the Maimonidean utterances is fully in agreement with the definition of Thomas Aquinas that the ultimate aim of economy is *totum bene vivere*. [31] Maimonides in various connections stresses the importance of a healthy body and such material goods as are necessary for the maintenance of a good physique. "It is one of the principles of the Torah that a man should engage in this world in either of two things: either in the study of the Law, so that his soul be perfected in its wisdom, or in work (also crafts or commerce) which should help him to maintain his livelihood." Maimuni stresses in particular the obligation of every Jew to earn a livelihood rather than become a public charge. Even the highly desirable devotion to intellectual pursuits is no excuse for economic inactivity, and "he who makes up his mind to engage in study exclusively, to have no other occupation and to live on charity, has desecrated the name of the Lord, depreciated the Torah, extinguished the light of the law, caused misfortune unto himself and shut himself out from the world to come." On the other hand, economic pursuit should be merely secondary; if at all possible, man should devote most of his time to study. Assuming a twelve-hour working day, Maimuni prefers the assignment of three hours to earning a living and of the remainder to the study of the Torah. But unlike the early Christians and some ascetic teachers of medieval Islam and Christendom, Maimuni finds no words of praise for poverty as such. [32] In exceptional cases, such as candidacy for the office of high priest, Maimuni accepts the talmudic requirement of wealth, together with physical strength, wisdom, and good looks. If the candidate is poor, his fellow priests ought to make proportionate contributions in his favor, so that he becomes the wealthiest of them all. Neither may men become high priests or kings if they have been engaged, be it only for one day, in the menial occupation of a butcher, barber, bathing master, or tanner, "because people will always hold them in low esteem." Moreover, as soon as a man is appointed to a leading position in the community, he must refrain from performing manual labor in the presence of three persons, "lest he become humiliated before them." In fact, no manual laborers, including master craftsmen, may be allotted places of honor ahead of scholars. Finding in the Mishnah the picturesque description of how the bearers of the first fruits arriving in Jerusalem were first welcomed there by the artisan groups, he states that this was a specific exception in honor of the visitors. [33] At the same time, he harshly condemns the exaggerated quest for material fortune, and finds sharp words of condemnation for the prevalent human greed. He even heatedly objects to those "foolish sensuous Arabs" who depict the glories of the world to come in terms of enjoyment of physical pleasures. [34]

When economic interest conflicts with religious duty, the former has to yield. If a Gentile army besieges a Jewish city and is exclusively bent upon pillage, the threatened financial ruin is not a legitimate excuse for breaking the Sabbath. If money used for idolatrous purposes gets mixed up with money belonging to a Jew, the Jew must abandon his share. Should anyone drop a coin in front of an idol, he must not bend down to pick it up, because he might give the appearance of bowing before the idol. [35] Discussing the problem of Jews forced to adopt another religion by royal decree, such as occurred under the Almohades, Maimuni commends voluntary exile; he argues that if people emigrate for purposes of earning a living, how much more necessary is voluntary exile when it offers better opportunities for learning or for the observance of the Torah. [36] The primacy of religion also comes clearly to the fore in his interpretation of the Sabbath idea, in which the social element of rest appears wholly subordinated to those of religious sanctification and historical commemoration. On the other hand, along with the geonim and Alfasi, he repudiates the extreme observance of the Sabbath even in the face of serious danger to life or limb, which observance was then advocated by some Karaite leaders. "The laws of the Torah are not for vengeance in the world, but for compassion and peace in the world." [37]

The social foundation of economics serves Maimuni also as a justification for the principle of economic leadership. Although nowhere discussing the problem of management versus labor in detail, Maimuni acknowledges the necessity of a leader and entrepreneur because of the great diversity of individual functions.

For the food which man requires for his subsistence demands much work and preparation, which can only be accomplished by reflection and planning, by the utilization of many utensils, and by the employment of numerous individuals, each performing a particular function. That is why they need one person who should guide and unite them, so that their group be properly organized and endure, and that they should coöperate with one another.

Such division of labor is also necessary for the provision of shelter and all other human needs. If, on the other hand, "in services and functions entrusted to many people, each were not assigned to a particular task, this would result in general neglect and laziness." Division of labor thus necessarily leads to combined efforts under some sort of authority. [38] Such statements clearly reflect those "aristocratic" leanings which Maimuni had taken over from the Muslim schools of philosophy, [39] but they do not offer any intrinsic justification for the existing economic inequalities. Maimuni, taking such inequalities for granted, sees in them primarily the expression of divine grace or reward. In a remarkable passage he contends that one who is rich today may be poor tomorrow and vice versa—a phenomenon particularly frequent in the semicapitalistic and autocratically governed Muslim states. While by no means advocating the abolition of class differences, Maimuni finds in them the reflection of a higher purpose; viz., the stimulation of efforts aimed at righting such inequities through charity and lovingkindness. Confronted with a Jewish society which, apart from its traditional egalitarian theory, had no permanent class distinctions and certainly no "estates" in the European sense, Maimuni could thus disregard the obvious differences which existed in income and social status. [40]

PRIVATE OWNERSHIP

The institution of private ownership is likewise taken for granted rather than justified by Maimonides. The Christian scholastics, writing against a background of early Christian communism (in consumption, if not in production) and Franciscan glorification of poverty, had to put up a staunch defense for the individual's right to own property. While Gratian in his Code had to admit that "according to natural law all things belong to all men; . . . only by virtue of custom or positive law this thing belongs to me and that to another person," Thomas Aquinas advanced mainly practical arguments for private ownership in production. Without such ownership, he contended, people would lack an incentive to efficient effort, there would be confusion rather than rational division of labor, and social peace would be threatened by constant feuds among collectivist owners. [41] Maimonides—as well as other Jewish and Arab thinkers— was less troubled. Starting with the Old Testament or the Qur'an, Judaism and Islam had accepted private property as an eternal and God-given institution under certain specific limitations. These limitations, rather than the basic institution, are hence the major subject of discussion. Of course, both faiths held that God is the ultimate master of all things and that his individual Providence determines the ultimate distribution of all property. But once acquired by an individual, such property is entirely his own and, subject to stated limitations, may be freely disposed of by him. Not even those who cherished poverty as an ideal, such as the Sufists and Al-Ghazali (and their Jewish followers), departed from this accepted pattern. They merely emphasized the inner virtue, and, to a certain extent, the personal bliss, of the man without property, as against the absorption in constant worry over possessions by the moneyed individual. Preference for public, as opposed to private, ownership, as a matter of principle, was not even characteristic of the semicommunistic, heretical trends within Islam, and found still less articulate expression among the heterodox groups in medieval Jewry. The prevalent maladministration by the Muslim bureaucracy; the abuses of that sort of state-socialism which existed, for instance, in the Egypt of Maimonides; the self-interest of Jewry as a whole, which prospered mainly in the domain of free enterprise, all operated against the rise of collectivist trends such as had existed among the ancient Rechabites and Essenes. [42]

The principle of private ownership remains unimpaired by the various types of public property. Following the talmudic doctrine, Maimuni recognizes, in the first place, the existence of the related groups of *hefker* and *reshut ha-rabbim*. Objects in the former group belong to no one in particular, until such time as somebody seizes them through one of the accepted methods of appropriation. This group includes objects freely available in nature, such as fish in rivers and lakes, or birds in the desert. Maimuni does not acknowledge the riparian rights of the neighboring landowners, and expressly states that all river banks to the extent of a four-ell strip are public. In contrast to RABD, he also denies the preferential rights of a tribe living in the neighborhood of the river or the desert. [43] *Res derelictae* likewise become *hefker*. It matters little whether the owner decides to relinquish his rights forever or merely for a limited period, except that in the former case he can retract only during the first three days; in the latter case, through the entire period. [44] The decease of a proselyte leaving behind no legitimate Jewish heirs—Gentile heirs are not recognized—places all his possessions in the *hefker* category, and entitles anyone who comes first to seize as much as he can.

There is one interesting exception, inasmuch as restoration of property robbed from the proselyte in his lifetime, and of an additional legal fine of one-fifth of its value, is to be made, if previously denied, not to the ownerless estate, but to the priests of that division to which the proselyte had belonged. [45] In all these aspects the state has no superior claim on account of its supposed "eminent domain." Of course, Maimuni is ready in this, as in all other branches of civil law, to respect the divergent legislation of the Gentile state. He can do so here with fuller complacency, however, as the Muslim state had often (for instance, through a decree of 923) recognized the right of the respective religious communities to inherit the estates of their deceased heirless members. From the standpoint of Jewish law, in any case, for Maimuni the only divine and eternal law, any accidental passer-by has the full right of appropriation. [46]

The *reshut ha-rabbim* ("public ground"), on the other hand, is permanently open to common use, but can never be appropriated by the individual. Maimonides defines such common property especially in connection with the observance of Sabbath laws, since the carrying of any object from private to public ground is forbidden on the Sabbath. Deserts, forests, and roads (sixteen ells wide or over) are examples of "public ground," while a city surrounded by walls whose gates may be closed at night is classified as "private ground." In between is the intermediate category of *karmelit*. Economically, however, these distinctions are less significant. An open city, for example, may at once become "private" by erecting a wall. Although Maimuni nowhere mentions it, there certainly existed in his day a public authority charged with the creation of new, and the maintenance of old roads. Such an authority could naturally regulate the width of the road at will, except perhaps for the limitations imposed by custom. Newly founded fortified cities would also naturally occupy an area which was formerly deserted or which in some other way belonged to "public ground." [47]

In short, there is, according to Maimuni, a complex variety of objects, either under direct public ownership or open to permanent public use, which come roughly under the following six headings: (1) public property belonging to no one and accessible to everybody for free use (e.g., deserts); (2) public property belonging to a corporate group, but open to general use (e.g., highways); (3) potentially private property belonging to no one, but available for free appropriation, namely all relinquished and some lost objects;

(4) private grounds belonging to the ownerless estate of a deceased proselyte, equally open to free appropriation; (5) private grounds not yet taken over by a Jew from a Gentile, open to appropriation with compensation; (6) private grounds in a walled city, open to everybody's use but not to appropriation. A seventh group, although not mentioned by Maimuni, is clearly implied by him: public property which at one time or another was taken over by a "private" body of men, such as a city, or even by individuals, but which has retained some of its public character. All these categories, which evidently do not fit into the Roman classes of *res nullius* and *res omnium communes*, have in common (except for the extralegal seventh group) that they are open to either free appropriation or free use on the part of any person, or at least any Jew.

There exists, however, a different type of property, owned by a king, a municipality, or a Jewish community, which can be neither appropriated nor used freely. This type of ownership does not differ in any essential from that by an individual. In general Maimonides distinguishes but little between the private estates of the king, acquired through the usual channels of civil law, and the funds received through the exercise of the royal prerogatives of taxation and legally delimited expropriation. The same applies to municipal or communal property. The public aspects of both royal and communal property will be considered by me in another connection.

Thirdly, there exists the "sacred" property (*heḳdesh*) of the Temple in Jerusalem. This type of property, similar to the Muslim *waqf*, has many peculiar characteristics, favorable as well as unfavorable. On the one hand, sacrilegious theft committed on such property is not to be prosecuted by earthly courts. Besides divine wrath, the criminal has to fear punishment only from the enraged populace, whose spontaneous reaction in this respect is encouraged by both the Talmud and Maimonides. [48] On the other hand, the accumulation of wealth by the *mortmain* is facilitated by the curtailment of its civil responsibility for damages and a greater freedom in making pledges in its favor. [49] Of course, for Maimuni, as for most of his rabbinic predecessors since the destruction of the Temple, this entire form of sacred ownership was a purely theoretical matter. Medieval Jewry had little to fear from the effects of such property accumulation upon public welfare; but such fears, combined with greed, inspired many Muslim rulers to lay hands upon the estates of the Mosque. The property of the medieval synagogue had none of that "sacred" character; it was but part and parcel of the usual private or communal property. [50] But even the Temple *hekdesh*, in the technical sense, was essentially subject to the usual laws governing private property and its modes of acquisition.

A fourth type of property consists in the negative group of objects placed *extra commercium* by the religious prohibition of their use in any form (*asurim behana'ah*). Maimonides, frequently at a loss to furnish adequate rational grounds for each prohibition, mentions a large number of objects outlawed by biblical-talmudic legislation. To a lesser extent, also excluded from commerce are those numerous foodstuffs which, while usable in other ways, may not be consumed by Jews (*asurim ba'akhilah*). Maimonides enumerates, for example, meat of dead or otherwise ritualistically unfit animals, insects, priestly portions of the first-born animals and agricultural crops, and the produce during the Sabbatical year. But he specifically allows trade in various prohibited fats and also of such articles as are outlawed for consumption not by biblical, but by rabbinic, law. [51]

A fifth type of property, of an entirely different order, consisted for Maimuni in the ideal claim of every Jew to four ells of land in Palestine. Assuming that God alone is the true lord of Palestine, and generally teaching that forcible seizure of land never deprives the real owner of his rights, Maimuni could not repudiate the geonic doctrine that the Jews still have an inherent claim to the Palestinian soil. From the practical point of view, this legal fiction served as an important vehicle in facilitating the transactions frequently required under the more advanced economy of the Muslim empires. Maimuni, not arguing against the principle as such, nevertheless rejects its practical application, because no contemporary Jew could prove his personal share in the claim (as Karo explains it, he might be a descendant of a proselyte or a liberated slave), nor was the property in his possession, possession being for Maimuni a necessary prerequisite for those particular transactions. [52] Even he insisted, however, upon the continued validity, under the necessary modifications imposed by the Exile and the seizure of Palestinian land by Gentiles, of the numerous commandments associated with Palestinian agriculture, notably those governing the observance of the Sabbatical year and the payment of tithes. [53]

Since the third and fifth of these classes of ownership were purely theoretical in Maimuni's time, and the fourth reflected but a religious postulate that owners abstain from the exercise of their otherwise undeniable right, Maimuni thus recognized essentially only two types of ownership: private ownership by individuals or public bodies, and the various forms of either *hefker* or *reshut ha-rabbim*. Some of the objects belonging to the latter categories were permanently ownerless, nontransferable, and merely open to public use. Others, however, could be appropriated by somebody and then instantly subjected to the usual private ownership. Most objects of *hefker*, moreover, originated from property privately owned, and were expected soon to be privately owned again. Their status was, so to speak, one of actual, though unidentifiable private ownership. They were, indeed, less ownerless than, for instance, the Roman *hereditas jacens*. [54]

Under these circumstances one might regard Maimonides and the other exponents of Jewish law as champions of private ownership. One might also consider them as identifying such ownership with "plenary control over an object," were it not for some very stringent limitations on the exercise of private ownership upon which they vigorously insisted.

In a general way ownership includes complete mastery over the object, with all its appurtenances. If people write into their contracts such specifications as that they will sell an orchard with its trees, fruits, and fences—which Maimuni encourages them to do—this is merely a formality which at best may serve to obviate judicial controversies. [55] Through the acquisition of an object, however temporary, one obtains the transfer of ownership of that object *quoad usum*, not the transfer of a right. A tenant, or even a borrower, becomes, for or without a consideration, a temporary owner, just as a purchaser or a recipient of a gift becomes its permanent owner. Like their Muslim confreres, the Jewish jurists had no term for the Roman institution of *servitus*. [56] Mere possession is of slight importance. An object unlawfully withdrawn from its owner remains his, as long as it lasts unaltered. Despite the importance generally attached to the psychological assertion of ownership, the abandonment of all hope of restitution in this case does not involve loss of ownership. According to law, in its strict sense, if someone forcibly appropriates a beam and puts it into a newly erected structure, the owner may insist upon the destruction of the whole building so that he get back his beam. However, in order to encourage repentance, says Maimuni, the sages have allowed the substitution of monetary compensation for the beam itself. [57] On the other hand, possession is significant, inasmuch as no one can sell an object which is not in his possession; this would be the transfer of a mere right. For the same reason one may not dispose of a future, as yet nonexistent, property, such as one's prospective inheritance or other expected acquisitions. The rabbis themselves had to grant dispensations in favor of the children of a dying person when the children tried to obtain money for funeral expenses on the security of their prospective estates, or to needy fishermen who tried to sell their prospective catch. [58]

All these regulations, emanating from the predominantly agricultural economy of the biblical-talmudic period, would have proved a serious handicap for the growing Jewish commerce in the Muslim caliphates, were it not for the extensive use made of deeds and various legal-commercial instruments. To be sure, Maimonides takes a rather conservative stand in interpreting the talmudic regulations concerning the transfer of deeds, which dispensed with many of the formalities usually required for the transfer of movable property. By declaring the transfer of commercial instruments to be but a rabbinic innovation, Maimuni reaches the extreme conclusion that if the original owner of a deed renounces his rights, the purchaser may not force a third person, such as the original debtor, to execute its provisions; he may only try to recover his damages from the man who had transferred the deed to him. Not only is this interpretation sharply rejected by Abraham b. David—who, like many contemporary scholars, wished to facilitate the transfer of deeds by the insertion of a clause in the deed itself, reading, "I am obligated to you and to your legal successors"—but Maimonides himself is forced to admit that a deed written in favor of an anonymous bearer may be utilized by any person possessing it. This is the more remarkable as the meaning of the talmudic passage referred to is rather equivocal. A mere perusal of the Maimonidean code reveals the tremendous significance attached by the author to transactions in all sorts of deeds, even though he may theoretically claim that "according to biblical law, it is the thing itself, rather than its proof, that is being acquired." [59]

More important are the following direct limitations of property rights: Ownership of a parcel of land does not automatically include that of the space underground or in the air above. In each case of transfer, these extensions have to be explicitly stipulated and the property disposed of as "from the bottom of the deep to the height of the sky." [60] In the discovery of treasure, Maimuni decidedly favors

the finder as against the owner of the ground or building in which
it was found. This preference was very important in the Muslim
countries, where treasures were frequently hidden away in order to
withdraw them from the grasp of oppressive governors, and where
caliphs themselves often professed to have unearthed ancient hoards,
in order to explain to the public the large monetary stocks accumulated through excessive taxation. [61]

Other limitations arise from considerations of public welfare,
which transcend individual property rights. A city may remove outside its boundaries members of certain trades—such as tanners,
because of the odors emanating from the exercise of their calling.
Characteristically, it may also remove all trees within a radius of
twenty-five to fifty ells from an open square; it has to compensate
the owners only, if such trees indubitably grew there before the
ordinance was issued. [62] One must also consider the interests of one's
neighbors. Nuisances, such as noises and smells, and undue infringe-
ments on privacy (insofar as they are resented by gregarious Orien-
tals), must be avoided. The neighbors may invoke the assistance of
the authorities to check them. [63] Moreover, every neighbor has an
inherent right to interfere in the case of a contemplated sale of
property; he may exercise the right of preemption, under the same
conditions as those offered by a strange purchaser. Maimuni, to be
sure, in the interest of greater liquidity, so necessary in the semicapitalist economy of his period, hedges on this "right of the neighbor" (בן המצר) by imposing severe limitations, such as the immediate
exercise of the option and the deposit of ready cash. He incidentally
thereby favors the wealthy neighbor, whose credit is good, as against
one whose word carries less weight. He also tries to restrict the rights
of neighbors whenever these are in conflict with a still higher social
aim, such as assistance to owners forced to dispose of their property
by liquidation, encouragement to the study of the Law, and protection for women or orphans. [64]

Another illustration of the supremacy of public over private interests may be found in those rabbinic regulations concerning trade in
stolen articles, regulations which, because of their divergence from
both the Roman and the Teuton laws, have aroused such widespread
comment. It is needless to state that Maimonides and the other
rabbis tried to discourage theft and its mercantile extensions with
all means at their disposal. Although deciding that one does not
technically become a thief until one acquires a stolen object by one

of the methods legally prescribed for the acquisition of movable property, Maimuni demands that even minors who commit this crime should not escape unpunished. Both minors and slaves, he declares, although free from the usual fines, should be severely beaten so as to discourage repetition of the offense. [65] He also emphasizes the great sin involved in trading in stolen articles, because it encourages the thief by furnishing a market for his exploits and induces him to continue his criminal pursuits. It is in the higher interest of society, however, that a bona fide buyer, especially the professional merchant, who cannot possibly check the origin of all his wares, be protected to the full extent of his investment. This law of the Talmud, which seems to have indirectly influenced various privileges granted to Jews in medieval Europe, and, through them, the development of a significant legal institution in Western lands, appears in Maimuni's *Code* with important reservations. On the one hand, the person of the criminal is to be considered. If he happens to be a notorious thief, no legitimate excuse of good faith can be advanced, and the purchaser must return the stolen object to its owner without compensation. He may merely seek whatever redress he can obtain directly from the thief. On the other hand, should the owner have given up all hope of restoration —usually after a considerable lapse of time—he has no claim upon the object itself and may demand only monetary compensation in the case of a notorious thief, and none at all in other cases. Such is the consequence of the loss, by the owner, of his psychological hold on the property—this, as we have seen, being an integral part of the rabbinic doctrine of private ownership. Maimuni stresses in all these connections that the laws, although somewhat in conflict with absolute ethics, have been enacted "for the benefit of the market." Indeed RABD and others find many a flaw in the Maimonidean interpretation, which, on the whole, favors the merchant against the original owner. It is evident, however, that Maimonides was prompted by consideration not of the interests of the individual merchants but of those of the "market" as a whole, i.e., of society. Similar considerations, based upon equally or even more complex trade relations in the large modern urban areas, gradually induced almost all Western legislators to adopt many of these rabbinic regulations. [66]

Custom, that all-pervading force in medieval civilization, likewise played a great role in limiting free ownership. Anybody may help himself, for instance, to dates strewn on the ground by the wind, unless the owner puts up a fence around his orchard, indicating his desire to keep out strangers. [67] Gifts sent to a man on the occasion of his wedding are based upon reciprocity; if he refuses to return a present when the donor's wedding takes place under exactly the same circumstances, the latter may lawfully take back his own gift. Expenses incurred by the groom in the preparation of a wedding feast, including payments to clerical assistants, must be repaid by the bride if she suddenly changes her mind and renounces the marriage. [68]

Though a man's right to give away his possessions, while he is alive or *mortis causa*, to whomever he wishes, cannot be limited except for the advice not to be ruinously charitable, his dispositions concerning the inheritance of his estate are under strict surveillance. In general "a man must not bequeath his possessions to one not called upon to inherit, nor disinherit a legitimate heir." Moreover, a pious person will refrain from witnessing a will which discriminates, through any of the admissible linguistic subterfuges, against a misbehaving son in favor of a learned and decent brother.

The Law has shown us to what extremes one is to go in the practice of this virtue of favoring one's relatives and of treating kindly those with whom one is bound by family ties, even if they happen to be offensive and hostile. A relative may prove to be extremely wicked, but nevertheless one ought to treat him with due compassion. [69]

In fact, all offices and appointments in Israel ought to be hereditary, provided that the son "can take the place of his ancestors by virtue of his wisdom and piety." [70]

On the other hand, an heir must not enter into any agreements to refuse an inheritance legally due him. A husband, for example, may arrange to forego an inheritance from his wife only before he marries her, i.e., before he becomes her legitimate heir. The reason for this limitation is the wish of the Torah that "no condition be valid in matters of inheritance regulated by biblical law, and the sages have strengthened their own regulations so as to place them on a par with the biblical law." [71] The heir is obliged to provide an appropriate funeral for the deceased; the court may forcibly collect the amount needed for hiring professional mourners, male and female. [72] All this is the more remarkable as the heir is by no means a continuator of the deceased man's legal personality. He is responsible for debts only up to the amount of the inheritance. All partnerships (overt or silent) of the deceased, even if entered into for a specific period, are immediately terminated; the heir must, if he desires to continue them, make a fresh start. [73] This compromise between the rigid laws of inheritance and the full liberty to give away one's property was necessitated by the conflict between the ancient residua of communal ownership and the considerable economic individualism in the semicapitalistic society of the early talmudic or the geonic period. Maimuni adhered to this compromise, even where a revered predecessor, Alfasi, was ready to pursue a more individualistic line of reasoning. Moreover, he emphasized the fact that "the sages have enjoined us that no one [even] in his lifetime should discriminate among his children to the slightest extent so that there should not arise among them rivalry and envy as among Joseph and his brethren." [74]

Most significant are the limitations upon free spending. Ethically, a man should spend only such moderate amounts as are necessary for the upkeep of his body and mind, because "the main design in the acquisition of wealth should be to expend it for noble purposes and to employ it for the maintenance of the body and the preservation of life, so that its owner may obtain the knowledge of God insofar as that is vouchsafed unto man." [75] Luxury of any kind, especially, to use a modern term, conspicuous consumption for the display of one's wealth, is to be curtailed. To be sure, the advice that a Jew, no matter how wealthy, should not marry more than four wives —this was also the prevalent law under Islam—was prompted mainly by the consideration that he be able to cohabit with each at least once a month. [76] But even a king ought not marry more than eighteen wives, have more horses than are absolutely needed for his carriage, or accumulate money beyond his usual expenses, except for certain reserves necessary for public expenditure in emergencies. [77] Reflecting the prevalent economy of scarcity, moreover, Maimuni strictly prohibits the waste of commodities of any kind. "He who unnecessarily burns a suit of cloth or breaks a vessel," as well as one who cuts down healthy trees, is subject to flagellation. Neither may one cause damage directly or indirectly to a neighbor, even though one is willing to pay for it. Indeed, mere compensation does not absolve one from the sin committed; the guilty person must repent, confess, and abstain from ever doing it again. [78] Fear of scarcity was undoubtedly also coresponsible for the great consideration given by Maimuni and the other Jewish leaders to all matters involving considerable monetary loss, to obviate which they were ready to interpret many older laws in a milder vein. [79]

All these limitations imposed upon private ownership merely stem from the far-reaching principle, adopted and even expanded by Maimonides, of the right of Jewish leadership to disregard private property rights when these conflict with the common welfare. The Talmud had already made use of the legal maxim "the court may declare anybody's property as belonging to none" (*hefker beit din hefker*) to justify certain departures from biblical law. [80] Maimonides asserts even more sweepingly: "A judge may always expropriate money belonging to whomsoever, destroy it and give it away, if, in his judgment, this would serve to prevent the breaking down of the fences of the law, to strengthen its structure and to punish a mighty offender." He applies this principle particularly to salvaging as much as possible of the property (or the rights thereto) of an apostate for his Jewish heirs. While acknowledging the basic right of a renegade Jew to inherit his father's estate, he insists that in practice the court should transfer the inheritance to the grandchildren, if they remain Jewish, or to other close Jewish relatives. The wife of an apostate may demand immediate payment of her marriage settlement, although, according to strict law, she is entitled to it only when she becomes a widow or divorcée. [81] Such "daily" practice was, indeed, but a necessary safeguard for a people whose very survival was threatened by recurrent waves of conversion under Islam. But it also revealed the inherent precariousness of "the plenary control over an object" by its private owner, in the face of the overwhelming social control of the medieval Jewish community.

Finally, there are certain peculiar legal-economic features attached to the ownership of land. In many ways characteristic of Maimuni's economic views is his high evaluation of land as against movable property. In his *Code* he gives the curious advice that a man

should not sell a field and purchase a house, or sell a house and acquire a movable object, or use the purchase money to engage in business, but should rather convert movables into landed property. In general he should aim to acquire wealth by converting the transitory into the permanent.

This sweeping statement, for which the commentators are at a loss to find a talmudic source or parallel, has a decidedly personal ring. It certainly goes far beyond R. Isaac's well-known advice that a man should divide his fortune so as to invest one-third in land, another third in commerce, and keep the last third ready at hand. While its tenor undoubtedly is in consonance with the conservative attitude of agricultural Jewry in talmudic Babylonia and echoes certain parallel teachings in Arabic letters, the sharp emphasis upon sound rather than profitable investments may well have been due to the serious business reverses sustained by Maimuni and his family during the first years of their settlement in Egypt. These reverses caused him to accept as the lesser evil both the heavy land taxes resting upon Jewish and other non-Muslim landowners and the bureaucratic chicaneries of the state-capitalist government in Egypt. [82] Contending, with the Talmud, that inexperienced minors are likely to prefer the glitter of ready cash to the steadiness of landed estates, Maimuni demands that the seller of land shall have attained not only the normal age of maturity in Jewish law (thirteen for boys, and twelve for girls), but also full understanding of the financial transactions involved. In the case of inherited lands, the minimum age of the seller is raised to twenty. At the same time, the sale of movables may be perfected by a child of six or more, if, not having a guardian, he must take care of his own resources and is economically mature for his age. Maimuni controverts, however, those of his teachers who wished to annul all land sales by boys under twenty, even if, upon reaching that age, they failed to protest the sale. To safeguard the rights of the purchasers, Maimuni considers such tacit approval legal reaffirmation of the original transfer. On the other hand, land acquired by a child through regular channels, without the intervention of a guardian, is to be retained as the child's property, "since we acquire rights in the absence" of the beneficiary. [83] Similarly, though hired workers may contractually renounce their right to consume some of the agricultural produce which they happen to be raising— and may even renounce this right in the name of their coworking adult family members or slaves, who, having full knowledge of the facts, are entitled to forego anything they please—they may not give up any such rights of minors, "because they consume something that comes neither from their father nor from their master, but from Heaven." In many other respects, too, land differs from other articles of commerce. Along with slaves and deeds and sometimes also "sacred" property and that belonging to Gentiles, land is subject to specific administrative regulations. Neither can man ever be forcibly deprived of his land, even if he relinquishes all hope of regaining its possession; at a favorable moment he may simply take it back, without any compensation, from the last possessor, who may have obtained it after a series of a thousand bona fide transactions. [84]

In short, land is not a simple commodity. Speaking in religious terms, it is, even more than any other object, under the direct overlordship of God. That is why, in Maimuni's opinion, the biblical lawgiver, by introducing through the Jubilee year a periodic *restitutio in integrum,* tried to forestall the permanent alienation of Palestinian land from its original owners. An irredeemable sale of Palestinian land constitutes a serious crime, although, for lack of effective enforcement, it is not punishable by flagellation. The seller may evade the law only by selling his land for a specified period of time, such as sixty years, but Maimonides urgently counsels Palestinian-Jewish property holders, even should the Jubilee year be in operation, not to rely upon its subsequent restitution, but to sell their houses or fields only in an extreme emergency. Although these teachings evidently have no bearing upon the realities of the Maimonidean age, they illustrate the philosopher's basic idea of what the Torah intended to achieve through the institution of a Jubilee year, besides "arousing sympathy with our fellow men and promoting liberality toward all men." Just as the Sabbatical year has the additional economic function of "the land's increasing its produce and improving when it remains fallow for some time," so it is the Jubilee year's objective to maintain a permanent social equilibrium. It is

to provide stability in securing for the people a permanent source of supply of the necessaries of life by converting the land into the inalienable property of its owners, so that it could not be sold in an irredeemable manner. . . . In this fashion the property of a person remains intact for him and his heirs and he can enjoy only the produce thereof.

Usufructus of, rather than plenary control over, Palestinian land was thus the ultimate aim of the lawgiver. [85]

This high estimate of land by Maimonides—largely a restatement of traditional views with a strong personal note—should not mislead us into assuming that he tried to emphasize rural as against urban economy. In fact, land is for him urban real estate just as much as tillable soil. In his own day the role of the Jews in urban occupations undoubtedly far exceeded their activity in agriculture. Although the forces which operated for the effective elimination of the Jews from the soil in the West were largely absent from the countries of Islam, the discrimination in taxation against the "infidels"—especially the burdensome land tax of some 20–50 percent of the harvest—combined with the vast industrial and commercial opportunities offered by the speedily expanding metropolitan economy under the Caliphate, led to the progressive urbanization of Jewry. [86] There still were a great many Jews who owned and tilled the soil, but for the majority the city opened much vaster fields of endeavor. No wonder that for both the Muslim and the Jewish jurists of the day, notwithstanding their heritage of a nomadically and agriculturally oriented scriptural law, the city appeared to be the focal point of all civilized life. Maimuni—who, incidentally, uses the word *medinah*, not only in his Arabic but also in his Hebrew writings, to mean "city" rather than "country" or "province" [87]—regards city life as the prevailing form of civilization. In his opinion, for instance, the lawgiver has no need to enumerate all the kinds of "forsworn animals," because they are rarely found in civilized regions and still less often in cities. Trying to explain the remarkable difference between the severe penalties imposed upon a thief in biblical law (two- to fivefold restoration) and the much milder treatment of the robber (only single restoration, plus one-fifth of the value for the forgiveness of the sin)—a fairly widespread distinction in primitive law, which frequently deprecates stealthy cowardice more than open attack—Maimuni particularly stresses the greater frequency of stealing. "Theft is possible everywhere, while robbery can be committed in a city only with some difficulty." Little wonder that, following the Talmud, Maimonides asserts his preference for a city neighbor over a country neighbor, if both wish to acquire property and neither has the statutory privilege of preemption. Moreover, such a privilege is forfeited if the neighbor intends to place the parcel under cultivation while the alien purchaser wants to use it as a building plot. The latter is to be preferred because of society's interest in human settlement. [88] This predominantly urban orientation, shared by the majority of Muslim jurists and philosophers, naturally colored the Maimonidean views in all domains of economic endeavor.

THE JUST PRICE

This urban orientation naturally renders trade and trade morals of primary significance in the economic outlook of Maimonides. As the son and leader of a people for whom the exchange of goods increasingly became the main basis of subsistence, and as a resident of Egypt, which in his day had become one of the main arteries of the world's commerce, he could not help acknowledging the socio-economic function of mercantile enterprise. He could but try to stem its excesses and subordinate it to the dictates of law and ethics. Once more he was not burdened by an anticommercial tradition such as found expression in the exclamation ascribed to St. Chrysostomus: "No Christian ought to be a merchant, or if he should wish to be one, he ought to be ejected from the Church of God." Nor did he have to contend with the genuine *hadith* of 'Umar I which, directed against the excessive speculation in grain in the Mecca of that day, assummed a tone of hostility to commerce in general. He seems to have had few, if any, compunctions such as those voiced by Augustine about the merchant's opportunities to live a life of virtue, or about his excessive mental absorption in his occupation. Maimonides, confronted with daily realities, saw clearly that apart from the inescapable necessity for most of his coreligionists to engage in trade, commerce offered better opportunities for carrying out his program of devoting a large part of the day to the study of the Law than did farming and industry, with their prevalently long working hours. It also extended considerable facilities for that silent partnership of scholars in business, which alone could stem the tide of commercialization of scholarship so vigorously denounced by Maimuni. That is why he never made the reservation, expressed by Thomas Aquinas, "that the perfect city ought but moderately to employ merchants," a reservation, incidentally, partly determined by the scholastics' deprecation of the merchant-patricians' military prowess. Rather, like most Arabic writers living under the more advanced economy of the Caliphate—for instance, the ninth-century philosopher Al-Jaḥiẓ of Baṣra, who wrote a treatise *On the Praise of Merchants and the Blame of Officials*—Maimuni accepts commerce as a necessary and unobjectionable human institution. [89]

To be sure, he realizes that in ancient times agriculture was far more important; he even discusses the original conflict between paganism and the patriarchs' monotheism in terms of their relative significance for the success of the agricultural harvest. He also knows that the much-revered patriarchs were shepherds and cattle breeders—a none-too-honorable calling in the later talmudic law, as restated by himself. But for his own day he chooses his examples largely from the domain of business, as when he discusses the effects of the accidental success of a business venture upon superstitious minds. [90] Without writing an apology for commerce, he merely tries to restate or refashion the traditional ethical standards so as to make them govern also all trade relationships. Here, too, the interest of society is paramount, and the individual Jew, while seeking to obtain a livelihood, must take into account the interests of his fellow tradesmen, of his customers, and of society at large.

Such a balance between opposing interests is unavoidable from the purely economic point of view as well. "Since financial cooperation is necessary for the people of every city, it is impossible to have these transactions without a proper standard of equity and without useful regulation." [91] That is why laws introducing order into the relations among men, and judges to administer these laws, are such universal features. Besides being one of the Noahidic commandments, the appointment of judges was, with the Sabbath, one of the first divine ordinances imposed upon the Israelites after their exodus from Egypt. When a legal principle is involved, it makes little difference, according to Maimuni, whether the subject of controversy amounts to a thousand denars or to one *peruṭah*. Not even the ethically important consideration of the relative economic positions of the litigants is to be taken into account. Maimuni reiterates the biblical admonition to the judge not to lean backward to extend even the slightest favor to a poor litigant only because he happens to be poor. The specific protection to be granted by society to its disinherited is a matter of charity and social work, but is outside the domain of the administration of justice. Even in the Exile, where the courts are devoid of the power of imposing the ancient Palestinian "fines," they are called upon to interfere in all matters involving financial losses, "so that the rights of the people, such as those arising from loans, sales, transfers, legal disputes, and damages should not be lost." [92]

It falls under the jurisdiction of both the civil and the judicial administrators carefully to supervise the weights and measures used in business transactions. Maimuni insists upon the rigid control of scales, weights, and measures at the very moment when these implements are manufactured. "The same applies to the measuring of land, where one ought to establish the figures relating to the survey of the land with full exactitude in accordance with the principles elucidated in the geometric works, since even a finger's width of land is to be treated as if it were a field full of crocus." It is also the duty of the Jewish administrators to appoint supervisors in every city and county to visit the shops, check the scales and measures, and, upon finding anyone in possession of faulty weights, to subject him to flagellation and a fine at the discretion of the court. In another connection, Maimuni declares that the use of measures below the standard agreed upon by the population of a particular city constitutes the breaking of a negative commandment, although it is not punishable by flagellation—the transgressor being obliged to pay damages. Even an unintentional miscalculation makes a transaction null and void, and the injured party may demand restoration of the precontractual status. The mere possession of a defective measure or scale in a private dwelling is a serious crime. Maimonides becomes rhetorical when, using a hyperbolical exclamation of R. Levi as a motto, he writes:

The punishment for [incorrect] measures is more drastic than the sanction on incest, because the latter is an offense against God, while the former affects a fellow man. He who denies the law concerning measures is like one who denies the Exodus from Egypt which was the beginning of this commandment. [93]

Society is also obliged to prevent excessive profits. Maimuni enumerates in the same breath the duty of the courts to appoint supervisors over weights and measures, and the obligation to fix prices. It is really in this field of economic regimentation that we can find a major criterion for the extent of his advocacy of active social control. Evidently at this point he comes very close to the doctrine of the just price, which played such an enormous part in the economic views of the Christian scholastics. Under the more advanced semicapitalistic economy of Muslim lands, the limitation of mercantile profits was less important. Nevertheless, Maimuni insists that

no overcharge is permitted in sales; only the known and customary rate of profit [must suffice]. The law has fixed the conditions under which a sale should be valid; and, as is well known, warned us even against verbal cheating. [94]

He refers here to those sections of his *Code* in which he had reiterated the talmudic regulations safeguarding the *justum pretium* for both the merchant and the customer. He realizes, however, as may be seen in several significant points, the necessity of adjusting the law to the novel economic conditions.

What is the just price? We shall search in vain for a full definition by Maimuni. He undoubtedly was familiar with Aristotle's penetrating analysis of the elements of value in the *Nicomachean Ethics*, a work quoted by him on several occasions. Nonetheless, we shall find in his presentation neither a clean-cut decision for the more objective criteria of the costs of production and the element of work, as emphasized, from the standpoint of the producer, by Augustine and Thomas Aquinas, respectively, nor one for the more subjective element of the need and utility on the part of the consumer, as seen by Aristotle himself and by Duns Scotus.[95] Like the Talmud, Maimonides merely insists that no one should obtain a profit, or incur a loss, exceeding one-sixth of the due price. While he thus seems to be leaning toward the criterion of cost, he qualifies this immediately by excluding from the operation of this law all transactions in which the seller frankly admits his original cost and intended profit. In such cases, the profit may far exceed one-sixth. The only requirement is that the merchant include in his calculations of the original cost only overhead, such as transportation and hotel expenses, but not, without express indication of so doing, the expected remuneration for his own time and efforts.[96] The law of "misrepresentation" (*ona'ah*) thus applies only to the usual transactions, in which the purchaser is not taken into the seller's confidence or vice versa. It is evident that for Maimuni, as for the rabbis generally, the prevailing price is based upon some sort of profit added to the merchant's own cost. To determine it he accepts two legitimate criteria: the market price and that fixed by the authorities. True to his urban orientation, he decides, on the basis of a rather incidental discussion in the Talmud, that it is the market price of the city rather than that established in a small town or village which really counts. He thereby assumes that the price, at least of agricultural produce, would be higher in the city than in the countryside, nearer the actual place of production, although this was not always the case in the Muslim cities. He also recognizes seasonal fluctuations.[97]

The acceptance of a freely established market price, however, would involve recognition of the uncontrolled operation of the law of supply and demand, which was, of course, repudiated by Maimuni, as by all other medieval thinkers. That is why, besides the limits of custom, he expects communal regulation to establish the prices of all important articles, in fairness to the producer, the distributor, and the consumer. Only in the necessities of life, such as wine, oil, and flour, however, does Maimuni insist upon price fixing to allow a margin of profit of but one-sixth for the merchant. With respect to all other merchandise, he leaves price regulation, if any, entirely to the discretion of the Jewish communal authorities, especially the distinguished leader of each city; clearly, he assumes that the authorities would take cognizance of the conflicting interests and adopt a middle-of-the-road policy in accordance with the demands of justice. In other words, one might accept for Maimonides the definition soon after formulated by Albertus Magnus: "Justum autem pretium est, quod secundum aestimationem fori illius temporis potest valere res vendita." [98] Such governmental "estimation" really corresponded to the prevalent practice of Egyptian state capitalism in Maimuni's day, which failed, however, to check all abuses arising from the excessive speculation in grain. Thus the subjective criterion of the court's opinion is substituted for the subjective element of the merchants themselves fixing the price in accordance with supply and demand. Maimuni is ready, however, to accept the latter, in case of the absence of authoritative regulation, which, under the conditions of his time, he hardly expected to serve as universal standards even with respect to basic commodities.

These subjective criteria of value evidently are in full consonance with the subjective character of the entire system of private ownership, as analyzed above. Even overcharging or underselling by more than one-sixth is discussed under the subjective term "cheating" the other party. We have seen that as soon as the injured party is informed of this excessive raise or fall in the price, the transaction is valid. The very fixing of one-sixth as the standard margin is due to the likewise "subjective" assumption that people are ready to forego their rights to that extent, and that the injured party would voluntarily renounce its due. That is also why "verbal cheating," consisting in willful misrepresentation entailing no financial loss whatsoever, is regarded as equally injurious. Indeed, since it affects personal integrity rather than property and since it does not lend itself to financial compensation, Maimuni denounces it with even greater vigor. [99]

In his elaboration of these principles Maimuni tries to meet the requirements of justice, but it is evidently justice in a psychological and judicial, rather than an economic, sense. In the case of the one-sixth overcharge, he is concerned principally with the prevention of willful or unconscious misrepresentation. As long as the case is correctly and clearly stated and no party can complain of having misunderstood the other, there is no legal redress, even though the injured party may have been compelled by urgent economic reasons consciously to concede to the other an undue advantage. In clarifying the case of "honest" trading, Maimonides states that the seller may either mention his own purchase price and the desired profit or else clearly indicate that the deal shall not be annulled on account of the stipulated overcharge. A condition phrased in general terms or stating the overcharge in obviously exaggerated terms (e.g., "this object sold to you for 100 denars is worth only 1 denar") is not valid, because it does not give the purchaser full information. But Maimuni would not accept—as did some Franco-German scholars— the purchaser's frank admission that he had realized the extent to which he had been overcharged, but that, being in need of the purchased object, he gladly overpaid by more than one-sixth so as to ensure the subsequent annulment of the contract. Such cynicism, if dictated by economic stress, could perhaps be tolerated in feudal northern Europe; it would play havoc with the widespread mercantile relations of the Jews under Islam. [100]

In other respects, too, the insistence upon merely "psychological" honesty often favors the merchant rather than the customer. In the first place, the very margin of one-sixth enables the seller to demand restitution if he sells the merchandise anywhere between 14.3 and 16.66 percent below the just price, while the purchaser can claim credit only if he pays from 16.66 to 20 percent over the just price. Above these percentages, the entire transaction becomes null and void at the request of the injured party. It has been estimated that any object worth, say, 210 denars can fetch up to 244 denars before the purchaser is entitled to challenge the sale, or down to 181 denars before the seller may do so. Actual annulment comes only if the price goes either beyond 252 or below 175 denars. In other words, a seller overcharging by 34 to 42 denars is in the same position as a purchaser underpaying by 29 to 35 denars. At the same time, a simple mistake in weight does not annul the transaction, but is to be adjusted by the merchant's either placing the additional weight at the disposal of the purchaser or receiving the excess back from him. [101] More important is the fact that according to rabbinic law the purchaser has the right to withdraw from a transaction only during a limited period of time; namely, until he has had a reasonable chance to show the merchandise to an expert or to one of his relatives, who might alert him to the excessive price. The merchant, however, can claim annulment (or restitution) at any future date, because it is assumed that, no longer being in possession of the sold object, he is in no position to ascertain its real value. To be sure, Maimonides tries somewhat to qualify this indefinite right. Although echoing R. Naḥman's evidently impulsive exclamation "forever," he states that if the seller happens to come across an identical object, he must immediately raise his claim. In the case of objects of unchanging quality, such as pepper, the claim expires as soon as the seller can obtain information in the market. Maimuni pays no attention, however, to the special need of protection for the usually ignorant customer as against the more experienced merchant, a need which undoubtedly had inspired the original legislators to enact this entire body of protective laws. [102]

Following the Talmud, moreover, Maimuni stipulates so many exemptions from the operation of the principle of the just price that its effectiveness is highly curtailed in an advanced economic system. While refusing to follow a gaon's opinion that the principle applies only to the sale of foodstuffs, he admits that such significant branches of economy as transactions in land, slaves, and commercial paper (apart from the more or less obsolete *hekdesh*) are generally exempt. [103] Since "land" included all types of rural and urban real estate, since a large number of Jews in Maimuni's age were still engaged in the slave trade, and since many important business transactions consisted in the transfer of sale and loan contracts or other deeds, one can easily understand that the ability to sell or purchase all these significant articles of commerce at the best price obtainable facilitated the unhampered development of trade. To be sure, here, too, Maimonides introduces a number of qualifications beyond those stated in the Talmud. Sales contracted on either side by plenipotentiaries, guardians of minors, or to a certain extent, by courts acting in behalf of minors (or of charitable funds) are subject to the laws affecting "misrepresentation." While contractual labor for wages, like slavery, is exempt, Maimuni was apparently the first jurist to demand the application of these laws to contractors and artisans undertaking a specific job. [104] But he could not repudiate those basic exemptions which had been granted by the talmudic authorities (evidently because they did not consider them as vitally affecting the rule itself). Those exemptions became immeasurably more important, however, in the days of Maimonides.

Another important talmudic exemption was granted to the non-professional seller of household articles, who was allowed to dispose of his property at the best possible price. Maimuni, like many other commentators, seems to have expanded this privilege to include the one-sided right of such a seller to claim restitution or annulment if he sold below the market price. This right is justified by the seller's frequent personal attachment to the sold objects, which, again psychologically rather than economically, modifies their value. [105] On similar grounds, Maimuni, taking his cue from an inconclusive talmudic analogy, postulates a general exemption for barter of specific objects. Barter in two kinds of fruit, he admits, is subject to "misrepresentation," because they possess an objective value. But "he who exchanges vessels for vessels or one animal for another, even if he exchanges a needle for a coat of mail or a lamb for a horse, has no claim of misrepresentation, because such a man may wish to have the needle rather than the coat of mail." [106] Whatever influence the endless Muslim casuistry concerning the unlawful increment—which was classified as "usury," whether obtained by a credit transaction or otherwise—may have exercised upon Maimonides, he remains true to his constant psychological interpretation of this law, with little, if any, regard for the economic realities.

Equally far-reaching qualifications are attached by Maimonides to his demand for official price fixing and related measures against unbridled speculation. Indeed, it was through a juxtaposition of these two lines of reasoning that he limited price fixing to the necessaries of life. The Talmud really postulated the suppression of all commerce in wine, oil, and flour in order that the consumer be able to obtain his food directly from the producer, without paying for the middleman's services. Maimuni, literally applying some statements of the ancient Palestinian sages, limits this prohibition to Palestine. Even there he admits the exception, stated previously in the tannaitic period, that when oil is plentiful a legitimate trader may draw profits from mediating between the producer and the consumer. [107] Maimuni seems to disregard geographic boundaries only for trade in eggs, when he demands that, whether in Palestine or elsewhere, the first purchaser alone be entitled to sell them with profit, whereas all subsequent buyers should resell them at cost.[108] To prevent an undue rise in prices, the Talmud had discouraged grain speculation through the storing up of grain and other necessaries for resale at a higher market price. Maimuni limits that prohibition to Palestine and to all other places where the Jews constitute the majority, "because from such practices suffering arises for Israel." The agricultural producer, however, may store up his own produce and sell it at the time most convenient to him. Before a Sabbatical year, everybody may accumulate the yield of harvests to provide for the needs of three years; namely, the year of fallowness, the year preceding, and the year following it. In emergency periods, however, when there is famine in Palestine, one must not store away even a measure of the cheapest food, such as St. John's bread, "because one thereby brings a scourge into the market prices." Another safeguard was the prohibition of exportation of such necessaries from Palestine, or even from one suzerainty to another in Palestine. In general, "he who raises prices [through speculation] or stores up produce in Palestine or in any other place where the majority consists of Israelites, is like a usurious moneylender." There is no evidence that Maimuni contemplated the practical application of most of these laws to his own time. [109]

Maimonides' indecisive views on competition are equally illuminating. He allows arrangements between members of an artisan group to divide up the working days so that they should not compete with one another. Any breach of such arrangements, which at most are subject to the approval of an outstanding communal leader wherever one exists, may be punished by a stipulated fine. A group of shipowners or members of a caravan may also agree upon a sort of mutual insurance for losses, in ships or donkeys, sustained by individual members. But this degree of regulation is far from that of a medieval guild, or even of such guilds as had existed in Sassanian Persia and in the declining Roman Empire. That is perhaps why Maimuni nowhere mentions that the general arrangements concerning working days must be agreed upon by all artisans in a city—as demanded, for instance, by the Spaniards Judah b. Barzillai and Nahmanides. [110] On the other hand, he does not object to underselling one's competitors or using other "fair" methods of competition. It is once more the psychological elements of frankness and clarity, rather than the consideration of a neighbor's economic rights, that are the criteria of fairness. Paraphrasing the liberal view of a majority in the Mishnah, he writes:

A merchant may distribute cakes and nuts among children and servant girls so as to induce them to frequent his shop. He may undersell the market price so as to attract more customers, and the members of the market may not prevent him from so doing. There is nothing underhanded in that. [111]

To be sure, he wishes to protect individuals well established in a certain craft against unfair competition. He regards it as one of the essentials of ethics "not to infringe upon the calling of a fellow Jew." In one notable case which was brought to his attention, he harshly condemned the revengeful proceedings of a wealthy citizen, who, to spite the *mohel* of the community, circumcised all newborn boys in the region and spent the fees on charity. "This is the fulfillment of a commandment arrived at through sin . . . because he interfered with the established livelihood of a poor and learned person." He here used the ancient phrase "the removal of a neighbor's boundaries" metaphorically—as did many other rabbis—even though he himself had taught that, in the strict legal sense, this biblical prohibition (superimposed upon the general prohibitions of theft and robbery) referred only to concrete land boundaries in Palestine. It was merely for the promotion of Jewish education that he welcomed competition among elementary teachers even when it interfered with such acquired rights. Nevertheless, in one practical case, he insisted that a newcomer in a community be excommunicated unless he desisted from engaging in elementary instruction without first obtaining the permission of the local teacher, who happened to be his superior in learning. [112] But apart from such general moral injunctions, the allowance of certain discretionary powers to Jewish courts and public opinion, and the recognition of customs wherever they exist, Maimuni nowhere consistently denies the legitimacy of competition in the furtherance of one's strictly commercial interests.

Similarly, there is full contractual freedom, according to Maimuni, with respect to leases of houses and shops. Legally a lease is but a sale for a specified or unspecified period. That this interpretation favors, from the economic point of view, the landlord rather than the tenant is of less concern to Maimuni than that there be full legal clarity. In fact, in every dubious case he is inclined to side with the landlord, since "the land is in the landlord's possession and we may not withdraw from him any rights without clear evidence." [113] No one is entitled to live in an unoccupied but habitable dwelling without paying rent. Such failure to pay rent, even if the landlord knows nothing about it, has some of the earmarks of robbery. [114] At the expiration of the contractual term of the lease, the tenant may be evicted "without an hour's delay." However, in indefinite leases, in summer either party must give thirty days' notice in the case of shops, and twelve months' notice in that of urban dwellings, while no evictions at all can take place in winter between the Feast of

Tabernacles and Passover. [115] However, the landlord may raise the rent, just as the tenant may reduce it, without warning, if the market fluctuates. If the landlord suddenly becomes homeless, or requires a new home on account of his son's unexpected marriage, he may evict the tenant without due notice. Maimonides, here largely restating traditional law, advocates only minor modifications in favor of the tenant, as when he insists upon the latter's right to sublease his place, to the same number of occupants, without the landlord's consent. The owner may still choose, however, an abrupt termination of the lease. [116] In any case, in the crowded civilization here envisaged, where urban rents—otherwise usually the first target of official regulation—are allowed to fluctuate freely, and where the landlord is generally favored, provided his behavior is psychologically correct, a regimented economy could hardly be more than an occasional pious wish.

The upshot of these Maimonidean norms governing the price structure is: (1) every community, if necessary with the cooperation of a great leader, may at its discretion fix the prices of all articles; (2) every community should fix the prices of necessaries, allowing for a total profit of but one-sixth; (3) wherever there are no communally fixed prices, the seller is wholly free to set his own price on land, slaves, free labor, and commercial paper; (4) a merchant may do the same with respect to movables, if he gives complete and candid information to the other party; (5) however, in case of failure to do so, he runs the risk that the injured party may choose to demand restitution of the balance of precisely one-sixth, or complete annulment of the contract if the difference exceeds one-sixth of the market price; (6) an error in weight or measure merely calls for the restitution of the difference; (7) the merchant is entitled to sell freely below the prevailing market price and to employ other "fair" methods of competition.

Under these circumstances, one can see that economic regimentation, as visualized by Maimonides, was left entirely to the discretion of the local authorities. In finding his way through a chaos of contradictory, and frequently purely theoretical, talmudic utterances, voiced in various periods by various individuals living under changing economic systems in both Palestine and Babylonia, he accepted from his immediate predecessors, and further elaborated, certain compromise formulas which left the way open to either comprehensive regulation or great legal latitude. We have practically no evi-

dence of the actual operation of these talmudic requirements in
the ancient period. We have still less convincing proof of their
practical application in the more capitalistically oriented Jewish
economy under medieval Islam. It is notable that the several hundred extant inquiries addressed to Maimuni himself—for many years
the recognized leader of Egyptian Jewry—do not refer to a single
instance of communal price fixing or to a complaint of "misrepresentation." [117] There must have occurred innumerable cases not only
of undue profiteering but of normal mercantile profits in excess
of 16.66 percent, but no one seems ever to have raised a legal issue
on this score. Much of what Maimuni here restates as a binding
legal norm appears unreal and bears the earmarks of an accepted
legal fiction.

Nevertheless, in his reformulation, adaptation, and modification
of the traditional law, we may perceive what he regarded as
desirable, and, to a certain extent, as feasible under the conditions
known to him. Two elements clearly stand out in his theory: the
communal will is supreme; it *may* regulate all prices, and *should*
regulate those prices which vitally affect the consumer. On the other
hand, there should be as little interference as possible in the fields
of land transfer, the acquisition of slaves, the hiring of labor, and
the trade in commercial papers, fields which are of direct concern
only to landowners, merchants, and other entrepreneurs. (Whatever
protection is to be extended to slaves and free workers shall be
afforded them, as we shall see, through a specific set of labor laws,
not through the operation of the law of the just price.) In other
words, a proper balance is sought between regimentation and freedom—another of those happy mediums which are the core of all
Maimonidean ethics. The basic aim of the Maimonidean, indeed of
the entire rabbinic, economic legislation, is to extend a well-balanced
protection to the consumer, the producer, and the middleman, each
acting within his legitimate sphere. In Christian scholasticism the
doctrine of the just price had to become the cornerstone of all economic thought, because, through the elements of labor and cost, it
offered a much-needed justification for mercantile profits, and
indirectly for private ownership as a whole. In Judaism, as well as
in Islam, where no such justification was urgently needed, this doctrine plays but a relatively minor role in the economic thinking of
the leaders, and is easily overshadowed by the complex doctrine of
"usury" and its extensive ramifications.

MONEY

Problems of money, and especially currency, are frequently discussed in Maimonides' writings. To be sure, he does not seem to have given much thought to the essence and function of money, and he followed rather closely the talmudic doctrine. But he realized that, since the currency of his day was in many ways different from that of the talmudic period, it called for considerable modification of the talmudic law.

He frequently goes to great lengths in explaining the talmudic references to the Roman and Persian currencies, and reiterates on several occasions that a *sela'* was the equivalent of four *denars*, a *denar* amounted to six silver *ma'ahs*, a *ma'ah* to two *pondions*, a *pondion* to two *issars* (asses), an *issar* to eight *peruṭahs!* There also existed at one time a *dareikon*, worth two *sela's*. In another connection he states that a Palestinian *sela'* was an alloy containing only one-eighth of a pure silver *sela'* and amounting to one-half of a silver *denar*, or three and one-half copper *denars*, and that consequently a fine of one hundred *sela's* was really the equivalent of only 12½ original silver *sela's*. Even in this Jerusalem currency, however, the *ma'ah* was still computed on the old silver basis as the equivalent of pure silver in the weight of 16 grains of barley. He warmly defends this computation against that of his teachers, whose method, he feels, he can prove to have been erroneous. He informs us elsewhere of the source of his statement that the ancient Palestinian currency was weighed in grains of barley. "It is a tradition with us from my father, blessed be his memory, who received it from his father and grandfather . . . and I do not know any reason for it." He then proceeds to explain that the ancient shekel, consisting of 24 drachmas of 16 grains each, amounted to 384 grains. Since the Egyptian dirhem weighs 61 barley grains, the shekel is equivalent to approximately 6⅓ dirhems. The 50 shekels referred to in the Bible (Lev. 27:3), for example, thus amount to approximately 314¾ Egyptian dirhems. There were also other monetary changes after biblical times. He insists that the biblical half-shekel was the minimum paid by the Jews at any time, while sometimes the payment rose with the introduction of a more highly valued unit of currency. For instance, when the unit was a *dareikon*, the payment amounted to a *sela'*; when it consisted of a *sela'* it declined to one-half of a *sela'*, the exact equivalent of a biblical half-shekel; but it was never allowed to fall below this amount. [118]

In this interpretation of the rabbinic sources, to which Abraham b. David seriously objects, we find an adumbration of the Maimonidean view on the nature of money. Money, for him, is evidently a medium of exchange, the value of which is determined by the two independent criteria of its metallic content and its legal value. The former is important insofar as the payment of the Temple tax can never amount to less than the content of one-half of the biblical silver shekel; if, however, the nominal value of the existing unit of currency is higher than that of the shekel, payment must be made in one-half of the higher unit. Abraham b. David accepts the former, but denies the latter, requirement, explaining the particular talmudic source as merely reporting a historic occurrence, without permanent legal obligations. Israelites may, he thinks, under some circumstances be asked to pay more as a voluntary contribution, but they cannot be forced to do so. While one may sympathize with RABD's distrust of the nominal value of coins in a country such as France, where in his day no less than eighty-odd feudal lords had unrestricted minting powers, Maimuni, living under the somewhat better-stabilized currency system of the Muslim lands, could express much more truthfully the spirit of the ancient rabbis. His combination of monetary nominalism, or *etatism*, with metallism underlies, indeed, all the numerous discussions in the Talmud. Both elements are also clearly discernible in the main Aristotelian discussion of money in the *Nicomachean Ethics*, with which, undoubtedly, Maimuni was also familiar:

Money has become by convention a sort of representative of demand; and this is why it has the name "money" [νόμισμα], because it exists not by nature but by law [νόμος] and it is in our power to change it and make it useless. . . . Now the same thing happens to money itself as to goods—it is not always worth the same; yet it tends to be steadier. [119]

The nominalist view becomes particularly significant in connection with the purchase of movable objects. Starting from barter, as the basic form of exchange, Maimuni, following the Talmud, regards a deal as completed if one of the parties takes possession through lifting or withdrawing the other party's merchandise. Money, however, being but the standard medium of exchange and the common denominator of value—one may perceive both these elements in the rabbinic doctrine—but not ordinary merchandise dependent on its intrinsic value, cannot serve as such an object of barter. The acceptance of the purchase price by the seller constitutes a moral obligation for both parties to consummate the sale, but legally each party may still withdraw. The only sanction upon such unethical withdrawal was the invocation, in open court, of divine wrath upon the malefactor, but the cancellation of the sale remained unaffected. Although this regulation was originally enacted by the rabbis for the protection of the purchaser, so that the seller, having received the money, should continue to take proper care of the sold object until it came into the purchaser's possession, it nevertheless emphasized the nominal value of money. [120]

What is "money" in this legal sense? In the first place, it consists of silver coins; in the second place, of gold and copper coins, which are made legal tender by their inscription and enjoy general acceptability in a certain region or period. "Bad moneys which the state or the city declares unfit, or coins which do not circulate in a particular city and are not being traded in until exchanged into other coins, are like fruits in every respect." Similarly, gold and silver bars are not money, but merchandise. Maimonides gives a similar definition of money in connection with the "redemption" of the second tithe, which the owner was allowed to convert into "money" before proceeding to Jerusalem. Besides stressing the importance of the silver coin, he reiterates the significant statement of the Tosefta (in the interpretation of the Palestinian Talmud) that coins of ancient kings, if still readily acceptable, could be used for such redemption. [121]

While with respect to other objects all valid coins in circulation are "money," it is the silver coin which serves as the main "unit of accounts." In comparison with it even gold and copper coins sink to the position of merchandise, rather than media of exchange. That is why an exchange of coins of different metallic content is completed when the gold or copper coin is given and accepted, although the equivalent amount in silver has not yet been returned. But if silver coins alone are transferred, both the seller and the purchaser may legally withdraw, because the "merchandise," namely the gold or copper coins, has not yet been appropriated. These assumptions, derived from the Talmud, were fairly justified in the Roman Empire. Although Roman currency was essentially bimetallic, the gold coin apparently was subjected to more frequent variations in weight than was the silver coin. In the predominantly agricultural Jewish settlements of Palestine, moreover, the relatively precious gold coins had a much smaller circulation than the silver coins. After a period of hesitation, the last Tannaim decided for the preferential treatment of silver. Once proclaimed as a general principle in the Mishnah and accepted by the Talmud and the early geonim, it had to be maintained even in the face of the transition from a preponderant silver standard, or the bimetallism of the early Caliphate, to the predominant gold standard of the tenth and eleventh centuries. Maimonides seems at first timidly to suggest that in his day gold coins were fully equal to those of silver. But in his *Code* he simply restates the explicit talmudic law. He fails, however, to draw from the talmudic discussion the evidently justified conclusion that copper coins, although inferior to silver, should be considered preferred currency with respect to gold. This conclusion, drawn by other rabbis such as Ibn Adret, undoubtedly reflected experience in ancient Palestine, where copper coins were widely circulated. It would have sounded starkly unreal under the advanced money economy of the Muslim lands. [122]

The same prevalence of the silver standard may also be seen in the rules governing "misrepresentation," as applied to money exchange. A simple mistake in counting, as in other transactions, does not nullify the exchange, but merely imposes restitution of the difference, even after the lapse of many years. [123] However, if the difference arose out of the rate of exchange agreed upon by the parties, it is considered a normal commercial transaction and subjected to the limitations of the just price. Maimuni gives the following example: "If at the time a gold denar was worth 24 silver denars and it was exchanged for either 20 or 28 silver denars, the difference is to be returned; if the difference was larger, the exchange is null and void; if smaller, we assume [the injured party's] acquiescence." Like Alfasi and others, he thus accepts R. Simon's opinion that there is no difference between coins and other movable objects with respect to the principle underlying the laws of misrepresentation: that an overcharge of less than one-sixth is not resented. R. Meir and R. Judah undoubtedly were more realistic when they tried to reduce the possible overcharge to one-twenty-fourth and one-twelfth, respectively. They clearly realized that people, relying upon the nominal value of coins, expect fairly exact rates of exchange. Indeed, Nahmanides and Asher b. Yeḥiel accept at least the reduction to one-twelfth. The general principle also applies, according to Maimuni, to damaged coins the metallic weight of which is below normal by one-sixth or more but which have not been withdrawn from circulation. Of course, if such coins are exchanged expressly on the basis of their weight, the slightest mistake calls for restitution. But so long as their nominal value alone is considered, a deficiency up to 16.66 percent may be disregarded. To diminish the injurious effects upon the recipient, Maimonides somewhat extends the talmudic time limit for claims. While generally repeating the talmudic statement that claims expire in villages on Fridays, when everybody is supposed to have a chance to exchange his money, and in cities as soon as one reasonably may consult a banker, "because the banker alone knows the coin, its deficiency and its monetary value," he qualifies the expiration date in the case of books, jewelry, or coins. If no expert is available, and the recipient must either bring the book or the piece of jewelry to another district or await the arrival of an expert in his own locality, he may raise the issue at such later date. Similarly, if a coin cannot be put back into circulation, the claim for restitution remains valid at any time; if it can be disposed of with some difficulty, the matter depends on the nature of the transaction and the question of whether or not it was expected to be scrupulously exact. [124]

Once more we find here the prevailing nominalist approach, but with due consideration of the metallistic element. It is evident that Maimonides does have in mind a bimetallic currency, where the relationship between gold and silver is fixed by law and where a difference in exchange would naturally be more in the nature of an error in counting. The price of gold coins is here allowed to fluctuate around some sort of market price, with a slight difference between the price paid and that received by the banker, which constitutes his legitimate profit. It is not included in the one-sixth differential, which might vitiate the transaction. As in other merchandise, consequently, the market price, rather than the merchant's cost, is taken as a basis. [125]

Modified monetary nominalism comes to the fore also in the following Maimonidean regulations: One may redeem the second tithe in coins which are known to be deficient, as long as the deficiency does not exceed one-sixth of the metallic content and the coins are circulating, certain difficulties in their transferability notwithstanding. The usual requirement of a purifying oath by the defendant, who admits part of the depositor's claim (*modeh be-miksat*), applies only to admissions referring to the same type of currency. If the plaintiff, however, claims that he has deposited a gold denar, and the defendant confesses only to the deposit of a silver denar, or if the claim is for ten Egyptian denars and the admission refers to ten Tyrian denars, the parties speak of different objects altogether, and no biblical oath is required. A robber who appropriates a good coin which subsequently disintegrates or is declared unfit by the government must return to the owner its full value at the time of the robbery. But if the coin, although declared unfit in one city, still circulates in another city, he may return it to the owner, regardless of the inconvenience accruing therefrom to the latter. [126] In all these respects the decisive criterion is the character of the coin as a circulating medium, whether or not it serves as universal legal tender and hence possesses easy transferability. The metallic content and the intrinsic value of the respective metals are of but secondary importance.

Special modifications of the nominalist doctrine became necessary in connection with loan contracts, on account of the lingering suspicion that the lender might derive therefrom some profit, which would be tantamount to usury. Maimuni joins the geonim in declaring that if the loan is stipulated in a currency subsequently declared unfit, the lender is obliged to accept payment in that currency only if it still possesses ready acceptability in a region within his reach. Otherwise he may insist upon payment in the new currency. [127] On the other hand, if the metallic weight of the coins borrowed is specified and subsequently the government increases their metallic content, the return of the same number of coins would yield a "usurious" profit to the lender. That is why a metallic increase of one-fifth or more unconditionally calls for a corresponding reduction in the amount due. A lesser increase may be disregarded, however, if there is no proportionate decrease in the cost of commodities. In other words, a fall in the prices of commodities, resulting from metallistic appreciation, as well as any appreciation of 20 percent or more, even if commodity prices remain stationary, calls for a readjustment of the loan to its original intrinsic value. This provision, adds Maimuni, also operates in favor of the lender if the currency is debased with respect to its metallic content in the period between the contracting of the loan and its repayment. [128] The significance of this Maimonidean extension may easily be gauged when one realizes that, throughout history, the metallic depreciation of currencies was much more frequent and gradual than their appreciation or revaluation.

BANKING

These discussions on the essence of money and its legal status as currency had considerable practical significance under later medieval Islam, where the circulation of a variety of coins was stimulated by the political dissolution of the Caliphate into many mutually hostile states and by the frequent inner upheavals. This monetary instability must have deeply affected the Jews, an increasing number of whom derived their livelihood from one or another form of the money trade. While far less one-sided in its economic exploits than the Jewries of contemporary Europe north of the Alps, with their growing concentration on moneylending, the Jewish population of western Asia and northern Africa, too, embraced a large number of bankers and their business associates. Indeed, after the tenth century the wealthiest and most influential leaders of the Jewish communities, next to the exilarchs and the rabbinic judges, belonged to this class of bankers and tax farmers, upon whose connections with the caliphs, sultans, and provincial governors frequently depended the welfare of their coreligionists.

The direct and indirect references scattered in Maimonides' writings to various phases of the money trade may conveniently be arranged under the following main divisions: (1) production of money, or minting; (2) money exchange; (3) money transfer or remittance; (4) deposits; (5) moneylending. We shall see that the last overshadowed in importance in the Maimonidean treatment all the other activities, not just because of its major economic role but largely on account of the problems of "usury." However, precisely because of the prohibition of usury, the extension of credit as such was, at least in theory, not considered to be the essential business of the banker. In the Maimonidean terminology, the *shulḥani* is still essentially the *trapezites* of antiquity, whose main dealings consisted in exchanging over the counter one coin for another. [129]

Jewish contractors for by-products of coins produced by the official mintmasters are often mentioned in the Maimonidean responsa and in other contemporary sources. Maimonides nowhere discusses the import of this activity upon the value of currency. Evidently he regards such pursuits as purely commercial and sees nothing objectionable in the private sale of gold or silver "dust" remaining after the coinage, apparently transacted with the tacit approval of state or city. Such dust was, indeed, utilized for commercial rather than minting purposes. The regulation of the value of currency and the modalities under which it was to be put into circulation, however, undoubtedly were governmental prerogatives, although in some instances the actual production may have been delegated to private citizens. To what extent Jews were employed in such official "mints" is of less concern to our subject of inquiry. As a matter of fact, the disputes mentioned in the Maimonidean *Responsa* arose from certain legal aspects of partnership, rather than from those involving minting by-products as such. [130]

Maimonides' views on the exchange of money have in part already been treated. We have seen that, like his talmudic predecessors, he believed the banker to be an expert in coins circulating not only in his own locality but in many other states and cities, and to possess more than ordinary knowledge of their metallic content. His services are remunerated by a fee, usually included in the margin between his bidding and his asking price. Maimonides evidently permits this margin to be freely established by the usual fluctuations in supply and demand; he does not include money among the necessaries of life, the price of which ought to be fixed by the community. An error in counting calls for restoration of the difference, but a conscious overcharge in the rate of exchange is subject to restitution or nullification of the transaction only if it equals or exceeds 16.66 percent of the market price. Even then, it appears, the money-changer still has an opportunity to forestall either effect by "honestly" informing the recipient of the discrepancy between his asking price and the prevalent market price. Since gold and copper coins, in relation to silver, were legally treated as merchandise, the banker obviously enjoyed a wide range of profit, even with respect to these essential parts of the currency circulating in his own country. We can see that, except for cases of fraud, his exchange business was subject to but few legal restrictions.

Connected with money-changing was also the expert appraisal of coins. On a banker's expert judgment, as we have seen, depended the claim of an injured party after an exchange of coins. Money-changers must have been consulted by laymen, particularly whenever new or unusual coins appeared in the market. It is only natural that bankers should charge a fee for such appraisals, in turn assuming responsibility for probable mistakes, and also that they should try to reserve this service to members of their profession. The rabbis lent them legal support in both endeavors, but also safeguarded the rights of their clients. Maimonides, amplifying the talmudic regulations in many significant points, states that an expert banker is responsible for damages arising from a mistaken appraisal only if he is paid for that service; a nonexpert is responsible even for freely offered advice, provided that its recipient directly or indirectly indicates that he is relying upon it. The burden of proof of his competence rests with the banker. We are nowhere told how large the fee was, but it may be assumed that it rose in proportion with the banker's risks, arising from a larger variety of coins in circulation or the prevalence of coin clipping, and sank with the increase in the number of competing experts. [131]

Money transfer over long distances became an urgent necessity through the vast expansion of Islam. A legal instrument was soon developed in the so-called *saftaja*, a sort of letter of credit, or draft, which enabled bankers to remit considerable funds without the inconvenience and danger of shipping coins. Notwithstanding certain legal scruples arising from the banker's fee for what might be termed a credit transaction, both Muslims and Jews made extensive use of this significant invention. [132] Maimonides did not directly discuss this new type of busines, probably because, in his general conservatism, he shared the talmudic distrust of all business dealings of an impersonal nature. Nevertheless, he admitted that if A sends an autograph letter to B, asking him to pay an amount owed A to C, B may do so and acquit himself of his obligation. Although B is also free to refuse payment, [133] Maimonides' comprehensive treatment of the talmudic laws concerning the power of attorney left enough loopholes for a fairly effective utilization of the new form of remittance.

On the whole, the rabbis disliked the power of attorney as a part of legal proceedings before the courts of justice. In order to prevent excessive legal technicalities and constant delay, Maimonides urges that the parties should always appear in court and personally state the case, without the intervention of tricky or influential intermediaries. Only in the case of a party's excusable inability to attend does he allow the use of substitutes. He is especially outspoken in denouncing this system in his *Responsa*. Like the Talmud, he also construes such power of attorney to be an actual transfer of rights, in full or in part, to the representative, who is then supposed to act in his own name. This theory operates against the defendant, who cannot appoint a substitute, since he has no rights to be transferred; neither can the plaintiff do so after his claim has been denied by the defendant. This legal theory is immediately abandoned by Maimonides, however, in the case of a representative exceeding his instructions or otherwise failing to take the proper steps to safeguard the plaintiff's interests. Even if the latter writes into the authorization in express terms, as demanded by Maimuni, "institute proceedings, obtain a judgment and collect it for your own benefit," all proceeds go to the real plaintiff, just as all expenses are charged to his account. [134]

With all these limitations, the power of attorney could be utilized to transfer to a third person funds available in a distant locality. By inserting a specific clause one could also authorize the recipient to transfer this power to a fourth person and the fourth to still other persons, and thus make it, to all intents and purposes, a negotiable instrument. The difficulty of assigning money, which, as we have seen, was not considered a proper object of barter, was evaded by the simultaneous grant of a parcel of land. It was in connection with such assignments that the geonim had devised the remarkable legal fiction that every Jew was able to use for such purposes his ideal claim upon four ells of land in Palestine. Maimuni, to be sure, frowns upon this legal fiction. But even he admits that it may be utilized as a psychological threat to bring a reluctant debtor or depository before the court. Neither does he contradict the geonic departure from talmudic law which permitted the assignment of loans, confirmed by deed or witnesses, even after their denial by the defendant. [135]

These discussions reveal a certain precariousness in the use of the *saftaja* if the person or firm on which it was drawn wanted to raise legal difficulties; but they did not prevent the smooth operation in the majority of dealings between more or less honest bankers in different cities. Maimonides may indulge in moral condemnation of those appearing with a power of attorney without a valid excuse, but he cannot definitely outlaw it. Neither can he condemn it on the ground of supposedly usurious gains, since it is the purchaser of the letter of credit who may be regarded as the lender and it is he who pays the fee. The saving to him of transportation charges and insurance against the risk of shipping coins can hardly be considered a usurious gain, in terms of Jewish law. Even the Muslim jurists, who did object to it on these grounds, were unable to prevent the triumphant march of this new commercial paper through all the lands of Islam. From there, evidently not without the assistance of Jewish intermediaries, it penetrated Italy and the other European countries, contributing a significant element to the rise of modern capitalism.

The deposit of funds with a banker, not only for safekeeping but also with a view to their gainful employment, was likewise widespread under medieval Islam. Neither the mosque nor the synagogue seem ever to have held a position similar to that of the ancient Babylonian or Greek temples or the medieval churches, which served as the main depositories, under the sanction of religion. It is evident that the ability to employ the deposited funds in their own business made it unnecessary for the bankers to charge a fee to the depositors. But there is no evidence that they paid any interest on such deposits. If they did, both Muslim and Jewish jurists would have qualified such interest as violating the prohibition of usury, unless paid to a member of another creed. [136] In Maimonides' *Code* we find the simple regulation:

A shopkeeper or money-changer who receives a deposit in cash must not make use of it, if it is handed to him bound up and sealed or tied in an unusual knot . . . . But if there is neither a seal nor an unusual knot he may employ these funds.

In other words, unless the depositor signifies his contrary will, deposits of this kind, which the Romans styled *deposita irregularia,* are freely disposable in the hands of businessmen, whereas other citizens have to obtain specific authorization by the depositors. Professional depositories, on the other hand, are immediately responsible for all preventable theft and loss; but, after employing the funds entrusted to them, they become simple debtors, responsible even for forcible losses. In another connection Maimonides prohibits deposits in Gentile firms with the understanding that the latter might lend the money at interest to another Jew. This would be but a clear evasion of the prohibition of usury, but evidently there is no objection to either a Gentile or a Jewish depository using deposits for lending money to Gentiles. [137] To what extent the Jewish depositor may participate in the ensuing profit will be seen later.

The most important branch of banking, the supply of funds on credit, is treated by Maimonides in terms of charity rather than business. Moneylending among Jews should yield no profits whatsoever to the lender, and should be transacted merely as a matter of courtesy and assistance to a needy coreligionist. We shall see, however, that enough loopholes were left, largely against Maimonides' will, to allow for extended and profitable credit transactions between Jews, and still more between Jews and Gentiles. Only so could Jewish law maintain a semblance of realism in a society in which numerous Jewish bankers were found among the outstanding citizens of their community.

In principle, Jewish law agreed with both Islam and Christendom that usury or, indeed, interest of any kind must not be charged to a coreligionist. Maimonides, summarizing talmudic regulations, declares that he who lends money on interest breaks six negative commandments; the borrower is guilty of two transgressions; the endorser, the witness, or any other accomplice in the transaction violates at least one biblical prohibition. Both the lender and the borrower, moreover, are guilty of moral turpitude, and by implication place themselves on a par with those who deny the God of Israel and, more specifically, his deliverance of the Jews from Egyptian bondage. [138] The ostracism of a usurious moneylender is pushed to the extreme of the treatment meted out to robbers. To be sure, to facilitate the moneylender's repentance Maimuni demands that his offer to restore the unlawful gain, like that of a robber, be refused. But to show sincere repentance he ought, on his own initiative, to tear up all the writs of indebtedness in his possession and abstain in the future from extending usurious loans even to Gentiles. [139] Both the usurious creditor and the debtor, being recognized as persons of inferior character, are disqualified from testifying in court. In any subsequent lawsuit against them, they lose the defendant's privilege in certain cases to take an oath denying the charges, and the oath devolves upon the plaintiff. They are still worse off if the plaintiff happens to be equally disreputable, because the oath legally reverts to the defendant, who, not being in a position to take it, must pay the entire claim, which he cannot otherwise disprove. [140]

On the other hand, gratuitous loans to needy coreligionists are to be highly encouraged. Following the Bible and the Talmud, Maimuni declares it to be a positive legal commandment to extend such disinterested loans if one is in a position to do so. Indeed "this is a

pious act greater than charity." In his well-known classification of
the eight degrees of charity, Maimonides actually mentions financial
support toward the rehabilitation of the productive capacities of the
recipient as by far the highest form of philanthropy. Even after
extending the loan, the creditor must consider the debtor's capacity
to repay. If he knows of the latter's inability to pay, his continued
demand of repayment is a violation of a strict biblical prohibition.

It is forbidden for a man to appear before, or even to pass by, his
debtor at a time when he knows that the latter cannot pay. He may
frighten him or shame him, even if he does not ask for repayment.

Under these circumstances, Maimuni is undoubtedly right when, in
referring in his *Guide* to his recodification of the laws governing
loans, he states that "on examination of these laws one by one you
will find them all to be filled with leniency, mercy and kindness
toward the needy; that no one be deprived of the use of anything
indispensable for his subsistence." [141]

What constitutes usury? Maimonides gives but a partial definition. However, he elaborates the principle in so many details that a
general theory may be abstracted therefrom.

Usury in the biblical sense is any kind of increment obtained from
any extension of credit. Its repayment may be obtained through
the courts . . . . Every other thing prohibited as usurious is forbidden by the sages, lest one be led thereby to charging the type of
usury prohibited by the Bible. This group is styled "a shade of
usury" and cannot be reclaimed through the courts.

Even considerations of a purely personal nature sometimes fall
under the term "usurious gain." A debtor, for instance, must not
greet his creditor first if he was not wont to do so before; he must
not praise him or be among his early callers; he must not teach him
the Bible or the Talmud unless he used to do it before. There are,
finally, contracts which, while permissible in themselves, are forbidden if they appear to be an "evasion of the laws of usury" (*ha'aramat
ribbit*). Despite this prohibition, such contracts, if concluded, are
valid and may even be enforced with the assistance of the courts. In
this terminology, presented in his *Code*, Maimonides seems to have
abandoned the distinction which he himself had suggested, in his
Commentary on the Mishnah, between the biblical terms *neshekh*
(being the type of usury prohibited by biblical law) and *tarbit*

(referring to usurious practices outlawed by talmudic law only). These practices are treated in the *Code* in the class of "shade of usury," which, as we have seen, constitutes a sort of *obligatio naturalis,* the fulfillment of which cannot be demanded by the creditor, but which, if fulfilled, cannot be reclaimed by the debtor. [142]

In further substantiation of this fourfold division into (1) biblically prohibited usury, (2) shade of usury, (3) verbal usury, (4) evasion of the laws of usury, Maimonides furnishes numerous detailed illustrations. The rabbinic term *ribbit* is clearly used in a much more comprehensive sense than the English term "usury," which as a rule applies only to excessive profits in moneylending. Besides including all interest, and even noneconomic gratuities in the form of "verbal usury," it embraces profits derived from a variety of transactions which may appear juridically as sales, leases, wages, and the like. Nonetheless, a certain element of credit extended to a borrower is concealed in every one of these transactions. Maimonides, to be sure, does not mention the drastic talmudic exception allowing a man to borrow a denar to meet an instantaneous obligation—without going home, where he possesses the equivalent amount in cash—and to pay a certain gratuity for this courtesy. According to the Talmud, this is not a "usurious" loan, but the exchange of a stipulated amount of money at home for a denar on the spot. But Maimuni expressly permits the analogous temporary borrowing of grain—if the borrower has some at home—regardless of the possible subsequent rise in prices. He regards such a transaction as a sale rather than a loan. On the other hand, the rabbinic *ribbit* is evidently less comprehensive than the Muslim *ribah,* which, although undoubtedly influenced by it, drew the line still wider to include almost every unlawful gain. Profit obtained through "misrepresentation," for instance, constitutes a separate talmudic transgression of *ona'ah,* but is part of the Muslim crime of *ribah.* The modern German term *Wucher* goes even further in including all forms of profiteering, wage exploitation, and so forth, but falls short of the rabbinic and Muslim "usury" by excluding "legitimate interest" and of course all forms of "verbal usury." The medieval references to *usura* oscillate between the exclusive emphasis upon income from moneylending and one approaching the Jewish use of the term. [143]

Maimonides evinces little concern about the theoretical justification of the prohibition of usury. For him it is a simple case of exploitation of another Jew's plight. "Why is it [usury] called *neshekh?* Because he [the lender] bites [*noshekh*] and afflicts his neighbor and eats his flesh." [144] One senses in the Maimonidean and all other rabbinic discussions of the problem of usury the underlying feeling that it conflicts with the principle of equivalence between what is given by the creditor and what is repaid by the debtor. But nowhere does Maimuni attempt an analysis of this aspect of the question, which occupies such a prominent place in the lucubrations of the Christian scholastics. Neither does he refer in any way to the well-known Aristotelian doctrine concerning the supposed "sterility" of money. At most he restates in his own fashion the talmudic law that

it is forbidden to lease denars, since this is not like leasing a vessel which is being actually returned, whereas these denars are spent and others are returned. That is why there is a "shade of usury" in the payment of rent for them. [145]

This emphasis upon the consumptibility of money—the Christian scholastics styled it *fungibilis*—is well in keeping with the prevailing monetary nominalism of the rabbinic doctrine. But it would have been sheer blindness toward reality or conscious opposition to it, such as had animated both Plato and Aristotle against the Attic banks of the fourth century B.C., for Maimonides and his confreres to invoke this principle of sterility in the face of the evident productive employment of capital in many branches of the semicapitalistic economy of medieval Islam. On principle they admitted, as we shall see, the productivity of money lent to Gentiles. It was precisely because money would normally "breed," i.e., be productive of income, that, according to Maimuni, the biblical lawgiver insisted that the moneylender forego this income and offer gratuitous loans as a matter of charity. Unlike most Christian Church Fathers and scholastics, having no compunctions about the principle of the return of the capital itself, and, unlike Aristotle, feeling no hostility toward commerce and mercantile profits, Maimuni was not impelled to search for deeper reasons in the prohibition of usury than the obviously adverse effects of the practice upon the needy borrower.

This emphasis upon the charitable aspects of moneylending had two vital effects. It facilitated a more lenient interpretation of the prohibition in cases where the borrower did not really require charitable credit, as in productive loans, or where the lender belonged to a class of persons requiring special protection. It also led to a series of protective regulations in favor of creditors, so "that you may not shut the gate before the borrowers." In either case it proved of great importance to the development of medieval Jewish banking.

In the first place, rabbinic law grants considerable exemptions to orphaned minors. If they become heirs to an estate which includes income derived from usury, they are obliged to make restoration only if their father voiced regrets before his death, and if the usurious gain consists in an extant specific object. The usual monetary gain is never subject to repayment. In managing a minor's estate, the court is also free to disregard the vast class of "shades of usury." What is more, even if the court happens to collect for the benefit of orphans regular usury in the biblical sense of the term, the debtor is urged not to reclaim it. [146] Another class of persons close to the heart of the rabbis were the scholars. Maimonides, in particular, sharply condemning the professional use of rabbinic learning, necessarily had to favor provisions for scholars to obtain some sort of unearned income. Next to that from silent partnership in business, which, as we shall see, likewise had its legal difficulties, revenue from money-lending offered the best livelihood for persons devoting their undivided attention to study. Interpreting more broadly than most other medieval rabbis a dubious talmudic passage, Maimuni denied the usurious character of credit transactions among scholars, followed by the repayment of higher amounts than originally borrowed. "Since the parties know the seriousness of the prohibition of usury, it is obvious that the debtor merely extended a gift" to his creditor. [147] As a matter of fact, Maimuni generally took a more lenient stand with respect to the "renunciation of his rights" (mehilah) by the debtor. Many geonim had declared the renunciation of usurious payments "made or to be made" by the debtor as null and void. They correctly argued that "every type of usury consists in the renunciation of the debtor's rights, but the Torah has not renounced these rights and has forbidden any such renunciation." Maimonides, however, repudiated this interpretation and insisted that even when the creditor is told to restore his usurious gain, the debtor is still at liberty voluntarily to forego its acceptance. [148] From the economic, not the juridical, point of view this opinion clearly enabled a creditor personally acquainted with his debtor, and relying upon his adherence to a sort of gentleman's agreement, to cash in all extra payments with practically no financial risks to himself. Even if neither of them was a scholar, and if the transaction was ultimately condemned by a court as usurious, the debtor, whose personal honor as well as future credit was involved, usually refrained from demanding restitution.

Much more important than these cases, where the payment of interest is clearly identified as such, are the various types of business transactions where such payment is concealed behind the screen of otherwise legitimate agreements. It is in these methods of circumventing the prohibition of usury, which was felt to be oppressive under the changed economic conditions, that the ingenuity of businessmen and jurists found ample means of fitting a vast and profitable credit system into the traditional legal structure. To be sure, following the Tosefta and the Talmud, Maimuni declares many such agreements, though in themselves permissible, forbidden because of their intrinsic purpose to evade the prohibition of usury (*ha'aramat ribbit*). But his illustrations refer only to such crude methods of evasion as few of his self-respecting contemporaries would have cared to apply. He mentions, for instance, the loan of merchandise and its subsequent repurchase for a smaller amount, which ultimately leaves the lender in possession of the entire merchandise and of an additional claim to the differential. Even such a clumsy contract, as we have seen, if properly executed, could not be legally annulled; but bankers in Maimuni's time could make much better use of the related *contractus mohatrae*, which, originating from an evasion of the Muslim prohibition of usury, was subsequently to play such a significant role in European moneylending. To be sure, the bankers would first have to overcome certain technical obstacles in Jewish law. They could not sell a fictitious object at one price and instantly buy it back at a higher price *for future delivery*, because such sales of nonexistent (or as yet nonexistent) objects were generally invalidated by Jewish law. Neither could they sell a particular object at a price higher than its actual value in the market without running the risk of recovering at the due date only the original market price. But what could prevent them from arranging for a sale below the market price of the moment, with immediate delivery, and an instantaneous resale at the market price with future delivery? The original owner evidently was free to dispose of his holdings below the market price and thus obtain the needed cash, under the promise of returning a higher amount at the stipulated future date. Such a twofold contract would in the interim also place in the hands of the creditor a pawn or mortgage in the form of the "sold" object.

Maimonides cites another illustration of the prohibited but none-theless legally valid evasion, viz., the leasing to the debtor of a field taken over by the creditor as security for his loan, the rental secur-ing the stipulated income. This method, closely related to the "purchase of rents," which came to play such an important role in medieval Europe, was reluctantly legalized by the canonists and, with further hedging, by the European rabbis. Maimonides himself tries to modify the laws directed against the creditor deriving income from property mortgaged to him. In opposition to some geonim, he draws a distinction between income from a house, a shop, and so forth—which, being more or less certain, is straight usury—and one coming from a field, which, dependent on a good or bad harvest, constitutes but a "shade of usury." Income from a field, moreover, is altogether permissible, if in return for it the lender dis-counts a stipulated amount, however small, from the debt. Neither does Maimuni apparently object to the lender leasing such a field to a third person for a higher rent than the discount. In the first exam-ple, too, there is nothing to prevent a merchant from extending to his neighbor a loan of a given sum of money in the form of merchan-dise, according to its supposed market value, and acquiring the same amount of merchandise elsewhere at wholesale prices. The usual span between the merchant's purchasing and selling prices, which Maimuni wished to see authoritatively fixed at 16.66 percent, but which, he admitted, could go much higher wherever there were no publicly fixed prices, would in this case clearly be mercantile profit in name, but substantial interest on a loan in its economic essence. [149]

Another important means of evasion was given by the permission to acquire deeds with a discount. Since the bulk of business in Mai-muni's time was transacted through the use of some commercial instrument, the flow of credit was greatly facilitated. For example, a merchant could sell merchandise on credit, at a price yielding him substantial profit, and obtain cash from the banker by discounting the bill given him by the purchaser. The underlying theory was that interest was prohibited only in direct relationships between lender and borrower. For the same reason one could pay a fee to an agent for his services in securing a loan. Since the law, according to Mai-muni, did not object if a third person, here the agent, paid a gratuity to the banker for the extension of credit to the agent's client, one can see how money could readily be diverted into profitable channels without exposing the lender and the borrower to public condemnation. [150]

The most important method of evasion under many antiusurious regimes was some sort of alleged silent partnership, in which capital was made to yield profit without work. While the rabbis strained their ingenuity to draw sharp juridical lines between real partnerships, going under the name 'iska, and concealed loan contracts, they could not entirely eliminate this means of securing income for money employed by others in a productive capacity. To be sure, the name "credit" was to be avoided. Even the early modern rabbis continued frowning upon the so-called contractus trinus, which came to be accepted by the later medieval canonists. This combination of contractual partnership with a sort of insurance for both capital and interest—hence the name—was regarded as admissible at best if the capitalist accepted the entire risk, which of course made it closely akin to the commenda, so widely accepted in the ancient and medieval Mediterranean world. The Arabs, too, recognized this institution, under the name of modarabat, and elaborated it in great detail in their great schools of jurisprudence. [151]

Maimonides, however, refers only casually to the usual commenda [152] and knows nothing of the contractus trinus. In restating the complicated talmudic regulations and cutting through a maze of controversial opinion accumulated in the centuries of juridical evolution, he clearly reveals his personal bent in two directions: he wishes to safeguard as far as possible the interests of the active partner. At the same time he insists upon great latitude in contractual dispositions. As a matter of principle, he forbids partnerships without active participation, unless the active partner receives a special compensation for his services. If he devotes himself exclusively to serving the company, he may legitimately expect an added remuneration in the amount of the wages which one normally would have to pay to an unemployed worker for doing the type of work which he (the active partner) had done before entering the partnership. As an alternative, he may be given a certain preference in the apportioning of gains or losses resulting from his business management. As a rule, he may be expected to participate in profits to the extent of two-thirds and in losses to that of only one-third. The parties are free, however, to make any other contractual arrangements, as long as the principle is maintained that the active partner be given some special remuneration for his labors. The parties may agree, for instance, that he share in the profits to the extent of one-ninth and in losses to that of only one-tenth. Maimonides argues specifically against his teachers, who recognized such agreements only if the active partner pursues another occupation on the side. If the active party, moreover, contributes a part of the capital, however small, the contract still is, in Maimonides' opinion, one of 'iska, rather than of ordinary partnership. By thus making the active worker an entrepreneur in his own right, even if his capital share be only one-tenth of one percent, the special compensation for his services may be reduced, without previous contractual agreement, to a nominal amount; e.g., one denar for the entire period of partnership. [153]

There is no doubt that most of the 'iska contracts entered into by Jews in the Maimonidean age were legitimate business agreements. They became of vital importance with the growth of international Jewish commerce, because they enabled merchants to entrust consignments of merchandise to fellow Jews traveling to foreign lands. After the disposal of these goods abroad, the merchants got back the invested capital and a stipulated share in the profits. We learn, for instance, from the Maimonidean Responsa that both India and the Mediterranean countries offered ample opportunities for this type of trading. However, one cannot deny that, notwithstanding all the obstacles erected by Maimuni and the other rabbis, such silent partnerships could be utilized also as means of evading the prohibition of usury. By letting the borrower participate with a farthing in the capital of the supposed partnership, one could arrange that most of the profits from the latter's employment of the borrowed money should go to the creditor. The only two deterrents, which Maimuni tries to fortify, were the lender's uncertainty of profit and the risk that he might lose one-half of the capital, which, according to the rabbinic theory, was to be treated as a deposit, and for which the borrower's responsibility was rather slight. The subsequent development of rabbinic law substantially weakened even these deterrents.[154]

The protective legislation for the creditor—arising from the principle of not shutting the gates to needy borrowers—likewise has many aspects. Apart from the general principle of formal justice that one must not favor the poor debtor against the rich creditor, even if the collection of the debt entails serious hardships for the debtor and his family, Maimonides, as we have seen, recognizes certain types of usury as forbidden, but collectible; and others as non-reclaimable if paid. In a talmudic controversy he also endorses the opinion that a deed containing usurious provisions remains valid as to principal and becomes void only with respect to interest. Other rabbis wished to condemn the entire deed, as a penalty for the inherent transgression. Maimonides also ethically advises all debtors to pay their bills promptly. [155] More important were the far-reaching departures from talmudic law which enabled creditors to collect outstanding debts from persons or properties which the Talmud had declared immune. According to the ancient law, only land could be seized for the satisfaction of creditors; the talmudic sages themselves, going beyond what they regarded as biblical law, enabled the creditors to seize land of medium quality, even where inferior land was available. The geonim, confronted with an increasingly landless Jewish population with a growing need of credit, extended the law to allow the seizure of movable property as well. Indeed, movables were to be disposed of first, and only if they were found insufficient was the land to be seized. The geonim made heirs of an estate, including orphans, fully responsible for the indebtedness of its previous owner. Creditors able to prove a claim derived only from an oral agreement were now entitled to execute it from the movable property included in the estate. Maimonides fully accepts these far-reaching modifications of talmudic law, merely expressing a personal preference for the insertion of a specific clause to this effect in the original contract, such as had become customary in Morocco. [156]

Maimuni takes a similar stand with respect to the Sabbatical cancellation of debts and its prevention through the so-called *prosbol*. Hillel had already motivated this abrogation of an ancient law by the need to stimulate charitable moneylending. Maimuni is somewhat in a dilemma. Personally, he would have liked to see the cancellation of debts by the Sabbatical year operative without restrictions. He becomes rhetorical in denouncing the judge who nowadays fails to apply the law as one who "does not fear God and robs the poor." Nevertheless, he admits the validity of the *prosbol*, because, since the discontinuation of the observance of the Jubilee year, the Sabbatical year has become a rabbinic rather than a biblical institution. While trying to discourage the indiscriminate use of the new instrument and insisting that only a court of very learned judges be given the right to issue it, he nevertheless accepts other protective measures for the creditor enacted long after the time of

Hillel. In his opinion, the creditor need not produce evidence that he obtained the *prosbol* before the Sabbatical year. A simple declaration that he had such a writ and lost it is to be accepted as true. That is why not only minor heirs of a deceased creditor, whose interests are always safeguarded by the courts, but all heirs have the legal presumption on their side that their ancestor had secured a *prosbol* for the debt due him, even if such a transaction is nowhere recorded. Under these circumstances, the Sabbatical cancellation of debts might occasionally have affected the uninstructed private citizen extending a charitable loan to a fellow Jew, but had practically no effect upon the professional moneylender who took the necessary precautions. [157]

Other alleviations were extended to the creditor in matters of judicial procedure. The creditor may force the debtor, says Maimuni, to follow him to a court of superior learning in another city, regardless of the old adage *actio sequitur forum rei*. [158] In order not to discourage prospective moneylenders, the witnesses in monetary transactions are not to be subjected to the usual rigorous cross examination, and certain allowances are to be made for deeds the witnesses of which are not available for examination in court. For the same reason the sages have accelerated the proceedings in favor of creditors appearing in court with a deed. If the debtor can be speedily summoned to present his case, this should be done. Otherwise the plaintiff is allowed to take oath and immediately seize any of the debtor's possessions. [159] Moreover, Maimonides accepts the doctrine of his "teachers," against that of some geonim, that a creditor presenting a properly attested deed is obliged to take oath only if the debtor contends that he has paid the loan, whereas other contentions, such as that the deed is forged or based upon a usurious claim, have to be proved by the debtor. To preclude controversies, Maimuni demands that all loans, even to scholars, be given in the presence of witnesses or else on a pawn or other security, and that preferably the transaction be recorded in a deed signed by witnesses. [160]

Maimonides rigidly objects to a Jew's bringing a lawsuit against a fellow Jew before a Gentile court; even if a Jewish court happens to commit the grievous error of sending the litigants to a Gentile court, the sentence of the latter is to be disregarded. But he allows the creditor and other plaintiffs who cannot force their opponents to repair to Jewish judges or where the Jewish court is powerless to carry out its sentence to invoke the help of Gentile authorities. Considering the changed conditions of his age, he tersely informs an inquirer that

he who is indebted to somebody according to Jewish law, may be forced by the creditor to sign a deed to this effect according to Gentile law. This deed may then be deposited with a trustworthy person, and when the debtor ultimately refuses to pay what had been imposed upon him by Jewish law, he may be forced to do so through Gentile courts.

This is in consonance with Maimonides' own view, in opposition to that of his teachers, that loan contracts properly executed before Gentile authorities establish valid claims in Jewish courts, provided there are Jewish witnesses to authenticate the signatures of the Gentile witnesses on the deed and to testify that the Gentile judge in question is not known to be accessible to bribery. [161] Only in case of a really impecunious debtor does Maimuni try to strike a balance between the legitimate interests of the creditor and the requirements of mercy toward the debtor. On the one hand, he states that the creditor, as the result of a geonic departure from ancient law, may demand from the debtor a solemn oath of manifestation that he posseses no concealed property and an equally solemn promise to apply all his future earnings (except for a month's food and a year's clothing for himself, but not for his family) toward the repayment of the debt. On the other hand, he demands that no such oath be administered to a debtor known to be poor and of good character, if this condition is recognized by both judge and public opinion. This liberating oath should be refused a well-known perjurer, who might readily take it in order to get rid of a debt. At the same time, neither the creditor nor the marshal of the court is entitled to infringe upon the privacy of the debtor's home in a search for hidden assets. [162] However, the biblical law demanding retention by the debtor (or constant restitution to him whenever needed) of all objects indispensable for daily use is interpreted to refer only to objects belonging to the debtor personally, not to those used by his wife and children. There are also recognized class differences, inasmuch as a defaulting debtor of the upper classes may claim, for instance, the retention of a regular mattress on his bed, one of the lower income groups only that of a mat. Finally, on grounds of sex morality Maimuni prohibits the seizure of such movables from a widow, since their repeated restitution by the creditor may lead to immoral relationships between them. [163]

These privileges of the plaintiff were, for the most part, limited to claims arising from loan contracts. Few of them were applicable to those other business transactions which, in order to secure income for capital, specifically avoided the term "loan." Nevertheless, one clearly sees that the Maimonidean restatement of talmudic law left sufficient means at the disposal of capitalists for the profitable employment of their funds in other persons' enterprises. The careers of the great Jewish bankers under Islam were little hampered by these prohibitive laws. Nonetheless these laws fulfilled their main function of extending a measure of protection to those needy borrowers who negotiated loans only for purposes of subsistence.

The prohibition of usury affected still less the vast domain of Jewish credit extended to Gentiles. To be sure, similar limitations weakened the Muslim and, to a certain extent, the Christian prohibitions of usury, but to Jews, the numerically smallest group, they opened the relatively largest range of "legitimate" activities. Let us assume, for the sake of illustration, that the population of a given district consisted of 70 percent Muslims, 25 percent Christians, and 5 percent Jews. A Muslim banker could deal more or less freely with only 30 percent of his compatriots, whereas his Christian colleague could extend credit on interest to 75 percent—a Jewish banker to 95 percent—of the population. The few obstacles to such trade, moral rather than strictly legal, could be overcome without much difficulty, as may be seen in Maimuni's attempt to harmonize the various biblical and talmudic regulations. As a son of the highly intolerant age of the Almohades and the Christian Crusaders, he quotes without qualification the Sifre's interpretation of la-nokhri tashshikh of Deuteronomy 23:21. Usually translated "unto a stranger thou mayest lend upon usury," the passage appears here as a positive commandment to extort interest from Gentile borrowers. This interpretation runs counter to the talmudic tradition, to such an extent that Maimuni's juridical predecessors and successors almost unanimously repudiated this view. He repeats, on the other hand, the talmudic injunction to refrain from lending money to Gentiles altogether unless one derives therefrom the only means of subsistence. Characteristically, he interprets in a restrictive rather than amplifying fashion the talmudic motivation that such transactions, because fostering the social relations between Jew and Gentile, may become prejudicial to the lender's orthodoxy. Instead of drawing the general conclusion that all other commercial transactions should be discouraged on the same ground—evidently a practical impossibility for the Jewish minority constantly living among Gentile majorities—he restricts even this regulation by exempting both a Jewish debtor and a scholarly creditor. There is no danger that the Jewish debtor, he says, would come under the social and intellectual influence of his Gentile creditor, because it is in the very nature of such relationships that the debtor avoids the creditor as much as possible. (One fails to see, however, why the Gentile debtor should not likewise avoid contact with his Jewish creditor and, being in an inferior position, fail to exercise any influence whatsoever.) A scholar may extend credit to a Gentile, because, being deeply imbued with the spirit of Judaism, he is immune from such outside heterodox influences. Maimonides does not even use moral suasion, such as demanded by Amram Gaon, to make scholars abstain from such trade. Every Jew, moreover, may freely collect from Gentiles all types of "shades of usury." [164]

Like the other rabbis, Maimonides is, of course, deeply concerned about the possibility of fellow Jews' evading the prohibition of usury by using Gentiles as intermediaries. Evidently nothing could prevent a Gentile borrowing from a Jew from lending that amount to another Jew at whatever rate of interest they might agree on. Maimonides declares that, if this is done with the connivance of the Jewish creditor, it is a full-fledged usurious transaction. He insists that a Jew who borrows money on interest from a Gentile should not transfer his indebtedness to another Jew under the same conditions, because the second debtor would appear to pay him the interest. He should rather repay his loan and let the Gentile creditor lend the amount directly to the new debtor. This regulation was evidently intended to prevent Gentile capitalists from making use of Jewish bankers to employ their funds profitably by lending them to Jewish merchants. Such practices were then fairly prevalent between the nobles and their Jewish agents in western Europe and were actually legalized by the western rabbis, such as Meshullam. The general prohibition against forming partnerships with Gentiles, however, fortified by similar Muslim laws directed against partnerships between Muslims and infidels, at least prevented the formation of banking companies in which the Jewish partner would become the creditor of Gentile borrowers and the Gentile partner would grant loans to Jews. [165]

Viewing the totality of the Maimonidean restatement of the Jewish laws of usury, one easily perceives that these legal precautions but slightly hampered Jewish moneylending to Gentiles, and were far from eliminating Jewish moneylending to Jews. Although the Oriental Jews never became so one-sided in their economic endeavor as did European Jewry in medieval England, France, and Germany, a Hebrew author, writing a century later, could nevertheless with but slight exaggeration contrast Palestinian Jewry, deriving its main livelihood from the cultivation of fields and vineyards, with the Babylonian and South-Italian Jews, "who can rely only upon usury." The prevailing high rates of interest of 30 percent and over per annum made this phase of banking, notwithstanding its economic as well as legal risks, most profitable and attractive in the period of Islam's great economic expansion. Despite its retrogression in the subsequent centuries, moneylending still was, together with the related field of tax farming, the main source of economic and political power for individual Jews on top of the social ladder, and through them greatly influenced the status of all Jewry in Muslim lands. Maimuni must have realized that the laws, as restated by him, served as but a slight check on "productive" forms of credit and that he was reiterating only a pious wish of the ancient sages when he counseled the Jews to grant gratuitous loans to coreligionists, rather than loans on interest to Gentiles. This advice was clearly in line with Maimonides' general ethical postulates, which he addressed to exceptional individuals, and could have little influence upon the economic behavior reasonably to be expected from the masses. It is, for instance, quite on the same plane as his demand that a scholar should be very exact in calculating his own obligations to others, but should be less exact about what others owe him; that in all his commercial dealings he should impose upon himself duties beyond those stated in the Torah and unfailingly keep his word, but be lenient and forbearing with others. "In general, he should be among the persecuted and not among the persecutors, among the offended rather than among the offenders." These ethical injunctions undoubtedly exercised some influence upon innumerable pious individuals who attempted to live up to these lofty expectations, but they could not serve as a foundation for normative compulsory laws. They were still less effective in the realm of hard and fast reality. [166]

SLAVERY

Like his Muslim, and most of his Christian, contemporaries, Maimonides takes the institution of slavery for granted. To the medieval Oriental, as to the ancient mind, "slavery was a fixed and accepted element of life and no moral problem was involved." Living in a world in which slaves supplied a part of agricultural and industrial labor and the bulk of domestic employment, Maimuni regarded slavery as a natural, though "accursed," state, inflicted upon the individual through God's will. He certainly saw no reason to depart from the well-established attitude of the biblical and talmudic legislators. Many of their laws, to be sure, like numerous other regulations embodied in his *Code*, have a purely theoretical import. He devotes about one-half of the entire section on slavery to the position of "Hebrew" slaves. At the same time, he clearly indicates that such slaves disappeared from Jewish life with the discontinuance of the observance of the Jubilee year; i.e., the end of the First Commonwealth. [167] Nevertheless, his restatement of these obsolete talmudic laws throws a characteristic light on his views concerning both Gentile slavery and Jewish free labor, between which Hebrew slavery occupies an intermediary position.

Maimuni does not consider at all the problem of philosophic justification of slavery, such as had been attempted by a few Graeco-Roman and Christian thinkers. For him it is simply a matter of positive legislation, inasmuch as the Bible had enjoined the Jews to exercise permanent dominion over the "Canaanite" slaves, and not to grant them freedom except in the case that serious bodily injuries were inflicted upon them by their masters. Like Plato and Aristotle, he cannot conceal his personal contempt for the slave, "the lowest among men." Discussing the various blemishes which, if discovered by a purchaser after the acquisition of a slave, make the sale null and void, he includes governmental requisition, but not many defects of character. "If a slave is found to be a thief, robber, kidnaper, constant fugitive, glutton, or the like, he cannot be returned to the seller, because all slaves are expected to possess all these bad traits." Nevertheless, Maimonides treats slaves juridically as human beings, rather than as chattels. Only with respect to minor slaves does he repeat a formalistic decision of R. Ashi that they are to be acquired through "drawing," like chattels. Adult slaves, possessing a will of their own, may be acquired in five different ways. [168] We shall presently see what important effects the slaves' independent will, as well as its legal limitations, had upon their economic function for Jewry under Islam.

How does one become a Gentile slave? Maimonides does not answer this question directly, but from various passages one may reconstruct the following possibilities: (1) birth from an unfree mother, regardless of the father (see below); (2) captivity in war, including piracy (these two sources of slavery were acknowledged in almost all slave-owning societies, including Islam); (3) captivity as the result of a royal decree imposing servile status upon the king's own subjects for various sins of commission and omission, and especially for tax defaults (Maimuni restates here the talmudic recognition of a practice which had been fairly prevalent in Sassanian Persia, but which had been wholly abandoned under the rule of Islam); (4) self-sale of the slave; (5) the sale of children by an impoverished father; (6) the sale, by the courts, of an insolvent thief who is unable to pay the prescribed fine; (7) the initiatory ablution of a kidnaped child or a foundling by a Jew, with the intent to use him as a slave. Maimonides seems to have omitted only one ancient source of slave supply: the seizure of an insolvent debtor by his creditor, directly or through the intervention of a court. This institution, recorded in ancient Israel, had come into disrepute in subsequent centuries, and Maimuni specifically repudiates it with respect to the Hebrew slave. His failure to mention it also in connection with Gentile slaves is very likely due to his feeling that the Jews would have to respect in these matters the legislation of those nations from which the slaves might be imported. Under Islam, in any case, all these methods, except the first two, had been suppressed by law. This consideration, indeed, may have influenced his reticence in discussing the origin of Gentile slavery, while he clearly states his views on the sources of Hebrew bondage. In practice the Jewish slaveholders undoubtedly derived their supply less through breeding—the reproductive power of slaves was probably as low under Islam as it was in other slave-owning communities—than through purchase. They bought them, directly or indirectly, from war lords operating along the Empire's frontiers from Turkestan and Ethiopia to France and Germany. The Cairo-Fusṭāṭ of Maimonides was speedily developing into the biggest slave market of the Middle East. [169]

As a matter of law a master is entitled to chastise his slave severely, but he must not kill him or injure him permanently. In the case of murder or manslaughter Jewish law extends to the slave the same protection as to an Israelite; namely, capital punishment for the offender. This is the more remarkable as a lesser punishment is to be inflicted upon a Jewish murderer of a free Gentile. Following the Talmud, Maimuni qualifies the difference between chastisement and murder by stating that if the injuries cause the slave's death within twenty-four hours, the master is guilty of murder, but if death occurs after a day or more the master escapes prosecution. Maimonides adds, however, as his personal opinion, that if the assailant used a knife, a sword, a stone, or merely a fist, with the clear intent to kill, the ensuing death of the slave even after a year is punishable by the master's death. [170] Permanent injury, insofar as it involves the slave's loss of an eye or a tooth (mentioned in the Bible) or any of twenty-four other "visible" members of his body enumerated in the Talmud, leads to his enforced emancipation. The purpose of the law is that he should not "suffer from slavery and mutilation at the same time." Here Maimuni makes the significant exclusion from the talmudic list of injuries of castration and the cutting off of the slave's tongue, both of which are included by Alfasi and other rabbis. One can hardly escape the conclusion that Maimuni is not guided here merely by strictly legalistic considerations such as the supposed invisibility of these injuries, which he himself emphasizes. The trade in eunuchs for the numerous Oriental harems was such an integral part of the flourishing slave trade that Jewish dealers would have been greatly handicapped in competition with their Muslim and Christian rivals if the performance of the requisite operation had entailed the loss of the slave. Maimonides offers further protection to the master or dealer by stating that the slave's liberation may be decreed only by a court of superior learning. One wonders how frequently an impecunious slave, as a rule unfamiliar with Jewish law, had a chance to appeal to such a court. There were also other procedural difficulties (e.g., the slave's inability to testify) which greatly weakened this type of protection extended to slaves. [171]

Legally the master is also entitled to impose the hardest type of labor upon a Gentile slave. Maimuni stresses the point, however, that both piety and wisdom dictate that a Jew be compassionate and charitable to his slave, not impose upon him too severe a yoke nor oppress him, but let him share in his own food, and treat him with dignity and humanity. Indeed Maimuni becomes rhetorical when he tries to emphasize the differences which ought to prevail between Jewish and Gentile slaveowners, because cruelty and haughtiness is to be found among the Gentiles only, while "the descendants of Abraham, i.e., Israel," have pity upon all creatures. Indeed he feels that all the precepts concerning slaves, as restated in his *Code*, "reflect only acts of pity, mercy, and kindness to the poor." [172]

Such consideration applies especially to the Sabbath rest. Although, unlike animals, slaves have their own mind and will, one ought to guard them against work on Sabbath. In a statement quoted in his name, Maimuni also stresses the moral obligation to refrain from disturbing their Sabbath even in matters not strictly prohibited by law. For example, one should not order a slave to fetch an excess of water or awake him from his sleep. Chastising a slave on the Sabbath is not only the foolishness of ignorant persons but also a great sin in the eyes of those who understand the intention of the Torah. It is characteristic of Maimuni that in this insistence upon the slave's Sabbath rest, as in his general injunction to treat slaves kindly, he advances merely ethical reasons. He totally neglects the economic arguments advanced by Bryson and his successors, who saw therein a great stimulus for the increased productivity of the slave's labor. [173]

A Gentile slave is, indeed, expected to observe a certain minimum of Jewish law. In the first place, every male slave should be circumcised as speedily as possible. If an adult slave refuses to be circumcised within twelve months after his acquisition, he must be disposed of to a Gentile master. This extreme solicitude of the rabbis was due less to outright conversionist motives than to the wish to increase the slave's attachment to the family of the master, and, in some cases, to prevent his turning informer to hostile outsiders. Maimuni allows, however, the keeping of an uncircumcised slave if this was made a condition by the previous Gentile owner. But the slave must in any case observe the seven Noahidic commandments, thus occupying in general the biblical position of a "resident alien." Refusal by the slave is punishable by immediate execution. Maimuni realizes, however, that this regulation was of little practical significance in his time, and that there were in Egypt and elsewhere numerous slaves belonging to Jews who adhered to their former pagan religion. The master could, in fact, find an easy subterfuge in the Muslim prohibition against converting any Muslim or "protected subject" to one of the non-Muslim religions. This prohibition could be interpreted as tantamount to a general condition, in advance of the acquisition, that the slave should not be converted to the master's creed. [174]

Once circumcised, a slave has in many ways the position of a free Jew, and the Jewish community is obliged to redeem him from captivity. An uncircumcised slave, however, does not enjoy this privilege, nor is he fully protected against murder or permanent injury. Even a circumcised slave, on the other hand, is not subject to all the obligations of a full-fledged Jew. Like a Jewish woman, he is exempted from many positive commandments, such as the duty to pray, to wear phylacteries, and to study the Torah. As a matter of fact, he must not be permitted to study the Torah, even if he is desirous to do so. [175]

On account of this partial conversion of the slave to Judaism, the ancient sages had adopted a series of safeguards of a religious as well as Palestinocentric nature, which Maimonides does not hesitate to restate in a fashion which makes them appear binding for his own day. One must not sell a slave included in the Jewish fold to a Gentile or a Jewish sectarian. In the case of contravention, the slave immediately becomes free. [176] The same sanction applies to the sale of a slave from Palestine to a Jew residing in a foreign locality, even to neighboring Akko. The Jewish purchaser abroad is to be forced by the courts to emancipate the slave. Furthermore,

if a slave declares his intention to emigrate to Palestine, we force the master to emigrate with him, or to sell him to another master who is willing to take him to Palestine. If a Palestinian master wishes to go abroad, he can take along his slave only with the latter's consent. This law is to be enforced at any time, even today when the country is in Gentile hands.

One can hardly imagine that such a law was at all operative in a period when an insignificant minority of the Jews resided in the country of their forefathers. Maimuni's Egyptian coreligionists would have been wholly at the mercy of their slaves' whimsical desires to settle in Palestine had it not been for the prevailing difficulty in obtaining court action in favor of slaves and the undoubtedly widespread practice of refraining from circumcising at least those slaves who were intended for resale to uncircumcised masters. [177]

Of great interest is the position of the slave in family matters. Although a member of the Jewish community, the circumcised slave is by no means a member of the Jewish *familia*. For Maimuni a slave is not fully human in matters of sex. While deciding in the affirmative the controversial point as to whether homosexuality and sodomy are capital crimes in the case of slaves, he nevertheless states peremptorily that legal matrimony may be established only between Jews or between Gentiles, not between slaves or between slaves and Jews. The prohibition of incest, consequently, does not apply to them and "as long as he is a slave he may marry his own mother." A master may freely give a female slave to his own or to another man's male slave; in fact, he may without scruple give her simultaneously to two slaves, "because they are like cattle." Children of slaves follow the status of the mother. If the mother is a full-fledged Jewess, the slave's paternity has no effect upon the civil standing of the child. But if the mother is a slave, the child likewise becomes a slave. In contrast to other illegitimate children, who in Jewish law enjoy full equality in regard to inheritance from their father, the child of a female slave and a free Israelite has no rights of inheritance at all. Moreover, such a child does not free the wife of its father (or its own mother after her liberation and lawful marriage) from the obligation of the levirate marriage, because the child is regarded as legally nonexistent. [178]

Through these harsh regulations, Maimuni, in some respects going beyond the talmudic law, tries to discourage sex relationships between the Jews and their Gentile slaves. This was particularly important in the Muslim countries, where slaves were generally included in the harems of the most prominent dignitaries of the state and the mosque, and where the majority of the caliphs themselves were descendants of female captives. Just as under Sassanian Persia Jews consistently fought for the preservation of their family purity by suppressing incestuous relations, which were widespread among their Persian neighbors, so also under Islam they placed cohabitation with female slaves under stringent sanctions. Public opinion often effectively interfered where the slightest suspicion appeared justified; an interesting case of this kind is recorded in a Maimonidean responsum. Maimuni must admit that the convicted lawbreaker cannot be sentenced to flagellation, according to biblical law. Nevertheless, he tries to impress the severity of the transgression upon the mind of the reader by pointing out that one thus despoils one's own offspring by making them slaves and infidels. Even with respect to the intermediary type of slave, the *shifḥah*

ḥarufah, whom he defines as "turning from the state of slavery to
the state of marriage," sexual intercourse is to be punished by
administering flagellation to the slave and forcing the Jewish male
to offer a sacrifice. This is, he points out in his *Guide,* one of the few
transgressions in which an inadvertent act is as severely punished as
one performed with premeditation, because of the great frequency
of the temptation. He well epitomizes his views in another connection in the following epigram: "slaves do not exist for sexual purposes, but for work." [179]

Thus having legally eliminated concubinage, one of the major
factors of almost all slaveowning societies, from Jewish slaveholding
—of course, not from the Jewish slave trade supplying concubines to
non-Jews—Maimuni centers his attention upon other, more strictly
economic functions of slaves. Unfortunately, the factual material in
his writings and in those of his predecessors under Islam is too
scarce to allow for a satisfactory explanation of the role of the slave
economy in the Jewish economic structure. Jewish slaveholders
could employ their slaves in agriculture and industry. But it seems
that, perhaps even more than their Muslim contemporaries, they
found it unprofitable to make extensive use of slave labor in these
spheres. Free labor was relatively cheap, the cost of slaves rather
high. Combined with the widespread scarcity of capital, it made the
investment of 200 dirhems and over for each slave even less remunerative to Jews, who could easily lend the equivalent amount to
their Gentile compatriots at a high rate of interest. The security of
investment in slaves suffered from widespread disease and high mortality, especially in the slave population. The responsibility for the
maintenance of a slave in his old age; in his years of illness; and, in
particular, during the seasonal inactivity in agriculture or in the
frequent industrial crises, made his productive employment profitable only in those exceptional periods when the wages of the free
laborers were considerably above sheer maintenance levels. The
absence of latifundia and large-scale industries in the Muslim world
generally prevented the rise of slave labor *en masse.*

It seems that the Gentile slaves belonging to Jews were somewhat
more extensively employed in commerce. The rabbinic principle
that "the slave is like the master's hand" (like the simile of the
Arabian economists which compared commercially employed slaves
to "legs" upon which rests the burden of the enterprise) made such
an unfree employee a most useful instrument in the transaction of

business. Any arrangements made by the slave in the name of his master were binding upon the other party, but could be repudiated by the master by a simple declaration to this effect. Unlike Roman and Muslim law, the rabbinic regulations did not allow a Gentile slave to manage an independent enterprise in his own behalf. Maimonides' intimation of the possibility of establishing a sort of *peculium* for the Hebrew slave merely puts into bolder relief his uncompromising insistence upon the talmudic principle that "all that the [Gentile] slave acquires is acquired for the master." Even gifts do not belong to the slave, unless the donor specifically stipulates that they shall not belong to the master. The slave's usefulness was further enhanced by the master's limited liability for damages caused by his slave to third persons. In most cases the slave alone was held responsible, even though the amount of the damage could not be collected from him until after he had obtained his freedom and amassed earnings of his own. On the other hand, damages inflicted upon the slave were immediately collectible for the benefit of his master. [180]

In general, however, slaves were principally used in domestic employ in Jewish, as well as in Muslim, houses. C. H. Becker is essentially right in stating that, under Islam, slavery as a whole was principally "a morally elevated solution of the problem of domestic help." In the case of Jews, we are informed by an earlier responsum that they favored the employment of Gentile slaves, because it kept the Jewish women away from the wells and other places where morally objectionable persons used to congregate. It was this prevalent domestic employment which made the partial conversion of the slaves to Judaism extremely desirable, and also served to arouse sexual appetites among the masters—solitary mistresses were not supposed to acquire any male slaves at all—appetites which had to be combated by the numerous legal and moral injunctions restated by Maimonides. [181]

It is also in the inheritance of such domestic slaves by more than one heir, rather than in their belonging to a commercial or industrial company, that we may see the origin of some of those partnerships in the ownership of slaves which gave rise to numerous complicated legal problems. This was particularly the case when one of the partners decided to liberate a slave, while the other partner or partners refused to do so. The result was a hybrid legal creature: a half-, three-quarters-, or five-eighths-free slave, and the like. The Mishnah had already considered the position of these complex beings and demanded that their masters be forced to liberate that part of them which was still enslaved. Perhaps under the influence of the extensive Muslim discussions on the *muba'ad,* Maimonides and his contemporaries debate rather frequently the legal consequences of such partial slavery in various walks of life. When one such complicated case was brought to Maimuni's attention, he answered in a strictly legalistic vein. [182]

The juridical features of slaveholding had many economic effects. Originally treated in the Bible as a sort of immovable property, the slaves were placed on a par with movables with respect to the new legal transactions introduced in the talmudic age. The result was that in Maimuni's treatment they have traits of both types. While basically treated as movable property, they are frequently exempted from the operation of the laws affecting this by being "compared" with land. That is why the theft of a slave is not subject to the usual fine of the double amount; robbery of a slave is not punished by the excess fine of one-fifth; a partial denial of a claim on a defendant's slaves need not be affirmed by a biblical oath. In principle, the regulations concerning the responsibility of a depository or guardian for property intrusted to him should not be applied to slaves given in trust. Nevertheless, Maimuni expresses his personal opinion, supported by that of his teachers, that the guardians should at least be responsible for overt negligence. More strictly adhering to the Bible and the Talmud, however, he declares that one who kills a slave must idemnify the master by paying him the lump sum of 30 *sela's,* regardless of the value of the slave. Since he had estimated an ancient *sela'* as the equivalent of 6⅓ dirhems, the total indemnity amounted to 190 dirhems. This sum was below the usual price of 200 dirhems and over for an unskilled slave, and was wholly incommensurate with the cost of a skilled worker or a beautiful woman, which sometimes went into thousands of gold denars.[183] Combined with the perennial problem of fugitive slaves, this weakening of the protective laws for the owner must have made slaveholding for purposes of commercial production even more precarious. Only in domestic employ, where the master's security was considerably enhanced by greater facility of surveillance, and where for obvious reasons the slave's permanence and his psychological attachment to the family added strong, noneconomic imponderables, did slave tenure remain a widespread feature of Jewish life. The wealthy Jewish bankers, landowners, and state officials, in particular, required the conspicuous display of a large retinue of slaves to impress their Gentile and Jewish compatriots with their superior status and power.

Still less significant was the economic role of the freedmen. Following the Talmud, Maimonides rather frequently refers to the legal status of the freedman and the freedwoman. On the whole, their position resembled that of proselytes. In almost all respects treated as full-fledged Jews, they were subject to certain limitations with respect to high offices and the *connubium* with priests. Other modifications of the law arose from their lack of legal family connections antedating their emancipation. Like proselytes, for example, they were not supposed to recite "the confession of the tithe," because it included a passage concerning the soil which God had "given us." But they were allowed by Maimuni to refer to the God of "our fathers" in their prayers over the "first fruits." If they did not leave offspring conceived after their manumission, their inheritance became *hefker*. Unlike Roman and Muslim law, Jewish law did not retain a permanent relationship between master and freedman in the form of patronage. The freedman was altogether a free citizen, largely equal in rights to all others. Economically, however, he had a struggle for existence. The humanitarian provisions of Deuteronomy 15:14, which had tried to offer the freedman a minimum of security by obligating the master to provide him with certain necessaries for the new start in life, referred only to the Hebrew slave. The manumitted Gentile slave was frequently worse off than while in slavery, especially if he was released at a period of reduced capacity for work. [184]

All these discussions seem to have had little relation to reality, however. Unlike the Muslim jurists, the rabbis viewed with disfavor the emancipation of Gentile slaves. Perhaps influenced by considerations of racial purity, they did not wish to see large-scale absorption of Gentiles into the Jewish community via slavery and emancipation. At any rate, Maimuni reechoes the talmudic statement that the Levitical lawgiver's injunction "They shall be your bondmen for ever" (Lev. 25:46) is to be regarded as a positive commandment, and that any uncalled-for manumission of slaves constitutes a violation thereof. To be sure, Maimuni countenanced the liberation of a female slave, with a view to subsequent marriage, as preferable to illicit relations. Neither was the liberation of slaves, after their master's death, as a reward for faithful lifelong service altogether discouraged. Like his predecessors, Maimuni insists that a testator's will to this effect be liberally interpreted in favor of the slaves. But, on the whole, his and the other rabbis' intrinsic opposition to the emancipation of slaves must have greatly diminished the number of freedmen in the Jewish community. That is probably why our sources have so few references to freedmen. They seem never to have attained a position or constituted a socioeconomic problem in medieval Jewry at all comparable with those of their brethren under Islam. [185]

There was one aspect of Hebrew slavery which was significant in the medieval period also: the redemption of captives. The Maimonidean statement that a Jew may become master over his fellow Jew if a royal decree allows the putting in bondage of an insolvent or recalcitrant taxpayer was of no practical significance. Apart from Maimonides' own qualification that such an appropriated Jew should be treated as a slave only when he misbehaves, there existed, to my knowledge, no such royal decree in any Muslim country. However, Jewish captives taken in the frequent wars or seized by Mediterranean pirates abounded, and here were applied those laws concerning the redemption of captives which Maimonides relates to Hebrew slavery. In the case of a Jew's self-sale to a Gentile, the nearest relatives were obliged to ransom him. If they were unable to do so, more distant relations, and finally all Jews, were obliged to redeem him. Those who paid the ransom were immediately to set him free. In another connection, Maimuni states that a Jew who sells himself or his children into bondage or is seized by a Gentile creditor for debts should be ransomed twice and no more. A circumcised Gentile slave is likewise to be redeemed, but he ranks below the ten categories of free Jews, who enjoy successive priority if the available funds prove insufficient for the redemption of all. Although, in a similar division into ten categories of Jews enumerated in the Mishnah in regard to *connubium* with full-fledged Jews, the freedman is placed sixth, he is but tenth in rank in the case of redemption. The free proselyte is ninth, because he never lived in the "accursed" state of slavery. In any case, the redemption of captives has precedence over any other form of charity, and "there is no greater commandment" than this. However, one must not pay a higher ransom for the captive than his market price, in order not to whet the appetite of pirates; nor should one help him to escape, because this would lead to increased vigilance over, and harsher treatment of, remaining captives. Numerous extant, more or less contemporary documents, especially from Maimuni's own community of Fusṭaṭ, unmistakably reveal that Jewry as a whole took these injunctions very seriously and time and again strained all its resources in order to redeem from captivity Byzantine and other coreligionists. [186]

FREE LABOR

Free labor, in contrast to slavery, appears to Maimuni to be almost exclusively Jewish. We have practically no reference to Gentile laborers for Jews. Even domestic service, which in medieval Christendom was predominantly in the hands of non-Jewish servants, seems under Islam, as in the talmudic era, to have been performed by Jews. This distinction is vital in the consideration of all Maimonidean views on the subject, because free labor is thus distinguished from unfree labor, not only as an economic class but also as an ethnic and religious group. Maimuni, indeed, places the employment of fellow Jews in domestic service among the highest forms of charity:

The sages have enjoined us to keep as one's domestics poor Jews and orphans rather than slaves; it is better to employ the former so that the descendants of Abraham, Isaac, and Jacob should derive the benefit of one's fortune, and not the descendants of Ham. He who increases the number of his slaves from day to day increases sin and iniquity in the world, whereas the man who employs poor Jews in his household increases merits and religious acts. [187]

Learning a trade and teaching it to one's children is declared by Maimonides to be one of the major obligations of every Jew. Commenting on the famous passage in the *Sayings of the Fathers:* "Love work and hate mastery, and make not thyself known to the government," he states that these three virtues have been juxtaposed here because they are vital for the welfare of religion and the world. "A man without work gets into difficulties and [ultimately] robs and cheats." In a style reminiscent of modern Jewish apologias, he emphasizes the fact that there were woodcutters and water carriers among the greatest sages of Israel, although his intention is to demonstrate that poverty and hard work should in no way diminish one's devotion to learning. Vocational education is placed on a par with that in the Torah and in wisdom. If a father exercising his "legitimate" right of chastisement accidentally kills an obstreperous son who refuses to be educated along any one of these three lines, he need not suffer exile to one of the asylum cities, the usual punishment for manslaughter. The obligation to work is coupled in rabbinic theory with a sort of moral, if not legal, right to work, emanating from the obligation of every Jew, as well as of the community at large, to supply employment to needy coreligionists. [188]

As a medieval man, Maimuni believes in the objective price of labor. Discussing the legal compensation for working time lost on account of physical injury, or the reward due to the finder for the time spent in returning a lost object to its owner, he states that payment is to be made in the former case to the extent of the *lucrum cessans,* in the latter case only in the amount which is necessary to induce this particular individual to abstain from his regular work for that period of time. While undoubtedly allowing for differences in local wages, he assumes that such compensation may be estimated in each locality with reference to the work in question and need not be computed on the basis of more individualistic considerations. He illustrates the operation of this principle by the example of a money-changer and a smith: their general earning capacity may be the same, but abstention from work is worth more to the smith. [189]

Nonetheless, he favors complete contractual freedom. Disregarding here, as often elsewhere, the pressure of economic inequality, he regards the parties to a contract as absolutely free and equal. That is why, in his opinion, one may employ a free Israelite to perform services which one must not impose upon a Hebrew slave. The ancient protective laws for the latter do not apply to the hired worker, "because he is doing the work of his own free will and on his own decision." With respect to the amount of wages, in particular, there are no legal restrictions upon either employer or employee. Either of them may also freely stipulate the conditions under which the contract should be operative, because all conditions are valid in labor contracts, as in sales contracts. Basically, "hiring is but a sale for a definite period." On the other hand, though assuming that there exists an objective price of labor, Maimuni exempts wage contracts from the operation of the laws governing the "just price." In regard to wages, free workers are placed in the same position as slaves, to whom, for reasons discussed above, the ancient laws of "misrepresentation" were never applied. That is why the underpay-

ment of wages by more than 16.66 percent of the market price does
not nullify a contract, whereas a similar underpayment (or overcharge) for the leasing of animals or vessels would immediately
have that effect. Bound by a long chain of historical evolution,
Maimonides could not radically alter these provisions. His own attitude, nevertheless, becomes apparent when he tries, as a matter of
personal opinion, to extend the protection of these laws at least to
artisans contracting with customers for a specific job. Artisan associations, moreover, are given the right to regulate their trade in
accordance with custom and under the supervision of the community as a whole. In another connection he expresses his moral rather
than legal conviction that workers "ought to receive their pay in
accordance with their work." [190] Two other significant restrictions of
the rights of employers, upon which all rabbis had agreed since the
days of the Mishnah, operated in favor of workers rather than
middle-class artisans. They referred to the hours of labor and the
entrepreneur's obligation to feed his employees in part or in full.
In both of these matters local custom was declared to be supreme,
except where there existed express stipulations in the contract. Even
if the employer agreed to pay wages higher than those customarily
paid to workers in that particular occupation, he could not exact
overtime work if the workers were unwilling. Neither could he
refuse them the type of food customarily expected from him, unless
he made his intention perfectly clear before the conclusion of the
contract.

Maimonides also describes at great length the mutual obligations
of employer and employee in the execution of such "freely" arranged
contracts. The employer's most important obligation, emphasized as
early as the biblical legislator, consists in the prompt payment of
wages. In this respect, says Maimuni, there is but slight difference
between a Jewish and a Gentile laborer. The withholding of due
wages for a single night constitutes a violation of one positive and
one negative commandment in the case of a Jewish laborer, and that
of one positive commandment in the case of a Gentile worker. In no
case is this transgression punishable by flagellation, however, because
it is subject to financial restitution. Permanent refusal to pay wages
constitutes a violation of four negative commandments and one positive commandment and is exaggeratedly likened to cold-blooded
murder. [191] To be sure, the employer may mitigate the harshness of
the law by hiring the worker for longer periods, such as a week, a

month, a year, or even seven years, since the wages fall due at the end of the contractual period, unless different dates are arranged in advance. Unfortunately, Maimuni's repetition of these talmudic laws gives us no indication of the contemporary practice, which probably ranged from daily to annual contracts. According to certain Muslim schools as well as some later rabbis, a triennial contract was the maximum allowed by law. An even more effective means of evasion is the hiring of workers through an agent, or manager. If the latter makes it clear to the worker that the employer is to pay the wages, he is not responsible for the delay, whereas the employer is not responsible because he himself did not do the hiring. [192]

For the protection of the worker, certain general rules are suspended with respect to both breach of contract and proof of the worker's claims. While the complicated regulations concerning withdrawal from a contract sometimes favor the employer, especially if unforeseen circumstances make the work unnecessary before it is started, it is the worker alone who may give up the work, without giving any reason, in the middle of the contractual period. The worker may even demand the proportionate payment of wages for the time he has worked or, if he is a contractor, the payment of the stipulated sum, proportionately reduced by the amount of work still needed for the completion of the job. Only in emergencies, such as threatened deterioration of material, or provisions for burials and weddings, may the employer engage another worker at higher wages and deduct them from the amount due to the first laborer, who has quit his work without legitimate excuse. The reason for this preferential treatment of the worker is offered through the ancient homily "because the sons of Israel are My slaves and not slaves of slaves." The usual rules of evidence, whereby the plaintiff must fully prove his claim, while the defendant need merely take the rabbinic type of oath that he had made the required payment, are reversed in the case of litigations over wages. A laborer hired in the presence of witnesses and claiming his wages at the proper time may obtain his due by swearing that he never received payment. The reason here given is that the employer is too busy with his numerous workers and may more easily make a mistake than the laborer, whose mind is set upon his earnings. [193]

The employer need not furnish food to the laborer, except when local custom prescribes it, but he must allow him, while working on the field, to eat from its produce. The worker ought not to be treated worse than one's ox or donkey, whose muzzling is strictly prohibited by the Deuteronomic lawgiver. To be sure, the original humanitarian intention of Deuteronomy 23:25–26 was to prevent starvation by enabling any passer-by to help himself from the agricultural produce. In the more capitalistic age of the Talmud or Islam, such infringement upon private ownership appeared untenable. That is why the law was first limited to apply only to workers employed in the cultivation of that particular parcel of land. It was then hedged by so many restrictions as to become practically meaningless. Restating talmudic law, Maimuni excludes orchards and most truck gardens, limiting this privilege of the worker to the consumption of grapes and grain. The latter could hardly be eaten without being baked into bread at home, but the laborer was forbidden to remove anything from the spot. Neither was he entitled to share it with his family, unless his wife or children happened to work together with him in the field. The employer was free, moreover, to curtail the laborer's right through contractual agreement. The law thus had a moral, rather than a practical, effect. Similarly, the waiter on table, says Maimuni, although not participating directly in the meal, should as a matter of humanity, be given a taste of every dish. That he considers it, however, a favor rather than a right, is clearly illustrated by the example of the benediction over wine which the waiter is to repeat before drinking each cup, since "his drink is dependent on their [the masters'] will and not on his." [194]

On the other hand, the laborer should be extremely careful in fulfilling his obligations toward the master. "He who interrupts his work in order to eat, or eats before the completion of his work, breaks a negative commandment." He is to work with all his strength, emulating the example of Jacob, who was ultimately rewarded with earthly fortune. He must neither starve himself by giving most of his food to his family nor do extra work at night and thus diminish the return of his labor during the day. "Just as the employer is enjoined not to rob the employee of his wages nor to delay their payment, so the poor [worker] is enjoined not to despoil the employer of the work due him, not to waste a moment here and a moment there and dishonestly spend the whole day, but to check his working time carefully." Indeed, the rabbis exempted the laborer from all benedictions before, and from some benedictions after, the consumption of food, so as not to interfere with the full utilization of his working time. [195]

Employment in certain activities does not in itself exempt the workingman from the general rules affecting his position as a citizen. Lay workers employed in the sanctuary, for example, are not entitled to consume any of the sacred food, although provisions for food may be included in their contract. In such cases the Temple administration is to pay them in cash the equivalent of their food. In building the Temple with the help of lay laborers, one ought not to use lumber or stones belonging to sacred property (hekdesh) nor devote the building in advance to sacred uses. In either case the workmen may find themselves guilty of the serious crime of sacrilege by making the slightest profane use of sacred objects, such as enjoying the shade of the structure on a hot day or leaning on a stone or a beam during their work. To safeguard the workers against unconscious sacrilege due to mistaken measurements, one ought to draw up a contract stipulating payment for each ell of twenty fingers, but actually to pay per ell of twenty-four fingers. The ensuing loss to the worker of 20 percent of his wages is infinitely less important than the possibility of unwittingly committing a grievous sin. Should a priest offer to his laborers (or guests) a meal of the heave-offering belonging to him, they are obliged, like other laymen mistakenly consuming sacred food, to pay a fine amounting to five-fourths of the value of the offering, but may demand compensation to the full value of their meal in ordinary food. Forestalling the objection that such a penalty would operate to the disadvantage of the innocent laborer, Maimuni argues from the economic standpoint, that nonconsecrated food would normally exceed in monetary value the heave-offering, the consumption of which is limited to a minority of citizens and hence creates but slight demand. [196]

These regulations referring to the sanctuary and priestly dues were of purely theoretical importance in Maimonides' day, and are cited here only because of the characteristic light they shed upon the Maimonidean views on the status of labor within the ceremonial system. Of more contemporary interest is, for example, Maimuni's acceptance of the talmudic assumption that many craftsmen and workingmen are frequently away from their families for a long time. Discussing their marital duties, he repeats the talmudic regulation that while men of leisure are expected to cohabit with their wives every day, artisans, such as tailors, weavers, and masons, are supposed to do so twice a week if their place of work is in the same town, and once a week if they work in a different locality. Donkey drivers are to comply with that duty once a week, camel drivers once a month, and sailors only once in six months. Scholars are advised, for the purpose of erotic self-control and for the conservation of their strength, rather than for reasons of economic stress, to refrain from exercising their marital rights more than once a week. That is why a woman may object if her husband wishes to change his calling to the disadvantage of his family ties or to undertake extended commercial journeys to distant localities. She must not object, however, if her scholarly husband finds it necessary for the pursuit of his studies to absent himself for a period of two or three years. Neither may she prevent her "rentier" husband from pursuing a scholarly career. [197]

Maimonides discusses various classes of labor, some of which offer peculiar legal problems. He refers, for example, to shepherds, supervising an entire herd, who employ assistants with various specific assignments. In such cases, Maimuni states, the responsibility for damages inflicted to a neighbor's property rests with the assistant in charge of the guilty animal, rather than with the general manager of the herd. The talmudic terms *sokher, hokher,* and *mekabbel* are illustrated by various forms of farm tenancy, insofar as the first two represent tenants who pay to the owner stipulated amounts in money or in kind, while the third term refers to sharecroppers. Sometimes applying the term *mekabbel* as a more generic denomination for all farm tenants, Maimuni goes to great length in expounding the talmudic laws governing their relationships with the landowners and their responsibilities toward outsiders. It is difficult to say to what extent these regulations reflected the economic realities in Maimonides' time. The material in his *Responsa* and in those of his predecessors is too meager to allow definite historical conclusions. In state-capitalistic Egypt, in particular, farm tenancy was largely a matter of state regulation. There was an increasing accumulation of crown lands on which the farmers served as "emphyteutic" tenants, paying a combination of rent and tax. There was more opportunity for the Jews to engage in large-scale tax farming and in collecting agricultural revenue in kind for the state than in leasing their own lands to Jewish or non-Jewish tenants. [198]

Some forms of labor connected with the performance of a civic duty constituted another sociological problem. Theoretically of a gratuitous nature, these civic labors often required all or most of the time of their devotees and before long became remunerative full-time occupations. Such was the case, especially, with teachers. Maimuni repeats the talmudic regulation that only the Written Law may be taught for a remuneration, in those places where payment is customary, but that instruction in the Oral Law should always be given without pay. This difference, which had probably originated from the need of paying for the services of the numerous elementary teachers after the spread of popular education in Jewish antiquity, was rationalized as a distinction between teachers of Scripture—who receive their pay only for supervising the children and keeping them out of mischief, and for the incidental instruction in accents and vocalization—and the intellectual élite giving academic instruction. Maimuni severely attacks those "great men whom greed had blinded and who denied the truth, permitting themselves to charge a fee for judging and teaching under false excuses." He nevertheless emphasizes the obligation of every father to pay for the elementary instruction of his son. In one of his *Responsa* we find a curious personal animus, revealing undisguised hostility to the entire teaching profession in the elementary schools of his day. Replying to an inquirer, he denies the right of elementary teachers to obtain a reward for appearing at court as witnesses, since "they waste so much time every day with futile matters." In contrast, the scribes of the court are entitled to charge for the time lost by appearing in court or rendering services such as writing deeds and the like. Maimuni argues that their reward is not for offering testimony, but for their notarial work. [199]

Reviewing the entire structure of rabbinic labor legislation as summarized by Maimonides, one can hardly escape the feeling that much more attention was paid to the problems arising from farm tenancy and contracting than to employee labor in the stricter sense. Undoubtedly, in the talmudic period the classes of farm tenants, artisans, and men engaged in some form of transportation numerically exceeded those of free wage earners. Subsequently, the first of these groups must have greatly declined, while the number of Jewish craftsmen of all kind, as well as of donkey and camel drivers, shipowners, and so forth doubtless increased steadily during the first centuries of Islam's marvelous expansion. There is every reason for assuming that the number of free Jewish employees in all these occupations, as well as in the manifold commercial undertakings, was likewise on the increase. Nevertheless, the medieval rabbis seem reticent in expanding the few talmudic regulations governing their economic status. Besides repeating the old laws, with minor adaptations to the new situation, the jurists are, on the whole, satisfied with general moral injunctions emphasizing justice as the paramount principle in the relationships between employer and employee. However, by removing these relationships from the realm of communal price fixing and the operation of the principle of the "just price," the road was opened to the largely uncontrolled fluctuations in supply and demand, with all the concomitant evils for the laboring masses. There was, of course, a major antidote: the force of custom. The prevention of glaring abuses by the force of unwritten laws may perhaps explain, in part, the extreme paucity of references to controversies over labor contracts in the Maimonidean or the geonic responsa. This paucity may also have been due, however, to reluctance on the part of laborers to go to court and air their grievances before the official judges. The rabbinic insistence upon the parties' personal appearance before the judges, although greatly enhancing the efficiency of Jewish courts, doubtless worked to the disadvantage of the employees. Their generally lower standard of education and slighter familiarity with the intricacies of Jewish law, coupled with their inability to go to court without losing some of their precious working time, must have encouraged more than one worker to forego his rights, rather than enter such an uneven contest. There may also be more than a grain of truth in the reiterated accusations, voiced by Sahl ibn Masliah and the other Karaites, that the judges, partly dependent upon the good will of the communal leaders, were not always above reproach in their dealings with poor plaintiffs against rich defendants. Did not Sherira Gaon himself attack those unscrupulous students of Jewish law who, literally applying the irate talmudic utterances concerning the 'am ha-ares, felt entitled to treat lightly the property rights of the uneducated masses? [200]

A definite answer to all these complicated problems must await the publication of many more sources, still hidden in the manuscript collections of the world's great libraries. It seems, nevertheless, that in Maimonides' day the inner Jewish class conflict was not so sharp as to require the direct attention of the Jewish leaders. Besides being overshadowed by the compulsory solidarity imposed upon a struggling religious minority, sensitive to all changes in Muslim society and exposed to the whims of its rulers, this conflict seems to have been greatly mitigated by the prevailing scarcity of labor, at least in periods of expansion. The rising prices paid for unskilled and skilled slaves, in the face of the prevalent shortage of capital and the high rates of interest, justifies the conclusion that the wages paid to free laborers must likewise have been comparatively high and the conditions under which the work was to be performed more or less tolerable. Maimonides, in restating the minimum protective laws concerning the immediate payment of wages, the relaxation of the strict rules of evidence, and so forth, and by generally invoking the sanctions of religion upon those who wronged the poor, undoubtedly felt entitled to leave the details to the deep-rooted respect for the customary and to the individual discretion of judges and elders in the Jewish community.

CONCLUSION

The present analysis of Maimonides' economic views lays no claim to being exhaustive. Entire branches of economic life, such as public finance and social work, which occupy a conspicuous place in Maimuni's legal-economic teachings, could not be dealt with here at all. Neither has the economic position of women and children in and outside the family been treated, although for Maimuni's contemporaries of the school of "Bryson" the status of women and children constituted, next to money and slavery, the chief topic of interest in the science of domestic economy. [201] It seems, nevertheless, that the present survey of the rabbinic doctrines concerning private ownership and just price, money and banking, slavery and free labor may give a fairly comprehensive idea of medieval Jewry's basic attitudes to economic endeavor. These attitudes, as reflected in the mind of the greatest medieval Jewish jurist and philosopher, were clearly the result of endless compromises between a powerful tradition, changing economic realities, and, to a certain extent, the exigencies of non-Jewish society and legislation.

One aspect of these compromises stands out boldly: the gap between certain phases of the accepted economic theory and those of the corresponding practice. In theory one might postulate comprehensive economic regulation by communal authorities, with price fixing for all commodities as its major objective; in practice one had to limit even the juridical demand to the field of necessaries and to

recognize the existing reality that the Jewish community under
Islam exercised no control whatsoever over the prevailing price
structure. In theory one might insist that, even in the total absence
of authoritatively fixed prices, producers as well a traders be satisfied
with the "legitimate" profit of one-sixth (in certain branches of
commerce, such as money-changing, some rabbis insisted upon a
maximum profit of less than one-sixth); in practice one had to allow
for the largely uncontrolled operation of the laws of supply and
demand, characteristic of the semicapitalistic economy of the period.
While the traditional view of the essence and function of money, as
accepted and amplified by Maimuni and his confreres, was already
a mixture of the nominalist and metallistic theories, various aspects
of the growing money trade called for increasing modifications of
legal theory and practice, in order to facilitate the flow of money
through the channels of bank deposits, transfers, and the extension
of credit. The undiminished theoretical resistance to "usurious"
credit transactions among Jews was, of course, no obstacle to the
development of extensive Jewish banking with a non-Jewish clientele.
Even moneylending to Jews on interest, however, was made possible
through various legal subterfuges, which, although largely ignored
in legal theory, effectively enabled numerous bankers and petty
moneylenders to evade the prohibition without serious inconvenience. Maimuni and his fellow rabbis might still deal with the
problem of slavery from the standpoint of unadulterated talmudic
law, but they put up no determined resistance to the increasing
transformation of certain segments of Jewry from slaveowning to
slave-trading communities. The talmudic legislation, which had well
met the needs of the predominantly rural Jewish mass settlements in
ancient Palestine and Babylonia, utilizing to some (though relatively
minor) extent the productive power of slave labor, evidently became
obsolescent in many details, as well as in its fundamental approach,
under the new social conditions of the Caliphate. But since, as in its
even more obsolete parts dealing with Hebrew slaves, it offered but
few practical hindrances to the growing employment of Gentile
slaves in the domestic service of the increasingly urbanized Jewries
under Islam, and to the commerce in slaves in which some Jews,
especially in the Western countries, began to participate even beyond their numerical strength in population, [202] it could be restated
by rabbis such as Maimonides without conspicuously clashing with
the existing reality. The talmudic provisions for free labor, on the

other hand, could be taken over and adjusted, with but few modifications, to the productive system under early Islam.

These modifications of a long-regnant theory and law, however camouflaged behind the veil of reinterpretation, rarely necessitated direct abrogation of the accepted talmudic norms. Such was the case, for example, in the new methods governing the issuance of powers of attorney and the 'iska partnerships. For the most part, adjustments were easily made by leaving open sufficient outlets into which the new economic stream could be diverted without undermining the existing structure. Moreover, the adjustment of law to life proceeded not only along the customary lines of scholarly and judicial interpretation but, curiously, sometimes also by a most literal adherence to the old regulations in the face of changing reality. Medieval rabbis merely had to restate, for example, the ancient talmudic exemption of sales affecting land, slaves, or deeds from the operation of the laws of "misrepresentation" and just price. By ignoring the vital difference between its original import and its significance for the contemporary world, they greatly facilitated untrammeled contractual freedom in three major domains of economic life. Originally land was not considered an ordinary commodity, but rather family property which was disposed of only in emergencies. Slaves, whether engaged in agricultural production or in domestic employ, were likewise in the permanent possession of their masters and were sold by them only under exceptional circumstances. To hamper these transactions, which as a rule had all the earmarks of forced sales, by restrictive price regulations would have injured rather than benefited those whom the lawmakers wished to protect. Deeds, too, were commercially insignificant in the relatively primitive economy of early tannaitic Palestine and served as instruments of court evidence much more than as media of business transactions. By simply *not* changing the existing law, the medieval rabbis succeeded in greatly liberalizing the restrictive provisions of *ona'ah* and in removing what otherwise would have become a serious barrier to the advanced mercantile relations of the semicapitalistic Caliphate. A final safety valve existed, moreover, in the elastic application of the ancient principle "the law of the kingdom is law." Just because this principle was subject to a great variety of interpretations, it could be invoked to support modification, or even temporary abrogation of the traditional law, whenever this conflicted with both the state laws and Jewish economic interest.

Since the major transformations in the economic system of the countries of Jewish settlement, which were largely responsible also for the changing economic needs of Jewry, were constantly reflected in the legislation of these countries, Jewish leadership had at its disposal a considerable mass of state laws which could be substituted for certain inconvenient vestiges of tradition. With all their insistence upon Jewish judicial autonomy, the rabbis professed respect for royal decrees, particularly in matters affecting taxation. Nonetheless, wherever Jewish interests conflicted with the interests of the state or its rulers, the nimble dialectical interpretation of the rabbis could easily fall back upon the supremacy of the divine law of Judaism over the human law of the kings. [203]

A combination of all these methods sufficed to maintain a sort of equilibrium between the universally accepted theory and the varying actual practices. Nor should one equate these endeavors with sheer opportunism. In the final analysis not only was it important for the very preservation of Judaism that the formalistic continuity of tradition and the authority of the ancient sources of Jewish law be strictly upheld, but the underlying purposes of this law in its economic aspects—namely, the preservation of a proper balance between the interests of society and the rights of the individual and the meeting of the exalted requirements of "justice"—could thus the more easily be realized. With all its compromises and enforced inconsistencies, the rabbinic solutions of the economic problems facing medieval Jewry proved to be astoundingly workable over a period of many generations. Thus equipped with a law and an economic theory which combined millennial continuity in fundamentals with great elasticity in details, even at the expense of logical consistency, the Jewish people was best prepared to face the constant changes in the outside world without losing its own identity. If, in the vast domains of its economic pursuits, even more than in those of its political and cultural evolution, the Jewish people had largely become the "object" of world-wide historical processes, it succeeded, mainly through the staunch adherence to its traditional but pliable law which permeated its self-governing communal organism, in salvaging a considerable measure of autonomous control over its historical destiny.

PART III

Medieval Europe

8

The Jewish Factor in Medieval Civilization[*]

THE SUBJECT of this paper reveals from the outset a number of ambiguities, which call for a few explanatory remarks. I am, for instance, painfully aware of the dichotomy inherent in it between the approach of a Western historian and that made from the standpoint of Jewish history. In its usual application, the term "medieval civilization" refers to the civilization of western and central Europe during the Middle Ages, excluding not only the vast areas under the domination of Islam but even Christian Europe of the Byzantine and eastern, Slavonic areas. While such a distinction may be largely justified by the more intensive interest of the West-European nations in their own history and, genetically, also by the subsequent unparalleled expansion of Western man and his culture, an expansion which carried his medieval heritage to the ends of the globe, it hardly corresponds to the realities of medieval Jewry. To the end of the twelfth century the overwhelming majority of the Jewish people lived under the domination of Islam. Even later its main numerical, economic, and cultural strength lay in countries such as Spain (with the adjoining southern French provinces), Portugal and southern Italy, upon which Muslim domination had left an indelible imprint. Any general term such as "medieval civilization," moreover, is likely to obscure tremendous differences in time and space. Despite all the uniformity established by the Catholic *Weltanschauung*—in itself a dynamic force, notwithstanding its strong traditional moorings—which permeated all Western countries throughout this entire period, there existed, of course, great differences between the civilization of Spain and that of Germany and, still more, between that of the

[*] This essay is based on a presidential address delivered at the annual meeting of the American Academy for Jewish Research on December 28, 1941, and later printed, in expanded and annotated form, in *Proceedings of the American Academy for Jewish Research* 12 (1942), 1–48.

eighth and that of the fifteenth century. On the Jewish side the height of medievalism was not really attained until the enforced ghetto, authoritarian community, and Lurianic Kabbalah of the sixteenth and seventeenth centuries, which coincided with Western Europe's deliberate separation from the *medium aevum* by the choice of this designation for an avowedly closed historical era.

Neither is the term "Jewish," used in this connection, entirely unequivocal. The racial concept of the Jew may have played but a minor role in the consciousness of medieval man. Yet there undoubtedly existed certain ethnic and social characteristics which, aside from his religion, set the Jew apart from his neighbors and caused him to "influence" them in a variety of often intangible ways. Even the religious influences emanating from the Jewish group were not of an easily definable type. With the Old Testament constituting in size about three-quarters of the Christian Bible and hence holding a preeminent position in the life and thought of medieval Europe, any change in emphasis from the New to the Old Law, especially among heterodox Christians, could be, and often was, classified as judaizing. This type of "judaization" sometimes took place without any active collaboration by professing or newly converted Jews. Often, however, it was directly stimulated by the presence of Jews of either type, little as the latter may have been aware of the impact of their strange, and therefore mysterious, folkways and even their most casual remarks upon the minds of thoughtful Christians.

Most questionable, however, is the designation "factor." Influences of one group upon another are generally hard to trace; parallels may too readily be mistaken for influences. The relative paucity of records concerning many important areas of medieval life increases the danger of such headlong conclusions. Bias, too, of more than the usual amount and intensity has opened many a pitfall before the investigator. From the beginning antisemitism and Jewish apologetics have colored far too many descriptions in both original sources and modern letters. Nevertheless, the term "factor" still seems preferable to the usual phraseology of "Jewish contributions to medieval civilization," which, without being less ambiguous, has decidedly apologetic overtones.

The purpose of this paper is not so much to describe the workings of the Jewish factor in detail as to point out the areas of research hitherto more or less extensively cultivated and to contrast them with those which have not yet been adequately treated. Much of this neglect is evidently due to the peculiar difficulties inherent in the available source material. Many a general medievalist, even if entirely devoid of bias, has conscientiously abstained from dealing with the Jewish factor because he does not consider himself competent to utilize the extensive Hebrew sources, only a small part of which are available in translation. Jewish historians, on the other hand, spent so many years in acquiring the necessary training in Hebrew letters, in rabbinics, philosophy, and so forth that they were unable to penetrate more deeply into the life of the contemporary non-Jewish environment. This is by no means an isolated phenomenon of Jewish research. It has long been realized, for instance, that concentration on the indispensable preparatory philological training in the Arabic language and literature has exhausted most of the available scholarly energies in this field and has been coresponsible for the relative absence of penetrating historical or sociological investigations of Muslim civilization. Despite repeated warnings, sounded over a period of many years, modern historiography has been dominated by two independent lines of investigation, cultivated by medieval historians on the one hand, and by students of Hebrew literature on the other, and even now the intermingling of the two streams is but in its incipient stages. [1]

DEMOGRAPHIC ASPECTS

The mere presence of a permanent Jewish minority amidst a more or less homogeneous majority exerted considerable influence on the latter's civilization. Positively and negatively, contacts between Jews and Christians added a characteristic tinge to the peculiar social and cultural life of each region. That is why a more thorough investigation of all localities where Jews were found, and of the number, absolute as well as relative, of Jews inhabiting them, would undoubtedly shed new light on the importance of the Jewish factor in their evolution. Unfortunately, the demographic studies of medieval Jewry thus far undertaken are woefully inadequate and, at best, fragmentary. While this situation may well be excused on the ground of the fragmentary nature of the extant sources and the general unreliability of figures quoted in them, a concerted, more vigorous attempt to ascertain the proportionate strength of the Jews in various parts of Europe over a period of many generations would doubtless yield some significant results. [2]

We know, for example, chiefly from Arabic sources, that the Jews constituted the popular majority of many cities throughout the Iberian peninsula before its complete reconquest by the Christians. This is true not only of the parts long dominated by Islam but also of some of those which had been recaptured by the Christians at an early period. From Al-Idrisi, the recently recovered Al-Ḥimyari, and other writers, we learn that Granada—that last citadel of Muslim culture in Spain—had long been called by the Muslims *Iğranāṭat al-Yahūd* ("Jewish Granada"), not only because of its very large Jewish population but also because of the Jews' apparently uncontroverted claim to having founded the city centuries before it became the capital of a Moorish kingdom. ³ From Menaḥem ibn Zeraḥ's description of neighboring Lucena, formerly the celebrated seat of Alfasi's and Ibn Megas' academy, we learn that "the entire township consists of Jews. According to tradition, they are descendants of the early exiles from Jerusalem who settled there and built the town." ⁴ This startling assertion seems to be borne out by the information supplied by Al-Idrisi and other non-Jewish writers. Even in northern Spain, which had long since reverted to Christian rule, Al-Idrisi calls Tarragona a *medinat al-Yahūd* ("Jewish city") with but a sprinkling of Christians. ⁵ Al-Ḥimyari informs us that Barcelona, the very center of Spanish Christendom before the reconquest of Toledo in 1085, had "as many Jews as Christians." ⁶ This numerical equality naturally changed in favor of the Christian population during the later periods. Nevertheless, at the end of the fourteenth century there still were more than a thousand Jewish families in Barcelona, as well as in each of several other Spanish cities. As medieval cities went, this might easily have been a ratio of one-fifth to one-third of the respective local populations as estimated by a conservative modern investigator. ⁷

Jewish numerical strength waned farther north. In northern France, Germany, and England, most Jewish communities were very slight in number, usually reaching, at best, but 1–2 percent of a city's population. However, even there, a more thoroughgoing analysis will detect the concentration of Jews in certain focal centers, which undoubtedly enabled them to exert an influence far beyond their numbers. Above all, the large majority of European Jewry lived in the nascent urban communities. The northern cities may have long embraced only a tiny minority of each country's population, but it was they who marched in the vanguard of medieval civilization; and, as has been noted, it is with good reason that the term "civilization" is derived from *civitas* ("city"). For one example, English Jewry at the time of its expulsion may or may not have counted the 16,000 souls who are recorded by contemporary chroniclers as having left the country in 1290. Even assuming the authenticity of this tradition and of a report that children were not allowed to leave and were forcibly converted, the total number of British Jews during the reign of Edward I could not possibly have exceeded 20,000, in a total English population of more than 2,500,-000. Very likely the proportion was less than 0.5 percent. This would seem an insignificant ratio, indeed. When one considers the geographic distribution of the Jews, however, these numbers assume a new meaning. One immediately realizes that after the Jews' exclusion from many English cities (Bury St. Edmunds, 1190; Leicester, 1231; Newcastle, 1234; Wycombe, 1235; Southampton, 1236; Berkhamsted, 1242; Newbury, 1244; Derby, 1263), and Henry III's express enactment in 1253 that they must not settle in towns in which they had not previously been established, their bulk was concentrated in a few areas (seventeen to twenty in all), such as York, Lincoln, Bristol, Cambridge, Oxford, and, especially, London. [8] From one-tenth to one-quarter of all English Jewry in the later years of Henry III and under Edward I must have congregated in London, in which case it may easily have constituted some 5 percent of the capital's population. [9] The influences emanating from this single, centrally located community, through its ramified business contacts with nobles, clerics, and burghers; its extension into rural England by virtue of frequent, though legally precarious, land tenures; and its manifold relations with the European continent, may have given many a stimulus to the rise of the medieval English civilization.

At the same time, on the Continent, tiny groups of Jews were scattered over a very large number of smaller localities, including villages. In a village embracing only one or two Jewish families, some fresh stimuli, perhaps irritants, were bound to be injected into the peasants' outlook and thinking, the cumulative value of which cannot easily be overestimated.

Apart from the needed statistical studies, which are still in their infancy, fuller consideration of personal relationships between Jews and Christians would elucidate many aspects of Jewish influence. Abraham Berliner and others who have casually discussed these personal contacts have largely limited their investigations to the few extant records of intellectual collaboration. Beyond such contacts between more or less superior intellects, however, there were innumerable instances of the daily exchange of ideas as well as goods between the two groups, exchanges which in their totality undoubtedly had even farther-reaching effects. Agobard, the well-known anti-Jewish archbishop of Lyons during the Carolingian age, speaks of his "almost daily" meetings with Jews. [10] Other, less prejudiced Christians, had still fewer objections to conversing daily with their Jewish neighbors. Positively or negatively, such relationships must have helped shape the medieval outlook in a direct, though often intangible, fashion. The very antagonisms which they often generated became a factor in the evolution.

These personal contacts may have diminished in both frequency and intimacy after the rise of official ghettos toward the end of the Middle Ages; but they were never completely severed, except through the physical removal of the Jews by expulsion. A general survey of medieval Jewish quarters, moreover, reveals that they were usually placed in the central districts of their respective towns. This situation is easily explainable. Medieval cities naturally grew along trade routes, which often went back to the period of Roman domination. It has been shown, for example, that the Paris Jewish settlements, reaching back to ancient times, clustered around such routes, which had doubtless been used by the first Jewish settlers coming with the Romans, whether as merchants or as soldiers. [11] Having settled in such quarters as a rule at the beginning of the city's evolution, the Jews lived in what, for the most part, was the original city area. When the population subsequently grew in number and affluence and inhabited an ever-increasing urban territory, the older sector usually remained in the center. The growing insecurity of Jewish life likewise made it advisable for the Jews to live in close settlements in the vicinity of baronial or episcopal castles, city halls, and other centers of government, which might thus be in a position to extend help during riots. These foci of government, too, were for the most part centrally located. [12] It was only during the last medieval century that the antagonistic legislation of both Spain and Germany forcibly removed many Jewish quarters from central to peripheral districts. Previously, the old Jewish quarter of Cologne, for example, had actually included in its area the city hall itself, which accounts for the curious regulation that when the municipal elders attended a night session the ghetto gates had to remain open long after official closing time. [13] In view of this peculiar circumstance, the Jew not only appeared more conspicuous to some of his Christian neighbors but also became more influential than was warranted by his numerical strength.

The closeness of social intercourse between medieval Jews and Christians often broke down the walls of segregation, even in the most obscure and outlawed domain of sex relations. Both Jewish and Christian legislators tried to suppress intimacies between Christians and Jews, with all the means at their disposal. Nevertheless, even in the face of the horrible death threatened by many city laws, if not by canon law itself, and of lynching, at least theoretically encouraged by Jewish law, intermarriage and, still more, illicit relationships, were far more frequent than is indicated in the sources. [14]

In the Mediterranean countries, particularly, the greater concentration of Jews and their lesser social and cultural segregation from the non-Jewish population greatly fostered intimate contacts. There undoubtedly is more than a grain of truth in the southern rabbi Solomon Duran's proud assertion that "among all nations you will find no nation so free of fornication as is Israel." [15] Nevertheless, casual court records and the utterances of rabbis, Jewish and Christian preachers, and moralists persistently inform us of the existence of numerous Spanish and Italian Jews who had Christian mistresses and concubines. Solomon ibn Verga and Abraham Zacuto actually tried to explain the catastrophic expulsions of the Jews from the Iberian peninsula and the previous century-long persecutions by the fact that the ancestors of Spanish Jewry had "taken Gentile women into their houses until they became pregnant. Their children became Gentiles and afterwards were among the murderers of their fathers." [16] The important conference of North-Italian communities held at Forlì in 1418 bitterly complained that "Gentile women appear permissible" in the eyes of many Italian Jews, and stated: "This is a very serious sin, indeed, aggravated by the possibility of their generating offspring outside the fold. That is why we have agreed that special officers in each town and city make careful investigations and searches for all such offenders." [17] The realistic background and apparent futility of these resolutions are well illustrated by M. Ciardini in his book on Florentine Jewish bankers, where he has analyzed the extant archival records of criminal prosecutions of Jews in that city during the fifteenth century. Compiling a statistical account from these records, I have reached the conclusion that, while we are familiar with the cause of less than half of these prosecutions, some 40 percent of all those known to have been condemned for a specified transgression relate to cases of sex relationships with Christians. True, Florence of the period of the Renaissance is by no means typical. It was an extraordinarily gay city, which did not even try to hide behind its beautiful artistic façade the prevailing laxity of public and private morals. Little wonder that the rather prosperous and Italianized Jewish community could not escape the general trend. But, what is more remarkable, the then extremely pious community of Ratisbon likewise witnessed, within a few years (1460-67), three cases of prosecution for the same transgression. The well-known accusations of Agobard concerning the seductions of Christian domestics by Jewish employers; the decisions of the Fourth Lateran Council to introduce the badge, allegedly as a preventive against mixed relationships; and the fulminations of Honorius IV in his epistles to England in 1286—"Yet Christians and Jews go on meeting in each other's houses. They spend their leisure in banqueting and feasting together and hence the opportunity for mischief becomes easy"—bear evident marks of exaggeration. Nevertheless, written by responsible leaders of the Church, these accusations must have sufficiently resembled reality to appear reasonably plausible to contemporary readers. [18] The establishment of houses of ill repute in or near the Jewish quarter was doubtless often dictated by anti-Jewish animus. Sometimes, however, they seem to have been placed there also for the convenience of Jewish patrons, who would thus not be forced to leave their quarter at night and expose themselves to danger of prosecution on this score. [19]

In short, this entire realm of sexual interrelations, extremely important not only for the racial history of both groups but also for their social coexistence; its impact upon mutual friendships or hatreds and upon the success of anti-Jewish propaganda; its influence on the guilt consciousness of the individuals involved and on the religious fervor of their repentance; the role played by the Catholic confession in its detection and prevention; and its contributions to Jewish and Christian asceticism—would all merit much more searching investigation than has been given it thus far.

More significant were the physical and spiritual contributions of the Jews to medieval Christian civilization through individual and mass conversion. In periods of great stress, the conversionary effort was greatly accelerated, but even in normal times the pressure exerted by the majority creed, its strong appeal as the foremost missionary religion, and the frequent political and social advantages looming beyond conversion, attracted many individuals, especially those weak in their Jewish faith. The story of the young Jew who, in trying to collect a debt owed to his father by the bishop of Münster, was lavishly entertained for weeks at the bishop's castle and was ultimately persuaded to join the Church, where he soon rose to the position of abbot of Scheda, has been told in picturesque detail by the distinguished Protestant theologian Reinhold Seeberg. [20] Some of these converts—for example, Petrus Alfonsi—became not only leading Christian polemists against Judaism but also most influential writers of their age.

We shall probably never know how many Jews were converted to Western Christianity in the course of the Middle Ages. That the numbers were very large goes without saying. If Isidore Loeb's estimates for Spain are at all correct, it would appear that, from some 900,000 who had lived there at the end of the thirteenth century, there remained only some 225,000 to be affected by the decree of expulsion in 1492. [21] While losses through pestilences and bloodshed —especially during the Black Death of 1348–49 and Martinez' "Holy War" against the Jews in 1391—undoubtedly were very great, it may readily be assumed that the Jews would have participated in the normal slight increase of the Spanish population, rather than have lost three-quarters of their number, were it not for the large-scale conversions which took place, especially in the years 1391–1415. Defection through baptism became so frequent a phenomenon among Spanish Jewry that, for instance, the community of Saragossa from 1415 on regularly figured budgetary deficiencies accruing from such losses. [22] Finally, the fatal blow of 1492, according to Loeb, brought about the mass conversion of some 50,000 Spanish Jews who preferred conversion to exile. On a lesser scale the same factors must have operated in other countries. Southern Italy, in particular, from the thirteenth century on, embraced a considerable number of converts, including some whose orthodoxy was so suspect as to create a full-fledged problem of *neofiti*. In some cases communal leaders themselves were seized by the mass psychosis; we learn, for example, about one Manoforte, elder of the Trani synagogue, who in 1267 was granted by the king an annual revenue of 6 ounces of gold in reward for his conversion and his promise to convert others. Little wonder that the number of baptized Jews at that time amounted in Trani alone to 310, and in all Apulia to about 1,300. [23] Moreover, the early mass conversions in Visigothic Spain, Gaul, and northern Italy, during the fateful seventh century must have injected a relatively large proportion of Jewish "blood" into the veins of the West-European nations.

Conversion undoubtedly stimulated the incursion of Jewish modes of thinking and living into the Western ways of life. Much as the Church demanded from each convert that he forget his past and consider himself newborn, [24] no adult Jew could escape the influence of his earlier environment and spiritual heritage. Consciously or unconsciously he influenced his newly acquired coreligionists by impressing upon them certain Jewish convictions and attitudes. The aforementioned Petrus Alfonsi, apparently one of the most sincere converts, could not help transmitting, in his *Doctrina clericalis*, not only to the Spaniards but also to the Englishmen among whom he lived later and to other Christians, much of the heritage of the Judeo-Muslim world, which he had left at the mature age of forty-three. Indeed, the *Doctrina* became one of the main vehicles of the diffusion of certain advanced Eastern cultural patterns among the Western nations. [25]

Some zealous Christians, indeed, resented the incursion of "foreign" ideologies. The orthodoxy of converts, especially in periods of mass baptism, which generated more or less segregated groups of baptized Jews and Jewesses, was often doubted by their fellow Christians. The problem of Marranism, coming to a historic climax in fifteenth-century Spain, had emerged on many previous occasions. Visigothic Spain in the seventh century, especially, had witnessed so extensive a legislation designed to absorb speedily the newly won adherents to the faith as to give a semblance of truth to modern allegations of its "racial" antisemitism. To be sure, "race" was still an unknown concept, and whatever racial feeling existed was latent rather than overt. Even the story told by Sir Thomas More of the English gentlewoman who, upon suddenly learning that the Virgin had been a Jewess, was deeply chagrined, and exclaimed "so help me God and halidom, I shall love her the worse while I live" mirrors only latent animosities. Nevertheless, the removal of children of Visigothic converts from their homes and the entrusting of their education to "old" Christians, as well as the encouragement of intermarriage between the old and the new groups, clearly expressed the instinctive desire of the majority of Iberian Christians to absorb the minority completely. [26] If this process was checked before long, by the Moorish conquest of Spain in 712, there undoubtedly remained in the country for generations thereafter a great many Christian descendants of Jews who, like the Mozarabs, helped furnish the nucleus for the subsequent Christian reconquest of the peninsula. These early ancestors of the Christian Spaniards, whose number must have been legion, were entirely forgotten by the time the new waves of conversion after 1391 began provoking a novel, almost irrational, quest for *limpieza* ("racial purity") and produced such extravagances as the *Libro verde de Aragón* or the *Tizón de la nobleza*. [27] There was, indeed, more than an overdose of bitter irony in Ibn Verga's ascribing to the Marrano interlocutor of a Spanish king the assertion that "Judaism is one of the incurable diseases." [28]

ECONOMIC FACTORS

The Jewish contributions to the economic development of medieval Europe have thus far been treated largely under the aspect of Jewish banking and international trade. There is no doubt that in both these economic domains the Jews played a role far in excess of their numbers. While a great many aspects of medieval Jewish commerce are still obscure—for example, the Jewish part in introducing certain advanced instrumentalities, such as commercial papers issued on bearers, is not yet fully clarified—there is no question that the Jews arriving in ever-increasing numbers from Middle-Eastern lands brought with them methods of trade theretofore unfamiliar in the West. [29]

It has long been rightly felt, however, although it could not always be fully documented, that the incursion of Eastern models through the instrumentality of Jews arriving from the Orient was not limited to international commerce and banking. In the local trade of the growing urban centers north of the Alps and the Pyrenees, the Jews must have performed certain pioneering services, not only as distributors of luxury goods brought by their coreligionists from the Orient, as salesmen whose persuasive powers stimulated the demand for new articles of consumption in the rapidly expanding markets of nobles and clerics, and as visitors to the regional fairs along the Rhine and in Champagne but also as petty traders and peddlers among the masses of the population in a period of extremely bad roads and insecure travel. [30] Their role as merchant explorers of the adjacent East-European areas and in drawing the western Slavonic peoples into the orbit of Western civilization is still shrouded in darkness, interrupted only by the few flashes of light cast by Ibn Khordadbeh's description of the Radanites, Ibrahim ibn Yakub's travelogue, the story of Ḥisdai ibn Shapruṭ's mediators in his correspondence with the Khazars, the Raffelstetten Toll Ordinance of 907, and the coins struck by the Hebrew minters of the early kings of Poland. In the few instances recorded in Sicily and southern France, we learn of Jewish artisans performing pioneering services in teaching new crafts to the Western nations. Moreover, the fact that in medieval England stone houses were considered "too expensive for anyone but aristocrats, or great ecclesiastics or Jews" has led to a theory, first timidly suggested by Joseph Jacobs, that it was the Jew who introduced stone masonry into England, both because he had long been accustomed to living in stone houses in Palestine and because he felt safer behind the shelter of stone walls. [31] It is also very likely that some of the new Jewish settlers from the East (who replenished the ranks of Spanish Jewry decimated by the protracted Visigothic persecutions), having learned the methods of intensive fruit growing and truck farming in the densely populated Eastern lands, took an active part in helping to convert the Iberian peninsula into a land of flourishing orchards and truck gardens under the Moorish domination. Radiating from Spain and Sicily, and in part transmitted by migrating Jews, similar Jewish influences upon the gradual intensification of northern agriculture are well within the realm of historical probability. The thrice-told story of the three Jewish purchasers of kermes trees in the Miramar district in southern France (1138) [32] may serve as an illustration of the stimulus given to agricultural production by Jewish traders and craftsmen, if not directly by Jewish tillers of the soil. The existence of the latter, too, is fully attested in the sources. Finally, the part played by the Jews in employing non-Jewish labor and in spreading, through it, a certain familiarity with some newer methods of production and new articles of consumption, must have been equally considerable, despite the constant reiteration of laws forbidding Jews to employ Christian servants. The few essays on Jewish slave trade hitherto published [33] have fallen far short of satisfying our scientific curiosity in this very important area of Judeo-Christian relations. Much research is still required to squeeze out of the recalcitrant body of documentary material all the available evidence about these vital Jewish functions in the medieval economy.

Even a fuller appreciation of the effects of Jewish moneylending still awaits elucidation from various angles. The relatively minor role, for instance, played by Jewish bankers in the growing deposit and transfer trade in the later Middle Ages, though fully understandable in the light of Jewish insecurity, ought not to blind us to the fact that the Jews may have been instrumental in popularizing pertinent new methods among the Christian nations. [34] Some negative contributions, too, ought to be considered. For example, the spread of the *montes pietatis* among the Latin nations was undoubtedly the result of Bernardino da Feltre's anti-Jewish animus and of his desire to replace the indispensable Jewish moneylender by supplying, through philanthropy, cheap credit to the local populations. [35] One ought also to examine more closely than has hitherto been done the effects of Jewish moneylending upon each nation's independence of foreign credit. It is a matter of record that the kings of England and France, particularly after the elimination of the Jews, were deeply indebted to Italian and other foreign bankers. Save in the case of bankruptcy, such as that of England, which ruined the Florentine firm of the Peruzzi, this meant the continual transfer of British and French funds to Italy in payment of the high annual interest. It may well have been the existence of a large and affluent Jewish banking group on the Iberian peninsula, as well as in early modern Poland, which made these countries relatively immune from the control of foreign bankers. The Jew, however exacting, was, after all, at the mercy of the local powers, and the interest paid to him not only remained within the country but ultimately reverted to the state treasury in the form of taxes or enforced loans. In fact, Aragon, apparently guided by such "mercantilist" considerations, on certain occasions insisted that the Jewish communities raise the amounts necessary for their forced participation in government financing by borrowing from coreligionists abroad, thus bringing fresh capital into the country. [36] Finally, fuller studies of the amounts paid by Jews in taxes to their respective governments, and of their importance in the fiscal structure of these countries, particularly in periods of economic and political crisis, are a major scientific desideratum and would doubtless reveal the extent to which the Jews helped buttress central or regional powers against the forces of the "estates," which otherwise were often in control of the country's purse strings. By such means, Jews greatly contributed to the gradual undermining of the feudal order. [37]

Along the same antifeudal lines undoubtedly operated also the concentration of Jews in those branches of the economy which were not sharply monopolized by guild restrictions. In the Mediterranean countries, as later in Poland, the mere existence of powerful Jewish guilds partly counteracted monopolistic extremes. Elsewhere, too, the Jews, forced out of the guild-dominated areas, had to exploit the few remaining opportunities more intensively and constantly be on the lookout for new openings. That they thus could serve, often unwittingly, as vehicles of economic progress, was due not so much to their forced breaches of medieval regimentation, for which Werner Sombart has adduced some rather tenuous documentation, as to the sheer force of necessity, "the mother of invention."

They were greatly assisted by having at their disposal both an economic tradition and a legal system which had originated in areas of more advanced economy. In the feudalistic medieval world the Jews were perhaps the most "liberal" economic group, not only as a result of their forced inventiveness in the struggle for economic survival but, paradoxically, also because of their staunch adherence to tradition. What the "reception" of Roman law at large meant to the German or French economies of the early modern period was accomplished on a minor scale by the Jews acting within the earlier medieval economy under the legal requirements of talmudic law, which was likewise basically formulated under the semicapitalist civilization of the Hellenistic and early Roman Empires. As a matter of fact, the teachings of the Roman schools of Labeo and Capito reached early modern Europe in the diluted form of the Code of Justinian, which in many ways reflected the increasingly feudal order of the Byzantine Empire. The norms of the schools of Hillel and Shammai and their early successors, on the other hand, were directly available to medieval Jewry through the Mishnah and other extant tannaitic collections. Even where they, too, had been modified by the Babylonian Talmud to meet the requirements of the semifeudal Persian environment, they had retained much of their pristine "liberal" orientation in the self-governing Babylonian-Jewish communities. Moreover, by the time Jews began to influence the European economy to any significant degree, talmudic law had undergone the reverse process of liberalization, by the Geonic teachers acting under the stimulus of the semicapitalistic evolution of the Great Caliphate. A great amount of sociological and rabbinic research is yet needed, however, to clarify medieval Jewry's ideological and practical stimuli in the many fields of economic endeavor. [38]

CULTURAL CONTRIBUTIONS

The Jewish factor in the development of medieval science and philosophy has frequently been treated from the point of view of the transmission of Eastern culture to the West through Jewish translators or Jewish collaboration with Christian translators. To be sure, even this aspect has, largely, been dealt with only bibliographically, i.e., by the enumeration of persons recorded in such a capacity in one or another medieval work. [39] However, a fuller evaluation of these contributions still awaits elucidation by thoroughgoing monographic treatment of each act of transmission and the relative share of the Jews in it. It is one thing to learn that such and such a Jew was helpful in the translation of a particular Arabic work into Latin, and another thing to estimate the relative importance of that work for medieval science and of the translator's peculiarities, which may have influenced or colored a particular scientific doctrine. Of course, the preliminary bibliographical work had to be done first. But it is high time now, several decades after Steinschneider, that the more quantitative approach be supplemented by a more significant qualitative evaluation and the ascertainment of, so to say, the specific gravity of each particular contribution.

Of equal importance are the innumerable personal contacts between Jewish and Christian scholars in the West. Whether or not they actually collaborated on a particular project, such scholars were always mutually stimulated by an exchange of ideas and very likely reciprocally influenced one another even in the interpretation of specific texts. True, a considerable body of evidence for such direct intellectual contacts has come down to us only from Italy in the thirteenth to the sixteenth centuries. But a more careful investigation of the extant sources will easily demonstrate that if, for example, Abraham bar Ḥiyya (Savasorda) worked together with Rudolph of Bruges on the translation of De Astrolabio, [40] it may readily be assumed that Rudolph received many a suggestion or differing point of view from the great Jewish astronomer in other fields of mathematics and astronomy as well. It is a matter of record that Leonardo of Pisa, perhaps the greatest medieval mathematician in the West, was deeply indebted to both Arabic and Jewish sources, which undoubtedly were transmitted to him in part by Jewish neighbors. Once more the problem of Jewish converts who carried over their intellectual heritage into their new Christian environment—for instance, Avendeath (Ibn Daud if, indeed, he was a convert and not a professing Jew)[41]—would merit further careful investigation.

Far less known are the intellectual relationships between Christians and Jews in the study of the Bible. It has long been recognized that the extremely influential Bible commentaries by Nicholas of Lyra were deeply indebted to both Rashi and Ḳimḥi. Herman Hailperin's studies on Rashi,[42] in shedding new light on many details of such indebtedness, fully bear out this general assumption. Further investigations are needed, however, to elucidate the indebtedness of the other medieval Christian Bible commentators (also preachers and moralists) to both the ancient Jewish tradition and the medieval Jewish Bible exegesis. The ancient tradition may have come to them primarily through their own patristic predecessors. It is nevertheless apparent that some elements of this tradition percolated into the medieval Christian world through contemporary Jewish students of the Midrash and the accepted Jewish commentaries. The collaboration of Moses Arragel with several Christian priests in the preparation of a new Castilian translation of the Bible (the so-called Alba Bible)[43] at the instance of Prior Luis de Guzman furnishes a striking illustration of how intimate such cooperation was at times. That relatively few instances of this type were recorded was undoubtedly due to the apprehensions of Church organs over the spread of Bibles in the vernacular; such Bibles not only seemed to diminish the authority of the clergy among the intelligent laity but also opened the gates to heretical interpretation.[44] However, one may take it for granted that in innumerable instances individual Christians, clerics as well as laymen, sought the advice of their Jewish friends in the interpretation of obscure passages in the Old Testament.

Moreover, the mere presence of a Jewish community exerted an influence on the medieval mentality which, though not easily recorded, was of incalculable importance. Thomas Huxley, himself rather an agnostic, extolled the influence of the Bible on Western civilization by pointing out that, among its other merits, "it forbids the veriest hind who never left his village to be ignorant of the existence of other countries and other civilizations, and of a great past stretching back to the furthest limits of the oldest civilizations of the world."[45] The international outlook and historical consciousness of medieval man, however rudimentary, were undoubtedly reinforced by the presence of Jews, who, through the very strangeness of their appearance and mores, appeared to him the embodiment of that ancient civilization.

The Jewish influences on the development of medieval mysticism and the magic arts are often hidden behind the veil of obscurity generally investing these occult domains of human life. We know from some specialized research that leading Christian mystics in Spain, Germany, and Italy—especially Jacob Böhme and Pico della Mirandola—were deeply indebted to Jewish philosophers such as Ibn Gabirol, and to the Kabbalah. We also know that the Christian populace frequently accused Jews of engaging in magic and witchcraft, [46] an accusation which, though not fully borne out by facts, nevertheless undoubtedly represented a kernel of historic reality. Here again personal contacts were far more widespread and effective than any form of literary transmission, which alone could be ascertained bibliographically.

One might mention in this connection, finally, the influence exerted by Jews and Jewish converts on the so-called Christian Hebraists. Throughout the ages Christians interested in the pursuit of Hebrew studies had recourse to Jewish teachers and other Jewish acquaintances. To be sure, the knowledge of Hebrew, especially before the Council of Vienne in 1311, was very limited even among Christian ecclesiastics. But there is little doubt that in addition to a few prominent writers such as Roger Bacon and, possibly, Sir Robert Grosseteste, [47] whose acquaintance with the Hebrew language may be gleaned from their writings, there were numerous other students of Hebrew, with varying degrees of accomplishment, who sought instruction and advice from their Jewish friends. The Council of Vienne, through its resolution to establish chairs for Hebrew at Oxford, Paris, Salamanca, and Bologna (following upon Clement V's decision of 1310 to institute regular instruction in Oriental languages in the papal capital), although prompted by missionary zeal and an attempt to convert the Jews to Christianity, undoubtedly fostered such personal relations between the Christian Hebraists and more or less learned Jews. [48] The full story of the Christian Hebraists and their relation to Jews, in the study of which the late George Alexander Kohut spent many years of his life, is yet to be told in illuminating detail.

Raymond Lull, the mastermind behind the decision of the Council of Vienne, unwittingly helped reinforce still another bridge between Christian and Jewish thinking. True to his general advocacy of exclusively spiritual means of conversion, he went further than his predecessors in instituting regular missionary sermons among Jews. [49] Such sermons which in the course of time tended to become caricatures through the use of enforced attendance and other routine methods of compulsion, were originally animated by the sincere belief that, if a Jewish audience were shown that the messiahship of Jesus was indicated not only by a correct interpretation of the Old Testament but also by the talmudic sources themselves, it would speedily recognize its error and accept the Christian religion. [50] Conversionist sermons of this type may quite early have degenerated into popular spectacles increasing the ill will between the two groups. Nonetheless, they must have stimulated the Christian preachers, ecclesiastics, and rulers, who supported them to devote considerable thought to those aspects of Judaism and those Jewish literary sources which could best be utilized in making Christian dogmas palatable to Jewish audiences.

On the other hand, we also have numerous records of Christians attending Jewish sermons. As early as the ninth century, Agobard had bitterly complained of some Christians in the archdiocese of Lyons who claimed "that the Jews preach better to them than our priests." [51] In Spain and Renaissance Italy, especially, where the social intercourse between Jews and Christians was more intimate and the Jewish preachers were in better command of the vernacular, Jewish sermons were often extremely popular among the educated classes. No one shall ever really be able to gauge the extent of the transmission of Jewish concepts to the Christian public through these oratorical performances.

Similarly, religious disputations between Jews and Christians often served to arouse the interest of the Christian debaters and onlookers in the Jewish side of the controversy, though not nearly as much as they helped to spread the teachings of Christianity among the Jews. We ought to bear in mind not only the great public quasi-gladiatorial combats (such as those in which Yeḥiel of Paris or Naḥmanides rather successfully defended the Jewish cause, or the long drawn-out Disputation at Tortosa), often attended by king and pope, which before long degenerated into the one-sided *informatio* of Joseph Albo and his associates by their Christian opponents. [52] In addition to these much-publicized events, there were innumerable semipublic or private debates between individual Jews and Christians, the majority of which undoubtedly never found their

way into written records. Those few of which knowledge happens
to have come down to us—such as the early disputation of Pavia
(about A.D. 800) or that between the proctor of Westminster Abbey
and a Mayence Jew (11th cent.)—demonstrate how often Jews
defended their cause candidly and overtly, despite the danger of
prosecution for blasphemy against the dominant creed. Such
debates undoubtedly enabled many a Christian to acquire some
familiarity with the religion of his Jewish neighbors. Even the most
pious Christians, moreover, were forced, by virtue of the contrast
presented, to reconsider their position toward their own creed. If
there is any truth in the old adage that one learns one's own language best by studying a foreign tongue, they evidently learned
much more about their own religion than if there had been no
Jews at hand to point out to them its characteristic peculiarities.

A great many, however, were not altogether confirmed in their
Christian orthodoxy through such contacts with Jews. Judaism may
have officially ceased to be a missionary religion for centuries past,
but it was nonetheless very difficult to dissuade all Jewish individuals from communicating to their Christian friends and employees
some Jewish beliefs or rituals. The unceasing stream of denunciation aimed at such Jewish influences, and the endless reiteration of
legislative enactments by Church and state bent upon their elimination, though doubtless grossly exaggerated, reflect a modicum of
reality which is rarely mirrored in the usual documents.

Of course, one need not take too literally the accusation of
"judaizing" hurled by orthodox Christians at their sectarian opponents, or by one Christian sect at another. Such an "invective" at
times may not have contained any truth at all and often was used
quite recklessly in discrediting an opponent before the uncritical
populace. In some cases a reversion to the Old Testament from the
New, as with the Franco-Italian Passagians, seemed to offer sufficient substantiation to the accusers. The insistence, particularly, on
observing the Sabbath on Saturday rather than Sunday appeared
to be the most obvious and obnoxious manifestation of Jewish
influence. Although a direct Jewish paternity at the resurgence
of such Christian currents, down to the Russian Subotniki and the
Anglo-Saxon Seventh-Day Adventists, can rarely be attested by
extant sources and must have been difficult to prove even for the
contemporary inquisitors, the underground persistence of such
currents through the ages may well have been linked in some

fashion with the tenacity of the Jewish people itself among the Christian nations. [53] There is no gainsaying that heretical trends must have been nurtured by the ever-present example of religious disparity offered by Judaism and, occasionally, also by the direct stimulus of professing or converted Jews who repudiated one or another teaching of the authoritarian Church. In the case of converted Jews, especially those forcibly baptized, there was great temptation for their former Jewish friends and relatives to try to regain them for their erstwhile creed. The frequent prosecutions of individual Jews, especially rabbis, accused of encouraging religious relapses of this type, bear somber testimony to the reality of such individual persuasion.

Finally, the anti-Jewish literature itself testifies to the vitality of the Jewish factor in medieval civilization. Much of that literature undoubtedly was stereotyped within a well-accepted genre, and could have been written even if no Jews had remained in Christian Europe at all. Jewish "perfidy" and "infidelity," or what was so designated by way of contrast with the Christian dogmas and practices which the authors wished to extol, could have been put up as an internal bogey before the Christian nations as a result of purely historical reminiscences. However, the force of the argument was increased many times over by the ever-present example of the well-known inmates of the Jewish quarter. Thus, in their very negation of Judaism, the Church and its medieval apologists were deeply indebted to the ubiquitous Jewish factor among them.

POLITICAL DICHOTOMIES

Politically and legally, too, the peculiar status of the Jews injected a new element into the political structure of medieval society, an element which, while often complicating the task of legislators and judges, added a particular hue to the multicolored pattern of medieval political evolution. Whatever one's judgment may be about the value of such a contribution, it is unquestionable that the presence of a Jewish minority added much to the richness and variety of public life.

There is a basic dualism in the political status of medieval Jewry which often baffles modern investigators and defies their attempts at clear-cut definitions. On the whole, the Jewish group was considered a corporate body within the corporate structure of medieval society. As a corporate body the Jews enjoyed a particular status of their own, with a peculiar system of rights and duties. It is easy to overemphasize the Jewish disabilities and burdensome duties, as was done during the Emancipation era. Any comparison with the legislation of Nazi Germany and fascist Italy will reveal that we are maligning the Middle Ages when we call the Nuremberg laws a reversion to the medieval status. Unlike the Jews under Nazism, who were the sole minority placed by law outside the framework of a population which enjoyed complete equality—be it only equality in subjugation—the medieval Jews at their worst were better off, both politically and economically, than the masses of villeins who usually constituted the majority in the European nations. I may be allowed to repeat here the paradoxical statement that medieval Jewry, much as it suffered from disabilities and contempt, still was a privileged minority in every country where it was tolerated at all. This was possible because, from the point of view of public law, it was considered but a corporate body like other bodies, its status being determined by a combination of specific legal enactments and customs born in times immemorial and carried along on the wave of medieval traditionalism. [54]

At the same time the Jewish community was a corporate body of a unique kind, consisting of a group of permanent "aliens," essentially living apart from corporate Christian society. Little as one is inclined today to subscribe to the older theories of medieval Jewish serfdom which traced the dependence of Jews on royal power back to the original Teuton "law of aliens" (*Fremdenrecht*), [55] there is no denying that, in the minds of most medieval men, the Jew appeared to be a permanent stranger. Whether or not this explains the vast extent of Jewish self-government, it undoubtedly helps us to understand the deep-rooted suspicions and frequent misunderstandings which permeated all Judeo-Christian relations. This alienage of the Jews was in itself unparalleled, inasmuch as, in contrast to other aliens, Jews were not expected to become "natives," except by conversion to Christianity; i.e., by the conscious act of separation from their own group. It made no difference how long a Jew lived in a particular country or whether he had actually settled there before the arrival of those ethnic groups who later claimed "native" rights on that soil. He was, moreover, an alien without a motherland. Much as the Christian world accepted the spiritual yearning of the Jews for the restoration to Palestine, and often considered such a return as a necessary prerequisite for the second coming of Christ—the equivalent of the Jewish messianic hope [56]—Palestine obviously was not the mother country of exilic Jewry in the normal sense. It could not threaten reciprocity, nor could its legislation in any way affect the changing personal law of the individual Jew or of his Western community. [57]

The ambiguity of Jewry's corporate status, which was at once like and unlike that of other bodies, and the divergence between its alienage and permanent residence, was tied up with still another dichotomy. Ever since the Christian Roman Empire, the Church preached the preservation of the Jewish people to the end of days, but demanded, at the same time, for the sake of both prestige and better "testimony," that it be kept in a status of submission and overt inferiority. The principle of toleration may have varied in its practical application, depending upon the period, the country and even the individual. In extreme cases, such as that of John Duns Scotus, a Franciscan living in the overheated atmosphere of pre-Expulsion England, it could mean merely the keeping alive of a few Jews somewhere on a distant island. [58] In other cases, as in papal Rome itself, it meant the preservation of the Jewish community in its historical continuity, without a single interruption through expulsion or large-scale massacre. The Jews' low social status was likewise subject to individual discretion and to the changing tempers of rulers and peoples. But it was the very contradiction between the principles of toleration and exclusion, which, by allowing for alternating emphases upon the one or the other, accounted for the great elasticity and adaptability of medieval legislation, and, in many ways, explains the unique destinies of the various segments of medieval Jewry.

Even Jewish serfdom was subject to equivocal interpretation. As successors of the ancient Roman Empire, which had subdued Palestine and had but conditionally liberated its Jewish population, the Holy Roman emperors claimed to own the Jews. The Church, on the other hand, demanded full control over Jewry because Jewish subjection was merely the effect of the Jewish repudiation of Christ. For this reason alone, it had long been foretold, "the elder shall serve the younger" and the Jewish people shall be *perpetuae servituti subacti.* [59] The various Christian kings and princes, however, interpreted the curse resting upon the Jews as the expression of the divine will to deliver up the Jewish people to the whims of their Christian sovereigns, whoever and wherever they might be. The struggle between kings and cities for control over the Jews merely added another disharmonious element to Jewish political allegiance and the general ambiguity of Jewish existence. [60]

In most cases, however, the Jews were pressed into an alliance with the powers that were, which often augured badly for them in periods of change. Living permanently under the protection of the kings, paying for such protection with enormous taxes and loans, and often directly supporting the royal power in their capacity as tax farmers, contractors, and administrative or diplomatic advisers (particularly on the Iberian Peninsula), they were easily associated in the popular mind with the forces of governmental and class oppression. Peasantry and urban proletariat were not apt to penetrate behind the surface and take note of the compulsion under which the Jewish puppets of their real oppressors had acted. They saw first of all the immediate agents of oppression and struck at them whenever conditions became unbearable. The defenselessness of these agents, moreover, as contrasted with the great power of the ruling classes, made them the obvious targets of popular resentment, the more so since religious antagonisms had long prepared the ground for Jew-baiting demagogues. Our understanding of the widespread medieval massacres of Jews is likely to gain much by a closer investigation of the motivating forces behind each outburst. It was easy for a Zunz to generalize that the mere existence of the Jews was "their sole really proven crime," but it was more than mere religious fanaticism which inspired the German peasants during the aforementioned revolts to attack Jews and clerics alike. Neither was mere religious fanaticism behind the social revolution of Majorcan peasantry. Aimed largely at the ruling classes, the revolution struck directly at the Jews because of the great indebtedness of the agricultural population to Jewish moneylenders and tax farmers. [61] The nexus between social revolution and anti-Jewish massacres during the Cossack rebellion has long been recognized. [62] Much research, however, is yet needed to clarify in detail the forces at work in the numerous pogroms, which increased in number and intensity in the three centuries beginning with the First Crusade.

In an entirely different fashion, and, in some respects, more profoundly, the Jews, by unwittingly becoming allies of the royal power, undermined their very survival in many European countries.

Because of insufficient detailed researches in the field of medieval Jewish taxation, we know very little about the extent to which the fiscal contributions of medieval Jewry helped the Western princes in gradually overcoming the resistance of their feudal lords. But there is little doubt that, through their loyalty to the Crown and their services as a "sponge," sucking up the wealth of the country for the benefit of the rulers (this figure of speech, first coined by Hessian theologians in 1538, [63] has since become a cliché), the Jews helped unify England, France, Spain, and Portugal. The unification of the country on a national basis held many evil portents for the Jews, however. As soon as a medieval country was converted into a "national" state—however unclear and often unconscious medieval nationalism still was—it began to resent deeply the presence of the only "alien" minority in its midst. I have long tried to unravel the deep connections between the processes of national unification and the growth of religious intolerance, which, as a rule, first manifested itself in undisciplined mob reactions, then was followed by severe anti-Jewish legislation, and, finally, culminated in complete exclusion *via* expulsion or enforced conversion. [64] But I readily concede the need of further searching investigations to explore the complex ramifications of this vital problem. [65]

The tragic nexus between loyalty to the Crown and ultimate self-destruction was mirrored on a different plane by a subtle interlocking of the interests of Jewry with those of the medieval Church. Overtly representing two hostile principles—in Christendom's public mind, in art, and in literature, Judaism was always envisaged as the "Synagogue of Satan," battling, though subdued by, the Church Divine—the two institutions nevertheless complemented one another; in a deeper sense, needed one another, for the full realization of their program on earth. It was interterritorial Jewry which, in a subtle way and quite unwittingly, helped the interterritorial Church to overcome nationalist disparities and to achieve the characteristic medieval supranational unity of culture. Reciprocally, the Church, despite the anti-Jewish leanings of many of its protagonists, and its unceasing denunciations of Jewish "perfidy," insisted upon a kind of limited toleration, which alone made it possible for the Jews to survive successive waves of persecution. [66]

This polarity of all Judeo-Christian relations was epitomized by the peculiar make-up of Jewish self-government. Outwardly resembling other corporate bodies in its autonomous features, the Jewish community was, as I have said, a corporate body of a unique kind. As a matter of fact, there existed a deep undeclared conflict in the very concept of sovereignty. From the point of view of state, Church, and city, the Christian ruler was the true sovereign, hampered solely by tradition and custom, and could, at his discretion, grant the Jews self-government or curtail and even abrogate it. Despite numerous Jewish professions of acceptance of these royal claims, however, the very core of Jewish self-government, the doctrines of Jewish law, was, in principle, diametrically opposed. According to Jewish belief, Jewish law in all its essentials was divinely ordained and could not be abrogated by any human power. The principle *dina de-malkhuta dina* ("the law of the kingdom is law"), which, by seemingly recognizing the royal point of view, tried to establish a *modus vivendi* between exilic Jewry and the Gentile powers, in essence merely reiterated and reinforced the sovereign claims of Jewish law. The gradual halakhic evolution of this principle may still be in need of more clarification and thorough monographic study,[67] but it appears certain that what was really meant was that royal law is to be respected, provided that it does not infringe upon any essential of Jewish law. If a king demands, however, that a Jew commit any of the ritualistically prohibited acts, the royal decree is not to be considered valid law and must not be respected. In the case of three major commandments, the Jew is even enjoined to resist royal force at the cost of his life. Some rabbis went so far as to claim, as did Mordecai b. Hillel, that, if a king tries to extort from Jews theretofore unaccustomed amercements, he is no longer acting as a legitimate ruler, and that, hence, his ordinance ought to be disregarded and all civil claims based on it entirely rejected. [68] Whether or not the regnant rabbinic opinion was ready thus to repudiate royal sovereignty in taxation, which is now so clearly recognized as the particular domain of statehood, the underlying philosophy of this decision, like others, was that it is up to the rabbinic judge to determine in each instance the validity and applicability of royal enactments regarding Jews, from the standpoint of Jewish law. In other words, it is the rabbinic exponent of Jewish law who reserves to himself the ultimate decision. This claim, superficially paradoxical, was fully justified under the assumption that the *jus divinum* of the Torah was subject to modification only by the internal evolution of the Jewish people and by the incursion of such new elements as were introduced into it by a divinely ordained fate. In the final sense, the Jewish people alone, acting through its representative spokesmen, the rabbis, was to determine the limitations of its sovereignty.

Neither side was interested in pressing this inherent conflict to its logical extreme. In practice, outward Jewish submissiveness, coupled with royal reluctance to interfere in the life of Jewish subjects outside the restricted areas of politics and finance, all but eliminated actual clashes. Certainly, if compared with the parallel claims of the Catholic clergy, the difficulties with the Jews appeared infinitesimal. That thoughtful Christians nevertheless dimly sensed the extraordinary position of Jewry may be noted from Augustine's semienvious observation, essentially repeated by Erasmus, on "the more tolerable condition of the Jews who, though they have not recognized the days of liberty, are yet subject to burdens of law, not to human presumptions." [69]

Such a unique concatenation of contrasts and conflicts, some of which were merely sensed and never clearly formulated by medieval man, undoubtedly introduced an element of instability into all social relations. But instability was perhaps favorable to medieval dynamics. To be sure, our traditional concept of a slow medieval progression has undergone considerable revision in recent years. We now realize the dynamism of medieval civilization, despite its earthbound and tradition-bound rhythm of evolution. There is no doubt, however—and further detailed research will undoubtedly make it ever clearer—that the tensions generated by the dichotomies of Jewish status added impetus to the speed of change and, if one may still use this term today, of human progress.

COMMUNITY OF THINKING

Viewing the problem as a whole, we may assert that the Jewish factor in medieval civilization can well serve as a criterion of that era's genuineness and inwardness. Despite the enormous Jewish sufferings during the Middle Ages, which not even the staunchest opponent of the lachrymose conception of Jewish history would wish to minimize, we must testify to the general fairness, or at least attempted fairness, of medieval man. Numerous exceptions notwithstanding—and exceptions to rules are characteristic of medieval life —one must admit that the prevailing legislation of practically all medieval countries tried to safeguard the legitimate interests of the Jewish minority. According to the dominant opinion, one was not to force a Jew to appear before the court of his Christian opponent; if the Jew was the defendant, he could insist upon repairing to his own court, or, more frequently, to a special mixed court or a generally less prejudiced superior court of the king or his highest officials. (At times such royal courts, acting in the interest of their masters and the latter's Jewish "serfs," were accused of consistently siding with the Jewish parties.) Neither were Jews to be condemned on the testimony of Christian witnesses alone. Their inclusion, along with clerics, women, and other defenseless groups, under the safeguard of royal "peace," was intended to grant them a higher degree of protection than could be ensured by mere paper privileges.

One must also always bear in mind that, despite the tremendous bloodshed from 1096 to 1391, we can find no instance of government-instigated pogroms. It was left to the Czarist government of the late nineteenth century, [70] and to its disciples among the Nazis, to introduce this new, anarchical feature into the relationship between a state and its Jewry. This is not to deny the Jewish role of "scapegoat" in the medieval, as well as in the modern, world. Indeed, this function of Western Jewry as an outlet for accumulated hatreds, a sort of safety valve within explosive societies, is yet to be investigated in detail. Nevertheless, one may readily acquit all medieval governments of acting in any way reminiscent of the Nazis in November 1938 and after.

Fairness also permeated relations between the Church and the Jews. Despite its all-embracing claims of supremacy, despite its overt attempts to penetrate all domains of public and private life, the Church imposed upon itself limitations in regard to Jews which are truly remarkable. An inquisitor such as Eymeric may claim that the pope has jurisdiction over the Jewish community even with respect to its internal affairs, and that he may prosecute Jewish heresies on a par with deviations from Christian orthodoxy. In practice, he admits, the popes will usually find it impolitic to exercise such jurisdiction. [71] As a matter of record, interventions of this kind were extremely rare and, when they occurred, were usually instigated by Jews. The very Inquisition, whose bloody record has contributed many a somber page to Jewish history, was, in principle, limited to Marranos and other professing Christians and only to such Jews as were accused of attacking Christianity or of proselytizing among Christians, including backsliding converts. Ecclesiastical censorship, too, as employed before the invention of printing and, outside of Italy, long thereafter, reveals far more self-restraint and respect for the legitimate disparity of minority opinion than one usually associates with medieval "intolerance." We may now resent the burning of Maimonides' *Guide* (incidentally, instigated by Jewish anti-Maimonists); we may even more deeply deplore the recurrent burnings of the Talmud, the results of which are still felt today, for, having deprived us of practically all older manuscripts, they greatly hamper any attempt at a critical edition of this monumental body of literature. We shall nonetheless have to admit that Church censorship has rarely interfered with the autonomous development of Jewish culture. A mere perusal of Eisenstein's *Oṣar ha-vikkuḥim*, whatever one thinks of the scholarly merits of this compilation, will show to every unprejudiced reader the great leeway given to Jewish apologetics. Not only orally but often in widely circulating pamphlets and treatises, the Jews were in a position to discuss frankly the differences between their own and the Christian attitude to life. [72] In few modern countries, not only totalitarian but all such as have seen in censorship a necessary safeguard, at least in emergency periods, would men be allowed to speak their minds so freely and in a way so clearly running counter to the established order and the interests of its dominant group.

Above all, despite the divergences between Judaism and Christianity, there was a basic unity of thinking, which made all conflicts a struggle between brethren, rather than a war between strangers. Only in the light of such unity of thinking was it possible for the greatest minds of the Christian world to quote freely the views of Maimonides and other Jewish teachers. [73] Only such unity made it possible for Gabirol to write a philosophic work so interdenominational in character as to prompt the mistaken notion that its author was either a Muslim or a Christian. The Christians may have had little use or understanding for the minutiae of Jewish law, [74] just as the Jews may have completely lacked an appreciation of the mysteries of the trinitarian dogma. The basic outlook of all Europeans was so much determined by the common Judeo-Christian heritage as to relegate these differences into the realm of nonessentials, however much heat was spent on their discussion.

In conclusion, it may be stated that this presentation has not been intended as a defense of the medieval civilization. Such a defense would be doubly unwarranted, as I am not at all convinced that the historian's task is to sit in judgment upon previous generations. But it is well worthwhile to remember now, in this period of epochal transitions, that, within the autonomous structure of a great era in human civilization, such as that of the Christian Middle Ages, the Jewish factor, in both its tangible elements and its imponderabilia, played a great role and left on the medieval era (and, indirectly, on Western civilization today) the indelible imprint of its remarkable historical career.

9

Rashi and the Community of Troyes[*]

THE POSITION of Rashi in the history of Jewish letters is full of obscurities. To a large extent these obscurities are due to the sudden emergence of an advanced type of Jewish culture in the Rhineland, under the leadership of Gershom b. Meir and his school, and in northern France, under the guidance of Rashi and his disciples. While the few extant medieval sources allow us occasional glimpses into the successive settlements of Jews in these regions, as well as into their political and economic status, from the Roman period to the beginning of the second millennium, their cultural history is almost totally unknown. Many riddles accompanying the achievements of Gershom, Rashi, and the Tosafists might be brought closer to clarification and ultimate solution if we knew more about the local backgrounds of the men. Any information which might be obtained in regard to the local conditions which affected the work of these leaders, in their Jewish, as well as their non-Jewish, environment, is likely to prove helpful in two respects: it will not only help elucidate a very significant phase in the history of northern European Jewry but, at the same time, will shed new light on the life and work of the great leaders.

TROYES FAIRS

It is known that Rashi was born and bred in Troyes, Champagne. Whether or not he was born in 1040, it is generally agreed that he was a mature man before he left for Mayence and Worms, where he spent several years studying under the disciples of Gershom. He seems to have interrupted his stay in the Rhineland at least once to go back to his native city, [1] where, after the completion of his studies, he resided until the end of his life. The influence of the environment of Troyes on Rashi's career can, therefore, hardly be overestimated.

Ever since Berliner's basic studies on Rashi, much ado has been made over the importance of the fairs which were held twice a year

[*] Reprinted from *Rashi Anniversary Volume*, American Academy for Jewish Research [Texts and Studies, I] (New York, 1941), pp. 47–71.

in Troyes and which attracted a host of merchants from Italy and
Flanders, from Provence and the Rhineland. In his *Blicke in die
Geisteswerkstatt Raschis* in particular, Berliner assembled a great
many illustrations to show how the experiences gathered at such
fairs, and the contacts with merchants of many nations not only
broadened Rashi's intellectual horizon, but enabled him to offer a
number of new interpretations of biblical and talmudic passages. To
be sure, a great many of the passages adduced by Berliner in support of his thesis are inconclusive, dubious, or even positively contradictory. For example, his citation of Rashi's comment on Ezekiel
27:3: "Such was their custom: when merchants arrived there [in
Tyre] from the North and the South, they were not allowed to trade
with one another, but the inhabitants of the city bought from one
and sold to the other" as a supposed reflection of a contemporary
fair in Troyes [2] is anything but convincing. It is certainly not in the
nature of most fairs to restrict foreign traders and force them to deal
exclusively with natives. As a matter of fact, there was a progressive
liberalization of commercial relations during all Champagne fairs,
which alone served to attract traders from far-flung commercial
centers. Later on, some reformers actually demanded "free" fairs,
unencumbered by even the usual taxes and fees. Neither does Rashi's
comment on a talmudic passage reveal any familiarity with the
operation of fairs beyond the periodic local markets where craftsmen
as well as farmers offered their wares directly to the consumers. [3]
Berliner also failed to explain the fact that Rashi apparently nowhere
refers directly to a fair in his native city. The only reference to a
fair which has come to my attention in any of the works of Rashi
and his school pertains to the fair of Cologne. [4] Nevertheless,
Berliner's contentions have been taken over without qualification
by nearly all writers on Rashi.

A closer examination of the available sources reveals the precariousness of the hypothesis. From all we know there were no fairs
in Troyes during the lifetime of Rashi. A superficial reading of
Bourquelot's penetrating study of the Champagne fairs during the
twelfth to fourteenth centuries, which appeared in 1865, led Berliner
to the assumption that the fairs in Champagne had an unbroken
history from the Roman period on. Indeed, a fair at Troyes was mentioned as far back as 427, by Bishop Sidonius Apollinaris. However,
there is absolutely no further reference to a fair until 1114, nine
years after Rashi's death. Bourquelot could still assume that there

may have been some continuity between the two dates; but sub-sequent researches have shown that, while the document of 1114 shows that the fairs had been in existence for some time, it is not at all likely that they were established on a regular basis during the eleventh century. Subsequently, our records speedily multiply. Con-temporary sources contain about half a dozen references to Cham-pagne fairs between 1114 and 1140, while from the second half of the twelfth century a score or more of documentary passages speak of fairs at Troyes alone. [5] Of course, in view of the general paucity of early source materials, one may not draw definitive conclusions from the mere absence of contemporary records relating to fairs; but other indications fully confirm the impression that those gatherings of foreign sellers and buyers at stated periods were still, at best, in their incipient stages. We have quite a number of sources referring to Troyes in the eleventh century, all of which give the impression of a rural community living on viticulture and farming, with very little craftsmanship or commerce. To be sure, periodic large-scale markets could also be held in rural centers, as was indeed the case in both Langry and Bar-sur-Aube, which, next to Troyes and Provins, played the greatest role in the fairs of Champagne during the thirteenth century. But before one postulates any direct influence of experi-ences gathered at such meeting places for merchants from distant lands upon Rashi and his commentaries, one must build firmer foun-dations than such slim probabilities.

Incidentally, the influence of a particular local craft, which has also been made much of in connection with the extensive literary activity of the Christian as well as the Jewish intellectual leaders of Troyes, likewise appears questionable. It has been contended that the tanneries of Troyes were responsible for a considerable output of parchment, which enabled scholars to acquire writing materials at much lower prices than those prevailing in communities which had to import this product. [6] For anyone familiar with the high prices of Hebrew books in the northern lands even in later periods, [7] such a reasoning appears quite plausible. The trouble is that the first reference to a tannery in Troyes dates from 1189. In 1233–36 we hear of two mills, the so-called *grande tannerie* and *petite tannerie*, operating in the city. While the conclusion that a craft of this kind developed slowly over a period of decades appears legitimate, there is no evidence that tanning was engaged in to any considerable extent in the days of Rashi. In fact, a passage in one of Rashi's responsa, recorded by his disciple Simhah of Vitry, seems to indicate that the synagogue of Troyes had but a single copy of the maḥzor at its disposal, although ordinary prayerbooks for Saturday and New Moon services were more readily available to the public. [8] If one wished to push the economic interpretation of history to absurd lengths one might contend that Rashi's exemplary brevity in his comments was due to a shortage in writing materials, whereas his grandson, Samuel b. Meir, having at hand a much ampler supply from the growing local tanneries, was able to indulge in lengthy expositions in his continuation of the commentary on Baba Batra.

When one considers the role of the Jews in the settlement and economic life of Troyes, the doubts about Rashi's connections with the local fairs become even more pronounced. We have records of two synagogues erected in medieval Troyes. One was located in the older, lower section of the city, and was subsequently replaced by the church of St. Frobert. Around it clustered the Jewish quarter, the *juerie*, *juiverie*, or the *broce aux Juifs*. Another synagogue, built at the extreme west of the upper city and subsequently replaced by the church of St. Panthaléon, is first recorded in 1216. [9] We need not doubt the antiquity of the earlier settlement, since it seems to have been situated in the vicinity of the ancient Roman trade route, named after Agrippa, which, connecting Milan and Marseilles with the North Sea, ran through Troyes. As Robert Anchel has shown in a paper on the ghettos of Paris, [10] the early medieval Jewish settlements often stuck close to such Roman trade routes. The synagogue in the upper city, however, was evidently added at the time this section was built up, in the course of the twelfth and thirteenth centuries, in connection with the fairs which were held there. Now, it is remarkable that, in the numerous sources mentioning foreign (including Oriental) merchants and their permanent or temporary quarters in the upper city, there is no reference to any Jewish settlement in that section prior to the above-mentioned record of 1216.

From the economic standpoint, the extant reference to a double tax paid by Jewish visitors to a Champagne fair pertains not to Troyes but to Bar-sur-Aube in the thirteenth century. Other documents, referring to merchants, moneylenders, and even pawnbrokers active at the fairs of Troyes, fail to mention Jews at all until the 1180s. The extensive transfer, exchange, and credit transactions which so greatly facilitated international trade evidently were concentrated in the earlier period in the hands of Italian visitors, as well as of some native Frenchmen. About 1200, however, we suddenly get a succession of records indicating widespread banking activities by the local Jews. [11] It does not appear unlikely, therefore, that the entrance of the Jews into the large-scale credit operations, and perhaps into the significant mercantile activities, of the Troyes fairs really dates from their return to the city after a brief absence resulting from their expulsion by Philip Augustus in 1180. Having been uprooted from their normal occupations and, especially, having lost whatever hold they still may have had on agriculture, the Jews upon their return very likely concentrated upon commerce and banking to a much greater extent. Before that time, however, we hear merely of an early decision by Joseph Bonfils (Ṭob 'Elem) of Limoges referring to a tax imposed by the community of Troyes upon the vineyard of a female member, and of Rashi and most of his disciples likewise deriving their livelihood from work in the vineyards. Even Samuel b. Meir is recorded as having owned a herd of cattle, his brother Jacob Tam alone apparently having been engaged in money-lending and perhaps also serving in the semimercantile position of governmental tax farmer. [12] In short, while the participation of Jews in the Troyes fairs in the second half of the twelfth century appears very likely, it is more than questionable whether there were any large fairs at all in Troyes before 1105, and, if so, whether Jews took any significant part in them.

This is not to say that the Jews of even rural Troyes had had no commercial or other relations with the Jewries of other lands. Situated at the intersection of many important highways, Troyes seems to have long maintained contacts not only with neighboring Franco-German territories but also with Italy, and especially with the papal city of Rome. The distance of some five weeks' journey from Troyes to Milan seems to have discouraged neither commercial travelers nor pilgrims. It is no mere accident that the Senate of Rome in 1158 coined currency of a type used in Provins, the city second in importance only to Troyes in the fairs of Champagne—evidently for the use of Roman merchants. These contacts also explain the relationships which indubitably existed between the schools of Gershom and Rashi, on the one hand, and the sages of Rome, on the other. One need not discount even the tradition that one of Rashi's teachers, Isaac b. Judah of Mayence, himself apparently a northern French Jew, had visited Rome. Moreover, just as Nathan b. Yeḥiel, the distinguished author of the 'Arukh, was thoroughly familiar with the exegetical work on the Talmud produced by the school of Mayence, and often cited Gershom by name, so Rashi was in a position to consult some manuscript comments on the Talmud assembled in Rome and known to him as the פירוש רומי or קונטרס רומי. While the 'Arukh as such seems to have remained unknown to Rashi (whose disciples, however, quoted it on more than one occasion), Rashi seems nevertheless to have maintained some contacts with its author, the recognized leader of the community of Rome. According to the testimony of Isaac Or Zaru'a and others, he even addressed several inquiries to Nathan and his brothers. By Rome's steady connections with the flourishing communities of Palestine, Egypt, and Kairuwan, the cultural isolation of both Champagne and Rhenish Jewry was greatly mitigated. [13]

SYNODS

The problem of the Troyes fairs may have much broader implications, especially with respect to the much-debated question of the medieval Jewish synods. The oft-heard contention that such gatherings of rabbis and laymen took place for the most part in connection with fairs, a contention undoubtedly prompted by observation of the impact of fairs upon the early meetings of the Council of Four Lands in Poland, seems justified with respect to the gatherings in Troyes under the leadership of the brothers Samuel and Jacob b. Meir in the second half of the twelfth century. In fact, Mordecai b. Hillel, in explaining a synodal regulation which prohibited the raising of objections to a writ of divorce after it had been properly handed to a wife, positively ascribed its authorship to Jacob Tam, his disciple Moses (of Pontoise), and other leaders, who had adopted it "in their gathering at the Troyes fair." [14] To be sure, the most important of these councils, meeting in Troyes in 1150–60, included representative rabbis from a fairly large area in northern France, but none from the Rhineland. Neither is it certain that all the districts enumerated were actually represented, since the four original signatories merely indicated the adoption of resolutions with a view to their subsequent acceptance by many of those who could not attend the meeting. Nevertheless, there is little doubt that many scholars were prompted to come, if not for the direct purpose of transacting business, at least in order to take advantage of the facilities and security of travel, and of the freedom of sojourn granted to strangers during the fairs. [15]

While the traditional view ascribing a synodal character to the ordinances issued in the name of Tam and his associates thus appears reinforced by the gradual development of the Troyes fairs after 1114, the doubts voiced concerning any synodal activity before Tam's generation seem equally justified. The documentary evidence in favor of Rashi's activities as a leader of a synod has, from the outset, been extremely weak. Even if we take Meir of Rothenburg's word that the text which he represents was "copied from R. Solomon of Troyes"—and there seems to be no valid reason for doubting it—the formulation "we the inhabitants of Troyes, together with the communities of its environs have decided . . ." is far from an indication of a synodal gathering. Whether or not we stress the term *kehillot* as representing full-fledged communities, rather than settlements dependent on Troyes, the decision here adopted seems to have had a decidedly local character. It is not at all unlikely that the community of Troyes, not only close to the seat of government but also in control of a cemetery of its own (which was finally disposed of in 1306), exercised some sort of jurisdiction over the surrounding area, which had more isolated Jewish settlers. In this case, the gathering presided over by Rashi would have resembled merely one of those regional gatherings which later became customary in fiscal matters, particularly between main and dependent communities of the Spanish *colectas,* or between the Polish *kahals* and their *przykahałki.* It is noteworthy that the Troyes gathering, too, was concerned primarily with various aspects of Jewish taxation. [16]

Another consideration, however insufficient in itself, adds force to this interpretation. It has long been suspected that the extensive synodal activity of Franco-German Jewry, which so obviously marked a complete departure from the long-established practice of the Mediterranean communities, owed its origin to the example set by the provincial councils of the Church. It may be worthy of mention that Troyes, long before 1150, had been the seat of several important gatherings of churchmen. Some of these councils had actually been called by the pope himself, were presided over either by him or by a papal legate, and counted among their participants several archbishops and many distinguished bishops, monks, and lay leaders. It is probably no accident that the first of these important councils took place in 1104, when, according to the above-mentioned document dated ten years later, some sort of fair had probably been established in the city. The council of 1104 was speedily followed by one in 1105 or 1106, and another in 1107, which, though not mentioning Jews at all, may have had some bearing upon the Jewish community, inasmuch as one of the main subjects of deliberation consisted in measures to be taken against the frequent disturbers of the "peace." While we have no direct documentary evidence that the Jews of Champagne enjoyed a protection similar to that extended to German Jewry by the *Landfrieden* agreed upon in 1103 by Henry IV and the German princes, the likelihood that they, too, benefited from a more efficient enforcement of any regional "truce" is very great, indeed. [17] Be this as it may, the stimulus given by the councils of Troyes, which assembled frequently during the following decades, to Jacob Tam and his associates to convoke a similar gathering of Jewish leaders seems rather obvious. No such local stimulus existed in the days of Rashi, however, unless it was in the very last year of his life.

SIZE OF THE COMMUNITY

From all we know, therefore, Rashi was the leader of a predominantly rural Jewish community, whose influence beyond the borders of the town was based partly upon its incipient commercial relations with more distant localities, partly upon the centralized power of the counts of Champagne residing in their Troyes castle, and, most of all, to Rashi's own intellectual preeminence. The community must have been very small, Rashi evidently serving as the principal spokesman by virtue of his learning, rather than by that of any recognized position. All data thus far assembled for the northern French communities, even in the twelfth and thirteenth centuries, clearly indicate that hardly any of them embraced much more than 100 families. Most of the larger settlements had a Jewish population of no more than 100 to 500 souls. [18] Rashi may actually have had no more than 100 to 200 Jewish fellow-citizens. After all, Troyes itself, although designated by a writer in 1188 as a "populous city, replete with fortune," probably did not have at that time more than 10,000 inhabitants. [19] A century earlier, the number must have been considerably smaller; and a community of 100 to 200 Jews by no means would have played an insignificant role in the city. We may visualize this tiny settlement as consisting of persons living in close quarters around their synagogue and constantly marrying among themselves. What Jacob Tam tells of the equally significant community of Orléans several decades later, namely, that, with the exception of the rabbi, all its Jews were related to one another by blood or by marriage, [20] undoubtedly also applied to the community over which Rashi presided. This constant mingling, incidentally, explains to us the otherwise strange phenomenon that almost all of Rashi's disciples and friends recorded in the sources appear to have been related to him in some degree or other.

The small size of the community makes it doubly likely that Rashi's leadership was nonprofessional, whether or not he served as the actual head of the community, as did his contemporaries Solomon b. Samson of Worms and Judah b. Kalonymos of Spires, recorded as the recipients of Henry IV's famous privileges of 1090. We merely have the intimation that, probably in his youth, he had been the tutor of one Joseph the son of Isaac, the local *parnas*. Neither are we aware of any scholarly attainments of the powerful leader Abraham (before 1210) and "Master" Jacob (in the 1220s) recorded in the annals of the community of Troyes. [21] The renowned academy, too, over which Rashi presided, need not have resembled in its externals any of the later regular Jewish institutions of higher learning. We may simply envisage Solomon Yiṣḥaḳi as the owner of a vineyard, which he cultivated with the assistance of his family, spending most of his free time—vineyards may allow for a good deal of free time—teaching a few pupils, mostly members of his own family, discussing with them the fine points in Bible and Talmud, and, perhaps with their assistance, compiling and revising his bulky commentaries. It is astounding with what vigor such a tiny community managed to pursue its independent intellectual career and spread its cultural influence over a vast area of northern France and western Germany.

The small size of the communities may help explain a number of legal decisions by Rashi, his contemporaries, and his disciples. For instance, an often-quoted responsum, referring to an occurrence in Mayence in 1093, clearly reflects this situation. The inquirers were deeply perplexed by the problem of accommodating two bridegrooms who happened to be *kohanim* and were to be called to the Torah on the same Sabbath. Not only does the inquiry seem to indicate that Mayence, one of the largest, if not the largest, Jewish community in Germany at the time, did not possess more than one synagogue, but it also shows that, because of the small population, no precedent was known to have been established for such an occasion. [22] Similarly, if Rashi or one of his disciples decided that a congregation which had no competent adult reader could entrust the leading of services to any boy aged thirteen and one day, such a decision is not so much proof of the low intellectual level of most of the congregations as it is of their small number. [23] Even a few decades later, Tam and his associates felt impelled to ordain (or at least to renew an ordinance attributed to Gershom) that "if there is exactly a quorum of ten in the synagogue and the reader begins to pray, none of those present may leave the congregation until the reader completes his service." The importance attached to this decision, which is placed at the head of a series of twenty-six ordinances in one of the recensions of the *Takkanot* of R. Tam, can be explained only by the frequency of such limited attendance. [24]

HEREM HA-YISHUB

If we thus visualize the Jewish community of Troyes, like the other contemporary communities, largely as a closed family group, we may better comprehend the significance of the regulations concerning admission of new members. It has long been recognized that the *herem ha-yishub* (later developing into the *hezkat ha-yishub*), which enabled local communities to determine whether and under what conditions they wished to admit newcomers, was the outgrowth of the prevailing economic regimentation. [25] The inbred familial relationships underlying some of these communities, however, must likewise have played a considerable part in shaping these communal ordinances. The author of the *Book of the Pious* (Nos. 1301, 1600, for instance) writes, in a typically medieval vein, that a Jewish settlement composed "of many families or of people hailing from different localities" is likely to reveal so many social and cultural weaknesses as to discourage a pious arrival from choosing it as a permanent residence. [26] A closer investigation of the available early sources, on the other hand, shows that this trend was not altogether uniform. One may perhaps contend that, generally, communities living under a more restricted or, at least, stable economy would be more likely to reveal antialien tendencies than those tending toward economic expansion and growing prosperity. This apparent correlation may also be illustrated by some of Rashi's teachings, as compared with those of his immediate predecessors and successors.

The origin of the *herem ha-yishub* in the northern countries has usually been ascribed to Gershom and his disciples in both France and Germany. While the sources concerning Gershom's enactment appear highly dubious, [27] there is some historical justification for attributing to Gershom some sort of initiative toward restrictive legislation in the Rhine districts. Such is not the case, however, with Rashi and his disciples, living under the different political and economic conditions of the Champagne communities. This difference may clearly be perceived in their respective attitudes to the main talmudic basis for the *herem ha-yishub;* viz., the discussion in Baba Batra 21b, where two Babylonian teachers, both named Huna, oppose the liberal legislation of the Palestinian Tannaim with wholly or partly restrictive interpretations. Their reasons are fairly obvious. The Tannaim, living under the semicapitalist civilization of the early Roman Empire, where changes of residence were extremely frequent and not often interfered with by law, had little incentive for making provisions against the settlement of new members competing occupationally with natives. Under the semifeudal civilization of Persia, however, the Babylonian rabbis, however highly they may have valued the precedents set by their Palestinian predecessors, were forced to enact a number of new, anticompetitive regulations which they thereafter sought to reconcile with the unequivocal utterances of the Tannaim. It was particularly the view expressed by R. Huna the son of R. Joshua, who as the *Amora* of a later generation is evidently cited with approval by the redactors of the Talmud, which greatly influenced the medieval rabbis. Says R. Huna:

It is quite clear to me that the resident of one town can prevent the resident of another locality [from setting up competition in his town]—not, however, if he pays taxes to that town—and that the resident of an alley cannot prevent [competition from] another resident of the same alley. R. Huna the son of R. Joshua then raised the question: Can the resident of one alley prevent the resident of another [from competing with him]?—This must stand over [and remain unanswered].

Around the qualifying phrase "if he pays taxes to that town . . . cannot prevent" (ואי שייך בכרנא דהכא לא מצו מעכב) centered the main subsequent discussions. In the commentary attributed to Gershom, which, though composed largely by his disciple Eliakim ha-Levi, reflects Gershom's opinions to a great extent, this phrase is translated as referring to men who "pay their poll tax to the same master," and who, consequently, may not be prevented from settling in the community. [28] If this passage reflects the genuine view of Gershom, we can see how, by way of interpretation, he had thus succeeded in insinuating into talmudic law the basic concept of the *herem ha-yishub*. It is obvious that this could not have been the meaning of the original passage, since Babylonia and the rest of Persia were under the domination of the same Sassanian king, to whom all Jewish subjects paid the poll tax. A regulation opening settlement to Jews from all over the Iranian plateau and Babylonia, and keeping out perhaps only new arrivals from the Roman Empire —however numerous those may have been at times—would have had little bearing upon the main purpose of preventing excessive competition. Whether merely unhistorical or biased, the author of the passage in "Gershom's" commentary, facing entirely different conditions, gave the talmudic statement a new, highly restrictive meaning by limiting the free admission of new members to the Jewish community of Mayence to such Jews as were paying taxes to the same sovereign (namely, the archbishop of Mayence). Since throughout the eleventh century the archbishopric had few Jewish subjects outside the community of the capital, this interpretation enabled the communal elders to keep out undesirable Jews arriving from practically any community outside of Mayence. To all intents and purposes, we have here a rationale giving free rein to the operation of the principle underlying the *herem ha-yishub* and granting the local or regional community full discretion in the admission or non-admission of new members.

Curiously, Rashi, by literally adhering to this interpretation of the school of Gershom, could, under the conditions of the community in which he lived, lend it a much more liberal meaning. In his *Commentary* on the passage, he gives exactly the same interpretation; viz., that men ready to pay the capitation tax to the "sovereign of that city" cannot be refused admission. [29] It so happens that Troyes was the capital of a rather large area dominated by the counts of Champagne. The number of Jewish settlements even under the sovereignty of Thibaut I (1048–*ca.* 1089) or Hugh (1093–1125), contemporaries of Rashi, must have been considerable. One need recall merely that the counts of Champagne at one time could have accepted, if they had wanted, the crown of England and Normandy to realize that Rashi, though technically adhering to the Rhenish interpretation, was giving the rabbinic law a much more liberal turn.

With the further expansion of the Jewish as well as the general urban population of northeastern France during the twelfth century, even these shackles were felt to be undesirable. The complexities caused by the operation of the *ḥerem ha-yishub* were such as to induce the teachers of Paris in 1130 to inquire of the Roman authorities (חכמי רומא) how to interpret the meaning of the ban in a specific case. The Roman rabbis legitimately expressed their astonishment at the "request that we take sides in a matter which, not being customary in our country, is unfamiliar to us." [30] Equally puzzling to the local administrators was a case later submitted to Jacob Tam. A member of an unnamed community had brought a teacher for his children from another locality. After five years they began quarreling, and the employer wished to compel the tutor not only to leave his house but also to give up his residence in that community. The tutor's reply clearly shows the complications arising from an as yet unsettled legal theory and practice. Said the tutor:

Thou hast not established the settlement, others have done it and have resided here before thee, which may be proved by numerous witnesses. Secondly, when thou didst bring me with thee thou gavest me the authorization and the power of *ḥazaḳah* to stay here forever. Thirdly, what greater rights hast thou in this settlement than I? There exists no ban in this settlement on anyone wishing to establish his residence here. Moreover, I belong to one of the best families in this country, whereas thou and thy father are newcomers with us here. Finally, I have lived here and established the right of sojourn over several years of *ḥazaḳah*.

The tutor's arguments found receptive ears among the communal leaders, but the power of the master and his influence with non-Jewish authorities were so great that the tutor had to agree "voluntarily" to leave the community for a stipulated period of time. Upon his return, before the period had expired, the controversy broke out afresh. Tam's reply, unfortunately, does not go into the merits of the original litigation, but merely tries to decide the question of whether the tutor's voluntary departure was contrary to a regular judgment by a qualified court. [31] Nevertheless, Tam's own opinion in the matter, once more with reference to the statement of R. Huna the son of R. Joshua, is given to us on the unimpeachable authority of one of his students. Going far beyond his grandfather, Tam wished to limit the right of the community to excluding only such newcomers as "are powerful, and denounce their brethren to Gentiles, or else refuse to assume their share in the tax burden of the community." [32] Evidently, only the second part is an interpretation of the ואי שייך בכרנא, the first merely being in line with the general endeavor of Tam and his associates to restrict the interference of Gentile authorities in the internal affairs of the Jewish community. His interpretation of the talmudic passage is so wide, however, as practically to nullify the entire restriction. It may readily be assumed that, with very few exceptions, newcomers were prepared to share in the fiscal burdens of the community in which they were going to settle permanently.

In the light of this decision by the French rabbis, reinforced by similar "liberal" interpretations by Spanish rabbis (especially Ibn Megas) living under the equally expansive civilization of the early Arab caliphates, the later German rabbis, such as Eliezer b. Joel ha-Levi, had to give up invoking the original talmudic source and restrict the validity of such regulation to the authority of a local communal ordinance or ban. Hence comes also their uniform use of the term *herem ha-yishub*, reflecting an innovation, rather than a continuity of talmudic tradition. [33]

This liberal trend in the leadership of the Jewish communities of Champagne was undoubtedly strengthened by the generally favorable political status of Champagne Jewry in the twelfth and early thirteenth centuries. It was especially in Troyes that the counts took a direct interest in their Jewish subjects and frequently extended immediate protection to them. The following curious incident of 1221 may serve as an illustration. A Jewish moneylender joined with several Italians to lend the substantial sum of 29,174 pounds to Countess Joan of Flanders for the ransom of her captive husband. To ensure the repayment of this sum, increased by some 5,500 pounds in interest, the counts of Champagne threatened to exclude all of Joan's subjects from their fairs in the case of default. [34] Even at a time when they, unlike most of their feudal confreres, embarked of their own free will upon a policy of extending the municipal autonomy of the burghers, which indeed was one of the contributory factors in the growing prosperity of the Champagne cities, they refused to subordinate the Jews to the burgesses. As late as 1230, in the famous privileges granted to the cities of Troyes and Provins, the Jews were specifically exempted from municipal jurisdiction, along with ecclesiastics, noblemen, and the counts' vassals. [35] The counts, on more than one occasion, also defended the Jews vigorously against the Church, sometimes provoking the wrath of the popes, such as Innocent III. On one occasion, Countess Blanche engaged in a protracted controversy on this score with local churchmen, who placed Troyes under an interdict; whereupon she appealed to Honorius III, who acknowledged the countess' right to act as she did in behalf of her Jews. [36] Moreover, the Jews appeared so precious to the counts and their neighbors that Blanche actually took over, for a sum of money, the Jewish subjects of the master of Ervy together with his other possessions (1214). [37] She, as well as other rulers, concluded treaties with the kings of France and many of their neighbors which provided that Jews who moved from one sovereignty to another be returned to their previous masters. Such treaties are recorded in rapid succession in 1198, 1201, 1207, 1210, 1218, 1224, 1228, etc. As a matter of fact, when the rich Jew Cresselin of Provins settled in the royal domain, he was forced by the king to return to Champagne. [38] Under such conditions, when every Jewish newcomer was considered an acquisition and apparently was welcomed with open arms by the various sovereigns, the Jewish communities could not really think of enforcing any restrictive bans on settlement. On the contrary, the Tosafists prided themselves on the fact that throughout Burgundy—and Troyes, though a fief in the hands of the counts of Champagne, technically belonged to that realm—the Jews, "like the nobles," could freely choose their residence, and that their rulers could not legally seize the property of even those Jews who had decided to move on to another locality. [39]

Like their overlords, the Jews themselves seemed much concerned with the effects upon the communal tax structure of the recurrent flights of capital and the emigration of wealthy members. The above-mentioned Troyes ordinance, said to have been promulgated under the leadership of Rashi, apart from defining the various possessions subject, in full or in part, to the communal property tax, specifically exempted temporary residents, insofar as they did not use the capital which they had brought in for business purposes. At the same time, capital given to children of residents for the purpose of trading elsewhere without giving up their residence was to be fully included in the tax computation. [40] Even this limitation, however, was a far cry from the complete prohibition of capital export which often served as the counterpart to the more rigid application of antialien laws. It was only under the different conditions of medieval Germany, with its steadily shrinking economic base for Jews, that the *herem ha-yishub* became a highly significant instrument of communal control over population movements and economic activities.

IO

"Plenitude of Apostolic Powers" and Medieval "Jewish Serfdom"[*]

THE QUESTION of "Jewish serfdom" (*servitus Judaeorum*) has occupied historians, both Jewish and non-Jewish, for decades. In Germany, especially, the Jews' status as "serfs of the Chamber" (*servi camerae*) exerted a tremendous influence on their political and cultural development until the nineteenth century. Among the important scholars who have investigated this problem is Fritz Baer, who treated the subject in the course of extensive studies. [1] I have also expressed my own views in my work on the history of the Jews in the Middle Ages. [2] In the last forty years, Guido Kisch has delved into the problem, endeavoring to trace in detail the development of the institution in Germany from the standpoint of general German law. [3] Nonetheless, many fundamental questions have remained unanswered, and one is justified, it seems to me, in devoting further attention to the problem in the light of present historical data. Much can be learned from a comparison of the development of the principle of "plenitude of apostolic powers" (*plenitudo potestatis apostolicae*) with the growth of the concept of "Jewish serfdom." [4]

THE VIEW OF THE CATHOLIC CHURCH

It is generally agreed that the phrase "serfs of the Chamber" first appears in the laws of Frederick II concerning the Jews of Sicily and Germany in the 1230s. However, the general subjection of Jews to their European rulers, and their particular relationship to the treasuries of the various countries, including Germany, are clearly indicated in many legal codes of the twelfth century and earlier. [5] The main question, therefore, is what prompted Frederick II to alter the accepted terminology, and how did this affect the legal status of German Jewry and perhaps that of other European-Jewish communities.

[*] Translated from the Hebrew essay in *Yitzhak F. Baer Jubilee Volume* (Jerusalem, 1960), pp. 102–24.

I believe that these changes can be best explained by the great crisis in the relations between Church and state, or between the Papacy and Empire, which reached its climax during the thirteenth century. Ever since Selig Cassel published his famous article on the Jews, in Ersch and Gruber's *Allgemeine Encyklopädie der Wissenschaften,* [6] scholars have realized the connection between the Church's historical explanation of the status of the Jewish Diaspora in the Christian world and the political concept of the Jews' serfdom to their rulers. It can be demonstrated, however, that it was the great debate about the relationship between the state and the priesthood (*regnum et sacerdotium*)—a debate conducted from the end of the twelfth century onward—together with the *realpolitik* behind this debate, which prompted new concepts of Jewish serfdom and opposing claims by European rulers as to the nature of their control over their Jewish subjects.

Among the various views expressed during that period, the position of the leaders of the Church was the simplest and the most traditional, although it, too, has recently received new interpretations. The classic form of this fundamental view had already been expressed by the Church Fathers during the Roman period, especially by Augustine. Essentially their view was in agreement with the Jewish opinion that the Jews were sentenced to exile and a life of servitude under foreign rule because of the sins of their ancestors. [7] The basic difference is that the Church emphasized one particular sin of the early Jews; namely, their rejection of Jesus as the messiah and their participation in his crucifixion.

Indeed, the weak political position of the Jews of the Diaspora, and their serfdom under foreign rule, served as proof positive in Christian apologetics that the scepter had departed from Judea upon the arrival of Shiloh (i.e., Jesus) and that thenceforth Isaac's blessing of Jacob, "the elder shall serve the younger" (Gen. 25:23), had been fulfilled, in that Israel, the firstborn, was enslaved to its younger brother, Christianity. Ever since Tertullian, the hermeneutic commentaries had included a homily about the relationship between Cain and Abel. Cain was regarded as symbolic of the Jewish people, who, because their sacrifice was not accepted, slew their younger brother, Jesus, whose sacrifice God had accepted. It was therefore decreed that "Cain" would wander until the end of days, or until the second advent of the Christian messiah.

From these beginnings developed the reigning view about the

Jewish people in the Diaspora, a view reflected in the opinions of their Christian neighbors in the Middle Ages. At first this view was accepted in theory but did not affect the Jews' legal status. In the Roman Empire, the Jews were not "serfs," at least no more than others who lived under the rule of this absolutist "evil kingdom." Even when the Christian emperors increasingly limited Jewish rights, and finally removed the Jews from every military and governmental post, the Jews' official status was still that of citizens of the Empire, essentially possessed of equal privileges, albeit limited in certain specific instances, with other citizens. When the Church attempted to act beyond its powers and compel the state to permit mobs to destroy Jewish synagogues in many places, it precipitated the famous split, in 398, between the powerful Bishop Ambrose of Milan and the Emperor Theodosius, although the latter was certainly not a friend of Jews. This split was a harbinger of the dangers that would face the Jewish people as a result of the constant friction between religious and political forces during the later Middle Ages. [8] But Jewish "serfdom" during the early Middle Ages was essentially a theologico-spiritual concept—as it was among the Jewish sages (as exemplified by Mar Samuel's famous remark that the Jews' enslavement to various governments would last until messianic times)— not a political or legal one.

It seems that the earliest efforts to introduce legal action against the Jews as a result of this general view were made in Visigothic Spain and in southern France in the seventh century. It was especially in the Church synods convened from time to time in the Spanish capital, Toledo, as political parliaments at the king's direction, that the problem of the Jews and their legal status was discussed from various points of view. After many unsuccessful attempts to compel the Jews to convert, and to ensure proper Catholic behavior on the part of secret Jews, the Seventeenth Toledan Council, which was convened in 694 with the participation of King Egica, decided to hand over all obstinate Jews as serfs to Christian masters who would obligate themselves to supervise their true Christian conduct. Since the Church authorities were not sure of the adults' complete conversion—even under these severe conditions—they decided, in addition, to seize all Jewish children above the age of seven and house them with reliable Christian families or in monasteries, and, in the future, to permit them to marry only pure Christians. To justify this cruel edict, the principle of "perpetual serfdom" (*perpetuae subiectae servituti*) was enunciated, a principle that was to be mentioned in later writings. [9] It must be noted, however, that the 694 edict was an unusual one. The Jews of Spain were punished then not primarily as disobedient serfs of the king or the Church but as traitors to their new faith. The decision of this synod is therefore to be considered an expedient for punishing wrongdoers rather than a permanent form of legislation with respect to all Jews living in Christian countries.

At first these persecutions did not exert a strong effect upon the central Church's attitude to the Jews; they began to be felt only when the Papacy extended its influence beyond Rome toward the entire Christian world. From the time of Gregory VII on, the political demands of the Church grew ever stronger. Its supporters among the jurists and statesmen of the twelfth and thirteenth centuries began to enunciate the principle that two swords, one temporal and the other spiritual, had been entrusted to the pope, but that he had voluntarily relinquished the temporal sword to the German emperor. This view was officially sanctioned in the bull *Unam sanctam* by Pope Boniface VIII in 1302.[10]

In these circumstances it was inevitable that the Papacy concern itself with the Jewish problem, which by its very nature was international in scope. For a considerable period, the central Church limited its activities to decisions, favorable or otherwise, in cases regarding Jews; as had been true of Gregory I. When Leo VII was asked by Archbishop Frederick of Mayence in 937–38 whether it was preferable to force Jews into conversion or exile, he permitted exile but categorically prohibited forced baptism. On the other hand, when several communities in France were subjected to harsh edicts, they sent their representative, Jacob b. Yekutiel, to Rome with a request for protection. Sometimes individuals, too, turned to the heads of the Church for favorable intercession with local rulers, especially bishops or other Church officials. Of their own accord the popes did not as yet interfere in the states' internal affairs, and kept silent even in the period of critical relations between Jews and Christians during the First Crusade. At best they began to extend, through their famous bull *Sicut Judaeis*, direct protection only to their Jewish subjects in Rome; the first pope to do so was Calixtus II. This bull became the cornerstone of the political and social structure of Jewish communities under the rule of the popes. [11]

However, as early as Pope Gregory VII's time a new approach can be discerned. When Gregory convoked a synod of Church elders in 1078 to discuss basic hierarchical regulations, the Jewish problem was brought to his attention. Among the synod's resolutions there appears one against the appointment of Jewish officials in Christian countries. While this resolution, *de Judaeis non praepondendis Christianis*, was a carry-over from previous generations, its announcement as a fundamental part of the great reform of the Church undoubtedly created a strong impression. This impression was strengthened three years later, when Gregory protested appointments of Jewish officials in Castile and Leon; in his letters to King Alphonso VI, he vehemently objected to such appointments, which in his opinion, would cause a submission of "God's Church" to "Satan's Synagogue." [12]

From that time on, the popes had no hesitation about issuing edicts in favor of the Church throughout the Christian world. Before the Second Crusade, the same Eugenius III who had renewed the bull *Sicut Judaeis* to protect the Jews decreed that Crusaders were not obliged to repay debts to Jewish lenders until they returned safely from their expedition. Now the popes decided to convoke several international assemblies in order to enact basic regulations for the entire Western Christian world. It is not surprising, therefore, that the Jews were fearful when they heard of the calls for councils to meet at the Lateran Palace in 1122, 1139, and 1179. According to Shem-Ṭob Sonzolo:

In the year 139 the Pope assembled all of his bishops from France and Spain [the reference is apparently to the Second Lateran Council of 1139] and all the Jewish communities were terrified. They fasted for three consecutive days. God showed them favor, however, and they [the members of the Council] spoke only kindly words about the Jews. [13]

Not so with the Third Lateran Council of 1179. Pope Alexander III, who presided, was not a Jew-hater. He not only renewed the *Sicut* bull but, according to the testimony of Benjamin of Tudela, paid no attention to the prohibition against Jewish officials, and appointed Yehiel, the grandson of R. Nathan (author of the *'Arukh*), to a governmental position. Nevertheless, the Council expressly prohibited the employment of Christian maids and nurses, excommunicated those who disobeyed this decree and lived in Jewish houses, encouraged the testimony of Christian witnesses against Jewish litigants, and ensured that Jewish converts would suffer no financial loss because of conversion. [14]

The Lateran Council employed expressions which reflected the new trends in ecclesiastical circles. In discussing the prohibition against preferring Jews to Christians as witnesses or in other matters, it stated the principle that "it is proper that they [the Jews] be subject to the Christians" (*eos subjacere Christianis opporteat*). The decision with regard to converts' property is also interesting. Many rulers basically objected to the conversion of their Jewish subjects because of the resultant loss to the royal treasury, which controlled Jewish property. Now the Council ruled that Christianity takes precedence over the demands of royal treasuries, and that in such cases the fate of Jewish property must depend upon the Church's wishes rather than on those of the kings. This was the logical outcome of the teaching that the serfdom of the Jews was a punishment for their "revolt" against Jesus Christ. However, while in 1146 Bernard of Clairvaux had taught that, on account of this sin, the Jews were dispersed among the nations and "suffer from harsh servitude under the Christian kings" (*duram sustinent captivitatem sub principibus Christianis*), i.e., that the kings are their masters,[15] the Church now began to demand that higher than the sovereignty of the various kings over the Jews shall be the universal hegemony of the Church.

This view reached a climax in the second half of the thirteenth century, during the reign of the powerful Popes Innocent III, Gregory IX, and Innocent IV. That period saw a renewal in Western Europe of ancient Roman law as well as of Aristotle's teachings. Under these influences, the canon jurists and, later, the popes themselves—many of whom had been trained in the revived Roman law—began to extend the meaning of the law of "plenitude of apostolic powers" to include not only unlimited control over all spiritual matters but also more-or-less direct control over all political problems. The lines of demarcation between these two areas were essentially blurred. Since the popes had the power to intervene in all matters relating to sin (*ratione peccati*), marriage, and justice, there was in effect no area about which they could not express an opinion if they so desired. Accordingly, Pope Innocent III claimed the right to abrogate the English Magna Carta, insisting that the king had been forced to sign it; to intervene in the election of the German emperor because he thought he had the right to investigate a candidate's ethics; and even to demand of the king of France a justification of his disagreements with the king of England. "The Church (i.e., the Christian world) is one body," wrote Alanus, an English jurist of that time, "and it is fitting that it have but one head [namely, the pope]." Innocent III himself announced this principle in one of his epistles, stating that "full apostolic sovereignty extends far and wide . . . to the ends of the earth." This view deepened in succeeding decades until the jurist Guillaume Durand publicly stated that the pope was "Peter's heir and Jesus Christ's vicar and thus the representative on earth not of man but of God . . . and accordingly sovereign of all, with the power of decree over all, according to his will." [16]

This extremist teaching was inevitably reflected in the popes' attitude toward the status of the Jews of Europe in general and their "serfdom" to their rulers in particular. The heads of the Church increasingly deemed it their privilege and obligation to establish international standards for the status of Jewish communities in the countries of their dispersion and to bring them under the authority of the Universal Church. Several months after his election, Innocent III issued a call to the churchmen of France, England, Hungary, and Sicily, urging them to influence their governments in favor of the Crusaders, not only to allow the warriors to postpone payment of their debts to Jews until they returned home but to compel Jews to return any interest which had been collected. The pope "commanded" (*precipimus*) the kings and the other temporal officers to carry out this order. In addition, he revalidated all the existing prohibitions on the employment of Jews in government service, on the employment of Christians as servants or nursemaids in Jewish homes, and on other social relations between the two faiths. With great force he sought to compel all Christian kings to ensure that the tithe which was in principle due the priests from all the inhabitants would be paid. The Jews had not previously been required to support the Church, but the pope now demanded that they pay the tithe from those properties and estates which had once belonged to tithe-paying Christians. Innocent was aware of the fact that he was thus interfering in a purely political matter, since it was the king's privilege to collect taxes from his Jewish subjects, all of whose wealth had been considered as belonging to him. In answer to an inquiry from Bishop William of Auxerre in 1207, Innocent stated that "the ruler must be convinced most emphatically that he must compel them [the Jews] to pay this tax, in view of his sovereignty, which was given to him [by God]." More novel was the decision of the Fourth Lateran Council (1215), headed by Innocent, to introduce—for the first time in the Western world—a comprehensive plan for separating Jews and Muslims from faithful Christians. This, of course, gave the Papacy an added opportunity to intervene in internal affairs in the area of daily living. On the other hand, the renewal, in the second year of his reign, of the *Sicut* bull, which was favorable to the Jews, also opened the way to all kinds of ecclesiastical intervention in internal affairs. He threatened Christians, especially the various officials, that "whoever dares to disobey this decree although he understands its purpose will suffer the loss of his post or will be excommunicated." Basic to these decrees was the realization that the principle of "plenitude of apostolic powers" gave the pope the ultimate right to supervise the status of Jews in the Christian world. While he needs them as witnesses to the truth of the Christian tradition, they are his "eternal serfs." In an epistle to the king of France in 1205, for example, the pope protested against those rulers "who place Jewish serfdom above the liberty of those who were freed by the Son of God, as if it were possible or desirable that the son of the handmaiden should inherit together with the son of the free mother." In the same year he wrote to Peter of Corbeille, archbishop of Sens and his former teacher, that the Jews, "because of their guilt in crucifying Jesus, were sentenced to eternal serfdom" (*quos propria culpa submisit perpetue servituti cum Dominum crucifiverint*). The pope thus hinted that, just as the Jews' sin was directed against the Church, their punishment was that they be enslaved forever to the Church and to its head, the pope. [17]

This view did not change under Innocent's successor, Honorius III. Since he was old and weak, he followed in the footsteps of his energetic predecessor and repeated his decrees without alteration. On the other hand, Honorius' successor, Gregory IX, was an ardent warrior in behalf of the Church's privileges and its international status. Although he was eighty when he ascended the papal throne, he continued, with even greater force, the imperialist policies of Innocent III, who had been his guide. His drawn-out battle against the famous Hohenstaufen dynasty and against its mighty head Frederick II helped to clarify the basis of the old struggle between Church and state and, at the same time, to crystallize the attitude of both to the Jewish problem.

Gregory emphasized Jewish serfdom more forcefully and more frequently than had his predecessors. His arrows were directed especially against Germany and Sicily, where his chief rival ruled. In an epistle to the German Church on March 5, 1233, he attacked the "arrogance" of the Jews of the Empire, who, in his opinion, not only held important public offices and dressed like their neighbors but also dared to mock Christianity publicly.

Neglecting to thank us for all the kindness we have shown them, the Jews return insult for goodness and reward our kind attitude with sinful scorn—they with whom we have dealt kindly because of our sense of mercy, they who should have realized that the yoke of eternal servitude was punishment for their guilt [*sue debere agnoscere jugum ex culpa propria perpetue servitutis*].

The pope demanded that the German bishops and priests, either with the aid of the temporal rulers or by the threat of excommunicating the Christian parties, prevent Jews from debating religious matters with Christians, "so that they will never lift their heads which are bent under the yoke of eternal servitude." About two months later the pope again employed the same expression—*Judei quos propria culpa submisit perpetue servituti*—in the opening of his epistle to Archbishop Bernard of Santiago de Compostela in Spain. In this letter he complained about the appointment of Jewish officials and about the Jews' usurious practices in Castile and Leon, and ordered Bernard to influence King Ferdinand III "to lower the pride of the unbelieving Jews and make them live in constant fear as slaves who suffer for their shameful sin" (*sed sub timore servili pretendant semper verecundiam culpe sue*). Gregory lifted the Latin sentences quoted here directly from Innocent III's letter to the archbishop of Sens on July 15, 1205. At the same time, he ordered the priests of France to protect the Jews against physical oppression and robbery by the officers of the various sections of this feudal country, "since the Christians must show to the Jews the same kind attitude that we desire to be shown to Christians by pagan countries [i.e., by Muslims]." Two years later he reissued the *Sicut* bull. Moreover, in 1236, when he heard about the massacres of Jews by French Crusaders, he firmly protested to King Louis IX and to the French Church. To the king he wrote: "We warn you and we demand in the name of God that you employ your God-given sovereignty to punish those who committed these despicable acts of evil against the Jews, desecrating God in Whose image they were created, and harming the Apostolic See, from which they obtained their privileges" (*in Apostolice Sedis injuriam cuius sunt muniti privilegis*). All this did not keep the pope from sending his well-known encyclical in 1239 to the rulers and priests of France, England, Spain, and Portugal (but not to Germany, for reasons which will be presented later), in which he began, for the first time in the history of the Church, to attack the Talmud and other rabbinic writings. In this, too, Gregory showed his power over the spiritual and religious life of Jews in all Christian countries. [18]

Innocent IV continued this political approach with great force, adding to it out of his extensive knowledge of ancient Roman law. He also frequently stressed the Jews' serfdom, although he usually intervened in their behalf, to protect their rights. Although at first he, too, ordered the Talmud to be burned (1244), three years later he accepted what was to become the approved practice, particularly in the Spanish Church: the censoring of rabbinic literature by Christian scholars (for the most part, converts), who removed only those statements which apparently maligned Christianity or its founder. In three epistles which he wrote in 1249 to the archbishop of Vienne and the leaders of the German Church, he strongly objected to the Blood Accusation and the resultant oppression of Jews by local rulers. He ordered the churchmen to attempt, after research and investigation, to undo "what the priests, nobles, and rulers had done to the Jews in their haste, to restore the *status quo ante,* and not to permit in the future that the Jews be injured in these and similar affairs without recourse to law." This matter was so close to the pope's heart that, although he had reissued the *Sicut* bull in October, 1246, he published it again nine months later, with a special supplement about the Blood Accusation, which had been spreading in the Christian world for a century. "No man may accuse them [the Jews]," announced the pope, "of using human blood for their religious needs, because their Law expressly states that they are forbidden to use any blood whatsoever and, especially, human blood." This law, which was announced to all "Christian believers," became the foundation for many similar announcements by other popes (e.g., Gregory X in 1272), sometimes with further additions. After approval by various rulers (among them King Rudolf I in 1275 and Duke Edward of Savoy in 1329), it also became part of the public law in a number of states. It seems, however, that this humane step was a link in a chain of acts whose purpose was to strengthen the "plenitude of apostolic powers," of which Innocent was a powerful proponent. Written in a similar vein were the pope's epistle to Thibaut IV, king of Navarre, with glowing praise for the king's kindness toward the Jews (1246), and his letter to Bishop Martial, which will be discussed later. It is not at all surprising that such pro-Jewish letters aroused suspicion among Jew-haters, and rumors were spread that the letters had been bought from Innocent at a good price. Essentially, however, this powerful statesman regarded defense of the Jews as a means of strengthening the hegemony of the Papacy over the entire Western world. Innocent was convinced that he had the right to intervene even in internal Jewish affairs, and expressed his pertinent views with a forcefulness which had not been known since the time of the Emperor Justinian. Writing as a jurist and interpreter of canon law, rather than as a legislator, he stated, in his *Apparatus ad quinque libros decretalium*: "Indeed we believe that the pope, vicar of Jesus Christ, has jurisdiction not only over Christians but also over unbelievers, even as Christ had jurisdiction over all mankind. . . . The pope, therefore, can judge the Jews whenever they behave contrary to evangelical law in moral matters, if their own leaders fail to punish them properly, or if they express heresies against their own Law. . . ." This doctrine might have endangered Jewish self-government in the Western world if the popes had really intended to meddle in the Jews' affairs, especially in connection with the Inquisition's investigations into Christian heresies. In practice, however, the popes were ready to limit the right of Dominican preachers to intervene in internal Jewish affairs only to cases of danger to the Church— namely, blasphemy, written or oral, against Christianity or Jesus, or attempts to convert Christians to Judaism, or to bring converts back to their ancestral faith. Such an approach can be seen even in the writings of Nicholas Eymeric, a leading inquisitor of the fourteenth century. [19]

During the time of Innocent IV and his successors, the affirmation of the "plenitude of apostolic powers" and the Church's control over its Jewish "serfs" reached a peak. As usual, the Church preferred not to clarify its new teaching in detail. It was obvious, however, that the concept of "Jewish serfdom" (*servitus Judaeorum*) ceased to be a merely theological term, and became a legal principle which could be interpreted in many ways. Not long after Innocent

IV, Thomas Aquinas, the greatest Christian theologian, announced this principle in his magnum opus, which became the cornerstone of future Catholic theology: "Since the Jews are the Church's serfs, it can do as it wishes with their wealth" (*cum ipsi Judaei sint servi Ecclesiae, potest disponere de rebus eorum*). However, even he did not clearly distinguish between the jurisdiction of the Church itself and the jurisdiction of the various Christian kings as "temporal" rulers of Christian nations. Indeed, in his famous reply to Duchess Aleyde of Brabant (later called "On Ruling the Jews"), he appeased her religious scruples, by telling her that she had the right to tax her Jewish subjects, although their income derived largely from usurious moneylending, since "they were punished with eternal serfdom for their own guilt, according to [canon] law; the rulers were therefore entitled to take the Jews' money as if it were their own." Thomas was of two minds about this matter, however, as he generally was about the relationship between royalty and the Papacy. It is clear, however, that he felt the authority of Christian rulers to be merely the offshoot of Jewish serfdom to the Church itself. [20]

IMPERIAL REACTION

Not much later, the emperors and their advisers, especially the experts in Roman law, gave a decisive answer to the authoritarian demands of the popes, including their attitude to the status of the Jews. It is unnecessary to review at this point the legal development of Jewish serfdom in Germany (or, as it was officially known, the Holy Roman Empire of the German Nation), a development which has been investigated by many scholars since Stobbe and Hoeniger. [21] The available documents have undergone thorough scholarly analysis; they are all gathered in Aronius's collection, which appeared at the beginning of this century. [22] It is the consensus among scholars that the root of this development can be found in the privileges given several Jews at the beginning of the ninth century by the Carolingian emperors Charlemagne and his son Louis the Pious. The relationship between these privileges in their subsequent development, on the one hand, and the *Fremdenrecht*, on the other, in all countries under Teutonic jurisdiction during the early Middle Ages (a matter which has been treated by J. E. Scherer [23]) is still, however, subject to discussion by students of the history of German law.

Nevertheless, attention should be drawn to an interesting phenomenon: all the important legal documents, especially the governmental laws written during the decisive period between 1090 and 1238, were issued by Emperors Henry IV, Frederick I, and Frederick II—rulers who were at odds with the Papacy. Henry, who fought for decades against Gregory VII, attempted, above all, to establish the principle that the power of the emperor did not depend in the least upon the Church but was a continuation of the old Roman Empire, and that the emperor ruled by divine right. In one of his arguments with Gregory, he stated: "He [the pope] has attempted to take the crown away from me, from me who received it as a divine right, while he was not divinely elevated to the Papacy. He has threatened to deprive me of my kingdom and (through excommunication) of my soul, neither of which I acquired from him, because he saw that I sought to retain my power by divine right and not by his favor." The king was assisted in his struggle not only by the new interest in the study of Roman law but also by the German bishops, who felt that the pope's demands endangered their power and their independence from the central authority in Rome. Nineteen German bishops joined the emperor at the Mayence assembly in 1080, where they stated their dissatisfaction not only with the "weakened status of the Church" but also with the "disturbances in the Empire and the attack upon the sovereignty of the king." [24]

These words were written by one of the chief spokesmen for the episcopacy, Rüdiger, bishop of Speyer. As is well known, four years later the bishop invited the Jews to settle in his city, "in order to enhance the glory of our area a thousandfold." In 1090 he took another interesting step by influencing his friend the emperor to validate the privileges of the Jews of his city, with the power of his royal sovereignty. Apparently, the bishop took advantage of some privileges which had been extended to Jewish settlers of the Kalonymos family in the Carolingian period; nonetheless, he thought it fitting to obtain the emperor's revalidation, so as to indicate that even in this matter he did not recognize Gregory's formal humiliation of the emperor, a humiliation which continued in effect even after the famous reconciliation at Canossa. Henry apparently agreed to take the entire community of Speyer under his protection (*tuicionem nostram*), and granted it many privileges in accordance with his royal sovereignty (*Unde regia nostre celsitudinis indictione praecipimus et iubemus*). Of the fifteen paragraphs in this document the most interesting is the permission granted the Jews of Speyer "to travel freely and peacefully throughout our kingdom, to carry on trade, to buy and sell; and no one may compel them to pay any toll whatsoever or any other payments, public or private." At the same time, the emperor extended similar privileges to the Jews of Worms, and here he stressed even more forcefully: "We desire that in all matters of law and justice they need look only to us" (*quia ergo volummus, ut de omni iusticia ad nos tantum habeant respicere, ex nostre regie dignitatis praecipimus*). Here the emperor added an explanation which utilized a vital expression—"because the Jews belong to our Chamber" (*ad cameram nostram attineant*). In order to emphasize his sovereignty even in matters concerning Christianity, he expressly prohibited the baptism of Jewish children without parental consent, decreed that all converts to Christianity would forfeit their property, and permitted the Jews to maintain Christian maidservants and nurses—in the last two matters, he was in direct opposition to Church law. In connection with the permission to employ maidservants, he added: "Let no bishop or priest oppose this!" [25]

It is not surprising, therefore, that after the tragic events of 1096, Henry once again rose in opposition to the accepted canon law and in 1097 permitted all Jews converted to Christianity during that year to return publicly to their ancestral faith. He made no distinction between those who had been forcibly and those who had been voluntarily baptized. This, of course, aroused the ire of the antipope Clement III. Recalling that he had been unable to protect the Jews during the great massacres, the emperor expressly included them (together with the Catholic Church, priests, monks, traders, and women) under his protection in the peace treaty he drew up with his nobles in 1103 for four years. In this manner he strengthened, of course, the power of the emperor over his Jewish subjects, and also cleared the way to prohibiting Jews from carrying weapons, since the Jews were to be protected by the government, like the other groups mentioned in the treaty. All this was part of his plan to strengthen the position of the imperial crown vis-à-vis the Church. [26]

This situation remained unchanged during the twelfth century, at least until there appeared on the scene two powerful opponents, Pope Alexander III and Emperor Frederick Barbarossa. It is interesting to note that, even during the Second Crusade in 1146, neither King Conrad III nor Pope Eugenius III interfered with those who massacred the Jews, but both men handed the task over to St.

Bernard of Clairvaux. One of the great leaders of the time, Bernard had gone to Germany to induce the emperor to lead the Crusaders to the Holy Land, and to reprove the monk Rudolph, the anti-Jewish rabble rouser. Both missions succeeded. At the same time, he strengthened the development of the law of "plenitude of apostolic powers." It was he who announced: "Jesus Christ appointed only one vicar [i.e., the pope], and he must lead not one nation but all nations." These words made a great impression, not only on Eugenius III, considered a leading disciple of Bernard, but even on Innocent III, who quoted them many times in his works. Bernard's intervention in Jewish affairs was an outcome of this point of view. On the one hand, he strongly objected to the election of Anacletus in 1130, not only because "Jewish offspring now occupies the see of St. Peter to the injury of Christ" but also because he saw in this election the cause of schism in the Church, whose unity was his constant aim. On the other hand, he reminded many cities, in his letters to them during the massacres, about the teaching of the Church concerning the dispersion of the Jews in their midst for the purpose of witnessing the truth of Christian tradition. "One day Israel will be redeemed." All this did not prevent him from mentioning "Jewish serfdom" in a theological sense, as a warning to Christians, claiming: "There is no uglier and harsher servitude than Jewish serfdom [*nulla turpior servitus graviorque quam servitus Judaeorum*]. Wherever they go it follows them, causing them to be despised by their masters." [27]

Frederick I would not accept these extremist views. In his attitude toward the Jews, he behaved more as their highest political ruler than as the executor of the Church's commands. In 1157, he unhesitatingly gave permanent validation to the Jewish privileges granted in the 1090s. He even made several minor changes which emphasized the emperor's jurisdiction over all the Jews in the Empire. When the Third Lateran Council met in Rome, in 1179, the emperor utilized the regional conference in Franconia to ensure the welfare of the Jews. The "peace" treaty of 1179 mentioned many more classes of people requiring protection, and assured them of peace four days a week. But "the Jews, who belong to the emperor's treasury, will enjoy peace every single day" (*Judei qui ad fiscum imperatoris pertinent . . . omni die pacem habeant*). In addition, in order to prove that jurisdiction over the Jews in Germany remained with him and not with a broad and representative council such as had met in Rome, he renewed, in 1182, the privileges which had been granted the Jews of Ratisbon in 1097, and added this rhetorical introduction:

It is the duty of Our Imperial Majesty, as well as a requirement of justice and a demand of reason, that We rightly preserve his due to everyone of Our loyal subjects, not only the adherents of the Christian faith, but also to those who differ from Our faith and live in accordance with the rites of their ancestral tradition. We must provide for their persevering in their customs and secure peace for their persons and property. For this reason We announce to all faithful subjects of the Empire, present and future, that, deeply concerned with the welfare of all Jews living in Our Empire who are known to belong to the imperial Chamber by virtue of a special prerogative of Our dignity (*quod nos solerter curam gerentes omnium Judaeorum in imperio nostro degentium, qui spetiali prerogativa dignitatis nostrae ad imperialem cameram dinoscuntur pertinere*), We concede to Our Ratisbon Jews and confirm with Our imperial authority their good customs which their ancestors had secured through the grace and favor of Our predecessors until Our time.

Such was the solemn announcement of imperial sovereignty over all the Jews of Germany! And indeed the emperor had the opportunity to prove his superior jurisdiction when the news arrived from Palestine in 1187 that the Muslims had captured Jerusalem from the Crusaders. According to a Hebrew writer of the period: "They had risen against the people of God to destroy and annihilate them, but God had mercy upon His people . . . And He influenced King Frederick to accept a small part of their wealth and to order the priests not to utter evil against them, and he protected them with all his might, aided by the Protector of Abraham their father, and he helped them against their enemies, and they were not harmed." [28]

After Barbarossa's tragic death at the head of an army of 100,000 Crusaders in Asia, the situation did not greatly alter, except for a general weakening of imperial jurisdiction in Germany because of internal warfare. At that time the power of mighty Pope Innocent III, who was also the guardian of young Frederick II, extended over all of Europe, from England to Hungary (both of these countries accepted the jurisdiction of Innocent) and as far as Constantinople, which had been captured in 1204 by the Latin Crusaders. During that period (1209–12), Emperor Otto IV transferred to the archbishop of Mayence the right to collect taxes from the Jews of Mayence, Erfurt, and the other cities of that sector. This was but the beginning of the general strengthening of the power of the lesser German rulers, religious as well as secular, at the expense of imperial authority, and it applied also to Jews and their taxes. Even Frederick II promised to entrust the collection of taxes from Jews and non-Jews to the bishop of Worms (1212). Only in 1216, on the occasion of the renewal of the privileges of the Jews of Ratisbon, did Frederick express himself in the manner of a powerful ruler, when he ordered that no one, officer or priest, ever interfere with Jewish rights in the future (*in perpetuum ab omnibus decernimus observare*). Elsewhere the emperor and his son, "King" Henry VII, limited themselves to protecting the Jews by means of "peace" treaties with the other German nobles (the Treaty of Saxony of 1223 and the so-called *treuga Henrici* of 1224), in which the Jews were specifically listed among those requiring special protection. [29]

All this was changed during the protracted struggle between Frederick II and the aged and obstinate Gregory IX. While Gregory continually emphasized the principle of "plenitude of apostolic powers," Frederick was occupied with the establishment of "the first modern kingdom" in Sicily, the heritage of the Normans. The pope regarded this plan with suspicion, because it increased the jurisdiction of the German Empire. Although Frederick was not guilty of the heresy of which his opponents accused him—he was undoubtedly truthful in his denial of the authorship of the tract about "the three liars" (a reference to Moses, Jesus, and Muhammad), and he occasionally even persecuted dissident Christian sects —he was primarily a secular statesman, who desired to establish a new state, free from the Church's influence. As a result, he came into violent conflict with Gregory, who excommunicated him twice (in 1227 and 1239), and vigorously opposed him, especially in later years. This struggle exerted a decisive influence on the development of the concept of "Jewish serfdom." [30]

Twelve days after becoming pope, Gregory hastened to assert himself—in particular, in the matter of the Ratisbon Jews. Without notifying the emperor, he ordered the abbot of St. Emmeram and other officials to review the right of the Jews to own property which had formerly belonged to the monastery and upon which they had built a synagogue and a cemetery. The pope did not specifically mention the early prohibition against building new synagogues, but demanded—in the event that those who had lodged the complaint were justified in their claim—the return of the property to the monastery (March 31, 1227). It is interesting to note that he did not mention, as was usual, that government officials would assist in enforcing the return, but ordered that the Jews be warned that their refusal to obey would result in the prohibition of all dealings between Christians and Jews. From another source we learn that this property had been purchased by the Jews at a high price seventeen years before, and that they were not inclined to give it up, in spite of the threats. In this they were apparently supported by the emperor and his son Henry, who, in his 1230 confirmation of the privilege of Ratisbon Jewry, expressly stated *autoritate regia* that any property which had been in Jewish possession for ten years or longer need not be given up. [31]

The disagreement between Gregory and Frederick was even more obvious in the Kingdom of Sicily and Naples. At first the pope accepted Frederick's jurisdiction with great reluctance, demanding a solemn recognition that he and his predecessors had taken possession of the kingdom only with the Church's consent (November-December, 1220). In 1221, perhaps to indicate that he recognized the Church's authority, Frederick ordered Jews and Muslims to wear a distinctive badge, as required by the Lateran Council of 1215. Those who disobeyed were threatened with confiscation of their property, while propertyless persons were to bear a white mark on the forehead. Some years later Frederick began to establish an autocratic state, employing Jewish assistance, especially in the monopolistic royal manufactories. In 1231 the basic Law of Melfi was enacted, despite the pope's objection that it was the work of one who "was persecuting the Church and destroying public freedom." This law guaranteed special protection to the Jews and Muslims in Frederick's kingdom, since "their different religions rendered them weak [*infestos*] and helpless." It is not surprising that in this law the emperor did not mention the badge. The following year a disagreement broke out between the pope and the emperor concerning the privileges of the Monastery of Monte Cassino, located on the Jews' street in nearby San Germano. According to Gregory, the entire suburb had belonged "from time immemorial" to the monastery, while the emperor's officers stated that "all the property and profits of the Jews' street belong to the emperor's Chamber" (*imperiali sit camere applicandum*). Shortly thereafter, Frederick carried his views to their logical conclusion: in the introduction to a privilege granted by him to two individual Jews he explained: "In view of the defenselessness of the Jewish people and the fact that all Jews as a whole and as individuals, throughout our jurisdiction, are the special serfs of our Chamber [*servi sunt nostrae camerae speciales*] under Christian law and by imperial power, we take our serfs K. and O., their children, and their property under our special protection and the protection of our Empire." In this connection, it may be noted, the emperor stressed the dual source of his jurisdiction, *christianae legis et imperii prerogativa.* The date of this document is uncertain, but it undoubtedly antedated the privilege granted by the emperor in 1237 to the Jewish physician Master Busach of Palermo, a renewal of which, in 1282, designated him as a "serf of our Chamber" (*servus camere nostre*). [32]

In both the earlier and newer formulations defining the Jews' relationship to the imperial Chamber, the obvious intention was not a lowering of their status, but rather an indication of the particular causes that impelled the emperors to offer them protection. Now, during the great crisis in Frederick's relations with the Church, he thought it especially important to place the protection of the Jews of Germany and southern Italy on a firmer and more permanent basis. As noted earlier, from 1233 on, Gregory had made frequent use of the concept of "Jewish serfdom" to the Church. Finally, in 1236, when he was preparing his denunciation of the emperor, in which he listed Frederick's sins against the Church, he mentioned that the ruler "had taken Jews away from certain churches." To this accusation Frederick responded simply: "According to common law, the Jews of Our Empire and of Our kingdom are Our direct serfs (*Iudeos autem etsi tam in imperio quam in regno nobis communi iure immediate subiacent*), and we have not removed them from the jurisdiction of any church which had claims upon them prior to Ours, according to common law." Two months earlier, he took advantage of his renewal of the privileges of the Jews of Worms to emphasize that he was responding to the request of "all the serfs of Our German Chamber" (*universi Alemanniae servi camere nostre*), and had renewed the privileges "for all the Jews of Germany." Indeed, about a year later (April, 1237), Frederick promulgated privileges for the city of Vienna in which he apparently limited the rights of Jews by forbidding them to hold official posts, in which they might be able "to oppress Christians." However, not only was this an ancient Roman law—and Frederick had thus introduced nothing new—but he argued in good ecclesiastical terms that "from time immemorial the imperial authority had imposed upon these Jews perpetual serfdom as punishment for their sin" (*cum imperialis auctoritas a priscis temporibus ad perpetrati iudaici sceleris ultionem eisdem Judeis indixerit perpetuam servitutem*). The same privilege was granted by Frederick to the Christian inhabitants of Wiener Neustadt and renewed by him again in 1247 and by Duke Ottakar in 1251. However, in order to lessen the anti-Jewish effects inherent in this formulation, the emperor issued in 1238 a special charter for the Jews of Vienna. "By means of this statute," he wrote in the introduction, "We wish to announce to the entire world that We take the Jews of Vienna, serfs of Our Chamber, under the protection of Ourselves and of Our Empire" (*quod nos Judeos Wienne, servos camere nostre, sub nostra et imperiali protectione recipimus et favore*).[33]

Frederick II took another step forward and began, at that time, to interest himself in the status of Jews living outside his realm. It is possible that the reason was the Church's constant intervention in the affairs of Jews of all Christian countries, in their behalf or otherwise. In July, 1236, Frederick utilized the occasion of the Blood Accusation in Fulda, which resulted in the massacre of thirty-two Jews by Crusaders, to dispatch messengers to all West-European rulers to request that they send him experts in Judaism chosen from converts living in their territories. The subsequent international conference concluded that there was no foundation for the Blood Accusation. On the basis of this conclusion, Frederick decreed that the Jews of Fulda, and of Germany in general, were innocent, and he forbade the airing of such accusations in churches and elsewhere. "Since the master is honored through his serfs," added the emperor, "we shall surely be pleased with those who show kindness and favor toward the Jews" (*cum in servis suis dominus honoratur, quicumque se Judeis servis nostris favorabiles et benevoles exhibuerint, nobis deferre non dubitent*). This dramatic step undoubtedly created a strong impression in all countries, particularly in Rome, and may possibly be the reason for Gregory IX's above-mentioned letters to the king and churchmen of France in which he urged them to protect the Jews in their country against the Crusaders' massacres. As stated earlier, the pope emphasized in these letters that forced baptism and persecution of Jews were in contravention of rights long granted them by the popes. In 1246–47 Innocent IV imitated the hated emperor and added to the *Sicut* bull a paragraph expressly denying the Blood Accusation. He also sent a letter to the German hierarchy, telling them to do all in their power to prevent the spread of this false accusation. It is not unreasonable to assume that the pope's rivalry with the emperor, who was apparently supported even by some Roman cardinals, prevented Gregory from acting rashly against the Talmud. As is well known, the apostate Nicholas Donin appeared before the pope in 1236 and presented a list of thirty-six accusations against the Talmud and rabbinic writings. These accusations undoubtedly impressed Gregory, yet he apparently did nothing for three years. In 1239, however, during the final split between the pope and the emperor, when Gregory excommunicated Frederick for the second time (March 20; the excommunication remained in force until the death of both), he decided to have the outstanding Catholic theologians at the University of Paris investigate the accusation. In his famous letters to the kings and churchmen of France, England, Spain, and Portugal (but not of Germany!), written in June, 1239, he ordered the seizure of all Hebrew books and the burning of those containing statements objectionable to the Church. The result of these letters, as well as of the famous debate with R. Yeḥiel of Paris in 1240 and the burning of the Talmud in 1242, are well known. [34]

The two factions strove to support their claims with historical proofs. In these ideological controversies, the scholars, especially the experts in canon or civil law, took precedence over the statesmen. The Church sought evidence in the Bible that the priestly miter was superior to the royal crown. According to Hugh of St. Victor, "the spiritual sovereignty established by Heaven is both older and higher." Innocent III elaborated on this subject in his addresses to the cardinals during the first year of his reign:

The two crowns, of royalty (*regnum*) and the priesthood (*sacerdotium*), were given to the people of God, but with this difference, that the priesthood was created at God's command, while royalty was established at man's request [here the pope contrasted Exod. 28:1 and I Sam. 8:7]. It is also true that the period of the Judges extended from Moses to Samuel and from the first High Priest Aaron to the first King Saul—a very long period.

It cannot be denied, however, that among other nations, particularly in the ancient Roman Empire, kings preceded priests. All this was changed by Emperor Constantine, who, realizing that his kingdom was not based on truth and justice, transferred his authority to the pope. This radical interpretation of the Donation of Constantine, the famous papal falsification, dates from the time of Gregory IX. In a letter to Frederick II of October 23, 1236, the pope expressed his considered opinion that Constantine had made the Donation with the consent of the senate and the people, not only of the capital but of the entire Empire. He decided "that, just as Peter's vicar has the control (*imperium*) over the priesthood and over the souls of the entire world, it is fitting that his authority extend also over all material things and bodies in the entire world." For this purpose, Constantine transferred to the pope of Rome the symbols and scepter of royalty and presented to him the imperial city and its environs, seeking for himself a new capital city in the East. In the course of succeeding generations the popes transmitted the crown of royalty, first to Charlemagne and then to the kings of Germany, "without diminishing in any way their own authority" (*nihil de substantia sue jurisdictionis imminuens*). From this we learn that if this is true of political matters, then jurisdiction over the "eternal serfs," whose enslavement is due only to their sins against Jesus and Christianity, must surely be in the hands of the popes! [35]

It is obvious that neither Frederick nor his allies among the civil jurists accepted these arguments. They believed that the emperor was the direct heir of the emperors of ancient Rome, and that, at least in secular matters, he was the ruler, by divine right, of the entire Christian world, having received the political sword from God Himself. Frederick II felt strongly that God had placed him "over all kings and kingdoms," as he stated in one of his laws. In a letter sent to Genoa in 1230, he argued that, since, in the time of Julius Caesar and the other pagan emperors, the Roman power had succeeded in occupying the entire world, including Judaea, the emperors who accepted Christianity had jurisdiction, *a priori*, over the entire world. During the imperial-papal crisis, especially in 1239, he invoked the aid of the German people: "Rise, O victorious Germany! Rise, O peoples of Germany! Fight alongside Us for the Empire, which arouses the envy of all the nations and which vests in your hands world authority and world office." Naturally, the German emperors also claimed as their heritage from ancient Rome hegemony over Western Jews and perhaps over world Jewry. In this connection we find in many German writings of the thirteenth century a legend, constantly growing in detail and form, about the relationship between Vespasian and Titus, on the one hand, and Josephus, on the other. This legend was apparently first mentioned by Eike von Repgow in his classic work, *Sachsenspiegel*, in connection with the legal status of German Jews. In one paragraph he describes the punishment of a Christian who murders a Jew and thereby breaks the king's treaty of peace with the Jews under his protection. He adds: "This peace was acquired for them by Josephus from Vespasian, because he had cured his son of gout." These words were written apparently in 1221–24, during a comparatively peaceful interval in the relations between the emperor and the pope. From the thirties onward, other writers expanded this story, until it received its final form in the *Schwabenspiegel*, written *ca.* 1274–75. In this book of laws the emphasis is on protecting the Jews not in the name of the king's "peace" but because they are the king's "serfs." The distinction is not as important as some recent scholars think, however. Essentially this legend only gave additional support to the opinion current among the German jurists that the German emperor's authority extended over all Christian countries. This doctrine, which was opposed by almost all the kings outside Germany and was specifically repudiated by Innocent III with reference to France, was upheld by several canonists, Hostiensis among them. Understandably, the principle of the emperor's authority over world Jewry—in theory if not in practice—was repeated and even accepted outside the Empire's boundaries. If we are to believe the Austrian chronicler Ottokar von Horneck, this view was apparently coresponsible for the exile of the Jews from France in 1306, since the king of France did not wish to retain in his kingdom people who were subject to the emperor, a foreign ruler. [36]

THE MEANING OF "JEWISH SERFDOM"

The extensive and complex subject of "Jewish serfdom" cannot be given exhaustive treatment here. In addition to the theories of the Church and the Empire, consideration should be given to the view of other Christian kings and their counselors, especially in England and Spain, where the centralized royal power was greater than in France or even Germany. A totally different view developed among the Jews themselves, who regarded their serfdom as part of their exilic life. Of greater importance is a consideration of the meaning of "serfdom," a concept involving many theological and legal aspects which separate it completely from "slavery" in the usual sense. It must not be forgotten, for example, that almost all the laws enacted by the German emperors in which the Jews are referred to as "belonging" to, or being "serfs" of, the emperor's Chamber were intended to benefit, not to humiliate, them. These aspects are treated by me in the next essay and, more fully, in Volumes IX and XI of my *A Social and Religious History of the Jews*.

II

Medieval Nationalism and Jewish Serfdom[*]

MUCH HAS BEEN written over the last century about the institution of
"Jewish serfdom" in the Middle Ages. Scholars have been particularly intrigued by the origin of the term *servi camerae,* which in the
1230s made its formal appearance in both a Sicilian and a German
decree issued by Frederick II, the last recognized Hohenstaufen
emperor of Germany and king of Sicily. However, even the German
"Chamber serfdom" and its connection with the ancient Church
doctrine of the Jews' subjection to the Christian world are far from
fully clarified, though I hope to have contributed something to their
clarification in the essay on " 'Plenitude of Apostolic Powers' and
Medieval 'Jewish Serfdom.' " [1] There the gradual unfolding of the
divergent papal and imperial interpretations of the origin and extent
of Christian overlordship over Jews is shown against the background
of the ever sharpening conflict between the Papacy and the Empire
from Gregory VII to Innocent IV and from Emperor Henry IV to
Frederick II. Jurists on both sides adduced a variety of legal and
historical arguments to support the claims of either the Church or
the Empire to supremacy over the Jewish communities, not only
within the areas of their respective political control but throughout
Christendom, if not all over the world.

Not surprisingly, the monarchs ruling over the other Western
lands were far from ready meekly to relinquish authority over their
Jews to these outside powers. Before long they insisted upon their
own wholly independent mastery over their Jewish subjects. But
their rationales likewise require further elucidation; doubly so, as
they were both reactions to and derivatives of the papal, and, to a
lesser extent, the imperial, doctrines. Of course, the kings could not
invoke the *translatio imperii,* [2] and had to fall back on the concept
of the general subjection of the Jews to Christian rule. But they
interpreted such rule as the dominion of all God-appointed monarchs.

[*] Reprinted from *Studies and Essays in Honor of Abraham A. Neuman*
(Philadelphia-Leiden, 1962), pp. 17–48.

MEDIEVAL NATIONALISM

Such Jewish allegiance to all rulers was only part of the general evolution of medieval nationalism. For a long time the leading thinkers of Christendom, recruited largely from among theologians and jurists, insisted upon the supremacy of the universal powers of the Papacy and the Empire over all Christian states. Whatever they thought about the relations between these two universal institutions, they had no doubt that the various kingdoms were but provinces of the same body of Christianity, entrusted to the leadership of pope and emperor. Such leading glossators as Bartolus and his pupil Baldus agreed that, to quote the former, "he who says that the Lord Emperor is not the lord and king of the whole world is a heretic, for he says it against the decision of the Church and against the testimony of the Holy Gospel." Baldus called such a denial an outright "sacrilege." [3] The emperor's universal power naturally extended over the Jews as well. Another leading jurist, Johannes Teutonicus, made this relationship explicit when he summarized the prevailing view: "The emperor is placed above all kings . . . and all nations are under him . . . the Jews, too, are under him." [4]

However, partly as a result of the weakening of the Empire in the course of its struggle with the Papacy from the eleventh to the thirteenth century, the Western nations and their rulers became ever more self-assertive. In England and Spain, where geographic distance made the imperial claims somewhat academic, national independence arose gradually. In fact, some Castilian kings started arrogating to themselves the title of emperor, and finally Alphonso the Wise entertained serious pretensions to the imperial throne of Germany itself. [5] Similarly, England's Henry III, after abrogating King John's submission to the Papacy, cast a covetous eye on the heritage left by the declining Hohenstaufen. He tried to place his brother Richard of Cornwall on the throne of the Holy Roman Empire, just as he sought the Sicilian crown for his son Edmund.

Not surprisingly, therefore, Vincentius Hispanus extolled Spain as being "wealthy in horses, celebrated for food, and shining with gold; steadfast and wise, the envy of all; skilled in the law, and standing high on sublime pillars." Understandably, addressing the aforementioned proimperial Johannes Teutonicus, the Spaniard exclaimed: "Make exception indeed, . . . of the Spanish, for they are exempt, by the law itself." [6] In England, John of Salisbury emphasized, in his *Policraticus*, written in 1159, the position of the *princeps* as against the emperor, an idea which was expanded by the subsequent English political thinkers, particularly Bracton. [7]

Somewhat more slowly this idea also gained ground in France, which, by geographic proximity as well as by the traditions of the Carolingian age, was more closely linked to the destinies of the Holy Roman Empire. The absence of a unitary monarchical rule extending over the whole country likewise militated against the full self-assertion of the Capetian kings, at least until the strengthening of the French Crown under Louis IX and his successors. But in the days of Philip the Fair, with the Empire humiliated by the Papacy, France took up the cudgels against the supremacy of Rome as well. The papal claims to universal power also in temporal matters, culminating in Boniface VIII's well-known bull *Unam sanctam* of 1302, exploded, so to say, in the pope's face. Within a few years France forced the popes to take up their residence in formerly French Avignon, reducing the supreme pontiffs, some of them Frenchmen by nationality, to mere appendages of French rule. These transformations found their theoretical counterpart in the political writings of such contemporaries as Pierre Dubois. [8] Some people began interpreting the term *francus* as being etymologically derived from the word for "free," that is, "free from imperial overlordship." [9] In short, the growingly accepted view now was that the king of France "has no superior," and that, more broadly, every "king is an emperor in his country."

Connected with this progressive emancipation of the Western kings from papal and imperial tutelage was their increasing self-assertion within their respective realms. While the Empire progressively lost its internal controls, and soon had to concede increased independence to the territorial princes, both lay and ecclesiastical, the English, French, and Iberian crowns succeeded in controlling ever more effectively the destinies of their countries. Only the English kings suffered some reversals through the Magna Carta and the rise of the parliamentary system. But they retained the essential unitarian controls over their possessions on both the British Isles and the Continent. The French and Spanish kings, on the other hand, increasingly overcame the resistance of feudal barons, and toward the end of the Middle Ages France and Spain tended to live under a concentrated, almost absolute, royal power. [10] The formerly debated question of whether the old Roman crime of *laesa maiestas* applied only to the emperor or also to the kings was now answered in favor of the latter by all competent jurists. [11]

On a more popular level, too, nationalism was gaining ground. At the growing universities, in particular, such as those of Bologna, Paris, and Oxford, which attracted pupils from many lands, the student bodies formed separate *nationes*. [12] Even the universal church councils, which, by their very nature, were intended to underscore the unity of Christendom, increasingly resembled a modern United Nations, with voting blocs of representatives of various states and nationalities. Ultimately, at the famous Council of Constance (1414–18), it was agreed to establish four geographic regions, called *nationes,* voting as single units. [13] In short, "from the beginning of the twelfth century, European nationalism has [had] a continuous history." [14]

All this unavoidably affected the Jewish status. In another context I have tried to explain how deeply the rise of the medieval national state, as well as the persistence of some multinational states, influenced the whole attitude toward the Jewish minority. [15] Here we need concern ourselves only with the impact of that growing national self-assertion upon the development of Jewish serfdom in the various Western kingdoms, in contradistinction to the teachings expounded by the canonists and the imperial jurists.

SPAIN AND PORTUGAL

The incipient transition from the ecclesiastical doctrine of Jewish serfdom as subjection to the Church, to the royal concept of Jews as serfs of the Christian kings, occurred in Visigothic Spain. It was in the Seventeenth Council of Toledo of 694 that the memorable phrase referring to Jewry as *perpetuae servituti subiecta* was used to justify regulations which cut across the lines of state and Church. [16] This canon was frequently quoted thereafter in the ecclesiastical literature and, being repeated in the Gregorian *Decretales,* became part and parcel of universal canon law. [17] At the same time it could also be used by legists to justify royal supremacy over Jews, inasmuch as the *Lex Visigothorum* remained the fountainhead of all civil law in the few remaining Christian provinces of the Peninsula not overrun by the Moors. It also greatly influenced the autonomous life of the Mozarab population in the Muslim parts of Spain. With the reconquest of the Peninsula by the Christian Crusaders many old Visigothic principles reasserted themselves and profoundly colored the whole legal structure of the newer kingdoms of Castile, Aragon, and Portugal. [18]

It was not surprising that the Spanish kingdoms early arrogated to themselves independent authority over their Jews. Even the pro-imperial Jacobus de Albenga had admitted that "the French, the Spaniards, and some other provinces, though *de jure* they should be subject to the Empire . . . yet *de facto* are not so subjected." [19] Of course, the Spanish kings, especially the Castilian emperors of the twelfth and thirteenth centuries, cast away such restraints. Their view was clearly expressed in the thirteenth-century *Libro de los Fueros de Castilla,* a distinguished collection of local Castilian custumals approved by the king. The pertinent passage read: "The Jews are the king's. No matter whether they live under the authority of all the dignitaries, the nobles, or others, or under that of monasteries, all of them belong to the king, live under his tutelage and for his service." [20] In another local custumal, the *Fuero* of Salamanca (about 1170), King Ferdinand II of Leon reached an agreement with the Jews and the city authorities in which he stated: "And the king places them [the Jews] in the hands of the Salamanca council so that they have no other master but the king. And the Salamanca council [promises] that it will govern them with justice." On the other hand, in the *Fuero* of Ledesma (another Leonese community), probably likewise issued by Ferdinand II, the king agreed to share his authority with the municipal organs, stating that "all the Jews shall be in the power of the king and the council." [21]

It was because of this particular relationship that the kings felt entitled to utilize their Jewish "serfs" in important administrative posts. The Jews could be trusted to safeguard the interests of the Crown, over those of the nobles, clergy, and burghers, in that strenuous period of the country's reconstruction during the progressive *reconquista.* This extensive employment of Jewish officials in high posts brought down upon the kings the censure of many powerful popes, including Honorius III. [22] But the need for Jewish assistance was so great that the papal bulls were simply disregarded. Only much later, after the consolidation of the royal power, could the assistance of Jewish administrators, if not also of Jewish fiscal advisers, be more readily dispensed with. The Jews, on their part, actually enjoyed their status under royal protection. In a remarkable report about the long-lasting controversies between the burghers and the abbot of Sahagun, an anonymous chronicler mentions the argument presented in 1255 by the local Jews, "that they in no way belonged to the jurisdiction of the Abbot, for they are serfs of the Lord King and are obliged to serve the royal power in all matters. They also claimed that the lord Abbot had in many ways aggrieved them without reason." [23]

This nexus between the kings and the Jews continued through the following centuries, the kings often unabashedly admitting their preeminently fiscal interest in this matter. During Ferrand Martinez' rabble-rousing propaganda in Seville, John I enjoined him from pursuing his hostile preaching. "You should know," wrote the king, "that it is Our will and grace that the said Jews be protected, defended, and maintained as Our and Our Chamber's property." [24]

Without any imperial aspirations, Aragon nonetheless followed suit. In fact, we find in its area one of the earliest formulations of royal authority over Jews. As early as 1176, the important *Fuero* of Teruel unequivocally assigned to the king the *wergeld* due for an assault on a Jew. Evidently brooking no contradiction, the author of that custumal wrote: "Be it known that the Jew has no part in the fine paid for an assault or homicide on him, but that it all belongs to the Lord King. For the Jews are serfs of the king and always belong to the royal Treasury [*nam iudei servi regis sunt et semper fisco regio deputati*]." [25] The kings upheld that principle particularly after James I threw off the Church's supremacy, which had been recognized by his father. Defying all the fulminations of local and Roman ecclesiastics, James employed Jewish bailiffs extensively in the service of the Crown. He considered Jewish leaders like Jahuda de Cavalleria and several members of the house of Ravaya the most effective agents in cementing the unity of his widely scattered possessions. [26] Not being able, however, to counterpose an imperial claim like that advanced by his contemporary Frederick II, he could only invoke the general principle that all Christian sovereigns enjoyed full authority over the Jews. In a remarkable order, addressed to the municipality of Montpellier in 1252, he opposed the attempt by the municipal council to impose local taxes upon Jews. He declared that such taxation then and at any future occasion would run counter to the royal jurisdiction and honor, "for the Jews in almost all lands are subject to the serfdom of Christian princes [*fere in terris omnibus Christianorum principum subiacent servituti*]." [27]

This point of view was maintained throughout the Jewish settlement in Aragon. Using a somewhat different terminology, the author of the *Fueros de Aragón* declared that "all the Jews . . . shall be . . . under the special protection of the Lord King." [28] As late as 1481, but eleven years before their decree expelling the Jews from Spain, Ferdinand and Isabella severely lectured the prior of the cathedral of Saragossa, who had issued an unauthorized public appeal seeking to confine the Jews in a quarter of their own. "It appertains to none," the king declared, "but Ourselves and Our own person to provide and ordain in matters relating to Jews, who are Our chests and Our patrimony." [29]

In Portugal, too, the kings made excellent use of Jewish officials, because of their greater reliability—or, as Queen Leonor observed concerning her deceased husband, Ferdinand, in 1383, because he "trusted them [the Jews] more than the Christians." In this sense, being "serfs" of the king—a term used in Portugal far less frequently than elsewhere—established a mutuality of interests and responsibility which for a long time accrued to the benefit of both. At times, to be sure, his high position at court misled one or another Jewish official into participating in court intrigues and political conflicts which might reflect adversely on the whole community. Yet, even in the crucial transition of the regime to John I in 1383–85, the danger resulting from such intrigues passed rather quickly, and other Jews continued "serving" the Portuguese kings in various capacities. [30]

ENGLAND

Nearly total dependence of Jews on the royal power was most evident in England. From the outset the English kings enjoyed considerable authority within and outside their country. As early as about 1100 an unnamed York monk contended that both the state and the Church ought to pay allegiance to the king enthroned by God. This doctrine was too radical, however, even for his English contemporaries, and was left dormant in a manuscript. It was later discovered and published by John Wyclif, when independence from the Papacy became a major battle cry of the religious reformers. However, the York doctrine was symptomatic of both the rising English nationalism and the quest for concentrated royal power. [31]

Under these circumstances, it was perfectly natural to attribute exclusive supremacy over Jews to the kings. Characteristically, it was during the mid-twelfth century, when Edward the Confessor was canonized—an event generally recognized today as an important step in the progress of English national self-realization—that a contemporary jurist attributed to this revered pre-Norman king a statute which stated bluntly:

It shall be known that all Jews, wheresoever in the realm they be, ought to be under the guard and protection of the king's liege. Nor ought any of them place himself under any mighty man without the king's license. For the Jews and all theirs belong to the king. And if any detain anything of theirs, let the king ask their money back as if it were his own. [32]

This did not mean that the property of the Jews could be readily expropriated by the king except for cause. In fact, the Charter of 1201, whose provisions went back to those enacted by Henry I, expressly stated that "when a Jew dies, his body shall not be detained above earth, but his heirs shall have his money and his debts." [33]

In the course of the thirteenth century the status of English Jewry greatly deteriorated. Yet the principle remained the same. Despite his numerous inconsistencies, even John Lackland upheld it. His attitude toward Jews varied much less than, for instance, that toward the Papacy, to which he first submitted as a vassal, but from whose tutelage he subsequently extricated himself more or less successfully. He so angered the domineering Innocent III that the pope excommunicated him, although he did not depose him, as is often asserted. While squeezing out of his Jewish subjects as much money as he could, John in his own interest endeavored to safeguard their commercial activities. In his aforementioned Charter of 1201 he provided, therefore:

And wherever Jews be, be it lawful for them to go wheresoever they will with all their chattels, as our proper goods [*sicut res nostrae propriae*], and be it unlawful for any to delay or forbid them. And We ordain, that throughout the whole of England and Normandy they be quit of all customs and tolls and prisage of wine, as our proper chattel [*sicut nostrum proprium catallum*]. And We command you and ordain, that you have them in ward and guard and countenance. [34]

While generally adhering to these principles, Henry III found himself so frequently in financial straits that he began exploiting his

Jewish resource with unprecedented severity. In 1255 he plaintively replied to a Jewish delegation which asked him for mercy in his tax assessment, "It is no wonder that I covet money, for it is dreadful to think of the debts in which I am involved. . . . I am a mutilated and diminished king. . . . I am, therefore, under the necessity of living on money obtained in all quarters, from whomsoever and in what manner so ever I can acquire it." [35] Finally, he had to pawn his Jews for a loan of £5,000 to his brother, Richard of Cornwall. Having surrounded himself, moreover, with a number of Continental advisers, whose ruthless exploitation antagonized all classes of society and greatly contributed to the unrest which ultimately resulted in the "Barons' War," he used some of these officials to administer all Jewish fiscal affairs. As early as June 28, 1232, he granted Peter de Rivaux (Rivallis) "the custody of the king's Jewry of England, so that all the Jews of England shall be intendant and accountable to him of all things belonging to the king." A month later he extended Peter's authority over the Jews of Ireland "for life." [36] Finally, Henry came to the sweeping conclusion that "no Jew remain in England unless he do the King's service, and from the hour of birth every Jew whether male or female serve Us in some way." This statement, included in Henry III's mandate to the Justices of the Jews in 1253, reflected both the growing dependence of Jews on the Crown and the latter's increasing reciprocal dependence on Jewish revenue. [37]

It was amid this general overassertion of the royal power, partly intended to counteract the growingly rebellious trend among the nobles, that the distinguished English jurist Henry de Bracton also overemphasized the royal authority over Jews. As a student of Roman law, this jurist was generally inclined to attribute to the kings of England some of the *auctoritas* of the ancient Roman emperors. Perhaps with unconscious humor, he observed, therefore, that "a Jew cannot have anything of his own, because whatever he acquires, he acquires not for himself but for the king; because they [the Jews] do live not for themselves but for others, and so they acquire for others and not for themselves." [38] This assertion, written in the 1250s, has led many modern scholars to view the status of medieval English Jewry in terms of total inferiority and "rightlessness." Even such eminent students of medieval English law as Frederick Pollock and Frederick William Maitland, who admitted that they had not found the actual term *servus* applied to Jews in any medieval text, nevertheless stated unequivocally that "the Jews' relation to the king is very much like the villein's relation to his lord." [39]

Such exaggerations have, to some extent, been rectified in more recent research. But the mere fact that Jews appeared to the public to be pawns of royal power sufficed to bring down upon them the wrath of the nobles, as well as that of the competitive burghers. Among the complaints voiced by the gentry before the Barons' War was that there was "collusion" between the Jews and the king, inasmuch as, through their loans to the much-indebted nobility, Jews had often foreclosed on the latter's landed estates and thus indirectly transferred them to the royal domain. For other reasons, the burghers likewise resented the alliance between the royal power and Jewry and often insisted that the kings grant their particular cities the right of not tolerating Jews at all. Ultimately, the Crown, in the person of Edward I, yielded to these ever-accumulating pressures, and in 1290 agreed to expel the Jews from the country. [40]

FRANCE

Across the Channel the situation was much more complicated. In those large sections of France which during the thirteenth century were under the suzerainty of the English Crown, the kings tried to establish royal supremacy over Jews, along the English lines. But the rest of the country was deeply divided. Some of the vassals of the Capetian kings—even the kings of England, in their capacity as dukes of Normandy, were, formally, vassals of the French Crown— were to all intents and purposes independent kings, more or less equal in power with their nominal overlords. Certainly the counts of Champagne or Toulouse could not be dictated to from Paris. But slowly and imperceptibly the royal family concentrated more and more power in its hands and, before long, transformed France into an even more unitarian monarchy than that of its Spanish or English neighbors.

This accomplishment came about only after a protracted four-sided struggle against papal supremacy, the pretensions of the Holy Roman Empire, and the self-assertion of French princes and nobles. In the case of the Jews, it was relatively easy for the French kings to affirm that in all temporal matters relating to the taxation of Jews and their judicial administration, the pope should exercise no direct authority. St. Louis and his successors were ready to go along with the papal demands in such spiritual matters as the defense of the Christian faith against the alleged "blasphemies" contained in the Talmud. If Gregory IX's assault on that Jewish classic was to some extent influenced by his critical struggle with Emperor Frederick II, [41] the French king was the only one among the European monarchs appealed to by the pope who responded quickly and effectively. The result was the well-known burning of the Talmud in 1242. Louis also actively promoted Jewish conversions to Christianity, although each conversion involved the loss of a taxpayer. In time, however, even in religious matters such as the relapse of a convert, or sexual relations between a Jew and a Christian woman, royal officials, acting upon the king's orders, often prevented the ecclesiastical inquisitors from exercising what they considered their legitimate jurisdiction. [42]

In its struggle with the Empire the French Crown had to overcome not only the imperial claims to universal overlordship but also certain specific rights enjoyed by the emperors within French territory. Not only was Burgundy a more or less permanent bone of contention between the two powers, but Frederick Barbarossa held direct seigneuries in southern France, which affected Jews as well. In 1177, for instance, he issued a privilege in favor of Archbishop Raymond de Bollène of Arles which read in part:

We generously add as a gift of Our benevolence the extension of his and his successors' power over the Jews residing in the city of Arles, who belong to Our Chamber. We firmly state that no one shall dare for any reason whatever to impose upon them his rule through any exactions without his [the archbishop's] consent and counsel. Anyone running counter to this statute and order of Our Majesty should know that he will without any doubt fall under Our ban, be peremptorily excluded from Our grace, and be subject to a fine of forty pounds of gold of the best alloy, of which one half shall be paid to Our Treasury, and the other half to the offended archbishop.

This privilege placed the ancient Jewish community of Arles on a par with those of many other feudal possessions of the kingdom. [43] Gradually the doctrine prevailed that "the king of France is the first [princeps] in his kingdom" (this phrase was used by Guillaume Durand, who otherwise considered the emperor "lord of the world"). Yet there still was sufficient lack of clarity concerning the ultimate dependence of French Jewry in the early founteenth century for an Austrian chronicler to explain, as we recall, the expulsion of Jews from France in 1306 as due to the French king's refusal to keep within his territory serfs of the imperial Chamber; that is, subjects of a foreign, often hostile power. [44] But these were ideological exaggerations, which by that time had hardly any tangible impact.

More serious were the difficulties encountered by the kings outside the Ile de France. In the twelfth century the monarchy was still weak enough for Philip Augustus to try to resolve them by mutual agreement. Prompted by greed, he ousted the Jews from the royal possessions in 1182, but he soon realized that his financial gain was short-lived and that the expulsion really accrued to the benefit of his vassals. For this reason he not only recalled the Jews in 1198, and made various efforts to attract them to his domains, but he also concluded remarkable treaties with Count Thibaut of Champagne and, somewhat later, with the counts of St. Paul and Nevers (1198–1210). The counts promised to restore to the king not only the Jews who had left France after the expulsion but also all future Jewish settlers from the royal domain. Reciprocally, the king promised to "extradite" Jews hailing from the other provinces. This policy of holding on to the royal serfs was also pursued by Philip II's successors, Louis VIII and Louis IX. These agreements culminated in the Convention of Melun of 1230, in which Louis IX and a very large number of French lords mutually pledged not to raid one another's Jewries. In contrast to the earlier agreements, this Convention was specifically extended to all the barons of the realm, and provided that "no one in the entire kingdom shall be able to retain a Jew of another lord. Wherever a master shall find his Jew, he may freely seize him like his own serf, no matter how long the Jew might have dwelled under the dominion of another lord, or in another kingdom." [45] This extreme type of allegiance particularly involved, of course, the lord's control over the Jews' property. It is not surprising, therefore, to find Count Thibaut requesting of Louis VIII a seven-year extension in the repayment of a substantial loan of 10,500 livres which he owed to three royal Jews. [46]

All this was but a stopgap, however. With the growth of royal authority, no further agreements were needed, particularly after the expulsion of the Jews from France in 1306 and their readmission in 1315. Philip the Fair and his successors not only fought off papal and imperial supremacy but also effectively consolidated the power of the Crown over all of France. In the few decades still allowed to the French Jews before their final expulsion in 1394, royal control extended over ever larger parts of France, and no one contested the king's authority over the Jews of that growing domain. Only a few vassal duchies remained on the periphery of royal France—such as Provence, Savoy, and Burgundy, where the Jews flourished during the fifteenth century. But the theory that the Jews were subjects of their respective sovereigns remained uncontested.

MEANING OF "SERFDOM"

This is not the place to analyze in any detail the range of the various doctrines of Jewish serfdom and their manifold legal ramifications. Understandably, modern scholars reading in medieval texts the term *servitus Judaeorum* have readily conjured up a picture of Jews as members of an unfree class, more or less on a par with the medieval villeins. This picture has been imbued with much color and vitality from the indubitable facts of the Jews' great insecurity, their frequent persecutions and expulsions. It has been further reinforced by the long-accepted "lachrymose conception of Jewish history," which has seen in the entire period of Exile an unending succession of unmitigated sufferings.

However, the attentive reader of the documents here cited will have noted, as has been mentioned before, that the term "serfdom" was, for the most part, employed by the medieval rulers when they wished to protect the Jews. True, they never clearly defined the meaning of that term. It was to the best interest of the monarchs and their juristic advisers to refrain from defining terms too clearly, since obscurity in legal terminology could play into their own hands. They could use, even abuse, the existing regulations to suit their own needs. But, on the whole, they sought to safeguard at least the economic well-being of that major fiscal preserve. Hence the kings found it necessary not only to intervene in behalf of Jews threatened by outside forces but also, on occasion, to stem internal disorders within the Jewish community. For one example, Infante John of Aragon consented in 1380 and 1384 to the enlargement of the Jewish communal council of Perpignan to twenty-three members, because, as he contended, the Jews being his and the king's "treasure," he was forced to take action "for the public good of that community and its preservation." [47]

Moreover, the medieval legislators as well as the Jews were perfectly aware of the distinction between Jewish "serfdom" and real slavery. The latter was actually threatened as a sanction for various transgressions committed by Jews, such as attempted illegal emigration. For instance, the crime of illicit circumcision of Moorish or Tartar slaves in Spain, or of an attempt to leave the country without specific royal authorization, was punishable by the confiscation of the transgressor's property and the real loss of his personal freedom, which he had theretofore fully enjoyed. [48] This characteristic distinction also clearly appears in the privilege enacted by the German king William in favor of the city of Goslar in 1252. The king promised: "The city's Jews shall suffer no undue molestation or *captivity* from Us, and We shall protect them amicably and benevolently as *special serfs* of Our Chamber; but as it is proper, they shall serve Us as their lord and Roman king." [49] With reference to the conditions in the Spanish kingdoms, the fourteenth-century jurist Martin Didaci d'Aux, observed:

A Saracen or a Jew cannot oblige himself by contract or loan to become anybody's slave. They must not do it even on account of hunger, for their persons belong to the king. Not even the king can sell them except in the case of a crime. Neither do they really deserve to be called captives or serfs in the sense that they may be sold, because according to law they have the liberty to move about [*liberum habent volatum juxta forum*], but they may be given away. [50]

Even the right to give Jews away or else pawn them as security for a loan—occurrences frequently recorded in the medieval sources —were really not transactions between private owners, but rather arrangements between lords, stipulated under public law. In this connection one must bear in mind that whatever the king's prerogatives may have been in theory, in practice they were severely circumscribed by custom and the generally prevailing sense of equity. As C. M. Picciotto has pointed out, even today "the King is the ultimate overlord of every yard of land in England . . . [he] can in law do innumerable things which he never does, such as attending Parliament, refusing his assent to a bill, or sitting in the Court of the King's bench. King Charles I lost his head for much less." [51] It was, indeed, this power of custom that the distinguished Tosafist Isaac b. Samuel of Dampierre (Rashi's great-grandson), invoked when he discussed the civil effects of Philip II's decree of expulsion. "For we have seen in the countries around us," R. Isaac declared, "that Jews have had the right to reside wherever they wished, like the nobles . . . therefore, if there is a regime which tries to alter the law and make a new law unto itself, this is not to be considered the 'law of the kingdom' for this is not a proper law at all." [52]

The very term *servitus* and its implication of lack of freedom had an entirely different meaning in the medieval theological and juristic terminology than they have today. Quite frequently *servitus* was used merely as the equivalent of our English word "service." For example, Bishop Hexilo of Hildesheim wrote to Emperor Henry IV in June, 1075, repeatedly reassuring him of his faithful services (*fidelis* or *fidelissima servitus*). [53] At times, the popes looked with jaundiced eyes on those monarchs or clergymen who arrogated to themselves the papal formula and signed themselves *servi servorum Dei*. More relevantly, as Otto Stobbe has already pointed out, the term *servi* was often employed in official documents with reference to the *Ministeriales*, at a time when these officials enjoyed not only a social but also a legal position high above that of the free burghers and peasants. [54]

Nor must we lose sight of the fact that the concept of liberty in the Middle Ages presupposed a certain measure of dependence. We need not accept such extreme formulations as that advanced in 1939 by Adolf Waas that "liberty exists [in the Middle Ages] only under dominion, whereas the nineteenth century saw liberty only in the absence of dominion." Yet the whole medieval outlook on life was colored by the ecclesiastical doctrine of liberty—which, until today, has never been able to grant to the individual full freedom of deciding about the truth of a religious tradition unequivocally stated in the revealed sources. Discussing the views of Gregory VII, A. Nitschke declared, "Under 'liberty' Gregory understands not the freedom of human decision but, on the contrary, man's freedom from purely human decisions by his full submission to the will divine." [55] Not surprisingly, therefore, medieval jurists, according to Eberhard Otto, defined the free man as "a protected individual. . . . Originally anyone who was not unprotected or rightless was called free. . . . The very idea of freedom necessarily presupposes a master who protects and safeguards." [56] It was, indeed, according to this widely accepted legal meaning of living as free men under royal protection that the Jews and most of their masters conceived their status as royal "serfs." The full implication of these doctrines and their practical applications can become manifest only from a detailed analysis of the complicated status of medieval Jewry in Western Europe.

12

Medieval Heritage and Modern Realities
in Protestant-Jewish Relations*

LIKE MOST REVOLUTIONS, the Protestant revolution of the sixteenth century changed the existing sociocultural realities far less than appears on the surface. To the reformers themselves and most of their contemporaries the new ideas sounded startlingly novel, and their realization promised to alter the existing social and political structures to their very foundations. In fact, however, except for the overt changes in certain dogmatic and ritualistic postulates, specifically advocated by the new champions of reform, life proceeded largely along accustomed lines.

In their basic outlooks, as has long been recognized, Luther, Zwingli, and Calvin were essentially medieval men with only such transformations in their general *Weltanschauung* as were generated by their specific reformist demands. Even their philosophy of religion was still deeply rooted in medieval scholasticism, and their calls for Reform sometimes appeared, even to their adherents, to be mere variations of the long-demanded reforms of the Church, such as had been debated a century before Luther at the universal councils of Constance and Basel and, in part, implemented early in the sixteenth century by the "Spanish Richelieu," Cardinal Ximénez, Grand Inquisitor of Castile.

The Protestant rank and file was even slower in abandoning its traditional ways of life and thought. As pointed out by Ernst Walter Zeeden, the formation of new denominational groups proceeded very slowly, the masses lagging far behind their leaders. [1] Nor was the Catholic reaction particularly novel. In the first flush of anger, in 1521, Luther's writings were burned in Germany, Italy, and England (in London at a public ceremony in the presence of Cardinal Wolsey and many ambassadors, while the king's absence was due only to illness). The Paris Parlement placed the mere possession of any work by Luther under the sanction of a severe fine or imprison-

* Reprinted from *Diogenes* no. 61 (January–March, 1968), pp. 32–51. Revised and annotated lecture delivered at the Divinity School of Harvard University, Cambridge, Massachusetts, on October 18, 1966.

ment. [2] These were the long-accepted methods of the "inquisition of heretical depravity," which were now reaching their climactic refinement in the Spanish Inquisition.

PERSISTENT TRADITIONS

In their attitudes to Jews and Judaism, the great reformers and their clerical as well as lay followers underwent an even less radical reorientation. Even the folkloristic accusations against Jews which had sprung from the masses and had often been repudiated by thoughtful Catholics in the Middle Ages were now frequently echoed by Protestant leaders. True, allegations of Host desecrations, which had deeply envenomed all Judeo-Christian relations in Central Europe, particularly in the fourteenth century, and were still believed by such an enlightened writer as Ulrich von Hutten, were now pushed into the background. But this restraint was due to the Protestant opposition to the Catholic doctrine of transubstantiation in all its ramifications, much more than to any skepticism about the willingness of Jews forcibly to penetrate the mystery of the Host. On the other hand, the belief that Jews poisoned individual Christians or entire communities because they felt an inveterate hatred for all Christians enjoyed widespread acceptance. With his usual penchant for exaggeration, Martin Luther once contended:

If they [the Jews] could kill us all, they would gladly do so; aye, and often do it, especially those who profess to be physicians. They know all that is known about medicine in Germany; they can give poison to a man of which he will die in an hour, or in ten or twenty years; they thoroughly understand this art. [3]

The Blood Accusation, too, although repeatedly and sharply denied by medieval popes and emperors, found spokesmen among Protestant as well as Catholic writers. The humanist historian Joachim Vadian (von Watt) calmly reported the accusations and tragic reprisals against Jews during the Black Death era and following the Blood Accusation of Trent, without any intimation of doubt or disapproval. If the distinguished reformer Andreas Osiander, from his superior knowledge (compared with that of other reformers) of Hebrew sources, ventured to deny the ritual murder accusation, he did it in a private memorandum, published anonymously and without indication of the date and place of publication, evidently because he feared reprisals from other leaders. It was only in the late nineteenth century that, in reissuing this memorandum for the benefit of the general public, Moritz Stern identified the author. None of the other reformers publicly denounced this obvious mass libel, notwithstanding its espousal by Johann Eck, the well-known anti-Protestant controversialist. [4]

Most remarkably, anti-Jewish prejudice so deeply permeated the whole Reform movement that converts from Judaism were rarely, if at all, admitted to clerical offices. We need but remember that the Ecumenical Council at Basel in 1434 had adopted a specific canon outlawing discrimination against former Jews in appointments to ecclesiastical offices. In contemporary Castile even a former rabbi, Solomon ha-Levi of Burgos, was able after his conversion to ascend to the bishopric of his home city, to be followed therein—an unusual spectacle indeed in the celibatarian Catholic priesthood—by his son Alonso, bishop of Cartagena and public defender of his fellow *conversos*. Interveningly, to be sure, the racialist drive toward *limpieza de sangre* had made sufficient headway to bar *conversos* from many higher posts in churches and monasteries. But, outside the Iberian Peninsula, the Church fought a strenuous battle against such discrimination. A well-known *converso*, Diego Laynez, served as Loyola's immediate successor in the post of general of the new Jesuit Order, and was a leading spokesman for the Papacy at the Council of Trent. In contrast, I can name only one Jewish convert to Protestantism—the sixteenth-century Protestant pastor Schaddäus— who was allowed to officiate in the relatively tolerant city of Strasbourg. Converts may have been admitted elsewhere to teaching posts at Protestant seminaries (even Luther's Wittenberg had to employ a Spanish convert, Adrian, as a teacher of Hebrew); but as distinguished a Protestant writer as Johannes Böschenstein repeatedly had to deny his Jewish descent against insinuations by ever suspicious colleagues, including Luther. The Calvinist clergy of Lausanne repudiated the appointment of Immanuel Tremellius to a teaching post because he was a convert from Judaism, although this notable Hebraist had already held influential academic positions in his native Italy and had no difficulty in securing appointments at the universities of Cambridge and Heidelberg. [5]

That this aversion to converts had certain racial overtones is not surprising, since many reformers, particularly those in German-speaking areas, in some ways reflected the rapidly expanding nation-

alist sentiments among the German middle class. Of course, German
Protestantism in turn stimulated German nationalism. It has long
been recognized that Luther's Bible translation ultimately served as
a major vehicle of German national unification, although in the short
run the Lutheran movement principally helped the various regional
authorities to establish more or less secular, absolutist states, under
the emperor's purely nominal supremacy. Understandably, therefore,
responding to the nationalist intolerance of their environment, the
reformers rarely objected to the total elimination of professed Jews
from their cities or states. When in 1536 Elector Frederick of Saxony,
Luther's chief protector, decided to expel the Jews from his electorate, he undoubtedly did so with Luther's concurrence. If Wolfgang
Capito, the far more tolerant Strasbourg preacher, was persuaded
by his personal friend Josel of Rosheim (who was in the habit of
attending Capito's sermons except when they referred to intimate
aspects of the Christian faith) to give him a letter of recommendation to Luther—in the hope that the Wittemberg reformer might
intercede with the elector in behalf of Saxon Jewry—Capito wrote the
letter in very guarded language. He clearly intimated that he was
not personally advocating the revocation of the Saxon decree of
expulsion but that he merely wished that Luther "either listen to
his [Josel's] complaint or read his petition." [6]

How little significance is to be attached to Capito's letter of
recommendation may also be noted from his assertion that his friend
Martin Bucer had approved it. Bucer himself was to have a more
direct opportunity to advance the religious toleration of Jews when
he entered a debate on the Jewish question in Hesse in 1538. The
famous landgrave Philip, who, together with the elector of Saxony,
was considered the main defender of Protestantism in German
lands, received from the Hessian clergy the so-called Cassel Advice,
doubtless prepared in cooperation with Bucer. Though not demanding total elimination of Jews, the writers unrealistically suggested
that Jews be made to give up all participation in commerce and
moneylending, as well as their traditional reliance on the Talmud.
The counterargument presented by the landgrave was controverted
by Bucer himself; his reply clearly betrayed that he had not completely outgrown his former experiences as a Dominican monk.
(Incidentally, it was in this connection that the Hessian clergy
coined the well-known simile of the sponge, which has since been
repeated in many variations, particularly by Jewish apologists.)

When the landgrave finally decided to follow his own counsel and, by his decree of 1539, to continue Jewish settlement in Hesse, he nevertheless yielded to many clerical postulates. The first three of its fourteen articles ordered the Jews not to follow the Talmud against the Prophets, not to blaspheme against Christ nor engage in disputations with Christian laymen, and to attend, with their wives and children, sermons preached by pastors. The other provisions included a maximum interest rate of 5 percent, the death penalty for intercourse with a Christian woman and for the acquisition of stolen objects, and the total exclusion of foreign Jews from trade in the country. [7]

Some of Luther's followers were not satisfied even with these harsh measures. For instance, Pastor Ehrhardt wrote in 1558: "We ought not to allow Jews to live among us, nor are we to eat or drink with them." He also recommended the burning of synagogues and the despoliation of all Jewish treasures, according to the "faithful advice and regulations given us by our divinely enlightened Luther." In the same year the clergy of Stettin likewise argued with the duke of Pomerania against the admission of a single Jewish person, advancing reasons "why Jews should by no means be tolerated among Christians." [8]

Nor were the Calvinist-oriented rulers of the German Palatinate more permanently tolerant. For a time, they admitted individual Jews to various localities, while they deported others. Documentary lists of 1548–50, still extant, show the presence of at least 155 Jewish taxpayers, contributing a total of 650 gold florins to the state Treasury. By 1556, however, the new Palatine, Otto Henry, perhaps stimulated by a court cabal against him in which some Jews were implicated, radically altered his hitherto moderate course. In his *Testament*, dated April 3, 1556, he wrote:

For this reason We have inescapably and necessarily been moved during Our reign to eliminate from the Palatinate the said Jews as public corrupters of the poor people, despoilers of the land, traitors, and dangerous operators. . . . Since such removal of Jews occurs for well-grounded motives and will accrue to the benefit of the whole country, We dispose, prescribe, and ordain that it is Our last will and opinion that henceforth and for all future times no unbaptized Jew be admitted to Our Electorate . . . under whatever subterfuge. [9]

While thus getting rid of his Jews, Otto Henry, a Hebraist in his own right, refused to let them take with them their accumulated

Hebrew books and manuscripts. Long interested in developing the Heidelberg Library into one of the most renowned book repositories in Europe, the Palatine, following an example set by his predecessor in 1391, now incorporated a considerable number of Hebraica into his priceless collection. It should be noted, however, that Heidelberg did not long enjoy the fruits of this despoliation. In 1623, during the Thirty Years' War, victorious Catholic armies transferred one hundred eighty-four cases of Hebrew manuscripts to Rome. Later removed by Napoleon I to Paris, this collection was restored to Rome in 1815, and, in the so-called Bibliotheca Palatina, it still forms an invaluable segment of the famous Vatican Library today. [10]

CALVINIST AMBIGUITIES

Calvin, too, was anything but a "modern" man. Although his native France had begun divesting itself of its medieval heritage, most of its intellectuals, including many humanists, still thought in medieval terms. In Jewish matters, Calvin argued like a typical medieval polemist, raising the same arguments against Judaism that had been voiced by Christian thinkers since the patristic age. This characteristic came particularly to the fore in a debate he had with an unnamed Jewish apologist. Elsewhere I have suggested that this debate, summarized in Calvin's *Ad quaestiones et obiecta Judaei cuiusdam Responsio,* may have taken place in Frankfort in 1539 before a large assembly of Christian princes and prelates, and in the presence of Emperor Charles V. I even proposed that the Jewish defender was none other than Josel of Rosheim, who nine years earlier had successfully taken up the cudgels for his ancestral faith against the convert Margaritha at the famous Diet of Augsburg. The Calvin-Rosheim debate centered around the traditional topics relating to Jesus' messiahship and divine character, the prophetic "testimonies" in their favor, and the role of the ancient Palestinian Jews in the crucifixion of Jesus. Of more contemporary interest, perhaps, were Calvin's contention that the abrogation of the Mosaic law in the messianic age had long before been predicted, and his insistence that the Jewish sufferings in exile were entirely owing to the Jews' obstinacy in repudiating Christ. [11]

Characteristically, it was Calvin's own legalism which subjected him to frequent accusations of judaizing. In particular, his enemy Miguel (Michael) Servetus, who combined attacks on the Trinitarian dogma—in many respects he was the progenitor of the modern Unitarian movements—with a sharp repudiation of the law of Moses, could, with some justice, accuse the Geneva reformer of "twisting that law to apply to us and violently agitating for its observance, as if he were dealing with Jews." Some four decades later Aegidius Hunnius wrote an entire tract, under the title *Calvinus Judaizans*. Conversely, it was precisely Servetus' repudiation of the Trinity which made it possible for Calvin to accuse the Aragonese reformer of himself being the true Judaizer. At the famous trial conducted by Calvin's associates against Servetus in 1553, a major article of the accusation read:

It is, indeed, an abomination to see how this wretched man excuses Jews' blasphemies against the Christian religion, and he approves and extols the miserable words of the Muslims that the three persons in the Trinity or, as he styles them, three gods, were unknown to the Fathers and are sons of Beelzebub.

Servetus—a truly extraordinary genius, equally distinguished as a scientist, a physician, and a theologian—was also accused of leaning too heavily upon the medieval rabbinic commentators. [12]

In part, to be sure, these mutual recriminations may be attributed to the long-practiced medieval trick of trying to discredit a religious opponent by attaching to him the label of "Judaizer," or even "Jew." Had not the Code of Justinian already included Roman imperial decrees, generally written in measured juristic phrases and yet calmly denouncing, "Nestorius, the Jew"? Clearly, the well-known founder of the great Nestorian sect, that pioneering movement which more than any other had helped spread Christianity in Central Asia and the Far East, seems not to have had any particular Jewish associations, nor even a drop of Jewish blood in his veins. Not surprisingly, therefore, in his letter of April, 1539, to Guillaume Farel, Calvin did not hesitate to refer to his criticism of the Lutheran liturgy as being excessively "Jewish," a criticism which he had defended before none other than Philip Melanchthon. [13]

MODERN TRANSFORMATIONS

Yet there was a basic difference between the two leading reformers. While Luther had both responded to and stimulated the growth of German nationalist feeling, Calvin's Genevan Republic was too small to serve as a cradle of Swiss or French nationalism. Switzerland was not even generally recognized as a political entity until the Peace Treaty of Westphalia of 1648. Even during the subsequent heyday of European nationalism the trilingual Swiss nationality was a somewhat abnormal phenomenon among Europe's ethnic groups. In France, the Calvinists never achieved majority status; they had to develop their confession in defiance of the state and national sentiment, ultimately falling prey to the drive for national homogeneity with the revocation of the Edict of Nantes in 1685. In other countries, too, Calvinists had to live side by side with other religious groups, both Catholic and Protestant, and hence had to draw a sharp line between religious and national allegiance. In fact, a good case has been made for the contention that even in the very citadel of Calvinist theocracy, Geneva, the basic principle envisaged by its founder was that the state had performed its major function in handing over the government to the Church, and that subsequently it was to withdraw into its own domain and cease interfering with ecclesiastical affairs. By a curious concatenation of circumstances one could thus view the Geneva experiment as presaging the future separation of state and Church. [14]

By thus counteracting the drive toward national homogeneity, Calvinism unwittingly undermined one of the major factors hitherto responsible for the total exclusion of Jews from many Christian lands. Moreover, by contributing its share to religious "dissidence," it laid the foundation for the development of multifarious sects which were in sharp conflict with one another. There emerged such radicals as the Anabaptist furrier Augustin Bader, who, defying the widespread popular dread of the "Turkish menace," expressed the hope that the Ottoman Empire would help erect a regime under which Christians, Jews, Turks, and pagans might live peacefully together. These premature internationalist views, looking forward to an era of mutual religious toleration, were then held by only a small, persecuted minority of the population. But they were ultimately to play an important role in the modern expansion of the Baptist denomination in the United States and, more recently, even in the Soviet Union. [15]

In the sixteenth century, however, these trends were sharply repressed by both Catholic and Protestant authorities. Their immediate impact upon Jews was thus very small. At most, the increasingly bloody clashes between the Christian sects reinforced the Jewish expectations of the coming of the Messiah. Not surprisingly, a few religious devotees were led to adopt certain Jewish teachings and rituals, or even to embrace Judaism outright. In that religiously enthusiastic age religious debates were very much in fashion. (This was indeed the excuse offered by some Portuguese humanists who had been accused by the Inquisition of debating religious issues too freely in France in the 1550s.) Not surprisingly, some articulate Jews ventured to defend their religion even in debates with Luther. The reformer's violent temper was aroused to a high pitch not only by the frustration ensuing from the debates themselves but, particularly, by a rumor that, after one such "dialogue," the three departing Jewish debaters had torn his letter of recommendation (which would have freed them from customs duties) to shreds because it contained the name of Christ. [16]

In some cases Jews seem to have been successful in persuading doubting Christians that Judaism was the true religion. To be sure, Marcin Bielski, the sixteenth-century Polish chronicler, grossly exaggerated when he wrote, about events in 1539:

When they saw that people began talking and fighting about their Christian faith as if they were doubting it, the Jews of that period seduced not a few Christians among us to the Jewish religion, and circumcised them. In order to prevent their relapse, they sent them to Hungary and subsequently to Turkey. When King Sigismund ordered the governor and captain of Cracow to institute an investigation among the Jews, the latter sent an agent to the Turkish sultan and asked his intercession with the king, that the road to Turkey might remain open. The sultan replied that there was no need for such action, for, if they waited a while, he himself would come there and expel the Christians, safeguard peace for the Jews, and open for them a free road everywhere.

Bielski here evidently confused rumors he had heard about the existing "underground railway" whereby Jewish communities helped Marranos escaping the grasp of the Spanish Inquisition in Western Europe to reach safety in Turkey. However, there were enough incidents of relapsed Jewish converts in other lands, and even of Old Christians adopting Judaism, to lend the chronicler's account a semblance of truth. It was about that time that in Bielski's own home town of Cracow an eighty-year-old woman of a patrician Christian family, Katarzyna Malcherowa, joyously underwent martyrdom on the stake, rather than yield to entreaties that she revert from Judaism to the Christian faith. While such proselytes were doubtless few and far between, and they filled most Jewish hearts with apprehension, the fact remained that the rise of numerous Protestant sects in many lands removed from the Jews the stigma of being the sole religious minority. Not only in Catholic countries forced to tolerate Protestants but also in Protestant lands having a variety of dissenters, the Jews were no longer the singular exception they had long been in the Middle Ages. [17]

HEBRAIC HERITAGE

Equally important were the long-range effects upon Jews of Calvin's legalism. Before long, many of his followers saw in the Mosaic law models for modern governments. The New England Puritans in particular tried to emulate the Old Testament legislation in organizing their own colonial regimes. In the raging eighteenth-century debates about the merits of monarchical versus republican forms of government, the protagonists of the former, as William Lecky has observed, usually cited the other-worldly passages in the New Testament in support of "rendering unto Caesar" whatever may be his due, whereas the spokesmen of republicanism almost invariably cited the antimonarchical statements in the Old Testament. Many New England divines agreed with President Samuel Langdon of Harvard when he declared, in his election sermon of 1775, that "the Jewish government, according to the original constitution which was divinely established, if considered merely in a civil view, was a perfect republic." Even earlier, the New England churchman John Cotton advocated, in his 1641 tract *Moses, His Judicials,* the adoption of a constitution fully based upon Mosaic law. [18]

Hand in hand with this political concentration on the Old Testament went a drive toward the acquisition of greater familiarity with the Hebrew language. True, the new appreciation of Hebrew originals of ancient texts was less the result of the Reformation than of the Renaissance. It is indeed hard to find among Protestant divines a counterpart to Cardinal Egidio da Viterbo's close association with the Jewish linguist and biblical scholar Elijah Levita, as described by the latter:

Now I swear by my Creator that a certain Christian (Egidio) encouraged me and brought me thus far. He was my pupil for ten years uninterruptedly. I resided in his house and instructed him, for which there was a great outcry against me, and it was not considered right of me. . . . When the prince [i.e., Egidio] heard my statement, he came to me and kissed me with the kisses of his mouth, saying "Blessed be the God of the Universe who has brought thee hither. Now abide with me and be my teacher, and I shall be to thee as a father, and shall support thee and thy house, and give thee thy corn and thy wine and thy olives, and fill thy purse and bear all thy wants." Thus we took sweet counsel together, iron sharpening iron. I imparted my spirit to him, and learned from him excellent and valuable things, which are in accordance with truth.

Evidently Levita was much more concerned about the unfavorable reaction among his coreligionists than Egidio was about the opposition of Christian divines to his entertaining a Jewish tutor at his home for many years. [19]

Yet, among Protestants, too, a quest for more information from Jewish associates about the interpretation of various *cruces interpretum* in the Bible promoted some mutual understanding and good will. Discounting Luther's usual exaggeration in his denouncing many Christian Hebraists for being "more rabbinical than Christian," there is no question that such associations accrued to the benefit of both parties. Luther himself could have avoided many pitfalls in his classic translation of the Bible had he consulted Jewish or converted experts more than he did during the thirty-two years he devoted to teaching the Old Testament in Wittenberg (as against the mere three or four years he spent teaching the New Testament). It was, we recall, under Andreas Osiander's pressure that the city council of Nuremberg exceptionally allowed a Jew to settle in the city, so as to give the Christian preacher the opportunity of improving his Hebrew knowledge. Similarly, Ezra Stiles, later president of Yale College, learned a good deal from R. Haim Isaac Carigal, the first Hebrew messenger to collect funds for Palestinian relief in America. So dedicated was Stiles to the study of Hebrew that he forced even the most unwilling Yale students to study that language. In his reminiscences, Jeremiah Mason, a Yale senior of 1778, wrote that Stiles had "insisted that the whole class should undertake the study of Hebrew. We learned the alphabet, and worried through two or three Psalms, after a fashion; with the most of us it was a mere pretense. . . . For the Hebrew he [Stiles] possessed a high veneration. He said one of the Psalms he tried to teach us would be the first we should hear sung in Heaven, and that he should be ashamed that any one of his pupils should be entirely ignorant of that holy language." [20]

Not that such a study of Hebrew was completely devoid of the old medieval conversionist aspects. In his inaugural address of 1838 as professor of Hebrew at Andover Theological Seminary, B. B. Edwards advanced, among his "Reasons for the Study of the Hebrew Language," the consideration that American missionaries throughout the world were busy translating Scripture into various primitive languages; for such translations a good knowledge of the original was indispensable. Further, some divines actually expected that their Hebraic studies would bring them closer to persuading Jews to join the Christian community. The outstanding colonial student of Hebrew Cotton Mather recorded in his diary on July 18, 1696, this fervent prayer:

This day, from the Dust, where I lay prostrate, before the Lord, I lifted up my Cries: . . . For the Conversion of the *Jewish Nation,* and for my own having the Happiness, at some Time or other, to baptise a *Jew,* that should, by my Ministry, be brought home into the Lord.

Nonetheless, scholarly interests prevailde in time over missionary quests, and collaboration on a purely intellectual level opened up new avenues for interdenominational amity. [21]

BROADER HORIZONS

All these ideological changes were secondary, however, to the basic transformations in society. Professor Roland H. Bainton may be right in asserting that "the Reformation at the outset brought no gain to liberty. Rather the reverse, for Protestantism arrested secularist tendencies and made religion again the preeminent concern of man for another century and a half. The spirit of persecuton was thereby aroused." [22]

Yet, in its ultimate effects the Protestant Revolution, coming as it did in the midst of the breakup of medieval feudal civilization and the transition of the new capitalist order, contributed much to the improvement of Jewish status. In some respects the Reformation was both the child and the mother of that new order. Max Weber's well-known theories [23] about the impact of the Protestant emphasis upon "calling," and of other Protestant doctrines, on the rise of modern capitalism have had to be modified in part in the light of our increased knowledge of the economic evolution of the fourteenth and fifteenth centuries. But there is no question that the general change from a closely controlled economy to one of private enterprise and competition was greatly facilitated by the new individualism in religion, reflected in the Protestant stress on individual conscience. The diversity of the Protestant sectarian movements likewise played into the hands of ambitious rulers seeking to establish modern states guided principally by *raison d'état*. The new independence from the universal Papacy, while couched in religious terms, also promoted the interest of German and other princes, who did not let the opportunity of "secularizing" the vast estates of the Catholic churches in their possessions escape them.[24]

These hints will suffice to make us understand why as early as the mid-sixteenth century the pious Protestant ruler Joachim II of Brandenburg overruled both public opinion and the wishes of Protestant clerics like the Berlin preacher Georg Bucholzer (supported by Luther), and recalled some Jews to his domain. This move opened up the era of the "Court Jew"—when, to use Werner Sombart's exaggerating phrase, "arm in arm the Jew and the ruler stride through the age which historians call modern" and build up the modern territorial state in Germany. [25]

Even more pronounced was the impact of the capitalist evolution on the West-European lands. Not by sheer coincidence, it was Hugo Grotius, equally eminent as an international lawyer and a Dutch Reformed theologian, who (as a member of a committee of two appointed by the city of Amsterdam to submit proposals for regulating the status of the newly admitted Jews) prepared in 1616 a memorandum which has been hailed in recent generations as the harbinger of Jewish Emancipation. While still advocating certain restrictions on Jewish rights, Grotius' approach was modern insofar as it assumed basic Jewish equality of rights, subject only to specific disabilities provided by law—in contrast to the medieval system of special rights and special duties of the Jewish "serfs." [26]

Later on, Oliver Cromwell, a devout student of the Bible (he never went to battle without reciting biblical verses; by coincidence all the recorded quotations were taken from the Old Testament), decided to open up his country to Jewish settlement, for economic as well as religious reasons. Religiously, he was easily persuaded by Menasseh b. Israel that, by refusing admission to Jews, England ("Angleterre") was an obstacle to the ingathering of the Jews from the four "corners" of the earth and was thus preventing the ushering in of the messianic era. Although Cromwell did not overcome all the traditional suspicions and anti-Jewish animosities, and hence could not secure the formal abrogation of the decree of expulsion of 1290, Jews began settling in the country. By 1697 the Protestant city of London prevailed upon Parliament to admit Jews formally to a privileged position among the members of the London Stock Exchange. Thenceforth that great Exchange was to consist of one hundred members enjoying the freedom of the city of London, twelve foreigners, and twelve Jews. The tiny Jewish community of England was thus permanently granted nearly 10 percent of the seats on the Exchange, which was soon to become the world's leading securities market. Lucien Wolf was not guilty of gross exaggeration when he called this act "the first stage of Anglo-Jewish Emancipation." [27]

Most decisive were, of course, also the subsequent developments in modern science and the European Enlightenment. The Protestant churches, as well as the Jewish communities, were both contributors to and beneficiaries of this new evolution, although some romantic adulators of the medieval system may consider them losers in a hopeless struggle against secularization. Certainly, as a result of the internal religious diversity promoted by the Protestant Revolution, the United States, even in its colonial period, no longer had a decisive religious majority. While Congregationalists may have dominated Massachusetts and Connecticut, Episcopalians played a major role in Virginia, and Quakers were dominant in Pennsylvania. Only complete religious freedom, and ultimately the separation of state and Church, could guarantee denominational peace in the country, which witnessed a constant proliferation of denominational groups. Suffice it to remember that in the single decade of 1926–36, the number of denominations counted by the United States Census of Religious Bodies increased from 212 to 256.

Under these circumstances, Jews had to be treated in modern states as individuals, rather than as members of a distinct corporate group. Sooner or later they were granted the rights of full-fledged citizens, integrated into the social fabric of their respective countries while worshipping their God in their own way. For, as I have pointed out in another context, Jewish Emancipation had become an even greater historical necessity for the modern state than for the Jews. [28]

In conclusion, it may be asserted that, contrary to the designs of its founders, Protestantism became one of several major factors in the removal of the Jews from the medieval ghetto and in the promotion of their amalgamation with their Christian neighbors. It is small wonder that, as in other vital areas of life, the resolution of certain problems raised new questions, some of which still await their historical answers. Today, one of the major issues confronting the Jewish communities in the Western world is whether they can survive such an amalgamation in an era of freedom and yet retain their Jewish identity. It is no longer the conversionist pressures of either medieval Catholicism or of early modern Protestantism which are the major threats to Jewish survival. But this is a problem which the Jews must solve for themselves.

13

John Calvin and the Jews[*]

UNLIKE MARTIN LUTHER and most other German reformers, John Calvin had few, if any, contacts with contemporary Jews. The first twenty-five years of his life he spent in his native Picardy, Paris, and Orléans, long after the expulsion of the Jews from France. Nor did he have many occasions to encounter Jews during the last quarter century of his life and his increasingly dictatorial regime in Geneva. Jewish sojourn in that Swiss city had been cut short by the city council's decree of expulsion of December 1490, which was carried out ruthlessly during the harsh winter season of January, 1491. So few Jews visited Geneva in the following decades that in 1547, when two travelers passed through the city on their way from Flanders to Venice, the council ordered a study of the regulations affecting such temporary sojourn, regulations which had evidently fallen into oblivion during the intervening years. While we do not hear of Calvin's personal participation in this debate, it stands to reason that nothing of such significance for religious conformity could have escaped the attention of Geneva's theocratic ruler. [1]

Nor did the issue of Jewish "usury," which so greatly embittered the relations between the two faiths throughout Western Europe, play a particular role in the Geneva reformer's attitude to the Jews. Apart from the absence of Jewish moneylending in Calvin's immediate environment, his view differed sharply from the traditional ecclesiastical rejection of charging any kind of interest. In his comment on the crucial passage in Luke 6:35, he stated clearly: "No Scriptural testimony exists which would totally condemn usury. For that sentence of Christ which the populace regards as most unequivocal—namely, *mutuum date nihil inde sperantes* (in Luke 6:35)—has been gravely distorted." [2] Not that Calvin altogether favored moneylending. True, many Genevans had long made a living from that occupation, and in several ordinances, confirmed in 1547, the city council of Geneva officially set the allowable maximum interest rate at 5 percent. Certainly no legislation adopted by the city during

[*] Reprinted from *Harry Austryn Wolfson Jubilee Volume*, American Academy for Jewish Research (Jerusalem, 1965), pp. 141–63.

Calvin's regime could have been promulgated without at least his tacit approval. Yet he refrained from clearly stating his position on this issue, which loomed increasingly large in that period of rising capitalism. Occasionally he indulged in gibes at contemporary Jewish greed and repudiated the Jews' privileged position with respect to charging interest to non-Jewish borrowers. In his comment on Isaiah 60:6–7, where the Jews are promised that the "abundance of the sea" and the "wealth of the nations shall come unto thee," Calvin observed: "Under the pretext of this prophecy, the Jews stupidly devour all the riches of the earth with their unrestrained cupidity." In a sermon of 1556 he also declared that the fact the Jews had once been allowed to charge usury to the heathen nations does not mean that "today they may aggrieve and molest God's children." [3] In any case, his attitude to moneylending was so ill-defined that it readily lent itself to divergent interpretations and opened the road for the subsequent Calvinist blanket approval of profits derived from banking. [4]

However, Calvin was undoubtedly impressed by the anti-Jewish teachings of most German reformers. True, Martin Luther's crudely anti-Jewish attacks of 1542–46 were not fully accessible to him because of his limited knowledge of German. He apparently studied only those works by Luther (whom he never met in person) which were available in Latin or French translation. [5] But during his sojourn in such German-speaking cities as Basel and Strasbourg, and particularly during his semipolitical appearances at the assemblies of Frankfort, Hagenau, Worms, and Ratisbon, Calvin must have discussed with German theologians various contemporary problems, including those related to Jews. In Strasbourg, in particular, the vaunted religious tolerance of minority groups by the city administration (greatly influenced by the humanist Jacob Sturm), if not by its famous theologians, attracted a great many religious persecutees and was conducive to sociopolitical as well as theological debates of all kinds. [6]

Among the German theologians it was Martin Bucer (Butzer) who exerted a particularly deep and permanent influence on Calvin's thinking. This generally rather gentle Strasbourg theologian had many harsh things to say about Jews, especially in connection with a debate between Landgrave Philip of Hesse and the Hessian theologians in 1538. Theretofore Bucer seems to have had but few direct relations with Jews. Several years later (in 1546) he was to remonstrate sharply against the imputation that he was of Jewish parentage. And, when approached by his Hessian theological disciples, he took a definitely anti-Jewish stand. He helped them prepare an extensive memorandum to answer the landgrave's seven-point program, which was rather friendly to the Jews. After claiming that it was the general duty of civil rulers to protect the true religion and that the Jewish people had been both dishonest and long condemned by God, Bucer and his associates stressed the country's losses occasioned by the economic rivalry between Jewish and Christian merchants; and, in the set of proposals known as the Cassel Advice, demanded both religious and economic safeguards. The Jews were to pledge themselves not to harm Christians, to have no religious disputations with them, to attend Christian sermons, and, most significantly, to discontinue their reliance on the Talmud. They were also to be forbidden to engage in moneylending, commerce, or industry, and were to be forced to make a living only from menial labor. In this connection the Hessian clergy coined that well-known simile of the spongelike function of Jewish moneylending, which first "sucked up" the country's wealth and was subsequently "squeezed dry" by the authorities. When the landgrave rejected the Cassel proposals as too extreme and argued against them on theological grounds, he received an urgent letter from Bucer, pointing out his alleged theological errors. [7] It was unavoidable that Bucer's anti-Jewish views should also affect Calvin, who happened to spend most of his involuntary exile from Geneva in close proximity to Bucer at Strasbourg in those very years of 1539–41. [8]

CALVINUS JUDAIZANS

Like other reformers, Calvin naturally had to take a stand on the differences between Judaism and Christianity. Not surprisingly, the late medieval and early modern sectarian struggles frequently resulted in each faction's accusing the other of "judaizing." This tendency, which in ancient times had led Roman emperors to speak in official decrees of Nestorius as the "new Jew," and which in the sixth century had made opponents of Patriarch Paul of Antioch call him "Paul the Jew," reappeared during the Albigensian revolt, and subsequently during the sectarian conflicts of the Protestant Reformation. [9]

Calvin and his associates were particularly prone to hurl that accusation at their opponents, especially at Miguel (Michael) Servetus, whose antitrinitarianism smacked, in fact, of Jewish as well as of Muslim teachings. [10] As was usual in such cases, the accusers did not have to be consistent. Almost in the same breath Calvin appears as the defender of the Old Testament against calumnies by Servetus (such as the statement that ancient Judaea had really been a very poor country) and as the denouncer of Servetus' too great indebtedness to Jewish Bible commentators. Indubitably, Servetus was a much better student of Hebrew than Calvin and most other reformers, and made good use of such Jewish commentaries as those of Rashi and David Kimhi, which enjoyed a great vogue among other Christian Hebraists as well. Curiously, Calvin often accused his enemy of having borrowed a "Jewish" interpretation from the commentary of a good medieval Catholic, Nicholas de Lyra. This denunciation was not completely far-fetched, however, for Nicholas had indeed borrowed extensively from Rashi's *Commentary*. [11] This series of denunciations constituted, of course, but a part of the Calvinist campaign against Servetus, which eventually resulted in the latter's burning at the stake in 1553—that permanent blemish on the dark, dictatorial regime of the Geneva reformer. [12]

Servetus had reciprocated in kind, however. Just as his antitrinitarianism had served as the main target for the Calvinists, so he turned the tables on his archopponent by pressing charges of Calvin's emphasis upon "Jewish legalism." There is no question, indeed, that Calvin, who had been trained for the practice of law rather than theology, and was building in Geneva what his fellow reformer John Knox admiringly called the "maist perfigt schoole of Chryst that ever was in the earth since the days of the Apostiliis," was greatly attracted to the Old Testament law, which he tried to imitate as much as possible in his new Christian republic. With his usual fervor, Servetus declaimed: "You [Calvin] place the Christians on a par with the vulgar Jews." Calling the Mosaic law an "irrational, impossible, tyrannical law" Servetus thundered: "And to that law you wish to make us adhere equally today." He further appealed to Calvin to desist from "twisting that law to apply to us and from violently agitating for its observance, as if you were dealing with the Jews." In another context he bluntly accused Calvin of overlooking that in the New Covenant a new and living way was inaugurated, an oversight which "shocked me with your true Jewish zeal." These accusations were not silenced by Servetus' death; and, in 1595,

Aegidius Hunnius published a polemical pamphlet under the characteristic title *Calvinus Judaizans*. Curiously, some of the main shafts were aimed at Calvin's doctrine of the Trinity. [13]

Perhaps goaded by such accusations, Calvin often went out of his way in attacking not only the ancient Jews but also his Jewish contemporaries, particularly in their persistent adherence to their traditional interpretation of the Bible. He did not hesitate to accuse Jews of fraudulently corrupting the biblical texts. True, he never budged from his insistence on the basic trustworthiness of the extant texts of the Law of Moses. Referring to contemporary queries as to how, after the burning of all books by Antiochus Epiphanes, the texts were again speedily available after the cessation of hostilities, Calvin exclaimed: "But even though all wicked men as if comspiring together, have so shamelessly insulted the Jews, no one has ever dared charge them with substituting false books." Nevertheless, some minor textual falsifications, especially in the books of the Prophets and the Hagiographa, were still possible. Calvin believed that Jewish scribes, even if supported by all extant Hebrew texts could not be trusted, particularly wherever the original reading might have had Christological implications. While suggesting, for example, an emendation in Psalms 22:17, he exclaimed: "I do not labor here in order to convince the Jews whose stubbornness is indomitable to the last ditch (*ad rixandum*). I merely wish to show how unjustly they have disturbed Christian minds because of their different reading of this passage." [14] In another context, he accused the Jews of knowingly denying the Old Testament's testimonies concerning Christ. "But they are not only foolish and stupid but also frenetic." All of this was, in his opinion, merely a sign that God had struck them with blindness, "and if I wished to persist in refuting their errors there would be no end." [15]

Understandably, it was the Book of Daniel, with its messianic predictions, which lent itself particularly well to Calvin's exposition of his general outlook on history and his delineation of the alleged differences between ancient Israel and post-Christian Jewry. Needless to say, the Geneva reformer unquestioningly accepted the traditional date of that book. In a long-overlooked brief statement of 1555, Calvin expressly stated that Daniel had accurately predicted the events unfolding during the following two centuries, "for he had so clearly specified the persons, the mores, and nature, as well as the circumstances of their actions, that one is bound to conclude that he was a true spokesman of God, before whom all matters are ever present." [16]

Here Calvin ran up against the commentary on Daniel by Don Isaac Abravanel, which had also attracted wide attention among Christians. It is possible that Calvin knew Abravanel's commentary only at second hand. In his first reference to Abravanel, he states that his friend Antonius Cevallerius suggested to him the name of "Barbinel who appears to be ingenious above all other" Jewish commentators. Here Calvin particularly attacked Abravanel's six arguments against the identification of Daniel's "fifth monarchy" with the reign of Jesus Christ. In various other comments Calvin attacked Abravanel with his accustomed vehemence, calling him an "impostor," "a dog," and the like. He denounced Abravanel's "hallucinations" in the reconstruction of ancient history. Apart from the usual theological and dogmatic controversies, Calvin went to great lengths in proving that Abravanel's repudiation of Josephus, whom he himself had avowedly not always followed, was completely unjustified. Of course, he rejected Abravanel's chronology (doubtless taken over from Ibn Daud's twelfth-century chronicle), in which two centuries were judged to have passed between the death of Christ and the destruction of the Temple. "How great is his ignorance!" [17] Elsewhere, Calvin also attacked the Jewish messianic expectation as too materialistic. In one of his sermons, he declared that the Jews imagined that the Messiah would "come into the world in order to bring an abundance of goods so that they may have a bellyful to eat, that there shall be no wars, that each should rest and indulge in various delights; this is how the Jews have depicted their savior." But he had to admit that the Apostles themselves were not completely free of that "fantasy." [18]

Not surprisingly, some homiletical interpretations of Scripture which were current among contemporary Jews served as special targets for Calvin's verbal arrows. Not drawing any distinction between what the Jews themselves considered the ordinary meaning of Scripture and the various folkloristic and homiletical elaborations by ancient and medieval rabbis, Calvin's logical mind could readily indulge in sharp attacks upon such Jewish "fantasies." In his comment on Isaiah 48:21, he declared that "according to their custom, Jews mix in here stupid fables and invent miracles which never occurred. This is the result not merely of their ignorance but of their audacity, for they easily allow themselves to invent whatever appears favorable to them even if it lacks all reason." In another context he derided the Jews' identification of the Canaanites with contemporary Illyrians, Germans, and even Frenchmen because the ancient Canaanites had allegedly migrated into Western Europe. "They even understand Zerphat to connote Spain" (Calvin had evidently received wrong information about the contemporary Hebrew use of Ṣarefat vs. Sefarad). These identifications, with a long folkloristic history behind them, furnished Calvin the opportunity of assailing the Jews, who, he wrote, "are not abashed by anything and incongruously bring together frivolous matters. . . . They are also garrulous about subjects unknown to them. They do it all without reason and discrimination (delectu)."[19] In all these matters Calvin drew no distinction between the ancient homilists, who tried to deduce moral lessons from Scripture through imaginative hermeneutics, and his Jewish contemporaries, who were perfectly aware of the difference between aggadic and allegorical interpretations, on the one hand, and the ordinary meaning of the biblical texts, on the other. As a matter of record, in the perennial Judeo-Christian polemics, Jews were often accused by their opponents of "materialism," precisely because of their rigid adherence to the literal meaning of Scripture.

The last-quoted passage, from Calvin's Commentary on Matthew, is exceptional insofar as, through drawing on the Jewish interpretation of Isaiah 7:14, Calvin had the opportunity of controverting a Jewish exegesis relating to the New Testament, an opportunity which rarely offered itself in connection with his commentaries on that Testament. Here he could only elaborate the differentiation between Israel before Christ and the Jewish people's repudiation of the Christian messiah as stated in the New Testament and in its interpretation by the Church Fathers. Like his predecessors, Calvin saw pre-Christian Judaism essentially as a preparation for the Christian message. "It ought to be known," he declared, "that to whatever places Jews had been expelled there was also diffused with them some seed of piety and the odor of a purer doctrine." But, as a rule, Calvin emphasized the anti-Jewish, and toned down the pro-Jewish, statements in the New Testament. Even the well-known pro-Jewish utterances of Paul in his Epistle to the Romans are twisted in Calvin's interpretation to convey an essentially anti-Jewish message. In this respect we find a considerable difference in emphasis between Calvin's Institutes and his commentaries. The former work (written before Calvin achieved domination in Geneva), though frequently revised, hews rather closely to the traditional interpretation. Discussing Romans 9 and 11, the reformer observes:

Nevertheless, when Paul cast them down from vain confidence in their kindred, he still saw, on the other hand, that the covenant which God had made once for all with the descendants of Abraham could in no way be made void. . . . Therefore, that they might not be defrauded of their privilege, the gospel had to be announced to them first. For they are, so to speak, like the first-born in God's household. Accordingly, this honor was to be given them until they refused what was offered, and by their ungratefulness caused it to be transferred to the Gentiles. Yet, despite the great obstinacy with which they continue to wage war against the gospel, we must not despise them while we consider that, for the sake of the promise, God's blessing still rests among them.

Against this deliberately cautious, but sympathetic, interpretation, we find that in his *Commentary* on Romans 11:28–32 he inconclusively argues the pro- and anti-Jewish elements in this passage, but finds its main meaning in the fact that "their [the Jews'] greatest crime consisted in their lack of faith [*incredulitas*]." Elsewhere, too, he contends that the Jews still "wish to have tangible [*ad oculos*] evidence of divine power in connection with every miracle." [20]

In his sermons Calvin could even more freely allude to contemporary Jews, while using historical developments or biblical interpretations as a foil. In the crucial matter of the Deuteronomic prohibition of interest, Calvin delivered, in 1555, an important sermon arguing that the distinction between the "brother," to whom no interest could be charged, and the "stranger," to whom one could charge it, no longer held true. But rather than contend that, after the advent of Christ, all men were brothers and hence usury was prohibited to all, Calvin, who had also rejected the underlying Aristotelian view of the unproductivity of money, taught that moderate interest could be charged to all borrowers except persons in utter penury. This classic tirade of the Geneva reformer included the following statements:

For God wished to withdraw the children of Abraham from the rest of the world; He had united them into one body and wished to be their chief. There was good reason, therefore, for their maintaining [that unity] and that they should be more inclined to support one another. From that condition the Jews took occasion to trap all those who have little, for they interpret all the Scriptural promises to their advantage. . . .

For example, when it is said "Ye shall rule over many nations" they conclude therefrom: It is permitted to us to exercise any kind of tyranny and to devour the heathens for they are uncircumcised, polluted, and in no way belong to God, and that we should extract from them everything possible without sparing them. Even the word of the priest [Deuteronomist] they understood as meaning that they create no difficulty for them [the Jews] to charge to a stranger as much usury as he can stand without any regard for equity. . . . [In contrast thereto] we [the Christians] should preserve equity and righteousness toward all men and have pity and compassion for all.

All of which did not prevent Calvin from teaching in the same breath that there may be a "special brotherhood" in a community of like-minded Christians. [21]

DEBATE WITH JOSEL OF ROSHEIM(?)

Among Calvin's writings there is a small but remarkable tract entitled *Ad quaestiones et obiecta Judaei cuiusdam Responsio*. Nothing is known about the circumstances which induced Calvin to write this noteworthy dialogue, nor about the date of its composition. [22] The content, too, raises many questions. In the first place the Jewish debater reveals an astounding familiarity with the New Testament. True, in the sixteenth century quite a few Jews, particularly before entering a religious disputation with a Christian, familiarized themselves with some of the classic Christian arguments and their scriptural backing. This is true of Don Isaac Abravanel, Abraham Farissol, and a number of other Jewish controversialists. Nevertheless, it is quite remarkable that the Jewish debater tried to persuade Calvin through arguments largely borrowed from Christian theology. As if to pay back in kind, Calvin's replies were based largely upon Old Testament passages. While neither debater drew a sharp line of demarcation between the two Testaments, this inverted emphasis by the two contestants is quite remarkable. [23]

Secondly, not only are the Jew's arguments given with much objectivity, a procedure rarely pursued by the Geneva reformer in his controversial pamphlets, but, despite their brevity, they often appear more forthright and logical than Calvin's much longer and quite involved replies. If this Jewish debater was a figment of

Calvin's imagination, as is assumed by most scholars, this discrepancy between query and answer would appear doubly remarkable. Even if logically able, and by his legal training perhaps fully prepared, to see two sides of any question, Calvin was temperamentally far from inclined to give any opponent an equal chance. It stands to reason, therefore, that Calvin had indeed heard such a presentation by a Jewish spokesman and tried to invalidate it by his replies. In that case, the most likely period for the composition of this tract would appear to be the time of Calvin's sojourn in Strasbourg in 1539–41, and particularly of his visit to Frankfort in 1539, where he may indeed have encountered Josel of Rosheim, chief defender of German Jewry at that time, who often sought direct contacts with the religious and political leaders of both warring Christian camps. Though primarily a businessman, Josel was a well-informed controversialist who could stand his ground in any religious disputation. In fact, in his *Diary* Josel records the "disputations he had held with many Gentile scholars [in Frankfort in 1539] to prove to them from our holy Torah against the words of Luther, Bucer and his faction" the groundlessness of the latter's anti-Jewish accusations. Among the Protestant controversialists, Josel informs us in another context, there arose one who attacked him in a "violent, angry and menacing" harangue. Josel replied calmly: "You, a learned man, wish to threaten us poor people? God, our Lord, has preserved us from the days of Abraham. He, in His grace, will doubtless preserve us also from you." It would quite fit Calvin's temperament to have made a menacing speech against a Jewish apologist of a type he had probably never encountered before in his life. [24]

Be this as it may, Calvin's replies are written without his customary rancor. We need not expatiate on the whole gamut of theological questions raised by the Jewish debater in the twenty-three queries reproduced. For the most part, they deal with the long-standardized arguments concerning the messiahship and divine character of Jesus, the early prophetic "testimonies" for it, and the Jewish participation in Jesus' crucifixion. Of more direct contemporary interest was the question relating to the perpetuity of Jewish law. Citing the Old Testament passages concerning the eternal validity of the law, which must not be added to, nor subtracted from, and illustrating it by the law of circumcision, the Jew pointed out that Jesus' assertion "I am not come to destroy, but to fulfill" the law (Matt. 5:17) was clearly controverted by the Christians' repudiation of circumcision. To which Calvin answered by referring to several Old Testament passages indicating that in the messianic age many laws would be abrogated. As is well known, the problem of the abrogation of the law in the messianic period had already been a subject of debate during the sectarian strife of the Second Commonwealth and remained a bone of contention in the medieval Judeo-Christian religious controversy. [25]

Another intriguing contradiction was pointed out by the Jewish debater. He referred to the contention that the messiah was to be the king of peace, whereas "from that [Jesus'] time on the world had not ceased from being at war." He also cited the contradiction between Isaiah's prediction "that the government may be increased, and of peace there be no end" (9:6) and Jesus' assertion "Think not that I am come to send peace on earth: I came not to send peace but a sword" (Matt. 10:34). To which Calvin could reply only by pointing out that many prophetic predictions concerning Israel's glorious future had not come true and that there could never be peace so long as there were stubborn evildoers. "Foremost among men are the Jews who through their perversity show that they wish to have no peace with God." [26]

Perhaps most relevant to the contemporary conflicts was the Jew's final query:

I ask those who contend that we are in this Exile because of Jesus' execution, but this is not true because we had been in Exile before his death. If it be true what is written that, in the hour of his death Jesus begged his Father and said, "Father, forgive them; for they know not what they do" [Luke 23:34] and if Father and Son are identical and both have the same will, then certainly that iniquity was condoned which he himself had forgiven.

In his reply Calvin could only harp on the theme of the Jews' obstinacy in persisting in their error and on the numerous sins their forefathers had previously committed, as is attested by the numerous prophetic denunciations. These cumulative sins over generations, he maintained, sufficiently accounted for the sufferings of the people of Israel since it went into exile. [27]

With all his fury, Calvin showed himself, on the whole, somewhat more merciful toward Jews and Muslims than toward Christian heretics. True, the passage in the first edition of his *Institutes* which had criticized the use of force to attract Jews or Turks to Christianity was omitted in later editions. Yet nowhere did Calvin advocate the use of fire and brimstone against Jews as he did against Servetus and other Christian heretics, in whom he rightly saw the real threat to his own position and the future of his Church. He seems to have been satisfied, on the whole, with keeping the Jews out of Geneva and with echoing the long-accepted anti-Jewish polemics. He certainly made no direct effort to undermine the position of those Jewries which still persisted in Germany. Nor did his correspondence with friends in Poland in any way interfere with the remarkable expansion—numerical, economic, and cultural—of Polish Jewry, then entering its golden age. He evidently was willing to let the Polish Protestants take care of their own Jewish question. [28]

IMPACT OF CALVINISM

John Calvin may thus be quoted as a classic example of a hero making history in a way unknown to, and unintended by, him. If Calvin's own tyrannical temperament often played havoc with his best intentions—he himself once admitted to having an irritable bent of mind, and conceded "here I have gravely sinned for I have been unable to keep moderation" [29]—and led to the establishment of his despotic theocratic regime in Geneva, the ultimate outcome of his reform work was the very opposite. Even as an immediate reaction to the execution of Servetus, many voices were heard in Switzerland and elsewhere condemning this first inquisitorial "act of faith" on the part of Protestants who believed in individual conscience. As a sequel to Servetus' martyrdom appeared, in particular, that distinguished collection of utterances, both old and new, concerning freedom of conscience which was assembled by Sebastian Castellio, another victim of Calvin's dictatorship. Castellio's *Concerning Heretics* sounded a clarion call for general liberty of conscience, which, though muted for a while by the clash of arms during the Wars of Religion, nevertheless ultimately helped to tip the scale for religious toleration in the Western world. [30] Needless to say, the Jews, whose position in sixteenth-century Europe might have been seriously endangered by the spread of Calvin's wrathful denunciations, unwittingly became major beneficiaries of the ensuing trend toward religious liberty.

Calvin's influence was even more directly felt in the new appreciation of religious "legalism." The statement in his *magnum opus* "Here is the function of the law by warning men of their duty, to arouse them to a zeal for holiness and innocence" could have been penned by any contemporary rabbi. His long elaboration of the Decalogue, to which he devoted fully fifty-nine chapters, and his emphasis that the intention behind the act is as important as the act itself, were also wholly in line with long-accepted rabbinic teachings. Perhaps the rabbis would not have followed him fully in the practical application of the lesson he derived from the last three commandments: "Murder that is of the soul consists in anger and hatred; theft, in evil covetousness and avarice; fornication, in lust." They certainly were not quite so ready to prosecute men for evil thoughts as was the Geneva dictator and his most zealous followers. But many of their teachings had a great affinity with those of a reformer who had, to all intents and purposes, abandoned Pauline antinomianism in favor of Old Testament legalism. In fact, so closely did Calvin adhere to the Jewish interpretation of the Ten Commandments that he reemphasized the Jewish prohibition of imagery in a way shared by few of his confreres. Unlike Luther, he left the second commandment intact, obviating the readjustment in subsequent numbers made necessary by Luther's compromise with Catholic imagery in worship. [31] It is small wonder, then, that the disciples of Calvin in many lands so eagerly turned for enlightenment to the Old Testament. With the newly awakened humanist recognition of the relevance of the original language for the understanding of any ancient text, Calvinist divines and scholars in many lands became some of the foremost Christian Hebraists of the following two centuries. Calvin's own commentaries on the Old Testament, with occasional asides concerning certain Hebrew words, and his admission that the rabbinical interpreters of Scripture were strong in grammar if not in theology, could not help but stimulate among his disciples interest in the Hebrew Bible and its rabbinic exegesis. [32]

If these spiritual bridges facilitated a rapprochement between Protestantism and Judaism, the effects of the Calvinist doctrines on the socioeconomic and political life of the Western world even more enduringly narrowed the chasm separating the two faiths. The original sweeping theses by Max Weber and Werner Sombart concerning the far-reaching relationships between the Protestant ethic, the Jewish spirit, and the rise and evolution of modern capitalism have rightly been toned down by the assiduous, more detailed work of later scholars. However, the historical fact that both Protestants and Jews contributed much more than their share to the rise of capitalist institutions and to the so-called capitalist spirit has remained unimpaired. These activities by bankers and merchants of both faiths may have stimulated competition and economic rivalries between them which at times created new tensions. But such tensions were more than counterbalanced by the ensuing opening of new lands and new economic avenues to the Jewish wanderers. [33]

No less paradoxical were Calvinist influences on the rise of Western democracy and the separation of Church and state. He who succeeded in establishing in Geneva a powerful dictatorship, which suppressed many democratic liberties, and in establishing a dominance of the Church over the state in a way unparalleled elsewhere in contemporary Europe, nevertheless became the fountainhead of much of the democratic and republican thought in Western Europe and America. Perhaps because of his very overstraining of the power of theocracy, Calvin helped bring into the world the doctrine of total separation of Church and state. It has been shown that his theory demanded the intervention of the state in religious affairs only once, for the purpose of suppressing heresy and establishing a righteous regime. Having accomplished this task, the state was to withdraw into its own sphere and leave the Church in exclusive control of all spiritual affairs. From here was only one step to the doctrine of total separation between the two institutions, a doctrine which was doubly necessary because of the growing sectarian discord within the Protestant camp. [34]

Last but not least was the fact that, equally unwittingly, Calvinism escaped the danger of becoming linked up with the rising European nationalism. If Erastianism became one of the greatest drawbacks of the modern Protestant evolution, and the involvement of the Lutheran churches in the increasingly authoritarian princely regimes and soon also in the German nationalist agitation, opened up threatening vistas for the universal teachings of Christianity in its Protestant reinterpretation, Calvinism avoided these pitfalls. In part his noninvolvement stemmed from Geneva's small size, which prevented it from forming a base for an independent national movement. More importantly, in its French Huguenot wing and in its large following among the English "dissenters," it commanded allegiance among persecuted religious minorities which refused to surrender their religious identity to national solidarity with the respective majorities. From the outset, therefore, Calvinism represented an international movement, in part an interterritorial diaspora, very much resembling in its socioreligious structure that of the persecuted Jewish minority. These deep affinities between the two groups far transcended the differences so harshly emphasized by the founder. [35]

In short, the total effect of Calvin's anti-Jewish preaching resembled that of the ancient prophecy of Balaam. The Geneva reformer had set out to curse the Jews, but in the end turned out to have blessed them.·

14

The Council of Trent and
Rabbinic Literature*

IN RECENT YEARS the Council of Trent has come under fresh scrutiny
by many scholars. Interest in the history of ecumenical movements,
including those represented by the Catholic Church's ecumenical
councils, has been greatly stimulated by the Second Vatican Council. Among these the Council of Trent, which met in a period of
great crisis for the Church and which for more than three centuries
gave it an undisputed sense of direction, has held a place of primary
importance. Although Trent and Vatican II greatly differed in their
attitude to ecumenicity—the original program of the Council of
Trent, which was to reunify the Church, then divided by the young
but rapidly expanding Protestant movement, was in fact abandoned
in the course of protracted sessions over the years—many problems
were common to both.

For one example, many who read in the daily press today about the
heated debates within the Church with respect to the independent
rights of bishops versus papal supremacy do not quite realize that
such a discussion had also arisen in the Council of Trent. Although at
that time the problem of the bishops' obligation to reside in their dio-
ceses loomed largest in the controversy, the issue assumed fundamental importance because it infringed in many ways on the popes'
authority to appoint bishops of their own choice. The dissension
became so far-reaching that, at the Council's final session of 1562–63,
it threatened to break up the entire assembly. The breach was
healed only by the compromise solution, proposed by the brilliant,
juridically and theologically eminent Diego (Jacobus) Laynez,
Loyola's successor as general of the Jesuit Order. Perhaps ironically,
the impending crisis was averted by the intervention of this Spanish
New Christian, who, if he had remained in Spain, would have been
barred from any higher ecclesiastical office. He would undoubtedly
have fallen victim to the discriminatory treatment of descendants of

* This essay was prepared for publication in the forthcoming Volume in
Memory of Rabbi Isidore Epstein of Jews' College, London.

Jews and Moors which was spreading like wildfire throughout the country, especially after the enactment of the statute of "purity of blood" by the archbishop and canons of the Toledan Cathedral in 1547. [1]

Apart from the growing interest in ecumenicalism, the four-hundredth anniversary of the conclusion of the Council produced in 1963 an outcropping of jubilee volumes and articles, some of which included new archival sources. The interpretation of the various steps taken by the Council in its three periods of 1545–47, 1552–53, and 1562–63 has also been rich and divergent, although, to the best of my knowledge, the few Jewish facets of the conciliar proceedings have not been subjected to renewed scrutiny. [2] There is general agreement, however, that the Council played a great historical role in helping to stem the tide of the Protestant Reformation, and reestablished the Catholic Church on new foundations. To be sure, Harold Stürmer has rightly observed that, "important as the decrees concerning the Faith may have been, Trent did not begin a victorious march of a new doctrine, but rather established a thoroughgoing practice in ecclesiastical discipline." [3] Nonetheless, the decisions of the three long assemblies, finally reconfirmed in the concluding meeting of December 4, 1563, marked a turning point in the history of the Church Universal.

PRELIMINARIES OF THE COUNCIL

When, under the leadership of Pope Paul III, the Papacy, long suspicious of ecumenical councils, took the initiative of convoking such an all-embracing assembly of high churchmen and theological experts, its program and contents were far from definitely laid down. The very place of the assembly was uncertain, as was its date. Under pressure from Charles V a locality under the control of the Holy Roman Empire had to be chosen, the final selection being Trent, because it was nearest for the Italian episcopate, which always predominated in the sessions of the Council and its committees, the so-called deputations. The date had to be constantly postponed because of the great power struggles of the time. Only after the Peace Treaty of Crépy between Charles V and Francis I could the first meeting take place, in 1545. No agenda was prepared by the Papacy; it was left to the discretion of the assembled churchmen to adopt one, naturally under the guidance of the papal legates. In the eighteen years of the Council's total duration, great changes took place on the European scene, both politically and religiously. When the Council first met, Luther was still alive. Eighteen years later, both Lutheranism and Calvinism had become established realities, and total reconciliation no longer appeared feasible.

It is not surprising that, on learning of the convocations of the Council, particularly in its final period of 1562–63, some Jewish leaders became quite apprehensive, lest the great ecumenical gathering adopt a resolution prejudicial to Jews and Judaism. Such fears were not completely unjustified, although Jews could hardly have learned about a memorandum submitted by the Bishop of Vienna, Friedrich Nausea (Gran), to Pope Paul III in June 1543. In his *Miscellanearum libri VIII* the bishop submitted a number of proposals for the Council's agenda which included a lengthy argument against Jews. Sharply accusing the Jews, of whom he had little first-hand knowledge—since the *Wiener Geserah* of 1421, Jewish individuals appeared but sporadically in the Austrian capital—of exploiting the Christian population through their usury and of undermining the Christian faith, particularly through baptized Judaizers, Nausea suggested that the Council deal decisively with the Jews' "abuses." He urged it to deprive them of "all their temporal goods which they had illicitly acquired through their usuries." [4]

However, filled as it was with destructive criticism of the established Church order, Nausea's memorandum antagonized the powers that were, and was completely ignored. Conciliar leadership was instead prepared to follow the advice of the experienced papal legate Girolamo Aleandro, who in a memorandum on the forthcoming council of 1537 proposed that the Council refrain from discussing matters pertaining to non-Christians. He would rather see the Council concentrate on healing the Protestant schism, with which he had become wholly familiar while serving as papal legate at various imperial diets. This advice was not prompted by Aleandro's alleged Jewish ancestry, as imputed to him by the ever-irascible Martin Luther, but rather because he followed the old advice given by St. Paul: "For what have I to do to judge them also that are without" (I Cor. 5:12). This apostolic injunction was indeed frequently heard in the theological circles of the period, particularly among those who favored the Jews' wide-ranging self-determination in their internal affairs. [5]

Not that the Council was to abstain permanently from missionary efforts among the Jews. Time and again Jewish conversions to Christianity were staged with appropriate pageantry before the Cathedral in Trent. It must have been an exciting spectacle for the city's small population to see princes of the Church, including papal legates, conduct such ceremonies or serve as godfathers to the new converts. But this was only a tangential activity of the assembled fathers and had little bearing upon the Council proceedings. Neither did the occasional references by speakers to Old Testament events or doctrines relate directly to contemporary Jews. As a result, the Council adopted but a few resolutions on matters pertaining even remotely to the "Jewish question." Apart from a brief reference to Jews in the important resolution concerning justification, the conciliar directives for a forthcoming reformulation of the Catholic Catechism could have had long-range effects on the popular Christian view about the presumptive Jewish share in the crucifixion of Christ. However, this matter remained unclarified until the full-scale debate and ensuing resolutions on the subject at the Second Vatican Council. The only issue, therefore, which really concerned the Jewish people arose after the Council decided, in January, 1562, to undertake the compilation of an authoritative Index of Prohibited Books, which could include the Talmud and other Hebraic writings. This aspect of papal thought control had apparently been raised during the first period of the Council's sessions, in 1545–47, but no action was taken, nor even extensively debated, until 1561–62. [6]

DIVERGENT REGULATIONS

The impetus for a serious consideration of the permissibility of owning and studying talmudic writings was given by the almost chaotic state of ecclesiastical censorship in the early 1560s. Because of the proliferation of Protestant books and pamphlets of various kinds, many provincial Church organs had long felt impelled to issue lists of prohibited books on their own. Even the first papal *Index librorum prohibitorum,* printed in 1557 under the sponsorship of the extremist Pope Paul IV, was not officially promulgated by him until after it had undergone extensive revision in 1559. Even that new papal Index did not enjoy universal validity. For instance, the Inquisitor-General of the Spanish Inquisition, Fernando de Valdés, considered it necessary to issue an Index of his own in the same year. Valdés did not even refer to Paul IV's Index, although he cited at length the pope's breve of January 4, 1559, in which Paul himself had admitted the need for an independent Spanish listing. In his Index, Valdés threatened anyone possessing or selling one of the outlawed books with an automatic excommunication *latae sententiae,* a fine of 200 gold ducats, and, what may have appeared more menacing, an inquisitorial investigation under the suspicion of heresy. [7]

Sometimes Indexes prepared by the same official body appeared in different editions. For example, that issued by the Spanish Inquisition in 1551 was ordered to be separately printed in each of four major cities. While the four editions were in agreement on most of the books which they wished to suppress, there were some interesting differences between them. As was pointed out by Israel Salvator Révah, a reader in Valladolid, Seville, or Valencia could own and study some books outlawed in Toledo. But all the Spanish editions agreed in including among the prohibited writings "all Hebrew books, or those written in any other language, relating to Jewish ceremonies," as well as those "belonging to the Old Law." At the same time they also forbade "any Bible translated into Castilian or any other vernacular language." [8] The Index issued by Paul IV likewise included a clause outlawing "the Hebrew Talmud and all its glosses, annotations, interpretations, and expositions." While it did not pronounce a wholesale prohibition against vernacular Bibles, it included a long list specifying the Bibles which were not to be used by pious Catholics. [9] This formulation remained intact, notwithstanding the subsequent *moderatio,* prepared by Paul himself, but not promulgated until two years after his death by his successor, Pius IV, on June 24, 1561. [10]

Paul's stringent censorship also extended to many books written by Christians with no heretical leanings whatsoever, and even included a number of secular publications which had no bearing on religion. The situation then prevailing in Rome and elsewhere in Italy is well described by Hubert Jedin, an outstanding student of the proceedings at the Council of Trent: "In 1560, the things finally came to such a pass that it was almost impossible to buy in the book marts a Bible that was not condemned, and scholars and preachers were greatly embarrassed. The prohibition of texts of the Fathers and of the classics, edited by heretical authors or published by heretical printers, practically paralyzed all scientific activity." There was a sharp reaction after Paul IV's death. In the public upheaval generated by the pope's extremism and by the inflation which was caused by the corrupt regime of Paul's nephews and was unbearable to the masses of the Roman population dissatisfaction with his Index became quite vocal. [11]

Jews had every reason to fear, however, that in the Council's revision of the papal Index the provision against Hebrew books might be retained. Such an ecumenical ruling could have catastrophic results for their rabbinic studies in all Catholic countries. They remembered all too vividly that, but a few years before, Paul IV, at that time still Cardinal Gian Pietro Carafa, Inquisitor-General of the Roman Holy Office, had persuaded Pope Julius III to authorize the Holy Office to issue, on August (September) 12, 1553, a decree ordering the Jews "of any of the Christian cities or lands" to deliver all copies of the Babylonian and Palestinian Talmudim to the local inquisitors. The autos-de-fé, staged in Rome's Campo de' Fiori, Venice, and other places, in which thousands of Hebrew books and manuscripts went up in flames, now served as a warning of what might happen if the Council were to adopt a similar provision and thereby universalize this outlawry under the combined authority of the Papacy and the ecumenical Council.

To be sure, papal attitudes toward the outlawry of the Talmud had not been consistent. They had been even less uniform in the various Christian countries during the Late Middle Ages and the early sixteenth century. It has been demonstrated above in another context that Gregory IX's encyclical of 1239 asking several European kings to confiscate all talmudic writings; the public debate between several Paris theologians and R. Yeḥiel and his associates; and, finally, the public burning of the Talmud in Paris in 1242 were not completely devoid of political bias. They were, in fact, but a phase in the historic struggle between the Papacy and the Empire, a struggle which reached a peak in 1239, when Gregory IX excommunicated Emperor Frederick II. [12]

Subsequently, burnings of the Talmud still occasionally took place, but the intervals between them grew longer and longer. Characteristically, in the Disputation of Tortosa in 1413–14 the convert Geronimo de Santa Fé (Joshua ha-Lorqi) tried to use talmudic literature as evidence for the messiahship of Jesus, which, he contended, the ancient rabbis had fully realized but had subsequently denied. In any case, the Christian world was familiar mainly with such excerpts from the talmudic and midrashic literatures—the authenticity of some of these excerpts still is debatable—as were presented by Raymond Martini, who had personally played a significant role in the prosecution of rabbinic works in Aragon. Not only was Martini's *Pugio fidei* (1278) often copied, but its texts were frequently cited in popular anti-Jewish works (such as those by Porchetus de Salvaticis and Petrus Columna Galatinus), almost invariably out of context and in slanted translations. [13]

During the Renaissance, Catholic opinion became somewhat more moderate. Despite the trials and tribulations which Johannes Reuchlin sustained because of his defense of the Talmud, he was not prevented from dedicating his *De arcano cabbalistico* to the humanistic Pope Leo X. The pope apparently went so far as to seriously contemplate printing the Talmud in Rome itself, and he certainly did not object to Daniel Bomberg's speedy publication of three successive editions of the Babylonian Talmud and of many other rabbinic works. This despite the pope's earlier approval of the canon adopted on May 4, 1515, by the Fifth Lateran Council (whose ecumenical character was under dispute) demanding precensorship of books because "in various parts of the world works translated from the Greek, Hebrew, Arabic and Chaldaean" helped spread errors. Neither the Council nor the pope, moreover, accepted the amendment suggested by Bishop Alexius of Melfi that censorship apply only to books to be newly issued, not to older publications. However, those moderate debates of the days of Leo X had long since passed and a much harsher spirit now reigned in Rome; it indiscriminately aimed at all unorthodox manifestations and began to embrace Jewish books as well. [14]

INDEX COMMISSION

The matter of a new Index appeared sufficiently urgent for the newly convoked third assembly of the Council to consider the preparation of the new catalogue of prohibited books one of its first duties. This matter had been hanging fire almost from the inception of Pius IV's regime (December 25, 1559). As early as March 2, 1560, Joannes Alphonso de Polanco, secretary of the Jesuit Order, informed Peter Canisius that the pope had invited the Order's general, Laynez, for a discussion of the Index problem, with the view of outlawing only outright heretical works and none other. In February, 1561, Laynez delivered an address before an assembly of cardinals and theologians in the presence of the pope, effectively arguing for major changes in Paul IV's Index. The task devolved now on the Council, which in February, 1562, elected a Commission of prominent ecclesiastics to review the existing materials and submit a proposal to the plenary session before the Council adjourned. The Commission initially consisted of four archbishops, nine bishops, two priors-general of monastic orders, and one abbot, but was subsequently enlarged. The members were assisted by a number of "theologians" who attended the Council as experts without the right to vote. Like most other "deputations," the Commission consisted of a majority of Italians and Spaniards, although it was headed, as we shall presently see, by the Archbishop of Prague, Anton Brus von Müglitz, who served as chief envoy of Emperor Ferdinand I. [15]

In the subsequent negotiations the Jewish "lobby" had access to some of the most influential members of the Council concerned with that problem. To begin with, Cardinal Ercole Gonzaga, chief papal legate and presiding officer of the whole Council, was by temperament and training of a rather tolerant disposition. Son of the famous lady humanist Isabella d'Este, he was raised, at the Gonzaga court in Mantua and in Bologna, where he studied for several years under the leading humanist teacher Lazzaro Bonamico, to appreciate classical learning, and had become a devoted bibliophile. The ever-critical Venetian ambassador Bernardo Navagero described him as a "most reverend and industrious father. . . . Apart from having a precise knowledge of Greek and Latin, familiarity with various sciences, and admirable judgment about a variety of subjects, he leads a most honorable way of life and cultivates most appropriate habits [costumi]." Although primarily a churchman—he was appointed bishop at the early age of sixteen, became cardinal at twenty-two, and, after Paul IV's death, was the leading candidate for the papal see—he had also acquired much practical experience by serving for many years as coregent of his duchy in behalf of two minor nephews. He had proved himself a very effective administrator, for in a short time he had brought a very difficult financial situation under rigid control. As a genuine humanist and booklover he must have resented the destruction of Hebraic treasures accumulated by the Italian communities over many generations. Moreover, in his correspondence with his nephew Cardinal Francesco Gonzaga, he agreed that it would not do to place all Protestant writings on the Index and then expect Protestant churchmen to participate in the

Council, a hope which he still cherished at that late date. A man of that character and approach could indeed prove helpful to those who tried to inhibit the Council from totally outlawing talmudic literature. [16]

In addition to Gonzaga (often called in the sources "the cardinal of Mantua" or, more briefly, "Mantua"), his friend and admirer Girolamo Seripando likewise served as a papal legate. Leading theologian and former prior-general of the Augustinian Order, Seripando had been, like his predecessor Egidio Canisio da Viterbo, a student of the Jewish Kabbalah. He was for a while a member of the Roman Inquisition, which, since its establishment in 1542, had become an instrument of sharp repression in the hands of such rigid inquisitors-general as Gian Pietro Carafa and Michele Ghislieri (later Popes Paul IV and Pius V). Seripando became quite critical of the operations of that office, and he once commented: "At first, this tribunal, in consonance with the pope's [Paul III's] inclinations, was moderate and mild, but later, as a result of the increase in its members and authority, it became imbued with Carafa's excessive severity. It was believed that no more terrible and awesome verdicts were passed anywhere in the world." Jews could legitimately expect that Seripando would follow Gonzaga in taking a more balanced view on rabbinic letters. Nor was a third legate, Cardinal Stanislaus Hosius, a determined foe of Jews or the Talmud, though he was an early leader of the Polish Counter Reformation. A leading literary controversialist, he concentrated his attacks on Protestantism, rather than Judaism. If, in the nine crucial months before the end of the assembly both Gonzaga and Seripando passed away (on March 2 and 17, 1563, respectively), the new chief papal legate and presiding officer of the Council, Cardinal Giovanni Morone, was likewise a moderate ecclesiastic. Not long before, he himself had faced an inquisitorial prosecution, instigated by his archrival Paul IV against his alleged philo-Protestant leanings. Through these representatives Pius IV managed to maintain strong control over the deliberations at the Council, so that, when it ultimately adopted a series of new resolutions and confirmed those passed at the first two assemblies in the 1540s and 1550s, the pope had no reason to alter them. [17]

Doubtless less friendly to, and less informed about, the Jewish cause was the new chairman of the Index Commission, Archbishop Anton Brus von Müglitz. In his earlier position as bishop of Vienna, Brus seems to have had few, if any, contacts with the tiny Jewish settlement in Austria. At the same time there is no evidence that he shared the strong anti-Jewish prejudices of his predecessor, Friedrich Nausea. His elevation to the archbishopric of Prague, where he might have met spokesmen of a long-established, prosperous, and culturally advanced Jewish community, came but shortly before his departure to the Council (the confirmation of his appointment by the pope was issued on September 5, 1561, and he left Prague for Trent on January 3, 1562). Nor did he evince any particular missionary proclivities such as were to lead his more famous successor, Cardinal Melchior Khlesel, to introduce, in both Vienna and Prague, missionary sermons among the Jews with a legally enforced attendance.

In any case, the German episcopate did not have behind it the long history of antitalmudic agitation which stimulated its Italian counterpart. Prosecutions of rabbinic literature, even of the kind attempted by Johannes Pfefferkorn, who, earlier in the sixteenth century, had secured from Maximilian I permission to seek out rabbinic books in Frankfort for censorial review, did not enjoy the unanimous backing of the German Church. Pfefferkorn's action was, indeed, countermanded by Uriel von Gemmingen, archbishop of Mayence, who forbade the priests of his archdiocese—which included Frankfort—to support that investigation. Although in the subsequent controversy over the Talmud Pfefferkorn found powerful backing among the Cologne Dominicans, the outcome was by no means a wholesale burning of rabbinic works such as was to be staged in many Italian cities later in the century. Nor was Ferdinand I personally involved in that controversy, as was his brother Charles V, who had taken a strong anti-Reuchlinian stand. Ferdinand may not have been a friend of Jews and, from time to time, may have issued decrees for their expulsion from both Austria and Bohemia (none of the decrees were completely implemented); he may also have invited the convert Antonius Margarita, after the latter's defeat in a debate with Josel of Rosheim at the Diet of Augsburg of 1530, to serve as instructor of Hebrew at the University of Vienna. But he apparently had no strong feelings about either seeking to convert Jews en masse, as his grandfather Ferdinand the Catholic had done in Spain, or suppressing rabbinic books of any kind. Moreover, both emperor and archbishop were facing a domestic situation fraught with great dangers for any attempt to establish religious conformity by force. There were too many Hussites and

Lutherans among both the nobles and the middle class in Austria and the lands of the Bohemian Crown for the episcopate or the monarchy to try to introduce any rigid censorship of "heretical" books. [18]

We are less well informed about the secretary of the Index Commission, the Portuguese Dominican Francisco Foreiro (Forerius). Before arriving in Trent in 1561 Foreiro had for several years served as court preacher to King Sebastian of Portugal, and also as a censor of books. He seems to have known enough Hebrew to publish in Venice, in 1563, at the time of his activities at Trent, a new translation (*ex hebraica versio*) of, and commentary on, Isaiah. He also wrote other commentaries on the Prophets and Job and compiled a Hebrew lexicon on which he claimed to have spent an "incredible" amount of time and effort. In this respect he was definitely superior to Gonzaga and Brus. Like the rest of his Portuguese confreres, he evidently came to Trent with a determined outlook on ecclesiastical censorship. On one occasion he quoted Ecclesiastes 12:12, "Of making many books there is no end," and drew a homely parallel to bankers. Just as the latter, he contended, select pure gold but reject adulterated metal, so ecclesiastical leadership should guide the people in the reading of only "good" books. Ultimately, he collaborated with two Roman colleagues on the final formulation of the new Index and, in behalf of the Council, wrote a Foreword to it. But there is no evidence that Foreiro, who served under members greatly outranking him in the hierarchy, did much more than execute their orders. This despite the warning, sounded by many theologians, including Francisco de Vargas (in a memorandum of 1551), that in matters of faith and dogma the opinion of experts should count for more than that of well-meaning but less-informed high dignitaries of the Church. [19]

The most influential member appears to have been the chairman. It was at his home that the Commission met from time to time. There seem to have been occasions when Brus used his own discretion as to whom he invited to one or another meeting. No lesser personalities than Laynez and his fellow Jesuit Alphonso Salmerón had reason to complain of not having been invited to a secret session which dealt with the alleged heresies of the Toledan Archbishop Bartolomé Carranza. At the same time, Brus himself accepted the assignment quite reluctantly, because he felt that, as the chief imperial delegate, he would have enough work in defending the interests of the Empire against French and other machinations without supervising the perusal of an endless number of books which might include heretical passages. However, he yielded to the entreaties of his colleagues. Even in March, 1563, when he asked the emperor for permission to resign from the Commission, Ferdinand pointed out to him that he, Brus, was the only German member of the group, and that only by his presence might he protect German literary interests. The emperor could have added that there were altogether too few German prelates in Trent to defend the position of German Catholics, whose country was the main battleground in the new sectarian strife. The archbishop obeyed, and skillfully saw the debates through to the end. Moreover, he apparently submitted a report to the final plenary session of the Council which was sufficiently comprehensive to serve as a basis for future action. [20]

Regrettably, the conciliar commissions did not keep regular minutes of their sessions. Hence, hardly any records of the negotiations in Brus' domicile have been preserved. Most reports which Brus and other delegates sent home dealt with the broader, dogmatic, ritualistic, and ecclesiological issues which were at the center of the Council's discussions. Only in a few letters did the Prague archbishop refer to his functions at the Commission. For the most part he emphasized that, as an imperial envoy, he considered it his duty to help remove from the Index, wherever possible, works by German authors of but questionable heretical content. He also complained that he did not have enough assistance in sifting the incriminated literature, particularly assistance from persons "familiar with German heresies and mores." When he asked the emperor to send him the Viennese expert Friedrich Staphylus, the latter declined. Nonetheless, on June 18, 1563, the archbishop assured the newly elected king, Maximilian II, that he had succeeded in deleting the names of certain German authors from the Index. However, his valiant efforts to spare many works by Erasmus of Rotterdam from wholesale outlawry proved unavailing, for the Italo-Spanish majority of the Commission proved inflexible in its opposition to the Dutch thinker. [21]

In contrast to Brus' concern about the possible outlawry of books written by fairly orthodox Germans, the Spaniards were mainly apprehensive that the elimination from the conciliar Index of certain books prohibited by the Spanish Holy Office might undermine its authority in their home country. To be sure, in a letter of June 8, 1563, to Ventura de Guzmán, chief representative of the Spanish Holy Office, Guzmán's confrere Francisco Sancho argued that the Commission could do no more than make a negative decision and fail to include a certain title or author in its list. Such an omission, in Sancho's opinion, would not prevent the Spanish Inquisition from adding the same title or name to its own compilation. Nevertheless, Guzmán and the Spanish members of the Commission unrelentingly continued to insist on the inclusion in the Index of the catechism prepared by their own primate, Carranza. Despite his high ecclesiastical office and the aid of many friends, including the Portuguese Archbishop of Braga, Bartolomeus de Martyribus Fernándes—a leading member of the Commission, Fernándes had from the outset proposed delegation of the entire Index revision to the Universities of Bologna, Paris, Salamanca, and Coimbra—neither Carranza nor his book escaped prosecution by his enemies. Ultimately, the Toledan archbishop died in a Roman prison, eighteen years after the initial indictment. [22]

Notwithstanding the professed ecumenical character of the Council, national interests and biases thus intruded into many of its discussions. Although the delegations at the Council of Trent were not formally divided into "nations" as had been those at the Councils of Constance and Basel in the fifteenth century, the papal legates in Trent realized from the beginning that they could not prevent divergent national viewpoints, even prejudices, from determining the attitudes of many prelates and their sovereigns. [23]

Under these circumstances the cards appeared stacked against the Talmud. Before long, some Italian-Jewish leaders began to realize the danger to their cultural evolution if the Council were to follow Paul IV's example and outlaw the use of the Talmud and all its commentaries without exception.

JEWISH INTERVENTIONS

Perhaps forewarned by someone in Ercole Gonzaga's entourage about the trends evolving in the Index Commission, Mantuan-Jewish leaders apparently sought to initiate a joint action with several other North-Italian communities. It probably took time to organize a formal petition to the Council, but before February 3, 1563, Jacob Bonaventura addressed a brief petition to the papal legates of the Ecumenical Council. Referring to the rumors about the Council's intention to review Paul IV's Index, he explained to Gonzaga and his colleagues the importance of the Talmud to all Jews in their daily social, political, and religious life. Bonaventura requested, therefore, that the voluminous work be carefully reexamined. He also reminded the conciliar prelates that many popes had for generations expressly permitted the use of that classic. But he added: "Should it be found that there are statements in it [the Talmud] which appear objectionable to the Christian religion, these can readily be deleted. After their expurgation the book should be allowed to be printed so that everybody be able to possess and study it without any scandal." Realizing that such a task would require much work and expense, Jacob expressed his readiness to assume the costs of these proceedings under whatever penalty the chairman of the Council might provide. [24]

Evidently this petition was sent on to the Index Commission, where it did not find a responsive echo. Even Brus merely submitted a copy of the petition to the emperor and complained that he and his colleagues had been "molested" by the Jewish representatives, who had "deservedly been rebuffed." To this report of February 3, 1563, Brus added talmudic excerpts, prepared by "some theologians," which were to illustrate the "myriads of fables and blasphemies found in the Talmud." In his reply, Ferdinand approved the position taken by his envoy. Other delegates to the Council, too, seem not to have subscribed to Bonaventura's views. In a vote submitted to the Council, one Magister Christophorus Patavinus discussed the alternatives open to the Council with respect to heretical Christian writings, if it wished to salvage them through the expurgation of objectionable passages. He drew a parallel with the Talmud, but emphasized the following difference: "Although Gregory IX and Innocent IV considered the Talmud to be subject to outright suppression rather than expurgation, notwithstanding its inclusion of innumerable obscure matters relating to the Holy Scripture, there is no similarity between the Talmud and other heretical books which include some nonconformist statements. For in the Talmud they [the rabbis] speak in such obscene and undignified terms about our Lord Christ that it is inappropriate to cite them, whereas the heretics who profess belief in, and the knowledge of, Christ do not act in the same way." Another undated memorandum submitted to the Council argued the pros and cons of a similar position. [25]

The Jews did not give up, however. On October 19, 1563, the Mantuan community elected a committee of five members who, together with the officiating elders, were to bend every effort to prevent an inimical decision by the Council. This committee was given wide discretion in disbursing funds. Two days later Samuel b. Moses Cazis and Solomon b. Ḥayyim Segal proceeded to Trent. They were told to appear "before the awesome Council" and try to prevail upon it to delegate the question of Hebrew censorship to papal decision. They were especially to seek permission to read and own expurgated talmudic and other rabbinic texts. By no means were they to pledge that the Jews would refrain from using outlawed rabbinic works. Moreover, neither delegate was to act without the other's consent. The delegates endeavored to enlist the cooperation of influential personalities wherever they could. For example, Bishop Pedro Gonzales de Mendoza of Salamanca complained that he had received a letter from Ferdinand's daughter, Duchess Eleanora of Mantua, asking him to support that petition. However regretfully, Mendoza, a member of the Index Commission, could not give vent to his indubitable antitalmudic bias. He doubtless was delighted to join his colleagues in suggesting delegation of the final issuance of the new Index to the Papacy. [26]

These few glimpses of the negotiations at the Council do not offer a complete picture of what happened. We know only that to the very end some matters relating to the Index remained unresolved. Overwhelmed as the members were by the immensity of their task, and subject to the many pulls and stresses of divergent national and theological interests, the Commission—and, following it, the final plenary session of the Council (on December 4, 1563)—decided to leave the ultimate decision to the pope. The Council voted to submit its assembled materials and records of discussions to the papal Chancery and to leave to Pius IV's discretion the final choice of what should be included in the forthcoming Index, to be published under the pope's name. The preparations were undoubtedly far advanced, however. They were summarized in ten basic rules (*regulae*) discussed by the Index Commission before November 27, 1563, and apparently adopted by it before its adjournment. Later these rules were taken over verbatim into the new Index. In fact, within less than four months (March 24, 1564) the pope was able to issue a brief promulgating the new Index, which appeared in print a few months later (August, 1564). In this brief the pope emphasized that the Index had been prepared after long and sustained labor by many prelates, "eminent for both learning and sound judgment," at the Council—an emphasis repeated by Foreiro in his Foreword to the new compilation. [27]

The Jews had every reason to be satisfied with the outcome. From the outset they had wished the Council to abstain from taking direct action and allow the pope to make the final decision. They felt confident that Pius IV would prove far more friendly to the Jewish cause. In addition, they must have learned that on August 31, 1563, the papal secretary of state had been induced by a Jewish representative of the Prague community to order the nuncio Zaccaria Delfino to intervene with the emperor in behalf of the Jews threatened with expulsion from Bohemia. True, the Index started on a menacing note. The very first of the Ten Rules stated succinctly: "All books which were condemned by popes or ecumenical councils before the year 1515 but are not found in this Index shall be considered condemned in the same fashion as they were once condemned." If that regulation were strictly interpreted, one could readily invoke the numerous papal enactments since Gregory IX which had outlawed the use of the Talmud and, as recently as 1553, had caused the burning of many thousands of rabbinic works. Yet by its specific reference to the Talmud in the third section dealing with anonymous writings, the Index precluded that interpretation. While adopting from Paul IV's Index the sentence outlawing the Talmud "and all its glosses, annotations, interpretations, and expositions," the new list added the clause: "If, however, the work should appear without the name Talmud and without any attacks and calumnies against the Christian religion, it shall be tolerated." [28]

The importance of the new Index for all of Western Christendom was underscored by none other than Francisco Foreiro. As secretary of the Index Commission, he provided the new Index with an extensive Foreword in which he characterized the list as the result of prolonged labor by the Commission. He thus put on the entire work the seal of approval of the great Tridentine Council, so that the Index would enjoy authority beyond the lifetime of Pius IV. Indeed, even after the demise of that pope and the assumption of the papal tiara by the Roman Inquisitor-General Michele Ghislieri (Pius V), the provisions of the Index remained unaltered. By continuing to publish the breviary, the missal, and the catechism as implementations of conciliar resolutions, Ghislieri indirectly expressed his approval for the Index as well. In some respects, Ghislieri and his associates had anticipated the universal validity of the new Index in their decree of May 13, 1562, relating to the treatment of heretical books. Though addressing themselves to the librarians, booksellers, and printers of the States of the Church, they spoke as "Cardinals, specially delegated by the Holy Apostolic See as general inquisitors against heretical depravity, for the entire Christian Commonwealth [*per tutta la Repubblica Christiana*]." Subsequent editions of the Index to the end of the nineteenth century constantly invoked the authority of the Tridentine Index, even if they made more or less substantial alterations in its text. [29]

AFTERMATH

When rumors about the decisions of the Council reached their ears, the Jewish leaders of many countries seem to have greeted it with rejoicing. No sooner did Brus von Müglitz return home than he was greeted by the Jewish community of Prague with a letter of thanks, most probably dated February 16, 1564. After asserting that they had heard that the archbishop "fought and struggled with all his strength to have the Talmud and other works well corrected and restored to their place," the Prague elders expressed to him their "immortal thanks" in their own and the entire community's behalf. [30]

This letter of thanks, if justified, reflects a considerable change in the archbishop's attitude after his anti-Jewish report to the emperor on February 17, 1563. We have no other information concerning Brus' activities during the last few months after his return to Trent (on May 19, 1563) from a trip home. He may have favored delegating ultimate responsibility for the new Index to the pope merely because he was tired and therefore happy to "pass the buck." But it is also possible that, during his visit to Prague in April, he had been approached by the Prague Jewish leaders and persuaded to play a more active role in the negotiations, an intervention which may have led to the addition of the clause allowing for the reprinting of an expurgated Talmud ultimately included in the new Index.

No conclusive documentary evidence is available. However, we know from Brus' own correspondence that his stay in Trent cost him much more than he could afford. A promised allowance of 600 florins a month from the emperor was admittedly insufficient to defray expenses (it compared unfavorably, for instance, with the monthly stipend of 500 scudi allotted to the papal legates). Brus was expected to supplement that allowance with revenue from his archbishopric. But even that modest imperial pledge was never kept; Brus received no more than 2,000 florins over a period of fifteen months. Yet the original promise may have given him enough confidence to rent expensive quarters in Trent, which had but few accommodations for the large number of delegates and visitors. Only so can we understand why his apartment served as headquarters not only for the Index Commission but also for meetings of representatives of other powers whenever some concerted action was indicated. Brus must also have expended considerable sums for clerical and domestic services and for entertaining colleagues and visitors in a style expected of the chief envoy of the Holy Roman Empire. As a result, he had to borrow much money. After the final session of the Council, on December 4, his Hungarian colleague Bishop Drascovič was able to leave Trent almost immediately. But as late as December 27 Brus wrote a pitiful letter to the emperor complaining that he had no funds for the expenses of his return trip. He even offered to forego all the back salary due him, if only the Imperial Chamber would take over the repayment of his debts. It is, therefore, not too venturesome to suggest that some of the Mantuan-Jewish representatives to the Council or the Jewish elders who, in the years 1558–62, had succeeded in publishing thirty-four Hebrew books in neighboring Riva di Trento, extended a helping hand to him during his stay at the Council. [31]

Leaving such speculations aside, it was doubtless with the authorization of the Commission that Foreiro, in his Foreword to the new Index, placed so great an emphasis on the international character of the work. This emphasis reminds one of a similar, though dubious, argument presented by Cardinal Morone, with special reference to the Index Commission, in response to Ferdinand I's complaint that prelates from the Mediterranean lands far outnumbered representatives from the other Christian countries. Nonetheless, the matter did not then come to rest as the Jews may have expected. To begin with, the decisions of the Tridentine Council, in general, highly significant as they appear in retrospect, were not speedily implemented even in Rome itself. In other countries, particularly France and Germany, their acceptance came only after long and arduous effort on the part of the Counter Reformation leaders. With respect to the Index, Spain made it quite clear that its local conditions might require the

outlawry of certain books which would seem innocuous elsewhere—
an attitude which caused Pius IV to exclaim that Rome is to dictate
to Spain, not Spain to Rome. The compilers of the Spanish Indexes
of the following years (including Cardinal Gaspar de Quiroga, archbishop of Toledo and Inquisitor-General of the realm, who, in collaboration with Juan de Mariana and other scholars, issued a new
Index in 1582–83) paid no heed to the Tridentine clause on talmudic
literature and continued to outlaw all rabbinic literature in terms
identical with those used in the Valdés Index of 1559. [32]

If outlawry of rabbinic letters in Spain was of but minor consequence to the Jewish people, since professing Jews had long
disappeared from the Iberian Peninsula, the situation elsewhere
remained in flux. In 1596 Clement VIII returned to the intransigent
position of Paul IV and, in his new "Sisto-Clementine Index,"
restored Paul's old formula, with a finality which seemed to defy
all Jewish communal efforts. Ironically, even the reading by high
churchmen of heretical works for purposes of condemnation was
made increasingly difficult. If Laynez and his associates had viewed
Paul IV's efforts as too severe and had sought to secure a blanket
authorization for the Jesuit Order's provincials to permit such reading to their subordinates when there was good reason, Laynez'
second successor in the leadership of the Order, Everard Mercurian,
insisted that licenses could be granted only by the general himself.
Such rigidity certainly militated against further progress in rabbinic
studies by Catholic scholars. Only the fact that the arm of the
Roman Inquisition did not extend beyond the boundaries of Italy
in any practical way prevented it from effectively outlawing the
publication of talmudic and other rabbinic texts in Germany and
Poland, not to speak of Protestant-dominated Holland. [33]

Notes

ESSAY 2

1. Javier Ruiz Almanza, "La Población de España en el siglo XVI," *Revista internacional de sociología*, III (1943), 115–38; *idem*, "Las Ideas y las estadisticas de población en España en el siglo XVI," *ibid.*, V (1947), 89–107; and Marcel R. Reinhard, "Histoire et démographie," *Revue historique*, CCIII (1950), 193–206. See also Karl Julius Beloch, "Die Volkszahl als Faktor und Gradmesser der historischen Entwicklung," *Historische Zeitschrift*, CXI (1913), 321–37. To be sure, there have always been pessimists who believe that trying to ascertain population figures for any period before the nineteenth century is a rather hopeless task. See, for example, Henri Sée, "Peut-on évaluer la population de l'ancienne France?" *Revue de l'économie politique*, XXXVIII (1924), 647–55. Only a bit less pessimistic was the report submitted by Carlo Cipolla, Jean Dhondt, Michael Postan, and Philipp Wolff to the IXth International Congress of Historical Sciences in Paris, 1950. See their "Rapport sur la démographie au moyen âge," in the *Actes* of that Congress, I, 55 ff. Yet the prevailing notion among medievalists now is that total despair is not in order and that patient research over many years, if attacked from various angles, would yield at least plausible approximations. See, for instance, Léopold Génicot's "Sur les témoignages d'accroissement de la population en Occident du XIe au XIIIe siècle," *Journal of World History*, I (1953–54), 446–62. Certainly, the very large, though incomplete, bibliography of pertinent studies in various lands, quoted in 1956 by Roger Mols, is mute testimony that a great many students believe in the worth of such research. See Mols's *Introduction à la démographie historique des villes d'Europe du XIVe au XVIIIe siècle*, 3 vols., Recueil de travaux d'histoire et de philologie of the University of Louvain, 4th Ser. Fasc. 3 (Louvain, 1956), III, pp. ix–lxix. The conviction that thoroughgoing demographic investigations pertaining to the history of the Jewish people are an urgent scholarly desideratum has been with me since my early historical studies and has grown deeper in the course of time. If I may be permitted a personal recollection, I still remember a discussion I had in the 1920s in the office of the late Dr. Stephen Wise with him and the late Dr. Judah Magnes. At that time I dreamed aloud about some day writing a book on "Jewish History in the Light of Numbers." However, I never got around to

publishing more than a first installment; see below, Essay 3. Hopefully this task will soon be undertaken by younger historians.

2. See the data supplied by Eduard Meyer in his *Geschichte des Altertums,* 3d ed., I, Part 2, p. 194; Ulrich Kahrstedt in his article "Bevölkerungswesen," in *Handwörterbuch der Staatswissenschaften,* 4th ed. (Jena, 1924), II, 656 ff.; K. T. von Inama Sternegg and R. Häpke, "Die Bevölkerung des Mittelalters und der neueren Zeit bis Ende des 18. Jahrhunderts in Europa," *ibid.,* pp. 670–86. See also Fernand Braudel's stimulating remarks on "La Démographie et les dimensions des sciences de l'homme," *Annales Economies, Sociétés, et Civilisations,* XV (1960), 493–523, with reference to such divergent new approaches as those advanced by Ernst Wagemann, Alfred Sauvy, and Louis Chevalier; Marcel R. Reinhard and André Armengaud, *Histoire générale de la population mondiale* (Paris, 1961); and particularly Josiah Cox Russell, *Late Ancient and Medieval Population,* Transactions of the American Philosophical Society, n.s. XLVIII, 3 (Philadelphia, 1958). Professor Russell, who has spent a lifetime of research in this field, is the author of many specialized studies relating to medieval demography, some of which will be mentioned in the following notes.

3. The problems connected with these biblical narratives, the way they were transmitted in the numerous extant Hebrew manuscripts and the ancient versions, as well as their evaluation against the background of other data available for ancient Israel and the neighboring countries of the period are examined by me below, "The Israelitic Population under the Kings" (Essay 3). Although this article was completed in 1928 and first published five years later, no substantial studies of any kind relating to this subject have appeared since that time.

4. Gregory Abu'lfaraj Bar-Hebraeus (Bar 'Ebhrāyā), *Ta'rikh mukhtaṣar al-duwal (Historia compendiosa dynastiarum),* edited in Arabic and translated into Latin by E. Pococke (Oxford, 1663), pp. 73, 116; new Arabic edition by Antun Salhani (Beirut, 1890), p. 115. Needless to say, the testimony of a chronicler writing some eleven centuries after the event cannot be considered very reliable. His statement has, indeed, been subjected to divergent interpretations; see below, n. 13. However, his testimony may, indeed, achieve greater authority if it is supported by a number of related facts or hypotheses.

5. In the absence of regular censuses, the teeming populations of the medieval Muslim countries have had to be "guestimated" on the basis of whatever chance records are available. Clearly, the larger a city was— and tenth-century Baghdad, for example, is sometimes assumed to have embraced as many as 2,000,000 inhabitants living in its more than 10,000 streets—the less familiar were even contemporaries with the size of its population, and the less dependable were the figures transmitted by them. Nevertheless, a number of sociological-minded scholars have attempted a variety of estimates for different periods and regions. As far as the Jews

are concerned Eli Ashtor (Strauss) courageously came to grips with these problems in his תולדות היהודים במצרים וסוריה תחת שלטון הממלוכים (History of the Jews in Egypt and Syria under the Rule of the Mamelukes), 2 vols. (Jerusalem, 1944–51), esp. I, 292 ff.; II, 429 ff.; and in his קורות היהודים בספרד המוסלמית (A History of the Jews in Muslim Spain), 2 vols. (Jerusalem, 1960–66), passim. It is to be hoped that with the publication of more and more Arabic and Hebrew sources this important area of medieval Jewish life will be further illuminated.

6. Francesco Bonaini, Statuti inediti della città di Pisa dal XII al XIV seculo (Florence, 1854), I, 5; and A. Rossi, "Lo Sviluppo demografico di Pisa dal XII° al XV° secolo," Bollettino storico pisano, n.s. XIV–XVI (1945–47), 5–61.

7. Edouard Baratier, La Démographie provençale du XIII⁰ au XVII⁰ siècle. Avec chiffres de comparaisons pour le XVIII⁰ siècle, Ecole pratique des hautes études, VI⁰ section, Démographie et sociétés, V (Paris, 1961), 60, 69 ff.; Robert Henri Bautier, "Feux, population et structure sociale au milieu du XV⁰ siècle (l'exemple de Carpentras)," Annales Economies, Sociétés, Civilisations, XIV (1959), 255–68; and Richard W. Emery, The Jews of Perpignan in the Thirteenth Century: An Economic Study Based on Notarial Records (New York, 1959), pp. 11ff. See also Josiah Cox Russell's review of "Recent Advances in Medieval Demography," Speculum, XL (1965), 90 f.; and on the general history of these and the neighboring communities, M. de Maulde, Les Juifs dans les Etats français du Saint-Siège au moyen âge: Documents pour servir à l'histoire des Israélites et de la Papauté (Paris, 1886), passim; and the extensive literature listed in SRH, X, 339 ff.

8. I. P. Donnazzolo and M. Saibante, "Lo Sviluppo demografico di Verona e della sua provincia dal sec. XV ai nostri giorni," Metron, VI, Parts 3–4 (1926), 56–180; Daniele Beltrami, "Lineamenti di storia della popolazione di Venezia nei sec. XVI, XVII e XVIII," Atti of the Istituto Veneto di Scienze, Lettere ed Arti, CIX (1950–51), 9–40; Karl Julius Beloch, Bevölkerungsgeschichte Italiens, 3 vols. (Berlin, 1937–61), especially the posthumously published vol. III, relating to Venice and other northern states. All these studies pay some attention to the Jewish segment of the population, although they are, of course, not adequate substitutes for more specialized research.

9. Albert Girard, "Le Chiffre de la population de l'Espagne dans les temps modernes," Revue d'histoire moderne, III (1928), 420–36; IV (1929), 3–17; esp. III, 420. See also Paul Mombert's review of "Die Anschauungen des 17. und 18. Jahrhunderts über die Abnahme der Bevölkerung," Jahrbücher für Nationalökonomie und Statistik, CXXXV (1931), 481–503.

10. Montesquieu, Lettres Persanes, cxii, in his Oeuvres, 5 vols. (Paris, 1796), V, 230 ff.

11. David Hume, "On the Populousness of Ancient Nations," in his

Essays, ed. by T. H. Green and T. H. Grose (London, 1875), p. 58. See more fully below, Essay 3.

12. Adolf Harnack, *The Mission and Expansion of Christianity in the First Three Centuries* (English trans. from the German), 2d ed., 2 vols. (New York, 1908), esp. I, 3 ff.; Arthur Ungnad, "Zahl der von Sanherib deportierten Judäer," *Zeitschrift für die alttestamentliche Wissenschaft,* LIX (1942–43), 199–202. Ungnad seems to have found no followers with his untenable emendation.

13. See Jean Juster, *Les Juifs dans l'Empire Romain,* 2 vols. (Paris, 1914), I, 209 ff.; and the various other sources cited in my *SRH,* I, 370 ff. n. 7. To the literature there listed, add Joseph Klausner, "How Many Jews Will Be Able to Live in Palestine? Based on an Analysis of the Jewish Population in Palestine in the Days of the Second Temple," *Jewish Social Studies,* XI (1949), 119–28; and Judah Rosenthal's note, "Bar Hebraeus and a Jewish Census under Claudius," *ibid.,* XVI (1954), 267–68. Even if we were to assume that Bar-Hebraeus mistook the reference by Eusebius to a Claudian census of Roman citizens for one intended to establish the size of the Jewish population in the Empire, the outcome as to the population figures derived from various other extant sources would not be much different. In any case, it stands to reason that after the fall of Jerusalem, when Vespasian transferred the Temple tax to the temple of Jupiter Capitolinus in Rome, the Roman office of the *fiscus judaicus* must have had a fair amount of information on the number of Jewish males over twenty who were supposed to pay two drachmas each. Such rolls, kept at the Roman headquarters of the *fiscus,* were indeed recorded in 236 and again when they were destroyed by Julian the Apostate in the following century. However, no detailed information from that source has reached us (although it might have influenced some contemporaries to assume a large Jewish population), and we are limited to the use of other meager sources for any kind of estimate of the Jewish population in the later Roman Empire. This neglect of demography is not limited to the Jewish subjects of Rome alone. It is noteworthy that, despite the publication of an enormous historical literature on classical antiquity, which includes a number of monographs on individual demographic aspects, the main comprehensive work on the general Graeco-Roman population still is Karl Julius Beloch's *Die Bevölkerung der griechisch-römischen Welt,* published more than eighty years ago (Leipzig, 1886).

14. K. T. Eheberg, "Strassburg's Bevölkerungszahl seit Ende des 15. Jahrhunderts bis zur Gegenwart," *Jahrbücher für Nationalökonomie und Statistik,* XLI (1883), 297–314; XLII (1884), 413–30, esp. XLI, 305 ff.; D. Beltrami, *Storia della popolazione di Venezia dalla fine del secolo XVI alla caduta della Repubblica* (Padua, 1954), pp. 10 ff.; *idem,* "La Composizione economica e professionale della popolazione di Venezia nei sec.

XVII e XVIII," *Giornale degli Economisti*, X (1951), 70 ff. These older censuses retain their relative usefulness despite the legitimate *caveats* sounded by Paul Mombert in his "Ueber die geringe Zuverlässigkeit älterer Volkszählungen," *Jahrbücher für Nationalökonomie und Statistik*, CXXXIX (1933), 745–51. See also Erich Keyser, *Bevölkerungsgeschichte Deutschlands*, 2d ed. enlarged (Leipzig, 1941), esp. pp. 285 ff., 342 ff., 355 ff., 435 ff. Despite its strong Nazi bias, this volume furnishes some useful demographic data about medieval German Jews as well.

15. See *SRH*, II, 185. Among the tax-dodging devices also was the false claim by the taxpayer that he was a rabbi and as such exempt from taxation. At one time 12,000 Babylonian Jews were denounced to the authorities for having wrongfully made such claims. It apparently was Rabbah bar Naḥmani who had certified the rabbinic profession of many of these claimants, and, as a result, he now had to flee from Pumbedita. After several changes of residence, he died in exile. *Ibid.*, p. 243. Not surprisingly, tax evasions on the part of both Jews and non-Jews were quite frequent elsewhere, too. In medieval Baghdad there was a popular saying that "a Jew will never pay his taxes till he has his head smacked." *Ibid.*, III, 167 f. Of course, the number of tax evaders, who do not appear on the extant tax lists, can no longer be ascertained. Wherever tax farmers were engaged to collect the taxes from Jews on a shared basis, the collectors, prompted by self-interest, were probably more efficient in curtailing evasions. If, as frequently was the case, the tax farmers themselves were Jews, we may take it for granted that they knew their fellow members of the community, and their respective possessions, much better than did any outsider–all of which added to the public's resentment of such *mokhsim* (publicans). Therefore, in evaluating tax rolls one must bear in mind in each case the peculiar local and personal situations before deciding the extent to which the records reflect reality.

16. The Chronicler wrote even more censoriously: "And Satan stood up against Israel, and moved David to number Israel" (I Chron. 21:1). While differing from the author of the Second Book of Samuel with respect to the results of the census, he agreed that 70,000 persons had died from the purported three-day pestilence. This folkloristic idea that the divine wrath was aroused by any population census and that a curse befell any people so counted probably antedated the biblical account. Nonetheless, because it was so blatantly stated in the biblical story concerning the most revered King David, it must have permanently discouraged pious Jews and Christians from conducting censuses.

17. Ya'qub ben Ibrahim Abu Yusuf, *Kitab al-Kharaj* (Le Livre de l'impôt foncier), French trans. by Edmond Fagnan, Bibliothèque archéologique, I (Paris, 1921), pp. 70 (Arabic), 189 (French); the anonymous "Vita Ludovici Quarti Imperatoris, 1312–1347" in J. F. Böhmer's ed. of *Fontes rerum germanicarum*, 4 vols. (Stuttgart, 1843–68), I,

156; Meir Wiener, ed., *Regesten zur Geschichte der Juden in Deutschland während des Mittelalters*, Part 1, pp. 44 f. Nos. 136–37; Solomon ibn Adret, שאלות ותשובות (*Responsa*) (Leghorn, 1778), III, 411; the resolutions of the Barcelona Conference of 1354 reprinted in Yitzhak Fritz Baer's *Die Juden im Christlichen Spanien* (Berlin, 1929–36), I, Part 1, 348 ff. No. 253, with the editor's notes thereon; and numerous other sources cited in *SRH*, III, 161 ff., 283 ff. nn. 43 ff.; XII, 198 ff., 341 ff. *passim;* and my *The Jewish Community: Its History and Structure to the American Revolution*, 3 vols. (Philadelphia, 1942), esp. Chaps. VIII and XV, *passim.*

18. See many illustrations furnished in my last-mentioned works, *passim.*

19. In the last four decades researches based upon city areas have considerably increased in number. In Germany alone, such works as Hans Planitz, *Die Deutsche Stadt im Mittelalter. Von der Römerzeit bis zu den Zunftkämpfen* (Graz, 1954); and Erich Keyser's voluminous *Deutsches Städtebuch. Handbuch städtischer Geschichte*, 4 vols. (Stuttgart, 1959–64), have taken full cognizance of the areal factor. See also Keyser's earlier work, *Bevölkerungsgeschichte Deutschlands*. At the same time, these and other scholars have paid full attention to demographic changes caused by biological or economic factors. See esp. Wilhelm Abel, "Wachstumsschwankungen mitteleuropäischer Völker seit dem Mittelalter," *Jahrbücher für Nationalökonomie und Statistik*, CXLII (1935), 670–92; *idem*, "Wüstungen und Preisfall im spätmittelalterlichen Europa," *ibid.*, CLXV (1953), 380–427; and several other studies by that author.

20. See P. Gras, "Le Registre paroissial de Givry (1334–57) et la peste noire en Bourgogne," *Bibliothèque de l'Ecole des Chartes*, C (1939), 295–308; John Saltmarsh, "Plague and Economic Decline in England in the Later Middle Ages," *Cambridge Historical Journal*, VII (1941–43), 23–41; and many additional data and literature supplied in *SRH*, XI, 160 ff., 365 ff. nn. 50 ff., as well as in various other contexts.

21. See below, Essay 3. The findings there have been largely confirmed by subsequent publications, especially by Samuel Klein and Père Félix Marie Abel.

22. No serious study is available about rural Jews in the Middle Ages. Generally speaking, even information about the peasant masses, who in most countries vastly outnumbered their urban compatriots, can to a large extent be reconstructed only from ecclesiastical and secular records preserved in towns. Understandably, there has been a growing interest in agriculture and the peasantry throughout the ages, particularly on the part of Marxist scholars. The number of publications in this field has, indeed, increased by leaps and bounds in the last few decades. But these studies have rarely paid attention to Jewish aspects of medieval rural life.

Even the scattered information available in either rabbinic or non-Jewish sources has thus far not been sufficiently brought together and analyzed. We are limited, therefore, to mere guesswork about the demographic aspects of rural Jews in the West before the early modern period, when, as a result of frequent expulsions from cities and a generally greater security of roads and rural habitations, the number of Jews living in villages (whether or not they were themselves tilling the soil) decidedly increased in both Poland-Lithuania and Germany.

23. See the numerous monographs on individual ghettos—such as Attilio Milano, *Il Ghetto di Roma* (Rome, 1964); Hermann Vogelstein and Paul Rieger, *Geschichte der Juden in Rom*, 2 vols. (Berlin, 1894), Vol. II, *passim;* Isidor Kracauer, "Geschichte der Judengasse in Frankfurt am Main," *Festschrift der Realschule . . . (Philanthropin)*, 2 parts (Frankfurt, 1904), Part 2, pp. 303–451; Karl Nahrgang, *Die Frankfurter Altstadt. Eine historisch-geographische Studie*, Rhein-Meinische Forschungen, XXVII (Frankfurt, 1939); Julius Hülsen, *Zwei Ansichten der Frankfurter Judengasse, mit Erläuterungen* (Berlin, 1931) and, more broadly, Kracauer's *Geschichte der Juden in Frankfurt am Main (1150–1824)*, 2 vols. (Frankfort, 1925–27); and many other local monographs. Regrettably, this method has thus far had little application in Jewish demographic studies; it has not even been used in a supplementary fashion. For example, the otherwise meritorious efforts to ascertain the size of the Jewish population in medieval Sicily (this problem had been discussed by scholars for many years) and in Italy during the Renaissance, by Attilio Milano and Moses A. Shulvass respectively, were based almost exclusively on deductions from scattered literary sources. See Milano, "The Number of the Jews in Sicily at the Time of Their Expulsion in 1492," *Jewish Social Studies*, XV (1953), 25–32 (also appeared in Italian); and Shulvass, "The Jewish Population in Renaissance Italy," *ibid.*, XIII (1951), 3–24, slightly revised in his Hebrew volume, חיי היהודים באיטליה בתקופת הריניסאנס (*Jewish Life in Renaissance Italy* [New York, 1955]), pp. 1 ff. See also F. Natali, "Problemi di una storia della popolazione siciliana medioevale," *Quaderni di geografia umana per la Sicilia e la Calabria*, II (1951), 20–31. This is not at all surprising, since the difficulties of this line of research are indeed very great.

24. Michael Adler, *Jews of Medieval England*, pp. 53, 123 f. App. xiv, 179 f., 249 f. App. xii. These studies reflect the general uncertainty about the size of the Anglo-Jewish population before the Expulsion of 1290. See the debates on this score mentioned in *SRH*, XII, 243 ff. nn. 2–3. Also of great value is, in this connection, the pioneering monograph by Alexander Pinthus, "Studien über die bauliche Entwicklung der Judengassen in den deutschen Städten," *Zeitschrift für Geschichte der Juden in Deutschland*, II (1930–31), 101–30, 197–217, 284–300; this study also appeared as a dissertation at the Technische Hochschule in Hanover,

under the title *Die Judensiedlungen der deutschen Städte, eine stadtbiologische Studie* (Hanover, 1931).

25. See J[osiah] C[ox] Russell, "A Quantitative Approach to the Medieval Population Change," *Journal of Economic History*, XXIV (1964), 1–21. Some limited information can also be derived from genealogical investigations. After carefully studying the records of some noble families in the district of Namur, Belgium, in the period from 1000 to 1250, Léopold Génicot reached the conclusion that the average number of children ranged from 4.30 to 5.75. See *Journal of World History*, I, 451 f. Somewhat similar calculations were made by Pierre Feuchère in his "Histoire sociale et généalogique: La Noblesse du Nord de la France," *Annales Economies, Sociétés, Civilisations*, VI (1951), 306–18. Some additional data were also yielded by archaeological excavations of medieval cemeteries. By reconstructing the ages of the extant skeletons some tentative conclusions were reached concerning the mortality rates of the local population. Such interesting discoveries, especially in Poland and Hungary, were mentioned by J. C. Russell in his article in *Speculum*, XL, 86. Unfortunately, few medieval Jewish cemeteries are preserved intact, although individual researches based upon the necropolises in Montjuich, Barcelona, and elsewhere, have been mentioned in my *SRH*, IV, 33, 249 n. 37, and in other contexts.

ESSAY 3

1. David Hume, "On the Populousness of Ancient Nations," in *Essays: Moral, Political and Literary*, ed. by Thomas Hill Green and Thomas Hodge Grose (London, 1875), p. 58.

2. Montesquieu, *Lettres Persanes* (1721), in his *Oeuvres complétes*, ed. by Edouard Laboulaye, 7 vols. (Paris, 1875–79), I, 351 ff. No. cxii.

3. In his aforementioned essay "On the Populousness of Ancient Nations." In fact Hume's attitude was not altogether negative. For example, in a letter to John Clephane on April 18, 1750, he stated that he had written "not altogether in opposition to Vossius and Montesquieu who exaggerate that affair infinitely; but starting some doubts, and scruples, and difficulties, sufficient to make us suspend our judgment on that head" (*The Letters of David Hume*, ed. by J. Y. T. Greig, 2 vols. [Oxford, 1932], I, 139 ff. No. 66).

4. Robert Wallace, *A Dissertation on the Numbers of Mankind in Ancient and Modern Times, with an Appendix Containing Observations on the Same Subject, and Remarks on Mr. Hume's Discourse on the Populousness of Ancient Nations* (London, 1753).

5. Julius Beloch, *Die Bevölkerung der griechisch-römischen Welt* (Leipzig, 1886), *passim*, (cited hereafter: Beloch); Eduard Meyer,

"Bevölkerungswesen," in *Handwörterbuch der Staatswissenchaften*, 2d–3d ed.; *idem, Geschichte des Altertums, passim.*

6. See, for instance, Frants Buhl, *Die socialen Verhältnisse der Israeliten* (Berlin, 1899), p. 52.

7. The official measurements of 1873 yielded 29,400 km^2, while those of 1879 counted only 24,197 km^2. Others have estimated 31,001 km^2 (see Beloch, p. 254). More recently the estimate was given as 12,023 square miles, or 31,137 km^2 (see the *New International Yearbook*, 1927, pp. 266 ff.).

8. See *Yearbook, ibid.*

9. See *ibid.*, p. 106. In his *Statistique générale de la géographie*, J. Birst estimates an average of 247 inhabitants per km^2 in Belgium in 1921, but assumes a larger figure, 410 inhabitants per km^2 in Egypt in 1922 on the basis of an area of 33,000 km^2.

10. *New International Yearbook*, 1927, p. 106. See also below.

11. In 1921, 242 inhabitants per km^2.

12. See Beloch, p. 254. Eugène Cavaignac, in his *Population et capital dans le monde méditerranéen antique* (Strasbourg, 1923), p. 1, estimates the habitable area of ancient Egypt at 25,000 to 30,000 km^2.

13. See Eugène Cavaignac, "La Milice égyptienne au VIe siècle et l'empire achéménide," *Revue Egyptologique*, n.s. I (1919), 194 ff.

14. See J. Sacharoff's essay in *Arbeiten der k. russischen Gesandtschaft zu Peking*, II, 127 f.; cited by Beloch, p. 253.

15. Even among late nineteenth-century scholars there were some opposed to that extreme approach. Ernst Kornemann was quite right in protesting against the method adopted by Beloch and Meyer: "He [Meyer] is too greatly influenced by the modern trend which dares to deny some well-attested facts in the sources on the basis of a thorough substantive criticism. It forgets that it thereby cuts off the branch on which we rest and opens the floodgates to any individual's untrammeled subjective opinion." ("Die römischen Censuszahlen als statistisches Material. Zum Streit Seeck-Beloch," *Jahrbücher für Nationalökonomie und Statistik*, LXIX [1897], 296.) This observation holds true despite Meyer's reply in "Die Zahl der römischen Bürger unter Augustus," *ibid.*, LXX (1898), 59–65.

16. See Beloch's remarks in *Die Bevölkerung*, pp. 7 ff.

17. In the survey made here, attention was paid only to numbers of inhabitants, cities, soldiers, laborers in public works, members of families, and the like—all of which are useful for the understanding of population problems. I have also mentioned, in exceptional cases, the number of sacrifices offered, the total amounts of taxation, and so forth. But I have omitted numbers relating to dates and measures (for instance, those recording the reigns of kings or the measurements of the Temple),

from which we can learn very little for the subject of our inquiry. Similarly, figures relating to the entourage of an individual—such as those pertaining to David's "men of valour"—have been ignored, except in one case where the matter was of special importance. Finally, in listing textual variants found in the hundreds of Hebrew manuscripts underlying the compilation of the Kennicott Bible, I did not record slight variants in a single manuscript, since for the most part, they arose from simple scribal errors.

18. See Josh. 4:13; 7:3–5; 8:3 (there is no need for Heinrich Holzinger's emendation in *Das Buch Josua* [Berlin, 1901]), 12, and 25; 15:36, 41, 51, 54, 59, and 60; 18:24; 19:6 and 7 (Arnold Ehrlich's emendation has no basis in either manuscripts or versions); 21:4–7, 16, 19, 22, 24–27, 29, 31–33, and 39–41.

19. See also Carl Steuernagel's commentary thereon in *Das Buch Josua, übersetzt und erklärt,* Handkommentar zum Alten Testament (Göttingen, 1899).

20. See Albrecht Alt, "Galiläische Ortsliste in Jos. 19," *ZAW*, n.s. IV (1927), 62 and *passim.*

21. See Steuernagel's commentary, *ad loc.* He unnecessarily assumes, however, that verse 19:30 is a later interpolation.

22. *Antiquities* 5.2.10. See also George Foot Moore's commentary thereon.

23. Kimḥi's observation may be quoted here in full: "The probable explanation is that those thousands fell in the first battles in which Israel was defeated, for it is impossible that no Benjaminites should have been killed in these encounters. But Scripture mentions only the number killed when Benjamin was defeated by Israel."

24. See Judg. 1:4 and 7; 3:29 and 31; 4:3 (part 1), 6, 10 and 13; 5:8; 7:3, 6–8, 16, 19, and 22; 8:10, 14 and 30; 9:2, 4, 24, and 56; 11:33; 12:6, 9 and 14; 14:11 and 19; 15:11, 15 and 16; 16:27; 18:11; 20:2, 16, 17, 21, 25, 31, 34, 35, and 44–47; 21:10 and 12.

25. Concerning the quality of these manuscripts see Kennicott Bible, I, 78, 95, 100.

26. Viktor Aptowitzer, *Das Schriftwort in der rabbinischen Literatur,* 5 parts (Vienna, 1906–15) I.

27. For instance, Abraham Krochmal emends the reading to "and fifty thousand," while Peters reads "and five *allufim* [heads of clans]."

28. For instance Karl Ferdinand Budde writes: "A senselessly exaggerating gloss, induced by the final phrase נדולה מכה [great slaughter], to which LXX adds 'very.' " See below, n. 42; and A. Ehrlich's commentary.

29. Samuel R. Driver (*Notes on the Hebrew Text of the Books of Samuel,* 2d ed. [Oxford, 1913]) observes correctly that "how it found

its way into the text must remain a matter of speculation." See also below, n. 43.

30. Johann Matthäus Hassencamp, *Erinnerung gegen die von Kennicott herausgegebenen Anmerkungen zu I. Samuel 6, 19* (Frankfort, 1770); cited by O. G. Tychsen, *Tentamen de variis codd. Hebraeorum vet. test. Mss. generibus* (Rostock, 1772), pp. 206 ff. I am grateful to the late Dr. Barnett A. Elzas for turning my attention to this passage.

31. See *ibid.* and the dictionaries.

32. Josephus, *Antiquities* 6. 5. 3. 78.

33. See also Nos. 27, 30–31.

34. See Alfons Schulz, *Geschichte und Erbauung im Alten Testament: Eine exegetische Untersuchung* (Braunsberg, 1912), p. 41; and his commentary on Samuel.

35. See also Aptowitzer, *Das Schriftwort,* II, 25.

36. Josephus, *Antiquities* 6. 12. 6. 260. On this point the Josephus MSS diverge greatly: one raises the number to 530. See Benedict Niese's note in his critical edition of *Flavii Josephi Opera,* II (Berlin, 1885), 61.

37. See I Sam. 22:11 and 16.

38. For instance Karl Ferdinand Budde: "As usual, LXX raises the figure"; and Alfons Schulz: "Perhaps to magnify Saul's misdeed."

39. See various modern commentators and especially Mosheh Zvi Segal's interpretation of I Sam. 23:13, in *Perush Madda'i,* ed. by Abraham Kahana, 2d ed. (Warsaw, 1922).

40. On the reasons why the Chronicler cites different numbers, see Wilhelm Nowack's Commentary (*Handkommentar zum Alten Testament,* I, 4). But it is also possible that the Chronicler used a different source.

41. Contrary to H. P. Smith's and W. Caspari's interpretations. It is doubly apparent that we cannot deduce that only the word *elef* ("thousand") was in the original source itself, as suggested by Budde.

42. To quote Karl Ferdinand Budde, *Die Bücher Samuel,* Kurzer Handkommentar zum Alten Testament (Tübingen, 1902).

43. It is very questionable whether the Chronicler would have consciously corrected the text—as Budde and others have proposed—if he had not found support for his version in another source. In any case, the reading in I Chron. 11:20 ולו שם בשלשה ("and had a name among the three"), which may be emended to ולא שם לו בשלשה ("and he did not have a name among the three"), as suggested by Stopford was more correct. See Driver, *Notes on the Hebrew Text,* and Aptowitzer, *Das Schriftwort,* III, 77.

44. See I Sam. 4:2 and 10; 13:2, 5 ("six thousand"), and 15; 14:2 and 14; 18:25; 22:2; 24:3; 25:13 (particularly important because of the variants in 23:13, etc.); 26:2; 30:10 (this passage, too, is important,

for the same reason) and 17; II Sam. 2:30 and 31; 3:20 (despite the grammatical difficulty which caused A. Ehrlich and W. Caspari to emend the text); 8:13; 9:10 (cf. Aptowitzer, *Das Schriftwort*, III, 128); 10:6 (!) and 18; 18:1; 19:18; 23:8, 18 ("three hundred"), and 39 (see Aptowitzer, III, 97); and 24:15.

45. See Rudolf Kittel's commentary in *Die Bücher der Chronik übersetzt und erklärt*, Handkommentar zum Alten Testament, I, 6 (Leipzig, 1901), *ad loc.*

46. In any case, there is no reason to deduce that all these numbers have been inserted by a later scribe, as proposed by Immanuel Benzinger in his commentary *Die Bücher der Könige*, Kurzer Handkommentar zum Alten Testament (Tübingen, 1899).

47. See I Kings 4:13; 5:25 ("twenty thousand"), 27–29; 9:11 and 14; 11:3; 18:19; 19:18; 20:29; 22:6; II Kings 3:4 and 26; 5:5; 10:1, 7, and 14; 13:7; 14:7; 15:19, 20, and 25; 18:14 and 23; 19:35; 24:14 and 16; 25:19 ("five").

48. Named after King Frederick August; see Constantin Tischendorf's edition of the *Codex Friderico-Augustinianus; sive fragmenta veteris Testamenti e Codici graeco* (1896).

49. See Johann Wilhelm Rothstein's and Johannes Haenel's commentary, *Das erste Buch der Chronik*, Kommentar zum Alten Testament, ed. by Ernst Sellin (Leipzig, 1927).

50. See I Chron. 2:22; 3:4, 5, and 8; 4:27 and 42; 5:18 and 21; 6:45–48; 7:2, 4, 5, 7, 8, 11, and 40; 8:40; 9:6, 9, 13, and 22; 11:20; 12:25–35, 37, and 38; 15:5, 6, and 8–10; 18:4, 5, and 12; 19:6, 7, and 18; 21:14; 22:14; 23:3–5; 24:4; 25:5, 7, and 9–31; 26:8, 9, 11, 30, and 32; 27:1, 2, 4, 5, and 7–15; 29:4, 7, and 21. II Chron. 1:2, 6, 14, and 17; 2:1, 9 (but see Kittel's commentary), 16, and 17; 8:10 and 18; 9:9, 13, and 28; 11:1 and 21 (three of the figures); 12:3; 13:3, 17, and 24; 14:7 (the first figure) and 8; 15:11; 17:11 (the first figure), and 14–18; 18:5; 25:5, 6, and 11–13; 26:12, 13, and 17; 27:5; 28:6; 29:32 and 33; 30:24; 35:7–9; and 36:3.

51. See above, Nos. 31, 34, 36, 37, 39, and 41.

52. It is difficult to accept the theory that the LXX scholars, too, derived their information from that "Midrash on Kings," the very existence of which is hypothetical, so long as we do not have convincing proof that the "Midrash" served as a direct course for LXX even where it was not accepted by the Chronicler. I have not found any such evidence. The three cases mentioned above—Nos. 31, 36–37—appear to contradict that theory.

53. Clearly, these questions are both complex and far-reaching; hence I can here refer to them only in very general terms.

54. See I Kings 11:3.

55. The number of wives kept by Solomon's father David and by

Solomon's son Rehoboam was relatively limited. Rehoboam had only eighteen wives and sixty concubines (according to LXX B; in Josephus only thirty concubines, as mentioned above). See I Chron. 3:4–9; 14:3–7; II Chron. 2:11 and 21.

56. Judg. 8:30. To be sure, Scripture adds the explanation "for he had many wives," which shows that the writer considered that number unusual. However "threescore and ten" children are so frequently mentioned in Semitic sources that the number appears to be a cliché, not to be taken literally.

57. See Judg. 10:4; 12:9 and 14; and above, No. 15.

58. See I Chron. 3:4–9 and 14:3–7.

59. See II Sam. 9:10 and 19:18.

60. See II Chron. 11:21.

61. See II Chron. 13:21.

62. See II Kings 10:1 and 7.

63. See I Chron. 26:8, 9, and 11.

64. See I Chron. 4:27.

65. See the observation made by Hume, in his *Essays*, pp. 385 f.

66. Eduard Meyer (*Sklaverei im Altertum*, p. 18) states: "The function of female slaves consists primarily of . . . the satisfaction of sexual desires. Slavery, in particular of the domestic variety, plays, under more primitive conditions, the role principally assigned in later societies to more or less well-regulated prostitution."

67. See II Chron. 2:34.

68. Even in Pergamum, with its slave-operated advanced industry, the slaves did not exceed one-third of the population. See Ulrich Kahrstedt, "Bevölkerungswesen," *Handwörterbuch der Staatswissenschaften*, 4th ed., 1924, II, 656 ff.

69. See my brief remarks in SRH I, 34 ff., 69 ff., 302 n. 5, 324 n. 12.

70. Enslavement could follow failure to pay either private debts or fines imposed by a public court (including the double, fourfold, or fivefold indemnities provided by Scripture in certain instances). For one such case, see especially II Kings 4:1.

71. See the Code of Hammurabi, arts. 227, 257, and 258.

72. This matter likewise requires elaboration. But it suffices to mention here that from the few records in extant sources we may deduce that the wages of a free worker barely exceeded his sustenance, since food prices were relatively high. Even in Rome, where slavery played a much greater role, the sources indicate that the maintenance of a slave was not much less expensive than that of a soldier. A slave annually consumed, on the average, upward of 4 or 5 hectoliters of grain, while the allotment for a soldier ranged from 4 to 8 hectoliters (one hectoliter =2.838 bushels).

73. During that period the ordinary rate of interest was 25 percent

in the Assyrian Empire and 20 percent in Nebuchadnezzar's Babylonia —not to speak of more exceptional cases, such as the Elephantine colony during the Persian period, in which the regular rate was 60 percent; see Meyer, *Der Papyrusfund von Elephantine*, 2d ed. (Leipzig, 1912), p. 30. We cannot assume that money was much less expensive in a poor country like Palestine under the last kings. Even if an Israelite refrained from extending loans on interest to coreligionists, he might easily have charged interest to the numerous non-Jews, many of them wealthy merchants, who lived in the country.

74. Deut. 15:18.

75. See especially Gen. 16:6; I Sam. 25:10; and I Kings 2:39.

76. Elsewhere, the treatment of slaves was much more severe. In Rome, for instance, a fugitive slave was returned to his master; if a slave became old or sick, his master could dismiss him without further responsibility (in the early period he could even kill him outright). The price of money, too, was much lower in Rome (in the period of the early emperors the legal interest rate was as a rule no more than 12 percent; later, in the Code of Justinian, only 6 percent). Even more important, while many wealthy men needed much domestic help, and numerous landowners required workers for their latifundia, Italy had but a small supply of free labor for hire; hence the number of slaves was unusually large there.

77. See Meyer, *Sklaverei*, p. 26. Starting from other premises, Meyer reaches the same conclusion, that the Middle-Eastern nations almost never employed large masses of slaves. M. Lurie's computation (in his *Studien zur Geschichte der wirtschaftlichen und sozialen Verhältnisse im israelitisch-jüdischen Reiche*, Beiheft of ZAW, XLV [Giessen, 1927], pp. 39 f.) that Israel had two hundred thousand slaves rests on very weak foundations.

78. See II Sam. 24:15.

79. See Deut. 17:16 and the Letter of Aristeas, ed. by Paul Wendland, Chap. XIII. See also Albrecht Alt, "Psammetich II. in Palästina und Elephantine," ZAW, XXX (1910), 295; and Meyer, *Der Papyrusfund von Elephantine*, pp. 33 f.

80. As against Josh. 11:19, see, for example, Josh. 16:10 and 17:12–13; and Judg. 1:21 and 28–33.

81. See I Sam. 15:3.

82. See II Sam. 12:31.

83. See Tacitus, *Histories* 2.44. See also David Hume, *Essays*, pp. 400 ff.

84. On the destruction of Nob, see also I Sam. 22:19, etc.

85. Frants Buhl, *Die socialen Verhältnisse*, p. 52. In fact, the ancients themselves used the ratio of 1:4 in their computation. That women constituted "half the *polis*" was mentioned by Aristotle in his *Politics*, I,

1260b; as well as in other sources quoted by Beloch, p. 42.

86. See Beloch, p. 472.

87. See Max Weber, *Gesammelte Aufsätze zur Religionssoziologie*, 3 vols. (Tübingen, 1920–21), III, 29.

88. On the biblical use of the term '*arim* ("cities") to refer to the country as a whole or in part, see Cyrus Sulzberger, "Polity of Ancient Hebrews," *JQR*, n.s. III (1912–13), 23 f.

89. Diodorus Siculus, *Bibliotheca historica*, xxxiii and xxviii, ed. with an English trans. by C. H. Oldfather *et al.*, Loeb Classical Library (London, 1933), apparently following Poseidonius.

90. See Beloch, p. 255.

91. This is indeed Beloch's opinion, *ibid.* As to the large number of "cities" (*nut*) in Egypt even in the earlier periods, see Meyer's observations in his *Geschichte des Altertums*, 3d ed., Vol. I, Part 2, p. 191. For Babylonia we have Sennacherib's reference to the conquest of 75 walled cities and 420 provincial towns, figures which other versions raise to 89 walled and 620 or even 820 other cities. See Bruno Meissner, *Babylonien und Assyrien*, 2 vols. (Heidelberg, 1920–25), I, 8.

92. Wilhelm Max Müller, "Die Palästinalisten Thutmosis III.," *Mitteilungen der Vorderasiatischen Gesellschaft*, 1907, No. 1, p. 34.

93. *Ibid.*, p. 37.

94. For all these matters, see Müller, *Egyptological Researches*, Publications of the Carnegie Institute in Washington, LIII, 3 vols. (Washington, 1906–20), I, 39 ff., 46 ff., 51 ff., and Tables 44–53, 60–63, and 75–87. See also his *Asien und Europa, nach altägyptischen ,Denkmälern*, with a Foreword by Georg Ebers (Leipzig, 1893), pp. 169 ff., 280 ff.

95. See Num. 21:32.

96. Eusebius Pamphilius of Caesarea mentions in one place (in his *Onomasticon urbium et locorum Sacrae Scripturae* [Greek with Latin commentary by St. Jerome], ed. by F. Larsow and G. Parthey [Berlin, 1862] 12:3) that Jazer ("Αζηρ) was eight Roman miles distant from Philadelphia, while in another (*ibid.*, 104:13) he speaks of it as ten miles from Philadelphia and fifteen from Heshbon ("Εσβους). A Roman mile equals approximately 1,480 meters (or about 1,614 yards).

97. See Sulzberger, "Polity," p. 15.

98. See *Sifre* on Deut. clxxx: "Cities, not hamlets; cities, not metropolises; cities, not villages." Similarly, Tosefta on Makkot 3, 8, speaking about the cities of refuge states: "They are not built as large cities or as small hamlets." Bab. Makkot 10a likewise says: "These cities are placed neither in hamlets nor in large cities but only in medium-sized towns." See also Gen. 25:17; Num. 31:10; etc.

99. See M. Megillah I, 1: "Large cities surrounded by walls from the days of Joshua, the son of Nun."

100. See Josh. 6:26 and I Kings 16:34.

101. See II Sam. 10:5; and Ernst Sellin and Carl Watzinger, *Jericho. Die Ergebnisse der Ausgrabungen* (Leipzig, 1913), pp. 173 ff., 182 ff. Similarly, Kiriath-sepher, which had been thoroughly destroyed by Othniel and Shishak, "even more than in the destruction of Nebuchadnezzar"— after the Babylonian occupation it really remained deserted until the Arab conquest—had nevertheless flourished again in the days of the Judean kings in a measure amazing modern archaeological excavators. See Melvin Grove Kyle, "Excavations at Tell Beit Mirsin, the Ancient Kirjath Sepher, 1928," *Bibliotheca Sacra*, LXXXV (1928), 381–408, esp. pp. 384 ff.; and his *Excavating Kiriath-Sepher's Ten Cities* (Grand Rapids, Mich., 1934).

102. I Kings 16:24.

103. See Erich Ebeling's translation in *Altorientalische Texte und Bilder zum Alten Testament*, ed. by Hugo Gressmann, 2d ed. (Berlin, 1926–27), p. 353. There is some support for this notion in the description—preserved in the Anastasius Papyrus I—by an ancient Egyptian traveler (13th cent. B.C.), who mentions fifty-six walled cities, thirty-eight of them south of Tyre. After all, more than five hundred years had elapsed between this account and Sennacherib's invasion.

104. See Valentin Schwoebel, *Die Landesnatur Palästinas*, Das Land der Bibel I, 2 parts (Leipzig, 1914). See above, Essay 2.

105. See Beloch, p. 29; but also *ibid.*, n. 2.

106. See *New International Yearbook*, 1927, pp. 266 ff. In 1926 the surplus amounted to only 1,875,000 Egyptian pounds.

107. See *Bulletin de l'Institut International de Statistique*, March, 1927.

108. See Martonne, "L'Egypte d'aujourd'hui," *Bulletin de la Société Géographique de Lille*, 1926, p. 28. This ratio is, in fact, larger, for not all the land under potential cultivation was actually tilled. During 1924, of the entire agricultural area of 8,070,186 feddans (one feddan equals approximately 1.038 acres), only 2,936,698 feddans were under general cultivation, whereas no less than 1,787,843 feddans, or more than one-third of the total, had been set aside for cotton growing. See *New International Yearbook*, 1926, p. 238.

109. Eugène Cavaignac's hypothesis (in his *Population*, p. 2) that annual cultivation in ancient Egypt did not exceed 10,000 km² is based entirely on the assumption that the total cultivable area amounted to only two-thirds of the inhabited land, and was cultivated only every other year. That half the arable land in the country would have lain fallow each year appears to be exaggerated. However, even according to this hypothesis, the annual cultivated area is quite close to the approximately 14,000 km² which were left in 1924 for the cultivation of produce other than cotton. See the preceding note.

110. To be sure, we have an ancient record concerning the produce

of one district. In telling about his conquest of Megiddo, Thutmes III states that his tax collectors had estimated the annual production of grain in the area at the equivalent of approximately 40,000 hectoliters. See James Henry Breasted, *Ancient Records of Egypt: Historical Documents from the Earliest Times to the Persian Conquest*, 5 vols. (Chicago, 1927), II, 188 ff. (Breasted's computation, based upon imperial bushels and cubic inches, seems slightly contradictory). However, since we do not know the size of the Megiddo district, we cannot obtain accurate estimates for the whole country. Nevertheless, Breasted's assumption that the farmers of that area harvested, on the average, about 20 bushels per acre or about 18 hectoliters per hectare, is not improbable. If we remember that in the Palestinian valleys one could harvest eight times as much wheat, and fifteen times as much barley, as was sown, and that the wholly extraordinary crop said to have been collected in Hauran amounted to sixty to eighty times the seed (see Immanuel Benzinger, *Hebräische Archäologie*, 3d ed. [Leipzig, 1927], p. 146), the hundred-fold return mentioned in Gen. 26:12 (see also Matt. 13:18) was rightly considered an exceptional blessing. As a matter of fact, barley, rather than wheat, was the staple foodstuff of the common man. Since Rome estimated a soldier's minimum annual consumption at but 4 hectoliters, it stands to reason that in Palestine, where the consumption of fruit was much higher, the general population, including women and children, could be satisfied with an average diet of less than 3 hectoliters of grain. If so, it appears that if only 20 hectares, or one-fifth of every km², was cultivated annually and if, according to the estimate above, their harvest yielded approximately 360 hectoliters, it would have been possible to maintain thereon 100 persons and still save about one-quarter of the crop for export. Moreover, much of the land was used for the much more intensive cultivation of fruit, which required still less space.

111. I Kings 5:25. See also the list of textual variants above, No. 36.

112. II Chron. 2:9.

113. See, for instance, Deut. 8:9.

114. It appears that throughout the Canaanite, as well as the Israelitic, period there was an ample supply of gold and silver in the country. See Ernst Sellin, *Eine Nachlese auf dem Tell-Taʻanek in Palästina . . . Nebst einen Anhange von F. Hrozný*, "Die neuen Keilschrifttexte von Taʻanek" (Vienna, 1906), Denkschriften der Österreichischen Akademie der Wissenschaften, LII, 3, p. 32.

115. See the story about King Mesha of Moab in II Kings 3:4, and a similar payment of tribute by Ammonites to Jotham in II Chron. 27:5. In the latter passage, Scripture expressly states that the Ammonites paid "a hundred talents of silver, and ten thousand measures of wheat, and ten thousand of barley. So much did the children of Ammon render unto him, in the second year also, and in the third." While the LXX version

gives the impression of but a single payment by Mesha, the Masoretic text makes quite clear that it was an annual tribute. It was thus understood also by the Targum.

116. *Geschichte des Altertums,* 3d ed., Vol. I, Part 2, p. 194.

117. See Kahrstedt (above, n. 68). In Greece, to be sure, no general census was instituted until the end of the fourth century B.C. However, in the earlier period the authorities kept fairly detailed records of those citizens who had to arm themselves at their own expense in time of war; see Beloch, pp. 3 ff.

118. The variants for the Chronicles passage in the manuscripts of LXX shed little new light. See the list above, No. 55. To be sure, according to Josephus (*Antiquities* 7.13.1), Joab's census yielded a total of 900,000 Israelites and 400,000 Judeans. But very likely the historian did not have a different version in his source, he but merely emended the figures himself because his historical sense made him doubt their accuracy in allotting to the ten northern tribes less than double the number of men given for the two southern tribes. However, as we shall presently see, the numbers given in Chronicles present no real difficulty.

119. See the related comments by Buhl, Meyer, Benzinger, Kittel, Driver, Lurie, and many others.

120. See also *A Critical and Exegetical Commentary on the Books of Chronicles, International Critical Commentary* (London, 1910) by Edward L. Curtis and Albert A. Madsen.

121. I Chron. 21:6.

122. See I Chron. 7:6–11.

123. I Chron. 23:3. To the "thirty and eight thousand" men over thirty, one must add more than 40 percent (or about 16,000 men) for those between twenty and thirty. But cf. the commentators' remarks on the contradiction with verses 24 and 27.

124. See various essays by William F. Albright in the *Journal of the Palestine Oriental Society.*

125. See *Pesiqta rabbati,* ed. by Meir Friedmann (Vienna, 1860), Chap. XI (43b). See also Louis Ginzberg, *The Legends of the Jews,* 7 vols. (Philadelphia, 1909–38), IV, 112; VI, 270.

126. The area within the stated boundaries—not extending to the Euphrates valley (to which at times the Davidic empire may have stretched)—was more than 400 kilometers long from the Red Sea to north of Kadesh and Dan. Its average width from the Mediterranean to the eastern borders of the territory of the two and a half Israelitic tribes —Ammon, Moab, and Edom—was more than 120 kilometers.

127. *Geschichte des Altertums,* 3d ed., Vol. I, Part 2, p. 382.

128. *Ibid.,* p. 31. See also Beloch, pp. 255 ff.; and Eugène Cavaignac in the *Revue Egyptologique* (above, n. 13).

129. Cavaignac, *ibid.* His statements, some of which he himself sub-

sequently revised (see his *Population*, p. 9), require a brief review here. Herodotus tells us about seven classes of the Egyptian population, one of which, the warriors, numbered 410,000 men. Although some scholars have doubted the accuracy of these figures (see Gaston Maspero, *Histoire ancienne des peuples d'Orient classique*, 3 vols. [Paris, 1895–99], III, 505; and Beloch, p. 257), it seems more or less confirmed by other statements in Herodotus and in Diodorus Siculus (despite Cavaignac's reservations in the *Revue*, p. 193). Cavaignac was right, however, in assuming that the 410,000 warriors—in actuality they were often much fewer in number—occupied about one-third of the area of Egypt given by Diodorus; that is, some 12,000 km^2, giving each man approximately 3 hectares. But Cavaignac is in error in deducing that, together with their families, they equaled one-third of the population. To begin with, most of them doubtless owned slaves and perhaps also employed some free workers on their land. It would appear, therefore, that if they and their families numbered at least 1,500,000 souls, that figure would have to be raised by a minimum of several hundred thousand slaves and free laborers. Moreover, it is very likely that in other districts, where the land belonged to either the king or the priests, the proportion of inhabitants was even larger. The methods of cultivating the soil at that time did not differ greatly from those of the early twentieth century, when, as we know, an Egyptian peasant family cultivated, on the average, only about one hectare. See Martonne (above, n. 108), p. 27. The peasantry alone thus seems to have numbered some 5,000,000 to 6,000,000 souls. To this figure we must add the members of the other six classes enumerated by Herodotus, and their total doubtless exceeded the number of the warrior class alone. Hence it is quite possible that the total Egyptian population exceeded 8,000,000 persons.

129a. In his *Natural History* (36.12) Pliny and Elder, referring to an earlier period, mentions that no less than 360,000 slaves had worked for twenty years on the erection of one pyramid. This is not an exaggeration, considering the enormity of the task of erecting such a monumental structure manually.

130. In antiquity the Tigris area had more canals than the environs of the Euphrates; today the opposite is true. See J. de Morgan, "Le Monde Oriental avant l'histoire, L'Asie antérieure et l'Egypte," *L'Anthropologie*, XXXIV (1924), 17–56, esp. pp. 48 f.

131. Cavaignac, in *Revue Egyptologique*, n.s. I, p. 196 n. 1.

132. Meissner, *Babylonien und Assyrien*, I, 8.

133. Cavaignac in *Revue Egyptologique*, n.s. I, pp. 195 f.; and Kahrstedt (above, n. 68).

134. Meissner, *Babylonien und Assyrien*, I, 13 ff.

135. This is not the place to elaborate this point, but see above, pp. 10 ff. We need but mention the earlier estimates, by several eminent

scholars, of Palestine's population in the first century: Beloch (p. 247) assumes approximately 2,000,000 persons, an estimate with which Meyer (see above, n. 5) concurs. Jean Juster (*Les Juifs dans l'Empire Romain,* I, 210 n. 2) raises the number to 5,000,000. If Adolf Harnack (*Mission und Ausbreitung,* I [1925], 10) lowers the number to 700,000, he clearly contradicts his estimate of 4,500,000 Jews in the whole Roman Empire. It is very unlikely that, before the destruction of the Second Temple, Palestine's Jewry amounted to but one-ninth of the Empire's total Jewish population. See also the other data discussed in *SRH* I, 167 ff., 369 ff.

136. I Chron. 7:2.

137. *Ibid.,* verses 1-5. In his commentary, I. Benzinger accepts this figure as far from exaggerated with respect to many a large clan (the original meaning of the term *mishpaḥah*). We know that similar Jewish clans in the Babylonian Exile were later able to send thousands of members back to Palestine. See Ezra 2:3, 6, 14, and 35; and Eduard Meyer, *Die Entstehung des Judentums* (Halle, 1896), p. 162.

138. Num. 2:6: "fifty and four thousand and four hundred"; Num. 26:25: "threescore and four thousand and three hundred."

139. See Rudolf Kittel's commentary trying to harmonize I Chron. 7:2 and 4.

140. Num. 1:41: "forty and one thousand and five hundred"; Num. 26:47: "fifty and three thousand and four hundred"; I Chron. 12:37: "forty thousand."

141. In any case, these statements do not appear to be wholly imaginary, as has been suggested by many commentators. One may indeed follow here the commentary attributed to Rashi: "you need not wonder why so few men came from the Judean tribes, for no one from Judah had to come to the coronation since that tribe had previously crowned him [David] in Hebron. But the other tribes, who theretofore had sided with Saul's sons, now had to come to Hebron for his coronation." See also Carl Friedrich Keil's *Commentary on the Book of Kings,* trans. into English by J. Murphy (London, 1854). The "four thousand and six hundred" Levites and "three thousand and seven hundred" priests mentioned in I Chron. 12:27-28, were not designated as "armed for war" or "mighty men of valour," as were the groups enumerated in the other verses. Though verse 29 speaks of Zadok as "a young man mighty of valour," the statement must not be generalized. Moreover, as is well known a "man of valour" was primarily a landowner obliged to supply his own equipment. Priests did not own land. It is quite possible on the other hand, that at that time both priests and Levites took part in wars and did not differ from other inhabitants except by their Temple services in peacetime. At any rate, some Levites and priests may well have attended David's coronation; it is even possible that the number quoted for them in Scripture is not quite so exaggerated as those of the follow-

ing categories.

142. See, especially, Kittel's commentary thereon.

143. I Sam. 13:5: "and people as the sand which is on the sea-shore in multitude." See also No. 23 in the list of variants above.

144. As in I Sam. 4:2; 13:2 and 15; 14:2 and 14; 24:3; II Sam. 6:1; 17:1.

145. See II Sam. 8:4, 5, and 13; 10:6 and 18; 1 Chron. 18:12; 19:7 and 18.

146. See I Sam. 11:8; 15:4.

147. Cf. I Kings 5:27–30; and II Chron. 2:1, 16, and 17. See also II Chron. 8:7–10; and No. 37 in the list of variants above.

148. Josephus *Antiquities* 8. 7. 3 ff.

149. See above, the list of variants, No. 41.

150. I Kings 20:15.

151. See Ebeling in *Altorientalische Texte*, ed. by Gressmann, pp. 340 ff.

152. I Kings 20:29 and 30.

153. In fact it is mentioned that while rebelling against David, the Ammonites paid "a thousand talents of silver" to hire 32,000 to 33,000 men from the kings of Aram. See I Chron. 19:6 and 7, which may be emended according to II Sam. 10:6.

154. See II Kings 14:7 and II Chron. 25:11.

155. II Chron. 25:12 and 13.

156. See also Meyer, *Geschichte*, I, 1st ed., *passim*. But after the appearance of that first edition Meyer changed his mind; see his article "Bevölkerungswesen."

157. See Meyer, "Bevölkerungswesen"; Buhl, *Die socialen Verhältnisse*, p. 53; M. Lurie, *Studien*, pp. 40 f.

158. II Kings 15:29 and Ebeling in *Altorientalische Texte*. See also Rudolf Kittel, *Geschichte des Volkes Israel*, 6th ed. (Gotha, 1923–1929), II, 362 ff., and the literature cited there.

159. See Ebeling, p. 349.

160. There is also some support to be found in Shalmaneser's report that several years before he had deported 208,000 captives from Aram.

161. See also Kittel in his commentary on I Chron. 2:21–23; and his *Geschichte*, II, 371 n. 3.

162. The political decline of Judah is manifest in the well-known wager offered by the Assyrian commander to Hezekiah: that he would give the king two thousand horses if he (Hezekiah) could find riders for them (II Kings 18:23)—an ironic contrast with the thousands of chariots and riders available to the earlier kings. Very likely Judah had suffered much destruction from its northern brethren shortly before Hezekiah's reign. Even if we do not accept the large numbers quoted in II Chron. 25:6, 8, the subsequent devastation of Judah by the north-

ern king Pekah the son of Remaliah must have played havoc with the well-being of the southern kingdom.

163. II Kings 19:35; Isa. 37:36.

164. Among the few extant epigraphic records relating to Assyrian soldiers, there is only one somewhat resembling that discussed here: the report that when Shalmaneser III went to war on Aram and her allies in 846 B.C. he commanded an army of 120,000 men. See Ebeling in *Altorientalische Texte*, p. 342; and more generally, Meissner, *Babylonien und Assyrien*, I, 101 f. But one cannot compare Hezekiah's forces with those of the earlier Aramaeans. Nonetheless, by his effective resistance the Judean king may have prevented a large-scale Assyrian invasion of Egypt such as that later staged by Asarhaddon.

165. On a similar speedy return after the war was over, in the days of the Destruction of the Temple, see Jer. 40:11–12 and 43:5.

166. In the El-Amarna period, too, Jerusalem seems for a time to have dominated Edom.

167. See Jer. 13:19; and Albrecht Alt in "Judas Gaue unter Josia," *Palästina Jahrbuch*, XXI (1925), 108. According to Julius Lewy in his *Forschungen zur alten Geschichte Vorderasiens*, Mitteilungen der Vorderasiastischen-Aegyptischen Gesellschaft, XXIX, 2 (Leipzig, 1925), pp. 37 f., all these events took place in 602–601. However, as we shall presently see (below, nn. 173–75), his hypothesis seems unacceptable.

168. See E. Forrer, *Provinzeinteilung des assyrischen Reiches*, p. 60; and Kittel, *Geschichte*, II, 363.

169. See especially Jer. 49:7–22; and Lam. 4:21–22. Ezekiel's accusations (35:5 and 10) against Edom: "Because thou . . . hast hurled the children of Israel unto the power of the sword in the time of their calamity" and "Because thou hast said: These two nations and these two countries shall be mine, and we will possess it" doubtless refer to the period of Samaria's destruction and Sennacherib's invasion of Judah, rather than to the days of Nebuchadnezzar. (The problem of the unity of the Book of Obadiah and its date may also assume a new aspect in this light. But this is not the place for further elaboration of this problem.)

170. Concerning Beth-el, cf. II Kings 17:28 and 23:15. That locality and Jericho are mentioned among the cities whose descendants were among the returnees from the Babylonian Exile (see Ezra 2:28 and 34 and Neh. 7:32 and 36), whereas the cities of the Negev are not mentioned at all. See also E. Meyer in *Die Entstehung des Judentums*, pp. 94 f.; and Alt in *Palästina Jahrbuch*, XXI, 108. But this matter can be understood only if in 597 (or 602–601) the inhabitants of the Negev either were not deported at all or else had not yet become sufficiently judaized for their descendants to join the returning exiles. Concerning Jericho, see also Sellin and Watzinger, *Jericho*, p. 177. For Megiddo we need but refer to the well-known encounter there between Josiah and

King Necho of Egypt. See also Kittel, *Geschichte*, II, 418, 444.

171. Jer. 52:28–30. Although these verses are missing in LXX, there is no doubt that they belong to that source. Possibly the Greek translators skipped these verses because they thought that they contradicted the statement in II Kings.

172. This explanation dates from the days of Bernhard Stade and Eduard Meyer; see their statements in "Miscellen, 6: Wie hoch belief die Zahl der unter Nebuchadnezar nach Babylonien deportierten Juden?" *ZAW*, IV (1884), 271–75; and Meyer's *Entstehung*, p. 113.

173. Among the modern commentators one may mention Julius Lewy (*Forschungen*, pp. 37 ff.). On the basis of ingenious speculations, Lewy concludes that the first battles between Babylon and Judah took place in 602–601, and thereby drastically changes the entire chronology of the Babylonian conquest of Judah. However, his conclusion ignores almost all the important verses in II Kings 24 and 25, as well as the essential words "in the . . . year of Nebuchadnezzar" in Jer. 52:29 and 30.

174. Jer. 52:28. The words "in the seventh year" can in this context mean only in the seventh year of Nebuchadnezzar's reign, notwithstanding Lewy's opinion to the contrary.

175. II Kings 24:15 and 16. The date mentioned in verse 12: "And the king of Babylon took him [Jehoiachin] in the eighth year of his reign" clearly refers to Nebuchadnezzar's reign. In order to advance the date of the first battles to 602–601, Lewy is forced to replace Jehoiachin by Jehoiakim. On the meaning of verses 13 and 14, see below.

176. Jer. 52:29.

177. II Kings 25:11; Jer. 39:9 and 52:15; II Chron. 36:20.

178. Jer. 52:30. The end of that verse: "all the persons, etc." is evidently an interpolation from a reader's marginal computation of the numbers previously cited.

179. See II Kings 24:7. To be sure Psammetichus II's journey in the year 592 (see Alt's essay cited above, n. 79) seems to contradict the beginning of the verse, but the fact itself is indubitably correct.

180. II Kings 24. See also Jer. 35:11. If some scholars emend Aram here to read Edom (the Hebrew *dalet* and *resh* being easily mistaken for one another), theirs is a mere conjecture seeking to find here a record of Edom's misdeeds which had contributed to Israel's defeat. But the aforementioned likelihood of the Edomites' early expansion in the Negev was sufficient cause for Israel's animosity.

181. II Kings 24:15 and 16.

182. See also Jer. 37:13 and 14.

183. II Kings 25:11; Jer. 39:9 and 52:15. See also Stade and Meyer (above, n. 172).

184. See Sellin and Watzinger, *Jericho*, p. 183.

185. Ezra 2:64 and 65; Neh. 7:66 and 67. According to LXX in

Nehemiah, however, the total number was "forty and two thousand three hundred and eight"; while MT has "two hundred and forty and five singing men and singing women."

186. II Kings 17:6 and 18:11. See also *SRH* I, 106 ff., 345 nn. 8–10.

187. Valentin Schwöbel in *Zeitschrift des Deutschen Palästina Vereines*, XXVII (1904), No. 50.

188. See also II Kings 18:13.

189. Josh. 15:63; 16:10; and others give a general impression of great antiquity. But A. Alt's hypothesis (*Palästina Jahrbuch*, XXI, 100 ff.) that the entire list (Josh. 15) relating to the southern cities was composed under Josiah makes very good sense. More serious doubts may be advanced concerning the list of northern cities, or at least those in Josh. 19. But Alt's theory (see his "Galiäische Ortliste in Jos. 19," *ZAW*, n.s. IV [1927], 80) that that list, too, dates from the days of Josiah likewise appears probable.

190. Josh. 19:1–9.

191. If we add the number included in LXX but omitted in MT after Josh. 15:59; see above, the list of variants, No. 4.

192. Josh. 18:11–28.

193. See Josh. 19.

194. Josh. 13:15 ff.

195. See above, the list of variants, No. 15.

196. See Josh. 16 and 17.

197. See Josh. 21.

198. One need not be surprised that the ratio of Judah to Israel appears here as only 1:2, whereas it is usually assumed to be 1:3. The author of Josh. 15 evidently extended Judah's boundaries beyond the two Judean tribes' ethnographic settlement, largely at the expense of the ten Israelitic tribes. We have already mentioned the Philistine cities. If the city lists were indeed compiled in the days of Josiah, his conquests in the north had substantially extended Judah's frontiers into the territories formerly occupied by David (this is, in fact, the most important proof for Alt's hypothesis). Incidentally, these observations seem to offer additional confirmation for the intrinsic consistency, if not for the historical authenticity, of the sources relating to David's census. If we have estimated above the presence of some 54,000 male Levites over twenty, or a total Levitical population of some 220,000, in that period, a multiplication of that number by eight—if the ratio of Levites to the general population corresponds to the ratio between the cities— would yield a total population of 1,760,000, which approximates the number of Israelites we suggested earlier.

199. Franz Heinrich Weissbach, "Das Stadtbild von Babylon," *Der Alte Orient*, V, 4 (Berlin, 1904), 14.

200. C. Schick, "Die Einwohnerzahl das alten Jerusalem," *Zeitschrift*

des Deutschen Palästina Vereines, IV (1881), 216; and Benzinger, *Hebräische Archäologie,* 3d ed., p. 36.

201. These matters likewise require further elaboration. Suffice it to mention here that, for instance, the excavations in Jericho have shown that most Israelitic houses—each house being intended for occupancy by a family of five or more persons—were of the kind of house A, the length of which was 5.10 and the width 5.20 meters. House C covered an area of 3.10 by 5.25 meters, E covered 3.80 by 5.25 meters, etc. See Sellin and Watzinger, *Jericho,* pp. 62 ff. In Taanach the houses were a bit smaller, none of them exceeding 4 meters in length or width. See Sellin, *Tell-Ta'anek,* p. 95; and Louis Hugues Vincent, *Etudes bibliques: Canaan d'après l'exploration récente* (Paris, 1907), p. 66. The streets, too, were extremely narrow. The assumption that the streets in the ancient town of Gezer were not wider than those in that village today, and that a man stretching out both arms could touch the walls on opposite sides (see Robert A. S. Macalister, *The Excavation of Gezer, 1902–1905 and 1907–1909,* 3 vols., Palestine Exploration Fund [London 1913], I, 167) is confirmed by all we know about the streets in ancient times. Even the main thoroughfare in glorious Babel, a street devoted to large processions in honor of the god Marduk in which tens of thousands of people participated, was not much wider than 10 meters; see Weissbach, *Das Stadtbild,* p. 27. On the other hand, there also existed some large and imposing structures. For instance the excavation in Taanach showed that the western cistern near the wall extended over an area of 20.08 by 18.60 meters. See Sellin, *Tell-Ta'anek,* p. 47. Omri's royal palace in Samaria included a courtyard of 8–9.5 by 17 meters. See George Andrew Reisner, Clarence S. Fisher, and David G. Lyon, *Harvard Excavations at Samaria, 1909–1910,* 2 vols., Harvard Semitic Series, I, II (Cambridge, Mass., 1924), I, 94. See also Vincent, *Canaan,* p. 53; Kittel, *Geschichte,* I, 133 ff.; Benzinger, *Hebräische Archäologie,* pp. 98, 101; Lurie, *Studien,* p. 38. Excavations in Kiriath-sepher have also shown that the majority of houses consisted of one or two rooms and that only a few included six to eight rooms. See Kyle, above, n. 101.

202. In Palestine the situation was different. There, even a two-story house, like that of the "great woman" in Shunem (II Kings 4:10), was apparently quite rare. See Robert A. S. Macalister, *A Century of Excavation in Palestine,* 2d ed. (London [Religious Tract Society], 1930), p. 211; and *The Excavation of Gezer,* I, 168.

203. See Kahrstedt (above, n. 68).

204. See Sellin and Watzinger, *Jericho,* p. 185; Sellin, *Tell-Ta'anek,* p. 10; Benzinger, *Hebräische Archäologie,* p. 111. In his *Canaan,* p. 27 n. 3, Père Vincent estimated the area of seven cities in ancient Palestine. The smallest, Tell Zakarieh, covered approximately 3.5 hectares, whereas the largest, Gezer, extended over a "maximum" of 9 hectares. The area

of Kiriath-sepher within the walls in the days of the Judean kingdom is estimated at approximately 3 hectares. See Kyle in *Bibliotheca Sacra*, LXXXIII, 392.

205. Alexander Knudtzon, ed., *Die El-Amarna Tafeln*, Vorderasiatische Bibliothek, II (Berlin, 1915), No. 239.

206. See Sellin and Watzinger, *Jericho*, p. 186.

207. Lurie, *Studien*, p. 36.

208. See Buhl, *Die socialen Verhältnisse*, p. 53; Lurie, *Studien*, p. 38; and others.

209. Most scholars offer much lower estimates, but I believe that my computation is justified by the sources (see above, p. 50 ff.).

210. Ancient Rome had an area of 1,230 hectares; Alexandria, 920 hectares; Babel, 889 hectares. According to Weissbach, *Das Stadtbild*, p. 7, Babel's area was "a maximum of 12 km²," that is, 1,200 hectares. These estimates are confirmed by the size of the walls. Rome's circumference, we are told, was more than 100 stadia. To be sure, within the Servian Wall the settlement was very dense: 1,162 persons per hectare; that is, about 9 square meters per person. The settled area extended, moreover, much beyond the wall. Alexandria's wall had a length of 80 stadia, according to Curtius, and 120 stadia, according to Pliny. Perhaps here, too, we may explain the discrepancy by the different definitions of the stadium measure. The wall of the metropolitan city of Antioch, with its several hundred thousand inhabitants surrounded an area of some 12,000 m²; thus it was more than 60 stadia in circumference. See Beloch, pp. 478 and 482; and Kahrstedt (above, n. 68).

211. See Josephus *Contra Apionem* 1.22. All these observations run counter to the accepted notions. See Beloch, p. 248; Lurie, *Studien*, p. 37; Meyer, Kahrstedt, and others. That is why Schick's "guesstimate" of 228,000 inhabitants (*Zeitschrift des Deutschen Palästina Vereines*, IV, 216) is not so grossly exaggerated.

212. The Chronicler expressly states (I Chron. 9:1): "They are written in the book of the kings of Israel." See also verses 2 and 3.

213. See the famous statement by Philo in *Legatio ad Caium*, No. xxxvi.

214. *Hebräische Archäologie*, p. 36.

215. In the first century A.D., Jerusalem's population of up to 200,000 compared with one of some 2,500,000 in the country at large. In addition, Jerusalem was in permanent contact with millions of Jews abroad, including countless pilgrims. At the time when Alexandria had some 500,000 inhabitants, all of Egypt had a population of about 8,000,000. Similarly, if in Nebuchadnezzar's days the city of Babel embraced some 400,000 people, Babylonia as a whole numbered many millions. Moreover, Babel was the capital not only of Babylonia as such but also of a vast empire. Neither was Rome with its 1,000,000 residents merely the

capital of 6,000,000 Italians; it was the seat of the far-flung Roman Empire. In general, it is difficult to find in antiquity a capital which embraced more than 10–15 percent of the population of its country, with the exception, of course, of cities which, together with their immediate environs, were independent states. Though Jerusalem had been such a city-state in the El-Amarna age and was again to assume some of the characteristics of one under the later Achaemenid regime, it was not so in the period of David and Solomon or even of the last Judean kings.

216. The excavations conducted under the sponsorship of Harvard University in the years 1909–10 (see the report thereon by Reisner, Fisher, and Lyon cited above, n. 201) failed to bring to light sufficient material for the investigation of this problem.

ESSAY 4

1. A. S. Tritton, *The Caliphs and Their Non-Muslim Subjects: a Critical Study of the Covenant of 'Umar* (London, 1930); *idem,* "Islam and the Protected Religions," *Journal of the Royal Asiatic Society,* 1931, pp. 311–28; *idem,* "Non-Muslim Subjects in the Muslim State," *ibid.,* 1942, pp. 36–40; S. D. Goitein, *Jews and Arabs: Their Contacts through the Ages* (New York, 1955; new impression, 1964); Antoine Fattal, *Le statut légal des non-musulmans en pays d'Islam* (Beirut, 1958); and other literature cited in my *SRH,* Vols. I–XIV, esp. III, 292 f. n. 9.

2. The examples cited in *SRH,* III, 159 ff., 308 nn. 45–46, can be readily multiplied.

3. Hai Gaon's responsum in *Teshubot ha-geonim* (Geonic Responsa), ed. by A. E. Harkavy (Berlin, 1887), No. 278; Moses b. Ḥanokh's responsum in *Teshubot geone mizraḥ u-ma'arab* (Responsa of Eastern and Western Geonim), ed. by Joel Müller (Berlin, 1888), No. 179. On the numerous Muslim sources attesting the widespread corruption among Muslim judges, see Émile Tyan, *Histoire de l'organisation judiciaire en pays d'Islam* (Paris, 1938), I, 428 ff. Not even the Genizah fragments are able to supply us with the necessary documentation, because, apart from their limitation in the main to one geographic area and a relatively short period, they stem for the most part from communal leaders, rather than from the rank and file. Nevertheless, we must be grateful to S. D. Goitein for having brought to light a number of such interesting illustrations in his various publications, including "The Muslim Government—as Seen by Its Non-Muslim Subjects," *Journal of the Pakistan Historical Society,* XII (1964), 1–13.

4. The *Tefillah* (Prayer) and *Nistarot* (Mysteries) attributed to R. Simon b. Yoḥai in Adolph Jellinek's compilation, *Bet ha-Midrash,* III, 78 ff.; IV, 117 ff.; and in Yehudah ibn Shemuel's (Judah Kaufman's) edition of the

Midreshe ge'ulah (Jewish Apocalyptic Writings from the Conclusion of the Talmud to the Beginning of the Sixth Millennium [Jerusalem, 1943]), pp. 161 ff.; Bernard Lewis, "An Apocalyptic Vision of Islamic History," *Bulletin of the School of Oriental and African Studies of the University of London*, XIII (1948–50), 308–38; Paul J. Alexander, "Medieval Apocalypses as Historical Sources," *American Historical Review*, LXXIII (1967–68), 997–1018, esp. pp. 1000 f.

5. Hamzah al-Isfahani, cited by Harold Bowen in *The Life and Times of 'Ali Ibn 'Isa, "The Good Vizier"* (Cambridge, 1928), pp. 177 f.; Jalalu'ddin as-Suyuti, *History of the Caliphs*, trans. by H. S. Jarret (Calcutta, 1881), p. 410, both cited below, pp. 434 f.

6. Cited in *SRH*, V, 83.

7. Maimonides' famed Hebrew "Epistle to the Sages of Lunel" in *Qobeṣ teshubot ha-Rambam*, ed. by A. L. Lichtenberg (Leipzig, 1859), II, fol. 44 ab.

8. *Seder Eliyahu rabbah*, ed. by M. Friedmann, pp. 113 f. See also *ibid.*, Chap. X, p. 54. While this Midrash has long been dated in the ninth century, the late Professor Mordecai Margalioth has made a case for placing it all the way back in the third century. See V. Aptowitzer, "Seder Elia," *Jewish Studies in Memory of George A. Kohut* (New York, 1935), pp. 5–39; and M. Margalioth, "On the Problem of the Antiquity of *Seder Eliyahu*" (Hebrew), *Sefer Assaf* (Jerusalem, 1953), pp. 370–99. Needless to say, all midrashic compilations include sayings, from various periods, which cannot be dated. But the idea was indeed shared by many rabbinic thinkers then and after.

9. See below, Essay 7, "The Economic Views of Maimonides."

10. Saadia's eloquent description of the advantages of attaining political power (in his *Beliefs and Opinions*, x.12), which, along with other emotions of this type, he deflates, offers some interesting tenth-century illustrations of the psychology of political domination, but has little bearing on political theory as such. Even Erwin Rosenthal's and Leo Strauss's valiant attempts in their respective essays on "Maimonides' Conception of State and Society," in *Moses Maimonides*, ed. by Isidore Epstein (London, 1930), pp. 189–206; and "Quelques remarques sur la science politique de Maïmonide et de Farabi," *REJ*, C^{bis} (1936), 1–37, succeeded in pointing up some Maimonidean insights into social philosophy, especially Plato's and Alfarabi's concepts of the ideal "republic." But they also showed that the Jewish philosopher held fast to the traditional notions about politics long accepted among his coreligionists.

11. Goitein, *Jews and Arabs*, p. 104.

12. Goitein, "The Muslim Government," p. 10; Maimonides, M. T., De'ot 6, 1; *Guide for the Perplexed*, II, 40.

13. Maimonides' *Maqalah fi-ṣina'at al-manṭiq* (Treatise on Logic; in Hebrew, *Millot ha-higgayon*), xiv, ed. by Israel Efros in *Proceedings of*

the American Academy for Jewish Research, VIII (1938–39), 63 (Ibn Tibbon's Hebrew version), 65 (English). See also my remarks on this passage, below, pp. 149 f and n. 3. It may be noted that, in contrast to both Maimonides and Averroës, Abu Bakr ibn aṣ-Ṣaij ibn Bajja (Avempace), failed to mention the divine law as the basic guide to government as well. See Erwin Rosenthal, "Politische Gedanken bei Ibn Baǧǧa," *MGWJ,* LXXI (1937), 162 f. See also my remarks on this passage, below, Essay 7.

14. See, for instance, David Corcos-Abulafia's recent Hebrew study, "The Attitude of the Almohadic Rulers Towards the Jews," *Zion,* XXXII (1967), 137–60. See also Nissim b. Reuben Gerondi, *Perush* (Commentary) on Bab. Talmud Nedarim 28a, with reference to a similar earlier statement by French Tosafists. On this distinguished scholar, see Leon A. Feldman's Columbia University dissertation (1967), *Studies in the Life and Times of R. Nissim b. Reuben Gerondi of Barcelona (ca. 1340–1380)* (typescript).

15. Thomas Aquinas, *De regimine Judaeorum,* in his *Opera omnia* (Parma, 1865), XVI, 295 f.; Maimonides' M. T., Gezelah va-abedah, 5, 17–18, with reference to the talmudic discussion of Mar Samuel's maxim in the Babylonian Talmud, B. Q., 113ab. See also other rabbinic sayings quoted in my *The Jewish Community: Its History and Structure to the American Revolution,* 3 vols. (Philadelphia, 1942; and later impressions), I, 170 ff., 213 ff.; and *SRH,* IX, 47, 262 f. n. 52; XI, 18 ff.

16. A. E. Harkavy, ed., "Neṭira and His Sons," in *Festschrift . . . A. Berliner* (Frankfort, 1903), Hebrew section, pp. 36 and 39.

17. *Teshubot ha-geonim,* ed. by Harkavy, No. 346. See also other data excerpted from these and other early medieval responsa by Jacob Mann in "The Responsa of the Babylonian Geonim as a Source of Jewish History," *JQR,* n.s. X (1919–20), 121 ff.

18. The ramifications of the maxim "The law of the kingdom is law" have but recently been subjected to more careful scrutiny. In addition to the studies listed in my *Jewish Community,* III, 52 n. 5, see Israel Moshe Horn, *Dina de-malkhuta dina* (The Law of the Kingdom Is Law) (Tel-Aviv, 1950); and Leo Landman's recent monograph, *Jewish Law in the Diaspora: Confrontation and Accommodation* (Philadelphia, 1968).

19. See Stephen P. Ladas, *The Exchange of Minorities: Bulgaria, Greece and Turkey* (New York, 1932), pp. 437 ff.; and, more generally, my *Modern Nationalism and Religion* (New York, 1947; and later paperback reprints), pp. 16 f.

20. Saadia Gaon, *Siddur* (Prayerbook), ed. by Israel Davidson *et al.* (Jerusalem, 1941); and other sources cited by me in "Saadia's Communal Activities," below, Essay 5.

21. Below, pp. 108 ff.; *Pirque de-R. Eliezer,* viii (also in Gerald Friedlander's English trans.); S. D. Goitein, "Congregation versus Community:

an Unknown Chapter in the Communal History of the Jews of Palestine," *JQR*, n.s. XLIV (1953–54), 291–304, esp. pp. 302 f. However, Maimonides' great emphasis upon the "perfect city," rather than the "perfect state" (as rightly pointed out by Leo Strauss in "Quelques remarques," pp. 12 f.), probably was less influenced by the diversity existing among the Islamic states than by the impact of Plato's teachings, which of course had been formulated in the period when the Greek city-states were still vigorous. The same influence holds true for Alfarabi.

22. A. Cowley, "Bodleian Geniza Fragments," *JQR*, XVIII (1905–1906), 401; *Biblia (Antiguo Testamento), Traducida del hebreo al castellano por Rabi Mose Arragel de Guadalfajara (1422–33?)*, ed. by Antonio Paz de Melia and published by the Duke of Berwick y Alba, 2 vols. (Madrid, 1920–22; English ed., 1918); and Antonio Dominguez Ortíz, *La Clase social de los conversos en Castilla en la edad moderna* (Madrid [1955]), pp. 213 ff. App. i; my *SRH*, XIII, 96 f. A similar praise of Spain by a thirteenth-century Muslim, Abul Walid Ismail ibn Mulan al-Shakundi, *Risala fi fadhl al-andalus*, was published with a Spanish trans. by Emilio García Gomez under the title *Elogio del Islam español* (Madrid, 1934). Clearly, such regional pride was conducive to a feeling of local independence and a preference for local and sectarian observances and customs over and above imperial enactments. This situation resembled that in the ancient Roman Empire, where, even after centuries of Roman rule, the imperial law was unable to uproot the well-entrenched legal practices in Syria, Egypt, and other provinces. See Raphael Taubenschlag, "Il diritto provinciale romano nel libro siro-romano," *Journal of Juristic Papyrology*, VI (1952), 119.

23. Tritton, *The Caliphs and Their Non-Muslim Subjects*, pp. 134 ff.; Goitein, *Jews and Arabs*, pp. 97 f.

24. Ignaz Goldziher, *Muhammedanische Studien* (Halle a. S., 1889), I, 143 ff., 158, 208 ff., 268 f.; *idem*, "Die Šu'ubijja bei den Mohammedanern in Spanien," *Zeitschrift der deutschen morgenländischen Gesellschaft*, LIII (1899), 608–20. See also such monographic studies as J. Lecerf, "La signification historique du racisme chez Mutanabbi," in *Al-Mutanabbi: Recueil publié à l'occasion de son millénnaire* (Beirut, 1936), pp. 31–43; and below, pp. 144 f.

25. Tritton, *Journal of the Royal Asiatic Society*, 1931, pp. 333 f.; Maimonides, *Iggeret Teman* (Epistle to Yemen): the Arabic Original and the Three Hebrew Versions, ed. from manuscripts with Introduction and Notes by Abraham S. Halkin, and English trans. by Boaz Cohen (New York, 1952), *passim;* and my "The Historical Outlook of Maimonides," reprinted in my *History and Jewish Historians: Essays and Addresses*, ed. by Arthur Hertzberg and Leon A. Feldman (Philadelphia, 1964), pp. 146 f., 389 f. n. 163.

26. Sa'īd ibn Ahmad al-Andalusi, *Tabakat al-umam*, trans. into French

by Regis Blanchère in *Le Livre des "Catégories des Nations"* (Paris, 1935), p. 37; Philip Hitti, *History of the Arabs*, 2d ed., pp. 526 f., 566; Goitein, *Jews and Arabs*, p. 100; and Werner Sombart, *Die Juden und das Wirtschaftsleben* (Leipzig, 1911), English trans. by M. Epstein, entitled *The Jews and Modern Capitalism* (London, 1913), *passim*.

27. Moses ibn Ezra, *Shire ha-ḥol* (Secular Poems), ed. by Heinrich (Ḥayyim) Brody, Vol. I (Berlin, 1935), p. 176 v. 7.

28. *Kitab al-Khazari*, in Hartwig Hirschfeld's ed. of the Arabic original (Leipzig, 1887), and his English trans., 2d ed. (New York, 1927), *passim*. The Hebrew trans. by Yehudah ibn Tibbon is best available in David Cassel's well-annotated edition with a German translation (Leipzig, 1853). On the popularity of Ibn Tibbon's version see Cassel's Introd., pp. xviii ff.; and B. D. Friedberg, *Bet 'Eked Sepharim* (Antwerp, 1928–31), pp. 284 ff. See also, more fully, below, Essay 6.

29. Maimon b. Joseph the Judge, *Iggeret ha-Neḥamah* (Epistle of Consolation), Hebrew trans. by Benjamin Klar (Jerusalem, 1945), p. 14.

30. Simḥah Assaf, ed., *Teshubot ha-geonim mi-tokh ha-genizah* (Geonic Responsa from the Genizah [Jerusalem, 1929]), No. 87. On the rabbinic laws related to protecting the property of neighbors, the so-called *Din Ben ha-meṣar*, see the Maimonidean interpretation of the pertinent talmudic passages and their application to the realities of Maimonides' time, as analyzed below, p. 166.

ESSAY 5

1. See S. Poznanski, "The Anti-Karaite Writings of Saadia Gaon," *JQR*, X (1897–98), 76: אלרגל הדא; Hartwig Hirschfeld, "The Arabic Portion of the Cairo Genizah at Cambridge," *JQR*, XIX (1907), 138 n. 4; *idem*, "Early Karaite Critics of the Mishnah," *JQR*, n.s. VIII (1917–18), 166; Israel Davidson, *Saadia's Polemic against Ḥiwi Al-Balkhi* (New York, 1915), pp. 36 f. Although opposing this view as too extreme, Henry Malter admits "that polemic against heresies in general and Karaism in particular, direct and indirect, is a very conspicuous feature in most of Saadia's writings." See his *Saadia Gaon*, p. 262 (cited hereafter: Malter). He certainly deserved the designation אלקראין כצם ("foe of Karaites") given him by a Karaite Bible commentator; see Jacob Mann, *Texts and Studies in Jewish History and Literature* (Cincinnati, 1931), II, 105.

2. This is repeatedly emphasized in both the Arabic and the Hebrew introduction to his first philological treatise, the *Egron*, written in 902–903, when he was twenty. Describing the variety of languages used by the Jews on account of their dispersion, he exclaims: ותלט עלנחם על שפר אמרינו ולאנכון כן . . . . יאתה לנו ולכל עם אלהינו לדרוש ולבין ולחקריהו תמיד גם אנחנו גם טפינו גם נשינו ועבדינו לא יזח מפינו כי בו נבון חקי תורת צורינו אשר המה חיינו חיתינו אורינו מקדושנו למעולם ועד עולם. The date which follows, 1214 Sel. era (A.D. 902–3), is of

course, to be retained in the light of our present knowledge that Saadia was born in 882. See A. Marx's note in *REJ*, LXXIV (1922), 222. See also the description of the general purposes of the *Sefer ha-Galui* in A. E. Harkavy's *Zikhron la-Rishonim* (Studien und Mitteilungen), V, 54 f., 155 f. (cited hereafter: Harkavy.) See also Neḥemyah Allony's recent critical ed. of *Ha'Egron* (Jerusalem, 1969), esp. pp. 25 ff., 159.

3. Ben-Zion Halper, "Jewish Literature in Arabic" (Hebrew), *Hateku-fah*, XXIII (1925), 269. See also *ibid.*, pp. 268 ff. for other Arabic versions of the Bible.

4. Although in his introduction to the Pentateuch (*Oeuvres complètes*, ed. by Derenbourg, I, 4) Saadia mentions only Jews who had requested him to undertake this work so that "they may understand the meaning of the Torah," his use of Arabic characters, attested by Abraham ibn Ezra (*Commentary* on Gen. 2:11), indicates that he wished to address himself to non-Jewish readers as well. See Malter, pp. 142 ff. The contempt in which Arab purists held Hunayn and his confreres, because, as one of them phrased it, they were "men, weak and imperfect in one tongue, who translated it into another, in which they were also weak and imperfect," was doubly justified in the case of the Bible translations made not from the original Hebrew but from the Greek and Syriac versions. On the other hand, there is little evidence that Saadia's translation made a dent in the prevailing ignorance of the Bible among the Arab masses or that even Arab authors who mention biblical topics (including Saadia's personal acquaintance Al-Mas'udi, who claims that he saw Saadia's translation and that it was "the most highly esteemed one among many of his [the translator's] coreligionists") ever used Saadia's version in their works. See A. S. Tritton, *The Caliphs and Their Non-Muslim Subjects* (London, 1930), pp. 170, 172; Al-Mas'udi, *Kitāb at Tanbiḥ*, ed. by De Goeje, pp. 112 f. (in French trans. by B. Carra de Vaux [Paris, 1896], pp. 159 f.).

5. See *Emunot*, Introd. (ed. by David Slucki [Leipzig, 1864; Berlin, 1928], pp. 3 f.): וכאשר עמדתי על השרשים האלה ורוע סעפותם כאב לי על מיני מן המדברים וכאשר עמדתי על השרשים האלה ורוע סעפותם כאב לי על מיני מן המדברים. והתעוררה נפשי לעמנו בני ישראל ... To conserve space, I shall cite, as a rule, the existing Hebrew translations of Saadia's writings, which are not always accompanied by English renditions, and shall refer to the Arabic originals only when a particular phrasing seems to be of special significance. See also below, nn. 134–38.

6. See *Siddur*, ed. by I. Davidson, S. Assaf, and B. I. Joel (Jerusalem, 1941), p. 10 (of text): לכן נחוץ לאסוף את התפלות והברכות שהן מסדר זמננו זה, ר'ל תקופת הגלות, ולרשמן, ובפרט משום מה שקורה בזמן הזה משלשה דברים, ההזנחה וההוספה וההשמטה, ויש בנללם לחשש לשכחה ולקביעת השינוי ... See also Simon Bernstein's comments on this work in *Bitzaron*, III (1941–42), 845–56.

7. *Siddur*, p. 117: ומותר ... ולעיין בעניני צבור; Harkavy, V, 227 (Ibn Sarjado said): וינרם הדבר להכות רבים מישראל בשבט השליטים ובחדשים ויחלל הוא את [i.e., Hasan-Josiah, השם גם את השבתות להביא משאות לפחות והסגנים ביום צאתו עם חסד

the antiexilarch] אל דאר מובבך. To be sure, such accusations in the heat of controversy need not be taken seriously; but this particular statement is reinforced by Ibn Sarjado's assertion that the act had been witnessed by many Jews of Baghdad. For the pertinent talmudic passages, permitting essentially verbal departures, and especially R. Jonathan's kindred ruling of Shab. 150a; Ket. 5a; and for the qualifications thereof see especially the comments of Don Vidal on M.T. Shabbat 24.5; and of Joseph Karo on Ṭur, O. Ḥ. 306.

8. See especially the quotation from Ibn Kutaibah in A. Mez's *Die Renaissance des Islams* (Heidelberg, 1922), p. 162 (in English trans. in *Islamic Culture*, IV [1930], 291).

9. G. G. Scholem, *Major Trends in Jewish Mysticism* (Jerusalem, 1941), pp. 85 f., 95 f., 110 ff.

10. It suffices here to refer to Malter's standard biography of Saadia and to Mann's reconstruction of the chronological sequence of the major communal developments of the period in his "Varia on the Geonic Period" (Hebrew), *Tarbiz*, V (1933–34), 148–79. There the important older literature is fully listed and analyzed, including the writings of numerous specialists who have discussed Saadia's work in philosophy, the Bible, etc. Among contemporaries one need but mention the numerous valuable contributions to Saadia research made by Moses Zucker during the last quarter century.

11. Philip K. Hitti, *History of the Arabs*, 2d ed. (London, 1940), p. 321, quoting Tha'alibi.

12. Quoted by Mez, *Renaissance des Islams*, p. 1 (*Islamic Culture*, II [1928], 92).

13. Jalalu'ddin as-Suyuti, *History of the Caliphs*, trans. by H. S. Jarret (Calcutta, 1881), p. 410.

14. *Ibid.*, pp. 402 f., 406, quoting As-Suli.

15. *Ibid.*, p. 411. See also the sympathetic characterization in *The Eclipse of the Abbasid Caliphate*, ed. by H. F. Amedroz and D. S. Margoliouth, IV (Oxford, 1921), 462; and Hitti, *History of the Arabs*, pp. 469 f.

16. Hitti, *ibid.*

17. These three viziers have frequently been treated by both medieval and modern historians. Harold Bowen's *The Life and Times of 'Ali Ibn 'Isa, (The Good Vizier)* (Cambridge, 1928) is more than a meritorious detailed biography; it is a good summary of all major events and a description of the workings of the imperial administration until 'Ali's death in 946, at the age of eighty-nine. It is supplemented by A. H. Harley's briefer sketch of "Ibn Muqlah," *Bulletin of the School of Oriental Studies, University of London*, III (1923–25), 213–29. Ibn al-Furat, the most colorful of them all, however, has not yet been the subject of a special biography. It must be borne in mind that the settlement of major Jewish communal conflicts depended just as much (or more) on the will

of the viziers as it did on the caliphs' whims.

18. As-Suyuti, *History of the Caliphs,* pp. 411, 413 f.; Reuben Levy, *A Baghdad Chronicle* (Cambridge, 1929), pp. 143 ff., 148 ff.

18a. Ed. by B. M. Lewin in *Ginze Ḳedem,* V (1934), 147 ff.; and, more fully, by Allony, see *supra,* n. 2.

19. S. Pinsker, *Lickute Kadmoniot,* II, 37: והספרים אשר כתב לא הוציאם בחייו מתחת ידו על בני מקרא ואחד מהם נפל ביד בן משיח . . . ואחרי מותו כמות נבל נפלו ספריו ביד בני מקרא בכל מקום ומקום וישיבו עליו תשובות בדברים נכוחים כמסמרות נטועים בספרים הרבה . . . . S. Poznanski minimizes the credibility of this statement; see *The Karaite Literary Opponents of Saadiah Gaon* (London, 1908), pp. 2 f. But his own work seems to offer partial confirmation. There is little doubt that the publication and wider distribution of Saadia's polemical works would have provoked an instant storm of protest among these highly articulate sectarians, as it did in the decades following his death. But Poznanski mentions only five Karaites who in Saadia's lifetime debated the issues with him. Of these, Ben Zuṭa disputed with Saadia orally, while the mysterious Ibn Saḳaweihi (whose identity with Salmon b. Yeruḥim, postulated by Geiger and, more recently, by Israel Davidson in *The Book of the Wars of the Lord* [New York, 1934], pp. 22 ff., 26, is rightly controverted by Mann in his *Texts and Studies,* II, 1469 f.) and Al-Ḳirḳisani covered many items of general Rabbanite-Karaite controversy, but as far as can now be judged nowhere refer to specific anti-Karaite works by Saadia. The only passage in Al-Ḳirḳisani's *Kitab al-Anwar* (written five years before Saadia's death) which Harkavy (V, 107 n. 3) suggested might refer to Saadia's polemic against 'Anan is too general to warrant such a conclusion. The objection that "for prayers (consisting of citations) from the Book of Psalms they [the Rabbanites] substitute some composed by themselves" (see Leon Nemoy's trans. in *HUCA,* VII [1930], 332) may have been repudiated by Saadia in many another work, including the lost portions of his introd. to the *Siddur,* the whole tenor of which is in clear contradiction to such a view. Al-Ḳirḳisani's calm and dispassionate tone in this and other passages, contrasting with the sharp polemics of his successors, likewise seems to indicate that he was not refuting any of the vigorous Saadianic attacks on Karaism. Ibn Mashiaḥ apparently knew only Saadia's *Kitāb al-tamyīz* (see Mann, cited above). Salmon alone indubitably refers to Saadia's pamphlet against 'Anan (Davidson's edition, pp. 106 f.: קרן סעדיה תנודע וחכמתו תבולע אשר בתשובתו על ענן התגלע although he, too, seems to have had difficulty in securing Saadia's אשא משלי; *ibid.,* p. 19) and is correspondingly vituperative. But both he and Ibn Mashiaḥ seem to have written in the last years of Saadia— Poznanski's suggestion of 940 for the composition of the *Wars* is more plausible than Davidson's earlier dating—when the latter's writings might have been somewhat more readily available. There is, indeed, a slight indication that even then Salmon was not fully familiar with the chronological setting of Saadia's anti-Karaite works. The accusation רוב מומו וטנוף נלמו בבעלי

מקרא ירשימו, ו י ר א כ י ל א י כ ו ל ל מ ו על ספר החכם המאור הגדול תפארת סגולת הי רבנו ענן הריק חרמו apparently betrays his ignorance of the fact that the *Refutation of 'Anan* was Saadia's first attack on Karaism. Moreover, the total disappearance of the *Refutation,* of which stray copies are recorded to the end of the twelfth century, but none later, would hardly be understandable if it had ever enjoyed wide popularity. Hai Gaon, a few decades after Saadia's death, no longer had access to most of Saadia's anti-Karaite writings. See Harkavy's comment in *Oeuvres complètes,* IX, xxxvi n. 18. The suggestion that this scarcity was due to the Karaites' destroying all copies of Saadia's polemical works on which they could lay their hands—a suggestion first timidly made by Pinsker, *Lickute,* I, 112, and then accepted by Hirschfeld and Malter—is not supported by any direct evidence; nor is it convincing at all in the light of the general observation that controversy usually increases rather than diminishes the circulation of a work.

20. This is clearly indicated by the only source of our information, Al-Ḳirḳisani, who, writing within half a century of Hai's death, knew of this rebuttal only from hearsay (וחכי ען האי). See Harkavy, p. 108; Poznanski, *JQR,* X, 238 f.

21. See Mann, *The Jews in Egypt and Palestine under the Fatimid Caliphs* (2 vols., London, 1920–22), I, 61 ff. Saadia's denunciation of 'Anan's motives in returning to actual observation of the new moon, in accordance with the Muslim custom, in order to curry favor with the government (reported by an unknown Karaite; see Pinsker, *Lickute,* II, 95: לבקש השררות ונעה אחריהם בעבור לעזרו . . .) may well have expressed more than a purely historical grievance.

22. Gregory Abu'lfaraj Bar-Hebraeus, *Chronicon ecclesiasticum,* ed. by J. A. Abbeloos and T. J. Lamy (Louvain, 1872–77), I, 366 f. See also Felix Lazarus, "Neue Beiträge zur Geschichte des Exilarchats," *MGWJ,* LXXVIII (1934), 279–88; and my *The Jewish Community* (Philadelphia, 1942), II, 179 f.; III, 40 f.

23. H. F. Amedroz, "Tales of Official Life from the 'Tadkhira' of Ibn Hamdun," *Journal of the Royal Asiatic Society,* 1908, pp. 447 ff., 467 ff. See my *Jewish Community,* III, 39 n. 13.

24. Mann, *Jews in Egypt,* I, 255.

25. S. Schechter, *Saadyana* (Cambridge, 1903), p. 20; Ḥayyim Yeḥiel Bornstein, "The Conflict between R. Saadiah Gaon and Ben Meir" (Hebrew), *Sefer ha-Yobel . . . Nahum Sokolow* (Warsaw, 1904), p. 104 (cited hereafter: Bornstein); A. Guillaume, "Further Documents on the Ben Meir Controversy," *JQR,* n.s. V (1914–15), 552: ונדחף מארץ מצרים ומת ביפו. The incredibility of the preceding assertion—allegedly supported by the testimony of reliable witnesses—that the father had been some sort of Muslim *muezzin* (מכה בפטיש בארץ מצרים לעבודה זרה ואכל מרק פינולים) need not detract from the veracity of this particular statement. As is well known, Saadia's forebears, particularly his father, were under constant attack in

the later controversy with David b. Zakkai (see Harkavy, pp. 225 ff., where not only Khalaf ibn Sarjado casts various aspersions on the father's occupation and character but the official denunciation by exilarch and fellow gaon constantly harps on Saadia's being an alien, the descendant of proselytes, and, generally, "an infamous fool" [נבל בן בלי שם, p. 232]). But nowhere do we find any clue to the reasons for the father's emigration from Egypt. There is not a shred of evidence for Malter's hypothesis (p. 63) that the father followed Saadia abroad, rather than vice versa. On the contrary, Ben Meir's invocation, in 922, of the testimony of witnesses for events affecting the father's life and death in Palestine—the היעידו undoubtedly refers to the whole statement—clearly indicates that the events had taken place several years before.

26. Pp. 57 ff.

27. As-Suyuti (*History of the Caliphs*, p. 398) reports succinctly that in A.H. 301 the Fatimid Mahdi who had "ravaged and slaughtered" in Alexandria "made himself master of Alexandria and Fayyum." This invasion has sometimes been mentioned in connection with Saadia's emigration from Egypt, but it presupposed the long-held date of 915 for this event. With the now recognized earlier birth date for Saadia (882 instead of 892) and, hence, an earlier date for the composition of his *Refutation of 'Anan* (905), the main prop for this hypothesis is lacking. In fact, Saadia's first communication to his Egyptian students, written in the winter of 922, clearly suggests that Saadia had left Egypt before 915—very likely much before. His complaint זה שש שנים ומחצה לא הגיעני מאתכם פתשגן אף לא גליון (Bornstein, p. 82) implies that he used to hear from them rather frequently for some time before 915.

28. In his review of Malter in *REJ*, LXXIII (1921), 106 f.; also *Tarbiz*, V, 157 ff.

29. Dunash, *Commentary* on *Sefer Yeṣirah*, Introd. (ed. by Grossberg [London, 1902], p. 17): לפי שכתבו פעמים רבות באו למדינתנו הידועה קירואן לזקננו רבינו יצחק בן שלמה ז'ל בשאילות מחכמות החיצוניות והוא עדיין בפיתום טרם לכתו ולבבל והיה רבינו יצחק מראה אותם לי ואנכי אז בן עשרים שנה והייתי מעמידו על מקומות טעותו ... (see the quotation from a Parma MS by Mann, *Texts and Studies*, I, 74 n. 25); Bornstein, pp. 81 ff.; B. M. Lewin's ed. of the *Iggeret R. Sherira Gaon* (Haifa, 1921), p. xxv no. 3; D. Revel, "An Epistle by R. Saadiah Gaon" (Hebrew), *Debir*, I (1923), 180–88, supplemented by J. N. Epstein's remarks, *ibid.*, pp. 189 f.

30. Al-Mas'udi, *Kitāb at-Tanbiḥ*, p. 113; Malter, pp. 32 ff. S. Eppenstein ("Beiträge zur Geschichte und Literatur im gaonäischen Zeitalter," *MGWJ*, LIV [1910], 315) suggests that Saadia's reference in his letter to the Egyptian students of 921—בעודני בחלב באו מקצת התלמידים מבעל גד—shows that he had been teaching in Palestine. However, the term תלמיד in Saadia's terminology is often the equivalent of "scholar" rather than "student." Nor is he likely to have failed to stress the fact that these were *his* students.

31. Mez, *Renaissance des Islams*, p. 182.

32. Bornstein, p. 83: ובלכתי מהמון אל האמון ובשובי מחיל אל חיל with obvious reference to Jer. 52:15; Ber. 64a. See Bornstein's n. 2, *ibid.*; and Simon Eppenstein, *MGWJ*, LIV, 314. See also Saadia's *Siddur*, p. 10: כי בארצות האלה שעברתי בהן ראיתי . . .

33. Tritton, *The Caliphs*, pp. 134 f.

34. A legal difficulty of this kind would best explain Saadia's apparent failure to return to Egypt even for a brief visit, a failure which perplexed Malter (p. 58) and others.

35. *Saadyana*, pp. 133 ff. The peculiarities of style, vocalization, and accentuation point to Saadia's authorship. Mann's main objection (*REJ*, LXXIII, 106 f.; *Tarbiz*, V, 158 n. 34) that the author's age is indicated by בן עשרים . . . (2 recto 1.2), whereas Saadia was thirty-three at the time of his emigration from Egypt, is removed if we date his departure several years earlier. We have seen that earlier dating is indicated for other reasons as well.

36. Mez, *Renaissance des Islams*, p. 465.

37. D. S. Margoliouth, *Lectures on Arabic Historians* (Calcutta, 1930), p. 7; Harkavy, V, 194 f. See also M. K. Ayad, *Geschichts- und Gesellschaftslehre ibn Halduns* (Stuttgart, 1930), p. 27. Incidentally, Dosa's biography of Saadia, sent to Spain at the request of Ḥisdai ibn Shapruṭ (see Ibn Daud's *Chronicle*, ed. by Neubauer, II, 66), seems to have met a demand awakening among the Jews under the stimulus of their Arab neighbors, of whom it was said: "when an eminent man died there was a market for biographies of him somewhat as is the case in the capitals of Europe in our time" (Margoliouth, p. 7).

38. The passage (. . . . כי נער אתה לא תדע צאת ובוא כי בן עשרים) raises far more questions than it helps solve. Apart from the dubious assumption that a man of twenty-odd years would heed warnings by friends concerning his utter immaturity—this may have been merely exaggerated advice against traveling alone in an inclement season—there is an obviously sharp change in style from the preceding passages. The text on fol. 1 recto and verso is entirely in the form of a prayer; that of fol. 2 is a consecutive narrative. The former seems to consist of semipoetic stanzas, each beginning with the word ועתה (lines 1, 11 of r., and 14 of v.); the latter is far more prosaic. In the former the author speaks in the first person; in the latter he uses the third person exclusively. It is possible that some missing lines or even folios between the two texts originally provided a transition—no opinion can be voiced on this score without consultation of the Cambridge Genizah fragment—hence we need neither insist that the two passages are disjointed fragments of two different writings nor impugn Saadia's authorship of either.

39. See below, especially n. 75. Malter's full analysis of the fragments here under review (pp. 59 ff.) has only partly been vitiated by his

assumption of its late date (winter 920/21) based upon his adherence to Ibn Daud's report of 892 as the year of Saadia's birth and by his interpretation of the crucial passage as referring to a journey from Egypt to Palestine and Babylonia, rather than vice versa.

40. Graetz, *Geschichte*, V¹, Note XII, pp. 446 ff.; Friedlaender, "The Arabic Original of the Report of R. Nathan Hababli," *JQR*, XVII (1904–5), 747–61; Ginzberg, *Geonica*, I, 55 ff.; Malter, p. 104 n. 234; Isaac Halevy, *Dorot ha-rishonim*, III, 249 ff.; Mann, *Tarbiz*, V, 149 ff.

41. According to Mann's reconstruction, Nathan, though well aware of the historical sequence of the events and the names of the two exilarchs, 'Ukba and David b. Zakkai, and the two bankers, Joseph b. Phineas and his son-in-law, Netira, is hopelessly mixed up in regard to the leaders of the two academies. The two predecessors of Saadia in the gaonate of Sura, Amram b. Solomon and Hai b. Kayomi, are of a wholly mistaken identity, since, according to Sherira, their names were Jacob b. Natronai and Yom Tob b. Jacob Kohen. Similarly mistaken are Nathan's references to Kohen Sedek as head of the academy of Pumbedita and main protagonist in the struggle against 'Ukba, and, for a time, also as the opponent of David. Mann believes that the gaon who deposed 'Ukba was Judah b. Samuel, Sherira's grandfather (d. 917), and that David's early opponent was Judah's successor, Mubashshir (or Mebasser), whereas Kohen Sedek was in fact a partisan of David and Mubashshir's opponent. Mann fails to explain why an author who, despite the picturesqueness of his narrative, is careful to mention that it is based [במקצת וספרו ושכצח] ממה שראה בבבל and that he knows of 'Ukba's reign merely that he . . . נהג שררה בבבל שנים רבות שלא עמד על מספרם, is very exact in his topography (see especially the Arabic fragment ed. by Friedlaender), and is quite correct in naming all personalities involved in the later controversy between Saadia and David, should have been so utterly careless or ignorant in regard to the geonic leadership of the preceding two decades. Neither is it at all likely that Sherira, who mentions other major conflicts over the exilarchic office and its relation to the academies (ed. Lewin, pp. 104, 105, 106, 107, 110 f., 113, 117 f., 119 f.) and seizes every opportunity to emphasize events involving his ancestors, should have completely passed over in silence his grandfather's major victory over the exilarch, a victory which he himself had witnessed as a child. Moreover, his own account of the succession in Sura during the crucial period of 'Ukba's deposition is not altogether satisfactory. Following the seven-year administration of Shalom b. Mishael, he tells us: ובתריה אדלדלא מלתא טובא במתא מחסיא ולא אשתיירו בה חכימי, ובתריה מניוה למר רב יעקב בר רב נטרונאי י[נ] שנה (*ibid.*, p. 116, the Spanish version; the German version is more definite only in regard to the thirteen years of R. Jacob). But Sherira fails to inform us as to how long Sura was deserted and when and how it was reorganized under R. Jacob's leadership. Evidently, all the reconstructions based upon a clear-cut superiority of Sherira's trustworthiness have thus far completely failed. But neither is the opposite

assumption—that Nathan's account alone is reliable—justified in the light of Sherira's generally proven exactitude, particularly in regard to events which took place in his native city during his lifetime, at the academy where his grandfather, father, and uncle had occupied leading positions.

42. By Ginzberg, *Geonica*, I, 61.

43. See Mann, "The Exilarchic Office in Babylonia, etc." (Hebrew), *Livre d'hommage . . . Poznanski* (Warsaw, 1929), p. 19; Alexander Goode, "The Exilarchate in the Eastern Caliphate, 637–1258," *JQR*, n.s. XXXI (1940–41), 163.

44. A. Marx, "Der arabische Bustanai-Bericht und Nathan ha-Babli," *Livre d'hommage . . . Poznanski,* pp. 76–81. The beginning of the Arabic fragment, and, to a lesser extent, that of the Hebrew translation, creates the impression that the entire story was told to satisfy the curiosity of the North-African Jews concerning 'Ukba and his deposition. The former exilarch, as we know from another source, had been received upon his arrival in Kairuwan with considerable pomp and ceremonial, appropriate to his former station. See Abraham ha-Yarḥi, *Sefer ha-Manhig,* ed. by J. M. Goldberg, fol. 32ab no. 58. It is not difficult to realize that such recognition of a deposed leader was stimulated by the Faṭimid counter-caliphs, who wished to disengage their Jewish subjects from the control of an official appointed by their rivals in Baghdad.

45. Marx (see preceding note), p. 77 n. 2, has sensed the difficulty of squaring the date of the composition of our account (about 960–70) with the author's presence at David's installation. Unfortunately, we are not quite sure when Ḥushiel opened his academy in Kairuwan. Leaving aside the problem of his Italian origin, and Mann's untenable hypothesis that there were two Ḥushiels, it appears that his Kairuwan activity began not earlier than 960. See V. Aptowitzer, *R. Chuschiel und R. Chananel* (Vienna, 1933); Mann's critique thereof in *Tarbiz*, V, 286 ff.; and Mordecai Margalioth's introduction to his Hebrew ed. of the *Halachot Kezuboth attributed to R. Yehudai Gaon* (Jerusalem, 1942), pp. 4 f., 9 n. 68.

46. Ed. Neubauer, I, 79: אבל ראש ישיבת סורא הנהיג אותו על עצמו וכתב לכל אנשי ...ישיבתו... ועכ"ז היה ממאן כהן צדק ראש ישיבת פומבדיתא ואינו רוצה בדבר עד ני שנים...

47. Although the introductory passage concerning "what he had seen in Babylonia" need not refer to the installation, his very minute description seems to indicate that he witnessed the events himself.

48. This assumption gains in probability when one considers the context of Nathan's description of the installation, which follows the brief historical survey ending in the vacancy in the exilarchic office and the appointment of Ibn Sarjado to the gaonate of Pumbedita, in 943, and obviously reflects the conditions of that late period. The reference to the equal division between Sura and Pumbedita of all unspecified donations is clearly a mirror of conditions after 926 (see below). The disrespect shown by the Jews of Persia to David's son, witnessed by Nathan (שראה is perhaps indicative

of his presence in David's son's entourage); the father's successful intervention, through the vizier, with the caliph; and the latter's communication to the "king" of Persia are all more likely to have happened in the anarchical 930s than before. The relatively insignificant annual revenues of the exilarch and the gaon of Sura (700 and 1,500 gold dinars [equivalent to $2,800 and $6,000] respectively)—incidentally showing that Nathan refrained from exaggerations—are best accounted for in the days of greatest imperial anarchy in the late 930s or early 940s and particularly during the two years between the death of David b. Zakkai and that of Saadia. These amounts certainly were a mere pittance as compared not only with private fortunes like the Baghdad jeweler Jauhari's self-assessed 20,000,000 dinars, and with Ibn al-Furat's reputed 1,000,000 dinars annual income before his first vizierate in 909, but also in relation to the much larger sums collected by the Baghdad exilarchs in the days of Benjamin of Tudela. They also compared unfavorably with the usual salaries of Muslim officials, recorded by Al-Makrizi, which ranged from 100 to 5,000 dinars monthly. See Amedroz-Margoliouth, *Eclipse*, IV, 39; Bowen, *'Ali Ibn 'Isa*, p. 103; Benjamin's *Itinerary*, ed. Adler, p. 41a (Hebrew); Tyan, *Organisation judiciaire*, I, 510 ff. Unsettled conditions may, finally, also help explain why Nathan enumerated only a few of the provinces from which the exilarch and the two geonim used to collect regular imposts. See Mann in *Tarbiz*, V, 167, for partial additions to the former Suranic area of control.

49. That is why he is so hazy about all earlier dates, such as the length of 'Uḳba's reign, the "four or five years" (the Arabic text speaks of only "about three or four years") which elapsed between his deposition and the elevation of David b. Zakkai, and even the beginning of David's controversy with Saadia (... ולא היה ימים מועטים עד שנפלה קטטה). He becomes more specific concerning Josiah's antiexilarchate, which lasted three years, and the reconciliation of the two protagonists after seven years. He is quite precise in stating that David's son lived only seven months more than David, and that the grandson was then twelve years of age. In the story of the Pumbedita academy Nathan gives thirteen months as the duration of the gaonate of Ṣemaḥ b. Kafnai, Kohen Ṣedeḳ's successor—in conflict with Sherira's version of two and a half years, and altogether fails to mention Ḥanina b. Judah, Sherira's father and Ṣemaḥ's successor. But one must bear in mind that many Sherira MSS date Kohen Ṣedeḳ's decease at 1247 Sel. era (936; it is so accepted by most modern scholars) and that of Ṣemaḥ at the beginning of 1249 (937), which would make Nathan more nearly right. The omission of Ḥanina, if not due to a copyist's *homoiote-leuton*, skipping from one ומלך אחר to another, may have been due to Nathan's desire to mention only the main facts relevant to his story; i.e., Kohen Ṣedeḳ's death and the ultimate succession of Ibn Sarjado.

50. As a parallel, one may cite the meek withdrawal, a generation later, of Sherira's maternal uncle Amram before the powerful and wealthy Ibn

Sarjado, while Nehemiah Gaon, militant Kohen Ṣedeḳ's militant son, did
not hesitate to defy Ibn Sarjado's authority despite his many years in office.
See Sherira, pp. 120 f. The revenue from Khorasan must have constituted
an important fiscal item, since we know from Muḳaddasi that the province
at that time contained "many Jews." Cited by Mez, *Renaissance des Islams,*
p. 34.

51. Some hesitation is, indeed, reflected in the Arabic and Hebrew versions. At the beginning, where the Hebrew (I, 78 f.) reads והיה ראש ישיבה בימיו
מר רב כהן צדק, the Arabic original (ed. Friedlaender, pp. 753 ff.) has, perhaps more precisely, ולי כהן צדק בן יוסף בן ישיבה בפומבדיתא (i.e., that Kohen Ṣedeḳ
b. Joseph was "in charge" of the academy in Pumbedita). Several lines
later, to be sure, Kohen Ṣedeḳ is called ראש ישיבת פומבדיתא. But apart from
the use of this Hebrew designation in an Arabic context in place of the
more frequent title ראס אלמתיבה, the appellation is doubly suspect because
the Hebrew here has merely ומנעו רב כהן צדק, without a title. The opposite is
true in the subsequent discussion of David's election, where the Hebrew
שהוא ראש ישיבה פומבדיתא has no equivalent in the Arabic text. It is
not impossible that only the first statement concerning Kohen Ṣedeḳ as
having been "in charge" of the Academy stemmed from Nathan himself,
while the subsequent use of the title ראש ישיבת . . . . is entirely due to the
Kairuwan rapporteur or to later copyists.

One could perhaps press the matter further and explain the meaning of
בפומבדיתא והי אלאנבאר as referring to Kohen Ṣedeḳ as in charge of a section of
the academy which was still in the city of Al-Anbar. While Mann has made
it plausible (see his "Responsa of the Babylonian Geonim as a Source of
Jewish History," *JQR*, n.s. XI [1920–21], 434 ff.·) that the main seat of
the Pumbedita school had been transferred to Baghdad about 890, the
continued functioning of a section in the original locality twenty-odd years
later is not unlikely. Such territorial separation may, in fact, be implied in
our principal source of information, Hai Gaon's responsum (cited *ibid.*),
which repeatedly stresses והוא [Hai b. David] תחלת מי ששכן מן הגאונים בבגדד
and והגאונים ששכנו אחריו בבגדד. It may also best account for the subsequent
reconciliation of David b. Zakkai and Kohen Ṣedeḳ and their followers at
a point half a day's journey from Baghdad (Neubauer, I, 80). The exilarch
evidently went part of the way to meet Kohen Ṣedeḳ, on his way from
Pumbedita, at a distance of 12 parasangs (some 36 miles) from the capital.
See Jacob Obermeyer, *Die Landschaft Babylonien* (Frankfort, 1929), p.
148; Graetz, *Geschichte*, V⁴, 444 n. 1. As against this factual reminiscence,
the story of Nissi's miraculous intervention with Kohen Ṣedeḳ, והיה פותח כל
מנעולי בבל בשם (*ibid.*, p. 79), carries less weight, since the locality is not given
in the Arabic original (*JQR*, XVII, 755). A division of the academy into
two sections may, finally, help explain the frequent coexistence of two rival
geonim at the Pumbedita academy in the course of the tenth century:
Mubashshir and Kohen Ṣedeḳ, Ibn Sarjado and Nehemiah, Nehemiah and

Sherira. Sherira's phrasing, too, might refer to just such a separation: ויתיב רב מבשר נאון ורבנן דיליה לבדם . . . ומר רב כהן צדק ורבנן דיליה לבדם (p. 120). But the verification of this hypothesis, however alluring it may be, would require a complete reexamination of all contemporary material, which would far transcend the scope of this investigation. See also Shalom Albeck's introd. to his edition of *Ha-Eshkol* (I [Jerusalem, 1935], 6 n. 18 and 73 n. 4) where the editor argues, on other grounds, for the simultaneous operation of three schools in Baghdad, Sura, and Pumbedita. Cf., however, Ch. Albeck's comment thereon, *ibid.*, p. 91 n. 1.

52. Schechter, *Saadyana*, p. 23; Bornstein, pp. 109 f. See also Saadia's *Oeuvres complètes*, IX, 149 no. 15, quoting from the *Sefer ha-'Ibbur:* ומצאנו הנאון ר"ס זכר המחלוקת הזה בחבורו הנקרא ספר ההכרה, referring to the year 926, two years before Saadia's elevation to the gaonate; the general Karaite usage of ראש הישיבה, without further designation, for Saadia (see Harkavy, V, 194 n. 1), despite the fact that most of his anti-Karaite writings antedated 928; the well-known anachronistic inscription concerning Hai ראש ישיבה נאון יעקב at the beginning of Sherira's *Epistle;* and many other instances.

53. It evidently does not suffice to gloss over Nathan's narrative in this respect and adopt Sherira's data instead, as is done by Graetz and Malter, despite their acceptance of Nathan's general superiority as a contemporary source. Halevy's correction of Amram b. Sheshna for Amram b. Solomon is impossible on chronological grounds, while the latter's simple identification with Jacob b. Naṭronai of Sherira's chronicle and the assumption that he and his father happened to have each two different names, obviously is a counsel of despair. It seems far more likely that Nathan's Amram was gaon at the time of Sura's eclipse, mentioned by Sherira (see the text cited above n. 41), which evidently caused an interruption in the succession of the Sura geonim, as reported by Nathan. Since, moreover, the chronology of this succession is obviously faulty (in the "century" beginning with R. Hillai's accession, allegedly in 1208 Sel. era and ending with either Saadia's appointment in 1239 or his death in 1253, he enumerates geonim who ruled a total of 159 or 173 years respectively) it is quite possible to place Amram b. Solomon during the intermission before the accession of Jacob b. Naṭronai in 914. The latter date may be computed backward from Saadia, if we read ten and four years respectively for his two predecessors. 'Uḳba's deposition, indeed, took place before 914 (see below). In the subsequent election of David b. Zakkai some three to five years later, it may have been Jacob who served as David's staunch adherent. It is to be noted that Nathan's account (both in Arabic and in Hebrew) speaks cautiously of a gaon of Sura, without mentioning his name. The same is true of his subsequent report of that gaon's death. However, his statement ומלך אחריו מר האיי בר קיומי והוא היה ראש דורו באותו זמן ונהג ישיבת סורא כ' שנה ומת וכהן צדק ראש ישיבת פומבדיתא עודנו חי evidently represented a bad slip of his memory. He may have

dimly recollected that the last outstanding leader of Sura before Saadia had been a Hai (b. Naḥshon; he may have confused his father's name with that of Mubashshir's father קיומי) who, according to Sherira, ruled there for ten years some three decades before Saadia. But this single demonstrable major error in a side issue ought not to shake our confidence in Nathan's over-all veracity any more than Sherira's general historical value is undermined by his glaring chronological miscalculations, which, if pedantically considered, would relegate his *Epistle*, a classic of medieval Jewish historiography and the most important source of our information for Muslim Babylonia, to the limbo of unreliable records.

54. See his *Jews in the Economic and Political Life of Mediaeval Islam* (London, 1937). For the Neṭira family, see especially the Hebrew description of the "Bene Neṭira," ed. by A. E. Harkavy in *Festschrift . . . A. Berliner* (Frankfort, 1903), pp. 34–43.

55. At-Tanukhi, *Nishwār al-Muḥāḍara*, ed. by D. S. Margoliouth (Damascus, 1930), II, 84 f. Three important excerpts therefrom are given by Fischel, *Jews in . . . Mediaeval Islam*, pp. 23 f., 28.

56. Amedroz-Margoliouth, *Eclipse*, IV, 22. Ibn al-Furat's second vizierate began in 917, a year after Neṭira's death.

57. Harkavy in *Festschrift Berliner*, pp. 36, 39. See also Siegmund Fraenkel's comments thereon in *JQR*, XVII (1905), 386 ff.; and above, p. 86.

58. Mann has rightly pointed out (*Tarbiz*, V, 155) that the passage in Saadia's letter (Bornstein, pp. 77 f.)—ויתנו את ידם לשלום בינימו לבלתי [ידח] נדח—refers to this reconciliation, which, according to Sherira, was effected in Elul, 1233. See below, n. 77.

59. See especially Bornstein (as cited above, n. 25); *idem*, "Latest Phases in the History of 'Ibbur'" (Hebrew), *Hatekufah*, XVI (1922–23), 228–92; A. Epstein's reply to Bornstein in *Hagoren*, V (1906), 118–42; Malter, pp. 69 ff., 168 ff., 351 ff., 409 ff.; Mann, *Jews in Egypt*, I, 64 ff.; *idem*, in *Tarbiz*, V, 154 ff., and the extensive literature listed in all these works.

60. See above, n. 21.

61. See the quotation in Abraham bar Hiyya's *Sefer ha-'Ibbur*, II, 5, and Bar Ḥiyya's expostulation thereon, cited in *Oeuvres complètes*, IX, 141 f. no. 50; also Saadia's radical view (*ibid.*, p. 169 no. 130): ב' י"ט של גליות אין ספק מעיקרו אלא הקב"ה צוה בארץ יהיה להם יום א' ובחוצה לארץ ב' ימים objected to by Hai Gaon. See also *ibid.*, p. xxxvi; Pinsker, *Lickute*, II, 95; Poznanski in *JQR*, X, 264; Davidson, *Wars of the Lord*, p. 15 n. 81. It very likely was Saadia's influence which induced one of his associates to write to Ben Meir: מפני שהחשבונות כולם כאחד נתנו מרועה אחד (Bornstein, pp. 88 f.; Guillaume, *JQR*, n.s. V, 547).

62. It has long been recognized that, like Hai Gaon and Abraham b. Ḥiyya, Maimonides had Saadia in mind when he wrote: ואלו העקרים שזכרתי לך

היא דרך החקירה בראיית הלבנה, ואני תמיה מאדם יכחיש הראות ויאמר כי דת היהודים אינה בנויה
על ראיית הלבנה אלא על החשבון בלבד והוא מאמין אלו הכתובים כולם ואני רואה שהרואה הזה
אינו מאמינו אבל היתה דעתו בזה המאמר להשיב אחור בעל דינו באי זה צד יודמן לו בשקר או באמת
כיון שלא מצא מציל לנפשו מהכרח הוכח. (Ccmmentary on M. R. H. II, 4). Of
course, Saadia's extremism made him an easy target for Karaite controversialists; see Poznanski, *Opponents, passim.*

63. Sherira, writing on various problems of the calendar, mentions: אחת
השאלות אשר שאל מר ר' סעדיה גאון עודנו בא"י טרם בא בבלה את אדונינו מר רב יהודה גאון זקנינו
זכרם שניהם לברכה. See Mann, "Gaonic Studies," *Hebrew Union College Jubilee
Volume,* 1925, p. 248.

64. Mann, *Jews in Egypt,* II, 42: ולעולם עליהון סמכינן דלא ליהוי ישראל אנודות
אנודות ואנא [the exilarch] וראשי מתיבאתא ורבנין וכל ישראל אסמכינן על עיבורא דאישתדיר
לקמי ח[ב]ירין; Bornstein, pp. 43 f. To be sure, among Ben Meir's opponents
were some extremists who altogether denied that the rule of the 642 parts
had any talmudic support: ואף מי [שבדאו מלבו] וכתבו לא היה יודע בטוב העבור בין ימינו
ושמאלו. The majority, however, apparently were satisfied with the contention that for "many years past" there had been agreement between the
rabbis of the two countries on a definitive computation וכבר בכל השנים האלה
עלה חשבונם אחד (*ibid.,* pp. 93, 88 f.)

65. Hirschfeld, *JQR,* XVI (1904), 292, 296 f. Nor was Saadia exaggerating when in his second letter to his former Egyptian disciples he warned
them: וחוסו על עם ישראל . . . לבל יאכלו חמץ בפסח, ובל יאכלון וישתון ויעשו מלאכה ביום
הכפורים (Bornstein, p. 84). See also the statement of the Karaite Sahl b.
Maṣliaḥ: ויש אנשים משוכני ארץ ישראל שהלכו אחרי הבבליים, וגם השוכנים בארץ שנער שהלכו
אחרי אנשי ארץ ישראל (Pinsker, *Lickute,* II, 36); and that of the Christian chronicler Elijah of Nisibis, quoted below, n. 81.

66. Bornstein, pp. 106 f.: אשר עבר[ו] עלינו צרות רבות ורעות וחבישת בית האסורים
וענוי הכבל ומ[כו]ח עד לצאת הנפש . . . מתחת יד בני ענן השונאים. ובאנו עליכם להיעזר
בי"י אלוהינו ובכם ועשיתם חסד ושכרם (read: ושכרכם) מי"י.

67. *Ibid.,* p. 105 (Guillaume, *JQR,* n.s. V, 553): עד אשר באו האגרות אשר
שלחם אלינו עטרת ישראל עדיינו . . . אהרן בירבי עמרם נ'ע מושיע הדור אשר לא הטה אזנו
. . . לסור מחוקי ה'. Mann (*Tarbiz,* V, 151 n. 18) rightly opposes a suggested
emendation to שלחתם, for undoubtedly a court banker had better means of
communication—not, as Mann thinks, because he used caravans, but because he had access to the excellent imperial postal services, which usually
carried only official mail. See Mez, *Renaissance des Islams,* pp. 464 f., 479 f.
See also below nn. 69, 76.

68. See Fischel, *Jews in Mediaeval Islam,* especially p. 12.

69. One ought not lay too much stress on Ben Meir's flattering comments, which might have been designed to capture Aaron's good will and,
perhaps, to strengthen his attitude of detachment. Even Aaron's opposition to David's election is purely hypothetical. His attitude at the time of
the controversy, however, is best revealed by his forwarding to Ben Meir
the warning and subsequently threatening and downright abusive com-

munications issued by the Babylonian leaders, including the exilarch. Eppenstein's attempted explanation (*MGWJ*, LIV, 456 n. 1) that Aaron had forwarded some *other* letters is controverted by the whole context. Aaron b. Amram may have served as a more or less neutral intermediary, but he certainly does not seem to have tried to check any of the repressive actions undertaken by his fellow Baghdadians.

70. This seems to be the meaning of Saadia's insinuations (Bornstein, p. 80): הספר בטבעת הנשיא . . . להרים מכשול מדרך העם . . . כי האכיל את חילם למלכיות. See also *ibid.*, p. 72: . . . שחד נוסו נודו מדעת חנף [מנותן] סורו, ואל ינקשו בפחזותיו. The parallel to the baits and flattery held out by Ben Meir is bribery given rather than one received by him as suggested by Bornstein's insertion [ממקבל]. Ben Meir, in turn, accused his opponents of soliciting outside aid, and invoked divine vengeance בכל מי שהוא מבקש עזרת השונאים (*ibid.*, p. 105). That some feeble attempt was made in this direction is also implied in the phrase ולא התעשתו used by Saadia in his statement cited below, n. 78.

71. Bowen, '*Ali Ibn 'Isa*, pp. 177 ff.

72. M. Sobernheim and E. Mittwoch, "Hebräische Inschriften in der Synagoge von Aleppo," *Festschrift . . . Jacob Guttmann* (Leipzig, 1915), pp. 273–85. See also E. N. Adler, "Aleppo," *Gedenkbuch . . . David Kaufmann* (Breslau, 1900), pp. 128–37.

73. Bornstein, p. 82: . . . דעו כי עודני בחלב באו מקצת התלמידים מבעל גד והנידו, p. 84: . . . כי בתוך הקיץ שעבר בהיותי בחלב שמעתי כי בן מאיר.

74. *Ibid.*, p. 82: וכסבור אני כי לא כתבתם אליו מבלעדי, בלתי כי דימיתם כי עד עתה . . . עודני בארץ ישראל כאשר שמעתם. וגם הוא אמר אולי כן חישבתם.

75. *Ibid.*, pp. 84 f.: וכתבתי אליו כמה אגרות להזהירו . . . ושבתי אני וירדתי בגדר, . . . והייתי סבור כי קיבל, עד אשר באה השמועה בבגדד כי הכריזם חסרין. It is quite inconceivable how, in the light of the context, Mann insists upon accepting Epstein's interpretation (*REJ*, XLII, 202 n. 1) of ושבתי as the equivalent of "I have resumed" or "I have reconsidered" (*Tarbiz*, V, 158 n. 34). Leaving aside the question of the authenticity of the aforementioned itinerary (see above, nn. 38–39; Bornstein, p. 185 n. 1; Malter, p. 56), the letters themselves indicate that Saadia now went to Baghdad for reasons other than the Ben Meir menace—which he had thought settled by his letters—and that he had expected his Egyptian pupils to use him rather than David b. Abraham as their intermediary with the Baghdad leaders. Obviously Saadia must have been living in Baghdad before his stay in Aleppo.

The prolonged sojourn in Aleppo, and perhaps also at some other centers of learning, doubtless was responsible for that long separation from his family to which Saadia refers twice in assuring his Egyptian pupils that he had not forgotten them (Bornstein, p. 82: וכאשר שמותימעת פרשי מן אהלי ומעל עוללי כן, p. 83: . . . [כ]זכרי טפי ועוללי לנגדי כן זכרכם תלמידי לא נגור; דאנתי על פרישתי מכם). The usual explanation hitherto given for these passages is that, like his disciples, Saadia's family was still in Egypt at that time; i.e., at least six and a half years, but in fact many more years, after his departure from his native land (see above). Though not altogether impossible, since Muslim travelers, too, often left their families behind for many years when they went out in search of some material or intellectual gain, this explanation is far less probable. Certainly Saadia's affection for his former pupils was no less vividly illustrated by a comparison with his longing for his wife and children in Baghdad, from whom he had been separated for a few months or a year, while his separation from his pupils may have already lasted a decade or more. If one may venture a guess, Saadia, after one or more brief visits, established his residence in the capital about 918–19. At that time he was also introduced to the leading Jews in the community, and came into contact with the scholars of the Pumbedita academy. That is probably why Ibn Sarjado, writing in 931–32 (see below, nn. 114, 116a), ironically inquired why Saadia had failed *thirteen* years earlier to reveal his descent from the tribe of Judah (Harkavy, pp. 164 f., 229)—i.e., upon his first appearance as a regular visitor or associate of the academy. Some such association during three or four years would also best explain why, within a few months after his return from Aleppo, Saadia could issue official documents as one of the highest ranking officers of the academy. See below, n. 85.

76. Since Bornstein (pp. 25 f., 63 f.), this has been the widely accepted interpretation of the following passage in Ben Meir's communication to Babylonia: כי בהיותינו בבגדאד אצלכם לא נמנענו מלעזור אתכם בכל לבבנו ובכל נפשנו על הקושרים עליכם . . . ובחזירתינו אל ארץ ישראל ארץ מולדתנו צוינו בכל מדינה ומדינה ועיר ועיר לחזנים והיו קוראים הפתיחים שלכם ומנדים שנאכם ומיכן נטרו איבה עלינו . . . . The statement is essentially repeated in Ben Meir's second letter (*ibid.*, p. 107). I have considerable misgivings concerning this interpretation. In the first place, this communication by Ben Meir has the character of an open letter, addressed to the entire Babylonian community and not to a particular faction: לכל המון קהלות אחינו ישראל הדרים במדינות שנער, הרבנים וזקנים וראשי כנסיות, ובתי אבות ופרנסי צבור, וגזברי עם ומרכולים ומלמד[ים] וחזנים, ויתר אחינו יש' . . . (*ibid.*, p. 60). It is to be noted that this rich verbiage refers neither to the exilarch nor to any head of the academies. If it were addressed to Mubashshir's faction, some reference to the Pumbedita gaon doubtless would have been inserted. Secondly, we have no information whatsoever that the Mubashshir–Kohen Ṣedeḳ rivalry had resulted in excommunications and bans which were read from the pulpits in every Palestinian township. Our only source is Sherira, whose description of the controversy does not seem to indicate any widespread repercussions or bitterness. In fact, the term פלונתא (p. 119) may mean a simple division into two factions, similar to that of Amram Gaon (p. 115: הוה פליג ליה) earlier, and that of Nehemiah vs. Aaron ibn Sarjado (p. 121: ובתר כמה פליג עליה) later. Even the exilarchic פלונתא between Daniel and David b. Yehudah (pp. 110 f.) evidently did not lead to such popular bans and counterbans as did the later conflict between Saadia and David b. Zakkai, for which Sherira uses the different terms ונצא and, in

some versions, מחלוקת (pp. 117 f.). One need not press this terminological distinction too strongly and still wish to have more reliable information concerning the extent of the Mubashshir–Kohen Ṣedeḳ conflict. Thirdly, the phrase הקושרים עליכם intimates some sort of secret intrigue, probably at the caliph's or vizier's court. It is questionable whether Ben Meir could have helped Mubashshir along these lines. If Aaron b. Amram intervened at all in Mubashshir's behalf, as Mann suggests, he did it out of opposition to David b. Zakkai, and not as a favor to Ben Meir, whom he may not have known before Ben Meir's arrival in Baghdad. Despite these misgivings, we have followed the regnant opinion in our presentation, simply for lack of an alternative, more satisfactory explanation. No records of other major controversies of that day have reached us (although several may have occurred in that turbulent age) except for those pertaining to 'Ukba's deposition, which do not seem to fit into this picture.

77. Saadia's initiative is indicated not only by the reiterated accusations of Ben Meir but also by numerous passages in his own letter: e.g., גם אנכי כתבתי עם אגרותיהם אל רוב המדינות (Bornstein, p. 82); וכה הסכים ראש הגולה וכתבתי אליכם אגרת ובתוך [ובתוכה] אגרות ראש הגולה יעזרהו קדושנו (ibid., p. 83); האדירות ו כ ל ראשי הישיבות יאמצם משגבנו (ibid., p. 84). See also Mann, Tarbiz, V, 275 (Saadia, writing in July, 922, as alluf of Pumbedita, states: כי באהבה רבה הוכחתים); Hirschfeld, JQR, XVI, 292, 297; Harkavy, V, 150 ff. Saadia constantly emphasized the full agreement of all Babylonian leaders, including "all" (i.e., the three) heads of academies. See, e.g., כי ראש הגולה יעזרהו קדושינו וגם ראשי ישיבות כ ו ל ם יתמכך משגבנו וכל האלופים וכל החכמים ותלמידיהם שוין בדבר הזה . . . ואין בינינו חלוקה (ibid., p. 84). See also above, n. 58. In his third letter to Egypt, however, he speaks twice of a communication by only one head of the academy (ראס אלמתיבה). See Hirschfeld.

78. Bornstein, p. 77: Saadia states, ויכתבו עליו בספר השני וגם בשלישי נבחרה לנו שופט. Ibid., p. 106 (Guillaume, JQR, n.s. V, 554): Ben Meir replies, והזכרתם כי נוסף יגון על מכאובכם . . . אין אנו [חפצים] להכאיבכם באיגרותינו ובנו ובכם נתקיים ולא יסף שמואל לראות את שאול (I Sam. 15:35). Ibid., p. 75: Saadia records, על כן ויחדלו עוד מענות אותו כי הבינו להם כי and finally declares (p. 79), הצמיתו אותו בזדון ובעקבה כל מעשיו, ויניחו אותו ליום נקם ועברה השמור לכל מדיח ולא התעשתו לקחת אגרות מאת המלך להסירו . . . ויאמרו לאמר לא נוכל לבער את כל כתביו מן החוק והחדר, אבל נכתוב ספר זכרון לדורותינו אחרינו בל יקומו מקצותם ויהבלו דבריו . . . See also Hirschfeld, JQR, XVI, 292, 296: ספר זכרון ומגלה לדורות. Many years later Sahl b. Maṣliaḥ likewise reports with glee only that וקללו אלו לאלו ונדו אלו לאלו (Pinsker, Lickute, II, 36). See above, n. 70.

The emphasis upon public opinion, noticeable throughout the correspondence, was apparently due not only to the evident deadlock in the balance of power between the leaders of the two countries but probably also to the influence of the Muslim doctrine of "catholic consent" (ijma') as a creative source of law. While Ben Meir stressed the importance of Jerusalem, the obedience due to its academy, and its acquired rights (e.g., pp. 61 f.:

אין רשות לאדם מישראל להשיג גבול ראשונים ... ומצוה לעשות עפ"י זקנים), Saadia and the
Babylonians insisted upon the preservation of what had been accepted by
"all" Israel (e.g., p. 75: והנה כל ישראל בכל הארצות לא כן חשבו ... וכמשפט וכחקה שמום;
p. 103 [Mann, כן כל בני ישראל אשר במזרח ואשר במערב ואשר בצפון ובאיי הים ....
Tarbiz, V, 273 f., proves Saadia's authorship]: כי כל ישראל אשר במזרח ובמערב
הסכמה אחת על זאת, חוץ מן מעט המקומות אשר סביבותיכם ....). It is in reply to these
assertions that Ben Meir also declared that וישראל בני יעקב הקדושים כולהם חוקת
אחת (*ibid.*, p. 104). The doctrine of *ijma'* also influenced Saadia in many
of his other teachings. He knew, for instance, of no other argument in
favor of the historicity of the Manna miracle than the catholic consent of
the people. See *Emunot*, Introd. (p. 50): ולא שיהיו המון בני ישראל מסכימים על
הענין הזה ומספיק זה בתנאי כל הגדה נאמנת; Jakob Guttmann, *Die Religionsphiloso-
phie des Saadia* (Göttingen, 1882), p. 147 n. 3. See also below, n. 114;
and, more generally, my *SRH*, I, 338, 344; III, 91 n. 21.

79. This is evidently the meaning of Ben Meir's dramatic exclamations:
שאבותינו הראשונים לא נהרגו אלא על ייחוד השם ... ואלו נהרגנו ואלף כמונו לא נשנה מנהג
אבותינו (Bornstein, pp. 106 f.).

80. See above, n. 69.

81. Bornstein, p. 105 (Guillaume, *JQR*, n.s. V, 552): ואמרתם שנעשתם חרפה:
בגוים וקלסה בין המינים. This statement is borne out by Elijah of Nisibis's well-
known description of the celebration of the New Year 4683 on Tuesday by
the Jews of Palestine and on Thursday by those of Babylonia. See Friedrich Baethgen, *Fragmente syrischer und arabischer Historiker* (Leipzig,
1884), pp. 84, 141.

82. Bowen, *'Ali Ibn 'Isa*, pp. 41, 170, 186 f., 209 f. If Bowen is right in
suggesting (pp. 191 ff.) that, despite great personal sympathy with the
famous mystic Al-Ḥallaj, 'Ali ibn 'Isa was unable to save him from execution, the vizier may since have become doubly sensitive about supporting
religious persecution. In fact, even Aaron b. Amram, who seems to have
taken care of Al-Ḥallaj during the trial, may have received an object
lesson in the effects of governmental suppression of religious dissent. See
Louis Massignon, "L'influence de l'Islam au moyen-âge sur la fondation
et l'essor des banques juives," *Bulletin d'études orientales de l'Institut
Français de Damas*, I (1931), 3.

83. Since all our documents, including the *Sefer ha-Zikkaron*, antedate
August 7, 923, we are in no position to state whether 'Ali ibn 'Isa's arrest
on that day and Ibn al-Furat's return to the vizierate had any effect on
the controversy. We know that Ibn al-Furat resumed his business relations
with Aaron b. Amram. The vizier ordered his banker, for instance, to pay
out of his account 2,000 dinars as a contribution to 'Ali ibn 'Isa's enormous
fine of 300,000 dinars ($1,200,000); this method of recapturing accumu-
lated state revenue from deposed officials had become such a routine
matter that it was customary for friends to contribute their share to the
fine, somewhat along the line of a wedding present. See Fischel, *Jews in*

Mediaeval Islam, p. 21; C. H. Becker, *Islamstudien* (Leipzig, 1924), I, 205. The professedly terroristic, extortionist new regime during Ibn al-Furat's final "year of perdition" may well have discouraged any appeal to the good offices of the vizier. Nor do we know whether the subsequent rehabilitation of 'Ali ibn 'Isa, and his appointment to the position of inspector general of taxes in Egypt, Palestine, and Syria in 925, had any bearing on the Jewish situation in the Holy Land.

84. Schechter, *Saadyana*, pp. 102 f.; Bornstein, pp. 48 ff. It seems, however, that the controversy stimulated the resurgence of a local Babylonian patriotism, such as had not been witnessed since the days of Yehudai Gaon and Pirḳoi b. Baboi. Such patriotism would best explain the extreme view voiced by Kohen Ṣedeḳ about Babylonian residents in Palestine, who, unlike other alien Jews, remained subject to the restrictive laws of both countries, even after several years of residence, provided they expected to return to Babylonia. See the identification of the author by Joel Müller in his ed. of *Teshubot geone mizraḥ u-ma'arab*, no. 39, despite the doubts expressed by Assaf in his essay on "Palestine in the Responsa of the Babylonian Geonim," *Ṣiyyon*, I (1926), 23. Similarly Saadia's sharp distinction between Palestine in the messianic age, the return to which all Israel ought to pray for fervently, and Palestine in ordinary times, which deserves no preferential treatment in Jewish liturgy, is best understandable in the light of the Ben Meir controversy. See Saadia's objection to the conclusion of the prayer ואור חדש על ציון תאיר because שלא תקנו חכמים, ברכה זו על האור העתיד לימות המשיח אלא על אור היום המאיר בכל יום, an argument repudiated by Sherira Gaon with the significant remark אלא בשתי ישיבות מעולם אומרים אותו. And Sherira's academy, Pumbedita, followed Palestinian prototypes in the *halakhah* less frequently than did Saadia's Sura! See *Siddur*, p. 37 n. 6, and Assaf's introd. thereto, p. 25; Ginzberg, *Geonica*, I, 127 f.; *idem*, in *Ginze Schechter*, II, 508 ff.

85. Schechter, *Saadyana*, p. 15; Bornstein, p. 72 n. 2; Mann, *Tarbiz*, V, 276; Malter, p. 64.

86. See the latest analysis by Menaḥem (Edmund) Stein in his "Ḥiwi-ha-Balkhi, the Jewish Marcion" (Hebrew), *Sefer Klausner* (Jerusalem, 1937), pp. 210–25; my *SRH*, I, 356 f.; 2d ed., Vol. VI, pp. 298 ff., 478 ff.

87. Harkavy, V, 177; Ibn Daud, *Sefer ha-Kabbalah* (Neubauer, II, 66): ואחד מהם חוי אלכלבי [אלבלכי] אשר בדה מלבו תורה והעיד ר' סעדיה שהוא ראה מלמדי תינוקות מלמדים אותה בספרים ובלוחות. Ḥiwi's only recorded earlier opponent was the sectarian Abu Imran al-Tiflisi. See also ed. G. D. Cohen, pp. 42 (Hebrew), 56 f. (English).

88. Davidson, *Saadia's Polemic*; republished, with an introduction and notes by S. Poznanski, under the title *Teshubot R. Saadiah Gaon 'al she'elot Ḥiwi ha-Balkhi* (Warsaw, 1916), in part restating Poznanski's opinions in his review of Davidson's edition in *ZHB*, XIX (1916), 2–8.

89. Ibn abi Usaybi'a, *Tabaḳat al-aṭibba'*, ed. by A. Müller (Cairo and Königsberg, 1882–84), I, 221; Ibn al-Ḳifti, *Ta'rikh al-ḥukama*, ed. by J. Lippert (Leipzig, 1903), pp. 193 f. See also Bowen, *'Ali Ibn 'Isa*, pp. 183 f.; Levy, *Baghdad Chronicle*, p. 142.

90. Nathan in Neubauer, I, 78. The curious miswriting of the date in my *Jewish Community*, I, 184, should be corrected accordingly.

91. Sherira, p. 117: ובתריה (after the "weaver" Yom Ṭob b. Jacob) אתמר ביני רבנן לבטולי למתא מחסיא ולמתייה מאן דמשייר בה לפומבדיתא.

92. See, e.g., the story of the negotiations which preceded the elevation of the youthful Al-Muḳtadir to the caliphate, as told by Bowen, *'Ali Ibn 'Isa*, pp. 84 ff. Nissi's refusal to accept the call is likewise more understandable in the light of the Shafi'ite opposition to blind judges. Since the Shafi'ite school of jurisprudence had great influence in Baghdad at that time, Nissi might have deemed it doubly wise not to expose the reorganized academy to their facile ridicule. See, however, below, n. 123.

93. See Sherira's oft-quoted statement (p. 117): ואתייה דוד נשיאה למר רבינו סעדיא בר רב יוסף ולא מבני רבנן דמתיבתא הוה אלא ממצרים וידיע בפתומי. The phrase מבני רבנן has a technical sound, reminiscent of the *aulād al-wuzara* ("sons of viziers") in the Muslim administration. Neither the vizierate nor the Babylonian gaonate was hereditary in the strict sense—as seems to have been, e.g., the leadership of the contemporary Palestinian academies—but the office was more or less kept within a limited number of families for a long period. Most Babylonian geonim, in fact, belonged to one of six or seven prominent families. See Mez, *Renaissance des Islams*, p. 83; my *Jewish Community*, III, 46 n. 34. Saadia's case was further aggravated by his nonnative origin, which irritated the deep-rooted antialien prejudice among both the Jews and the Muslims of the period. See Tyan, *Organisation judiciaire*, I, 249 f., 462 ff. Even Al-Mas'udi (*Kitāb at-Tanbih*), discussing Saadia's controversy with the exilarch, emphasizes that many Jews chose "the Fayyumite" as their chief. No wonder that, unfamiliar with this specific background, Ibn Daud misunderstood Sherira and believed that David brought Saadia directly from Egypt to Sura, thus misleading generations of scholars until the discovery of the new Genizah materials. Saadia's unusual oath is later summarized by the exilarch: אשר השבעתיהו באמונת שמים שלא יעבור על דברי ולא יעשה עלי קשר ולא יקרא ראש גולה זולתי ולא יהי עם מי שחולק עלי (Harkavy, V, 232).

94. See Harkavy, in *Festschrift Berliner*, pp. 38, 40; and S. Fraenkel's revised translation in *JQR*, XVII, 388. There is nevertheless an undercurrent of resentment in Saadia's comment on the advantages of great wealth: ואין ההליכה אל בתי העשירים וחלות פניהם כי אם בעבורו (*Emunot*, X, 8, p. 151).

95. See Harley's biographical sketch of Ibn Muḳlah (above, n. 17); Bowen, *'Ali Ibn 'Isa*, Index, s. v. Ibn Muqlah; Amedroz-Margoliouth, *Eclipse*, IV, 210. There may have been a special relationship between the Al-Aḥwaz tax farmers and the academy of Sura, inasmuch as that province

lay within the academy's sphere of control. See Mann, *Tarbiz*, V, 171.

96. Nathan the Babylonian in Neubauer, I, 87: ‏ופעמים שיהיה לישיבת ראש גלות‎
[i.e., Sura, according to the context] ‏צוק הזמן ושולחים כתבים לכל קהלות ישראל‎
‏ומודיעים להם עניים ולחצם וכל קהל וקהל שולחים להם מתנות כפי כחן וכפי השנת‎
‏ידן, וכמו כן מנהג ראש ישיבת פומבדיתא בכל רשויותיו.‎

97. The extant fragment, first published by Ginzberg (*Geonica*, II, 86 ff.), has frequently been reprinted. Nevertheless, because of its intrinsic significance to the subject of our inquiry, we shall quote in full the following passage from the revised text as given by Lewin (*Ginze Kedem*, II, 1923, 35): ‏וכן כל חפץ ושאלה אשר יהיה לכם מצד המלכות הנד תגידוהו לפנינו כי אז נצוה את‎
‏בעלי בתים חשובים אשר בבגדד אשר אנחנו יושבים ביניהם בני מ'ר נטירא ובני‎
‏מ'ר אהרן זכר הנאספים לברכה וזכרון פליטיהם דקימה ואז ישיבו לכם מאת המלך כאשר יספיק יי'י‎
‏מעוזנו בידם כן תעשו ואל תטשו. ואחרי זה אנו מצווים עוד וכתבים אליכם כתבי הזהרות ותוכחות‎
‏לעורר את לבותיכם ולהקיץ את שרעפיכם על מצות יי'י אדונינו מה תעשו ותחיו בו וממה תסורו ולא‎
‏תמותו כי כן חייבין אנחנו אולי נצא ידי חובתנו בדבר הגדול הזה אשר‎
‏קבלנו וכן יום ביום תבשרונו משלומכם כי שלום נפשנו הוא כי אם אין צבא אין‎
‏מלך ובאפס תלמידים אין הוד לחכמים ויהי יי'י בכסלכם וינהב עמכם‎
‏ועמנו ב[רבו]ת רחמיו וחסדיו הרבים. ושלומכם וברכותיכם וטובותיכם וכל הצלחותיכם ירבו לעד.‎
The passages underscored here show that Saadia considered it part of his newly assumed obligation to enlist a following, without which no academy could operate fruitfully. For this purpose he did not hesitate to combine political promises—in the style of the age these may actually have been a form of political pressure—with ethical and religious exhortations, which, too, as we shall presently see, were not wholly devoid of worldly aspects.

98. It was published by Dob (Bernard) Revel in *Debir*, I (1923), 183–88, and was immediately reinterpreted and connected with the first letter, in J. N. Epstein's comments thereon (*ibid.*, pp. 189 f.). Neither of these two scholars, nor any of their successors, however, has fully perceived the undercurrent of financial solicitation running through the second letter.

99. See pp. 186 f. fol. 2a l. 24: . . . ‏בני ישראל אל תפרשו מן העדה‎; 2b ll. 6–7:
‏ב'י. כל העמים בוטחים אלה ברכב ואלה בסוסים ואתם רכבכם וסוסיכם תורת ה' וחכמיה‎;
‏ב'י. כל העמים יקבצו כסף וזהב באוצרותיהם ואתם כספכם וזהביכם התורה והמדרש‎: 8–9. ll.
‏ב'י. הכינו צידה‎: 11–12. ll; ‏ב'י. אם תזנחו תורה ה' יזניחכם ביד אויביכם‎: 10. l.
‏ב'י. בתכם נדבותיכם ליי'י תנו אותה‎: 17. l; ‏להוגי תעודה למען יחזיקו בתורת ה'‎
‏ב'י. כי תצטרכו לדעת דברי תורה אל תעצלו מלשאול ותעשוהו‎: 1–2. ll 3a–26. l; ‏מן המובחר‎
‏בספק כי לא לרצון יהיה לכם אלא שלחו ושאלוהו מלפנינו ואנחנו נהיה אתכם נהיה ולא נכלה דבר‎
‏שפתינו . . .‎

100. See, e.g., p. 185 fol. 2a ll. 3–4: ‏בני ישראל. אם לא תראו את יי'י ביום טובה‎
‏את מי תקראו ביום צרה וישמעכם‎. The editor's suggested emendation to ‏תיראו‎
misses the main implication of the parallel to ‏שלש פעמים בשנה . . . ולא יראה את‎
‏פני ה' ריקם‎ (Deut. 16:16). See also fol. 1b ll. 16–17; 2b ll. 12–13, 15, 18–20, 24–26.

101. See the last passage quoted above, n. 99, and the editor's note thereon, showing that other geonim also encouraged inquiries. The finan-

cial import is made clear by Nathan's description of the contemporary
status of the academies: ואין לראש גלות בנדרים ונדבות שמשגרין קהלות ישראל אל הישיבות
כלום כי אינם משגרים אותם אלא עם שאלותיהם ובשאלות אין לראש גלות עסק בהם (Neubauer,
I, 86). It is also confirmed by other sources.

102. See my *Jewish Community,* I, 180 f., 200 f., III, 41 n. 20, 50 n. 39.

103. Ibn Daud, *Chronicle,* ed. Neubauer, II, 74. See Mann, *Texts and
Studies,* I, 67 n. 11. Neither content nor date is given, and the term גליון
would seem to indicate a circular letter of the kind sent out during the
subsequent controversy. It is, nevertheless, possible that it pursued more
pacific communal objectives. On the variants in the names of the Spanish
cities, see Ibn Daud, ed. G. D. Cohen, pp. 59 (Hebrew), 79 (English).

104. Harkavy, V, 232: נם הכביד עלו על מקום שהמשלתיהו עליו לרדות את העם במקל
ולהכביד עלו לצרום באוז ישראל ולהפילם על פניהם ולהלקותם בלי משפט ולהכותם על
הלחי ולמרוח אשך . . .

105. *Oeuvres complètes,* IX, 91 no. 4: ולאלחר משמתין את שניהן עד שיצא . . .
מביחה וכמו כן האנשים שהיו שם בעת שידוכי אשת איש והתירו דבר זה כולם חייבי נידוי ואפי' היו
חכמים כמו ר' שילא with reference to Yeb. 121a. See also *ibid.,* nos. 3, 5–6, 35,
where Saadia takes throughout the more rigid stand. His sense of justice,
however, was strong enough to annul certain vows in favor of the academies because compulsion had been used in obtaining them. *Ibid.,* pp. 124 f.
no. 37. Few of these and other responsa, collected by Müller, are dated;
some are of doubtful authorship. Nevertheless, they fit best into Saadia's
first two years in the gaonate, when he lived in comparative peace and
security. Less likely, though not impossible, is a provenience from the five
years 937–42, after his return to power. Nos. 32–33, in fact, either are
specifically dated with an equivalent of Sivan, 929, or from their context
reveal an origin before Saadia's break with the exilarch.

106. *Siddur,* p. 155. It is cited by the correspondents of Hai Gaon in
Teshubot ha-geonim mi-tokh ha-genizah, ed. by S. Assaf (Jerusalem,
1929), p. 212 no. 34, as found in Saadia's "commentaries."

107. See I. H. Weiss, *Dor dor ve-doreshav,* IV, 97 ff. Strictness in the
interpretation of the Law must have appeared doubly meritorious to
Saadia, as on frequent occasions he had to take issue with Karaite accusations of Rabbanite leniency. See especially the fragment of his poem *Esa
meshali,* ed. by H. Brody in *Alumah,* I (1936), 49–58; and M. Seidel's
note thereon, *ibid.,* p. 156.

108. *Oeuvres complètes,* IX, 113 f. nos. 22–23. Saadia's authorship is
doubtful, however. Nor do we possess more than a brief, rather uninform-
ative fragment of Saadia's special "Treatise on Usury." See Hirschfeld,
JQR, XVIII, 119 f. For the contemporary adjustments of the talmudic
doctrine of usury to the realities under early Islam, see below, Essay 7,
esp. pp. 197 ff., for the service which Saadia's monograph on the "Laws
on Pledges" may have rendered to the banking profession. The later quotations from the book under the title ספר הפקדון imply that much of it

was devoted to a consideration of the laws governing deposits, the handling of which had become a major function of the bankers under Islam.

109. S. Assaf, *Teshubot ha-geonim mi-kitbe yad she-be-ginze Cambridge* (Jerusalem, 1942), pp. 29 f. no. 22.

110. Harkavy, V, 155. My translation is in part a variation of the motto to Malter's work. See also Harkavy, pp. 158, 160, etc.

111. *Siddur*, p. 431: בשבת שמת בה חכם מפטירין נלה כבוד מישראל. See also *Oeuvres complètes*, IX, 155, no. 55 n. 1. Quite outspoken is his *Commentary* on Ps. 2:2, ed. by S. Eppenstein in *Festschrift Harkavy*, p. 158 (with some corrections by I. Goldziher in Eppenstein's "Beiträge," *MGWJ*, LIV, 312 n. 1; and others, less harsh, in the German trans. by J. Cohen in *Magazin für die Wissenschaft des Judenthums*, VIII [1881], pp. 81 ff.), where Saadia develops the theory that rebellion against God's anointed (kings, high priests, prophets) is like rebellion against God himself and that, in view of the Scriptures' brevity, God entrusts their specific interpretation to the sages of every generation. Hence the words of the sages are like those of the divine lawgiver himself. Unfortunately there is no way of telling when this passage was written, but it has all the earmarks of the first years of Saadia's gaonate.

112. *Emunot*, III, 7, p. 115.

113. Hirschfeld, *JQR*, XVII, 722, 724 (despite its clumsiness, Hirschfeld's English translation renders Saadia's ideas on this point far more accurately than does Ibn Tibbon, *Emunot*, III, p. 60 [in the Arabic original, ed. by Landauer, p. 115]; Ibn Tibbon not only toned down Saadia's more daring formulation to the level of generally accepted Jewish ethics but, by translating the two Arabic words as ככהן והנביא, virtually eliminated the deeper implications of the term *imam*); *Sefer ha-Galui* (Harkavy, V, 158): וכמו שהיו הנביאים בזמנסמנהינים אותה כן יוליכוה הצדיקים בדורותיהם. Al-Khazari, I, 95, 115; IV, 15; Abraham b. Ḥiyya, *Megillat ha-megalleh*, III, 213b, 22b; Bernhard Ziemlich, "Abraham bar Chija und Jehuda Halevi," *MGWJ*, XXIX (1880), 369 n. 4; Julius Guttmann, "Ueber Abraham bar Chijja's 'Buch der Enthüllung,'" *ibid.*, XLVII (1903), 465. There seem to be, however, no direct traces of this Muslim doctrine in Saadia's own theory of prophecy. On the contrary, in his philosophic treatise he emphasizes, almost above everything else, that the ancient prophets were ordinary persons, distinguished from all others only by the *occasional* faculty of performing miracles at God's command (*Emunot*, III, 4, pp. 62 ff.). Similarly, in characterizing the revival and universality of prophecy in the messianic era, he merely states that any Jew arriving in a foreign country will be able to identify himself by foretelling the future or guessing some secret event in the past (*ibid.*, VIII, 7, p. 125). One can easily see that such a divinely imposed faculty did not elevate its bearer to a position of intrinsic superiority over the great sages of the intervening generations. See also

below, nn. 134–38.

114. See Ibn Sarjado's accusation, Harkavy, V, 229: ויכתב מגלה להדמות בנביאים כאחד נביאי השקר; *Sefer ha-Galui* (*ibid.*, p. 160), while explaining the reasons for his translating this work into Arabic, Saadia retorts: ואומר כי רשעים כאשר ראו שחברתי בספור אודותם ספר בעברית מופסק לפסוקים מסומן ומוטעם אחזו ברכילות מנונה ואמרו שזה תביעה לנבואה . . . כי שם הקדמתי לומר בשני מקומות שכבר פסקה הנבואה . . . . Eppenstein (*MGWJ*, LIV, 224 n. 4) translates instead of the poetical תביעה לנבואה more precisely: כי בזה לוקח הנבואה לעצמו. Of course, this attack very likely did not originate with the composition of the Hebrew version of this work (probably in 930–31; see Mann, *Tarbiz*, V, 165 n. 59), but could have been directed at many of Saadia's earlier pamphlets published in the same form during the Ben Meir controversy, his *Refutation of Ḥiwi*, etc.

115. See, e.g., *Emunot*, II, 5, p. 47: ואינני מכוין בתשובה הזאת עמי הארץ שבהם . . . . ולא אטריד ספרי בתשובתם . . . .

116. Harkavy, p. 158: והתבוננתי . . . במה שיהיה לעתיד וכמה שנים נשאר עוד עד עד קץ הישועה. See also *Emunot*, VIII, 3, pp. 120 ff.; and the relatively moderate and weighty assertions of David b. Zakkai and Kohen Ṣedek in the booklet (וכחזקתו) accompanying Saadia's excommunication (*ibid.*, p. 232): כתב עברה גבה לב[ו] . . . [והתחיל ללכת] בגדולות ובנפלאות [כמו] . . . ונביאי הבעל לאמר אני אתקן בעם תקנות ואני אעצור מנפה נם הכביד עלו . . . . One would expect something like נביאי השקר before ונביאי הבעל, rather than ירבעם בן נבט as suggested by Harkavy. These citations are all taken from the subsequent period of strife, but they evidently refer to occurrences and assertions made during Saadia's untrammeled administration in 928–30. There is little doubt that at least the text of the excommunication here cited originated in the very early stages of the controversy. But the other pamphlets, too, were written soon thereafter. See above, nn. 110, 114. Moreover, Saadia expounded his views in some of his commentaries on the Bible. While that on the Book of Daniel seems to have been written late in Saadia's life, that on Genesis is quoted in the *Emunot* and may well have appeared before the conflict with David. According to Salmon b. Yeruḥim's accusation ובו נתהללה לדעת בו קץ הגאולה some such statement was included in the Genesis commentary. See Davidson, *Wars of the Lord*, p. 49; and, more generally, S. Poznanski, "Die Berechnung des Erlösungsjahres bei Saadja," *MGWJ*, XLIV (1900), 400–16, 508–29.

116a. Harkavy, V, 229: Ibn Sarjado asked לם לם תנתסב אלי שבט יהודה מנ י"ג סנה ("Why have you not claimed descent from the tribe of Judah for the last thirteen years?" See above, n. 75). Saadia answered lamely (*ibid.*, p. 164): שאנכי לא בארתי זה היחוס כל זמן שלא היה נצרך לי זה וכשהוצרכתי אליו הודעתיו; Abraham ibn Daud (Neubauer, II, *loc. cit.*); B. M. Lewin, "אשא משלי" of R. Saadia Gaon" (Hebrew), *Tarbiz*, III (1931–32), 159: דוסא זקיני המשיבי אל קוני. The two aggadic utterances of Rab here cited are recorded Ber. 17b, 61b. See also above, n. 25. Some such premonition, or perhaps better information concerning Saadia's views, may have determined Nissi's counsel against the appointment of Saadia, which, if we are to take Nathan's phrasing seriously, consisted of the strange combination of reasons for the candidate's adamant nature: מפני רוב חכמתו ורוחב פיו ואריכות לשונו ויראת חטא (Neubauer, I, 80).

117. S. Assaf, "Letters of R. Samuel b. 'Ali and his Contemporaries" (Hebrew), *Tarbiz*, I, Pt. 2 (1929–30), 65 f.

118. S. Pines, "Une notice sur les Rech Galuta chez un écrivain arabe de IXe siècle," *REJ*, C (1936), 71–73.

119. One such case, affecting the estate of one Bahlul b. Naṭir (possibly identical with Isaac, the younger son of the banker Neṭira—although Saadia's reference to the *Bene Neṭira* in 928, and Nathan's report that the same family assisted Saadia in the controversy with the exilarch, somewhat militates against this assumption), was settled by the exilarch and then brought to Saadia for confirmation, apparently in 929. Saadia found that ופסק ראש נלותא נטריה רחמנא דינא מן הלכתא נבאראתא וטעמי ברירי. *Oeuvres complètes,* IX, 119 f. no. 32.

120. Nathan the Babylonian mentions only fees to be paid to exilarchic judges: ומהכתובה (וכל כתובה :MS) ונט ושטר חוב ושטר מתנה ושטר מכירה (Neubauer, I, 85). But these refer only to payments—incidentally quite substantial payments, of 4⅓ dirhems each—for the *writing* of deeds, the judges being interested in sharply controlling this monopoly, established for them and apparently shared by the exilarchs. It is evident that separate fees had to be paid for the administration of estates or for decisions in disputes over hereditary claims.

121. Tyan, *Organisation judiciaire*, I, 438.

122. Of the three main chroniclers of the event, the closest and fullest witness, Nathan the Babylonian, does not conceal his leanings toward the great gaon. While Sherira is far more circumspect, almost neutral, Ibn Daud violently condemns the exilarch's cause. Were it not for the few stray records recovered by Harkavy, mainly from Karaite sources (in his *Zikhron*, V), we would have practically no testimony stemming from the exilarchic party. As it is, most of the arguments, and, hence, the relative merits, in the controversy, and its various stages, are still very obscure. M. Auerbach in his "Der Streit swischen Saadja Gaon und dem Exilarchen David ben Sakkai," *Jüdische Schriften Josef Wohlgemuth . . . gewidmet* (Frankfort, 1928), pp. 1–30, stands out among modern writers for his attempted fairness to David, but otherwise offers little more than a restatement in German of the main narratives.

123. In many periods of human historiography, from Livy through the Arab middle ages to the Renaissance, rhetorical amplifications were considered a legitimate means of conveying to the reader the main ideas of the acting personalities. None of these historians ever pretended, nor were the readers supposed to believe, that the speeches were actually

delivered in the form given. For the later use of this technique by Ibn Verga and Joseph Hacohen, see my *La Méthode historique d'Azaria de Rossi* (Paris, 1929; reprinted from *REJ*, LXXXVI–VII), p. 18; and in the English trans. entitled "Azariah de Rossi's Historical Method" in my *HJH*, pp. 214 f. One wonders whether too much attention has not been bestowed by modern scholarship on the conversational matter inserted decades after the events into Nathan's picturesque chronicle.

124. Amedroz-Margoliouth, *Eclipse*, IV, 55 f. Accusations of bribery were very frequently combined with those of pederasty (see Tyan, *Organisation judiciaire*, I, 442 ff.); hence, the hair-raising denunciations of Saadia by Ibn Sarjado (Harkavy, V, 230) merely followed the fashion of the age.

125. Saadia's early authorship of the *Sefer ha-Yerushot,* postulated by Joel Müller in the introd. to his ed. of this work (*Oeuvres complètes*, IX, p. xvii), and accepted by Ginzberg (*Geonica*, I, 165 n. 3), is rejected by Malter, pp. 164 f., on the ground that its obvious indebtedness to Muslim prototypes indicates an origin in Babylonia. As if Egypt had not likewise been an important center of Muslim jurisprudence! Moreover, Saadia left Egypt so early in his literary career (see above) that his treatise *On Inheritance,* even if written in the period of his wanderings through western Asia, might still have been his earliest halakhic monograph. It is barely possible, however, that it owed its origin to Saadia's controversy with the exilarch and that, despite its impersonal tone, resembling that of his main philosophic work (see below), it offered him the opportunity of casually expounding his views as to why David's decision had been wrong.

126. Al-Mas'udi, *Kitāb at-Tanbiḥ,* evidently using the term *wazir* rather loosely. Mann's hesitant suggestion (*Tarbiz,* V, 167) that Ibn Sarjado's attack on Saadia's associates included Mu'nis under the designation of סריס אדם אוכל בשר חזירים (Harkavy, V, 227) is quite unacceptable. Among the innumerable eunuchs of the imperial harem—Al-Muḳtadir is supposed to have had eleven thousand eunuchs—there must have been many lesser personages who may have sided with Saadia. In fact, even the presence of a Jewish eunuch enjoying some influence at court does not appear out of the question. Not only would a Jew fit better into the context, but the accusation of pork-eating would be far more pointed if it were aimed at the violation of a Jewish commandment.

127. Bowen, *'Ali Ibn 'Isa,* pp. 292, 300, 302.

128. It has been pointed out that David's excommunication of Saadia had already mentioned: וחרחר ריב ושלח מדנים ביני ובין חסן אחי (Harkavy, p. 232), indicating Saadia's *first* move in the deposition of the exilarch. See Auerbach, pp. 15 f. The remarks (*idem,* p. 11 n. 45) are pointless, inasmuch as Harkavy's emendation (p. 233) [עם ראשי הישיבות] והסכמתי is to be corrected to [עם ראש הישיבה], parallel to the [וא]ב בית דין, and refers only to the officers of the academy of Pumbedita.

It is noteworthy that throughout the controversy we nowhere find aspersions cast on David b. Zakkai's reputed descent from Bustanai's Persian wife, which, in the opinion of some rigid legalists, invalidated the claim of the entire line to the exilarchic office. Of course, Saadia labored under a double restraint, since he had supported David's brother Josiah, of the same parentage, and had for years, ever since the Ben Meir controversy, fully cooperated with David himself. But it is also quite possible that descent from a Persian princess was at that time not considered a stigma, inasmuch as the Persians themselves, out of national pride, were making much of the alleged marriage of the Prophet's grandson Ḥusayn with Shahr-Banu, another captive daughter of Yezdegerd III, the last Sassanian "king of kings." See Edward G. Browne, *Literary History of Persia*, I, 130 ff., citing the ninth-century historian Al-Yaḳubi. The Jewish legend, while uncertain about Yezdegerd, ascribed the marriage to Ḥusayn's father 'Ali or to 'Umar I. Among the contemporary writers, Aaron ibn Sarjado seems to express approval rather than condemnation, while Nathan, Saadia's partisan, though noting that Baghdad Jewry hated the descendants of Bustanai, admitted that there were no other exilarchs available. See H. Tykocinski's careful examination of the extant records in his Hebrew essay on "Bustanai, the Exilarch," *Debir*, I (1923), 145–79 (with some notes by J. N. Epstein); Marx, in *Livre d'hommage . . . Poznanski*, pp. 78 ff.

129. Al-Mas'udi, *Kitāb at-Tanbiḥ*; Bowen, *'Ali Ibn 'Isa*, pp. 298 *ff.*; Harkavy, pp. 228 ll. 9–10, 154 ll. 10–11: ספור מה שבא עלי מן האנשים הנקראים שם ... בשמוחם מן הצרות והמשטמה ובקשת הנפש. If we may take a clue from Nathan's obvious exaggeration, וכל עשירי בבל (Neubauer, I, 80), it appears that a large segment of the upper classes sided with Saadia, while in the lower classes the exilarchic party seems to have been in the majority. This is to some extent conceded by Saadia himself when, among the reasons for the issuance of the *Sefer ha-Galui*, he mentions: מפני שאלה ההמונים [Arabic אלאנאס התנגדו אלי משנאתם להחכמה ומחפצם שלא יהי בין אומתנו לא דעת ולא משפט צדק [Vulgus=] (Harkavy, pp. 152 f.). The emphasis upon the lower classes' enmity to wisdom is heightened by Saadia's use of the Hebrew terms לשנאתהם ללחכמה in the Arabic context. He may well have had in mind the popular opposition to his particular conception of wisdom and of the role of its bearers in the Jewish community. On the other hand, by a strange concatenation of circumstances, Saadia's supporters seem to have included the Karaite *nesi'im* of Jerusalem, David and Josiah *bene Boaz*, as has been convincingly demonstrated by Mann in his *Texts and Studies*, I, 132 ff., on the basis of Ibn Sarjado's attack. Although it is not altogether impossible that, out of sheer enmity to the Rabbanite exilarch, they were ready to bury the hatchet with Saadia, it appears far more likely that they were not fully cognizant of Saadia's anti-Karaite polemics. Saadia, then in greatest jeopardy, was in no position to reject support, from whatever quarter. See above, n. 19,

and below, n. 138.

130. If Nathan is right that Josiah lived only three years after his appointment (Neubauer, I, 81: ונהג ג' שנים ומת), Josiah may have suffered both banishment and death during the same year, 933. In fact, it was not unusual for guards of deposed officials to be instructed to see to it that their charges should not long survive the journey. See, e.g., the fate of Ibn Muḳla's fellow-exiles, in Bowen, 'Ali Ibn 'Isa, pp. 226 f. This may, indeed, be the reason why Nathan fails to mention Josiah's stay in Khorasan, known to us only from Sherira's equivocal ואדחי יאשיהו לכרסאן (p. 117). Nonetheless, as often occurred in the history of the Muslim dynasties, the defeat presaged the ultimate recognition of the candidate's line, and it was not very long before Josiah's descendants succeeded those of David in the exilarchic office. See above, n. 43.

131. Fischel, Jews in Mediaeval Islam, p. 42 n. 1. See also Amedroz-Margoliouth, Eclipse, IV, 393 f. The identity of Sahl b. Nazir with Sahl b. Neṭira is supported by the story told by Sahl to At-Tanukhi. In this story he appears as a Jewish collector of the clerk of Shiraz and the narrative refers to his grandfather, likewise a collector, who had been involved in a game of power politics. See D. S. Margoliouth's translation of "The Table Talk of a Mesopotamian Judge, Pt. II," Islamic Culture, V (1931), 181 f. According to Margoliouth, this grandfather lived after A.H. 247, which would readily correspond to Joseph b. Phineas' early period of activity. There is, of course, no use in sentimentally rebelling, a millennium after the events, against such hard and fast realities, and still less in trying to deny them, as does Mann, Tarbiz, V, 164 n. 57. For the military mutiny and assassinations in Al-Aḥwaz in 936, see Amedroz-Margoliouth, Eclipse, IV, 381 ff. Bachkam, the governor of the day, was certainly ruthless enough to execute even his banker for money. See below, n. 141.

132. Siddur, pp. 182 f. See also above, n. 6. It is noteworthy that, despite his great emphasis on learning and on the importance of the Jewish scholars, Saadia failed to include in his prayerbook a special prayer for the welfare of the academies, such as the Yeḳum purḳan. Although first given in the Maḥzor Vitry (ed. by S. Hurwitz, pp. 172 f.), and apparently nonexistent in the various recensions of the Seder R. Amram, the prayer has been detected, in nuclear form in a ninth-century manuscript (after Amram), by Charles Duschinsky in Livre d'hommage . . . Poznanski, pp. 182–98. Saadia's antiexilarchic bias cannot serve as an explanation, inasmuch as various early recensions of this prayer lack the blessing for the exilarch; and, in the state of flux in Saadia's day, such an omission should not have proved too difficult. See A. Marx, "Studies in Gaonic History and Literature," JQR, n.s. I, 63 n. 1. It may not be too venturesome to suggest that for Saadia, if not for Ṣemaḥ, Amram's assistant, the Aramaic formulation of this prayer may have appeared to be

a serious deterrent. Other Babylonian geonim, under the stimulus of the Aramaic speech prevailing in the local population (both Jewish and non-Jewish), preferred prayers in that language. As late as 922, Sherira informs us that . . . . כולהו רחמי ובעיי דאתו לאבותינו זכ' לב' ממתיבתא קדישתא כולהו בלשון ארמית הן ורוב ברכות דכתבי גאונים בין ליחיד ובין לציבור הם בהאי לישאנא כתבי. See *Teshubot ha-geonim*, ed. by Harkavy, no. 373 end, p. 372; and, more generally, J. N. Epstein, *Der gaonäische Kommentar zur Ordnung Tohoroth* (Berlin, 1915), pp. 53 ff. No such incentive existed for Saadia, whom Egyptian-Palestinian origins and vital Hebraic interests predisposed in favor of Hebrew prayers. This ramified problem merits further investigation.

133. See especially the second morning prayer (*ibid.*, pp. 64 ff.) evidently intended to replace, or at least to be superimposed on, the first liturgical composition of an earlier date. The first prayer is still written calmly and with some philosophic detachment, while the second is correctly characterized in the heading as containing "harrowing matters, heart-rending and inspiring humility." Various passages seem, indeed, to reflect their author's harrowing experiences during the perilous years of his hiding. See, e.g.: ונפשי יודעת מאד כי חסדך גדול עלי והצלת לנפשי משאול תחתיה צר ומצוק מצאני ואתה הושעתני. זדים קמו עלי ומידם פדיתני פעמים רבות הגעתי עד שער מות והחייתני (p. 69). There are other poems reflecting Saadia's utter despondency, but since they are undated and, in fact, are not even an integral part of the prayerbook, they may belong to almost any period of suffering and mental depression in Saadia's turbulent life. See especially below, n. 142.

134. *Emunot*, I, 4, pp. 37 f. See also Landauer's introd. to his edition of the Arabic original, p. vi.

135. Landauer, *ibid.*, p. xx; Malter, pp. 194 n. 456, 248 n. 530.

136. See Isaac Husik, *A History of Medieval Jewish Philosophy* (New York, 1930), p. 25.

137. See especially *Emunot*, X, 12, p. 155: כי סדור העולם לא יהיה כי אם בחכמה, והם הפילו מעלת החכמה ושמוה לשררה לעצמה. וצריך שאזכור מה ששכחו אותו מנקי הגאוה והשררה, מהם כי האדם כשיתגאה ותגדל נפשו בעיניו יצא משטתו ויתגאה על הקרובים והרחוקים, ויראה עצמו כאלו הוא יחיד בדורו, ויבוא לעצת כל אדם ויתעקש וידחה כל מאמר . . . וחלק על הזקנים במה שנסוהו בארך ימיהם . . . These were precisely the arguments voiced by Saadia in his controversy with David. See Harkavy, V, 152: . . . . מה שיקרה מפני שכל מי שהם: p. 190; במדינה כאשר ישתדל איש עריץ להיות עליה לראש המה נערים ונקראו זקנים ללא אמת [with David b. Zakkai] עמו.

138. *Emunot*, X, 2, p. 145: וכח הכעס הוא אשר יביא האדם אל התגברות; X, 17, p. 159: . . . ואל יחפוץ במאומה מן השררה והנקמה, etc. Note also the formulation of the book's objectives: וראיתי בני אדם כאלו טבעו בימי הספקות . . . והיה אצלי ממה שלמדני אלהים מה שאוכל לסמוך אותם בו וביכלתי ממה שחנני מה שאשימהו להם למסעד, וראיתי כי הועילם בו חובה עלי והישירם אליו מן הדין עלי . . . ותתקיים אמונתם בעסקיהם ותמעט קנאת קצתם בקצתם על עניני העולם ויבאו כלם לפני אנשי החכמה ולא יטו אל דבר אחר (*ibid.*, Introd., p. 3). Despite the intervening professions of limited knowledge, ואינני חכם מכל בני דורי, etc.,

which, apart from following fashion may have been intended to allay some of the hostile accusations, these objectives become undeniably transparent when read in the context of Saadia's sustained efforts to proclaim the supremacy of the intellectual leaders, including himself.

A remarkable illustration of the devious ways of human thought is offered by the inverse effects of some of Saadia's teachings upon later generations. In X, 4, he made a special point of combating the doctrine of love as the supreme human motivation and the highest of all values. It has been suggested that he thereby opposed a doctrine expounded by Al-Zahiri in a work published in Baghdad in 910. See Georges Vajda, "Une source arabe de Saadia: Le Kitab al-Zahra d'Abou Bakr ibn Dawoud (Al-Zahiri)," *REJ*, XCII (1932), 146–50. But it was precisely Saadia's concise but fair summary of Al-Zahiri's views, in the enthusiastic old paraphrase of the *Emunot*, which so greatly influenced the kabbalistic ideas of mystic love. Similarly, Saadia's insistence on the moderate application of the ten positive mainsprings of human behavior was aimed directly at the extremism, however well-meant, of religious enthusiasts. Nevertheless, his description of such an extremist, the *hasid*, as given in the old paraphrase, was zestfully adopted as a model for the best human conduct by the later medieval *hasidim*. See Scholem, *Major Trends*, pp. 95 f., 368 n. 60 (giving an excerpt from the Vatican MS).

The relative absence of anti-Karaite polemics in Saadia's philosophic work has likewise puzzled modern investigators. See Poznanski, *JQR*, X, 257 f. The various reasons suggested (*ibid.*) for this unexpected reticence are far from satisfactory. In the light of Mann's hypothesis (mentioned above, n. 129), however, that in his struggle with David b. Zakkai, Saadia was deriving important aid from Karaite circles, his reluctance to antagonize influential allies in the midst of battle would be the more humanly understandable as it did not require the abandonment of any previously cherished convictions. It was a matter of tact and strategy rather than of a substantive change in attitude. The same considerations may have influenced Saadia's evident reluctance to discuss in detail the major issues in the age-old Judeo-Muslim controversy. The brief hints given here must suffice for the present, since a fuller analysis of the political implications of Saadia's philosophic work would far transcend the scope of this study.

139. Nathan, in Neubauer, I, 82. The phrase ונתן אותו בבית הספר does not necessarily mean that Saadia sent the boy to a regular school. It was probably age which at that time militated against his election to the exilarchic office and caused a search to be made for a more distant relative in Nisibis. There is some likelihood, however, that the entire exilarchic house, in the quarter Al-'Atikah (see Mann, *JQR*, n.s. XI, 434), was too much exposed to pillage and murder and that, hence, Saadia removed the young heir-apparent to his own residence at Sura, an out-of-the-way locality.

140. Sherira, pp. 120 f.

141. As-Suyuti, *History of the Caliphs*, pp. 413 f.; Bowen, *'Ali Ibn 'Isa,* pp. 364 ff.; Tritton, *The Caliphs*, p. 130. See above, n. 131.

142. Neubauer, II, 66. The term *melancholia* seems to have here a technical connotation; hence, Steinschneider's translation as "in" rather than "an" *Melancholia* (see his *Arabische Literatur der Juden* [Frankfort, 1902], p. 47; accepted also by Malter, p. 128 n. 278) is hardly justified. The vindictive reference of a hostile Karaite to Saadia's death (cited above, n. 19) likewise indicates some serious aggravations, which were all that could be expected under the circumstances. The date of May 16, rather than the usual May 15, or 18, here given is justified by the statement of Saadia's son that he died ... בליל שני בסוף האשמורת התיכונה. The hour of 1:00 to 2:00 A.M. of Monday, Iyar 26, was on May 16, 942. See J. N. Simḥoni's review of Malter's biography in *Hatekufah*, XXII (1924), 499 f.

It is not unlikely that in this mood of utter despondency Saadia wrote some of the best poems of his life. Among his undated elegies, the one beginning אתא היום אשר ינורתי (published in the Appendix to the *Siddur*, pp. 412 f.) seems to reflect both his sufferings and his resignation particularly well. See especially vv. 12 ff.: למלך ולנבירה השך ושח עם חדל מאדון, אוי לי אמי כי ילדתיני איש ריב ואיש מדון, מדון ונציון בכל ערי מגרשי, הייתי לשכני כי אדוני נטשי, נתיפחתי בנועל ולא מצאתי נפשי, אוי נא לי כי עיפה נפשי ...

143. Mann, *Tarbiz*, V, 171.

ESSAY 6

1. Hartwig Hirschfeld in the introductions to his ed. of the Arabic original of Halevi's *Kitāb al-Khazari* (Leipzig, 1887) and to his English trans. of this work (2d ed., New York, 1927), pp. 26, 29, 31; David Cassel in his ed. of the Hebrew text (trans. by Judah Ibn Tibbon), with a profusely annotated German trans. under the title *Das Buch Kuzari* (Leipzig, 1853), pp. xviii ff.

2. Cassel, *ibid.*; B. Friedberg, *Bet Eḳed Sepharim* (Antwerp, 1928–31), pp. 284 f.

3. The paucity of reliable biographical data has made the reconstruction of Halevi's life and work an extremely arduous task for his biographers, among whom one ought to mention, in particular, David Kaufmann and Ḥayyim Yefim Schirmann. Kaufmann's essay "Jehuda Halevi," originally written in 1877, was reprinted in revised form in his *Gesammelte Schriften* (Frankfort, 1910), II, 99–151; Schirmann's fuller analysis of the "Life of Yehudah Halevi," a Hebrew essay in *Tarbiz*, IX (1937–38), 35–54, 219–40, 284–305 (with a few additional corrections, *ibid.*, XI, 125), has been supplemented by his note, *ibid.*, X, 237–39, where he has suggested that the recorded birthplace of Halevi was Tudela rather than Toledo. More recently, Shelomo Dov Goitein, with the aid of newly discovered Genizah documents, has shed much new light on the last years

of Halevi's life. See esp. "The Last Phase of Rabbi Yehuda Hallevi's Life in the Light of the Geniza Papers" (Hebrew), *Tarbiz*, XXIV (1954–55), 21–47, 468; and other studies by him *et al.*, cited in his essay mentioned *infra*, n. 57.

4. Unfriendly critics among the Jews under Islam were inclined to overemphasize the political element in Muḥammad's achievement. Maimonides, for instance, bluntly accused him of having contributed little to religious thought, and of having taken over the doctrines of his predecessors with a new purpose, "namely the quest for power and for making people subservient to him"; see Maimonides' *Iggeret Teman* (Epistle to Yemen), ed. by David Holub (Vienna, 1875), p. 19; ed. by Abraham S. Halkin (New York, 1952), pp. 14 f. (Arabic and Hebrew), iv (English); my "The Historical Outlook of Maimonides," reprinted in *HJH*, pp. 146 ff.

5. Hrotsvitha of Gandersheim *Passio Sancti Pelagii* v. 12, in *Opera*, ed. by Karl Strecker, 2d ed. (Leipzig, 1930), p. 54; P. K. Hitti, *History of the Arabs*, 2d ed. (London, 1940), pp. 526 ff.

6. Hitti, *ibid.*, pp. 537 ff.; Ramón Menéndez Pidal, *The Cid and His Spain* (London, 1934), pp. 32 ff. Menéndez Pidal's important work has, in part, been supplemented and revised, especially in the light of new documents found in the Great Mosque of Fez, by E. Lévi-Provençal in his "Le Cid de l'histoire," in *Revue historique*, CLXXX (1937), 58–74.

7. E. Lévi-Provençal, ed., *La Péninsule Ibérique au Moyen Âge d'après le Kitāb ar-Rawḍ al-miʿtar fi ḫabar al-aḳṭār d'Ibn Abd al-Munʿim al-Ḥimyari* (Arabic text with French trans. and notes)(Leiden, 1938), no. 66, p. 64 (Arabic), 80 f. (French); *idem*, "Tudela," in *Encyclopaedia of Islam*, IV, 819.

8. Menéndez Pidal, *The Cid*, p. 35.

9. This estimate by Menéndez Pidal (*ibid.*, p. 44) is admittedly based upon the questionable reference to "more than a million men" among the Castilian and Leonese subjects in Pope Gregory VII's letter to Alphonso VI written in 1081. On the other hand, Menéndez Pidal's calculation of the entire peninsular population from the relative density in the respective areas of Spain and Portugal today does not seem to take cognizance of the evident shifts of the population northward since the *reconquista*. In the eleventh century, the southern areas, under Muslim domination, were undoubtedly much more populous. If the figures of 113,000 houses, twenty-one suburbs, and 3,000 places of worship in Cordova (about the year 960), cited by the Muslim historians Ibn Idhari and Maqqari, are at all correct, the population of that city alone could not have been much less than 500,000. The possibility of such a large population need not be discredited since the two rival capitals of Muslim civilization, Baghdad and Cairo-Fusṭaṭ, counted an even larger number of inhabitants. Baghdad's population in the ninth century was exaggeratingly

estimated at 1,500,000 males by a contemporary Arab chronicler; see A. Mez, *Die Renaissance des Islams* (Heidelberg, 1922), p. 389. Even in its period of decline during Benjamin of Tudela's visit in the 1160s it still was a very populous city; see my *SRH*, 1st ed., III, 78.

10. Al-Ḥimyari (see above, n. 7), nos. 19, 42, pp. 23, 42 f. (Arabic), 29 ff., 53 ff. (French); Idrisi (Edrisi), *Description de l'Afrique et de l'Espagne*, Arabic text ed. with a French trans. and notes by R. Dozy and M. J. de Goeje (Leiden, 1866), pp. 191 (Arabic), 231 (French).

11. On the events of 1066, see Ḥayyim Schirmann's Hebrew essay on "Yehosef ha-Nagid: The Tragedy of a Jewish Statesman," in *Moznaim*, VIII (1938–39), 48–58. For the status of Jewry in eleventh-century Granada, see also the same author's Hebrew study of "The Wars of Samuel ha-Nagid" in *Zion*, I (1935–36), 261–83, 357–76.

12. Idrisi, *Description de l'Afrique*, pp. 205 (Arabic), 252 f. (French). The Hebrew author Menaḥem b. Aaron ibn Zeraḥ (in his *Ṣedah la-derekh*, introduction [Sabionetta, 1567–68 (?)], fol. 15a) goes further and states that "the entire township consists of Jews, who, according to tradition, are descendants of the early exiles from Jerusalem, who had settled there and built the town." See also Kaufmann, *Gesammelte Schriften*, II, 105 n. 2; and Halevi's *Diwan*, I, nos. 62, 95, 114, 130.

13. See especially F. Codera, *Decadencia y desparicion de los Almoravides en España* (Saragossa, 1899), pp. 208 ff., 215 ff., 357 ff.; E. Lévi-Provençal, "Réflexions sur l'empire almoravide au début du XIIᵉ siècle," in *Cinquantenaire de la Faculté des Lettres d'Alger (1881–1931)* (Algiers, 1932), pp. 316 ff.

14. See F. Fernández y González, *Estado social y político de los Mudejares de Castilla* (Madrid, 1866), pp. 42 f. (based on Ibn al-Khaṭīb's history of Granada). Not only is the number of Jewish combatants greatly exaggerated—one may even doubt whether the total of the Castilian army reached that figure—but the participation of the Jews to any significant extent in the military exploits of Alphonso VI appears somewhat doubtful. F. I. Baer, in particular, has pointed out that the *Poema del Cid* and other Spanish sources of the period mention Jews as agents, ransomers of Muslim captives, and the like, but not as soldiers; see his Hebrew essay on "The Political Status of Spanish Jewry in Yehudah Halevi's Generation," in *Zion*, I (1935–36), 9 ff. This *argumentum a silentio* is considerably weakened, however, by the fact that the *Poema* was written some forty years after the death of the Cid and that, on the other hand, a century later the Viennese rabbi Isaac b. Moses mentioned as a matter of course that "it is still customary in Spain for the Jews to go to war together with their king"; see his *Or Zaru'a* (Zhitomir, 1862), I, no. 693.

15. Menéndez Pidal, *La España del Cid* (Madrid, 1929), I, 163 ff. (omitted in the English trans.); F. Baer, *Die Juden im christlichen Spanien* (Berlin, 1929–36), II, 5 no. 12, 9 f. no. 18; *idem*, in *Zion*, I, 7 ff.

16. Halevi's *Diwan*, ed. by H. Brody, 4 vols. (Berlin, 1894–1930), IV, no. 58, vv. 7 ff. This theme occurs in several other poems, e.g., *ibid.*, no. 99, vv. 9 ff.

הלמוני שעיר וערב ואני בקבורתי . . . | זה יחלוש או זה יחלוש תמיד עלי פוקח . . .

17. Hitti, *History of the Arabs*, p. 541. The frequent rapid changes in individual fortunes, characteristic of all periods of great crisis, are often alluded to in Halevi's poems. See, e.g., *Diwan*, III, no. 49, vv. 132:33: קבוצת טלטלות הון יקרנו | רוח עברה בו ואיננו. The general implications of these changes and the apposite consolation of speedy redemption are beautifully expressed by the poet, *ibid.*, no. 70, vv. 3–7.

18. The following passages in Moses ibn Ezra's *Shire ha-ḥol* (Secular Poems), ed. by H. Brody, I (Berlin, 1935; only the first of these poems is included in the *Selected Poems of Moses Ibn Ezra*, ed. by Heinrich Brody and trans. into English by Solomon Solis-Cohen [Philadelphia, 1934], pp. 2 ff.) well illustrate the poet's state of mind during the years of his exile (nos. 67, vv. 1, 31): רגלי ועוד לא מצאו מנוח . . . | עד אז בגלות שלחו שלוח 13, v. 23: דרכי יצלחו צלוח .הדיחני זמני מהמונם | אם עוד ישיבני אלהים אל הדר רמון (Granada) 143, v. 23: הם הם בעיני | והפקיד בי שכון מדבר פראים אל תדאני נפשי לדבריהם חכי 176, v. 7: ובין חוחים כשושנה קטופה | כל ונתגו נחנו .נתנני כציץ נובל ביער. At the same time Ibn Ezra claimed that he was not of those who always complain against fate; see his *Shirat Israel* (Hebrew Poetry), trans. from the Arabic into Hebrew by Benzion Halper (Leipzig, 1924), pp. 83 ff. For Halevi's advice to him, נר מערבי שוב למערבך, see the *Diwan*, I, no. 66, v. 7. In general, see also Brody's introduction to the *Selected Poems*, pp. xxiv f., and the notes thereto, pp. 185 ff.

19. Sa'īd ibn Aḥmad al-Andalūsi, *Tabakat al-umam*, trans. into French by Regis Blanchère, *Le Livre des "Catégories des Nations"* (Paris, 1935), p. 37; Hitti, *History of the Arabs*, pp. 526 f., 566. The section in this work referring to the Jews of Spain has been translated into English with a brief introduction by Joshua Finkel, "An Eleventh-Century Source of the History of Jewish Scientists in Mohammedan Lands (Ibn Said)," in *JQR*, n.s. XVIII (1927–28), 45–54. See also above, p. 91.

20. Maimonides, "Epistle to the Sages of Lunel," in *Ḳobeṣ teshubot ha-Rambam*, ed. by A. L. Lichtenberg (Leipzig, 1859) II, 44a–b.

21. *Kitāb al-Khazari*, iv, ii; see also *ibid.*, ii, 72, 78; and *Diwan*, III, no. 72, vv. 29–30: צור תעודה בריתם נצרם מדתות שונות | תצפנם בסוכה מריב לשונות.

22. This circumstance seems clearly indicated in his poetic allusions, such as: כי | לא אפרשה כפי פני אל זר | ואט אלי על סבלו שכמי | ואסבלה סבל עון עמי או: גם את בריתי לא אפירה | אם נעבדתי על דתך לא אבדתי זולתך (Diwan, IV, no. 138, v. 13 ff.); לא בזולתך אני נעזר | אחי אמונה לא אמירה (ibid.); see also *ibid.*, II, no. 23, vv. 29–32; IV, no. 24, v. 5; and Kaufmann, *Gesammelte Schriften*, II, 128 f.

23. The convention between Alphonso I of Aragon and the capitulating Moors of Tudela, signed in 1115, provided that Jews should not be given

any control over Muslims, not be allowed to acquire Muslim captives or to insult Muslims. See Baer's *Spanien*, I, nos. 27, 569, pp. 15 f., 919 f. Our presentation of Halevi's activity as centered in Muslim rather than Christian Spain seems to be borne out by all the important biographical data which have come down to us and, even more so, by his entirely Judeo-Arabic mode of thinking and writing, which reveals no traces of the contemporary Christian civilization. To be sure, several strong indications of Halevi's Castilian origin have been brought forth by modern scholars, but none of them is sufficiently conclusive, nor would they, in any case, prove his indebtedness to Castilian culture. That some medieval manuscripts expressly designate him as a Castilian (see Leopold Zunz, "Mitteilungen aus hebräischen Handschriften," in *Zeitschrift für hebräische Bibliographie*, XIX [1916], 142 n.), and that Moses ibn Ezra once hails him as an arrival from Christian parts (*Shire ha-ḥol*, no. 17, v. 14: הן משעיר זרח לאיר), may be due either to the copyists' and the poet's confusion owing to Tudela's location in the vicinity of Christian lands even before its incorporation in them in 1115, or else to Halevi's subsequent prolonged stay in Toledo which was probably terminated during the upheaval of 1109. Halevi himself describes his origin as העולה משעיר (in his letter to Moses ibn Ezra, published by I. Davidson, *Ginze Schechter* [New York, 1928], III, p. 319) or, perhaps more correctly, as קצות ארץ בני שעיר (*Diwan*, III, no. 58, v. 38). His familiarity with the Spanish dialects of the day and his composition of a few Spanish verses (*Diwan*, I, no. 126, etc.) proves very little, as "few Muslims were ignorant of the *aljamia* or *latinia*, as they termed the Romance language of Spain; and most of the Mozarabs knew Arabic"; see Menéndez Pidal, *The Cid*, p. 42. In view of the close socioeconomic and cultural relations between the peninsular communities, Ibn Gabirol's statement that among his coreligionists in Spain "one half speaks Idumean [a Romance tongue] and the other half the language of the children of Kedar [Arabic]," is understandable only if we assume widespread bilingualism. See Gabirol's *Shire*, ed. by Ch. N. Bialik and I. H. Ravnitzky (Tel Aviv, 1927–32), I, p. 173. Considering also the aforementioned suggestion that Halevi was born in Tudela and not in Toledo (which, although conquered by the Christians in 1085, also retained its fully Arab character long after Halevi's death; see C. A. González Palencia, *Los Mozárabes de Toledo en los siglos XII y XIII*, 4 vols. [Madrid, 1926–30]), the assumption of his Castilian background as a determining force in his world outlook rests upon very shaky foundations. This assumption vitiates in part the otherwise very informative study by Baer in *Zion*, I; and his "Jehudah ha-Lewi und seine Zeit," in *Almanach des Schocken Verlags 5699* (Berlin, 1938), pp. 74–91.

24. Moses ibn Ezra's condemnation of Ibn Gabirol's excitable temper, which often "dominated his reason" and made it "easy for him to disparage great men and to write about them in derisive and insulting terms" (*Shirat*

Israel, p. 71), is fully borne out by many of his extant sharp and caustic poems. It is doubly remarkable, therefore, to hear him pray: "Thou art God and all things formed are Thy servants and worshipers. Yet is not Thy glory diminished by reason of those that worship aught besides Thee, for the yearning of them all is to draw nigh Thee," *Selected Religious Poems*, trans. by I. Zangwill (Philadelphia, 1923), p. 86.

25. Typical of the mood of that period doubtless are poems like ואשריכם בחלק שירשתם | וטוב לכם ביפי נחלתכם (*Diwan*, II, no. 2).

26. The idea of the *galut* undoubtedly played a major part in the world outlook of Ibn Gabirol. Karl Dreyer, in *Die religiöse Gedankenwelt des Salomo ibn Gabirol* (Leipzig, 1930), pp. 36 ff., has brilliantly analyzed the numerous pertinent passages in the poet's works. By placing it on a par, however, with the idea of sin as conceived by Ibn Gabirol, by lending it a modern tinge, and especially by giving it a feeling of utter urgency, the author seems to have overstressed his point. He readily concedes, nevertheless, the difference between Ibn Gabirol and Halevi: "What meaning does the term *galut* possess for Ibn Gabirol? It is not a purpose, a problem, something filled with significance and meaning, as it is for Yehudah Halevi. For Ibn Gabirol it is a negative entity, a limitation, a 'privation'" (p. 155); see also the pertinent remarks of Isaak Heinemann, "Die Erforschung des jüdischen Denkens im Mittelalter, iii," *MGWJ*, LXXVI (1932), 473.

27. Solomon ibn Parḥon, *Maḥberet he-'Arukh*, ed. by Salomo Gottlieb Stern (Pressburg, 1844), p. xxii, 5a–b; Halevi, *Diwan*, I, no. 14, v. 53–54: חיו הרוי שיר קצפיה | אם היתה חכמה ברכת ים. See Kaufmann, *Gesammelte Schriften*, II, 147 f. It is noteworthy that, despite the great bitterness which must have grown in Halevi's mind against the oppressors of Israel, and of which we get occasional glimpses in his poetic works (e.g., *Diwan*, IV, no. 8), he never abused his talent for the composition of vindictive *seliḥot* like those attributed to the great teacher Rashi under the impact of the anti-Jewish massacres of 1096. The text of this poem, beginning התנם לחרבה, was published by A. H. Freimann in *Tarbiz*, XII (1939–40), 70–74. It is not unlikely that, having soon been incorporated into the liturgy of French Jewry for the Day of Atonement, "Rashi's" *seliḥah* came to the attention of Yehudah Halevi.

28. Kaufmann asserts that this was regular practice in Spain; *Gesammelte Schriften*, II, p. 131 n. 3.

29. Halevi, *Diwan*, III, no. 87, v. 1012: מאלף באדמת זר | טוב יום על אדמת אל ידידות חרבות הראל מארמון כל מנור | כי באלה אנאל ובזה אעבר אכזר; see Schirmann in *Tarbiz*, IX, pp. 229 f., 239 f., 284. The prevalence of a pro-Palestinian sentiment among Halevi's contemporaries is well illustrated in a responsum by Joseph ibn Megas (no. 186) mentioning the case of a Jew who vowed not to eat meat or drink wine until he had journeyed to the Holy Land. From a Genizah letter, dated 1053, published by S. Assaf in "Sources for Jewish History in Spain" (Hebrew), in *Zion*, VI (1940–41),

38 ff., and other sources cited there, we also learn that there actually existed regular colonies of Spanish Jews in eleventh-century Palestine. The motives for Halevi's decision, however, long interpreted in exclusively individualistic terms (the fulfillment of a lifelong yearning, the sense of obligation to do as one preaches, and particularly the quest of expiation for personal sins), have been explained along strongly nationalist lines by Ben Zion Dinaburg in his Hebrew essay, "Yehudah Halevi's Journey to Palestine and the Messianic Ferment in his Day," in Minḥah le-David (David Yellin Jubilee Volume [Jerusalem, 1937]), pp. 157–82.

30. This was a far from unusual occupation for a poet in the Islamic world. "Every merchant was a poet," explains Alfred Guillaume, "and as likely as not any poet a merchant"; see his "Philosophy and Theology," in Legacy of Islam (Oxford, 1931), p. 281.

31. An echo of the persuasive arguments raised by his Spanish and Egyptian friends against his Palestinian journey is found not only in numerous poems addressed to them on this score but also in the following imaginary discourse of the king of Khazaria to his rabbinic interlocutor (Al-Khazari, v, 22): "What can be sought in Palestine nowadays, since the divine reflex is absent from it, whilst, with a pure mind and desire, one can approach God in any place. Why wilt thou run into danger on land and water and among various people?"

32. Halevi, Diwan, II, no. 6 (p. 164), vv. 53–54; Selected Poems, p. 51. In Al-Khazari, v, 2, the rabbi, evidently referring to Halevi's own intellectual development, comments on the fact that, with the exception of a few natively endowed individuals "to whom belief comes naturally," man is rarely "strong enough not to be deceived by the views of philosophers, scientists, astrologers, adepts, magicians, materialists, and others, and can adopt a belief without having first passed through many stages of heresy."

33. For a well-balanced analysis of the close relationship between the thinking of the two philosophers, see especially D. H. Baneth, "Jehuda Hallevi und Gazali," in Korrespondenzblatt . . . Akademie für die Wissenschaft des Judentums, V (1924), 27–45. M. Ventura's complete denial of any influence of Al-Ghazali on Halevi, on the other hand, is decidedly too far-reaching; see his Le Kalām et le péripatétisme d'après le Kuzari (Paris, 1934), pp. 89 ff. See also David Neumark's remarks, "Jehuda Hallevi's Philosophy in its Principles" (1907), reprinted in his Essays in Jewish Philosophy (Cincinnati, 1929), pp. 292 ff.

34. Al-Khazari, i, 67 (the quotation here and, as a rule, those elsewhere in this essay are taken from Hirschfeld's English translation). The basic rationalism of Halevi's approach is rightly emphasized by Julius Guttmann, "Das Verhältnis von Religion und Philosophie bei Jehuda Halewi," in Festschrift . . . Israel Lewy (Breslau, 1911), pp. 327–58; his Philosophie des Judentums (Munich, 1933), pp. 139 ff.; and in the English

trans. by David W. Silverman, entitled *Philosophies of Judaism* (New York, 1964), pp. 122 ff. It is not intended here to review the entire philosophic system of Halevi, on which see the extensive literature quoted *ibid*. We are concerned here merely with the philosophic background of those sociopolitical doctrines of Halevi which are both the most original part of his teaching and most directly related to the critical status of Jewry in his day.

35. Differences of opinion as to the unity of tradition are emphasized by Halevi as being also the major weakness of the Karaite schism. "Should Karaite methods prevail," he declares through the mouthpiece of the king of Khazaria, "there would be as many different codes as opinions. Not one individual would remain constant to one code. For every day he forms new opinions, increases his knowledge, or meets with someone who refutes him with some argument and converts him to his views. But whenever we find them agreeing we know that they follow the tradition of one or many of their ancestors" (*Al-Khazari*, iii, 38). Halevi pays no attention to the Karaite counterargument that Rabbanite opinion was often likewise divided, which in a creed invoking the exclusive authority of tradition was, of course, a much more serious drawback than in a sect whose founder publicly proclaimed the principle of free individual interpretation of Scripture. While it was still possible for Naḥshon Gaon to insist that all inquiries be addressed to either the academy of Sura or that of Pumbedita, not to both, since differing replies might lead to "the disgrace of the name of God," i.e., to the reinforcement of the Karaite attack (J. Mann, *Texts and Studies in Jewish History and Literature* [Cincinnati, 1931], I, 584), in Halevi's day any such attempt at centralization would have been utterly hopeless. On the other hand, the Karaite movement had traveled far in the opposite direction and had replaced the 'Ananite principle of חפישו באורייתא שפיר with an increasing "burden" of tradition.

36. *Al-Khazari*, i, 4, 9, 10.

37. *Ibid.*, i, 67, 89.

38. See Harry A. Wolfson, "Maimonides and Halevi," in *JQR*, n.s. II (1911–12), 323: "Halevi accuses the Greeks of lacking historic sense, of considering the history of man as beginning with himself . . . . [The Greek philosophers] reflected upon the purposiveness of nature, but saw no teleology in the flux of history; Halevi, on the other hand, denies the purposiveness of nature, but asserts the onward march of history to a clearly defined end."

39. *Al-Khazari*, iii, 73; ii, 50.

40. *Ibid.*, iv, 6, 13; v, 16.

41. Anticipating the usual objection to the superiority of Hebrew over other languages—"Do we not see distinctly that the latter are more finished and comprehensive"—Halevi tries to explain some of the deficiencies of Hebrew historically by its sharing "the fate of its bearers,

degenerating and dwindling with them"; nevertheless, in a lengthy philological discourse, he points out some of its superior qualities (*Al-Khazari*, ii, 67 ff.). These evidently strained arguments were, in part, rationalizations, not only of his nationalistic sentiments but also of his life-long personal experience. Though all his life he spoke and wrote Arabic, and though this very discourse was composed in Arabic, he undoubtedly had a much greater command of the fine points of Hebrew.

42. *Al-Khazari*, i, 80–81.

43. *Ibid.*, i, 27, 115; iii, 63. Here, as in the case of the preeminence of the Holy Land, Halevi attempts to furnish a rational explanation: it is because so many of their ancestors had striven toward the light of true prophecy and because all of them had been exposed to direct contact with the genuine prophets of ancient Israel that the Jewish people acquired a native predisposition toward prophecy, absent among other nations. Cassel in a note to his translation (p. 72 n. 1) has rightly pointed out that Halevi's extremist views are controverted not only by the well-known biblical narratives concerning non-Jewish prophets, such as Bileam, and talmudic legends referring to Obadiah as an Edomite proselyte (Sanhedrin 39b), etc., but also by express statements such as that of the author of *Seder Eliyahu Rabba:* "I invoke the testimony of Heaven and Earth that whether Israelite or Gentile . . . in accordance with the deed done thus the Holy Spirit rests upon him" (ed. by M. Friedmann [Vienna, 1902], p. 48). That this was the author's well-considered point of view is emphasized by Max Kadushin, *The Theology of Seder Eliahu* (New York, 1932), pp. 125, 167 f.

44. See my *SRH*, 1st ed., I, 140 ff.; III, 36 n. 11; *Al-Khazari*, i, 115.

45. *Ibid.*, ii, 33–36. There is but slight exaggeration in Neumark's contention (*Essays in Jewish Philosophy*, p. 262) that Halevi used the figure of the heart not merely in a metaphorical sense but that he actually believed that "the blood of Israel, *blood* literally, achieves the most subtle chemical composition" and that, hence, "Israel is the center of the blood-circulation of mankind."

46. *Al-Khazari*, i, 113 ff.; iv, 21 ff. In his poems, too, Halevi often emphasized this affirmation of Jewish powerlessness. See, e.g., *Diwan*, III, no. 75, vv. 3–4: הדרך והודך עבוד אל בעודך | ולעזוב הדר הזמן לאחרים; IV, no. 19, pt. 9, vv. 18 ff. (pp. 51 f.), where the "enemy's" assertion: הנח עם מפורד ומפוזר | ומכסא מלוכה נזר | בשל קציר | ויבש חציר | לכו ונכחידם מגוי is countered by God's assurance that like his covenant with the universe כן בריתי עם בני | לבל יכרתו מלפני מחיות גוי. Finally, taking a cue from the well-known passage in Zech. 4:6, Halevi even elevated powerlessness to a cosmic principle and extolled the greatness and eternity of God, as לא בכוח כי ברוח יצר כל היצורים; *Diwan*, III, no. 38, vv. 30–32. Of course, for the individual Jew, his exilic destiny should serve as a permanent reminder and give him considerable pause for meditation. But just as in contemplating his

individual sins and transgressions he shall not despair of divine forgiveness and ultimate salvation, so also, "if his mind is disturbed by the length of the Exile and the Diaspora and the degradation of his people, he finds comfort first in 'acknowledging the justice of the [divine] decree,' as said before; then in being cleansed from his sins; then in the reward and recompense awaiting him in the world to come, and the attachment to the Divine Influence in this world" (*Al-Khazari*, iii, 11, end). Neither the individual nor the collective sense of guilt must result, however, in asceticism, withdrawal from society or the shirking of social responsibility. For Halevi's "organistic" view of society and his acceptance of full social control, see especially *ibid.*, iii, 3, 19.

47. *Ibid.*, ii, 30 ff., 66; iii, 11, 23; iv, 30 f. See also the passage cited below, n. 51.

48. Julian Ribera y Terrago, *Disertaciones y opusculos* (Madrid, 1928), I, pp. 12 ff., 109 ff.

49. This emphasis upon the contributions to civilization made by the non-Arab peoples was the chief argument in this type of apologetical literature, such as the works of Ḥabib, the spokesman of the Spanish *saklaba* and of the Eastern *Shu'ubiya*. Very likely Halevi was also familiar with the famous ninth-century forgery by Ibn Wahshiyya entitled *The Nabatean Agriculture*. Often cited as an authentic ancient source by Maimonides and others, this book extolled the merits of the ancient Babylonian culture—for Halevi, too, a most significant link between ancient Israel and Western civilization—with overtly anti-Arab implications. Halevi may also have known of the numerous Persian attacks on the Arabic language and its alleged superiority over other languages. It is also possible that his distinction between the "white and the black man" in the above-cited passage (from *Al-Khazari*, i, 27) was meant to differentiate between non-Arabs and Arabs. See, in general, Ignaz Goldziher's *Muhammedanische Studien* (Halle a.S., 1889), I, 143 ff., 158, 208 ff., 268 f., and his "Die Šu'ubijja bei den Mohammedanern in Spanien," in *Zeitschrift der deutschen morgenländischen Gesellschaft*, LIII (1899), 608-20. The specific relation between Halevi and the writings of the Shu'ubiya and cognate movements, however, would deserve special investigation by a competent Arabist.

50. The use of this term in writings by such Jewish leaders living in Islam as Sherira Gaon and Maimonides, although they were somewhat protected against reprisals by the unfamiliarity of Arabs with Hebrew, clearly indicates its prevalence in Jewish circles. See also above, pp. 90 ff.

51. *Al-Khazari*, ii, 48; iii, 7. There was, of course, the additional gain that, by observing the Torah, Israel is separated from the Gentiles (*Diwan*, III, no. 72, v. 11: טוב אשר תאחוז בפקודי להבדילכם מכל העמים) and finds an antidote to those forces of assimilation of which Halevi so often complained. See also his poem on the Sabbath, claiming the superiority of the Jewish

day of rest and sanctification over its imitations among Christians and Muslims, and culminating in the exclamation וקדשתו ויהי מבדיל בין ישראל לגויים ירמו עדים לעדיים והמתים אל החיים | (ibid., IV, no. 1, v. 2 ff.). Unrestricted compliance with the Law does not, however, involve any renunciation of worldly pursuits or even of legitimate worldly pleasures. "The contrition on a fast day does nothing the nearer to God than the joy on the Sabbath and the holy days, if it is the outcome of a devout heart . . . . Neither is diminution of wealth an act of piety, if it is gained in a lawful way, and if its acquisition does not interfere with study and good works, especially for him who has a household and children. He may spend part of it in alms-giving, which would not be displeasing to God; but to increase it is better for himself," Al-Khazari, ii, 50. See also iii, 1 ff., where the ethical "golden mean," achieved by complete self-control, is compared with the just social control by a benevolent monarch who assigns his due to each member of society. For the general medieval rabbinic-philosophic attitude, especially to economic endeavor, see below Essay 7: "The Economic Views of Maimonides."

52. *Al-Khazari*, iv, 23.

53. *Diwan*, IV, nos. 40, 51, 62, pt. 14, etc.

54. Jacob Mann, "The Messianic Movements in the Period of the First Crusades" (Hebrew), in *Hatekufah*, XXIV (1928), 355 f. (from the Arabic original of Maimonides' *Epistle to Yemen*); also available in the Arabic original and in Hebrew and English translations, ed. by A. S. Halkin; see above, n. 4; Fritz Baer, "Eine jüdische Messiasprophetie auf das Jahr 1186 und der dritte Kreuzzug," in *MGWJ*, LXX (1926), 119 ff.; Dinaburg, in *Minḥah le-David*, p. 181.

55. *Diwan*, III, no. 121, v. 5. Halevi's expectation concerning a catastrophe to be expected in 1130 (*Diwan*, II, no. 86: ושנת תתץ תתץ לך כל נאוה), often adduced as proof that Halevi, too, was one of the "computers of the end," refers merely to a dream and is too equivocal to allow for such a definite conclusion. Nor does the repetition of the mystic number 1335 from Dan. 12:12 (*ibid.*, IV, no. 130, v. 10) seem to indicate more than a pious restatement of a traditional hope.

56. *Selected Poems*, pp. 14 ff.; *Al-Khazari*, v. 23, 27; see also *Diwan*, IV, no. 149, etc.

57. See, however, Shelomo Dov Goitein's final observation in "The Biography of Rabbi Judah Ha-Levi in the Light of the Cairo Geniza Documents," *PAAJR*, XXVIII (1959), 41–56.

ESSAY 7

1. Ibn Khaldun, *Prolegomena to History*, ed. in Arabic with a French trans. in *Notices et extraits des manuscrits de la Bibliothèque Imperiale* in Paris, XVI/1, 56 (Arabic); XIX/1, 71 (French). See also, in general,

M. Kamil Ayad, *Die Geschichts- und Gesellschaftslehre Ibn Ḥalduns* (Berlin, 1930); and Sobhi Mahmassani, *Les Idées économiques d'Ibn Khaldoun* (Lyons, 1932), with a brief sketch of the preceding history of economic doctrines under Islam.

2. *Treatise on Logic* (*Millot ha-higgayon*), Chap. XIV. See also Harry A. Wolfson, "The Classification of Sciences in Medieval Jewish Philosophy," *Hebrew Union College Jubilee Volume* (1925), p. 309. Although the Arabic original of this passage was long unavailable in any extant manuscript (see M. Ventura's and Israel Efros's editions of the manuscript fragments of the original, entitled *Makālah fi-ṣinā'at al-manṭiḳ* [Paris, 1935; New York, 1939]), this phrasing, upon which there is practically no disagreement in the numerous Hebrew manuscripts and editions, seems fully to render the meaning of the original. It does not enable us, however, to answer definitely the intriguing question of whether Maimonides was familiar with the rather meager economic literature of the Arabs, and especially with the Arabic translation of the Hellenistic treatise the *Oikonomikos*, by Bryson. Since the writings of Aristotle and his school on this subject apparently were never translated into Arabic, this rather platitudinous booklet was the only fairly comprehensive Greek work which had exercised some influence on economic thinking under medieval Islam. See its recent edition with a Hebrew translation of the fourteenth century and an incomplete Latin translation of about A.D. 1300, in M. Plessner's *Der Oikonomikos des Neupythagoräers "Bryson" und sein Einfluss auf die islamische Wissenschaft,* Orient und Antike, Vol. V (Heidelberg, 1928). See also R. Gottheil, "A Genizah Fragment of a Treatise on the Sciences in General," *JQR*, n.s. XXIII (1932–33), 171, 178, where Bryson's work is characterized as "the most renowned book" on the subject of domestic economy, while Avicenna's (the Head Sheikh's) similar treatise is said to give but "the quintessence of the book" by Bryson. Shem Ṭob ibn Falakera, in his *Reshit ḥokhmah* (p. 58), mentions economics as the second of the three practical sciences (next to ethics and politics) and describes it by saying that "it acquaints man with the way he is to govern his household which is common to him, his wife, children and servants, so that it be arranged in such order as to achieve success. All this is found in Bryson's work on Economics and I have referred to it in my *Epistle on Ethics*." See Israel Efros, "Palquera's Reshit Ḥokmah and Alfarabi's Iḥṣa al'Ulum," *JQR*, n.s. XXV (1935), 227–35; and Leo Strauss, "Eine vermisste Schrift Fârâbis," *MGWJ,* LXXX (1936), 96–106.

3. The meaning of this passage, which has led to many disputes, becomes clear when we insert, with most manuscripts, the word היא before בענינים אלהיים (see Ventura's edition, p. 120) or, with one manuscript, the word אלא before הנהגת האנשים. See Efros's introduction to his edition, pp. 18 f. It has been correctly interpreted, also with reference to Alfarabi, by Leo

Strauss in his "Quelques remarques sur la science politique de Maïmonide et de Fârâbi," *REJ, C^{bis}* (1936), 8 ff. For the meaning of the complex term נמוסים, see Wolfson, *Hebrew Union College Jub. Vol.* (1925), pp. 311 f.; supplemented in *HUCA*, III (1926), 374 f. See also Falakera's statement, directly connected with economic matters and incidentally rather obviously dependent on Bryson, והיה שם הנימוס נדר אצל היונים מההנהגה, in his *Sefer ha-Mebakkesh* (The Hague, 1772), p. 47. This work, being a poetic elaboration of *Reshit hokhmah,* is also greatly dependent on Alfarabi.

4. M.N. III, 27–28.

5. See especially *Al-Khazari*, IV, 19; V, 14.

6. This expression, fairly common in contemporary Muslim letters (see Ibn al-Jauhar's works under this title, the reference thereto in the aforementioned Muslim classification of sciences, ed. by Gottheil, in *JQR*, n.s. XXIII; and other references in Chaim Neuburger's *Das Wesen des Gesetzes in der Philosophie des Maimonides* [Danzig, 1933], p. 114 nn. 304–5) is used by Maimonides to characterize ethics rather than the entire field of practical philosophy, in C.M. on Abot Introd. (=Eight Chapters), III–IV. Here, too, he invokes the supreme authority of the Mosaic Law in all fundamentals of ethical conduct, including such ethical aspects of economic behavior as excessive liberality. There is no reason, consequently, to exclude ethical science from Maimonides' negation in his logical treatise, as suggested by Strauss in the *REJ, C^{bis}*, 11 f. Like Alfarabi and Ibn Daud, Maimuni sees the whole of "practical philosophy" as adequately covered by the religious law.

7. *Emunah ramah*, p. 98. Ibn Daud repeats (*ibid.*, p. 101), with special reference to domestic economy, which he defines as "the government of wife, children, and slaves" (see above, n. 2), that "this, too, is found in the Torah." He proceeds to explain it with the biblical laws concerning wives and children, but fails to mention slaves, except in connection with the political law governing the discharge of Hebrew slaves after six years. See below.

8. See, for instance, M.N., Introd., end, where in explaining the general similarity between his exegetical method and that of the talmudic sages, he also stresses the difference between the rabbis' attempt to reconcile prophetic utterances concerning laws and moral behavior and his endeavor to eliminate apparent disagreement in scriptural passages referring to opinions and beliefs. See also M.N. III, 8, end.

9. M.N. III, 27, 35, 39–42; M.T. Yesodei ha-torah 4, 13.

10. Samuel Rosenblatt, ed., *The High Ways to Perfection of Abraham Maimonides* (New York, 1927), I, 91. See the equally sweeping statement by Ibn Khaldun in his *Prolegomena*, XVI, 220 (Arabic); XIX, 254 (French).

11. See Thomas Aquinas's comment: sed quia hoc videtur repugnare

documentis S. Scripturae, Rabbi Moyses Judaeus volens utrumque concordare posuit quod . . . secundum Aristotelem . . . ad salvandam Scripturam. . . . (*Summa theologiae*, I, 50, 3). See my "The Historical Outlook of Maimonides," reprinted from *PAAJR*, VI, in *HJH*, pp. 109 ff., 161 ff. That the phrase of philosophy as a "maidservant of theology" is exaggerated to a large extent also in the case of the Christian scholastics has been rightly pointed out by Martin Grabmann in *Der Gegenwartswert der geschichtlichen Erforschung der mittelalterlichen Philosophie* (Vienna, 1913), p. 28.

12. The conflict between the powerful political realities of medieval Christendom and its essentially nonpolitical biblical heritage left a permanent imprint upon the social teachings of the Church. "From the first century of the Christian era until the later years of the eighteenth century, political theory presents itself to us as dominated in form by the conception that the great institutions of society, and especially the institution of government, were artificial or conventional not 'natural' or primitive." Not even the adoption of the basic political teachings of Aristotle by Thomas Aquinas could prevail against this evasive compromise. See R. W. Carlyle and A. J. Carlyle, *A History of Medieval Political Theory in the West* (Edinburgh, 1928), V, 441. Islam, starting from basically political Scriptures, had less difficulty in squaring the political institutions of the Caliphate with both the Qur'an and Greek politics. Although the superiority of the divine teachings over the philosophers' writings on economics, political science and ethics is also intimated by the Muslim author of the above-mentioned Genizah fragment (see n. 2), his pious endings for the three series of descriptions are rather vague in regard to the practical superfluity of this type of scientific literature. The deep affinities, on the other hand, between medieval metaphysics and the psychology and social structure of medieval man—so convincingly demonstrated by Wilhelm Dilthey (*Einleitung in die Geisteswissenschaften* [Leipzig, 1883], I, 453)—were much less obvious. Maimonides, for one, could readily believe in the universal validity of metaphysical doctrines and their intrinsic roots in human reason as such.

13. Saadia, *Beliefs and Opinions*, X, 8; Bahya, *Duties of the Heart*, VI, 4, in the Hebrew edition of Zifroni (Jerusalem, 1928), p. 179.

14. M.N. III, 37, 40, 54; M.T. De'ot 1, 4. For a similar contention of Abraham Maimuni, see his *High Ways to Perfection*, ed. by S. Rosenblatt, p. 90.

15. M.N. III, 33.

16. See also Max Weber, *Wirtschaft und Gesellschaft* (Tübingen, 1922), pp. 395, 424.

17. See Alfarabi, *Ueber den Ursprung der Wissenschaften* (*De ortu scientiarum*), ed. by Clemens Bäumker (Münster i.W., 1916), pp. 12, 20. Mahmassani (*Les Idées économiques*, p. 61) rightly emphasizes the main

preoccupation of Arabian economists before Dimashki and Ibn Khaldun with domestic rather than national economy. See also, in general, my *SRH*, 1st ed., I, 307 ff.; III, 75 ff.

18. M.N. II, 40; III, 41; Aristotle, *Nicomachean Ethics* 1097[b]; Ibn Khaldun, *Prolegomena*, XVI, 62, 66, 68 ff., 72 ff. (Arabic); XIX, 78, 83, 86 ff., 89 ff. (French). Ibn Khaldun himself, however, could not refrain from using the Aristotelian ζῷον πολιτικόν as a starting point. See also Ayad, *Die Geschichts- und Gesellschaftslehre*, pp. 165 ff., 175. Of course, for Maimuni the נטאם אלמנאזל, "domestic order," is the object of study for the תדביר אלמנזל, "the science of domestic economy," which, as we have seen, is included in the teachings of the Torah.

19. M.T. De'ot VI, 1. While the postulate that a Jew associate only with pious and learned men is based upon talmudic injunctions (e.g., M. Abot I, 6–7; IV, 14; Ket. 13a, 111b, and so forth; see also C.M. on the passages in Abot), the general formulation of the motive of imitation is Maimonides', under the influence of Alfarabi. So is the extreme demand that "if all the cities he knows, or has heard of, follow a bad course as in our day . . . he ought to withdraw into a cave, an abandoned field, or a desert" (M.T., *ibid.;* and above, Essay 4, n. 12). To be sure, this demand, emphasized by the sweeping denunciation of all contemporary civilization, is purely theoretical. But Maimonides was undoubtedly in earnest when in another connection he argued that a Jew threatened in the free exercise of his religion should instantly repair to more hospitable regions. See *Iggeret Teman*, ed. by Holub, p. 27 (*Ḳobeṣ* II, 3c); ed. by A. S. Halkin, pp. 34 ff. (Arabic & Hebrew), vii f. (English), See also M.N. III, 33, discussing the desirability of man's accommodation to his fellows' wishes.

20. M.N. III, 39, 43, 49. The various types of "love" are further defined by Maimuni, again with special reference to Aristotle, in C.M. on Abot I, 6. For the influence of the *Nicomachean Ethics* upon Maimonides, see David Rosin, *Die Ethik des Maimonides* (Breslau, 1876), pp. 6 ff.

21. M.N. II, 40. Maimuni evidently does not think in this connection about the various economic needs of humanity and the necessity of a variety of callings to satisfy them as the main motive for the rise of organized society, as suggested by the two leading commentators, Falakera and Efodi, *ad loc.* Maimonides rather emphasizes the psychological disparity among individuals, for which Crescas, *ad loc.*, tries to supply mainly physiological reasons. Nevertheless, Maimuni himself describes elsewhere (M.N. I, 46) how the peaceful coexistence of a physically weak, but wealthy, banker and a powerfully built beggar presupposes the existence of an organized state. Discussing the needs of man for food, dwelling, bath, and so forth, he states: "one man alone cannot procure all this; it is impossible for an individual to reach this goal except within

a social group, since man, as is well known, is by nature a social being" (M.N. III, 27. The expression כן may mean "dwelling," but it may also mean "clothing"; see Munk's translation, III, 212 n. 2. Both were regarded, next to food, as the most vital needs of man. See for instance, Plato's *Republic* 369d and Al-Ghazali's *Ihya 'ulum ed-din*, III, 155 ff. It is notable that Maimonides, the physician, places the need for a bath in the same category). We shall see that Maimuni, in other aspects, too, fully recognized the social import of the division of labor. It is not impossible that, like Plato, he regarded the division of labor as derived largely from different human aptitudes—hence, from basic characterological differences. See *Republic* 370b and Zevi Diesendruck's n. 59 to his Hebrew trans. thereof. It is also remarkable that, in contrasting the social propensities of man with the asocial nature of animals, Maimonides pays no attention whatever to the gregariousness of ants, bees, and flocks of birds, which was emphasized by both Aristotle and Alfarabi. See F. Dieterici and Paul Brönnle, *Die Staatsleitung von Alfarabi* (Leiden, 1904), p. 50, and the Hebrew trans. by Samuel ibn Tibbon, ed. by Filipowski in *He-Asif* (Leipzig, 1849), p. 32.

22. M.N. III, 54. It is precisely this last chapter of the volume, ending in the intense hope "may He grant us and *all* Israel with us to attain what He promised us . . . ," which, if read in its full context, shows how greatly overstressed is the allegedly "asocial" ultimate goal set up by Maimonides. See Isaac Husik's *History of Medieval Jewish Philosophy* (2d ed., New York, 1930), pp. 299 f., and Neuburger, *Das Wesen des Gesetzes*, pp. 13 ff., 86 f. Like almost all of his philosophic predecessors, from the mystic Philo to the rationalist Ibn Daud, Maimonides, in all his works, including his *Guide*, remained the exponent of the preeminently social orientation of biblical and rabbinic Judaism. His chief philosophic teachers, Aristotle, Avicenna, and Alfarabi, likewise being social-minded, Maimonides, with his profound distrust of sufistic asceticism, would have been led to the strong affirmation of social action and responsibility even if he were not simultaneously a distinguished jurist and the semipolitical leader of his people.

23. M.N. III, 39, 42 (see also Munk's note in his translation, III, 336 n. 2); M.T. De'ot 6, 3. The latter passage is a typical Maimonidean amplification of Hillel's negative golden rule (Shabbat 31a) and other talmudic statements. In C.M. on Abot II, 11 (13), Maimuni renders עין הרע as "greed," which, together with excessive desire and misanthropy stemming from pathological "melancholia," leads to man's self-destruction. This type of greed, however, consists primarily in the mere negativistic envy of other men's possessions, which drives the person so obsessed into solitude. While this interpretation is not at all certain in the Arabic original of C.M. ed. by E. Baneth, it was so understood by the Hebrew translator. See also *ibid.*, II, 9 (11).

24. M.N. I, 46; III, 27 (see Munk's notes, *ibid.*, III, 211), 35–40.
25. M.T. Melakhim 9, 1 based on Sanh. 56–57; *ibid.* 8, 11; Gezelah, 1, 2, 4, 13, based on B.Ḳ. 113a; B.M. 111a, and so forth; M.N. III, 41. For Maimonides' attitude to "booty," see below. See also "Outlook," in my *HJH*, pp. 115 f.; and George Foot Moore, *Judaism in the First Centuries of the Christian Era*, 3 vols. (Cambridge, Mass., 1927–30), I, 274 f.; III, 86. The emphasis אע״פ שכולן הן קבלה בידינו ממשה רבינו, והדעת נוטה להן, מכלל דברי תורה יראה שעל אלו נצטווה is significant for Maimuni's realization that there is no plain scriptural authority behind these laws (see Karo's comments *ad loc.*), but that, while in agreement with the general tenor of Scripture, they are based upon a combination of Mosaic tradition and human reason. In this sense it is possible for him, on the basis of talmudic statements, to include under the term "robbery" by Gentiles a variety of violations of property rights which, in the case of Jews, constitute different, mostly lesser, crimes, and to demand for all of them much harsher punishment and a greatly simplified prosecution. M.T. Melakhim 9, 9, 14. The omission of a part of 9, 14, in certain manuscripts, such as the Codex Trivulzio, is evidently due to a copyist's regard for Gentile sensitivities. See J. Feigenbaum, שנויי נוסחאות (Frankfort, 1889), p. 147. See also Naḥmanides' citation in his *Commentary* on Gen. 34:13. It is clear that, side by side with tradition, reason is mainly responsible for this vast extension of the two Noahidic commandments concerning "robbery" and "laws." In "idolatry," on the other hand, the position of a Gentile in a Jewish country is roughly similar to that of a Jew. With respect to "blasphemy," "murder," and consumption of "living flesh," too, there are but minor aggravations due to removal of talmudic minima, and so forth, whereas in "incest," as a result of the low rabbinic estimate of pagan family life, the prohibition for Gentiles is less severe. While in general this old, universal human law appears crude and Draconian, because it lacks the fine nuances of the more highly developed Mosaic legislation, the distinction is nowhere drawn by Maimonides as sharply as in the endless variety of crimes against property and in the legal procedure designed to safeguard society against them. His extreme stand in interpreting stray talmudic passages referring to these Noahidic commandments has aroused widespread objections. See Naḥmanides (cited above). But it is precisely this extremism which reveals the decisive role ascribed by Maimuni to criminal legislation in economic matters within the framework of organized society, however primitive. For the general kinship of the "Noahidic commandments" with "natural law," see the remarks of Nathan Isaacs in "The Influence of Judaism on Western Law," *The Legacy of Israel* (Oxford, 1928), pp. 383 ff.; and of M. Laserson in his *Ha-Pilosofiah ha-mishpaṭit shel ha-Rambam* (The Maimonidean Philosophy of Law [Tel Aviv, 1939]), pp. 11 f.

26. M.N. III, 35. Maimuni repeats (*ibid.*, 39) the idea that "mercy on sinners is cruelty to all creatures," and rejects the opposed principle of

indiscriminate hospitality toward visitors, which had found frequent expression in Arabian poetry, especially of the pre-Islamic era. See Munk's translation, III, 304 f. See also Abraham Maimuni's objections to the protection of criminals in Rosenblatt, ed., *The High Ways*, p. 95; and Th. W. Juynboll, *Handbuch des islamischen Gesetzes nach der Lehre der schafi'itischen Schule* (Leiden, 1910), p. 285.

27. M.T. Sanh. 11, 5. It is characteristic that instead of quoting Deut. 13:9, the original injunction concerning the heresiarch (also cited in Maimuni's direct talmudic source, Sanh. 37a), he prefers verse 18, which, although referring rather to a condemned town, better expresses the idea that the punishment of sinners is not refusal of mercy, but its truer application.

28. M.T. Sanh. 2, 7. While in general agreement with the opinions expressed in various connections by the ancient sages, this interpretation of Exod. 18:21 is largely Maimuni's own contribution. If Abraham de Boton finds a source for it in the Palestinian Talmud, this is due to his mistaken reading of Moses of Coucy's *Sefer miṣvot ha-gadol*, Positive Commandment 97, where this citation from Maimonides (without mention of the name) is preceded by another passage from j. Sanh. II, 1, 19d. See *Leḥem mishneh, ad loc.*; and *Sefer miṣvot* (Venice, 1547), fol. 286c.

29. A brief reference to the penetrating analysis of the biblical-rabbinic criminal law by Maimonides in M.N. III, 40, must suffice here. See also *ibid.*, III, 35, and the entire section "Neziḳin" in M.T. For the idea of "correction," see, for instance, *ibid.*, Gezelah 1, 13, where, on the basis of B.Ḳ. 94b, the advice is given that, if a repentant robber, after the loss of the original object of the robbery, wishes to indemnify the owner, such a restoration be refused and the sinner be fully rehabilitated, without any financial liability to himself. Of course this advice went beyond the bounds of strict law, and is given by both the Talmud and Maimonides in very cautious terms. See also Saadia, *Beliefs*, X, 13. The Maimonidean theories of criminal law deserve special investigation; the apologetical essay of Solomon Funk, *Das Grundprinzip des biblischen Strafrechts nach Maimonides und Hofrat Müller* (Berlin, 1910), has not even scratched the surface. See also Chaim Neuburger, *Das Wesen des Gesetzes*.

30. M.T. De'ot 6, 7; Roṣeaḥ 1, 14–16; and 'Akum 5, 9, based on Shab. 54b, Sanh. 73–74, and so forth. See also C.M. on Sanh. VIII, 7; S.M. Commandment 247; Prohibition 297 (quoting Sifre; see also Ch. Heller's introd. to his ed., p. 12, and p. 68 n. 3); M.N. III, 40.

31. Maimonides speaks of the pursuit of happiness as essential, especially in connection with political science in the stricter sense. In his *Treatise on Logic*, Chap. XIV, he describes it as "a science which imparts to its adepts the knowledge of true happiness . . . and . . . the relinquishing of illusory happiness." He follows therein Alfarabi. See Harry A. Wolfson,

"Note on Maimonides' Classification of Sciences," *JQR*, n.s. XXVI (1935–36), 374; and Strauss in *REJ*, C^{b^{i^s}}, 10 ff. The same Tibbonian term הצלחה (Aḥitub's trans., ed. by M. Chamizer in the *Hermann Cohen Festschrift Judaica* [Berlin, 1912], p. 449, and by Efros, in his ed. of the *Maḳālah*, p. 99, has the colorless טובה) is used by both Ibn Tibbon and Alḥarizi in their translation of the idea of "felicity," which may be obtained, according to Maimonides, by purely human, political legislation (M.N. II, 40). We have seen that he regarded at least national economy as part of "politics." Maimonides himself incidentally uses הצלחה in his Hebrew writings more in the prevalent sense of success, especially economic success. See M.T. Deʿot 5, 10: . . . תלמיד חכם אוכל ושותה וזן את אנשי ביתו כפי ממונו והצלחתו; Teshubah 9, 1: והצלחת מעשה והפסדו, and so forth. See also his use of the Hebrew phrase הצלחת יוסף בבית המצרי in the Arabic context of M.N. II, 45 (ed. Munk, fol. 94a).

32. See especially C.M. on Sanh. III, 3; Abot *passim;* and M.T. Deʿot *passim.* See also *Iggeret shemad*, 1a, and M.T. Talmud torah 1, 12; 3, 10. Maimonides becomes rhetorical here and quotes a number of equally exaggerating talmudic utterances, because he thereby tries to stem the tide of the growing commercialization of learning under the semicapitalistic conditions of early Islam. See also his sharp denunciation of professional learning, written, on second thought, in C.M. on Abot IV, 5, and his overoptimistic assurance that God rather than men will take care of the pious in time of need. M.T. Matenot ʿaniyim 10, 19; Zekhiyah u-mattanah 12, 17.

33. M.T. Klei ha-miḳdash 5, 1, based on Yoma 18a, and so forth; Melakhim 1, 6, based on Ḳidd. 82a; Sanh. 25, 4 based on Ḳidd. 70a; C.M. on Bikkurim III, 3. It is to be noted that in the second passage Maimuni ignores the talmudic motivation of possible sexual licentiousness and selects, among all the occupations there listed, only those four which seem to have had a low socioeconomic status in his time. See also Karo's comments *ad loc.*, and Yom Ṭob Lippman Heller's *Tosefot Yom Ṭob* on ʿEduyot I, 3. See also M.N. III, 8; and, for similar views of Abraham Maimuni, in his *High Ways*, ed. by Rosenblatt, I, 82–106. The importance of ornate and even expensive attire for any person of standing in the Orient is well known. It is also stressed by Abraham Maimuni, *ibid.*, p. 94, and by Judah ibn Tibbon, who urgently advised his son, "take off from your belly and put it on your back." See his Ṣavaah, in Israel Abrahams, *Hebrew Ethical Wills* (Philadelphia, 1926), I, 66. Maimonides, too, stresses cleanliness and beauty in one's dress, but demands that it be worn with moderation. M.T. Deʿot 5, 9. For the frequent deprecation of the working classes among the Arabs, see, for instance, the violent tirade of an Abbasid courtier, Al-Fadl ibn Yahya, who, after stating that only the four upper and middle classes count at all, dismissed all others: "The remainder are filthy refuse, a torrent of scum, base cattle, none of whom

thinks of anything but his food and sleep." Quoted from *Kitab al-Buldan* by Reuben Levy, in *An Introduction to the Sociology of Islam* (London, 1929–31), I, 96. See also Al-Ghazali and Abul Fadl, quoted by Mahmassani, *Les idées économiques*, p. 83; At-Tusi, quoted by Plessner, *Der Oikonomikos*, pp. 65, 131. The antiquity of this deprecation, which may be pursued in a straight line from Panaetius and Cicero to the medieval scholastics, is stressed by Otto Schilling in his *Die Staats- und Soziallehre des heiligen Augustinus* (Freiburg i.B., 1910), pp. 227 f. Had not Aristotle already declared that artisans and wage earners could not possibly devote themselves to a life of virtue? See his *Politics*, III, 5. See also E. Troeltsch, *The Social Teaching of the Christian Churches* (New York, 1931), I, 317. As to Jews in the manual crafts, mentioned by Maimonides, see the statement of an Arab writer, Abû Nu'aim, concerning the Jews of medieval Isfahan in Persia, quoted by A. Mez in *Die Renaissance des Islams* (Heidelberg, 1923), p. 36 n. 3. For the general attitude of Maimonides to labor, see below.

34. See especially C.M. on Abot Introd. (Eight Chapters), V; M.T. Teshubah 8, 6; 9, 1; M.N. III, 39–40.

35. M.T. Shabbat 2, 23, based on 'Erubin 45a; 'Akum 3, 7 and 7, 10 (see also RABD and Karo, *ad loc.*), based on 'A.Z. 12a, Zeb. 74a; M.N. III, 37. Similarly, decency in matters of sex and in speaking thereof should be maintained, even when one faces financial losses on this score (M.N. III, 49). On the other hand, Maimuni, following B.B. 9a, relaxes the general prohibition against emigrating from Palestine except in case of absolute need, although he believes that a really pious man would hold out to the end (M.T. Melakhim 5, 9). Evidently this was sheer theory in Maimuni's time, whereas his tannaitic source reflected sincere, but futile, endeavors of the Palestinian leaders to stem the rising tide of emigration, especially after the fall of Jerusalem.

36. *Iggeret Teman*, ed. by Holub, p. 27 (*Kobeṣ*, II, 3c); above, n. 19. Baḥya goes further and objects to emigration on purely economic grounds, because it implies lack of reliance upon God. See *Duties of the Heart*, IV, Introd., p. 119.

37. M.N. II, 31; III, 32. See also Ibn Ezra's comments on Deut. 5:14. In the long section on the Sabbath in M.T., climaxed by an enthusiastic finale on the great significance of the Sabbath observance, Maimuni discusses many detailed regulations governing compulsory rest, but refrains from explaining the underlying social reasons. The accent here, too, is evidently upon sanctification rather than recreation. However, when confronted with an important economic problem, such as navigation on rivers, Maimuni leans toward the milder interpretation and advocates the application of the less stringent rules governing the operations of the merchant marine on salt-water seas. See the extended correspondence in Resp. Nos. 67–69, supplemented *ibid.*, pp. 361–67. For the controversy over

the permissible breaking of the commandment, see M.T. Shabbat, 2, 3, based on Yoma 84b; B. M. Lewin, *Otzar ha-Geonim*, VI (Jerusalem, 1934), pp. 30 ff.; and my *SRH*, 1st ed., I, 348.

38. M.N. I, 72; III, 45. See also III, 40, and above, n. 21. The enormous significance of the division of labor was a commonplace in ancient and medieval philosophy from Plato's *Republic* (369–70) on. Bryson had derived therefrom an interesting theory concerning the rise of the city and the necessity of money. See Plessner's ed., pp. 148–49 (Arabic and Hebrew; not extant in Latin). For a specific religious motivation of the role of the entrepreneur, see Baḥya, *Duties*, IV, 133. See also the rather biased discussion of Fr. M. Robert in his "Hiérarchie nécessaire des fonctions économiques d'après St. Thomas d'Aquin," *Revue thomiste*, XXI (1913), 419–31.

39. M.N. Introd. and M.T. Talmud torah 6, 10, where the motivation כדי שלא יתבזו בפני עמי הארץ is a typically Maimonidean rationalization of the existing privileges liberating Jewish scholars from the public *corvée* which had been demanded, and largely attained, in B.B. 8a. See also Eppenstein in MbM, II, 29 f., and above, n. 33.

40. M.N. III, 35. See also above, n. 14. For the conflict between theory and practice in medieval Islam and Christendom, see R. Levy, *Sociology of Islam*, I, 80 ff.; Ayad, *Die Geschichts- und Gesellschaftslehre*, p. 190; Carlyle and Carlyle, *Medieval Political Theory*, I, 6 ff.; V, 443 ff.; and Edmund Schreiber, *Die volkswirtschaftlichen Anschauungen seit Thomas von Aquin* (Jena, 1913), pp. 8 f.

41. Gratian, *Decretum*, VIII, 1, in *PL*, CLXXXVII, 43–46; Thomas Aquinas, *Summa theol.* II, 2, 66, 2. See also J. B. Kraus, *Scholastik, Puritanismus und Kapitalismus* (Munich, 1930), pp. 24 ff.; R. H. Tawney, *Religion and the Rise of Capitalism* (London, 1926), pp. 3 ff.; and Richard McKeon, "The Development of the Concept of Property in Political Philosophy," *Ethics*, XLVIII (1938), 297–366.

42. On medieval Egypt, see especially C. H. Becker's *Islamstudien* (Leipzig, 1924), I, 146–233. It may be true that Ibn al-Rawandi, the leading exponent of Arab heterodox collectivism, was the son of a heretical Jew, as is claimed by one of his opponents, Ibn al-Jauzi. See H. Ritter, "Philologica, VI," *Der Islam*, XIX (1930–31), 9. But there is no evidence for the penetration of these ideas into the Jewish sects of that time, which, as in the case of most Karaite groups, were, on the contrary, more radical exponents of individualism than the traditionalist Rabbanites. Even the ascetic groups of "Mourners for Zion," Karaite as well as Rabbanite, showed little predilection for communal ownership. The individualistic coloring of the Karaite schism is by no means controverted by Raphael Mahler's attempt to demonstrate its "national-social character." See his Yiddish essays in *Jiwobleter*, Vols. VIII–IX (1935–36); and my *SRH*, 2d ed., V, 393 f. n. 14.

43. M.T. Zekhiyah u-mattanah 1, 1: ‏ההפקר כל המחזיק בו זכה, וכן המדברות‏
‏והנהרות והנחלים כל שבהן הפקר‏ . . . where Maimonides clearly distinguishes between the *res ommium communes*, which never belonged to anyone in
particular and cannot be appropriated, and the objects which potentially
belong to everybody and frequently had had a former owner. Only such
he classifies as *hefker*. This legal clarity is the more remarkable as we find
the talmudic sources frequently applying a looser terminology. See, for
instance, Sanh. 49a: ‏מה מדבר מופקר לכל אף ביתו של יואב מופקר לכל‏. See also
Shulḥan ʿArukh, H.M. 273, 12, where Karo gives preference to this exact
Maimonidean formulation over the looser phraseology of Jacob b. Asher;
Asher Gulak's *Yesodei ha-mishpaṭ ha-ʿibri* (The Principles of Jewish Law
[Berlin, 1923]), I, 97; RABD's objections and Ibn Gaon's and Don Vidal's
comments on M.T., *ibid.* Don Vidal correctly points out that Maimuni in
this connection accepts certain limitations on the rights of the Palestinian
landowners, imposed upon them by a specific ten-point agreement among
the original Israelitic settlers under Joshua. For these fairly comprehensive
limitations, see *HJH*, pp. 128 f. Unlike Isserles in his note on H.M. 274,
Karo evidently shares Maimuni's view that this agreement affected only
Palestinian land, and not land owned by Jews outside that country. That is
why, considering the agreement obsolete in his day, Karo fails to mention
it in his Code. See also M.T. Genebah 8, 2; and below, n. 46, for further
clarification of the difference between the terms *hefker* and *res nullius*. On
Islam, see *Qurʾan* II, 27, and Von Tornauw, "Das Eigentumsrecht nach
moslimischem Recht," *ZDMG*, XXXVI (1882), 291. It may not be re-
dundant to state that for the purposes of our present discussion the purely
juridical aspects of private ownership are pertinent only insofar as they
color the economic views of the writers.

44. M.T. Nedarim 2, 14–19, based on Ned. 43–44 and j. Ned. IV, 10,
38d. See also C.M. on Peʾah VI, 1, and Ned. IV, 8. Gulak (*Yesodei*, I,
138 ff.) stresses the difference between the Roman *res derelicta* and
relinquished property in Jewish law: while the Romans demanded an act
of overt abandonment, the Jews were satisfied with the mere expression
of a wish on the part of the owner. To be sure, Gulak somewhat exag-
gerates the Maimonidean repudiation of the validity of such acts. Maimuni rejects only inconclusive acts; but where they take place under
circumstances which clearly indicate the owner's desire to relinquish his
property—or merely his conscious abandonment of hope to recover it
(‏יאוש‏)—it has all the effects of an expressed wish. See M.T. Gezelah
va-abedah 11, 9–11, and H.M. 261, 4, where Karo once more gives preference to the Maimonidean terminology, even though the Talmud (B.M.
21a, and so on) clearly discusses such "conscious losses" under *hefker*.
See also Judah Ashkenazi's comments on the controversy between Karo
and Isserles, *ibid.*, and 260, 11. Although from the *economic* point of
view the effects of the Roman action and the Jewish wish are practically

the same, this distinction further illustrates the importance attached by the Jewish jurists, including Maimonides, to the psychological assertion of property rights.

45. M.T. Zekhiyah u-mattanah 1, 6; 2, 1; Gezelah va-abedah 8, 5, 14, based on M.B.B. III, 3 (see also C.M. thereon), B.Ḳ. 109ab, and so forth. No mention is made here or elsewhere of heirless estates of native Jews, because Maimonides assumes that by tracing his genealogy back far enough a Jew will always detect some lawful heirs. See M.T. Naḥlot 1, 3. In the somewhat analogous situation of land acquired by a Jew from a Gentile, before the purchaser takes regular possession, the occupant must indemnify the purchaser for the full amount of the purchase money. M.T. Zekhiyah u-mattanah 1, 14; 2, 1, based on B.B. 54b. See however, Samuel b. Meir's comments thereon and H.M. 194. See also below.

46. M.T., ibid. 1, 15. For the edict of 923, see Mez, Renaissance des Islams, p. 106. Safra (pseud.) in his brilliant Hebrew essay on "Private Property in Jewish Law," Ha-Mishpaṭ ha-'ibri, II (1927), 25–73, emphasizes the importance of the idea of hefḳer for the relativity of private ownership in biblical and talmudic law. Starting with the idea of the common use of the agricultural produce during the Sabbatical year (see the dominant opinion of the school of Hillel in M. Pe'ah, VI, 1; C.M., ibid.), hefḳer was not altogether ownerless, but was merely open to everybody's use. This theory, to be sure, accounts mainly for the various types of hefḳer resulting from dereliction, the estate of a proselyte or Gentile land already sold to a Jew, all of which originally had owners; it does not, and need not, explain the real res nullius, such as deserts, which had never belonged to any individual. Although, with the majority of the rabbis, Maimonides rejects the opinion of R. Jose that relinquished objects remain the property of their original owners until their definite acquisition by somebody else (for the connection of this controversy with that in M. Ned. IV, 8, see the Palestinian Talmud and C.M. on that Mishnah), he still retains the three-day period for reconsideration. This is not a period of grace, but is intended to serve mainly as a check on fraudulent dereliction followed by immediate reappropriation, which would enable the owner to get rid of all legal obligations resting on the "relinquished" object.

47. The main Maimonidean discussions on the subject of רשות הרבים are to be found in C.M. on Shab. I, 1, and M.T. Shabbat 14, 1. Both texts agree that deserts and highways "running through" (מפולשים) are public grounds, but the emphasis מפולשים להן is evidently intended to exclude the extreme opinion of R. Simon b. Lakish, לעולם אין רשות הרבים עד שתהא מפולש מסוף העולם עד סופה (j. 'Erubin VIII, 8, 25a), which, if consistent, would lead to the direct negation of such public grounds. For the different types of roads, ranging from the "private road" (2½ ells wide), through the

"country road" (between two cities, and 8 ells in width), to the "regular highway" (at least 16 ells), see M.T. Mekhirah 21, 9, based on B.B. 100ab. The paving and maintenance of roads, and the provision of other facilities for travel and transportation are regarded by Maimuni as the foremost duties of municipal government. See M.N. III, 40. See also M.T. Nizkei mamon 13, 26, based on B.M. 107b, on the facilities to be extended to boatmen on rivers. The "markets" (שוקים) in M.T. Shabbat 14, 1, are perhaps in the same class with "highways," provided they are situated in "open" cities. The reading עיירות ("towns") in certain editions of M.T. is undoubtedly a corruption of יערות or יערים ("forests") as stated in C.M.; the Amsterdam edition of 1702; and the main commentaries. In M.T. 'Erubin 1, 1–5, Maimuni takes great pains to assert that a township, with its streets and markets, if surrounded by a wall ten handbreadths high, is "private ground," and that King Solomon instituted 'erubin in such cities only in order to counteract popular misapprehensions. See "Outlook," in my HJH, pp. 132 f. In contrast to Maimonides, Solomon ibn Adret, also quoted by Don Vidal, placed deserts and forests in the intermediate class of karmelit. See also M.T. Bet ha-behirah 7, 14; Biat ha-mikdash 3, 8, and so forth, on the differences between Jerusalem and other walled cities.

48. M.T. Sanh. 18, 6, based on Sanh. 91b–92a. While in C.M. on Sanh. IX, 6, Maimuni states, at least with respect to the analogous case of sex relations with Gentiles, that "we do not advise" lynching, in M.T. he refers to all these cases of popular violence as meritorious deeds: וכל שהורגן זכה. See also ibid., Issurei biah 12, 4, and "Outlook," in my HJH, pp. 124 f. In Muslim law, too, most crimes against religion, as such, were not punished by earthly courts, but left to divine judgment. See Josef Schacht, "Zur soziologischen Betrachtung des islamischen Rechts," Der Islam, XXII (1935), 209.

49. M.T. Nizkei mamon 8, 1, 4, based on various passages in B.K. The reciprocal liberation of civil offenders for damages to sacred objects was mitigated by the strong incentive for every owner of a damaging animal to donate it to the Temple and thus escape all further responsibility. M.T. Mekhirah 22, 15: hekdesh acquires rights from the donation of an as-yet-nonexistent object, because man ought to keep his sacred pledges even if they are considered void in commercial transactions. The rabbis extended special legal protection to "sacred" institutions in their character of depositors. M.T. Sekhirut 2, 1–2. For the encouragement of both vows and pledges to "sacred" causes, see especially M.T. Maaseh korbanot 14. See also Gulak, Yesodei, I, 98 f.

50. The use of the term hekdesh to designate contemporary charities was fairly prevalent in Maimuni's time, however. See, for instance, Sha'arei teshubah, No. 145; Alfasi, Responsa, No. 6; Joseph ibn Megas, Responsa, No. 207. Maimonides, too, at least in reply to an inquiry using that term, makes use of it in its new meaning, see Resp. No. 80; but in

M.T. Mekhirah, 15–17, he uses it in contradistinction to charity. In any case, he deals with objects of philanthropy, here and elsewhere, as with usual civil property, except for certain legal peculiarities which will be discussed by me in another connection. For the Muslim *waqf*, see Becker, *Islamstudien*, I, 62 f.; and Levy, *Sociology of Islam*, II, 84 f.

51. See especially M.T. Ishshut 5, 1; Ma'akhalot asurot 8, 15–18; Sheluḥin ve-shutefin 5, 10, based on Pes. 24b, Ḳidd. 56b, and so forth. In this connection Maimuni demands that Jews should generally refrain from raising animals, such as pigs, whose consumption has been prohibited by biblical law. C.M. on B.Ḳ. VII, 8. Curiously, in M.T. Nizḳei mamon 5, 8, he prefers to advance the original tannaitic reason, that pigs are likely to become obnoxious to neighbors. He may have been influenced here by the consideration that, through such reasoning, one could outlaw the raising of, and trade in, these undesirable creatures, not only by Jews but by Gentiles as well. On Islam, see G. Bergsträsser and J. Schacht, *Grundzüge des islamischen Rechts* (Berlin, 1935), p. 44. See also C.M. on Ḳidd. II, 9; M.T. Ma'akhalot asurot 10, 6, 9; 14, 10–13, and so forth; and M.N. III, 46, 48.

52. M.T. Sheluḥin ve-shutefin 3, 7, in conjunction with *ibid.*, Gezelah va-abedah 8, 14. See also *Haggahot Maimuniot*, Karo's and Abraham de Boton's comments on the former passage, and Adolf Schwarz's article in MbM, I, 382 ff. For the geonic sources and especially the conflicting opinions of the academies of Sura and Pumbedita in regard to this claim, see Simḥa Assaf, *Teshubot ha-geonim min ha-genizah* (Jerusalem, 1929), p. 31 and n. 3; Louis Ginzberg, *Genizah Studies*, II (New York, 1929), 11, 38, 632; and H. Tykocinski, *Die gaonäischen Verordnungen* (Berlin, 1929), pp. 117 ff. This controversy may originally have been actuated by the Palestinophilism of the academy of Sura and the more "Babylonian" self-assertion postulated by the academy of Pumbedita; but Maimuni, despite his own devotion to the Palestinian ideal, does not hesitate to follow the lead of Pumbedita in this respect.

53. Maimuni not only devotes entire sections in his *Code* and long passages in M.N. to a discussion of these commandments but also writes several responsa to explain certain details in their contemporary operation. See Resp. Nos. 133, 136, and so forth. See also "Outlook," in my *HJH*, pp. 137 f.

54. See Safra, in *Ha-Mishpaṭ ha-'ibri*, II, 70.

55. M.T. Mekhirah 24, 14, a translation of R. Judah's statement B.B. 96b, with an additional motivation.

56. See especially *ibid.*, 22, 14; 23, 1; She'elah u-piḳḳadon 1, 5. This is not contradicted by the statement in M.T. Terumot 1, 17, concerning the liberation of the Jewish coloni and tenants of Gentile land in Syria from the tithes לפי שאין לו בגוף הקרקע כלום, which is merely a reference to the peculiar situation of Syria. See the more precise explanation given in C.M. on

Ḥallah IV, 7. See also Safra, in *Ha-Mishpaṭ ha-'ibri*, II, 44; and Von Tornauw, in *ZDMG*, XXXVI, 329.

57. M.T. Gezelah va-abedah 1, 5; 2, 1, based on B.Ḳ. 94b, and so forth.

58. M.T. Mekhirah 22, 1, 5–6, based upon several rather controversial talmudic passages. See also Don Vidal's comments *ad loc.* For Muslim parallels, see Levy, *Sociology of Islam*, II, 85.

59. M.T. Mekhirah 6, 11–12; Malveh ve-loveh 24, 9 based on Ket. 86a; B.B. 76b–77a, 172b; RABD, and Abraham de Boton's comments on the first, and Judah Rosanes's comments on the second, passage. The latter rightly points out the inconsistency in Maimuni's view, which evidently arose from his attempt to reconcile his conservative interpretation of ancient sources with his recognition of a widespread contemporary practice. See also the related controversy among post-talmudic authors in Ginzberg's *Genizah Studies*, II, 109 ff. For the economically significant question as to whether or not such easily negotiable instruments were to be found in the talmudic period, see L. Auerbach, *Das jüdische Obligationsrecht* (Berlin, 1871), I, §13, answering the question in the affirmative; and Gulak, *Yesodei*, pp. 140 f., giving a negative answer. In any case, however, there was enough talmudic material for Maimuni to derive therefrom his moderately liberal interpretation, and for his perennial opponent RABD to go several steps further. For the relatively inferior position of deeds in Muslim law, on the other hand, where they were accepted merely as subsidiary to the testimony of witnesses, see Schacht, in *Der Islam*, XXII, 213.

60. M.T. Mekirah 24, 15, based on B.B. 63b. See also Don Vidal's comments thereon and the formulas for a deed of sale in the *Sefer ha-Sheṭarot* (Book of Deeds) of Hai Gaon, ed. by S. Assaf (Jerusalem, 1930), pp. 26 f.; and in that of Judah al-Barceloni, ed. by S. J. Halberstam (Berlin, 1898), pp. 45 f.

61. M.T. Gezelah va-abedah 16, 7–11; C.M. on B.M. II, 3, based upon B.M. 25b–26a. The stronger emphasis upon שאני אומר של עכו'ם הקדמונים הן is probably due to the provisions of Muslim law, which recognized the finder's right only with respect to treasures dating from pre-Islamic days. See Bergsträsser-Schacht, *Grundzüge*, p. 51. While Maimuni generally tries to protect owners, even beyond the talmudic requirements, and cautions finders not to touch treasures which might belong to the house owner, he draws no distinction, such as suggested by RABD, between houses guarded by their owners and such as are not watched, in which latter alone the finder has presumptive rights. To justify this infringement upon the rights of ownership, Maimuni construes a rather unconvincing conclusion *a fortiori* from objects lost in the sea. See also Ibn Gaon's and Don Vidal's comments, and *Haggahot Maimuniot, ad loc.* Despite the obvious precariousness of such hiding places, C.M. on B.M. III, 10; and M.T. She'elah u-piḳḳadon 4, 4, mechanically repeat the injunctions of

B.M. 42a that a depository ought to conceal all money entrusted to him one handbreadth below the surface of the soil or, in a wall, below the ceiling. See also M.T. *ibid.*, 7, 8. Neither does Maimuni pay any attention to the fact that, if such advice, prompted by certain specific conditions in third-century Babylonia, were to be generally followed, it would merely facilitate the search by thieves. He adopts, moreover, a suggested extension of these injunctions to include all valuable objects which would not be damaged by preservation in the soil, and does not seem to exonerate a paid depository from responsibility for theft, even after he has taken all these precautions. See Don Vidal's comments and *Tosafot* on B.M. 62a s. v. אמר. He adheres to these stringent postulates also in the actual case recorded in his Resp. No. 290, relaxing them slightly only in the case of gold and silver objects other than money (and possibly gold or silver bars), which, he admits, according to custom could be kept in a tower or a hidden chest. This literal acceptance of practical advice given in the Talmud is the more remarkable as Judah al-Barceloni, one of Maimuni's Spanish predecessors, had stated, in terms of an old tradition, that the talmudic injunctions were conditioned by the prevalence of thieves in the ancient period, but that subsequently one was entitled to hide deposited money in any normal receptacle used for the safekeeping of one's own funds. See *Tur* H.M., 291, and *Haggahot Maimuniot* on M.T., *loc. cit.* For the prevalence of "treasures" under medieval Islam, see W. Björkmann, "Kapitalentstehung und Anlage in Islam," *Mitteilungen des Seminars für Oriental. Sprachen . . . Berlin*, XXXII (1929), 91, 95; D. S. Margoliouth, *Lectures on Arabic Historians* (Calcutta, 1930), p. 135; Walter J. Fischel, *Jews in the Economic and Political Life of Mediaeval Islam* (London, 1937), pp. 13 f.

62. M.T. Shekhenim 10, 1–4, based on B.B. 24b–25a. More explicit is C.M. on B.B. II, 7–9, where Maimuni advances two reasons, rather than one, for the removal of tanners, as well as of brush, to a distance of fifty ells from the city. In his *Code* he has evidently reconsidered both statements, undoubtedly because in the meantime he realized that east winds were not so uncommon in Palestine as he had first thought; and that thorny bushes should really be counted among trees. It is uncertain, however, whether he likewise dropped the intimation in C.M. on B.B. II, 9, that these laws, essentially militating against all city parks, applied to those Babylonian and other non-Palestinian cities where the Jews formed the majority of the population. Rashi and Solomon ibn Adret clearly decided that they were valid only in Palestine. See Don Vidal's comments on M.T. *loc. cit.* With respect to the exclusion of the parks from Jerusalem, see also M.T. Beit ha-behirah 7, 14, based on B.K. 82b, both strangely contrasting with Kohelet 2:5. Perhaps it was the Hellenistic character of the Palestinian gardens which aroused rabbinic antagonism with respect to the Holy City; but Maimuni is also conspicuously

silent about the removal of truck gardens to a distance of 1,000 ells, this being logically derived from the talmudic discussion by the Tosafists on B.B. 24b s. v. מרחיקין. This deduction would also have been in full agreement with Maimuni's own acceptance of the idea underlying that discussion in M.T. Shemiṭṭah ve-yobel 13, 2. See Abraham de Boton's comments on M.T. Shekhenim 10, 1. As a physician he certainly realized that walking in beautiful parks is one of the more effective remedies for men stricken with melancholy. C.M. on Abot, Introd., Chap. V. One cannot escape the conclusion that through his silence Maimuni modified the stringent talmudic regulations, in order to meet contemporary needs in the Muslim environment, where flourishing parks, suburban orchards, and truck gardens were very common.

63. Maimuni discusses an endless variety of mutual rights of neighbors in his M.T. Shekhenim, 3 ff., culminating in the general principle that in "all matters where one person benefits without any loss to another the latter is forced" to comply with the former's request. *Ibid.* 7, 8. The opposite behavior is stigmatized as that of Sodom.

64. M.T., *ibid.* 12, 4–5, 9, 13–14; 14, 1–3, based on B.M. 107; C.M. on B.B. II, 4. Maimonides frequently goes beyond the literal meaning of his talmudic sources in trying to reduce the burden of this law. For example, he excludes from its operation all leases (*ibid.* 12, 8), and explains the equivocal passage הני ציירי והני שרי as referring to ממהרים לצאת יותר מזווי, thus enabling the purchaser by depositing especially good currency to spring a surprise upon the hapless neighbor. There is also a slight shade in the meaning of Maimonides' אמור שיש לו against the talmudic אי גברא דאמיד הוא דאזיל ומייתי זוזי. Like Alfasi and Rashi, however, he refuses to go all the way toward the liberalization of these laws in favor of the owner's free disposal of his property where no superior social interest is involved. That is why he evidently would have repudiated the decision of Jacob Tam that no right of preemption may be exercised with respect to urban real estate. See *Tosafot* on B.M. 108b s.v. ארעא. See also the extensive geonic responsum in *Teshubot geonim ḳadmonim*, ed. by David Cassel, No. 9; and, with respect to land sales to Gentiles, *Sha'arei ṣedeḳ*, IV, 8, 1; 21–22 (fol. 30a, 33b); and below, n. 88.

65. C.M. on B.Ḳ. VII, 7; M.T. Genebah 1, 10. The commentators are here at a total loss to find a talmudic source or precedent.

66. M.T. Genebah 5, 1–7, based on B.Ḳ. 114b ff. RABD's objection, if it refers to 5, 2 (so in the printed editions; Ibn Gaon and Don Vidal take it to be aimed at a misreading of 5, 3), is evidently based upon an inclusion of Raba's statement in the concluding passage in the Talmud: והלכתא בכולהו, and so forth. Maimuni, like the Tosafists, *ad loc.*, excludes it, thus further obstructing fraudulent trade. For divergent views of Hananel and Hai Gaon, see *Haggahot Maimuniot, ad loc.* See also Resp. No. 148 and, for a similar treatment of articles forcibly taken away from

their owner, M.T. Gezelah va-abedah 5, 7. For other geonic material, see Jacob Mann, "The Responsa of the Babylonian Geonim as a Source of Jewish History," *JQR*, n.s. X (1919–20), 131 ff.; and, for the so-called *Hehlerrecht* in medieval Jewish privileges, Moses Hoffmann, *Der Geldhandel der deutschen Juden während des Mittelalters* (Leipzig, 1910), pp. 64 ff.; G. Kisch, "Research in Medieval Legal History of the Jews," *PAAJR*, VI (1934–35), 244; *idem.*, "The 'Jewish Law of Concealment,'" *Historia Judaica*, I (1938), 3–30. The objections raised by I. F. Baer (in his review of Raphael Straus's *Die Judengemeinde Regensburg im ausgehenden Mittelalter*, in *Kirjath Sepher*, XII [1935–36], 463 f.) against the alleged nexus between the tannaitic law and medieval legislation are very inconclusive. The nexus here postulated is not between "two laws which had been enacted under totally different social conditions and from totally different juristic considerations," but between a talmudic law vigorously restated by Maimonides and other medieval rabbis, and fully practiced in commercial transactions among Jews, and a privilege repeatedly granted to Jews by medieval rulers. Prompted by existing economic need, the Jews, in their negotiations with the authorities, were in a position the more readily to insist upon such a privilege, as they could stress its actual operation in the Jewish quarter over a period of many generations. See also *SRH*, 2d ed., XII, 120 f., 299 f. n. 58.

67. M.T. Gezelah va-abedah 15, 16, based on B.M. 22b. For the special rights of a worker to help himself to the fruits of his employer, to which the original Deuteronomic injunction (23:25–26) had been reduced by the Talmud B.M. 87b, see below. For the significance attached to custom by Maimuni's predecessors, see the material assembled by J. L. Fishman in his "'Custom' in Geonic Literature" (Hebrew), *The B. M. Lewin Jubilee Volume* (Jerusalem, 1939), pp. 132–59.

68. M.T. Zekhiyah u-mattanah 7, 1 ff., based on B.B. 145; *ibid.*, 6, 24, in the name of his teachers. See also RABD's objections and the commentaries. Maimuni also accepts (*ibid.* 6, 21–23) his predecessors' opinion concerning the customary return of gifts exchanged between fiancé and fiancée, if the engagement is broken. Even the food consumed in the meantime in each other's houses is to be paid for. For a practical application, see the interesting Resp. No. 225. See also M.T. Gezelah va-abedah 12, 11, 14; Sheluhin ve-shutefin 5, 1, and so forth.

69. M.T. Nahlot 6, 1 ff., 11; M.N. III, 42, based on M.B.B. VIII, 5, and so forth. For the ramified Jewish inheritance laws in general, see Gulak, *Yesodei*, II, 71 ff.; and M. Mielziner, *The Rabbinical Law of Hereditary Succession* (Cincinnati, 1900). We are here, of course, concerned only with those phases of the law which throw light on the economic aspects of private ownership.

70. M.T. Melakhim 1, 7, based on Sifre, and so forth. See *Haggahot Maimuniot, ad loc.*

71. M.T. Ishshut 12, 9; 23, 5–7, based on M. Ket. IX, 1, in conjunction with b. 83a and B.B. 49ab (see also C.M. on Ket., *ibid.*); Resp. No. 319, where he combats an attempted distinction by Alfasi. Maimuni seems to believe, however, that the heir may refuse the inheritance after it falls due, against his teacher Joseph ibn Megas' contrary opinion. Both agree, however, that the heir may relinquish his rights by making them *hefker*. See also Freimann's notes on Resp., *ibid.*

72. M.T. Ebel 12, 1, based on Sanh. 46–47b. See also M.T. Zekhiyah u-mattanah 11, 24, and Ket. 48a.

73. M.T. Sheluhin ve-shutefin 5, 11: "so did the geonim teach." See also Schwarz in MbM, 1, 385.

74. M.T. Nahlot 6, 13, somewhat stronger than Shab. 10b. For Alfasi, see above, n. 71.

75. C.M. on Abot, Introd. (=Eight Chapters) Chap. V, trans. by Joseph I. Gorfinkle (New York, 1912), p. 70. See also M.T. De'ot 2, 7; M.N. III, 39, and so forth.

76. M.T. Ishshut 14, 4, based on Yeb. 44a. See also C.M. on Yeb. IV, 11.

77. M.T. Melakhim 3, 12–14, based on Sanh. 21ab. See also C.M. on Sanh. II, 4, and S.M. Prohib. 363–64. In all of these Maimuni goes beyond his talmudic sources in emphasizing the right of the king to use cavalry and to accumulate financial reserves for future emergencies. As to the contrast between the limitation to eighteen "wives" in S.M., which allows for an additional unlimited number of concubines, and the total of eighteen wives and concubines of M.T., to which RABD objected, see the variants in the latter text reported by Ibn Gaon, *ad loc.;* and Heller's comments in his edition of S.M., p. 135 n. 5.

78. S.M. Prohib. 57; M.T. Nizkei mamon 5, 1; Teshubah 1, 1. Maimonides' more radical interpretation of B.K. 23b called forth a sharp rebuke by RABD and caused embarrassment to friendly commentators on Nizkei mamon. The Talmud evidently had in mind only legal protection against possibly unrecoverable future damages; Maimuni thinks of the ethicoeconomic implications of waste. He also finds the same motives underlying the prohibition of raising small cattle in Palestine; B.K. 79b. See M.T., *ibid.*, 5, 2, and C.M. on B.K. VII, 7. For different interpretations, see SRH, 1st ed., I, 279 f.; III, 69. Through the psychology of scarcity we may also explain Maimuni's rhetorical denunciation of those who put precious silk or gold-woven garments as shrouds upon the corpses of wealthy personages before interment. "They should be given to the poor rather than thrown to the worms." M.T. Ebel 4, 2; 14, 24, going beyond the ancient sources listed by Michael Higger in his edition of the *Treatise Semahot* (New York, 1931), pp. 81, 178 n. 87.

79. See M.T. Shehitah, 11, 15, and so forth.

80. For the ramifications of this principle, see Shekalim 3a, Yeb. 89b

and 90b, Giṭṭin 33a, 36b, B.B. 48b, and so forth. These cases include the juristic fiction of a retroactive annulment of marriage by the court's expropriation of the money originally used for the betrothal. This fiction sometimes appears without the psychological motivation of the supposed implicit consent of the bridegroom that his betrothal be valid only with the rabbis' approval. See especially Rashi and *Tosafot* on Giṭṭin 33a and B.B. 48b.

81. M.T. Sanh. 24, 6; Naḥlot 6, 12; Resp. Nos. 202, 302. For certain geonic rather than talmudic antecedents of these decisions of Maimonides, see the sources quoted by Freimann on Resp. No. 202; Lewin, *Otzar ha-Geonim*, IX, 30 ff. Characteristically, Maimuni is once more careful in the use of the term *hefḳer*. In the first of the above passages he uses it correctly, in reference to the judge's action to declare any man's property as *hefḳer;* in the second, where he deals merely with the transfer of an inheritance from one heir to another, he says but לאבד את ממונו; in the third he uses the term merely in quoting the talmudic formula; in the fourth he subscribes to a decision of others based upon a similar quotation. See above, n. 43. Such interference by Jewish judges with the inheritance of a Jew converted to Islam was by no means hampered by state legislation. On the contrary, it was a fairly accepted principle that no Muslim, Christian, or Jew should inherit the estate of a member of another creed. See Mez, *Renaissance des Islams*, pp. 30, 106; Juynboll, *Handbuch des islamischen Gesetzes*, p. 243; Bergsträsser-Schacht, *Grundzüge*, p. 45. See also Juster, *Les Juifs dans l'empire romain* (Paris, 1914), I, 259 ff.; II, 90 f.

82. M.T. De'ot 5, 12; Letter to Yefet b. Elijah in *Ḳobeṣ* II, 37d. See also M.T. Naḥlot 11, 6; Eppenstein in MbM, II, 36. R. Isaac's advice (B.M. 42a) was evidently prompted by his opposite predilection for cash, quite understandable in the light of the economic precariousness and the fiscal burdens of land tenure in both Palestine and Babylonia at the end of the third century. For the opinions of Arab economists, see Bryson's advice to a man to sell movable property quickly, but to delay the sale of land, "even though the profit may be slight in the disposal of merchandise and substantial in that of land," echoed, as elsewhere, almost verbatim by Maimonides' contemporary Abul-Fadl al-Dimashki. See Plessner, *Der Oikonomikos*, pp. 158–59 (Arabic and Hebrew; not in Latin); and Mahmassani, *Les Idées économiques*, p. 87 n. 82.

83. M.T. Mekhirah 29, 1, 6, 11–16, based on Giṭṭin 59a, B.B. 195–96, and so forth. For a practical illustration, see Resp. No. 220. Maimonides' opinion that legal obstacles be placed in the way of the squandering of any of a youth's inherited land, and not only his direct patrimony, is shared by Maimuni's teacher Ibn Megas, but contradicted by others. See Don Vidal's comments on 29, 13.

84. M.T. Sekhirut 12, 14, based on B.M. 92b–93a; Gezelah va-abedah

8, 14, based on the implication of B.Ḳ. 116b–117b (see also C.M. on B.Ḳ. X, 5). For partly divergent opinions of scholars, see Rosanes's comments thereon; and *Teshubot geonim ḳadmonim,* ed. by Cassel, No. 41. See also M.T. Sekhirut 2, 1; Genebah 2, 2; Zekhiyah u-mattanah 1, 14, and so forth.

85. M.T. Shemiṭṭah ve-yobel 11, 1–3; M.N. III, 39. See Munk's translation and notes, III, 301 f. See also S.M. Prohib. 227; Rosanes's comments on M.T.; and Abraham Maimuni's *High Ways,* ed. by Rosenblatt, I, 112. It goes without saying that Maimuni did not attach practical significance to the Jubilee year. S.M. Comm. 136 states that it is observed only "under the condition that every one of the tribes be settled in its place, i.e., in its portion of Palestine, and that they should not be mixed up with one another." This seems to indicate that he did not expect the revival of the Jubilee year even in the Messianic age. See also "Outlook" in my *HJH,* pp. 150 ff.

86. For the early land flight of the non-Muslim peasants, see Edgar Probster, "Privateigentum und Kollektivismus im mohammedanischen Liegenschaftsrecht, insbesondere des Maghrib," *Islamica,* IV (1931), 431; Ben Zion Dinaburg, *Israel ba-Golah* (Tel Aviv, 1926), I, 58. One may hear an echo of the contemporary situation in Saadia's disparagement of landed property because it gives its owner constant worries. The farmer is dependent not only on God's will with respect to the weather, and the like, but also on "the fiscal burdens of the kings and the imposts of their servants, so that the entire yield goes to them and the owners receive nothing at all." *Beliefs and Opinions,* X, 10. In the Egypt of Maimonides, particularly, the position of the peasantry, which had sunk into a state of villeinage, was anything but enviable. See Becker, *Islamstudien,* I, 209 ff.

87. C.M. on Shabbat I, 1; B.Ḳ. I, 5, etc.; M.T. 'Akum 7, 6; Shabbat 5, 18; 12, 3; Niẓḳei mamon 5, 3; Malveh ve-loveh 9, 4; etc.; M.N. *passim.* The Christian scholastics, too, speak of *civitas,* "the city." Thomas Aquinas thus renders the original Aristotelian *polis*—which helps us to understand some of his teachings. See Schreiber, *Die volkswirtschaftlichen Anschauungen,* p. 24.

88. M.N. III, 41; M.T. Shekhenim 14, 1, 5, based on B.M. 108b, in general following Alfasi's (and Rashi's) interpretation. Maimuni generally champions these social measures in favor of neighbors, scholars, and relatives, against the more "liberal" view taken, for instance, by the Tosafists on B.M. 108b s. v. שכיני. See above, n. 64. See also M.N. III, 46, concerning magic in urban centers. For the dominant Arab opinion, see, for example, Alfarabi's statement that "the villages exist only for the service of the city" (*Staatsleitung,* p. 51). Ibn Khaldun made the distinction between urban and nomadic civilizations one of the cornerstones of his sociological interpretation of history. See also Becker, *Islamstudien,* I, 55. Thomas Aquinas, following Aristotle, claims that, by nature, man

lives in cities (*civitates;* see above, n. 87); the rural economy is for him but the effect of misfortune and want. See Troeltsch, *Gesammelte Schriften,* I, 298, 318.

89. Pseudo-Chrysostomus *Opus imperfectum in Matteum,* hom. 38 (Migne, *Patrologia graeca,* LVI, 839 f.); Plato *Laws* 743 D, 918 DE; Augustine *De opere monachorum* 15 (Migne, *Patrologia latina,* XL, 561); Thomas Aquinas, *De regimine principum,* II, 3; Björkmann, in *Mitteilungen des Seminars für Oriental. Sprachen . . . Berlin,* XXXII, 85 f., 89; [O. Rescher], *Exzerpte und Uebersetzungen aus den Schriften des Philosophen und Dogmatikers Čahiz aus Basra (150–250 H.)* (Stuttgart, 1931), I, 186–88. See also Mez, *Renaissance des Islams,* pp. 442 ff.; Becker, *Islamstudien,* I, 186, 213 f.; *Encyclopaedia of Islam* s. v. Egypt; Mahmassani, *Les Idées économiques,* pp. 82, 184; Schreiber, *Die volkswirtschaftlichen Anschauungen,* pp. 4 ff.; Kraus, *Scholastik,* pp. 45 ff.; H. Coutzen, *Geschichte der volkswirtschaftlichen Literatur im Mittelalter* (2d ed., Berlin, 1872), p. 63; Schilling, *Augustinus,* pp. 249 ff. The occasional anticommercial statements of M. Ḳidd. IV, 14, and so forth, had been so thoroughly disposed of in the talmudic and geonic periods that Maimuni had no compunction about leaving that Mishnah without comment.

90. See M.N. III, 30, 37, 39, as against M.T. 'Edut 10, 4, and so forth. See also below.

91. M.N. III, 3, 35.

92. *Ibid.* III, 32; M.T. Sanh. 20, 4, 10; Malveh ve-loveh 1, 4; Melakhim 9, 1, 14; S.M. Comm. 177; Prohib. 277; C.M. on B.Ḳ. VIII, 2. See also above, n. 25. Personally, Maimuni would have liked to see class distinctions between scholars and illiterate persons carried into the courtroom to the extent of seating the former and merely perfunctorily inviting the latter, too, to be seated. But he had to admit that, since the close of the Talmud, all courts of justice indiscriminately invited all parties and even witnesses to be seated, "in order to obviate controversy." This is because, he adds with a sigh, "we have no power to carry the requirements of the Law into full effect." M.T. Sanh. 21, 3–5. See also C.M. on B.Ḳ. VIII, 6; and Tykocinski, *Die gaonäischen Verordnungen,* pp. 167 f.

93. M.T. Genebah 7, 1–3, 12; 8, 1, 20; Mekhirah 15, 1; S.M. Comm. 176; Prohib. 271, where mathematical surveying is contrasted with the "illusory proceedings possessing no truth whatsoever in which most people indulge." In many of these passages Maimuni goes beyond his talmudic sources, as when he gives a scientific turn to B.B. 89b or when, in M.T. Genebah 7, 12, he contrasts a statement of R. Levi (*ibid.* 88b) with one in Sifra Ḳedoshim 8, 12, giving both a personal, metaphysicosocial motivation. See Don Vidal's comment, and *HJH,* p. 358 f. n. 51. For כרכום, see j. Sanh. II, 5, 20c. The distinction between שופט ("judge") and שוטר ("police supervisor") corresponds to that of the Arab functionaries *ḳadi*

and *muḥtasib*. See also *Qur'an*, Sura 7, and Björkmann in *Mitteilungen des Seminars für Oriental. Sprachen . . . Berlin*, XXXII, 93.

94. M.N. III, 42. For the general rabbinic legislation concerning the just price, and numerous ancient and modern parallels, but with practically no reference to Jewish, Muslim, or Christian scholasticism, see P. Dickstein, "The Just Price and Misrepresentation" (Hebrew), *Ha-Mishpaṭ ha-'ibri*, I (1926), 15–55. The author makes it appear quite plausible that the rabbinic law had exercised considerable influence upon these phases of Western legislation ever since the days of Diocletian. (See, however, the opposing view of H. F. Jolowicz, in "The Origin of Laesio Enormis," *Juridical Review*, XLIX [1937], 53 ff.) Heinz Grünwald, in *Die Uebervorteilung im jüdischen Recht* (Göttingen, 1933), offers a careful analysis of the juridical aspects of the law of *ona'ah* (but cites little comparative material except in occasional brief remarks on Roman and canon law). Neither author pays any attention to that law's economic causes and effects, nor to its operation within the entire framework of Jewish economy.

95. For Aristotle's views, see the careful analysis by W. Gelesnoff in "Die ökonomische Gedankenwelt des Aristoteles," *Archiv für Sozialwissenschaft und Sozialpolitik*, L (1922–23), 1–33. The Christian scholastics are treated especially in Kraus, *Scholastik*, pp. 45 ff. where it is shown that they, too, were oscillating between objective and subjective criteria of value.

96. M.T. Mekhirah 13, 5–6; 14, 1, based upon Maimuni's interpretation of B.M. 51b, which agrees in the main with that of Alfasi, Ḥananel, and Tosafot, against that of Rashi. However, his explanation אלא מפרש ואומר לו כך וכך אני משתכר is hardly borne out by the text of the Talmud. See Don Vidal's and De Boton's comments. Maimonides' intention thus to withdraw numerous commercial transactions from the operation of the law of one-sixth appears undeniable. Rashi, on the other hand, frequently more typically "medieval," tries to shift the impact of the more liberalistic Baraita to the different sphere of a merchant and his agent, which would leave the main law intact.

97. M.T. Malveh ve-loveh 9, 4, 7, amplifying the discussion of B.M. 72b, notwithstanding the considerable difficulties of such interpretation. See Don Vidal's comments and *Haggahot Maimuniot, ad loc.* The contrary phenomenon of lower prices of grain in large cities, as the result of a larger supply, is mentioned by Ibn Khaldun, *Prolegomena*, ed. Paris, XVII/1, 239 ff. (Arabic); XX/1, 282 ff. (French). See also M.T. Mekhirah 21, 4; Ma'aser sheni ve-neṭa reba'i 4, 22, and so forth; and below.

98. M.T. Mekhirah 14, 1–2, 9, 11, based upon a peculiar interpretation of B.B. 8b, 90a, and so forth. On the one hand, Maimuni fails to mention the price fluctuations between the acquisition of the merchandise by the merchant and its sale, such as were stressed by Samuel b. Meir on B.B.

90a s. v. המשתכר. It may be assumed that Maimuni left this decision to the court at the time of its price fixing. On the other hand, by placing it in connection with a subsequent unrelated discussion, he reduces the requirement of one-sixth to life's utmost necessaries, namely wine, oil, and flour. Meat and bread, for instance, are no longer in this category. See also Don Vidal's comments and *Haggahot Maimuniot, ad loc.* On Albertus Magnus, see Kraus, *Scholastik,* p. 52; and, more generally, Wilhelm Endemann, *Studien in der romanisch-kanonistischen Wirtschafts- und Rechtslehre* (Berlin, 1883), II, 36 ff.

99. C.M. on B.M. IV, 10; M.T. Mekhirah 12, 3; 14, 12–18, based on B.M. 49b, 58b–59, slightly expanding here the talmudic homily on Lev. 25:17, rather than repeating that on Amos 7:7. See also S.M. Prohib. 250–51; M.T. Deʿot, 1, 6, and so forth. Maimuni admits, however, that verbal cheating is not subject to prosecution by earthly courts. It is needless to say that if the legitimate profit from the sale of the most important commodities amounts to no more than 16.66 percent, the assumption that people gladly renounce a slightly smaller difference is hardly realistic. But this merely adds emphasis to the "subjectivity" of the motivation and of the underlying general outlook.

100. M.T. Mekhirah, 13, 4–5; 15, 11. The latter is a Maimonidean extension of B.M. 51b. The extreme Franco-German opinion was expressed by Eliezer b. Joel ha-Levi, as quoted by Mordecai b. Hillel on B.M. 51b and by Isserles on H.M. 227, 7.

101. M.T. Mekhirah 12, 1–4; 15, 1–2, based on Maimuni's interpretation of B.M. 51ab, B.B. 83b–84a, Ḳidd. 42b, and so forth. For the computation of the actual range of possible misrepresentation, see Dickstein, in *Ha-Mishpaṭ ha-ʿibri,* I, 52 f. This list shows the paradoxical result that the sale of an object worth 210 denars for 175, 180, 245, or 252 denars would be valid and would merely require indemnification of the injured party in the amount of 35, 30, 35, or 42 denars, respectively; whereas its sale for 176–79 or 246–51 denars would completely nullify the transaction. Don Vidal and De Boton, who wish to explain Maimuni's opinion in a less casuistic way, must ultimately resort to textual emendation—a desperate expedient, indeed. This is but another illustration of Maimonides' main concern with the formal, judicial—rather than the economic —effects of these laws. The same formal, psychological slant may also be seen in his exclusion of a conspicuous discrepancy between price and value which far exceeds one-sixth of the latter. Like Naḥmanides and Ibn Adret, he believes that "if the discrepancy is very large, there is neither misrepresentation nor annulment; because of the large discrepancy, one is not likely to err in such matters. This is a basic principle, and remember it, since we may assume that he [the purchaser] consciously gave him [the seller] a present." C.M. on B.B. V, 2. Similarly, in M.T. Mekhirah 27, 3, Maimonides disregards the price difference as long as the term

employed is, according to local usage, clearly indicative of the range of the sale. That is why "he who sells a yoke, sells the cow" along with it. We have here once more the precedence of the formal, psychological factor over the economic. See also Don Vidal's and Rosanes's comments on 12, 4. In all discrepancies exceeding one-sixth, moreover, the injured party alone has the choice of either retaining the object, *without* compensation, or annulling the contract. Against the opinion of other jurists, Maimuni does not concede the right of annulment to the misrepresenting person, because he does not regard the contract as intrinsically void, but merely as one which may become void through the psychological decision of the injured party. He wholly disregards the economic reality that annulment might be either impossible, if the object has been disposed of in the meantime, or more injurious than the overcharge. Restoration of the difference can, nevertheless, be demanded only in the exceptional case that the discrepancy amounted to exactly one-sixth of the price, neither more nor less. On the other hand, following his teacher, Ibn Megas, but against the opinion of RABD and others, Maimuni demands payment of the difference, rather than annulment, in the case of a mistake in the weight or measure. This realistic view merely puts into bolder relief the sheer casuistry of most of his discussions on "misrepresentation."

102. C.M. on B.M. IV, 3; M.T. Mekhirah 12, 5–8, based on an interpretation of B.M. 50b which is not shared by all rabbis. See Don Vidal's comments.

103. C.M. on B.M. IV, 9; M.T. Mekhirah 13, 8, based on B.M. 56b– 57b. By emphasizing אפילו מכר שוה אלף בדינר ושוה דינר באלף, Maimuni, like Alfasi, rejects the recurrent attempts in the talmudic and geonic periods, as well as in some modern legislations, to limit the permissible overcharge (as opposed to the *laesio enormis*) on land to 100 percent. See Don Vidal's comments, Hilai Gaon's responsum in *Sha'arei ṣedek,* IV, 6, 24, 28, fol. 83ab; *Teshubot ha-geonim,* ed. by Harkavy, Nos. 77, 435; Lewin, *Otzar,* IX, 116. On the other hand, again following Alfasi, Maimuni includes in C.M. on B.M. IV, 9; M.T. Mekhirah 13, 13, all movable objects, such as cattle, jewels, swords, and scrolls of law, which some sages had tried to exempt from the operation of the law. See also Dickstein in *Ha-Mishpaṭ ha-'ibri,* I, 45 ff.

104. M.T. Mekhirah 13, 9–18, based upon various talmudic passages. In Resp. No. 144 Maimuni applies these regulations in favor of a court acting in behalf of an estate bequeathed to charity. He goes to the extreme of allowing the court to revoke the sale of a house simply because it had been "unnecessarily" (ללא הכרח) sold, and even to deduct the amount of rent collected in the meantime by the purchaser. In the case of mistakes involving the loss of one-sixth or more, Maimuni insists that sales contracted by guardians or courts should be annulled only in their favor, not in that of the purchasers—thus establishing another unusual disparity between the contracting parties. This disparity is justified by

the purely formalistic consideration that the purchaser's status as such remains the same, whether he buys directly from an adult owner or from the local representative of a minor. Maimonides refuses, however, to extend this privilege to a plenipotentiary acting in behalf of an adult; it would, he realizes, merely have the undesirable effect of encouraging land sales through substitutes. RABD, more consistently, objects to any disparity. With respect to the courts, Maimuni himself qualifies their right of retraction to cases where they did not regularly estimate the property and duly advertise it or where no such public announcement is legally required. M.T. Malveh ve-loveh 12, 11. Since in the case of slaves and deeds an announcement is not needed at all, and in that of land is required only in an emergency, this qualification has little practical value, except in land sales effected by the court for the satisfaction of creditors. Only in the case of movables the court seems to be placed on a par with ordinary sellers. In extending all these one-sided privileges, Maimuni, undoubtedly guided by the humanitarian motive of furthering the protection of minors, readily overlooks the economic effects of the ensuing legal uncertainty for the purchasers. If, in acquiring slaves, commercial papers, or many parcels of land belonging to minors, they could not rely upon the court's official estimate and advertisement, but had to accept the price as final for themselves though not for the court, and frequently not even for the guardian, one can hardly see any incentive for them to negotiate such dubious purchases. That, with price concessions beyond 14.3 percent being equally precarious, this discriminatory treatment might greatly curtail the demand and ultimately entail hardships for the orphans themselves, does not seem to trouble Maimonides or most of his fellow jurists. But he realizes that he is not voicing an accepted opinion when on both crucial points (M.T. 13, 9, 11) he inserts the personal נראה לי. The same remark precedes his statement in 13, 18, removing the contracting artisans from the class of workingmen and placing them on a par with merchants. For Maimonides' views on the general relationship between the contractor and the laborer, as well as for his equation here of free labor with temporary slavery, see below. See also ḤM. 109; 247, 30, 48–49, and the commentaries thereon.

105. M.T. Mekhirah 13, 2. See Don Vidal's comment, and Joseph ibn Megas, *Responsa*, No. 104.

106. M.T. 13, 1. For the difficulties of reconciling these views of Maimonides (as well as of his teacher, Ibn Megas) with the talmudic sources and the opposing interpretation of RABD, see Ibn Megas, *Responsa*, No. 107, and the ingenious, though not altogether satisfactory, explanations of Ibn Gaon, Don Vidal, and De Boton, *ad loc.* For Muslim law, see Bergsträsser-Schacht, *Grundzüge*, pp. 62 f.

107. M.T. Mekhirah 14, 1, 2, 4, based on a combination of passages in B.B. 90b–91a. See Don Vidal's and Karo's comments.

108. M.T. *ibid.*, 14, 3, based on B.B. 91a by evidently ascribing it to

Samuel, against Don Vidal's opinion. However, Karo is hardly right in regarding eggs as merely an example of food in general. Maimuni adheres strictly to the talmudic classification; eggs in ancient Palestine were certainly much less of a necessity than oil, which Karo evidently misunderstands. He also overlooks the fact that both meat and bread appear in 14, 9, outside the realm of life's necessaries. Under "bread" Maimuni very likely understands here the bread of barley, the unleavened bread, or that baked in oil, as against the white bread which he probably includes in the term סלת. The former types of bread, indeed, as well as many meats, are regarded by him as bad for digestion. See M.T. De'ot 4, 9–10. The denial of any profit to the second merchant undoubtedly has the same practical effect as prohibiting the first merchant to sell eggs for purposes of resale, as it appears in the more literal interpretation of Samuel b. Meir on B.B. 91a s. v. תגר.

109. M.T. Mekhirah 14, 5–8, based upon B.B., *loc. cit.* Contrast these moderate limitations with the sweeping condemnation of contemporary storing of wheat and barley as well as wine and oil, for speculative purposes, by Naṭronai Gaon in Ginzberg's *Geonica,* II, 117 f. (despite poor preservation, this is clearly the meaning of the responsum). There was no need of specifically legislating against the purchase of agricultural futures for speculative purposes, since no transaction was valid if it involved as yet nonexistent crops. See M.T. Mekhirah 22, 1, and n. 58 above. The acquisition of future crops in orchards, where this argument would not hold true, is prohibited, on the ground that it leads to usurious gains, in M.T. Malveh ve-loveh 8, 5.

110. M.T. Mekhirah 14, 10 (also Don Vidal's comments); Gezelah va-abedah 12, 12–15. Characteristically, there is no mention here of price fixing by such interested groups. Only the community at large is entitled to do this. Of course Maimuni also acknowledged governmental price regulation, but there was little opportunity for monopolistic practices of individuals or corporations. Both Muslim and Jewish law failed to develop legal facilities for large mercantile companies, so that we possess but occasional references to a sort of monopolistic control over a certain branch of the economy by a large and wealthy family. There also were, under medieval Islam, associations of artisans; but, notwithstanding their strong Persian and Byzantine antecedents, they possessed few of the extreme price-fixing powers of the medieval European guilds. For the medieval Jewish professional associations and their relation to early Muslim guilds, see my *JC,* I, 364 ff.; III, 94 ff.; and Mark Wischnitzer, *A History of Jewish Crafts and Guilds,* New York, 1965.

111. M.T. Mekhirah 18, 4, based on M.B.M. IV, 12.

112. M.T. De'ot 5, 13; Talmud torah 2, 7; Genebah 7, 11; Resp. Nos. 103, 386; S.M. Prohib. 246. Similarly, in M.T. Ma'aser 6, 15, he restates the law of M. Pe'ah I, 6 (see also C.M. thereon) and j. Pe'ah I, 6, 16c,

that a *kohen* or Levite who acquires produce from an Israelite after the ingathering must himself pay the tithe and the heave-offering to another priest and Levite. In restating this regulation, intended as a deterrent against sharp practices by unscrupulous Levites, who otherwise would buy up all such untithed crops, to the detriment of their slower or more conscientious colleagues, Maimuni denies its application to produce, the harvesting of which is not completed, because at that time the grains or fruits are not yet legally subjected to a tithe. Once more the criterion for the unfairness of the competition is the formalistic date of the obligation to pay tithes, rather than the economic power of the richer Levite and his ability to invest money in the early acquisition of grain.

113. M.T. Mekhirah 13, 14, 17; Sekhirut 7, 1–2; C.M. on B.M. VIII, 8, based on B.M. 56b, 102b. The first source is incidental, the second controversial.

114. M.T. Gezelah va-abedah 3, 9, based upon Alfasi's rather arbitrary distinction with reference to B.K. 21a. See the difficulties of this interpretation, as pointed out by the commentators, *ad loc.* This is the more remarkable, as Maimonides rejects the opinion of R. Judah in M.B.M. X, 3. See C.M. thereon and Resp. No. 361.

115. M.T. Sekhirut 6, 6–8, based upon Alfasi's interpretation of B.M. 101b and j. VIII, 8, 11d. It is notable that Maimuni here withdraws his decision in C.M. on B.M. VIII, 6, which had favored the professional bakers and dyers with the requirement of an extended notice of three years. See also Don Vidal's comments on M.T. and Bertinoro's exposition of that Mishnah. Some rabbis have also contended that the tenant need not give an equally long notice. See *Haggahot Maimuniot, ad loc.*

116. M.T. Sekhirut 6, 9–10, based upon B.M. 101b. The vital point of fluctuating prices is stated in the Talmud merely as an escape from an embarrassing question of R. Naḥman, whose opinion is usually accepted as authoritative. Maimuni is in general satisfied with the formal equality between landlord and tenant, even though the former has precedence in the case of unavoidable conflict. He does not mention even the tenant's safeguard against eviction on account of the landlord's sudden need, if the term of the lease has been stated and has not yet expired. See Don Vidal's comment.

117. See Resp., *passim.*

118. C.M. on B.M. IV, 5; Bekhorot VIII, 10, and so forth; M.T. Ḥobel u-mazzik 3, 10, based on Ḳidd. 11a; B.K. 36b; Shekalim 1, 3–6, based on M. Shekalim II, 4; j. *ibid.*, 46d; To'en ve-niṭ'an 3, 1–2, based on Shebuot 39b (see also Karo's and De Boton's comments, and C.M. on Shebuot VIII, 1), Bekhorot 50ab. In C.M. on Ḳidd. I, 2, he likewise identifies a denar with 24 issars and 192 peruṭahs by stating that a denar equals 96 grains; an issar, 4 grains; a peruṭah, ½ grain. He adds here the significant identification of a drachma, equal to 4 issars (and consequently also to one

ma'ah), with the Arabian dirhem. In C.M. on Ma'aser sheni II, 9, he pleads ignorance as to the value of an *asper*, although he believes that it is a *ma'ah* in Greek. In M.T. Ishshut 10, 8, he uses this computation for an estimate of the minimum amounts stated in M. Ket. I, 2, as indispensable in each marriage settlement. Allowing only one-eighth of the silver content for the 200 and 100 denars, respectively, he figures with an equivalent of 25 and 12½ pure silver *zuzim*, each containing 96 grains (=6 ma'ahs of 16 grains each). One can easily perceive the importance of this computation for contemporary practice. See Irving A. Agus, "The Development of the Money Clause in the Ashkenazic Ketubah," *JQR*, n.s. XXX (1939–40), 221–56. See also M.T. 'Erubin 1, 12, and Don Vidal's comments on both passages. In C.M. on Bekhorot VIII, 10, he cites in the name of his father a responsum of a Babylonian gaon, from which it appeared that 5 biblical shekels amounted to 33½ dirhems, or about 2 dirhems more than according to his own computation. But he explains this discrepancy by the likely difference between the former Babylonian and the contemporary Egyptian dirhem. The differences existing between the coins circulating in Egypt, Babylonia, and Persia are, indeed, emphasized in the interesting responsum in *Teshubot hageonim*, ed. by Harkavy, No. 386, discussing the views of Saadia, Sherira, and Hai on the conversion of talmudic coins into contemporary currency. For another, rather obscure, geonic responsum, see Ginzberg, *Genizah Studies*, II, 156 ff. See also Lewin, *Otzar*, IX (Part 2), 66 ff.; *Tosafot* on Bek. 49b. s. v. רבי אמי and רבי יוחנן. That he was generally very exact in computing the ancient weights and measures is stressed by Maimuni himself in C.M. on Menaḥot Introd.: "and I have scrutinized it as carefully as I possibly could," referring also to other passages in C.M. See also Immanuel Löw, *Die Flora der Juden*, IV (Vienna, 1934), 202, 204. For his generally successful attempts at exactness in calculating the data with respect to the related field of historical chronology, see "Outlook" in my *HJH*, pp. 150 ff. In Resp. Nos. 213, 217, 277, 285, 287, 289, 293, 379, the coin in circulation is called פרחים. From the last two responsa, particularly, it appears that Maimuni had in mind the silver dirhem rather than the usual gold coin (denar or "florin"). Perhaps the later Oriental translators or copyists of these responsa (all except No. 397 come from MS Oxford) confused this coin with one subsequently circulating in Turkey. For modern estimates of the value of the talmudic coins, see also Samuel Krauss, *Talmudische Archäologie* (Leipzig, 1911), II, 404 ff., 712 ff. The rabbinic theories on money and banking in general have been treated by Eliezer Lambert in "Les Changeurs et la monnaie en Palestine du Ier au IIIe siècle de l'ère chrétienne," *REJ*, LI (1906), 217–44, and by Simcha Ejges in *Das Geld im Talmud* (Giessen, 1930).

119. *Eth. Nic.* 5. 5. 1133ab (trans. by Ross); see also *Politics* 1. 8–11,

1256a–59a, and so forth. For a discussion of the complicated problems of the Aristotelian theory, see Giuseppe Majorana, "Le teorie della moneta e del valore in Aristotele," *Giornale degli economisti,* LXVI (1926), 49–61; Gelesnoff, in *Archiv für Sozialwissenschaft,* L, 1 ff.; and, in general, René Gonnard, *Histoire des doctrines monétaires dans ses rapports avec l'histoire de monnaies,* Vol. I (Paris, 1935). As usual, the Oriental theories, ancient as well as medieval, are passed over here in silence. For the Talmud, see Ejges, *Das Geld.* Bryson and the Arab theorists following him assigned the entire first section of their treatises to a discussion of money and its functions.

120. C.M. on B.M. IV, 2; M.T. Mekhirah 5, 6; 6, 1; 7, 1–2, based on the extensive discussions in B.M. 44–49. There seems to be a slight difference between C.M. and M.T. with regard to the invocation of divine wrath. C.M., more in accordance with the talmudic text, does not specify where the curse should be uttered, and leaves it to the injured party to pronounce it anywhere in the presence of the offender. M.T. demands its proclamation by the court in open session. The latter naturally offers better protection to the party withdrawing on account of newly arisen, unforeseen circumstances. See also C.M. on Ḳidd. I, 7; *Sha'arei ṣedeḳ,* IV, 2, 26–27, fols. 40b–41a; Lewin, *Otzar,* IX, 75 ff.; H.M. 204, 1, and the commentaries thereon. For a somewhat related opinion of the Roman jurist Javolenus—that the value of merchandise may be estimated in money but the value of money cannot be estimated in merchandise—see *Corpus juris civilis* L. 42, D. 46, 1. That this is at variance with the views expressed by modern economists such as Adam Smith, at least with respect to the value of precious metals, has rightly been pointed out by Gonnard, *Histoire des doctrines monétaires,* p. 53 n. 6. For some Arab views, see Plessner, *Der Oikonomikos,* pp. 63, 152 f., 277 f.

121. C.M. on B.M. IV, 1; Ma'aser sheni I, 2; M.T. Mekhirah 6, 2, 6, Ma'aser sheni 4, 9–10, based upon B.M., *ibid.,* and Alfasi's interpretation thereof; j. Ma'aser sheni I, 2, 52cd; Tosefta, *ibid.,* I, 6, 86. Maimuni's interpretation of אסימון evidently agrees with that of Rashi and not that of Jacob Tam. It is etymologically more correct. See also Ginzberg, *Geonica,* II, 2 ff. In M.T. Ma'aser sheni 4, 14, Maimuni adds that the redemption must be performed in local currency, regardless of its acceptability in the place where the money happens to be. For instance, a man redeeming the second tithe in Tiberias may use Tiberian currency which he possesses in Babylonia, but not Babylonian currency at his disposal in Tiberias. This statement is at variance not only with B.Ḳ. 97b but apparently also with j. Ma'aser sheni I, 2, 52d. It called forth a sharp objection from RABD and caused difficulties to the commentators. See Karo's comments, *ad loc.,* and Moses Margolis's lengthy discussion on j., *loc. cit.*

122. M.T. Mekhirah 6, 3–5, based on B.M., *ibid.* C.M. on B.M. IV, 1,

somewhat equivocally states that "there is no difference" between gold and silver coins, which may be but a pointed repudiation of Hai Gaon's statement that gold coins are always in the class of merchandise. See *Teshubot ha-geonim,* ed. by Harkavy, No. 78; Ginzberg, *Geonica,* II, 229, 231. In view of the prevalent gold standard in Hai's day (see the sources quoted by Fischel, *Jews in Mediaeval Islam,* pp. 3 f.), one may perhaps see in this decision of Hai without talmudic backing only the gaon's attempt to free commercial transactions from the shackles of the Talmud's "protective" laws for the purchaser. For the relation between gold and copper, see H.M. 204, 6, and the commentaries thereon. The Maimonidean view of the redemption of the second tithe in gold, which he permits because it facilitates transportation to Jerusalem, and in copper, which he tries to restrict to the minimum necessary for spending, are in consonance with this general sequence of (1) silver, (2) gold, (3) copper. See M.T. Ma'aser sheni 5, 13–14; C.M. on Ma'aser sheni II, 7–8. In contrast, for instance, to the explanation of Samson of Sens, he selects here from the discussion in B.M. 44b–45a only that which involves no denial of the character of currency to either gold or silver, and translates הפורט סלע by the exchange of silver into copper, rather than the opposite as was done by Rashi and others. See also Moses Margolis's comments on j. Ma'aser sheni II, 7–8, 53c.

123. M.T. Mekhirah 8, 6; 15, 1–2, following Ibn Megas' interpretation. See also RABD's objection and the comments of Ibn Gaon, Don Vidal, and Rosanes, *ad loc.*

124. C.M. on B.M. IV, 6; M.T. Mekhirah 12, 8–12. See Don Vidal's comments. For divergent opinions of other rabbis, see H.M. 227, 16–17, and the commentaries thereon. To illustrate the operation of the law of one-sixth, Maimuni here places the value of a gold denar as equal to 24 silver denars, although elsewhere he usually assumes a relation of 1:25. See, for instance, M.T. Mekhirah 6, 4. But this is merely another illustration of the variations in the value of other coins with respect to the basic silver currency. See also the next note. The regulation concerning books and jewelry, in 12, 11, is apparently influenced by Muslim economic thought. That it is not a mere denial of R. Judah's statement in M.B.M. IV, 9, as explained by some commentators, *ad loc.,* and on H.M. 227, 15, may be deduced from Maimuni's previous rejection of R. Judah's view as a matter of course in 12, 8; his failure to reject R. Judah b. Batira's opinion concerning the exemption of war implements in B.M. 58b; and his emphasis here upon the rarity of, and the need of expert knowledge in, these articles, which is nowhere discussed in the Talmud. On the contrary, he seems to agree with R. Judah that scrolls of law and jewels attract certain individuals more than others, but denies their having, for this reason, no market value at all. One is reminded of Bryson's advice to investors not to put their money into merchandise for which there is no

widespread demand, "such as precious stones which are needed only by kings and scholarly books which are only sought for by scholars." Plessner, *Der Oikonomikos*, p. 158. Curiously the Hebrew translator (p. 159) adds another example: "such as weapons which are needed only for a limited time." It is not likely that he had found it in any Arabic version (although it might have been part of the Greek original), since in the Arab world implements of war evidently were easily marketable. Perhaps it is not altogether venturesome to assume that the translator was influenced here by the above-mentioned juxtaposition of B.M. 58b. Bryson's advice, in any case, was reechoed by many Arab writers, among them Abul Fadl. See Mahmassani, *Les Idées économiques*, p. 87. In M.T. To'en ve-niṭ'an 8, 10; Resp. 336, Maimuni places great emphasis upon the legal presumption that books as a rule are neither lent nor leased to anybody else. This interpretation, shared by Rashi on Shebuot 46b s. v. מיתמי, is contradicted by Ḥananel and the Tosafists on Shebuot, *ibid.*, s. v. וספרא, B.B. 52b s. v., דברים, and so forth. Judah ibn Tibbon, in his "Ethical Will" (Abrahams, ed., *Hebrew Ethical Wills*, I, 82), merely advised his son to register every book lent out of the house and properly to enter its return. For the trade in both books and jewelry in Maimuni's time, see also the two interesting Resp. Nos. 287, 293.

125. See M.T. Ma'aser sheni 4, 18: ונותן המעות כמות שהשולחני פורט לא כמות שהוא מצרף, based on M. Ma'aser sheni IV, 2 (see also j., *ibid.*, 54d). In C.M. thereon we find, indeed, the illustration of 24 denars bid and 25 denars as the asking price. One may perhaps see in the figure 24, in M.T. (see n. 124), not only a convenient amount divisible by 6, but also the influence of the prevalent custom among bankers of charging one silver dirhem for the exchange of one gold denar. See Fischel, *Jews in Mediaeval Islam*, pp. 21 n. 2, 25 n. 2. It must be borne in mind, however, that the dirhem amounted to more than 4 percent of the gold denar. See also *Tosafot* in Bek. 50 s. v. דמוזבנא end, where the differential of one silver denar is suggested as the fee of the mintmaster to coin 24 silver denars out of 25 denars worth of bullion. If there really was such a disparity between a 24-silver-denar bid and a 25-denar asking price, the result, according to the above example, would have been that the banker could claim nullification of the transaction if he paid more than 28 denars; i.e., more than 3 denars above his purchasing price. The customer's claim would be valid only if he received less than 20 denars, which is more than 5 below the banker's purchasing price. See also *Teshubot ha-geonim*, ed. by Harkavy, No. 73; and n. 101 above.

126. M.T. Ma'aser sheni 4, 19, based on B.M. 52ab; To'en ve-niṭ'an 3, 8, based on Sheb. 39b–40a; Gezelah va-abedah 3, 4, based on B.Ḳ 96b–97a. See also C.M. on Ḳidd. I, 5; Ket. XIII, 4; B.Ḳ. IX, 2; and the next note.

127. M.T. Malveh ve-loveh 4, 12, based on B.Ḳ. 97ab. Although Mai-

muni repeats here the equivocal talmudic phrase המלוה את חברו על המטבע which has given rise to endless discussions, by later specifying נותן לו ממטבע שהלוה, he clearly refers to a loan of money. Rashi, *ibid.*, explains it as referring exclusively to an obligation arising from an ordinary commercial transaction with the price computed in money. There is no evidence that Maimuni would wish to exclude such a transaction from this regulation. More likely, like the Tosafists, *ibid.*, he had in mind both types of credit; so does, indeed, Don Vidal, *ad loc.*, explain the passage. The difficulty raised by the Tosafists as to why a robber and not a debtor should be entitled to return the original coins is obviated by Maimuni's aforementioned decision that the robber's privilege applies only to money still circulating in another locality. This decision seems to have been overlooked by the author of *Haggahot Maimuniot, ad loc.* The additional qualification here, ויש לו דרך לאותה מדינה, is not of far-reaching significance. In this generic term Maimuni seems to include the difficulties placed by different states in the way of transfer of depreciated coins from one country to another. This problem undoubtedly loomed large in the frequent commercial conflicts between ancient Rome and Persia and then again in medieval Europe. That is why the Talmud and, still more, Jacob b. Asher and his satellites in H.M. 74, 7, attach greater significance to this issue than do Maimuni and the other rabbis under Islam. For the views of the geonim, see the statement of Ṣemaḥ Gaon, quoted by Eliezer b. Joel ha-levi and published by V. Aptowitzer in his "Fragments from Geonic Literature" (Hebrew) in the *Samuel Krauss Jubilee Volume* (Jerusalem, 1937), p. 103, as well as the geonic responsa cited there. See also the sources cited by Freimann in his ed. of Resp. p. 218, line 25.

128. M.T. Malveh-ve-loveh 4, 11, based on B.Ḳ. 97b–98a. See also Ibn Megas, *Responsa,* No. 195. By adding here, and not in 4, 12, the significant qualification ופירש משקלו (apparently referring to both loan and marriage contracts), Maimuni considerably reduces the range of that talmudic discussion. It means that failure to specify the weight in the original contract makes a subsequent increase or decrease of the metallic content wholly irrelevant, since the nominal value of the currency is the same. Evidently this qualification likewise favors the lender, who is usually in a position to lay down the terms of the loan so as to include such specifications, if he fears devaluation of the currency, or to omit it, if an appreciation should be in sight. See Karo in Y.D. 165, repeating verbatim Maimuni's statement, but eliminating this qualification, which he may have interpreted as referring only to the *ketubah.* Maimuni evidently accepts the statement of R. Ṣemaḥ Gaon that a fall in the prices of commodities, without change in the metallic content, does not diminish the nominal indebtedness, even though the creditor is thereby allowed to receive more than he has lent in terms of goods. Such a "real" increment could not be regarded as usury, since the creditor

might legitimately contend that the money would also have appreciated in value, if it had remained in his possession. See Aptowitzer (above, n. 127). This is, indeed, the burden of R. Ashi's distinction in B.Ḳ 97b–98a. See also *Teshubot ha-geonim*, ed. by Harkavy, Nos. 424, 518. We have a further illustration in the characteristic Resp. of Maimonides (No. 230) concerning a loan in a currency withdrawn from circulation. In the locality of the inquirers, the main circulating medium consisted originally of a standardized paper bag of a certain foodstuff; it was then successively replaced by two different units of silver dirhems. Nevertheless, after the introduction of the last dirhem, the two older units did not disappear, but on the contrary appreciated in value. Maimuni, citing Ket. 110b, decided that the borrower should "pay back in the same currency, if it still exists, or in its equivalent in the new currency, if the former no longer exists." It goes without saying that the same principle operates to the creditor's disadvantage in the case of currency inflation and rise of commodity prices. The geonim and Maimuni failed to discuss this aspect, chiefly because it had no bearing upon any likely usurious gain for the lender. It may be of incidental interest to note that Maimuni, in repeating in M.T. Roṣeaḥ u-shemirat nafesh 12, 4, the prohibition of j. Terumot VIII, 4, 45d, against placing coins in one's mouth, amplifies the hygienic motivations as to the ensuing dangers to health. But he also reiterates verbatim the talmudic distinction between perspiration of the face, which is innocuous, and that of the rest of the human body, which is "mortal poison."

129. See, for instance, the definition given in C.M. on B.M. II, 5.

130. Resp. Nos. 269, 274, 277. See also S. Assaf's note, *ibid.*, p. 377. The fact of governmental approval becomes evident when one considers the refusal of the defendant in No. 277 to divulge the name of the person to whom he was supposed to have given the amount due the plaintiff, "because the matter depends on the state, and by making it public, we shall sustain a loss." The fact that two of these three cases had some connection with partnerships, if more than accidental, may perhaps sustain the conclusion that this was a large-scale business which required greater resources than could be marshaled by a single entrepreneur. For geonic sources referring to Jews trading in bullion, supplying it to mints, and grinding the gold and silver dust, see Mann in *JQR*, n.s. X, 331. See also Ginzberg, *Genizah Studies*, II, 49 ff.

131. M.T. Sekhirut 10, 5, largely based upon Alfasi's interpretation of B.Ḳ. 99b–100a. Other medieval rabbis wished to strengthen the banker's monopoly either by extending the responsibility of the nonexpert to cases where the inquirer failed to indicate his reliance upon the judgment of the appraiser, as suggested by the Tosafists (*ibid.*, s. v. אחוי; see also SeMaG, Comm. 89), or by wholly relieving even the paid expert from responsibility for errors, as taught by Ibn Adret, Luria, and so forth. See

Don Vidal's comment, *ad loc.;* H.M. 306, 6, and the commentaries thereon. For a different type of controversy between the money-changer and his client, arising from contradictory claims as to whether the other party had fulfilled his part of the contract, see C.M. on Shebu'ot VII, 6; M.T. Mekhirah 20, 9. Maimuni reduced the tannaitic regulation to the unlikely case that the money in dispute is placed on public ground; i.e., is in neither party's possession. He was forced to do so, because of his general theory that all the oaths mentioned in the Mishnah are of biblical origin. See C.M. on Shebu'ot VI, 1; M.T. Shebu'ot 11, 7, and so forth, and the commentaries on M.T. Mekhirah, *ad loc.* Very likely, however, Maimuni accepted Ḥananel's suggestion that the regulation of the Mishnah should also be applied to cases in which both the banker and the client held the coin in their hands. For an interesting record of a partnership in profits from money exchange, see *Teshubot ha-geonim,* ed. by Harkavy, No. 592 (Hebrew trans. and notes, pp. 340 f.).

132. See the numerous Muslim and Jewish sources quoted by Fischel, *Jews in Mediaeval Islam,* pp. 17 ff. While the author is right in stating that the *saftaja,* as used by Jews, is mentioned only in some Arabic responsa of the rabbis, one must bear in mind that the Jews could obtain somewhat similar effects by expanding their long-established legal instrument, the *harsha'ah.*

133. M.T. Sheluḥin ve-shutefin 1, 8, largely following Alfasi's interpretation of B.Ḳ. 104b. According to one version, Alfasi went even further and accepted the "contemporary practice among merchants" to the extent of regarding such a note as legal even if the recipient (or messenger) was not named therein. This would make it an altogether negotiable instrument issued to the bearer. Maimonides insists that the recipient's name be included in this type of draft. See Don Vidal's comments; *Tosafot* on B.Ḳ. 104b s. v. ורבי; and numerous sources quoted in the commentaries on H.M. 121, 4–5. It is the difficulty of forcing B to pay, and the risk involved for him in the intervening decease of A, that made the rabbis turn to the power of attorney for remedy. See H.M. 122, 1. This is also the meaning of the conservative distinction in M.T., *ibid.,* 3, 5. For drafts on a local banker to pay certain regular wages to the client's employees, see below.

134. M.T. Sheluḥin ve-shutefin 3, 1–2, 5; Resp. Nos. 300 and 301, based on B.Ḳ. 70a; Shebu'ot 33b, and so forth. The contemporary formulas for the writ of authorization quoted in M.T. are very likely similar to those contained in the *Sefer ha-harsha'ot* of Samuel b. Ḥofni, cited by the inquirers of No. 300. See also *Teshubot ha-geonim,* ed. by Harkavy, No. 467 (Hebrew trans., p. 327). For the general problem of substitution in court, see the notes to Resp. *loc. cit.,* and S. Assaf, *Batei ha-din ve-sidreihem* (The Courts and Their Organization after the Conclusion of the Talmud [Jerusalem, 1924]), pp. 95 f.

135. M.T., *ibid.*, 3, 7–8. This section has given rise to many opposing interpretations. For our purposes the most crucial question is whether Maimonides accepted the innovation of the geonim concerning the assignment of loans. It is evidently to be answered in the affirmative. See Karo's, De Boton's, and Rosanes's comments. The latter correctly cites in confirmation M.T. Malveh ve-loveh 20, 7. Maimonides still tries to salvage from the sweeping geonic reversal of talmudic law at least the invalidation, by speedy denial, of the assignment of debts orally contracted, or of deposits. He thereby disregards the well-established custom, reported by Ḥananel, of ruling out the debtor's denial from the consideration of the validity of a *harsha'ah*. While this eleventh-century Kairuwan scholar is still puzzled about the reason for such a deviation from a clear talmudic statement, Jacob Tam supplies one through a long casuistic discussion. See *Tosafot* on B.Ḳ. 70a. s. v. אמטלטלין and on Shebu'ot 336 s. v. היכא. Even Maimonides' sweeping condemnation of this practice on moral grounds, which, although quoted from Shebu'ot 31a, evoked a sharp attack by RABD (see also M.T. De'ot 5, 13), was toned down in Resp. Nos. 300–1, where he appears to be in agreement with his opponent (and probably also with *Tosafot* on Sheb., *ibid.*, s. v., זו). His qualification that such an assignment is justifiable in the case of debtors or depositories living in other cities was all that was needed to make the remittance of funds truly operative. All these Maimonidean scruples were increasingly swept away by the commercial needs of the people, and four centuries later both Karo and Isserles mentioned assignment of all claims, whatever their provenience and whether or not they were denied, as a prevalent usage in their time. See H.M. 123, 1. See also Ginzberg, *Geonica*, II, 290 f.; Schwarz in MbM, I, 382 ff.; B. Z. Halper's notes to his ed. of Resp. No. 300, in *JQR*, n.s. VI (1915–16), 225 ff.; H. Tykocinski, *Die gaonäischen Verordnungen*, pp. 117 ff. One must also bear in mind that there was another, somewhat more clumsy method of assigning money, which consisted in endorsing, in the presence of two witnesses, the writ of indebtedness itself in favor of a third person and handing it to the beneficiary. Even the *saftaja* in the technical sense apparently was never forbidden. The geonic responsum which deals with it, although unable to offer any support from Jewish law, approves it, because it had become a widespread mercantile usage. See *Teshubot ha-geonim*, ed. by Harkavy, No. 423 (Hebrew trans., p. 316). One wonders whether this timid recognition did not pave the way for those sweeping modifications in the talmudic laws governing "authorization" which, apparently unknown to the early geonim, are here willy-nilly accepted by Maimuni. See *ibid.*, Nos. 181, 200, 279 (the authorization may also be given to a Gentile), 467; Schwarz, in MbM, I, 384 n. 1. Unfortunately, the paucity of the available source material offers but little substantiation either for or against such a hypothesis. For the Muslim *saftaja* and the related *hawala*, as well

as for the juristic objections to them, see Bergsträsser-Schacht, *Grundzüge*, pp. 66 f. See also Björkmann in *Mitteilungen des Seminars für Oriental. Sprachen . . . Berlin*, XXXII, pp. 89 f.

136. Fischel (*Jews in Mediaeval Islam*, pp. 14 ff.) has shown that the important position of the banker in the field of deposits under Islam was due largely to the possibility thus given of withdrawing possessions from the immediate reach of rapacious government officials. That is why bankers not only were preferred to sanctuaries but also were able to obtain funds without paying for them, the usual risks of business failure notwithstanding. The frequency of deposits among Jews seems also to be attested by the fact that Saadia Gaon felt prompted to write a special monograph on the laws governing them. See *Teshubot ha-geonim*, ed. Harkavy, No. 454 (Hebrew trans. and notes, p. 322). Even assuming that this קצור הפקדון was but an excerpt from Saadia's more comprehensive monograph *On Pledges* (see Henry Malter, *Saadia Gaon: His Life and Works* [Philadelphia, 1921], pp. 163, 345), the evident interest of jurists in such a brief compilation can be explained only as the reflection of an existing social need. See also *supra*, Essay 5 nn. 54–56.

137. C.M. on B.M. III, 11; M.T. She'elah u-piḳḳadon 7, 6–7, largely based on Alfasi's interpretation of B.M. 43a; Malveh ve-loveh 5, 5, based on Tos. B.M. V, 19; b. 61b. Like Alfasi, Maimuni reads rather than interprets בנכרי as ביד נכרי, making the Gentile the immediate creditor. See Rosanes's comment. For the actual reading, see Rabbinowicz's *Diḳdukei Soferim*, XIII, 175 n. 10.

138. S.M. Prohib. 235–37; M.T. Malveh ve-loveh 4, 2, and 7, based on B.M. 61b, 71a, 75b. See also C.M. on B.M. V, 13. For Maimuni's reading of B.M. 75b, referring to two rather than three prohibitions of borrowing money on interest, see Alfasi's and Asheri's version, cited in the note to Don Vidal's comment. Rabbinowicz, *Diḳduḳei*, XIII, 210, mentions no variants. See David ibn abi Zimra's *Responsa*, II, 313. The reason, according to Maimuni, why only a private transaction without witnesses implies a denial of the Exodus is clearly based upon the nexus between such secret moneylending and negation of the individual divine Providence manifested in the Exodus. See Rosanes's comments, *ad loc.;* "Outlook," in my *HJH*, p. 122; and n. 93 above.

139. M.T., *ibid.*, 4, 5, based on B.Ḳ 94b, B.M. 61a; 'Edut 12, 5, based on Sanh. 25b. See also C.M. on Sanh. III, 3. In the first passage Maimuni limits the refusal to accept restoration to usury paid in money and other replaceable articles, but permits the return of a specified object still in the creditor's possession. He seems, on the other hand, to include all usurious moneylenders and robbers, however casual, in the same category —many other rabbis applied the category only to professional usurers and robbers—and hence the restoration presupposed in 'Edut 12, 5, evidently refers only to specified objects, to money accepted by the debtor in

defiance of the rabbis' displeasure, or else to usurious income spent on charity. For the divergent interpretations of the other rabbis, see *Tosafot* on B.Ḳ. 94b s. v. ביט, which also refer to Jacob Tam's opinion that the talmudic refusal to accept restoration was but an emergency measure enacted by R. Judah the Patriarch and applicable only to his generation. See also H.M. 34, 29; 366, 1.

140. C.M. on Sanh. III, 3; Shebu'ot VII, 4; M.T. 'Edut 10, 4; Ṭo'en ve-niṭ'an 2, 2, 4 based on Sanh. 24b–25a; Sheb. 47a. For Maimuni's version (following that of Ibn Megas and some MSS) of the controversy between R. Meir and R. Jose in M. Sheb. VII, 4, see Rabbinowicz, *Diḳ-duḳei*, X (Part 3), 100 n. 9. This Maimonidean interpretation of the controversy, in which he follows Alfasi against Hai Gaon and others, goes so far in punishing the usurer as to make him an easy target for another usurer's lawsuit. It thereby disregards the encouragement it lends to the latter, to counteract which the other rabbis demanded a division of the claim into two halves.

141. M.T. Malveh ve-loveh 1, 1–3; Matenot 'aniyim 10, 7; De'ot 5, 3; S.M. Comm. 197; Prohib. 234, quoting Mekhilta 22, 24, ed. by Hoffmann, p. 151; Shab. 63a; B.M. 61a, 75b, etc.; M.N. III, 39.

142. C.M. on B.M. V, 1; M.T. Malveh ve-loveh 4, 1, 6; 5, 12–13, 15; 6, 1, supported by numerous illustrations mostly based on B.M., Chap. V. The difference between M.T. 4, 1, and C.M. may perhaps be explained by the difficulties of interpreting B.M. 62b, such as pointed out by De Boton, *ad loc.*, which induced Maimuni in C.M. to declare *tarbit* to be usury prohibited by the rabbis only. On second thought, he placed all such rabbinical prohibitions in the class of "shades of usury," which, having different legal effects, could not be identified with the definitive biblical prohibition of *tarbit* or the later Hebrew equivalent, *marbit*. For the original meaning of these two terms, see the biblical dictionaries and Meyer Lambert's note in *REJ*, XXXVI (1898), 294. The expression ויוצאה בדיינין in the Maimonidean decision, in favor of R. Eleazar's view as against that of R. Joḥanan in B.M. 61b, evidently means the forcible collection by the court of any amount paid in excess of the original loan. Several of Maimonides' Spanish successors limited the court's intervention to the application of personal sanctions to force the recalcitrant creditor to return the usurious gain, but eliminated direct seizure of his property. See Y.D. 161, 5. It is notable, on the other hand, that Maimonides does not seem to approve of the sanction proposed by Sar Shalom Gaon for lending on a "shade of usury." The gaon demanded that such a creditor be forewarned not to negotiate a similar loan for a second time, under the penalty of a fine and the forcible return of the unlawful profit. See *Sha'arei ṣedeḳ*, IV, 2, 3, fol. 34a.

143. C.M. on B.M. V, 10; M.T. Malveh ve-loveh 10, 3–4, based on B.M. 75a. See Y.D. 173, 6, with reference to B.M. 46a. Thomas Aquinas

deals with *usura* principally in some connection with *mutuum*. But we find a close resemblance to the rabbinic doctrine in the definition given in a medieval manual and quoted by Du Cange in his *Glossarium*, s. v. *usurarii* (Paris, 1846; VI, 892): "Et note quod usura non solum se extendit ad pecuniam mutuandam, sed ad quicquid ultra sortem accipitur, sive honoris, vel gagerii, vel comestione equorum, vel de illicitis venditionibus, et hujus modi." See, in general, the two keen analyses of Jewish and Muslim law by Emil Cohn in his "Der Wucher im Talmud, seine Theorien und ihre Entwicklung," *Zeitschrift für vergleich. Rechtswissenschaft*, XVIII (1905), 37–72; and "Der Wucher im Qoran, Chadith und Fiqh," *Berliner juristische Beiträge*, Part 2 (1902); as well as Robert Salomon's monograph *Le Prêt à intérêt en la législation juive* (Paris, 1932). These investigations are concerned only with the juridical cohesiveness of the theoretical prohibition, and pay no attention to its effects upon economic practice.

144. M.T. Malveh ve-loveh 4, 1.

145. *Ibid.*, 5, 15, based on B.M. 69b. Maimonides emphasizes the fact that by merely calling the transaction a "lease," the responsibility of the borrower is not diminished in the case of money, which, being usually intended for spending, makes the recipient responsible also for forcible losses. See n. 137 above, and Rashi on B.M. 96b s. v. זוז. Nevertheless, this simple formal expedient eliminates for the creditor the danger of subsequent reclamation of the fee paid by the debtor. If the same money is physically returned, moreover, Maimuni would evidently accept the term "lease" at its face value and regard the fee as permissible. See Don Vidal's comments and *Haggahot Maimuniot, ad loc.*, with reference to Tos. B.M. IV, 2. It is worthy of mention that, in contrast to the other Church Fathers, Augustine objects to usury on grounds of humanity, but not because of the "sterility" of money. See Schilling, *Augustinus*, pp. 246 f.

146. M.T. Malveh ve-loveh 4, 4, 14; Naḥlot 11, 1; Resp. No. 113, partly based on B.M. 62a, 70a. Maimuni accepts here the talmudic modifications of Mar Samuel's sweeping statement that "one may lend on interest money belonging to orphans." By מותר ליתן he undoubtedly wishes to express that a court or its representative may do so. He disregards, however, the numerous detailed difficulties arising from the comparison of B.M. 62a with B.Ḳ. 94b, as pointed out by *Tosafot* on the latter passage s. v. אי. Neither does he amplify the complicated minutiae of this important exception in favor of orphans, for which see the material assembled in Rosanes's comments, *ad loc.* In Resp. No. 112 he merely restates his opinion that the court may try to collect for orphans various kinds of income ordinarily prohibited by the rabbis, against the view of those medieval jurists who wished to open to minors only the otherwise prohibited form of partnership, with a full share in profits and but slight

responsibility for losses. There is no evidence, however, that he also placed communal funds in the same privileged position, a view expounded by many medieval rabbis. See *Or Zaru'a*, I, 30; Menaḥem Recanati, *Piskei Halakhot*, No. 65; Y.D. 160, 17, and the commentaries thereon.

147. M.T. Malveh ve-loveh 4, 9, based on B.M. 75a. While Maimuni excludes here only advance arrangements for such extra payments, other rabbis, ever since Amram Gaon, proposed more far-reaching qualifications. Many applied the fiction of a gift only if the creditor's profit was negligible; others, ready to concede fully 20 percent of the original amount, limited it to loans consisting of articles of food. See Don Vidal's comments; *Tosafot* on B.M. 75a s. v. מתנה; Y.D., *loc. cit.* Maimuni's desire to favor the scholarly creditor appears undeniable.

148. M.T., *ibid.*, 4, 13. Asher b. Yeḥiel on B.M. 61a states the source for this difference of opinion, finally agreeing with Maimonides. See also *Haggahot Maimuniot* and De Boton's comments, *ad loc.*; Y.D. 160, 5. See also Thomas Aquinas, *Summa theologiae*, II, 2, 78, 2: "Si vero accipiat aliquid hujus modi [money or money's worth] non quasi exigens, nec quasi ex aliqua obligatione tacita vel expressa, sed sicut gratuitum donum, non peccat."

149. M.T., *ibid.*, 5, 15; 6, 7–8; 8, 1–2, based on B.M. 62b, 67b–68a. See nn. 59, 109 above. For the operation of the *contractus mohatrae* in Muslim law, see Joseph Kohler's remarks in Cohn's *Der Wucher im Qoran*, pp. 32 ff.; Björkmann, *Mitteilungen des Seminars für Oriental. Sprachen . . . Berlin*, XXXII, 85. According to Don Vidal's interpretation of M.T. 8, 1–2, such evasion was greatly facilitated if the object so sold and resold was a parcel of land, since land is not subject to the limitations of the market value. Don Vidal's concluding sentence (8, 1) well characterizes his intention: "Every contract under the form of sale is permissible so long as it does not look like usury." In both illustrations of "the evasion of usury" in 5, 15, Maimuni runs counter to the opinion of many other rabbis. Naḥmanides regards all profits through the loan of merchandise as actually noncollectible, while the leasing back of the field to the debtor is declared by Rashi (on B.M. 68a s. v. ולאו) to be straight usury. Nevertheless, the main trend in medieval Jewish law was in the direction of further liberalization of the law, as evidenced by the sources assembled in the commentaries on Y.D. 163, 3; 164, 1; 172, 1. That Maimuni is right in saying (6, 8) that only some of the geonim opposed his view is evidenced by those quoted in Isaac b. Abba Mari's *Sefer ha-'Ittur* under letter 'פ No. 1, who were, in part, even more liberal. Indeed, we learn therefrom that there existed an early and widely prevalent practice of allowing the creditor to collect all revenue from the field after granting a nominal discount to the debtor. Only Jacob Gaon demanded the fixing of the discount at 25 percent or more of the loan. See also Schwarz in MbM, II, 389 f. In M.T. 7, 1–5, Maimuni is ready to respect even

farther-reaching infractions of the prohibition, if sanctioned by local usage. For the merchant's profit, see above, n. 97; and below, n. 154; and Resp. No. 118, where the sale of merchandise on credit with 25 percent profit on the merchant's purchasing price is declared as "the usual run of business without which the source of livelihood would be destroyed."

150. M.T., *ibid.*, 5, 14, based upon Tos. B.M. V, 16, 382; b. 69b. There is no indication that, like Naḥmanides, Maimuni legalized the sale of deeds with a discount only if the seller declined all responsibility. See Don Vidal's comment. On the contrary, it appears that in accordance with M.T. Mekhirah 6, 11–12; Ḥobel u-mazziḳ 7, 9, he wished to retain the precariousness of such a sale by maintaining the right of the seller to renounce his claim. Under these circumstances, the seller, after having properly endorsed the deed, became responsible for the full face value of the deed, and not merely for the amount he had received. Neither do we find in Maimuni's formulation any of the restrictions upon the payment of a fee to the intermediary, or by the latter to the lender, such as were postulated by other medieval rabbis. On the other hand, he does not countenance the flagrant evasion of the law through allowing a "messenger" to contract a loan and pay interest for it, since such interest does not come directly from the borrower. This subterfuge, suggested by Rashi, found powerful support among the European rabbis confronted with the overwhelming reality of medieval Jewish moneylending. See *Haggahot Maimuniot*, Don Vidal's and Rosanes's comments, *ad loc.;* Y.D. 160, 13; and the commentaries. See also n. 59 above.

151. For the complicated rabbinic laws of *'iska*, see E. E. Hildesheimer, "Das Recht der 'iska," *Jahrbuch der jüdisch-literarischen Gesellschaft in Frankfurt*, XX (1929), 337–77; reprinted in the same author's *Das jüdische Gesellschaftsrecht* (Leipzig, 1930), pp. 87 ff. The *contractus trinus*, evidently discussed in Y.D. 177, 6, is briefly compared with the Jewish שטר עסקא by Moses Hoffmann in *Festschrift . . . David Hoffmann* (Berlin, 1914), pp. 383–86.

152. Resp. Nos. 267, 275, and 276 reflect a rather widespread use among Jews of the Muslim type of *commenda*, in which all the risks of the enterprise rested with the capitalist, in return for which the manager received but one-third of the profit. See also the sources quoted by Hildesheimer (above, n. 151), pp. 366 n. 157, 369 n. 165 (pp. 122, 124); and Bergsträsser-Schacht, *Grundzüge*, pp. 75 f.

153. C.M. on B.M. V, 5; B.B. X, 4; M.T. Sheluḥin ve-shutefin 6–7; Malveh ve-loveh 5, 8–9; Resp. Nos. 214, 265–76, 294, and so forth. It may be noted that the presumptive share of the active partner, where there is no special agreement, is given, in M.T. Sheluḥin 6, 3–4, as two-thirds in profit and one-third in losses. Maimuni expressly rejects as erroneous the opinion that the share may be lowered to one-half of the profits. In C.M. and Resp. No. 268 Maimuni himself voices just that

opinion, which, like that of RABD concerning the two-thirds share in profits and one-half in losses, seems more in agreement with the talmudic source in B.M. 68b. The proportion of one-half and one-third is also the prevalent doctrine of the geonim. See Hildesheimer (cited above, n. 151), p. 348 n. 65 (p. 101). The geonic responsa offer, however, a number of illustrations of different special agreements. For example, one silent partner, contributing 60 percent of the capital, agreed to share in the profits only to the extent of seven-twelfths. See *Sha'arei ṣedeḳ,* IV, 8, fol. 93a ff. (especially Nos. 6 and 12); and other sources quoted by Mann in *JQR,* n.s. X, 332 f. Maimonides' interpretation of Abbaye's statement in B.M. 68ab concerning the compensation כפועל בטל של אותה מלאכה דבטל ממנה, offering a sort of *lucrum cessans* to the active partner for work which he otherwise would normally have done, is contradicted by Maimuni's distinguished predecessors Hai Gaon, Ḥananel, Alfasi, and Rashi, who offer different explanations. See the commentaries on M.T. 6, 2; *Tosafot* on B.M. 68a s. v. ונותן; and Hildesheimer, pp. 345 f. (p. 98). See also below, n. 189. While Maimuni in 6, 1, emphasizes the fact that the criterion for 'iska is the exclusive work done by one partner, with or without capital investment on his own part, Alfasi and others insist that the contribution of even the slightest amount by the active associate converts the arrangement into a straight partnership not subjected to the limitations of the 'iska contract. See, however, C.M. on B.B. X, 4, where Maimuni apparently accepts Alfasi's view. Such discrepancies between C.M. and M.T. are not altogether unusual, in particular when Maimuni decides, after more mature consideration, to repudiate the opinion of a revered predecessor. See his own remarks in another instance, Resp. No. 240, and the literature cited there by the editor. To what extent Maimuni may also have been influenced, in the two instances cited here, by the growing trend toward restrictive state capitalism in Egypt, to abandon views held by himself and his predecessors under the somewhat more "liberalistic" regimes of the earlier caliphates cannot be fully ascertained on the basis of the available evidence. See also Y.D. 177, 3, and the commentaries thereon.

154. All medieval rabbis agreed with the talmudic principle that half of the money invested in 'iska should be treated as a gratuitous loan and the other half as a deposit from which the depositor might draw an income. But opinions differed on the extent of the "depository's" responsibility. Maimuni believed that he was responsible only for willful mismanagement, since he was receiving no direct remuneration for safeguarding the deposit. RABD and others, viewing his income more realistically, made him responsible for robbery and theft, if not for enforced losses. The trend to facilitate profitable employment of capital became ever stronger, and the latter opinion prevailed. See Y.D. 177, 2, 5. M.T. Malveh ve-loveh 5, 17, affirming the right of any third person to pay a

coreligionist's defaulted head tax and place him in bondage, although
his work may yield the creditor a higher income than the original outlay,
is but an antiquarian reminiscence of conditions prevailing in Sassanian
Persia, as reflected in B.M. 73b. It illustrates, nevertheless, the extent to
which Maimuni is ready to respect the law of the kingdom, even in matters of usury. One must bear in mind, however, that he had little choice,
since the talmudic source is altogether unequivocal. The variant eliminating the word טפי, and thereby all excess income, is suggested by *Tosafot,*
ibid. s. v. משתעבדי, but apparently has no support in talmudic manuscripts. In Resp. No. 114, on the other hand, Maimuni is forced to deal
with a contemporary problem arising from the equally drastic penalties
imposed by the Muslim administration upon taxpayers in arrears. The
dread of these penalties in the Great Caliphate had led many subjects to
incur loans at the enormous interest rate of 1,000 percent per annum. See
Mez, *Renaissance des Islams,* p. 454 (*Islamic Culture,* VII, 322). A similar case was brought to Maimonides' attention when a Jew unable to
secure an ordinary loan for the payment of his overdue head tax had to
"purchase" on credit three garments worth thirty-nine dirhem for sixty
dirhem. Maimonides simply decided that the "purchaser" should pay only
the equivalent of the market price of the garments and not the face value
of the deed. Of course, as elsewhere, he did not object to the usual mercantile profit already included in the normal market price. See n. 149
above.

155. M.T. Malveh ve-loveh 1, 4; 4, 6; 5, 14; Yesodei ha-torah 5, 11.
For the underlying reasons, as well as the various qualifications, of 4, 6,
see *Tosafot* on B.M. 72a s. v. קונסין, and Y.D. 161, 11–12.

156. C.M. on B.Ḳ. X, 2; Gittin V, 1; M.T. Ishshut 16, 7; 17, 6; 19,
17–18; Nizḳei mamon 8, 10–12; Gezelah va-abedah 5, 6; Malveh ve-
loveh 11, 11; 19, 1. The innovation of the geonim was introduced about
787 because of the structural changes in Jewish landownership, and was
solemnly proclaimed to the world at large. See Sherira Gaon's *Iggeret,*
ed. by Lewin (Haifa, 1921), pp. 105, 108; *'Ittur,* fol. 77d. While an early
gaon tried to limit the new law to countries in which the Jews had few
landholdings, Amram Gaon, and after him Sherira Gaon and Maimonides,
emphasized the fact that it was applied in the courts throughout the
world. See also Schwarz, in MbM, I, 345 f., 372 ff., 391 f.; Mann in
JQR, n.s. X, 310; and Tykocinski, *Die gaonäischen Verordnungen,* pp.
34 ff.

157. C.M. on Shebiit X, 3; S.M. Comm. 141; M.T. Shemiṭṭah ve-yobel
9, 2–3, 15–18, 24; Resp. Nos. 233–41, based primarily on Giṭṭin 36–37.
M.T., *ibid.,* 9, 14: debts contracted on the security of land or pawn are
not canceled by the Sabbatical year; and 9, 27: scholars need not go to
court, but may simply declare in the presence of their pupils their intention that their claims should not be canceled. No wonder that with so

much hedging the entire institution of debt cancellation gradually disappeared, causing no little embarrassment to the later medieval rabbis. See H.M. 67, 1, and the commentaries thereon. For Maimuni's computation of the Sabbatical cycles, brought down to his own day, see "Outlook" in my *HJH*, pp. 150 ff. See also n. 85 above.

158. M.T. Sanh. 6, 7–9, based on Maimuni's interpretation of Sanh. 23a, 31b, and the contemporary "daily" practice in Spain. Other rabbis interpreted the respective passages differently, Jacob Tam, for instance, extending the same privilege to the defendant. This procedural chicanery had to be altogether abandoned in the subsequent generations because of the growing independence of the local community, as opposed to the more centralized regional bodies such as the *negidut* of Muslim Egypt. See H.M. 14, 1–2, and the commentaries thereon.

159. M.T. 'Edut 3, 1, 4, based upon various talmudic passages (see Karo's and De Boton's comments, *ad loc.*); C.M. on Ket. IX, 6; M.T. Malveh ve-loveh 13, 1–2, based on Ket. 88a. Maimonides does not specify the time limit of במהרה, leaving it to the judge's discretion to choose a reasonable period. Alfasi seems to have demanded that, if the court's messenger could reach the defendant and report back within thirty days, the hearing should be postponed. See Karo's and De Boton's comments, *ad loc.*, and the sources quoted by the commentaries on H.M. 106, 1. Maimuni, however, apparently refuses to encumber this protective measure in favor of the creditor by any hard and fast rule. In Resp. No. 311 he does not inquire at all into the defendant's place of residence, but favors immediate action.

160. M.T. Malveh ve-loveh 14, 3; Resp. No. 117. See also RABD and commentaries, *ad loc.*, and Schwarz, in MbM, I, pp. 393 ff. Maimonides' decision was accepted by the majority of the later rabbis. See H.M. 82, 10. M.T., *ibid.*, 3, 7, amplifying the statement in B.M. 75b.

161. M.T., *ibid.*, 27, 1; Resp. 294–98. See also the note to Resp. No. 155, quoting the text of a regulation enacted by a college of Egyptian rabbis, headed by Maimonides, that Jewish parties should refrain from repairing to Gentile courts. This, of course, was an old law, which apparently had to be vigorously restated in the face of frequent violations by Maimuni's contemporaries in Egypt. See also Ginzberg, *Genizah Studies*, II, 118, 127 f.; and the excerpt from Hai Gaon's *Book of Judges' Morality*, ed. by S. Assaf, *Tarbiz*, VII (1935–36), 217 f.

162. M.T., *ibid.*, 2, 1–4; Resp. Nos. 204, 228, 312. According to Moses of Coucy's SeMaG, Comm. 93, and *Haggahot Maimuniot, ad loc.*, the originators of this oath were the Saboraim. See Tykocinski, *Die gaonäischen Verordnungen*, pp. 67 ff. That this innovation was widely accepted by the Jewish communities is emphasized by Maimuni: וכזה דין ישראל בכל מקומותן. Maimuni amplifies it in many significant details: (1) the oath is to include the promise of payment from future earnings; (2) the burden of proof lies

with the debtor that money found with him thereafter does not belong to him (Maimuni quotes his "teachers'" opinion to this effect; but it is not mentioned, for instance, in Alfasi's *Responsa* No. 259); (3) only one oath is to be taken against the claims of many creditors; (4) it is left to the discretion of the judge to free an obviously honest debtor from an oath and to refuse it to a notorious perjurer. It is questionable whether Maimuni wanted a period of ninety days, during which the debtor would live under ban to reveal his assets, to precede the administration of the oath, as demanded by Hai Gaon and others; see Tykocinski. The statements אבל מחרימין and ומחרימין תחלה are inconclusive, inasmuch as the former may have been replaced by the oath, and the latter is addressed to the public at large. Neither is any time limit set. At any rate, in Resp. Nos. 204, 228, 312, no bans are mentioned. In Resp. Nos. 177 and 203 a wife was protected against being divorced by an impecunious husband who, through such an oath, tried to free himself from her marriage settlement. Curiously, Maimuni, in his desire to protect the innocent debtor in the case of insolvency, states in Resp. No. 299 that if threatened by the creditor to be dragged before a Gentile court, where a declaration of bankruptcy would lead to his imprisonment, the debtor may swear that he is not indebted to the plaintiff at all. He should only make the mental reservation that he means to say that he owes him nothing until such time as he may have money to repay him. See also M.T. Shebu'ot 3, 3, and the qualifying statements of Naḥshon Gaon quoted by *Haggahot Maimuniot* thereon.

163. C.M. on B.M. IX, 15; S.M. Comm. 199; M.T. Malveh ve-loveh 3, 1, 4–6, based on B.M. 113a–116a. See also Resp. No. 177. The principle of differentiating between debtors according to rank, here (M.T. 2, 2) and elsewhere, is in keeping with the general medieval rabbinic concept of giving a poor man the things to which he has become accustomed. Lujo Brentano, in his stimulating lecture on "Ethics and Economics in History," has rightly pointed out that this doctrine of making allowances according to rank opened many a door for shady practices and concealed many legal subterfuges behind a cloak of respectability. See *Der wirtschaftende Mensch in der Geschichte, Gesammelte Reden und Aufsätze* (Leipzig, 1923), p. 46 n. 2.

164. C.M. on B.M. V, 7; S.M. Comm. 198; M.T. Malveh ve-loveh 5, 1–2; Resp. Nos. 115–16, based on Sifre on Deut., ed. Friedmann, No. 263 and B.M. 70b–71a. See also RABD, *Haggahot Maimuniot* and the other commentaries, *ad loc.*, and Y.D., 159. Amram Gaon's responsum is printed in *Sha'arei ṣedeḳ*, IV, 2, 20, fol. 40a. See also *ibid.*, No. 7, fol. 35b, where the gaon takes pains to persuade his inquirers not to excommunicate a creditor lending on interest to Gentiles.

165. M.T., *ibid.*, 5, 4–5, based on B.M. 70b–71. Other rabbis were more lenient; see the commentaries and Y.D. 169. For Meshullam's opinion, see Ginzberg, *Genizah Studies*, II, 200, 220. See also Hoffmann, *Geld-*

handel, p. 84. The rigid prohibition of partnership with Gentiles in M.T. Sheluḥin ve-shutefin 5, 10, is based on Bek. 2b, Sanh. 63b, but fails to take cognizance of those contradictory statements in the Talmud which induced some Tosafists to take a more lenient view. See *Tosafot* on Bek. 2b; Sanh. 63b s. v. אסור; *Haggahot Maimuniot;* SeMaG Comm. 82 (Venice, 1547; fol. 167d); *Oraḥ Ḥayyim,* 156. Maimuni's unqualified prohibition in M.T. (not so in C.M. on Bek. I, 1), in which he follows Sar Shalom Gaon and Alfasi, may have been influenced by a similar rigidity of the Muslim prohibition; see *Encyclopaedia of Islam,* s. v. "Naṣara"; Bergsträsser-Schacht, *Grundzüge,* p. 45. Many geonic sources show, however, that these prohibitions by both religions' laws were widely honored in the breach. See Mann in *JQR,* n.s. X, 331 f. M.T. Malveh 5, 5, forbids a Jew to serve as guarantor for a debt contracted by another Jew from a Gentile on interest, because, if forced to pay, the guarantor would become the usurious creditor of a fellow Jew. This interpretation of B.M. 71b insofar corresponded with the practice under Islam that the creditor actually had the choice of first approaching the debtor or the guarantor. See Eduard Sachau, *Mohammedanisches Recht nach schafi'itischer Lehre,* Lehrbücher of the Seminar für Orientalische Sprachen, of the University of Berlin, XVII (Stuttgart, 1897), p. 395. It is likely, therefore, that Maimuni understood the prohibition to cover such a contingency, and not merely that in which the Gentile laws prescribed that the guarantor be sued first. See De Boton's correct reply to Don Vidal's remarks, *ad loc.*

166. M.T., *ibid.,* 5, 7, based on B.M. 70b; De'ot 5, 13, based on B.Ḳ. 93a; Yoma 86a, and so forth. The statement of Kalonymos ben Kalonymos in his *Massekhet Purim,* IV, 13: אבל בני בבל ואיטליה של יון אין להם על מה שיסמכו אלא על הרבית (*c.* 1300) is partly borne out by numerous earlier sources quoted by Mann in *JQR,* n.s. X, 310 ff.; Björkmann, in *Mitteilungen des Seminars für Oriental. Sprachen . . . Berlin,* XXXII, p. 89; Fischel, *Jews in Mediaeval Islam;* Louis Massignon, "L'Influence de l'Islam au moyen âge sur la fondation et l'essor des banques juives," *Bulletin d'études orientales de l'Institut français de Damas,* I (1931), 3–12.

167. *Encyclopedia of Social Sciences,* s. v. "Slavery," by W. L. Westermann *et al.;* M. T. 'Abadim 1, 10, based on Ḳidd. 69a, 'Arakhin 29a, etc. The talmudic laws of slavery have been treated by Zadoc Kahn in his *L'Esclavage selon la Bible et le Talmud* (Paris, 1867); David Farbstein, *Das Recht der unfreien und freien Arbeiter nach jüdisch-talmudischem Recht* (Bern, 1896); Robert Salomon, *L'Esclavage en droit comparé juif et romain* (Paris, 1931). For Islam, see Juynboll, *Handbuch des islamischen Gesetzes,* pp. 202 ff., 234 ff.; Sachau, *Mohammedanisches Recht,* pp. 121 ff.; Bergsträsser-Schacht, *Grundzüge,* pp. 38 ff.; Mez, *Renaissance des Islams,* pp. 152 ff.; and, for the Jews under Islam, Mann in *JQR,* n.s. X, 144 ff.; S. Assaf, "Slavery and Slave Trade among the Jews during the Middle Ages" (Hebrew), *Zion,* IV (1938–39), 91–125. It is notable that,

although Maimuni was undoubtedly influenced by Alfarabi's condemnation of the primitive tribes, whom he, too, considered as "below the rank of men and above that of monkeys" (M.N. III, 51; see Strauss in *REJ*, C*bis*, 27 f.), he evidently did not adopt the Arab thinker's "natural" justification of slavery on this score. The fact that many slaves, including Jewish victims of Mediterranean piracy, hailed from civilized countries clearly militated against the facile equation of slave with semihuman barbarian.

168. S.M. Comm. 235, based on Giṭṭin 38b; M.N. III, 39; M.T. Mekhirah 15, 13, based on Tos. B.B. IV, 7, 403; M. Abot II, 8; Ḳidd. 11a, and so forth. See also Ginzberg, *Geonica*, II, 106. Maimuni not only adds several categories to the talmudic designations of thief and קוביוסטוס but also translates the latter by the harsh גונב נפשות ("kidnaper"). This explanation, although given also by Gershom and Rashi, is evidently incorrect. Etymologically, it can mean only a dice player, as translated by Ḥananel and the Tosafists, *ad loc.* See also Alexander Kohut, *Aruch Completum* (Vienna, 1926), VII, 56; Samuel Krauss, *Griechische und lateinische Lehnwörter* (Berlin, 1898), p. 501. Maimonides hesitated neither to attach to the slave the opprobium of professional kidnaping, instead of the milder charge of professional gambling, nor to add, on his own initiative, the generalization that all slaves are like that. M.T., *ibid.*, II, 1–4; Matenot 'aniyim 8, 17; 'Abadim 5, 1; C.M. on Ḳidd. I, 3, based on Ḳidd. 22b., and so forth. The משיכה of adult slaves is described, in accordance with talmudic law, as forcible seizure. In M.T. Zekhiyah u-mattanah 2, 17, based on Ḳidd. 23a, Maimuni explains the effect of the decease of an heirless convert to Judaism upon the status of the latter's slaves. Adult slaves, able to make use of the free right of appropriation in such an ownerless (*hefḳer*) estate, immediately become free. "But minor slaves are like cattle and he who seizes them acquires them." Karo, in Ḥ.M. 275, 29, repeats Maimuni's statement verbatim, but omits the comparison with cattle. Muslim economists—for instance, Abul Fadl—sometimes enumerated slaves among the household animals. See Mahmassani, *Les Idées économiques*, p. 80.

169. M.T. 'Abadim 8, 20; 9, 1–4, in conjunction with *ibid.*, 1, 1–2, 5, based on numerous talmudic sources. The latter passages referring to a Hebrew slave undoubtedly allow the deduction *a fortiori* for Gentile slaves. Only the sale of an insolvent debtor (practiced in ancient Israel, but abolished under the Second Commonwealth; see, for instance, II Kings 4:1, and Asher Gulak's *Toledot ha-mishpaṭ ha'ibri bi-teḳufat ha-Talmud* (A History of Jewish Law in the Talmudic Period [Jerusalem, 1939], I, 149 f.), which is here strictly prohibited, may still have been regarded as permissible in a country which generally tolerated it. The reference in 1, 5, to the right of the Jewish community to enslave a misbehaving Jew, based on B.M. 73b, is evidently tied up with Hebrew slavery and has no practical importance for Gentile slaves. For 8, 20, see

C.M. on Makhshirin II, 7; M.T. Issurei biah 13, 7; 15, 26, and De Boton's question, *ad loc*. See, in general, also Y.D. 67, 14–18, where this method of acquisition is totally ignored. To facilitate the transfer of Gentile slaves to Jewish masters, Maimuni interprets (in M.T. 'Abadim 8, 19; 9, 5) the equivocal discussion in Yeb. 45b–46a in a sense enabling the Jews to acquire full ownership over the slaves, although the "title" of their previous Gentile owners is necessarily limited to the latter's output alone. He must warn his coreligionists, however, that, if their newly acquired slaves hastened, immediately after the completion of the sale, to be initiated into Judaism for the purpose of obtaining their freedom, they would become free, unless the masters took the necessary precautions. But how should slaves know of this provision of Jewish law? According to M.T., *ibid.*, 8, 18, the slave, even while in the service of a Jewish master, must not be taught the Torah at all. See *Sha'arei ṣedeḳ*, III, 6, 29; 36 (fol. 26b, 27b); and Karo's and De Boton's comments on M.T.

170. M.T. Roṣeaḥ u-shemirat nafesh 2, 10–14, based upon Mekhilta ed. Hoffmann, 21, 14, 20; Sanh. 52b, 86a, and so forth. This discrimination between the murder of a Jew and that of a Gentile reveals less tolerance than the doctrine of the Ḥanafite school of Muslim jurisprudence, which demanded full retaliation for the murder of a *dhimmi* by a Muslim. But the other Arabian schools of Shafi'ites and Ḥanbalites and, to a certain extent, of Malikites likewise demanded different sanctions for the slaying of a believer and that of an infidel. See Bergsträsser-Schacht, *Grundzüge*, p. 46. Maimuni explains the preferential treatment of a Gentile slave over a free Gentile or a "resident alien" (*ger toshab*) by the fact that "the slave has accepted Jewish commandments and joined the heritage of the Lord." He personally (ירָאה לִי) emphasizes the psychological element of the intent to kill, rather than the time elapsing between the fatal injury and death. See also David Hoffmann's note (ק׳) to his edition of the *Mekhilta*, p. 129.

171. C.M. on Ḳidd. I, 3; M.T. 'Abadim 5, 4–5, 17; M.N. III, 39, based on Ḳidd. 24–25. See also C.M. on Nega'im VI, 7. The inclusion of castration is clearly outside the controversy of Ḳidd. 25a. It is so understood by Rashi and Alfasi, but Maimonides chooses to interpret it into the text and thus out of the list, without, of course, wishing to encourage the performance of such an operation, which he himself declares to be strictly prohibited by biblical law. See S.M. Prohib. 361; M.T. Issurei biah 16, 10–11, based on Shab. 110b–111a. Asher b. Yeḥiel suggests a compromise formula with respect to an outwardly recognizable or unrecognizable form of castration. See Karo's comments on 5, 4, and Y.D. 267, 28. For this reason the Jewish slave traders preferred to acquire slaves from Gentiles with the understanding that they be castrated before delivery. This procedure was specifically permitted by one of the geonim; see *Teshubot ha-geonim*, ed. by N. N. Coronel (Vienna, 1871), No. 78. See

also Assaf's remarks in *Zion,* IV, 100 n. 62, and the question raised by De Boton, *ad loc.,* with respect to the cutting out of the slave's tongue. Karo's interpretation of 5, 17, in a way favoring the slave, is hardly tenable in the face of the final פטור מלשלמו, which shows that the first פטור does not refer to sacrifice, but to the obligation to liberate the slave. The milder view is taken by Naḥmanides and others. See *Haggahot Maimuniot, ad loc.;* and Y.D. 267, 40. Further procedural aggravations for the slave are the requirements of a deed of manumission on the part of the master, instead of automatic liberation; and the provision that the Gentile slave must prove that he has already been properly circumcised and subjected to the required ablutions.

172. M.T. 'Abadim 9, 8—a dramatic finale of the section dealing with slaves; M.N. III, 39. The emphasis upon Israel's exclusive descent from Abraham is, of course, a pointed denial of the equality in rank of the descent of the Arabs. See "Outlook" in my *HJH,* pp. 118 ff.

173. M.T. Shabbat, 20, 14; Ḳobeṣ 53a; Plessner, *Der Oikonomikos,* pp. 168 ff. For Maimuni's emphasis upon the obligation to enforce Sabbath observance upon a fully converted slave only, see *Teshubot ha-geonim,* ed. by Harkavy, No. 11. See also the next note.

174. S.M. Comm. 215 (see Heller's n. 6); M.T. Milah I, 1, 6; Melakhim 9, 2, based on Ḳidd. 29a, Yeb. 48b, 'A.Z. 64b, Sanh. 56b. The fear of disloyal slaves is well reflected in the geonic responsa printed in *Teshubot ha-geonim,* ed. by Harkavy, Nos. 11, 431. See also *Sha'arei ṣedeḳ,* III, 6, 1; 20–21 (fols. 23a, 25b, 26a); Ginsberg, *Geonica,* II, 74, 81, 189 f., 197; Assaf, in *Zion,* IV, 92 f. RABD's excited objection "we cannot now execute anybody" is beside the point, not only on strictly legalistic grounds as stressed by Karo, *ad loc.* It seems that by immediately adding "we accept 'resident aliens' only when the Jubilee year is being observed" Maimuni himself indicated clearly that the required observance of the seven Noahidic commandments had little bearing upon reality. See also M.T. Issurei biah 14, 7–9, where Maimuni makes it perfectly clear that a slave purchased from a Gentile should be circumcised and, like a proselyte, taught the fundamentals of Judaism, provided he freely consents to it. The period of twelve months is granted to obtain such consent, but where it is clearly stipulated that he should not be converted at all, he ought to be immediately resold to a Gentile. RABD objects to that, too; and other rabbis, such as Naḥmanides, take cognizance of the undeniable existence of numerous pagan slaves among Jews. Don Vidal, in his comment on M.T. Shabbat 20, 14, excuses his lengthy harmonistic discourse by the fact that this third type of unconverted slave "is constantly found." In M.T. 'Abadim 8, 12, Maimuni himself seems to relax his stringent demands and to compromise with facts. The equation of governmental prohibition with a general stipulation in advance was subsequently made by Mordecai b. Hillel ha-Kohen on Yebamot No. 41, and adopted by

almost all rabbis. Some later rabbis went a step further and expressed the opinion that, if a third person initiated a female slave, through ablution, into Judaism without the master's permission, he became personally responsible for the damage accruing therefrom to the master. This opinion was later recognized as authoritative by Isserles and others. See Y.D. 267, 4, 11.

175. M.T. Matenot 'aniyim 8, 14; 'Abadim 5, 5; Talmud torah 1, 1, and so forth, based on Gittin 37b, Kidd. 25a, 29b, Ket. 28ab, and other passages. With respect to the study of the Torah, see the somewhat less rigid stand of the geonim in Sha'arei ṣedek, III, 6, 29; 36, fol. 26b f.; Ginzberg, Geonica, II, 75 f., 83 f. The vital distinction between the circumcised and the uncircumcised slave with respect to both redemption and freedom as a result of permanent injury seems to be derived from Maimonides' own interpretation of the sources.

176. M.T. 'Abadim 8, 1–5, based on Gittin 43b–44a. Of course, the rabbis realized that the Gentile purchaser would hardly respect the Jewish demand that the slave be given freedom. Maimuni therefore added the provision that the former Jewish master should try to repurchase the slave at a price up to ten times the amount which he had received. Through this interpretation he greatly limited the practical effect of this talmudic penalty. According to some of his geonic predecessors, a regular tenfold fine was to be imposed upon the transgressor, and the amount diverted to charitable causes within the Jewish community. See Sha'arei ṣedek, III, 6, 5; 19; 37 (fols. 23b, 26a, 27b); and Mann, in JQR, n.s. X, 145. Following some geonic teachers and Alfasi, moreover, Maimuni declared this penalty to be operative only if imposed by an ordained court. This provision nullified the entire sanction and removed a serious obstacle from the way of the Jewish slave traders who wished to dispose of their wares to Gentile masters, thus evoking, for example, Asher b. Yehiel's vigorous protest. See Karo's comment, ad loc. Of course, the uncircumcised slave could freely be sold to a Gentile or into a foreign country; and, hence, most slaves were apparently uncircumcised. Another method of evasion was to mortgage the circumcised slave as security for a loan from a Gentile, with the understanding that in case of the master's refusal to pay the debt at a stipulated date, the slave should remain in the "creditor's" possession. To be sure, Jewish law demanded that the borrower stipulate that the new slaveholder should own merely the slave's products, and not the slave himself. But since, according to that law, all Gentile ownership of slaves was theoretically reduced to such control over the revenue, this condition was purely nominal. In practice, the Gentile who acquired slaves through such credit transactions would pay little attention to these minutiae of Jewish law. One wonders whether אפילו לכותי in 8, 5, refers to a real Samaritan, as interpreted by Karo. According to ibid., 6, 6, the Samaritans are to be treated altogether like

Gentiles. It is more likely that Maimuni wished to prohibit the sale of circumcised slaves to Karaites, whom he placed practically on a par with the ancient Samaritans. He thus incidentally answered in the affirmative a question left open in the Talmud.

177. M.T., *ibid.*, 8, 6–9, based on Gittin 43b–45a and Ket. 110b. Maimuni interprets the לאחוי עבדים in Ket. in a subjective rather than objective sense (as Rashi and others understood it), thus making masters dependent on their slaves' wishes. He decides also, in S.M. Prohib. 252–55; M.T., *ibid.*, 8, 10–11, that a fugitive slave from abroad should be treated in Palestine as a full-fledged proselyte and merely made to promise to indemnify his master when able to afford it. This interpretation is also given by Jacob Tam, notwithstanding Joseph b. Yom Tob's self-evident objection that, in this case, "all slaves could get rid of their masters by fleeing to Palestine." See *Tosafot* on Ket. 110b s. v. הכי. However unrealistic this interpretation may be, it helped to explain away the still more radical demand of the Deuteronomist (23:16) that no fugitive slave be returned to his master. The rabbis reduced this highly humanitarian postulate to the case of either a slave fleeing from a Gentile owner or one deserting a Jewish slaveholder abroad, after a pledge to make good the loss. See Onkelos' translation of, and Rashi's, Ibn Ezra's, and Nahmanides' comments on, that biblical passage. It is to be noted that Maimonides' extreme views are shared by most of his successors; see Y.D. 267, 82–85, and the commentaries thereon. The evidence collected by Mez (*Renaissance des Islams*, p. 162) indicates that the masses of runaway slaves constituted a serious problem in the tenth-century Caliphate. It is not likely that the conditions were vastly different two centuries later. See also Mann, *Text and Studies*, II, 91; and Raphael Mahler, "Studies in the Socio-Political Conditions of the Babylonian and Persian Jews in the So-Called Geonic Period" (Yiddish), *Jiwobleter*, XI (1937), 178 n. 14.

178. C.M. on Temurah VI, 2; Kidd. III, 12; M.T. Issurei biah 12, 11–14; 14, 17–19; 15, 3; Yibbum va-halisah 1, 4; Ebel 2, 3; 'Abadim 9, 1, based upon Sanh. 58b, Niddah 47a, Yeb. 45ab, 78ab, Kidd. 68ab. In M.T. Ebel 12, 12, based on Berakhot 16b, Maimuni states generally that one does not mourn a deceased slave in the usual way, nor does one console his master through the recitation of the usual formula, "but one says to him, as one would say over the loss of his ox or donkey: may the Lord replenish thy deficiency." In 'Abadim 9, 1, he emphasizes the fact that it makes no legal difference whether the mother of the master's child is his own or somebody else's slave. This is in line with M.T. Gerushin 10, 19; Nahlot 4, 6, where he expressly combats various opinions of his predecessors, who wished to establish some such difference. They evidently tried to compromise on a social phenomenon which they did not wish to encourage, but some hardships of which they tried to mitigate. They were

also concerned with the effects of such extramarital relations upon the laws of divorce and levirate marriage. Maimuni declines to follow even the intermediary solution suggested by Alfasi. See Don Vidal's comments on Naḥlot 4, 6, and the sources quoted by Schwarz in MbM, I, 351 f. See also the conflicting opinions discussed in the commentaries on Y.D. 267, 69, and, for punishments far transcending in severity the rabbinic type of flagellation suggested by Maimuni, Shaʻarei ṣedeḳ, III, 6, 13; 38; 42 (fols. 25a, 27a, 28b); and the sources cited by Tykocinski, Die gaonäischen Verordnungen, pp. 174 ff. Maimuni himself cannot quite escape the impact of reality, however. In Resp. No. 154 he advises his inquirers to induce a young Jew suspected of illicit relations with one of his female slaves to liberate and marry her, although he clearly realizes that he thereby runs counter to a talmudic law. He does it, he contends, merely "for the welfare of the penitents." That the Jewish public was not inclined to rely wholly upon these legal prohibitions is evidenced by several extant marriage contracts (from a Muslim environment of a later age) in which the bride makes the bridegroom promise that during her lifetime he will not take another wife, wife-slave, or concubine, except with her consent, and that he will not "have in his employ a female slave that is objectionable to her." See Louis M. Epstein, The Jewish Marriage Contract (New York, 1927), pp. 272 f., and, for the connection between these safeguards and the Maimonidean views on concubinage, the same author's "The Institution of Concubinage among the Jews," PAAJR, VI (1934–35), 182 f.

179. Resp. No. 154; see the last note; C.M. on Keritot II, 4–6; M.T. Issurei biah 3, 14–17 (insisting upon the rabbinic type of chastisement for the adult male offender); 12, 13; M.N. I, 39; III, 41, based upon Ker. 10b–11b, and so forth; M.T. Mekhirah 15, 12, possibly paraphrasing Mar Samuel's homily on Lev. 25:46: לעבודה נתתיו ולא לבושה in Niddah 47a. See also the sources quoted by Assaf, in Zion, IV, 98 ff.

180. C.M. on B.M. VIII, 3, based on B.M. 99a, and so forth; M.T. Mekhirah 30, 2, following Hai Gaon's interpretation of the often-reiterated talmudic principle "all that the slave acquires is acquired for his master," Pes. 88b, and so forth, which is literally the same as Justinian's quodcunque per servum acquiritur, id domino acquiritur. See also M.T. Sheluhin ve-shutefin 2, 2, based on M. ʻErubin VII, 6; Ḳidd. 41b, and so forth. M.T. ʻAbadim 2, 7 end; 5, 2, in conjunction with ibid., Gezelah va-abedah 17, 13; Zekhiyah u-mattanah 3, 12–15; C.M. on Ḳidd. I, 3, based on B.M. 12ab, Ḳidd. 23ab, and so forth. M.T. Ḥobel u-mazziḳ 4, 21–22, repeating B.Ḳ. VIII, 4, and adding the comparison with an insolvent debtor.

181. C. H. Becker, Islamstudien, I, 60; Shaʻarei ṣedeḳ, III, 6, 6, fol. 23b; Teshubot ha-geonim, ed. by Harkavy, No. 431; Assaf, in Zion, IV, 107 n. 113; M.T. ʻAbadim 1, 2; 9, 6, based on B.M. 71a. Maimuni's personal view that a woman should be allowed to acquire male slaves below the age of nine is rejected by Jacob b. Asher and his successors, on

the ground that this purchase might be preparatory to illicit relations sometime later. See Y.D. 267, 19. But they evidently did not object to her raising male slaves born in her household, and possibly allowed her to keep such slaves as she might have inherited from somebody else.

182. See, for instance, C.M. on Pes. VIII, 1; IV, 5; M.T. Ḥobel u-mazziḳ, IV, 12; ʿAbadim 7, 4, 7–8, based on Pes. 87–88; Gittin 41–43; Resp. No. 317. See also Ibn Gaon's, Karo's, and De Boton's comments on M.T.; Y.D. 267, 60, 62–63; Levi ibn Ḥabib, *Responsa,* No. 85; and, for Islam, Juynboll, *Handbuch des islamischen Gesetzes,* p. 205.

183. M.T. Mekhirah 2, 1–4 (C.M. on Ḳidd. 1, 3); Ṭoʿen ve-niṭʿan 5, 1; 10, 4; Genebah 2, 2; Gezelah va-abedah 8, 14; Sekhirut 2, 1; Nizḳei mamon 11, 1, based on numerous talmudic sources. See also *Teshubot ha-geonim,* ed. by Harkavy, Nos. 435, 536 ("The slave resembles land and resembles movables"); Gulak, *Yesodei,* I, 38, 92 ff.; and n. 103 above. The prices of slaves seem to have been rising from the eighth to the tenth centuries, when a Nubian female slave was valued at 300 gold denars and a white slave girl at 1,000 denars and over. See Mez, *Die Renaissance des Islams,* pp. 153 f. In the recorded cases of redemption of Jewish captives, the price paid in the eleventh century averaged about 25–33½ gold denars each. See Jacob Mann, *Jews in Egypt,* I, 87 ff., 244; II, 316 f.; idem, *Texts and Studies,* I, 136 ff., 348 f., 366 ff. In the case recorded in the Maimonidean Resp. No. 379, the undoubtedly exceptional sum of 100 denars was agreed upon between the community of Alexandria and the captive's owner. See also n. 186 below.

184. M.T. Issurei biah 13, 12; 14, 11, 19; 19, 15–16, based on Yeb. 47b–48a; Ḳidd. 69ab, and so forth. M.T. Maʿaser sheni 11, 17; Bikkurim 4, 3; C.M. on Maʿaser sheni V, 14; Bikkurim I, 4. The last, referring to the milder decision in j. Bik. I, 4, 64a, mentions only the proselyte, but undoubtedly also includes the freedman. M.T. ʿAbadim 3, 14; 5, 3; 6–7, based upon numerous talmudic sources. All money owned by the slave and even all his clothes except those worn by him at the time of his manumission were adjudicated to his master by a gaon in *Shaʿarei ṣedeḳ,* III, 6, 31, fol. 27a. The complex regulations concerning the deed of emancipation are explainable in the light of the high legal status enjoyed by the freedman. To eliminate all disputes, especially in family matters, this deed had to be issued, like a writ of divorce, by Jewish rather than Gentile courts (M.T. 6, 5). Various legal sanctions increased the self-interest of the liberated slave in obtaining a proper legal deed. For example, a manumitted slave was open to assault without being able to collect damages, as long as he could not produce his deed of manumission. Neither could his former master raise the claim, since he had lost his ownership over the slave through his declaration, however informal. M.T. Nizḳei mamon 11, 1; Ḥobel u-mazziḳ 4, 11, deciding an open

question in Giṭṭin 42b against the freedman. See Don Vidal's, Karo's, and De Boton's comments.

185. S.M. Comm. 235; M.T. 'Abadim 6, 4; 9, 6, based on Giṭṭin 38b, 40a, Soṭah 3a, and so forth; Resp. No. 154, discussed in n. 178 above. The explanation here suggested—viz., fear of the influx of too many foreign elements—seems to be more satisfactory than that based upon the assumption that the legal curtailment of the owners' right to emancipate their slaves under the Roman Empire influenced the ancient rabbis. See Krauss, *Archäologie*, II, 98, 497 n. 677. Only so can we understand the consistent approval of the alleged biblical prohibition by Jewish teachers both in Persia and under Islam. Their attitude is, indeed, in striking contrast to the injunctions of Muḥammad and the leading Muslim jurists, who favored, morally as well as legally, the manumission of slaves. See Qur'an 4, 94, and so forth; Juynboll, *Handbuch des islamischen Gesetzes*, p. 205; Bergsträsser-Schacht, *Grundzüge*, p. 41. For Maimuni's realization of the importance of the ethnic element in connection with slavery, see n. 187 below. Characteristically, in M.T. 6, 4, Maimuni repeats the talmudic phrase פלונית שפחתי, thus leaving somewhat unclarified the position of the male slave similarly liberated through the will of his master. Like Alfasi, Maimuni interprets the קורת רוח in the Talmud in a rather restrictive sense. Rashi on Giṭṭin 40a s. v. ועושין is still more liberal. See also De Boton's comments. For some geonic sources, see Mann, in *JQR*, n.s. X, 149 f.

186. C.M. on Giṭṭin IV, 6; Horayot III, 7; M.T. 'Abadim 1, 8; 2, 7; Matenot 'aniyim 8, 10–18, based on Giṭṭin 45a, Horayot 13ab, etc. For the ransom of captives, see n. 183 above. We also possess an autograph letter of Maimonides addressed in 1173 to various communities and requesting their leaders to assist a special messenger dispatched for the collection of such funds. See S. H. Margulies, "Zwei autographische Urkunden von Moses und Abraham Maimuni," *MGWJ*, XLIV (1900), 8 ff. See also Resp. Nos. 223 and 379.

187. M.T. Matenot 'aniyim 10, 17; C.M. on Abot I, 5, based on Pes. 60b. See also "Outlook," in my *HJH*, pp. 154 ff. Although Maimuni here expresses but a commonplace opinion of the medieval commentators of that Mishnah in Abot, such as Meshullam, Rashi, Jonah Gerondi, and Simon Duran, he formulates it more sharply and evidently wishes to warn his readers against an existing evil. Apart from this general moral injunction, Maimonides, following Tos. Pe'ah III, 1, 20; and j. Pe'ah II, 7, 17a, states that one must not employ Gentile laborers during the harvest, because they are not familiar with the laws concerning the gleanings and corners which are to be given to the poor, see M.T., *ibid.*, 2, 10. The reference to corners seems to be Maimuni's own addition, evidently in reference to the latitude left the owner in assigning the corner, according

to *ibid.* 1, 15. Here and in C.M. on Pe'ah I, 2, Maimonides demands that the owner should leave more than the legally required one-sixtieth of the area whenever the "corner" would be too small to be of any use, when the number of the poor in the community is very large, or when the crop is unusually bountiful. The exercise of such discretion naturally was to be left to the owner himself or, if necessary, to his Jewish employees, but not to his Gentile workers.

188. C.M. on Abot I, 10; Makkot II, 2–3; M.T. Talmud torah 1, 9; Roṣeah u-shemirat nafesh 5, 5, amplifying Ḳidd. 30b, Makkot 8b, and so forth. See also Rosin, *Die Ethik des Maimonides,* p. 125. For somewhat similar teachings of Avicenna, Al-Ghazali, and others, see Plessner, *Der Oikonomikos,* pp. 47, 86; Mahmassani, *Les Idées économiques,* pp. 67, 83. Nowhere in Maimuni or in these Arabian thinkers do we find a theoretical evaluation of labor as a basic element of value, such as visualized by Aristotle before and Ibn Khaldun after them.

189. There is a characteristic difference in Maimonides' formulation of the following passages in his Code: M.T. Ḥobel u-mazziḳ 2, 11, discussing the compensation for enforced idleness caused by physical injury, and in Sheluḥin ve-shutefin 6, 2, referring to the compensation for the active partner (see n. 153 above), we find the phrase כפועל בטל של אותה מלאכה שבטל ממנה, which evidently indicates the loss of all earnings by an average worker of this type and is a literal repetition of Abbaye's statement in B.M. 68ab, and so forth. A similar reasoning is expressed, *ibid.* 8, 1, by שכר עמלו ומזונו בכל יום כפועל בטל. In M.T. Gezelah va-abedah 12, 4, however, Maimuni changes the same statement in B.M. 31b to read: כפועל בטל שיבטל מאותה מלאכה שהיה עוסק בה, and explains it specifically to mean that a man returning lost property has no right to demand full compensation for his normal earnings during the time so consumed, but must deduct the difference between the value of time spent in work and that spent in idleness. C.M. on B.M. II, 9, may be interpreted in the same way. In M.T. Sanh. 23, 5, Maimuni completely rephrases Abbaye's identical statement in Bekhorot 29b as ואמר להן תנו לי מה שיעשה תחתי עד שאדון לכם או תנו לי שכר בטלתי, indicating that a judge who is forbidden to charge anything for his judicial function may nevertheless demand compensation to the extent of either the cost of a substitute or that of his own idleness. The latter formula being rather equivocal, one may best explain it in the light of Maimuni's own interpretation in C.M. on Bek. IV, 6. After mentioning the controversy over the meaning of Abbaye's statement, he advances the following explanation (which he underscores as being "wonderful and true"): (1) One must not make such estimates on the basis of the particular individual's capacity for work and daily earnings, but on that of the customary earnings in his line of employment. (2) One must also take into consideration the amount of labor usually required in that occupation and the ensuing benefit of idleness. Since the labor of a smith is incomparably harder than that of a money-changer, the benefit of

rest to the former is so much the more substantial. Assuming that both earn on the average two drachmas a day, you would have to pay for enforced idleness perhaps as much as a drachma and a half to the money-changer, and only one-half a drachma to the smith. It is evident that Maimuni here follows a clear line of demarcation: the compensation (unless otherwise stipulated in advance) should be reduced to a minimum if the time is spent in the pursuit of a pious cause, such as the administration of justice or the return of a lost object to its owner; but it should make good the entire loss in earnings sustained by an innocent victim of assault or by an active partner devoting all his time to the company's business. The latter provision was doubly necessary to counteract evasions of the antiusury legislation, which might have been the original purpose of those silent partnerships. In this interpretation Maimonides runs counter not only to the obviously uniform meaning of Abbaye's statement in all four connections but also to the opinions of his predecessors, including Hananel, Alfasi, and Rashi. See also *Tosafot* on Bek. 29a s. v. כפועל; the commentaries on M.T.; H.M. 9, 5; 265; Y.D. 177, 2 (generally following Maimonides) and the commentaries thereon.

190. M.T. 'Abadim 1, 7; Sekhirut 7, 1; Mekhirah 13, 15–18; 14, 10– 11, based on B.M. 56b, and so forth. See nn. 104 and 110 above. Maimuni's inclusion of the contracting artisans in the class of those subject to the laws of "misrepresentation" was accepted by the subsequent codifiers as authoritative, despite the objections raised by Nahmanides and Ibn Adret. See Don Vidal's comments on M.T. Mekhirah 13, 15; and H.M. 227, 36. For Maimonides' personal view, see M.N. III, 42. His insistence upon the validity of contractual conditions beyond and above custom comes to the fore also in the following provision of M.T. Sekhirut 5, 6: when hiring a beast of burden, one must not load upon it more than the stipulated weight, even if an animal of that sort usually carries heavier loads. An excess load of but one-thirtieth of the contractual burden calls for special remuneration to the owner of the animal, while a greater excess makes the contractor responsible if the animal breaks down. Nahmanides and others argue that such responsibility exists only where the overloading exceeds the customary (not the contractual) load by more than one-thirtieth. See Don Vidal's comment, *ad loc.;* and H.M. 308, 5–6.

191. M.T. Sekhirut 9, 1; 11, 1–2, based upon B.M. 73a, 111ab. While in both passages Maimuni merely repeats the Mishnah's protective laws, we find in them curious deviations. He evidently agrees with *Tosafot* on B.M. 73a s. v. השוכר that contracts may abrogate custom, but ignores the problem of legal presumption concerning the hours of labor where there is no clearly established local custom. Like Alfasi, he fails to repeat Simon b. Lakish's statement, in B.M. 73b, that the normal hours of labor extend from sunrise to sunset and that the laborer's walking time to his

place of work is included in that working time, but not his walk home after work. This provision was subsequently included by Jacob b. Asher and Moses Isserles in H.M. 331, 1. The explanation frequently offered (for instance, by Moses Rivkes in his comments thereon) that Maimuni would not mention such a rare case is rightly rejected by Rosanes, *ad loc.* It is much more likely that Alfasi and Maimuni disregarded this passage because it so obviously conflicted with the system prevailing under Islam. Maimuni may also have had in mind his pet advice to all Jews to devote as little time as possible to earning a living and as much as possible to the study of the Torah. See n. 32 above. The apparently innocuous repetition in 11, 1, of the Mishnaic phrase with respect to the *ger toshab*, assumes different meaning in the light of Heller's comment on S.M., p. 63 n. 3. It may perhaps be explained by Maimuni's contention that the *ger toshab* had disappeared from Jewish life since the discontinuation of the Jubilee year observance. See M.T. 'Akum 10, 6; Issurei biah 14, 7–8, based on 'Arakhin 29a, and so forth, and the objections to this interpretation raised by RABD and others. Since uncircumcised Gentile slaves, to some extent falling into this category (see M.T. Milah 1, 6; n. 174 above), could not be considered by the Mishnah in connection with hiring free labor, Maimuni was induced to extend its range to cover all free Gentile workers.

192. M.T. Sekhirut 11, 2, 4, based on B.M. 110b–111a. See Isserles H.M. 333, 3; Farbstein, *Das Recht der Arbeiter*, pp. 43, 57.

193. C.M. on B.M. IX, 12; Shebu'ot VII, 1; M.T., *ibid.*, 9, 4; 11, 6, 9, based on B.M. 76b, 112b, Shebu'ot 45ab. Maimonides' decision that the worker's oath is of the biblical kind is in line with his general conviction that all oaths recorded in the Mishnah are of that type. See n. 131 above. The homily on Lev. 25:55 is given as the reason for the worker's privileged position in B.K. 116b, B.M. 10a. See *Tosafot* on the latter s. v. יכול. Nevertheless, some of Maimuni's predecessors took a stand less favorable to labor even in cases where the work could suffer delay. See Ginzberg, *Geonica*, II, 157, 164 f.

194. C.M. on B.M. VII, 2–7; Ma'aserot III, 1–3; M.T. Sekhirut 12, 1–14; Ma'aser 5, 9–13, based on B.M. 87a–93a, and so forth; M.T. Berakhot 7, 7, based on Ket. 61ab, Hullin 107b. See Karo's comments, *ad loc.*, and Orah Hayyim 169; 170, 18, 21.

195. M.T. Sekhirut 12, 3; 13, 6–7; Berakhot 2, 2, based on Tos. B.M. VIII, 8–9, 388; Berakhot 16a. See Don Vidal's and Karo's remarks on these passages. See also S.M. Comm. 19; and "Outlook," in my *HJH*, p. 119.

196. C.M. on Kelim XVIII, 9; Terumot VI, 3; M.T. Me'ilah 8, 1, 4; Terumot 10, 10, based on Me'ilah 13a; Men. 98a; j. Terumot VI, 3, 44a. The latter passage is quoted by Samson of Sens in his commentary on M. Terumot VI, 3, as a question of fact, while Maimuni in M.T. interprets it as referring to the economic effect of a diminished demand. In his own remarks in C.M., he merely points out the additional religious responsi-

bility of the priest for misleading his laborers. In his zest to forestall all possible sacrilege, on the other hand, he fails to mention the economically important exception permitting the use of larger measures in contracts affecting precious workmanship by gold- and silversmiths. This exception, stated in Men. 96a, had scriptural backing in Job 37:22, according to *Tosafot, ibid.*, s. v. הדא. See Karo's comments, *ad loc.*

197. C.M. on Ket. V, 6; M.T. Ishshut 14, 1–2; De'ot 5, 4; Issurei biah 21, 11, based on Ket. 61b–62b, etc. Maimuni's decision in favor of the majority opinion, against the evident context of the Talmud and the interpretation of Alfasi, merely adds another illustration to his glorification of · scholarly pursuits. See Don Vidal's comment on 14, 2. It is interesting that taking his cue from מפנקי דמערבא in Ket. 62a, Maimuni renders the class of טיילים of the Mishnah as "the strong pampered persons who have no work to do which would weaken their bodies, but eat and drink and sit at home." Jacob b. Asher adds the characteristic "and do not pay taxes," while Karo reverts to the original undefined term "men of leisure" in the Mishnah. See *Eben ha-'Ezer* 76, 1. All these definitions clearly are reflections of changing contemporary conditions.

198. C.M. on B.K. VI, 2; B.M. IX, 2; M.T. Sekhirut 8, 1–14, and so forth. See Becker, *Islamstudien*, I, 211 ff.

199. C.M. on Nedarim IV, 3; M.T. Talmud torah 1, 3, 7, based on Ned. 36b–37a; j. Ned. IV, 3, 38c; Resp. No. 194. Maimonides, true to his general opposition to 'the growing commercialization of learning, does not allow the teacher of Oral Law to charge even the accepted minimum wage for time spent in teaching. This is doubly remarkable since he was forced to permit such charges to judges for the time spent in the exercise of their function. See n. 189 above. Other medieval rabbis were more lenient. See the commentaries on M.T.; Nissim's comments on Ned. 37a; Y.D. 246, 5.

200. S. Pinsker, *Licḳute ḳadmoniot* (Vienna, 1860), Appendix, pp. 31 f.; *Sha'arei teshubah*, No. 23.

201. I intend to deal with some of these problems in another essay on "The Political Theories of Maimonides."

202. Eugen Täubler has rightly emphasized the fact that the role of the slave trade in the nascent Jewish communities of the Merovingian and Carolingian empires has been greatly exaggerated, but he seems to have gone too far in the opposite direction. See his "Zur Handelsbedeutung der Juden in Deutschland vor Beginn des Städtewesens," *Festschrift Martin Philippson* (Leipzig, 1916), pp. 381 ff.; *SRH*, 1st ed., III, 95 f. n. 3; and, more fully, in 2d ed., IV, 187 ff., 332 ff.; and the data assembled by Assaf, in *Zion*, IV, 109 ff.

203. An analysis of the complex problems of the rabbinic recognition of *dina de-malkhuta* and its limitation, which played a vital role in the political theory of the rabbis, must also be relegated to the forthcoming essay mentioned in n. 201 above.

ESSAY 8

1. For several decades Eugen Täubler and others have preached such a unity of approach, but in practical execution these demands were heeded by only a few Jewish historians. Fritz Baer's writings on Spanish-Jewish history are a noteworthy example of a successful blending of the two approaches. In general historiography, the assignment of a separate chapter on Jews and the nearly complete silence on them in other chapters, in the *Cambridge Medieval History* still had the earmarks of a reluctant compromise. G. G. Coulton's *Medieval Panorama: the English Scene from Conquest to Reformation* (Cambridge, 1938), however, is an illustration of far more effective integration. Nazi historiography, on the other hand, despite its overemphasis on the Jewish question, failed to produce any worthwhile collections of new archival materials, which alone might have proved to be of more permanent value.

2. The difficulties of such an undertaking are, of course, very great, since even the general demographic studies in medieval history are as yet far from satisfactory. For a brief discussion of the pertinent problems, see the two essays by Josiah C. Russell on "Medieval Population," *Social Forces*, XV (1937), 501–11; and "Medieval Demography," in Caroline F. Ware's (ed.), *The Cultural Approach to History* (New York, 1940), pp. 291–93. See also *supra*, Essay 2.

3. E. Lévi-Provençal, *La Péninsule Ibérique au moyen-âge d'après le Kitāb ar-Rawḍ al mi'ṭar fī ḥabar al-akṭār d'Ibn 'Abd al-Mun'im al-Ḥimyari*, ed., trans. into French, and annotated (Leiden, 1938), no. 19, pp. 23 (Arabic), 30 (French).

4. Menaḥem ibn Zeraḥ, צדה לדרך, Introd. (Sabionetta, 1567–68), fol. 15a. See also David Kaufmann, *Gesammelte Schriften* (Frankfort, 1908–15), II, 105 n. 2. In a much earlier responsum, of Naṭronai Gaon, we likewise read: שאליסונה מקום ישראל ויש בה ישראל הרבה...ואין ביניכם נוי כל עיקר. See *Ḳebuṣat ḥakhamin* (Vienna, 1860–61). The exaggeration of the latter assertion is evident. It becomes even more dubious in the light of the following claim that similar conditions prevailed in the capital, Cordova, where, too, the author states, וישראל מרובים וישמעאל מעט.

5. Muḥammad ibn al-Idrisi (Edrisi), *Description de l'Afrique et de l'Espagne*, ed. and trans. into French by R. Dozy and M. J. de Goeje (Leiden, 1866), pp. 191 (Arabic), 231 (French). The same designation is used for Lucena; *ibid.*, pp. 205 (Arabic), 252 (French).

6. Lévi-Provençal, *Al-Ḥimyari*, no. 42, pp. 42 f. (Arabic), 53 ff. (French). This passage seems, like the following, to have been lifted by the author from Al-Bakri, who had evidently copied at least the story of Raymond Berenguer I's romance from a contemporary eleventh-century source. See the word اليوم on p. 42 l. 15. See also the editor's remarks in the introduction, pp. xxii ff., and his notes to the trans., p. 54. For the general

Spanish population of the period, see my remarks above, in Essay 6, "Yehudah Halevi: An Answer to a Historical Challenge."

7. Fritz Baer, "Probleme der spanisch-jüdischen Geschichte," *Korrespondenzblatt* . . . *Akademie für die Wissenschaft des Judentums*, VI (1925), 8.

8. B. Lionel Abrahams, "The Expulsion of the Jews from England," *JQR*, o.s. VII (1894–95), 90, 245; *idem*, "The Condition of the Jews of England at the Time of their Expulsion in 1290," *Transactions of the Jewish Historical Society of England*, II (1894–95), 97 ff. (the list on p. 85 enumerates twenty localities). If the royal decree of 1253 stating "quod nullus Judaeus recepetur in aliqua villa sine speciali licentia Regis nisi in villis illis in quibus Judaei manere consueverunt" (Thomas Madox, *History and Antiquity of the Exchequer of the Kings* [London, 1769], I, 249) left open the loophole of royal license, there is no evidence that Jews availed themselves of that opportunity to any significant extent. From the point of view of population figures the exceptions, if any, may be entirely disregarded. On the other hand, the trend toward concentration was intensified in 1269–84, when successive decrees all but eliminated the Jews from towns which did not possess chirograph offices. See Cecil Roth's *A History of the Jews in England* (London, 1941), pp. 82, 91 ff. See also *ibid.*, pp. 272 f., for a brief discussion of the general problem of Anglo-Jewish population.

9. No reliable information concerning London's general and Jewish populations in 1290 seems to be available. But even if the poll tax record of 1380 indicating the existence of 20,397 persons over fifteen years of age (see Charles Pendrill, *London Life in the 14th Century* [London, 1925], p. 105) is an understatement (see Ephraim Lipson, *The Economic History of England*, 7th ed. [London, 1937], pp. 122 f.), we may readily assume that a century earlier the city embraced only about 30,000 to 40,000 inhabitants. In this case, too, it would have exceeded in size most Continental metropolises. To be sure, "Jew Street" ("Old Jewry"), first recorded in 1115, was not disproportionately large; but it certainly could have accommodated 2,000 Jews or more. Moreover, there is no evidence that all London Jews lived in the ghetto. The municipal ordinance of 1276–78 forbidding the burghers to lease houses from or to Jews, because the latter were to remain within their quarter (quoted from the *Calendar of Letter Book A* by Martin Weinbaum in his *London unter Eduard I und II: Verfassungs- und Wirtschaftsgeschichtliche Studien* [Stuttgart, 1933], p. 85) seems clearly to indicate the opposite practice. In Oxford, on the other hand, during the thirteenth century, the Great and Little Jewries occupied between them a fairly large section of the town area. See the map of Oxford adapted by Sarah Cohen in her essay on "The Oxford Jewry in the Thirteenth Century," *Transactions of the Jewish Historical Society of England*, XIII (1936), 295. It may be readily assumed that the population density in the Jewish quarter at least equaled that of the remainder of the city.

10. "Quotidie pene cum eis loquentes." *De judaicis superstitionibus,* IX, end, in *PL,* CIV, 86.

11. Robert Anchel, "The Early History of the Jewish Quarters in Paris," *Jewish Social Studies,* II (1940), 45–60. See also my "Rashi and the Community of Troyes," below, Essay 9; and, especially, Alexander Pinthus, "Studien über die bauliche Entwicklung der Judengassen in deutschen Städten," *ZGJD,* II (1930–31), 101–30, 197–217, 284–300.

12. The central location of the Jewish quarters is evident on the map of almost any medieval city. See, for example, the aforementioned map of Oxford, where Jewry Hall appears at but a short distance from Gild Hall, and where St. Edward's Church is not far from the New (?) Synagogue. As is well known, the forced removal of the famous Frankfort Jewish quarter to the town's periphery in 1462 originated largely in the resentment of many pious Christians, including the rather humane emperor Frederick III, toward the close proximity of Jewish settlers and worshipers to the city's cathedral, which in many respects served as the imperial church of Germany. See, e.g., A. Freimann and F. Kracauer, *Frankfort* (Philadelphia, 1929), pp. 38 ff. Similarly, in the smaller Sicilian town of Savoca, the viceroy ordered, in 1470, the transfer of the synagogue from "centro et meliori loco" to the periphery, because the Jews "maxime die sabati semper canunt eorum officium alta voce eorum more," disturbing neighboring Christians. See B. and G. Lagumina, *Codice diplomatico dei Giudei di Sicilia* (Palermo, 1884–95), II, pt. 1, no. 533.

13. See Adolf Kober, *Cologne* (Philadelphia, 1940), pp. 83 f., 88.

14. Some data have been assembled by Louis I. Newman in his brief essay on "Intermarriage in the Middle Ages," *Jewish Institute Quarterly,* II (1926), January, pp. 2–8; March, pp. 22–28. See also Israel Abrahams's *Jewish Life in the Middle Ages,* 2d ed. (London, 1932), pp. 109 ff.; my *SRH,* 1st ed., II, 42 f.; III, 108 f.; and *JC,* II, 311 ff.; III, 205.

15. Solomon b. Simon Duran, מלחמת מצוה (Leipzig, 1856), p. 14.

16. Abraham Zacuto, ס', יוחסין השלם, ed. by Filipowski, 2d impression (Frankfort, 1925), fol. 225a; Solomon ibn Verga, ס', שבט יהודה, ed. by M. Wiener, 2d impression (Hanover, 1924), p. 95. See also M. Golde, "Familienleben der spanischen Juden vor ihrer Vertreibung 1492," *Jüdische Familien-Forschung,* II (1929), 110–14; H. J. Zimmels, *Die Marranen in der rabbinischen Literatur* (Berlin, 1932), pp. 60 ff. For Portugal one might also mention the complaints of the Cortes of Évora in 1481 that Jewish tailors, cobblers, and other craftsmen in their journeys through the villages and mountain settlements had illicit intercourse with the wives and daughters of farmers while the latter were working in the fields. See M. Kayserling, *Geschichte der Juden in Portugal* (Leipzig, 1867), pp. 85 f. The repeated royal decrees forbidding Jewish women unaccompanied by men to visit Christian houses for business, and parallel prohibitions forbidding Christian women to enter Jewish dwellings alone, reveal, in their

very reiteration, their ineffectiveness. See *Ordenaçoens do Senhor Rey D. Affonso V* (Coimbra, 1792), II, 80.

17. L. Finkelstein, *Jewish Self-Government in the Middle Ages* (New York, 1924), pp. 286 f., 294.

18. The passage from Honorius IV's bull is given here in the English trans. of B. L. Abrahams in his aforementioned essay, *JQR*, o.s. VII, 442. The Ratisbon records are cited from the documentary Appendix to Raphael Straus's *Judengemeinde Regensburg im ausgehenden Mittelalter* (Heidelberg, 1932), nos. 44–47, 56, 168, item 24. The Ratisbon case, which resulted in the expulsion of a Christian cobbler and his wife from the city (1467), was based upon the following characteristic confession of the shoemaker: ". . . und mer so han ich meiner hausfrauen vergondt, das sy eynen J., der vormalen umb sy gepult, haym in mein haus . . . gezilt hette, und als derselbig J. zu ir in die kamer kame, da kame ich mit ungestym an die kamer . . . , da nottet wir baide dem J. 10 gulden r. ab. . . ." This appendix was available to me in one of the few copies of page proof which had escaped suppression by the Nazi regime; it is now readily accessible in Straus's *Urkunden und Aktenstücke zur Geschichte der Juden in Regensburg, 1453–1738* (Munich, 1960), pp. 11 ff., 46. See also the earlier censure of the behavior of Ratisbon Jewish women in an inquiry addressed to Meir of Rothenburg יען כי נברו בנות ריינשפורק על בעליהן מאז ומקדם וכ"ש עתה. See his *Responsa*, ed. Prague, no. 946. See also Marino Ciardini, *I banchieri ebrei in Firenze nel secolo XV* (Borgo San Lorenzo, 1907).

19. The few extant rabbinic discussions on the subject, to be sure, refer to purely Jewish institutions of this kind. But their defenders justified them on the ground that they were needed to counteract adultery and illicit relations with Gentiles. See, e.g., Isaac Arama's עקדת יצחק, I, 20 (Lwów, 1868, fol. 162a); Judah Menz, *Responsa*, no. 5 (ed. Fürth, 1766, fol. 7b). But the numerous accusations against Jews for prohibited relations with Christian *meretrices* point to the frequent interdenominational use of such houses.

A large, hitherto almost unexplored, body of materials on mixed amorous relationships may be culled from medieval belles-lettres; though fictional in nature, these sources undoubtedly reflect life's daily realities at least as much as the normative sources. For example, the frequency of the literary theme of the seduction of Jewish girls by Christian suitors, heard ever since the days of Caesarius of Heisterbach (1170–1240), indicates a certain recurrence of such episodes. See Caesarius' *Dialogue on Miracles*. English trans. by Scott and Bland (London, 1929), I, 102 ff. (the generally anti-Jewish author explains these amorous ventures by referring to one of the young ladies as one "who like many of her kind was a very beautiful girl"); and Fritz Aronstein, "Eine jüdische Novelle von Grimmelshausen," *ZGJD*, V (1939), 239 ff. Similarly, the presentation, in the popular fifteenth-century Italian play *Agnolo Ebreo*, of an extremely benevolent Jew who, long before his ultimate conversion, was married to a Christian wife, must have had enough probability to be acceptable to contemporary audiences. See the text in Alessandro d'Ancona's *Le sacre rappresentazioni dei secoli XIV, XV, XVI* (Turin, 1872), III, 485 ff.; and Heinz Pflaum's remarks in his essay on "Les scènes des Juifs dans la littérature dramatique du moyen âge," *REJ*, LXXXIX (1930), 125 f. The possible deeper correlation between the very frequent representation of Jews under the guise of a scorpion in medieval art and the ancient use of the scorpion to symbolize sex might also bear investigation. See Marcel Bulard's fascinating monograph on *Le scorpion, symbole du peuple juif dans l'art religieux des XIVe, XVe, XVIe siècles* (Paris, 1935), especially p. 66 n. 7.

20. In his *Hermann von Scheda, ein jüdischer Proselyt des zwölften Jahrhunderts* (Leipzig, 1891). See also Julius Aronius, "Hermann der Prämonstratenser," *ZGJD*, o.s. II (1888), 217–31; and, more broadly, Leopold Lucas, "Judentaufen und Judaismus zur Zeit des Papstes Innozenz III," *Festschrift . . . Martin Philippson* (Leipzig, 1916), pp. 25–38; Michael Adler, *Jews of Medieval England* (London, 1939), pp. 277–379 (on the London *domus conversorum*).

21. I. Loeb, "Le nombre des Juifs de Castille et d'Espagne au moyen âge," *REJ*, XIV (1887), 161–83. These estimates, insofar as they relate to the period of 1492, have been essentially confirmed by the data made available by Alexander Marx in his essay on "The Expulsion of the Jews from Spain: Two New Accounts," *JQR*, o.s. XX (1908), 245 ff. See also my *SRH*, XI, 20 ff., 254 ff.

22. See Manuel Serrano y Sanz, *Orígenes de la dominación española en América* (Madrid, 1918), I, 466; and F. Baer's review of this work in *MGWJ*, LXIX (1925), 57 ff. In the will of a local widow of 1443 provision is made that, in case the community of Saragossa should "for whatever reason be destroyed or depopulated or else change its religion," the legacy be transferred to the largest Jewish community in Aragon. See Serrano y Sanz, p. 186 (Baer, p. 60).

23. G. Carano-Donvito, "Gli Ebrei nella storia economica di Puglia," *Rivista di Politica Economica*, XXIII (1933), 838. For the problem of the *neofiti*, which was very much akin to that of the Spanish Marranos, see U. Cassuto, "Un ignoto capitolo di storia ebraica," *Judaica, Festschrift . . . Hermann Cohen* (Berlin, 1912), pp. 389–404; *idem*, "Iscrizioni ebraiche a Trani," *Rivista degli studi orientali*, XIII (1932), 172–78. It may also be noted that in 1280 the London *domus conversorum* alone accommodated ninety-six inmates, in addition to many more outside the establishment. See Michael Adler, *Jews of Medieval England*, pp. 288 ff., 306, 308 f.

24. The Church therein followed the well-known principle of the rabbis: גר שנתגייר כקטן שנולד דמי (Yeb. 62a, etc.), causing thereby considerable difficulty to those Jewish jurists, who, invoking the opposite adage for Jews: ישראל אע"פ שחטא ישראל הוא (Sanh. 44a), insisted, e.g., that the wife of a con-

verted Jew must obtain from him a regular writ of divorce. The Church consistently preached the automatic annulment of such marriages. For a somewhat strained defense of the Jewish position, see, e.g., Isaac 'Arama's עקדת יצחק, IV, 97 (Lwów, 1868, fol. 89ab).

25. That Petrus was also a distinguished and influential astronomer is emphasized by J. M. Millás in his Hebrew essay devoted to this subject in *Tarbiz*, IX (1937–38), 55–64.

26. Sir Thomas More, "A Dialogue concerning heresyes and matters of religion (1528)," in *English Works* (London, 1557), p. 137 (also in the facsimile edition thereof with a modern version by W. E. Campbell [London, 1923], p. 56 of the trans.); Councils of Toledo, IV, cans. 57–64 (633); XVII, can. 8 (694); in Mansi's *Sacrorum conciliorum collectio*, X, 634 f.; XII, 102. See *Lex Visigothorum*, XII, 2, 17 (reporting the *placitum* of the baptized Toledan Jews to King Receswinth in 654): "We will not on any pretext, either ourselves, our children or our descendants, choose wives from our own race; but in the case of both sexes we will always link ourselves in matrimony with Christians." Quoted here in the English trans. by James Parkes in *The Conflict of the Church and the Synagogue* (London, 1934), p. 394. See also, in general, Jean Juster, *La condition légale des Juifs sous les rois visigoths* (Paris, 1912), pp. 14 ff., 36 ff., 45; Solomon Katz, *The Jews in the Visigothic and Frankish Kingdoms of Spain and Gaul* (Cambridge, Mass., 1934), *passim*.

27. See Amador de los Rios's edition of the "Green Book of Aragon" in *Revista de España*, CV (1885), 547–78; CVI (1885), 249–88, 567–603; and Cardinal Francisco Mendoza y Bobadilla's *Tizón de la nobleza española*, 3d ed. (Barcelona, 1880). Proof of "purity of blood" was often demanded even from artisans applying for admission to a Christian guild. See Julius Klein, "Medieval Spanish Guilds," in *Facts and Factors in Economic History*, in honor of E. F. Gay (Cambridge, Mass., 1932), p. 184. Sporadic manifestations of enmity toward converts also came to the fore in Spain in periods of less frequent conversion. For instance, in 1118, hardly three decades after the reconquest of Toledo by the Christians, and some nine years after a bloody anti-Jewish riot there, the local burghers forced Alphonso VII of Castile to promise them that "no Jew, not even a converted Jew, shall exercise any jurisdiction over any Christian in Toledo or its territory." See Baer's *Juden im christlichen Spanien* (Berlin, 1936), I, pt. 2, no. 18.

28. שבט יהודה, ed. by Wiener, p. 97.

29. Before this problem can be brought to a satisfactory solution, however, we have to know much more about the economic history of the Jews under the Great Caliphate and its successor states. It is to be hoped that the beginning, limited in scope and area, made by Walter J. Fischel in his *Jews in the Economic and Political Life of Mediaeval Islam* (London, 1937); and by my study of "The Economic Views of Maimonides," above, Essay

7, will be followed by many detailed researches. It must be conceded, however, that the significant Jewish contributions during Europe's "dark" ages before the First Crusade will probably remain full of obscurities. Even the few glimpses warranted to us by Eastern sources are of largely a legalistic and ritualistic, rather than economic, nature. See, e.g., Aron Freimann's brief summary, "Verbindungen von Juden in Deutschland mit denen in Babylonien und Palästina während des Mittelalters bis zum ersten Kreuzzug," ZGJD, I (1929), 165–67.

30. Despite the work done by Caro, Schipper, and the students of special phases of medieval Jewish economic history, much material, particularly outside Germany, still awaits thorough investigation. For instance, the economic data supplied by the early German מעשה הגאונים 'ס, ed. by A. Epstein and J. Freimann (Berlin, 1909), and those scattered in the *Tosafot*, have been but briefly summarized by I. Elbogen in his "Hebräische Quellen zur Frühgeschichte der Juden in Deutschland," ZGJD, I (1929), 39 ff.; and by Louis Rabinowitz in *The Social Life of the Jews of Northern France in the XII–XIV Centuries, as Reflected in the Rabbinic Literature of the Period* (London, 1938). An interesting approach, though based on only partial evidence, is exemplified by Isaac A. Agus's analysis of "The Value of the *Ketubah* as a Standard of the Economic Position of the Jews in Medieval Germany" (Hebrew), *Ḥoreb*, V (1939), 143–68. See also my *SRH*, IV, 150 ff., 312 ff.; XII, *passim*.

31. Coulton, *Medieval Panorama*, p. 310; Joseph Jacobs, *The Jews of Angevin England* (London, 1893), pp. 383 ff. See also Roth, *Jews in England*, pp. 11, 15, 123.

32. See Georg Caro, *Sozial- und Wirtschaftsgeschichte der Juden im Mittelalter*, I, 2d ed. (Frankfort, 1924), p. 250.

33. See especially the data assembled by Eugen Täubler in his "Zur Handelsbedeutung der Juden in Deutschland von Beginn des Städtewesens," *Festschrift . . . Martin Philippson* (Leipzig, 1916), pp. 381 ff.; and by Simḥa Assaf in his "Slavery and Slave Trade among the Jews in the Middle Ages" (Hebrew), *Zion*, IV (1938–39), 91–125; V (1939–40), 271–80. See also the extensive study of "L'ésclavage dans le monde ibérique médiéval" by Charles Verlinden in *Anuario de historia del derecho español*, XI–XIII (1934–36), which includes material of Jewish interest.

34. Some pertinent information on this subject may be found in Moses Hoffmann's *Der Geldhandel der deutschen Juden bis zum Jahre 1350* (Leipzig, 1910); and in the manifold discussions elicited by Werner Sombart's *Die Juden und das Wirtschaftsleben* (Leipzig, 1911). The literature of these discussions is most conveniently listed in A. Philips's "antikritisch-bibliographische Studie" under the same title, which appeared, under Sombart's auspices, in Berlin, 1929. Further light on the subject may be obtained from the views of European rabbis, incidentally analyzed by me in Essay 7 above, "The Economic Views of Maimonides"; and, as sum-

marized and adjusted to the new conditions by the sixteenth-century banker-scholar, Yeḥiel Nissim da Pisa, in his *Ḥayye 'olam*. See the brief excerpt therefrom published by A. Marx in *Ha-Ṣofeh*, VI (1922), 19–23; and in English trans. in the *American Economic Review*, VI (1916), 609–14; and the complete ed. of that work, *Banking and Finance among Jews in Renaissance Italy*, with an introd., trans., and notes by Gilbert S. Rosenthal (New York, 1962). However, the study of this entire ramified problem, both in its theoretical and practical implications, is still in its incipient stages.

35. See, especially, H. Holzapfel, *Die Anfänge der Montes Pietatis (1462–1515)* (Munich, 1903); Maurice Weber, *Les origines des monts-de-piété* (Rixheim, 1920).

36. See Pierre Vidal, "Les Juifs des anciens comtés de Roussillon et de Cerdagne," *REJ*, XV (1887), 50; Fritz Baer, *Studien zur Geschichte der Juden im Königreich Aragonien* (Berlin, 1913), p. 45.

37. Of course, Jewish loans could also be used by feudal lords to strengthen their baronial control. In fact, the lesser barons of England bitterly complained at the Parliament of Oxford in 1258 that the bigger lords (and the Crown), aided by Jewish bankers, appropriated their estates. See William Stubbs, ed., *Select Charters and Other Illustrations of English Constitutional History*, 9th ed. revised by H. W. C. Davis (Oxford, 1913), p. 377. There is also little doubt that Jewish assistance, through banking and revenue farming, was in part responsible for the extensive *Bauernlegen* by the German nobles in the late medieval period. It was largely this factor which so greatly endangered the Jewish population of southwestern Germany at the outbreak of the Peasant Wars in the early sixteenth century; though the danger was in part averted by Josel of Rosheim's courageous intervention. See Alfred Stern, "Die Juden im Grossen Deutschen Bauernkriege, 1525," *Jüdische Zeitschrift für Wissenschaft und Leben*, VIII (1870), 57–72; Josel's *Diary*, no. 11, published by Isidor Kracauer in *REJ*, XVI (1888), 89; and Ludwig Feilchenfeld, *Rabbi Josel von Rosheim* (Strasbourg, 1898), pp. 101 f., 209 f. Nevertheless, the centralizing effects of Jewish banking doubtless far exceeded its incidental strengthening of centrifugal forces.

38. A clearer knowledge of the social teachings of rabbinic Judaism in their historical development seems to be one of the urgent tasks for contemporary scholarship. The difficulties of such a study, or rather series of studies, though considerable, are not insurmountable. See my brief remarks in *JQR*, XXXII (1941–42), 324 f. The extent to which Jewish legal concepts and practices influenced non-Jewish jurists, especially in countries where Christian judges and administrators had frequent occasion to apply the teachings of Jewish law to Jewish parties, would likewise merit consideration. Pedro IV's order, in 1383, to the communities of Barcelona, Gerona, and Perpignan speedily to prepare for his use a Catalan trans-

lation of the Maimonidean Code (see Antonio Rubio y Lluch's *Documents per l'historia de la cultura catalana migeval* [Barcelona, 1908–21], I, no. 338) dramatically illustrates that it was necessary for some Christian leaders to familiarize themselves with the intricacies of Jewish law. Once acquired, such a familiarity, reinforced by the parties' disputes over controversial matters, must have made a permanent impression upon the legal thought of many an influential non-Jewish judge. Clear vestiges of such influences in the subsequent development of English law have, indeed, been found by F. Ashe Lincoln in his *The Starra: Their Effect on Early English Law and Administration* (London, 1939).

39. The enormous contributions in this field by Steinschneider are still unexcelled in either factual information or method of approach. Needless to say, many specific data have since been supplied by a great many specialists in various fields. Good, readable summaries of more recent knowledge may be found in Charles and Dorothy Singer's survey of "The Jewish Factor in Medieval Thought" in the *Legacy of Israel*, 2d impression (Oxford, 1928), pp. 173–282; and in A. Marx's "The Scientific Work of Some Outstanding Mediaeval Scholars," *Essays and Studies in Memory of Linda R. Miller* (New York, 1938), pp. 117–70.

40. See Solomon Gandz, "The Astrolabe in Jewish Literature," *HUCA*, IV (1927), 470 n. 4.

41. Fritz Baer, "Eine jüdische Messiasprophetie auf das Jahr 1186 und der dritte Kreuzzug," *MGWJ*, LXX (1926), 119. Neither were Jewish contributions in the realm of European belles-lettres, though far less conspicuous than in the field of science and philosophy, altogether negligible. The transmission of Oriental songs and tales, in both literary and oral form, must, in some part at least, have been accomplished by Jewish arrivals in the West. For their general importance in medieval literature, see H. A. R. Gibb, "Literature," in Th. Arnold's and A. Guillaume's *Legacy of Islam* (Oxford, 1931), pp. 180–209. A thorough investigation, by specialists, of the stray records, and an examination of the Jewish ingredients and contributions to the literature of the type of *El Cid* or to the works of Boccaccio might yet reveal unsuspected interrelations. Once more the role of translations, such as John of Capua's thirteenth-century rendition of the *Kalila ve-dimna* into Latin, under the title *Directorium humanae vitae*, comes first to mind. But here, too, one ought to avoid concentration on the literary masterpieces, which legitimately absorb most of the attention of literary historians, and descend to the broad expanses of the popular literature of every age. Whatever the literary quality, the popular appeal of the works is of primary concern to the student of social factors. Similarly, the Jewish assistant who helped two German poets continue the famous epic poem of Wolfram von Eschenbach on the basis of a French work evidently was not an entirely exceptional phenomenon even in the countries north of the Alps and the Pyrenees. The career of the German-Jewish *Minnesänger*, Süsskind

von Trimberg, though far more unique, likewise presupposes a degree of literary contact which could not possibly be suspected from the more formal, legalistic, official records. Although Süsskind's difficulties amidst a hostile environment undoubtedly were very great, we need not take too seriously the mood of resignation in his poem (in modernized German):

> Nach alter Judensitte will ich fortan leben
> Und stille meines Weges ziehen
> Der Mantel soll unfahn mich lang
> Tief unter meinem Hute
> Demütiglich sei nun mein Gang,
> Und nie mehr sing ich höfischen Gesang,
> Seit mich die Herren schieden von dem Gute.

From this poem Wilhelm Grau (in *Die Judenfrage in der deutschen Geschichte*, 2d ed. [Leipzig, 1937], p. 9), deduces the complete breakdown of the poet's attempted assimilation. For a more balanced analysis, see Meier Spanier, "Der Spruchdichter Süsskind von Trimberg," *Jahrbuch für jüdische Geschichte und Literatur*, XXXI (1938), 124–36.

42. "Nicolas de Lyra and Rashi: The Minor Prophets," *Rashi Anniversary Volume*, pp. 115–47; *idem, Rashi and the Christian Scholars* (Pittsburgh, 1963). Certain points of contact at the very beginning of Franco-German Bible exegesis are indicated, but not elaborated, by Israel Lévi in "Un commentaire biblique de Léontin le maître de R. Gershom (vers l'an 1000)," *REJ*, XLIX (1904), 231–43. These remarks have been but partially vitiated by A. Epstein's subsequent demonstration that the author of the commentary lived several generations later. See his "Leontin und andere Namen in den מעמים של חומש," *MGWJ*, XLIX (1905), 557–70.

43. *Biblia (Antiguo Testamento)*, published by the Duke of Berwick y Alba (Madrid, 1920–22). The fact that such a public collaboration was possible within a decade or two after the severe anti-Jewish reaction in Spain which lasted from 1391 to 1415 and culminated in the bitter disputation of Tortosa is doubly noteworthy.

44. For this reason, e.g., James I of Aragon in 1233 ordered all laymen to surrender Bibles *in Romancio* within eight days to their respective bishops. There were also other instances of such repressive legislation. See Louis I. Newman, *Jewish Influence on Christian Reform Movements* (New York, 1925), p. 316.

45. Quoted by Albert S. Cook in "The Authorized Version and Its Influence," *Cambridge History of English Literature* (Cambridge, 1919–31), IV, 43.

46. See the instances cited by Joshua Trachtenberg in his *Jewish Magic and Superstition* (New York, 1939), pp. 1 f., 271; Rubio y Lluch, *Documents*, no. 247; Baer in *Juden im christlichen Spanien* (Berlin, 1929–36), I, pt. 2, no. 352; and Roth in *Jews in England*, p. 121.

47. See Lee M. Friedman, *Robert Grosseteste and the Jews* (Cambridge, Mass., 1934); Roth, *Jews in England*, p. 129.

48. See A. Kleinhaus, "Der Studiengang der Professoren der hl. Schrift im 13. und 14. Jahrhundert," *Biblica*, XIV (1933), 381–99. A curious illustration of such extended contacts, from a slightly later period, is offered by the career of the well-known reformer Andreas Osiander. Living in Nuremberg, which by that time had excluded Jews from residence in the city, Osiander persuaded the city council to allow a Jewish schoolmaster from neighboring Schnaittach to visit him there for purposes of Hebrew instruction (1529). The knowledge so acquired the reformer then utilized for missionizing among Jewish pupils, on the one hand, and for the preparation of his remarkable pamphlet against the blood accusation, on the other. See Emanuel Hirsch, *Die Theologie des Andreas Osiander* (Göttingen, 1919), *passim*. See also, in general, the selected writings cited in my *SRH*, 1st ed., III, 136 ff.; 2d ed. VI, 272 ff., 462 ff.; and my *Bibliography of Jewish Social Studies* (New York, 1941), pp. [109 ff.].

49. See especially James II's decree of 1299 enjoining Jewish audiences in all synagogues of Aragon to listen attentively to Lull's sermons, delivered at the latter's choice on any Saturday or Sunday. The Jews, however, were given an opportunity to reply, and, if we may judge from the large controversial literature circulated by the Jews of Spain, they undoubtedly availed themselves of it often and effectively. See the text published by M. Kayserling in his "Notes sur l'histoire des Juifs en Espagne," *REJ*, XXVII (1893), 148 f. For Lull's preeminent role at the Council of Vienne (his indebtedness to Yehudah Halevi's *Kuzari* may be mentioned here in passing) and for his sponsorship of the resolution calling for the establishment of Hebrew chairs at the leading European universities, see Ewald Müller's *Das Konzil von Vienne, 1311–12* (Münster, 1934), *passim*. See also, in general, Berthold Althaner, "Glaubenszwang und Glaubensfreiheit in der Missionstheorie des Raymundus Lullus," *Historisches Jahrbuch*, XLVIII (1928), 586–610; E. A. Peers, *Ramon Lull* (London, 1929), *passim;* and Fritz Baer's brief remarks in the *Korrespondenzblatt . . . Akademie*, VI (1929), 19.

Another aspect of the polemical literature, worthy of consideration, is the stimulus indubitably given by it to the rise of vernacular literature. It is easily understandable that both attacks and apologias, addressed to the masses, had to be written in a language accessible to them, as is evidenced by the history of the later Protestant-Catholic controversy. We learn, indeed, that Isidore of Seville's *Defense of the Catholic Faith against the Jews* was translated into German in a monastery near Strasbourg as far back as the eighth or the ninth century, thus becoming one of the earliest documents of German literature. See James Parkes, *The Jew in the Medieval Community* (London, 1938), p. 32. Raymond Lull's major contribution to the vernacular Catalan literature, in which his philosophic works truly pioneered, may also have been influenced largely by his missionary interests.

50. Cecil Roth has called attention to the persistence of this paradoxical argumentation on the part of Christian disputants and polemists. See "The Mediaeval Conception of the Jew: A New Interpretation," *Essays and Studies in Memory of Linda R. Miller*, pp. 171–90. The truth of this contention is borne out by any general summary of Christian polemical literature, such as A. Lukyn Williams's *Adversus Judaeos: A Bird's-Eye View of Christian* Apologiae *until the Renaissance* (Cambridge, 1935).

51. In the tract cited above, n. 10; *PL*, CIV, 74 f.

52. See especially the searching analysis of these debates in Fritz Baer's "The Disputations of Yeḥiel of Paris and Naḥmanides" (Hebrew), *Tarbiz*, II (1931), 172–87; and "Die Disputation von Tortosa," *Spanische Forschungen der Görresgesellschaft*, 1st ser., III (1939), 307–36. Together with his fascinating study of the arguments of the baptized anti-Jewish polemist Abner of Burgos, in the *Korrespondenzblatt . . . Akademie für die Wissenschaft des Judentums*, X (1929), 20–37, these essays whetted the appetites of readers looking forward to the long-delayed publication of the special volume of Baer's *Juden im christlichen Spanien*, which was to be devoted to Judeo-Christian polemics. In the meantime, see also Bernardo Sanvisenti, "Un documento sobre la luche antijudaica en la España del siglo XV," *Boletín de la Academia Argentina de Letras*, VII (1939), 137–50. Much more preliminary work of this kind is yet needed, however, before a fuller understanding of the mainsprings and objectives of the religious controversies between Jews and Christians or Muslims, an understanding auspiciously inaugurated by the works of Steinschneider and Isidore Loeb, can be attained. See also my *SRH*, IX, Chaps. XXXVIII–XXXIX.

53. Many instances of the allegation of "judaizing" in Christian sectarian conflicts have been assembled by Louis I. Newman in his *Jewish Influence;* see the passages listed in the Index under this term. See also P. Alphandéry, "Sur les Passagiens," *REJ*, LXXXII (1926), 353–61. For the Christian Sabbath observance in the Carolingian age, see the sources cited by Solomon Katz in his study of "Pope Gregory the Great and the Jews," *JQR*, XXIV (1933), 120 n. 45. These instances could easily be multiplied.

54. These obviously unorthodox views were first expounded by me in a brief essay on "Ghetto and Emancipation," *Menorah Journal*, XIV (1928), 515–26. They were expanded in various other connections, such as my essay on "Jewish Emancipation," *Encyclopaedia of the Social Sciences*, VIII (1932), 394–99; and *SRH*, 1st ed., Vol. II, *passim*. It was a foregone conclusion that they would not be readily accepted by the majority of Jewish scholars. However, the criticism expressed in this respect by Fritz Baer in his extensive Hebrew review of *SRH*, or rather in his statement of dissenting opinions, in *Zion*, III (1937–38), 291, seems entirely beside the point. His remark that it was antisemites who first contended that the

Jews had no just reason for complaint and that Jewish authors merely followed them in denouncing the "lachrymose conception of Jewish history" is certainly erroneous insofar as I am concerned. I am still unable to locate any antisemitic forerunners; and, to the best of my knowledge, I was the first to coin the term "lachrymose conception" (in the aforementioned essay in the *Menorah Journal*), when my scholarly conscience (perhaps also, subconsciously, pride in the Jewish heritage) made me impatient with the eternal self-pity characteristic of Jewish historiography. I have fully acknowledged, however, the venerable antecedents of the doctrine of Jewish martyrology and have even tried to explain them sociologically, as reaching far back into the early stages of social control in the Diaspora community. See especially *SRH*, 1st ed., III, 5 f., 42 f., 104 f. It is high time, in any case, to divorce the indubitable reality of the general insecurity of medieval Jewish life from an objective consideration of the Jews' political and, especially, legal status in the medieval countries where they were tolerated by law.

55. This theory, once effectively championed by J. E. Scherer (in *Die Rechtsverhältnisse der Juden in den deutsch-österreichischen Ländern* [Leipzig, 1901]; further studies in this field promised by the author have unfortunately remained unpublished), has in part been abandoned by subsequent writers. The pendulum seems to have swung too far to the other side, however. See G. Kisch, "Research in Medieval Legal History of the Jews" in *PAAJR*, VI (1934–35), 240 n. 15; and his "The Jewry-Law in Medieval German Law-Books," *ibid.*, VII (1936), 64 ff.

56. A careful analysis of the deeper interrelations between medieval Jewish and Christian messianism is still a desideratum. It may be hoped that certain phrases of this interplay of ideas will be clarified by a study in preparation by my former pupil, Abraham Berger.

57. The difference between the generally accepted Palestinocentric doctrine and the far more realistic appreciation of Palestine's actual remoteness from the medieval scene by the rabbis themselves may well be observed in the examples cited by J. H. Zimmels in his study of "Erez Israel in der Responsenliteratur des späteren Mittelalters," *MGWJ*, LXXIV (1930), 44–64. That, nevertheless, the impact of the doctrine was felt in many walks of private and communal life goes without saying. See especially Fritz Baer's *Galut* (Berlin, 1936); his "Palestine and Exile in Medieval Conception" (Hebrew), *Ṣiyyon*, VI (1934), 149–71; and the few illustrations cited in my *Jewish Community*, II, 339 ff.; III, 215 f.

58. *Sententiae*, IV; dist. 4, qu. 9 in *Opera omnia* (Paris, 1891–95), XVI, 489: "Unde sufficeret aliquos paucos in aliqua insula sequestratos permitti legem suam servare, de quibus tandem illa prophetia Isaiae [10:22; quoted by Paul, Romans 9:27] impleretur."

59. This homiletical interpretation of רב יעבוד צעיר (Gen. 25:23) is used by Augustine in his *Quaestiones in Heptateuchum*, I, 83 (*PL*, XXXIV,

567: "solet et sic intelligi quod dictum est, ut in Esau figuratus sit major populus Dei, hoc est Israeliticus secundum carnem; per Jacob autem figuratus est ipse Jacob secundum spiritualem progeniem") to justify the doctrine of Jewish serfdom developed by himself and the other Church Fathers. See especially Leopold Lucas, *Zur Geschichte der Juden im vierten Jahrhundert* (Berlin, 1910), pp. 90 ff.; Jean Juster, *Les Juifs dans l'Empire Romain* (Paris, 1914), I, 44 ff., 46 n. 8, 226 ff. This doctrine found expression in the anti-Jewish legislation of the various councils of Toledo (note especially the term referring to all Hebrew persons as *perpetuae subiectae servituti*, employed by the Seventeenth Council of Toledo in 694 [can. 8 in Mansi's *Collectio*, XII, 102], which later found widespread application) and laid the foundation for the medieval doctrines of Jewish serfdom. Because of the equivocal nature of the Jewish status and the corresponding ambiguity of the legal enactments, this concept has long puzzled jurists and historians. See the remarks and the literature cited in my *SRH*, 1st ed., II, 22 ff.; III, 100 ff. Further progress has been made in the study of this complex subject by Guido Kisch and other recent writers. See especially his "The Jewry-Law in the Medieval German Law-Books, II," in *PAAJR*, X (1940), 151 ff.; and the literature quoted there. However, the vast majority of these studies have been limited to the German areas. A real resolution of the existing difficulties may be expected only from the application of similarly rigid standards to the investigation of the Jewish status, and of the juristic literature (both civil and canonical) thereon, in medieval Italy, Spain, France, and England. See *infra*, Essay 10.

60. The general attitude of the medieval cities to the Jews, despite innumerable monographs pertaining to local conditions of various Jewish communities, is yet to be fully examined. Herbert Fischer's *Die verfassungsrechtliche Stellung der Juden in den deutschen Städten während des dreizehnten Jahrhunderts* (Breslau, 1931) is, considerable reservations by critics notwithstanding (see G. Kisch's remarks in *PAAJR*, VI, 264 f., 268 f.), a step in the right direction. Similar studies for other periods and countries, not only from juridical but also from economic and sociological angles, would help lay the foundation for a real understanding of one of the vital factors in shaping the destinies of medieval Jewry. For the time being, see, particularly, my remarks (with special reference to Jewish self-government) in *JC*, I, 274 ff.; III, 63 ff., and the literature cited there; and, especially, my *SRH*, XI, Chap. XLVII, *passim*.

61. See Alfred Morel Fatio, "Notes et documents sur les Juifs des Baléares," *REJ*, IV (1882), 38 f.

62. See, e.g., the study of Jacob Shatzky in his Supplement to the Yiddish trans. of Nathan Neṭa Hannover's יון מצולה (Vilna, 1938).

63. L. Munk, "Die Judenlandtage in Hessen-Cassel," *MGWJ*, XLI (1897), 507.

64. See my "Nationalism and Intolerance," *Menorah Journal*, XVI

(1929), 405–15; XVII (1929), 148–58; *SRH*, XI, Chap. L, *passim*. None of the criticisms or differing opinions which have come to my attention have in the least shaken my conviction of the validity of this theory.

65. In Germany and Italy, particularly, the operation of these factors was greatly complicated by the conflict between Papacy and Empire; the struggle between the imperial and the territorial powers; the growing independence of the north-Italian states, as opposed to the rule of foreign dynasties in southern Italy; the growth of the Venetian Empire; and, finally, the rise of an individualistic and commercial civilization in the age of the Renaissance. Nevertheless, some phenomena akin to those in Western Europe manifested themselves in these Central-European areas.

66. These interrelations, long sensed, and, as is usual, gravely distorted by racial antisemites (see, for one example, Herman de Vries de Heekelingen's *Juifs et Catholiques* [Paris, 1939]), require much further elucidation in detail. Two authors who have contributed a good deal to the discussion of this problem—namely, Solomon Grayzel (see the introduction to his *The Church and the Jews in the XIIIth Century* [Philadelphia, 1933]) and James Parkes (see *The Conflict of the Church and the Synagogue* [London, 1934], covering the first eight centuries of the Judeo-Christian controversy; the third volume of this series, to be devoted to the same subject in the later Middle Ages, never appeared)—seem to have blocked their own way by their unqualified acceptance of the traditional view, which has blamed most of the misfortunes of medieval Jewry on the Church and its teachings. See also Grayzel, "Christian-Jewish Relations in the First Millennium," *Essays on Antisemitism*, ed. by Koppel S. Pinson (New York, 1942), pp. 25–44; and Parkes, "Christian Influence on the Status of the Jews in Europe," *Historia judaica*, I (1938), 31–38. This view, born from the stress and strain of the struggle for Emancipation, especially in Protestant countries, was even then justifiable on psychological, not scholastic, grounds. Today, when the entire Judeo-Christian world outlook is under a many-sided attack, it is high time that a calmer and more dispassionate view of these internecine conflicts replace a scholastically long-outworn conception.

67. The two brief essays on this subject by Leopold Löw in his *Gesammelte Schriften*, III (Szeged, 1893), 347–58; and by Abraham N. Z. Roth in *Ha-Soker*, V (1937–38), 110–26, have merely scratched the surface. See also my *JC*, I, 214 f.; II, 210 ff.; III, 52.

68. Mordecai b. Hillel on B.K., no. 152 (quoting a London rabbi, probably Elijah Menaḥem; the author distinguishes between מתנה, an amercement whose royal collection is illegal, and legal taxes, מסים). Similarly, Meir of Rothenburg, denouncing, as did many other medieval rabbis, arbitrary royal grants of tax immunities to Jewish favorites without a corresponding reduction of the fiscal burdens on the community as a whole, declared: המלך הבא לשנות את הדין אין שומעים לו ולא אמרינן בכה"ג דינא דמלכותא דינא דלאו דינא דמלכותא הוא. See his *Responsa*, ed. Prague, no. 134; my *Jewish Community*,

II, 274 ff.; III, 192 f. This view appears less paradoxical when one considers the general medieval reverence for custom and opposition to sudden change injurious to an entire class. This attitude, as applied to unaccustomed Jewish taxation, also dominates the well-known views of Thomas Aquinas, as they were, somewhat hastily, formulated in his epistle *De regimine Judaeorum*. For the latter's origin, see particularly Henri Pirenne, "La duchesse Aleyde de Brabant et le 'De regimine Judaeorum' de Saint Thomas d'Aquin," *Bulletin de l'Académie royale de Belgique*, Classe des Lettres, 5th ser., XIV (1928), 43-55; and *SRH*, IX, 47, 262 f. n. 52.

69. Augustine, *Epistolae*, LV (*Ad Inquisitiones Januarii*, II), 19, in *PL*, XXXIII, 221; Erasmus of Rotterdam, *Opera* (Leiden, 1703-6), VI, 64, on Matt. 11:30.

70. See M. Paléologue, "L'antisémitisme, moyen du gouvernement sous Alexandre II et Alexandre III," *Annales politiques et littéraires*, CXII (1938), 19-22; Mark Vishniak, "Antisemitism in Tsarist Russia," *Essays on Antisemitism*, ed. by Pinson, pp. 79-110.

71. Nicholas Eymeric, *Directorium inquisitorum*, ed. and annotated by F. Pegna (Venice, 1607), fol. 353b.

72. Of course, individual Christians, even ecclesiastics, may not always have approved of such latitude. The preacher Berthold of Ratisbon recommended to his listeners that they avoid religious disputations with Jewish Bible experts or else that they settle the argument quickly by thrusting a "sword into a Jew's belly as far as it would go." Cited by G. G. Coulton in his *Ten Medieval Studies* (Cambridge, 1930), pp. 35, 120. A similar story of a Christian debater in Paris, who made short work of the argument by killing his Jewish opponent, is told with much gusto by the leading preacher Caesarius of Heisterbach in one of his homilies. See *Wundergeschichten*, ed. by Alfons Hilka (Bonn, 1933-37), I, 1212. But such extralegal incidents are no more proof of the official attitude than are, for example, sanguinary preelection riots in America.

73. A most glowing description of this unity of thought, with an implicit appeal for emulation today, may be found in Étienne Gilson's "Homage to Maimonides," in *Essays on Maimonides*, ed. by me, pp. 19-35.

74. The utter misunderstanding, for instance, of the nature of the Jewish Sabbath, despite basic acceptance of the Sabbath idea by Christianity, was reflected in numerous folktales told and retold for the amusement of Christian audiences. According to one such incredible story, reflecting the crudity of medieval humor much more than Jewish attitudes, a Jew who had fallen into a sewer on a Saturday refused to be rescued on his day of rest, whereupon the prince (in one version it was the count of Champagne) ordered that he be left there during Sunday as well. See Caesarius of Heisterbach, *Wundergeschichten*, I, 151 f. and the editor's note thereto.

ESSAY 9

1. *Sefer Pardes,* ed. by H. L. Ehrenreich (Budapest, 1924), p. 161: וכשבאתי לעיר[י] . . . שמרתי הדבר בלבי עד שחזרתי לוורמישא. See also V. Aptowitzer, *Mabo le-Sefer Rabiah* (Introduction to Sefer Rabiah [Jerusalem, 1938]), p. 405 n. 20.

2. Abraham (Adolf) Berliner, *Geisteswerkstatt Raschis* (Frankfort, 1905), p. 6.

3. Rashi, on B.B. 22a s. v. ולעלמא states: יומא דשוקא הוא והרבה באין ממקום אחר לקנות מן השוק לפיכך אין בני העיר מעכבין גם על המוכרים להביא אומנותם ולמכור לנקבצים לשוק. Contrast with this the evidently more "advanced" mercantile relationships underlying the comments of the Tosafists (*ibid.*): מכאן משמע דביומא דשוקא היה מותר להלוות לבני אדם הבאים ממקומות שם לשוק לנכרים דאתו מעלמא אבל לבני המקום לא. The authorship of this statement is ascribed to the famous Isaac of Dampierre (a Champagne scholar living a century after Rashi), by Mordecai, on B.B., No. 519.

4. *Pardes,* p. 73, referring to a decision by Gershom in a reply to Rashi's teacher Jacob b. Yaḳar concerning the unlawful practice in which merchants of Mayence and Worms would borrow, before their departure for the fair of Cologne, a silver mark weighing 12 ounces but would pay back 13 ounces when they returned. That even before 1096 the Cologne fairs played a considerable role in the evolution of the Rhenish communities is evidenced also by the chronicler (Solomon b. Simson?) who showers praise on the martyr Judah b. Abraham: יועץ וחכם ונשא פנים וכשהיו כל הקהילות באים לקולוניא לשווקים ג' פעמים בשנה והיה הוא מדבר בראש כולם בבית הכנסת . . . *Hebräische Berichte über die Judenverfolgunsen während der Kreuzzüge,* ed. by A. Neubauer and M. Stern (Berlin, 1892), p. 20.

5. Félix Bourquelot, *Etudes sur les foires de Champagne, sur la nature, l'étendue et les règles du commerce qui s'y faisait aux XIIe, XIIIe et XIVe siècles,* 2 vols. (Paris, 1865); T. Boutiot, *Histoire de la ville de Troyes et de la Champagne méridionale,* I (Troyes, 1870), 191; Elisabeth Bassermann, *Die Champagnermessen. Ein Beitrag zur Geschichte des Kredits* (Tübingen, 1911); Elizabeth Chapin, *Les Villes des foires de Champagne des origines au début du XIVe siècle* (Paris, 1937), pp. 25, 29.

6. Berliner, *Beiträge zur Geschichte der Raschikommentare* (Berlin, 1903), p. 6: "For Troyes, where Rashi lived, possessed at that time widely known tanneries; hence the manufacture of parchment for writing materials was quite familiar there"; *idem, Geisteswerkstatt,* pp. 10 f.

7. See the data assembled by Leopold Zunz in his *Zur Geschichte und Literatur* (Berlin, 1845), pp. 211 ff.; and by S. Assaf in his " 'The People of the Book' and the Book" (Hebrew), *Reshumot,* I (1918), 309 ff.

8. Chapin, *Les Villes des foires,* pp. 81, 85; *Maḥzor Vitry,* No. 321 (p. 358): כי לא ראיתי נוהגין במקומינו בשום יום טוב הזכרת מקראות של מוספין, לפי שאין שגורין בפה, חוץ ממוספי שבת וראש חדש שהן תדירין ושגורין בפה.

9. Boutiot, *Histoire de Troyes*, I, 249; M. A. Gerson, "Les Juifs en Champagne," *Mémoires de la Société académique d'agriculture, des sciences, arts et belles-lettres du département de l'Aube*, LXIII (1899), 183; Chapin, *Les Villes des foires*, p. 31 and Pl. II. According to a local tradition, Rashi's house stood on a site later occupied by butcher shops (such shops still existed in the nineteenth century in the same neighborhood). This circumstance gave rise to a legend attributing to a blessing by Rashi the remarkable absence of flies from these shops, a phenomenon which the Christian population had long ascribed to a miraculous intervention of St. Loup, while modern rationalists explained it as the result of strong natural air currents. See J. J. Clément-Mullet, "Documents pour servir à l'histoire du rabbin Salomon fils d'Isaac . . . ," *Mémoires de la Société . . . de l'Aube*, XIX (1855), 159.

10. "The Early History of the Jewish Quarters in Paris," *Jewish Social Studies*, II (1940), 45–60; also in the French version in his *Les Juifs de France* (Paris, 1946), pp. 59–77.

11. Bourquelot, *Etudes sur les foires*, II, 159 ff., 191; Arsène Darmstetter, "L'Autodafé de Troyes (24 Avril 1288)," *REJ*, II (1881), 247; Bassermann, *Die Champagnermessen, passim;* Chapin, *Les Villes des foires*, pp. 105 f., 125 ff. The observation of the Tosafists quoted above, n. 3, may indeed be a reflection of this new status.

12. *Mordecai*, on B.B., No. 481; *Sefer ha-Orah*, ed. by S. Buber, II, 108; I. Elbogen, "Les 'Dinim' de R. Pereç," *REJ*, XLV (1902), 212; Meir of Rothenburg, *Responsa*, ed. Prague, No. 795; Jacob Tam, *Sefer ha-Yashar, Responsa*, ed. by F. Rosenthal (Berlin, 1898), p. 26, No. 15. See also Aptowitzer, *Mabo*, pp. 360, 423 ff. For Troyes in general, see Chapin, *Les Villes des foires*, pp. 29 ff.

13. Bourquelot, *Etudes sur les foires*, I, 447; René Bourgeois, *Du mouvement communal dans la comté de Champagne aux XIIe et XIIIe siècles* (Paris, 1904), p. 35; Mordecai, on Shabbat, No. 398; Alexander Kohut, *Aruch completum*, I, Introd., pp. xi f.; VIII, Supplement, pp. viii ff.; I. H. Weiss, *Toledot Rabbenu Shelomoh b. Yiṣḥaḳ* (A Biography of Rashi [Vienna, 1882]), p. 15; Berliner, *Beiträge*, pp. 5 f.; *Or Zaruʿa*, II, 52, 104. The explanation sometimes offered, that אני שלמה בר יצחק and שלמה היצחקי here mentioned was a rabbi other than Rashi, seems still less justified when one considers that fairly good roads connected Troyes with Italy. See the discussion in Aptowitzer's הוספות ותקונים לספר ראבי״ה (Addenda and Emendations to Sefer Rabiah [Jerusalem, 1936]), pp. 5 f. (showing that Nathan b. Yeḥiel and his brothers answered Rashi's inquiries on at least three occasions); *idem, Mabo*, pp. 371 f., 403 f.; and, for the communications between Troyes and Italy, Chapin, *Les Villes des foires*, p. 233. It was on the ancient road of Agrippa, or a variant thereof, that Count Hugh, for example, journeyed to Palestine in 1114. Neither, for that matter, does Kalonymos of Mayence seem to have encountered any serious difficulties in dispatching,

in 1095, a messenger to Henry IV, then in northern Italy, to inform him of the early disturbances in the Rhineland. See Neubauer and Stern, eds., *Hebräische Berichte,* pp. 3, 87 f. These cultural links with Italy were doubly significant, since the southern French center of Jewish learning, in and around Narbonne, gravitated exclusively toward Spanish Jewry, which as yet had few commercial or cultural relations with the communities of northeastern France. By 1160, however, the example set by Narbonne could serve as a model for a synodal ordinance in Troyes and its environs. See Tam's *Sefer ha-Yashar* (Vienna, 1811), No. 579; Louis Finkelstein, *Jewish Self-Government in the Middle Ages* (New York, 1924), pp. 43, 163 ff.

14. Mordecai, on Giṭṭin, No. 455: כך החרים ר׳ת והסכים רבינו משה תלמידו עמו וכל הגדולים גזרו בכנופיא של שוק טרוייש באלה חמורה... . See also Henri Gross, *Gallia Judaica* (Paris, 1897), pp. 444 f.; Moïse Schwab, "Manuscrits hébreux de la Bibliothèque Nationale," *REJ,* LXIV (1912), 281, referring to MS No. 1408, fol. 89a, on the decision adopted בכינופיא של שוק טרוייש; Finkelstein, *Jewish Self-Government,* pp. 44 f., 105 f.

15. Finkelstein, *ibid.,* pp. 41 f., 150 ff. Since the identification (*ibid.*) of חכמי גבול ריינס with "the Sages of the Rhine country" has rightly been rejected by both his predecessors and his successors (see, e.g., Gross, *Gallia judaica,* pp. 234 f.; Moritz Stern in *Monatsblätter für Vergangenheit und Gegenwart des Judentums,* 1890–91, p. 30; and Fritz Baer's review of Finkelstein's book in *MGWJ,* LXXI [1927], p. 396 n. 1), his assumption that Eliezer b. Nathan of Mayence and Eliezer b. Samson of Cologne participated in the deliberations has no support in the original record. The mere mention of their names in Meir of Rothenburg's *Responsa,* ed. Prague, No. 1022, need not even indicate their immediate approval of the resolutions adopted in Troyes, as suggested by Selig Auerbach in *Die rheinischen Rabbinerversammlungen im* 13. *Jahrhundert* (Würzburg, 1932), p. 13. In fact, there is no way of telling how many leaders, apart from the four signers, attended the conference. The resolution itself reads: יש שכבר הסכימו ויש.אשר לא שמענו דבריהם כי היה הדבר נחוץ וסמכנו על אשר ידענו גדולים נשמעים לקטנים ובדין דין אמת.

16. Meir of Rothenburg, *Responsa,* ed. Berlin, pp. 320 ff. No. 866: אנחנו שוכני טרוייש עם קהלות אשר סביבותיה... הועתק מר׳ שלמה מטרוייש. See Finkelstein, *Jewish Self-Government,* pp. 36 f., 148 ff.; and below, n. 40. The term שוכני, too, conveys the idea of a plenary assembly of all adult male members rather than of a meeting of a few representative leaders. On the other hand, the extant records concerning some forty-three Jewish settlements under the reign of the counts of Champagne (assembled by Gerson, in *Mémoires de la Société . . . de l'Aube,* LXIII, 221 ff.), although mostly dating from a much later period, clearly indicate the great diffusion of the Jewish population in that section of the country.

17. Boutiot, *Histoire de Troyes,* I, 180 f., 195 ff.; Mansi, *Concilia,* XX, 1218 ff. (concerning the "universal" Council of Troyes in 1107 in the

presence of Paschal II): "Omnes eos excommunicaverit, qui pacem vio-
larent, et praecipue eos qui res ecclesiasticas usurparent, vel personas in
aliquo injuste laederent, ut nec in vita, nec in morte, ecclesiae communi-
onem haberent, nisi digna satisfactione prius recipiscerent." Ever since
the Carolingian Empire the Jews had enjoyed the protection of some sort
of royal "peace," which in a feudal territory such as Champagne must have
been extended to them by the counts. The "truce" proclaimed in Mayence
in 1103 by virtue of an agreement between Henry IV, his son, and the
feudal lords (see Aronius, *Regesten*, No. 210), though undoubtedly
prompted by the breakdown of royal protection during the massacres of
the Crusaders, was novel in its method of enforcement, not in its substance.
See e.g., J. E. Scherer, *Die Rechtsverhältnisse der Juden in den deutsch-
österreichischen Ländern* (Leipzig, 1901), I, 84.

18. L. Rabinowitz, *The Social Life of the Jews of Northern France in
the XII–XIV Centuries* (London, 1938), pp. 30 ff. These figures confirm
my independent estimates on the basis of some extant tax records from
France and Germany.

19. Robert of Auxerre *Chronicle*, in *MGH*, Scriptores, XXVI (Hanover,
1882), 253, referring to a conflagration which had destroyed a large part
of the city. There is some evidence that Provins, which the same author
likewise includes in the *urbes populose opulentesque*, had a population of
less than 10,000, which, after all, compares favorably with Frankfort's
estimated 8,719 inhabitants in 1440 and Basel's population of some 8,000
in 1450. See, e.g., Henri Pirenne, *Les anciennes démocraties des Pays-Bas*
(Paris, 1910); Chapin, *Les Villes des foires*, pp. 53, 62 f.

20. *Sefer ha-Yashar*, ed. Rosenthal, p. 63 No. 36: ובעירנו אין מי, כי כלם אחים
וקרובים לבד רבנו שלמה ב'ר יצחק. See also *Sefer ha-Yashar*, ed. Vienna, 1811, No.
595: מי ינור לנו מוקדי עולם כי בושנו ונכלם על מקום רבינו שלמה ועיר קברות אבותי אשר קלקלו
... בה לבייש חתניו ובני בנותיו.

21. Gross, *Gallia Judaica*, pp. 226, 239, quoting the MS of *Shibbole ha-
Leket*, II; Meir of Rothenburg, ed. Prague, No. 546 (referring to a decision of Isaac of Dampierre allowing a change in venue on account of the
great power of Abraham of Troyes, שהיה ראש העיר וכלם נשענים עליו); Ulysse
Robert, "Catalogue d'actes relatifs aux Juifs du moyen-âge," *REJ*, III
(1880), 213 (in 1222, Count Thibaut confirmed a receipt for 160 livres
given to Jacob, "master of the Jews of Troyes"). See also Bourquelot,
Études sur les foires, I, 160 f.; Aptowitzer, *Mabo*, pp. 387, 420 (giving
variants to Meir of Rothenburg's report). Even if we assume that Rashi
held in his community a position similar to that of Salmann (Solomon b.
Samson) in Worms and that of Judah b. Kalonymos and his associates in
Spires (see Moses Frank, *Kehillot Ashkenaz u-bate dinehen* [The German
Communities and Their Courts from the Twelfth to the Fifteenth Century],
Tel Aviv, 1938, pp. 2 f.), there is absolutely no evidence to support the
hypothesis voiced by Wilhelm Bacher: "dass ihm, der wohl auch als das

religiöse Oberhaupt seiner Gemeinde tätig war, die niederen Sorgen des Lebens erspart blieben." See his essay on "Raschi" in *Jahrbuch für jüdische Geschichte und Literatur*, IX (1906), 91.

22. See the text, in the relation of Menaḥem b. Makhir, published by A. Epstein in his *Schemaja, der Schüler und Sekretär Raschis* (Berlin, 1897; reprinted from *MGWJ*), pp. 22 f. Under the circumstances, it appears rather dubious whether "the number of Jews in the community [of Cologne] during the last quarter of the eleventh century could not have been less than six hundred," as stated by Adolf Kober in his fine monograph on *Cologne* (Philadelphia, 1940), p. 13. Kober seems to rely too much upon the casualty figures quoted by the chroniclers of the massacres. See, e.g., Neubauer and Stern, eds., *Hebräische Berichte*, pp. 20, 121, concerning the three hundred Cologne Jews slain in Altenahr. Apart from the probable inclusion in this number of refugees who had found temporary shelter in Cologne (the designation of that community as עדר האסוף, *ibid.*, p. 17, was probably due to this circumstance), the natural exaggerations in all such cases, and the general unreliability of medieval chroniclers in regard to numbers, the authenticity of Solomon b. Simson's report has been subjected to serious doubts by I. Sonne's "Nouvel examen des trois relations hébraïques sur les persécutions de 1096," *REJ*, XCVI (1933), 133–56.

23. *Sefer ha-Orah*, I, 31. This law may have been derived from an earlier decision in *Seder R. Amram Gaon*, but its actuality was greater in the early Franco-German communities than in the populous Jewish settlements of the ninth-century Middle East. The use here and in the following paragraph of the term ש"ץ rather than חזן may well be explained by the phrasing of the geonic sources. Otherwise Rashi seems familiar with the medieval usage of the term *ḥazzan*, as well as with its older meaning of "sexton." While in his *Commentary* on Berakhot 53a and Yoma 68b (M. VII, 1) he correctly renders the term by the word שמש, in his comments on M. Shabbat I, 3 (11a), he explains the same term as המקרא את השבעה מהקוראים בתורה. The second, obviously more authentic, identification with מלמד תינוקות is probably a later gloss, possibly added by Rashi's son-in-law, Judah b. Nathan. See J. N. Epstein, "The Commentaries of R. Judah ben Nathan and the Commentaries of Worms" (Hebrew), *Tarbiz*, IV (1932–33), 17, 32. Judah b. Nathan is probably also the author of the statement on Makkot 22b pleading ignorance of the etymology of the term *ḥazzan* as applied to the שמש הקהל. See *ibid.*, pp. 15, 183 f. More significant, however, is that, without prompting by the talmudic text, Rashi on his own uses the term חזן as equivalent to ש"ץ in his comments on Ber. 34a s. v. אם and on Ta'anit 15a (M. II, 1) s. v. ורגיל, calling forth objections by the Tosafists on the former passage and by Joel Sirkes on the latter. Rashi's authorship of the commentary on Ta'anit, however, is rather doubtful. See the literature cited in E. M. Lipschütz's Hebrew biography of *Rashi* (Warsaw, 1912), p. 68 n. 4. In any case, the conclusion does not seem warranted that the Franco-

German congregations during the eleventh century could afford to maintain a salaried "reader," unless he combined with this office the services of a sexton and other functions.

24. Finkelstein, *Jewish Self-Government*, pp. 124 f., 137 f., 192, 196 f.

25. *Ibid.*, pp. 14 f., 376 f.; Asher Gulak, *Yesodot ha-mishpaṭ ha-'ibri* (Principles of Jewish Law), I (Berlin, 1923), pp. 172 ff.; Rabinowitz, *Jews of Northern France*, pp. 255 f.; *idem*, "The Talmudic Basis of the Ḥerem ha-Yishub," *JQR*, XXVIII (1937–38), 217–23; *idem*, "The Medieval Jewish Counterpart to the Gild Merchant," *Economic History Review*, VIII (1937–38), 180–85.

26. *Sefer Ḥasidim*, ed. Wistinetzki, No. 1301: ויש מקומות שהנויים דנים באמת ולא היהודים, מפני שמעט תלמידי חכמים שם או ממשפחות מרובות או ממקומות מרובות מלוקטין מהרבה משפחות, ואותם שבאו ממקום אחר שתרבותם רע מתעים אותם אחריהם. See also *ibid.* Nos. 1300, 1600, etc.

27. The first direct reference to such a *takkanah* seems to have been made four centuries later by Jacob Weil in Isserlein's *Pesaḳim*, No. 126. The text quoted here from *Or Zaru'a*, however, evidently refers only to the comment attributed to Gershom. See next note. Unfortunately, our text of *Or Zaru'a* (III, Pt. 3, p. 8) contains no comments on this passage of Baba Batra.

28. The English translation of the talmudic passage here cited largely follows the rendition of Maurice Simon in the complete translation of the Babylonian Talmud issued by the Soncino Press in London. The text of Gershom's commentary on B.B. 21b reads: ואי שייך אכרנא להתם שפורעין מס גלגולתם לאדון אחד דמי מכאן דהוה תרווייהו מאותה העיר ולא מצו מעכב ליה. For its authorship see A. Epstein's penetrating investigation, "Der Gerschom Meor ha-Golah zugeschriebene Talmud-Commentar," *Festschrift . . . Steinschneider* (Leipzig, 1896), pp. 115–43.

29. Rashi, *ibid.*, s. v.ואי, translates it: שנותן מס גלגלתו למושל העיר הזאת כבר מתא.

30. S. D. Luzzatto in *Bet ha-oṣar*, I (1847), 57a–60. This inquiry is also briefly mentioned by Mordecai, on B.B., No. 517, as having been found in a collection of responsa brought from "distant islands." The Roman teachers are said to have considered a temporary residence permit a definite departure from the *ḥerem* and hence the equivalent of a permanent right of sojourn. Of course, Mordecai b. Hillel could not subscribe to this view, which would evidently deprive the leaders of the German communities of all discretion in admitting visitors.

31. *Sefer ha-Yashar*, Responsa, pp. 167 f. Nos. 71–72. Whether or not Tam, in writing this responsum, already lived permanently in Troyes, whither he moved from Ramerupt toward the end of his life (see H. Gross, "Étude sur Simson b. Abraham de Sens," *REJ*, VI [1882], 175 n. 4, 183), the inquiry very likely came from one of the smaller settlements in northern France.

32. This interpretation, handed down by Jacob Tam's student Eliezer of

Orléans, is mentioned in *Or Zaru'a*, I, 115: אליעזר ר' הרב של תשובה לי ויש טרוייש של מביה"כ כשיצא תם רבינו מפי העדות כן ששמע זצ"ל מאורליינוש. See also Meir of Rothenburg's *Responsa*, ed. Lwów, No. 11. This tradition has all the earmarks of authenticity.

33. See Alfasi on B.B. *loc. cit.*; Joseph ibn Megas, *Ḥiddushe Baba Batra* (Amsterdam, 1702), fol. 5d f.: כמוניה כל לאו ללוקחים הרווחה דאיכא כיוון הלכך לאחרינו ויפסדו לנפשייהו דמתקני דמוכרים; Maimonides, *Mishneh Torah*, Shekhenim, VI, 8–12, and the comments of Don Vidal and *Haggahot Maimuniot* thereon; Eliezer b. Joel ha-Levi quoted by Meir of Rothenburg, Responsa, ed. Lwów, No. 77; and by Mordecai, on B.B., No. 519. See also the annotations *ibid.* Similarly, the only text of a *ḥerem ha-yishub* extant from medieval England, with its relatively expanding economy—the so-called Canterbury Treaty of 1266—withheld the right of settlement only from a "liar, improper person and slanderer." See the text in the English trans. by J. M. Rigg, reprinted and annotated by L. Rabinowitz in *Miscellanies of the Jewish Historical Society of England*, III (1937), 76–79. It may be worthy of mention that the Tosafists commenting on those passages in B.B. 21b subscribed to Rashi's view that we are to accept the decision of R. Huna the son of R. Joshua as law, but at the same time decided that the inhabitants of a particular quarter might nevertheless keep out competing craftsmen or traders from their quarter. These two decisions evidently reflected conditions in communities where the Jews were not yet legally limited to a single quarter, and where a newcomer could erect a competitive establishment in one of the unrestricted areas. It might, indeed, correspond to the situation in Troyes, with its two Jewish streets and, possibly, even Jewish residences outside of both.

34. H. d'Arbois de Jubainville, *Histoire des ducs et des comtes de Champagne*, V (Paris, 1863), pp. 175 f. No. 1398.

35. The great municipal charters of Troyes (dated in 1230) and of Provins (dated in 1252), known for many decades, have been reprinted from the original documents by Chapin, *Les Villes des foires*, pp. 288 ff. They show to what length the counts were ready to go in encouraging municipal liberties. A significant difference may be detected in regard to the two cities, however: In Provins the count unreservedly retained full, direct jurisdiction over the clergy, the nobility, and the Jews, while in Troyes he promised that the amends due him from all such cases shall be adjudicated "in accordance with the usage and customs of Troyes by the mayor and the jurymen of Troyes." See *ibid.*, p. 289. See also the observation in the *Chronicle* of the monk Albericus, p. 531: "Comes Campaniae communas burgensium fecit et rusticorum in quibus magis confidebat quam in militibus suis"; and, in general, Bourgeois, *Du mouvement communal*.

36. See Solomon Grayzel, *The Church and the Jews in the XIIIth Century* (Philadelphia, 1933), Nos. 18, 39.

37. Boutiot, *Histoire de Troyes*, I, 285. Incidentally the term "sale" of

Jews, used in this as in many other medieval documents, has little bearing upon the significance of medieval Jewish serfdom. For instance, see also the characteristic phrase in Asher b. Yeḥiel's *Responsa*, VI, 15:והם חקרו ודרשו כי מכרוהו קהל ולדוליד לקהל קריאון ואינו חייב לפרוע מס לקהל ולדוליד. See also, in general, *SRH*, XI, 3 ff.

38. Robert in *REJ*, III, 212 f.; Grayzel, *The Church and the Jews*, pp. 351 ff.; Bourquelot, *Etudes sur les foires*, II, 167 f.

39. Tosafot on B.Ḳ. 58a: כי ראינו במדינה שסביבותינו שמשפט היהודים לעמוד כמו פרשים בכל מקום שירצו, ובדין מלכותא היו תופשין שלא יחזיק המושל בנחלת היהודים כשיצאו מעירו, וכן היו נוהגין בכל ארץ בורגוניא.

40. Meir of Rothenburg, *Responsa*, ed. Berlin, p. 321, no. 866 (Finkelstein, *Jewish Self-Government*, p. 149): אכל שמענו שכך מנהג הקדמונים שאחד מבני העיר שיש לו ממון שהוציא מן העיר שיתן מן הכל, לבד אם כא לגור ולא להכניס ממונו בעיר לא יתן עד שיכניסם וישא ויתן בהם, ואם היה צרור ומונח לא יתן עד שישלח בו יד, ואם מן הדרים באן נותנים מתנה לבניהם או לבנותיהם והוציאו מן העיר כל זמן שהבנים בעיר או הלכו מן העיר לפי שעה ודעת האב להחזירם בעיר יתן בעול צבור מאותו ממון ... Later these restrictions were both multiplied and made more severe by numerous local ordinances. Even in more "liberal" thirteenth-century Spain, Ibn Adret mentions a local ordinance prescribing that any Jew marrying off a daughter or a sister to a nontaxpayer should pay the regular capital flight tax on the amount of dowry given her, "as if he had left the city to settle in another locality." See his *Responsa*, III, 406.

ESSAY 10

1. Y. F. Baer, ארץ ישראל וגלות בעיני הדורות של ימי הבינים (Palestine and Exile in the View of Medieval Generations), *Zion*, VI (1934), 153 ff.; *idem*, *Galuth* (New York, 1947), pp. 16 ff.; and, regarding Spain, *idem*, *Studien zur Geschichte der Juden im Koenigreich Aragoniem während des 13. und 14. Jahrhunderts* (Berlin, 1913), pp. 11 ff.; תולדות היהודים בספרד הנוצרית 2d ed. (Tel Aviv, 1959), pp. 49 f., and in the English trans. by Louis Schoffman entitled *A History of the Jews in Christian Spain* (Philadelphia, 1961), I, 85 ff.

2. *SRH*, 1st ed., II, 22 ff.; III, 100 ff.; 2d ed., IV, 36 ff., 48 ff., 58 ff., 70 ff., and 79 ff.; XI, 3 ff; as well as relevant notes to these pages. See above, Essay 8, "The Jewish Factor in Medieval Civilization."

3. Guido Kisch, "The Jewry-Law of the Medieval German Law-Books," *PAAJR*, X (1940), 130 ff.; and, enlarged in book form, *The Jews in Medieval Germany* (Chicago, 1949), pp. 129 ff. and 421 ff. Here and in my work above n. 2 the reader will find an extensive bibliography pertaining to earlier research on this problem.

4. Because of limitations of space, I will confine my discussions to this involved and difficult problem only, without reference to the various opinions and controversies around this theme.

5. See below.

6. Selig Cassel, "Juden (Geschichte)," *Allgemeine Encyklopädie der Wissenschaften und Künste*, ed. J. S. Ersch and J. S. Gruber, Vol. II, 27, (Leipzig, 1850) pp. 86 ff.

7. Augustine *Civitas Dei* iv.34; *Sermones* 374, 2; in *PL*, XXXIV, 567; XXXIX, 1666 ff., and additional references cited in Bernard Blumenkranz, *Die Judenpredigt Augustins* (Basel, 1946); and in my *SRH*, 2d ed., III, 168 ff. and 298 ff.

8. Augustine *Quaestiones in Heptateuchum* 1. 83; Tertullian *Adversus Judaeos* 3; *idem, Apologeticus adversus gentes*, in Migne, *PL*, XXXII, 567; I, 451; II, 637; and in my *SRH*, II, 136 f., 381 f. n. 10.

9. The decisions of the Seventeenth Council of Toledo, in Mansi, *Sacrorum conciliorum collectio*, XII, 102 ff.; see also *Leges Visigothorum*, xii.2, 18, ed. Zeumer, pp. 426 ff. and 481 ff.

10. The political theories of the Church which evolved during this period of tension between the Papacy and the Empire are still the concern of scholars of the history of the European Middle Ages. Suffice it to mention these important works: Walter Ullmann, *Medieval Papalism* (London, 1949); *idem, The Growth of Papal Government in the Middle Ages* (New York, 1954); Ernst H. Kantorowicz, *The King's Two Bodies: A Study in Medieval Political Theology* (Princeton, 1957); and the rich material assembled by Ewart Lewis in his *Medieval Political Ideas*, 2 vols. (New York, 1954).

11. Leo VII *Epistolae et privilegiae*, in *PL*, CXXXII, 1084 ff.; the excerpt published by Abraham Berliner, מעשה נורא, *Ozar Tov*, III (1877), 46–48; and my references in *SRH*, 2d ed., III, 27 ff., 224 ff.; IV, 5 ff., 235 ff., 265.

12. The decisions of the Lateran Council of 1078, par. 10, in Mansi, *Collectio*, XII, 384 ff.; XX, 507, Introduction; the letter of Gregory VII to Alphonso VI, dated August 25, 1081, in Philip Jaffé, *Monumenta Gregoriana*, pp. 331 and 472.

13. The brief list by Shem-Ṭob Sonzolo was reproduced in Ibn Verga's *Shebeṭ Yehudah*, ed. M. Wiener, p. 112; ed. Shohet, p. 146. The date of this Council is uncertain and has been discussed by various scholars. See my interpretation in *SRH*, IV, 11 ff. and 238 n. 9.

14. *The Itinerary of Benjamin of Tudela*, ed. M. A. Adler (London, 1906), p. 6; the decisions of the Third Lateran Council of 1179, in Mansi, *Collectio*, XII, 355 ff. Included here is the confirmation of the *Sicut* bull by Alexander III, which is the earliest extant copy of this bull. Together with the other decisions of the Council, this edict is included in the collection of canon laws by Gregory IX, known as the *Decretales*. See *Corpus juris canonici*, ed. Emil Friedberg (2d ed.), II, 322 and 773.

15. St. Bernard of Clairvaux in Letter 363 of his *Epistolae*, in *PL*, CLXXXII, 567 ff. and 570 ff. This well-known letter, which favorably influenced the Crusaders toward the Jews during the Second Crusade, was sent

not only to France and Germany but also to England, where the attitude toward the Jews was more benevolent. On the variants in the text of the Paris Bibliothèque Nationale MS, see the English trans. by B. S. James, *St. Bernard of Clairvaux Seen Through His Selected Letters* (Chicago, 1953), pp. 268 ff. Bernard's general attitude toward the Jews is discussed in my *SRH*, IV, 121 and 300 n. 41.

16. See especially the letters of Innocent III, in his *Epistolae*, part I, no. 495; part III, no. 22; in *PL*, CCXIV, 458 and 779; Alanus, cited by Ullmann, *Medieval Papalism*, pp. 147 ff.; Guillaume Durand, *Speculum judiciale*, ed. Basel, 1574, I, 51; the other sources, quoted by Ullmann, *loc. cit.*; and in his *Growth of Papal Government*, pp. 413 ff.; R. W. Carlyle and A. J. Carlyle, *A History of Medieval Political Theory in the West*, especially part II of Vol. VIII; and by E. Lewis, *Medieval Political Ideas*, Vol. II.

17. Innocent III, *Epistolae*, *PL*, CCXIV, 312 and 864; CCXV, 502, 694, and 1166; the decisions of the Fourth Lateran Council, par. 68, in Mansi, *Collectio*, XXII, 1055. All these sources are reproduced and newly translated into English by Solomon Grayzel, *The Church and the Jews in the XIIIth Century*, pp. 86 ff., 92 ff., 104 ff., 112 ff., 125 ff., and 308 ff. In all these matters Innocent went beyond his predecessors and even farther than did his teacher in Roman law, Ugoccio of Pisa, who had likewise taught that the pope may interfere in any legal matter involving sin (*ratione peccati*), as well as in any case where the law is not properly observed. See, particularly, M. Maccarone, *Chiesa e Stato nella dottrina di papa Innocenzo III* (Rome, 1940); Friedrich Kempf, *Papstum und Kaisertum bei Innocenz III*, Miscellanea Historiae Pontificae, Vol. IX (Rome, 1954); Alfred Hof, " 'Plentitudo potestatis' and 'Imitatio imperii' zur Zeit Innocenz III," *Zeitschrift für Kirchengeschichte*, LXVI (1954–55), 39–71. Concerning the Jewish aspects of the widespread and fateful activities of this pope, see especially M. Elias, "Die römische Kirche, besonders Innocenz III und die Juden," *Jahrbuch der Jüdisch-Literarischen Gesellschaft, Frankfurt a.M.*, XII (1918), 37–82.

18. The letters of Gregory IX, ed. by Lucien Auvray, *Les Registres de Grégoire IX* (Paris, 1899–1908), nos. 1159, 1216, 1426, 2525, 3308, 3312. On the Talmud, see Jacques Quétif and Jacques Eckard, *Scriptores Ordinis Predicatorum* (Paris, 1719–21), I, 128 ff.; Heinrich Denifle and G. Chatelaine, *Chartularium Universitatis Parisiensis*, I, 201 ff.; the letters of Innocent III of July 15, 1205, in *PL*, CXV, 694 no. 121. All these sources are also to be found in Grayzel, *The Church and the Jews*, pp. 198–207 f., 218, 226, and 238 ff. See below, n. 34. Much has been written on the burning of the Talmud in France and the orders issued by earlier and subsequent popes. Nevertheless, there still remains room for further research if we desire to understand these developments in the light of the international controversies and the expansion of ecclesiastical versus imperial power during that epoch.

19. See Elie Berger, *Registres d'Innocent IV* (Paris, 1884–1911), nos. 682, 2838, 3077. The 1246 letter to the bishop of Marseilles was published again by Carl Rodenberg, *Epistolae saeculi XII*, in *MGH* (Berlin, 1883–94), part II, p. 175 no. 236, and see below, n. 34. The important declaration of Innocent IV on the power of the pope to intervene in the internal affairs of nonbelievers ("heretics"), including Jews, is to be found in his *Apparatus ad quinque libros decretalium*, iii.34, 8. All these sources but the last are in Grayzel, *The Church and the Jews*, pp. 250 ff., 258–265, 268 ff. and 274 ff. See also Nicholas Eymeric, *Directorium inquisitorum*, ed. Venice, 1607, p. 353b; and the works of Morits Stern, *Urkundliche Beiträge über die Stellung der Päpste zu den Juden* (Kiel, 1893–97), I, 5 ff. nos. 1 and 2 (the confirmation of the *Sicut* bull by Gregory X in 1272, the inclusion of references to blood libels, and the privilege of Edward of Savoy of 1329); and *Päpstliche Bullen über die Blutbeschuldigung* (Munich, 1900). On the general political ideas of Innocent IV, see the interesting summary by R. W. Carlyle and A. J. Carlyle, *Medieval Political Theory*, V. 318 ff. The attitude of this pope to the Jews also needs further investigation.

20. Thomas Aquinas *Summa Theologica*, bk. 2, pt. 2, q. 10, par. 10, etc., in the large Rome edition (under the patronage of Pope Leo XIII) of all his works, VIII, 93; *De regimine Judaeorum ad ducissam Brabantiae*, beginning of sect. 1, ed. Parma, 1865, XVI, 292 ff. The question of whether this celebrated philosopher, who also influenced some medieval Jewish thinkers, was an antisemite or not is a topic which has occupied both Christian and Jewish theologians and historians for many years. See especially Jacob Guttmann, *Das Verhältniss des Thomas von Aquino zum Judentum und zur jüdischen Literatur* (Göttingen, 1891); Abbé Hippolyte Gayraud, *L'Antisémitisme de St. Thomas d'Aquin* (Paris, 1896); and the controversy between B. Mailloux, *St. Thomas et les Juifs*, which is part of his *Essais et bilans* (Ottawa, 1935), pp. 217–35; and Samuel S. Cohon, *St. Thomas et les Juifs* (Montreal, 1935). However, with regard to Jewish "serfdom," the "Doctor Angelicus"—as many generations of admirers called him—neither contributed anything new nor at all clarified the concept. On the contrary, the equivocal notions of canon law, which emanate from its teachers and interpreters, crept into his writings as well.

21. Otto Stobbe, *Die Juden in Deutschland während des Mittelalters*, 2d ed. (Leipzig, 1902), pp. 8 f. (see the notes by Guido Kisch in *Otto Stobbe und die Rechtsgeschichte der Juden*, which was reprinted in his *Forschungen zur Rechts- und Sozialgeschichte der Juden in Deutschland während des Mittelalters* [Zurich, 1955], pp. 199 ff.); R. Hoeniger, "Zur Geschichte der Juden im frühern Mittelalter," *ZGJD*, I (1887), 65–97, 136–51. See also some additional bibliography in my *SRH*, IV, 272 ff.

22. Julius Aronius with the collaboration of Albert Dresner und Ludwig Lewinski, *Regesten zur Geschichte der Juden im Fränkischen und Deut-*

schen Reiche bis zum Jahre 1273 (Berlin, 1902). There are several new editions of these documents; but, in reality, no important changes in the text itself have been made, though differences in interpretation do exist. Since most of the material has been preserved only in later copies, it is not astonishing to find in them numerous "emendations" by the copyists.

23. Johannes E. Scherer, *Beiträge zur Geschichte des Judenrechts im Mittelalter*, I: *Die Rechtsverhältnisse der Juden in den deutsch-österreichischen Ländern* (Leipzig, 1901), especially pp. 62 ff.

24. See the letter of Henry IV, reprinted in C. Erdmann, *Die Briefe Heinrichs IV.* (Berlin, 1939), p. 19 no. 13; and the letter by Bishop Rüdiger to the clergy of Lombardy, in *MGH, Constitutiones*, I, 118 no. 69. See also *ibid.*, p. 112 no. 63; and, in more detail, the chapter on "Royal Reaction and Episcopal Resistance," in Ullmann, *Growth of Papal Government*, pp. 344 ff.; and Lewis, *Medieval Political Ideas*, II, 430 ff.

25. Aronius, *Regesten*, pp. 69 ff. nos. 168, 170, and 171, also the bibliography given there. Regarding the questions of whether the texts of these privileges have been changed by copyists, whether the charter concerning the Jews of Speyer was based on earlier Roman privileges, and whether Henry IV issued a similar law in favor of the Jews of Ratisbon in 1097, see the notes and comments of Eugen Täubler in his "Urkundliche Beiträge zur Geschichte der Juden im Mittelalter," in *Mitteilungen des Gesamtarchivs der deutschen Juden*, IV (1913), 31 ff.; Sarah Schiffmann, in her dissertation *Heinrich IV. und die Bischöfe in ihrem Verhalten zu den deutschen Juden zur Zeit des ersten Kreuzzuges* (Berlin, 1931), especially pp. 44 ff.; and D. von Gladiss, in his new edition of *Die Urkunden Heinrichs IV.*, in *MGH, Diplomatica*, VI (Weimar, 1952–53), 543 ff.

26. Aronius, *Regesten*, pp. 93 ff. nos. 203, 204, and 210. Since Stobbe (*Die Juden in Deutschland*, p. 10), this peace treaty was regarded, together with the other steps taken by the emperors, as the beginning of "Jewish serfdom." It is self-evident that the great crisis of 1096 considerably lowered the status of the Jews in the realm. However, "serfdom" was not at the beginning interpreted as a decline of the legal status of the Jews, but only as a special, strong relationship with the imperial power.

27. St. Bernard of Clairvaux *De consideratione*, i.3; ii.2, 84, in *PL*, CLXXXII, 732 and 752; also his *Epistolae*, nos. 363 and 365, in *PL*, CLXXXII, 567 and 570 ff. See my *SRH*, IV, 10 f., 120 f., 237 n. 8, 300 f. nn. 40–42.

28. Aronius, *Regesten*, pp. 123 no. 280, 139 ff. no. 314a (see also p. 147 no. 325); and the Frankish peace treaty of 1179 in *MGH, Constitutiones*, I, 380 ff. no. 277. See also Täubler, in *Mitteilungen des Gesamtarchivs*, IV, 32 ff. and 44 ff.; and Raphael Straus, *Regensburg and Augsburg* (Philadelphia, 1939), pp. 9 f. The events of 1187–88 are retold in detail in the chronicle of R. Ephraim of Bonn, newly published by A. M. Habermann, ספר גזירות אשכנז וצרפת (Records of Anti-Jewish Persecutions in Germany and

France [Jerusalem, 1946]), p. 130. See also the story of R. Eleazar b. Yehudah (*Roḳeaḥ*), *ibid.*, pp. 163 ff.; and in my *SRH*, IV, 304 n. 52. See my discussion, *ibid.*, p. 274 n. 92, concerning the question of whether the historical introduction of 1182 was part of the original privilege renewed by Barbarossa or, which is more likely, was added by the emperor in order to stress that his authority over the Jews was supreme. See also the analysis of H. Karge, *Die Gesinnung und die Massnahmen Alexanders III. gegen Friedrich I. Barbarossa* (Greifswald, 1914); and, on the general and particular background of the controversy, the biographies of the two leaders in R. Wahl, *Kaiser Friedrich Barbarossa* (Munich, 1950), and Marcel Pacaut, *Alexandre III: Étude sur la conception du pouvoir pontifical dans sa pensée et son oeuvre* (Paris, 1956).

29. Aronius, *Regesten*, pp. 167 no. 379, 171 nos. 384 and 385, 180 no. 403, 187 f. nos. 422 and 428. The politics of Henry can be clearly seen from his transfer, to the duke of Jülich, of the right to treat the Jews who settled in his duchy (1277) as he saw fit. It is also noteworthy that thirty years after he had reconfirmed the important privilege of the Jews of Ratisbon, he gave his income from them to Bishop Siegfried as a reward for his past and future services (1230–33). Aronius, *Regesten*, pp. 195 no. 441, 197 no. 448, and 201 ff. no. 459.

30. The controversy between Frederick and Gregory IX, followed by Innocent IV, has been dealt with many times. See especially Carlyle and Carlyle, *Medieval Political Theory*, Vol. V; Ernst Kantorowicz, *Kaiser Friedrich der Zweite* (Berlin, 1927), and in the *Ergänzungsband* thereto (Berlin, 1931), or, in English trans., *Frederick the Second, 1194–1250* (New York, 1931); also in his *The King's Two Bodies*. See also the biography by D. C. Einstein, *Emperor Frederick II* (New York, 1949); and, on the papal side, J. *Felten, Papst Gregor IX.* (Freiburg, 1886); and F. Podesta, *Papa Innocenzo IV* (Milan, 1928).

31. Aronius, *Regesten*, pp. 194 no. 440, 197 no. 448; Grayzel, *The Church and the Jews*, p. 178 no. 57. It is obvious that the popes intervened most in matters more directly relating to the Christian faith. When the bishop of Strasbourg brought before Gregory the case of a father who had converted to Christianity and wanted to gain custody of his child from the Jewish mother, the pope decided (in 1229) in favor of the apostate. This decision was shortly thereafter incorporated into Gregory's *Decretales*, thus becoming part of official canon law. See Aronius, p. 196 no. 445; Grayzel, pp. 180 ff. no. 59; and *Corpus juris canonici*, ed. Friedberg, 2d ed., II, 588. In matters such as these, the popes did not consider it necessary to secure the consent of the imperial officials.

32. See *MGH, Constitutiones*, II, 84, 87; Bartolomeo Lagumina and Giuseppe Lagumina, *Codice diplomatico dei Giudei di Sicilia*, I (Palermo, 1884), 17 ff. nos. XIX, XX; pp. 26 f. no. XXX; Grayzel, *The Church and the Jews*, pp. 193 ff. no. 65; Aronius, *Regesten*, p. 205 no. 468 (the date of

Frederick's privilege is 1234; the privilege granted the two Sicilian Jews is surely of an earlier date; see Täubler, in *Mitteilungen des Gesamtarchivs*, IV, 186). The basic Law of Melfi is reproduced in full by J. L. A. Huillard-Bréholles, *Historia diplomatica Frederici Secundi*, 6 vols. (Paris, 1852), IV, p. 1 f. The strong opposition of Gregory on the Monte Cassino affair can be seen from his letter of July 5, 1231, which was reprinted anew in *Epistolae saeculi XIII*, ed. by Carl Rodenberg, I, 445. The pope's anger is understandable, not only because the legislation involved the clergy but especially because the king requested that the investigation of heretics should be vested only in the state officials. See the comments in Carlyle and Carlyle, *Medieval Political Theory*, V, 258 n. 1. The Melfi constitution underscored the king's aim to strengthen his position and independence of any outside power, including the Church. From this tendency also sprang, in subsequent years several letters relating to Jews, written at a time when his relations with the pope had deteriorated to the breaking point. It is noteworthy that the term *camera* was used by Frederick and his Sicilian advisers not only in the ordinary sense of "royal treasury" but also in the broader sense of "royal court." See Wilhelm E. Heupel, *Der sizilische Grosshof unter Kaiser Friedrich II.: Eine verwaltungsgeschichtliche Studie* (Stuttgart, 1952), pp. 110 ff.

33. Gregory's letter of August 17, 1236, in his *Registres*, ed. by Aubrey, no. 2482; Frederick's reply of September 2, 1236, in Huillard-Bréholles, IV, 912; a shorter version in Grayzel, *The Church and the Jews*, p. 224 no. 566. From the entire exchange between Gregory and Frederick, and especially from explicit statements by the emperor in 1236, one can clearly see how closely related were the affairs of the Jews of Sicily with those of their German coreligionists. This interdependence has eluded many historians who tried to clarify the institution of "Jewish serfdom" solely on the basis of the legal developments in Germany.

34. Aronius, *Regesten*, pp. 207 no. 472, 242 no. 568; Grayzel, *The Church and the Jews*, pp. 226 nos. 87–88, 238 nos. 95–98, 250 ff. no. 104, 260 ff. no. 111, 113–14 and 116; 274 ff. no. 118. As if doubly to ensure his supremacy over the German emperor, Innocent IV confirmed, in 1244, the right of the bishop of Marseilles to rule over all Jews of his city (notwithstanding its division between neighborhoods under the control of the viscount and those belonging to the bishop), as well as the Jews of Arles. This privilege had been issued to the bishop of Marseilles by Frederick I in 1164 and was reconfirmed by Frederick II in 1222. Nevertheless, the pope felt compelled to confirm it again, because "We believe that the kindheartedness of the kings needs strengthening by the emphatic support of apostolic power." See *Epistolae saeculi XIII*, ed. by Rodenberg, II, 175 ff. no. 236. It must be remembered, however, that around 1236 Gregory was not too sure of support from the citizens of Rome and the College of cardinals. On occasion, Frederick turned to this highest body of

the Church and tried to prove to them that they alone, and not the pope, were appointed by Jesus to be "heirs of the apostles." See especially his letter of March 10, 1239, in Huillard-Bréholles, *Historia diplomatica*, V, 282; additional sources are cited by Ferdinand Fehrling, *Kaiser Friedrich II. und die römischen Cardinäle in den Jahren 1227 bis 1239* (Berlin, 1901). There is support for the fact that those hesitations which caused Gregory not to issue a ban on the emperor until 1239 were the cause for his delay in ordering the Talmud investigated and burnt—a delay of three years, which was misinterpreted by those who studied the history of the burning of the Talmud and the debate of R. Yeḥiel (A. Lewin, Kisch, Graetz, and others). See my *SRH*, IX, Chap. XXXVIII.

35. Hugh of St. Victor *De sacramentis*, ii.2, 4, in *PL*, CLXXVI, 418; Innocent III's statement in *Regestum Innocentii III papae super negotio Romani imperii*, ed. by Friedrich Kempf (Rome, 1947), p. 45 no. 18; Gregory IX in his letter to Frederick II of October 23, 1236, in *Epistolae saeculi XIII*, ed. by Rodenberg, pp. 694, 703. See the references cited in previous notes and in the following works: Friedrich Kempf's interesting collection, *Sacerdozio e regno da Gregorio VII a Bonifacio VIII* (Rome, 1954); P. van der Baar, *Die kirchliche Lehre der Translatio Imperii Romani bis zur Mitte des 13. Jahrhunderts* (dissertation submitted to the Gregorian University in Rome, 1954); Alfons M. Stickler, "Imperator Vicarius Papae, die Lehren der französisch-deutschen Dekretistenschule des 12. und beginnenden 13. Jahrhunderts," *Mitteilungen des Instituts für österreichische Geschichtsforschung*, LXII (1954), 165–212; P. Sambin, "Problemi politici attraverso lettere inedite di Innocenzo IV," *Istituto Veneto di scienze morali, Memorie*, XXXI (1955), 1–71.

36. *MGH, Constitutiones*, II, 197–224; J. F. Boehmer, J. Ficker, E. Winkelmann, *Regesta imperii* (Innsbruck, 1881–1901), V, 1773; Eike von Repgow, *Sachsenspiegel Landrecht*, iii.7, 3, ed. by Carl Gustav Homeyer, 3d ed. (Berlin, 1861), pp. 306 ff.; *Schwabenspiegel*, ch. 214, ed. by Heinrich Gottfried Gengler (Erlangen, 1875), pp. 174 f.; Aronius, *Regesten*, pp. 200 ff. no. 458, 327 ff. no. 771; Hostiensis, *Summa super titulos decretalium* 13; and *In decretalium libros commentarius*, i.6, 34 ("Unus enim est imperator super omnes reges . . . et omnes nationes sub eo sunt . . . etiam Judaei"), quoted by Carlyle and Carlyle, V, 143; Ottokar von Horneck, *Österreichische Reimchronik*, esp. lines 91276–78, ed. by Joseph Seemüller, II, 1186 ff. Regarding Ottokar's statement, see what Pope Boniface VIII said, as quoted by Lewis, *Medieval Political Ideas*, II, 450. In *The Jews in Medieval Germany*, pp. 34 ff. and 53 ff. Kisch provides a detailed analysis of the German legal codes and other sources relating to the legend of Josephus and its influence upon the concept of Jewish serfdom in Europe. See also *idem*, "A Talmudic Legend as the Source for the Josephus Passage in the 'Sachsenspiegel,'" *Historia Judaica*, I (1939), 105–18; Hans Lewy, "Josephus the Physician: A Medieval Legend of the

Destruction of Jerusalem," *Journal of the Warburg Institute*, I (1938), 221–42. The earlier sources cited by these authors are too far removed from the days of Eike von Repgow to have served as his direct sources. He doubtless took his information from intermediate medieval sources, some of which may have been composed in the days of Frederick I in order to justify the emperor's claim of being the supreme ruler over all Jews in the world. Generally, writers of that era did not hesitate to invent "historical" sources and events to justify the political claims of their rulers.

ESSAY 11

1. See above, Essay 10.

2. See especially the comprehensive analysis by Werner Goez, *Translatio imperii: Ein Beitrag zur Geschichte des Geschichtsdenkens und der politischen Theorien des Mittelalters und in der frühen Neuzeit* (Tübingen, 1958). Goez also quotes some of the enormous literature on this subject, supplementing in part our references given in the aforementioned essay.

3. Bartolus de Saxoferrato in his *Commentary* on the *Corpus iuris civilis*, Dig. xlix.15, 24: "Si quis diceret dominum imperatorem non esse dominum et monarcham totius orbis, esset hereticus, quid diceret contra determinationem ecclesiae, contra testimonium S. Evangelii . . ." (with reference to Luke 2); Petrus Baldus de Ubaldis in his *Consilia*, III, cons. ccxviii: "Quia imperator est dominus universalis . . . Nam in dubio omnis temporalis jurisdictio sua est . . . et contrarium dicere est sacrilegium" (ed. Venice, 1609, III, fol. 62a). The meaning of these extreme statements within the general political theories of these outstanding jurists will become clearer in the light of the analyses by Walter Ullmann, "The Development of the Medieval Idea of Sovereignty," *English Historical Review*, LXIV (1949), 1–33; and Francesco Calasso, *I Glossatori e la teoria de la sovranità: Studio di diritto comune pubblico*, 2d ed. (Milan, 1951). Ullmann subsequently restated his views in his comprehensive analysis of *The Growth of Papal Government in the Middle Ages: A Study in the Ideological Relation of Clerical to Lay Power* (New York, 1953). His general theories, which are also pertinent to our subject, have stood the test of various criticisms, such as voiced by another well-informed student, Friedrich Kempf. See the latter's "Die päpstliche Gewalt in der mittelalterlichen Welt: Eine Auseinandersetzung mit Walter Ullmann," in *Saggi storici intorno al Papato*, Miscellanea historiae pontificiae, XXI (Rome, 1959), pp. 117–69.

4. Johannes Teutonicus in his *Apparatus* to Compilation III: "Est autem imperator super omnes reges . . . et omnes naciones sub eo sunt . . . . Etiam iudei sub eo sunt . . . . Neque aliquis regum potuit eximi ab imperio quia illud esset acefalum." See the improved version, cited from MSS by Gaines Post in his "Two Notes on Nationalism in the Middle Ages," *Traditio*, IX

NOTES TO PAGES 309–310

(1953), 281–320, esp. p. 299 n.10. The absence of a single "head" of all Christendom appeared, indeed, as utterly unnatural to many legists, as well as canonists. A similar statement by Hostiensis is quoted above, Essay 10 n. 36.

5. One of the clearest equations of royal and imperial power and, by intimation, also an assertion of the independence of kings from emperors, is found in the famous Castilian code *Las Siete Partidas*, ii.1, 1 and 5, ed. by Gregorio Lopez, new impression, 5 vols. (Paris, 1847), II, 3 ff., 11. Here Alphonso X stated succinctly: "Vicarios de Dios son los reyes, cada uno en su regno, puestos sobre las gentes para mantenerlas en justicia et en verdad quanto en lo temporal, bien asi como el emperador en su imperio." It is to be noted that Alphonso VII had been crowned in Leon in 1135 under the title of "Emperor of Spain and King of the men of the two religions"; that is, of Christians and Muslims. One of his successors, Ferdinand III (1217–52), went further. Despite his Christian piety, which later earned him the designation "Saint," he styled himself "King of the three religions"; that is, of Jews as well as of Christians and Muslims. On the Spanish quest for empire, see Ramón Menéndez Pidal, *El imperio hispánico y los cincos reinos: Dos épocas en la estructura política de España* (Madrid, 1950), esp. pp. 155 ff.; and Hermann J. Hüffer, "Die mittelalterliche spanische Kaiseridee und ihre Probleme," *Saeculum*, III (1952), 425–43. See also my *SRH*, IV, 28, 245 f. n. 30.

6. The passage *excepto regimine hyspanie*, however, attributed to Johannes himself, is missing in many MSS and may be but a later insertion. See G. Post's observations in *Traditio*, IX, 299, 307.

7. That John of Salisbury exerted considerable influence on the thinking of jurists even in Italy was shown by the extensive data assembled by Walter Ullmann in "The Influence of John of Salisbury on Medieval Italian Jurists," *English Historical Review*, LIX (1944), 384–92. The political ideas of Bracton have likewise frequently been studied. See especially Fritz Schulz, "Bracton on Kingship," *ibid.*, LX (1945), 136–76. In view of Bracton's importance for the royal doctrine of medieval Jewish serfdom, his political theories will have to be briefly mentioned again, below, n. 38.

8. See Hellmut Kämpf, *Pierre Dubois und die geistigen Grundlagen des französichen Nationalbewusstseins um 1300* (Leipzig, 1935).

9. Ullmann, in *English Historical Review*, LXIV, p. 12.

10. Perhaps the clearest expression of the French monarchy's self-assertion may be found in Philip the Fair's sharp repudiation of the order given him by Boniface VIII to suspend hostilities with both the emperor and the king of England. We are told that he "ordered and commanded . . . that such protests as the following be made: namely, that the government of the temporality of his realm belongs to him alone, as king, and to no one else, and that he recognizes no superior in it, and that he is not obliged and does not intend, in matters pertaining to the temporal

government of the realm, to submit or subject himself in any way to any living man; but he rather intends to do justice over his fiefs, to defend his kingdom continually, and, with his subjects, his allies, and his warriors, to further the right of his kingdom in every way."

See Pierre Dupuy, *Histoire du différend d'entre le Pape Boniface VIII et Philippe le Bel Roy de France* (Paris, 1655), pp. 27 f.; cited here in the English trans. by Ewart Lewis in his *Medieval Political Ideas,* 2 vols. (New York, 1954), II, 529. See also other recent literature reviewed by Alfonso M. Stickler in his "Sacerdozio e regno nelle nuove ricerche attorno ai secoli XII e XIII nei decretisti e decretalisti fino alle decretali di Gregorio IX," in *Sacerdozio e regno da Gregorio VII a Bonifacio VIII* [ed. by Friedrich Kempf], Miscellanea historiae pontificiae, XVIII (Rome, 1954), pp. 1–26.

11. An interesting illustration was furnished in 1259, when a French baron was condemned by the royal court for the crime of *lèse-majesté*. See Count Beugnot, *Les Olim, ou registres des arrêts rendus par la cour du roi, sous les règnes de St. Louis, de Philippe le Hardi, de Philippe le Bel, Louis le Hutin et Philippe le Long,* 3 vols. (Paris, 1839–48), I, p. 460 no. iv.

12. Pearl Kibre, *The Nations in the Mediaeval Universities,* Publications of the Mediaeval Academy, XLIX (Cambridge, Mass., 1948).

13. George C. Powers, *Nationalism at the Council of Constance (1414–1418),* Diss. Catholic University of America (Washington, D.C., 1927); and Heinrich Finke, "Die Nation in den spätmittelalterlichen allgemeinen Konzilien," *Historisches Jahrbuch,* LVII (1937), 323–38.

14. Halvdan Koht, "The Dawn of Nationalism in Europe," *American Historical Review,* LII (1947), 279.

15. See my "Nationalism and Intolerance," *Menorah Journal,* XVI (1929), 405–15; XVII (1929), 148–58 (also reprint); and, more generally, my *Modern Nationalism and Religion,* The Rauschenbusch Lectures for 1944, Colgate-Rochester Divinity School (New York, 1947; 2d impression, 1960); and *SRH,* XI, Chap. L.

16. J. D. Mansi, ed., *Sacrorum conciliorum nova et amplissima collectio,* XII, 102 can. 8. On the background of this phrase, see my *SRH,* 2d ed., III, 42 f.

17. For one example, in his letter to the archbishop of Sens and the bishop of Paris of July 15, 1205 Innocent III used the phrase *ne cervicem perpetue servitutis jugo submissam presumant erigere*. Solomon Grayzel, *The Church and the Jews in the XIIIth Century* (Philadelphia, 1933), pp. 114 ff. no. 18. Like many other statements by that powerful pope, this epistle was taken over into the *Decretales,* v. 6, 13 in the *Corpus iuris canonici,* ed. by Emil Friedberg, 2d ed., II, 775 f. It may be noted, however, that in the earlier compilation, the *Decretum Gratiani,* some of the most extreme resolutions of the Toledan Councils, including that here cited, were omitted. See my *SRH,* IV, 241 n. 19.

18. To be sure, the later Spanish *Fueros* often diverged from the Visi-

gothic law. But this was owing in part to the ever-present conflict between the local customs and the royal laws in Spain. For the Visigothic period see esp. Theofil Melicher, *Der Kampf zwischen Gesetzes- und Gewohnheitsrecht im Westgotenreich* (Weimar, 1930). Nevertheless, the persistence of Visigothic tradition has long been recognized. In fact, a good case has been made for the assumption that medieval Spanish nationalism had its roots in the doctrines of Isidore of Seville of the Visigothic age. See José Antonio Maravall, "Sobre el concepto de monarquía en la edad media española," *Estudios dedicados a Menéndez Pidal*, 7 vols. (Madrid, 1950–57), V, 401–17, esp. pp. 406 f., 410; and, more generally, W. Reinhard, "La Tradición visigoda en el nacimiento de Castilla," *ibid.*, I, 535–54.

19. Jacobus de Albenga in his *Apparatus* to Compilation V (*Decretales* of Honorius III), cited from a British Museum MS by Post in *Traditio*, IX, 302.

20. *Libro de los Fueros de Castilla*, art. 107: "Esto es por fuero: que los judios son del rey; magüer que sean so poder de ricos omnes o con sus cavalleros o con otros omnes o so poder de monesterios, todos deven ser del rey en su goarda e para su servycio." Cited from Galo Sanchez's edition (Barcelona, 1924), by Fritz Baer in *Die Juden im christlichen Spanien*, 2 vols. (Berlin, 1929–36), II, 36 no. 60. The translation here of *ricos omnes* as "dignitaries," rather than "rich men," follows the etymology of *ricos* as derived from a root similar to the German *Reich*.

21. *Fuero of Salamanca*, art. 341: "Esto faz conceyo de Salamanca con los iodios, alcaldes e iusticias e iurados, por manos del rey don Fernando. E metelos el rey en manos del conceyo de Salamanca que non ayan otro senor se non el Rey. E el conceyo de Salamanca quelos ampare con derecho." *Fuero of Ledesma*, art. 399: "Todos elos iudios seyan en poder del rey e del conceyo." Both in the *Fueros Leoneses de Zamora, Salamanca, Ledesma y Alba de Tormes*, ed. by Américo Castro and Federico de Onís (Madrid, 1916), pp. 201 f., 286; and Baer, *Die Juden*, II, 30 ff. nos. 57–58. Such a division of authority between the king and municipal council or baron was not unusual in medieval Spain and other countries. Of interest may also be Nilda Guglielmi's Buenos Aires dissertation, *La Administración regia en León y Castilla de Fernando I a Alfonso X*. Unfortunately, the brief summary published in the *Revista* of the University of Buenos Aires, II (1957), 141–43, does not give a sufficient inkling of the author's treatment of the royal administration of Castilian-Jewish affairs.

22. See especially Honorius' circular letters, addressed on March 20, 1220, to the Spanish kings and bishops and relating to the employment of Jewish diplomats. An earlier protest had been dispatched by Innocent III to Alphonso VIII of Castile (May 5, 1205). Here the pope contrasted several forms of favoritism extended by the king to Jews while the clergy was being oppressed, the result being: "ut synagoga crescente, decrescat ecclesia, et libere preponatur ancilla." Grayzel, *The Church*, pp. 112 ff.,

no. 17, 158 ff. nos. 45–46. See also Demetrio Mansilla Resyo, "Inocencio III y los reinos hispanos," *Anthologica annua*, II (1954), pp. 9–50. On the extensive employment of Jewish officials by medieval Spanish kings, see the data assembled by Abraham A. Neuman in *The Jews in Spain: Their Social, Political and Cultural Life during the Middle Ages*, 2 vols. (Philadelphia, 1948), II, 221 ff.; and by Yitzhak Baer, in his *Toledoth ha-Yehudim bi-Sefarad ha-noṣrith* (A History of the Jews in Christian Spain), 2d ed. (Tel Aviv, 1959), *passim*. See also below, n. 26.

23. The anonymous monk of Sahagun in his *Chronicle*, ed. by Julio Puyol y Alonso in "Las Crónicas anónimas di Sahagun," *Boletín* of the Academia de la historia, LXXVII (1920), 151–92, esp. pp. 181 f.: the Jews "afirmavan que en ninguna manera pertenescian a la jurisdición del abad, ca siervos eran del senyor rey e eran tenudos en todas las cosas de servir al poderio real. Decian aun quel señor abad los agraviaba a sin raçon en muchas maneras." See also the comments thereon by Fritz Baer in *Die Juden*, II, 56 no. 70.

24. John I's letter to Ferrand Martinez of March 3, 1382, published from a Toledo MS by Baer, *ibid.*, pp. 214 f. no. 221. The crucial passage reads: "E sabed que nuestra voluntad e merced es que los dichos judios sean guardados e defendidos e mantenidos como cosa nuestra e de la nuestra camara."

25. Fuero of Teruel (*Forum Turolii*), art. 425, reproduced from Francisco Aznar Navarro's edition by Baer in *Die Juden*, I, 1043; in the Romance trans., ed. by Max Gorosch, *Leges hispanicae medii aevi*, I (Stockholm, 1950), p. 320 no. 568. Although this *Fuero* was extremely influential and widely imitated in other local custumals, this text is by no means necessarily original. None of the extant MSS antedates the late thirteenth century, and especially the phrase *fiscus regius* (*real bolsa*) may have been a subsequent interpolation. See Gorosch's introd., pp. 11 ff.

26. See the data assembled by Jerome Lee Shneidman in "Jews as Royal Bailiffs in Thirteenth-Century Aragon," *Historia Judaica*, XIX (1957), 55–66; and above, n. 22.

27. Salomon Kahn, "Documents inédits sur les Juifs de Montpellier," *REJ*, XIX (1889), 259–81, esp. p. 261 n. 2. See also the other sources cited by Baer in *Studien zur Geschichte der Juden im Königreich Aragonien während des 13. und 14. Jahrhunderts*, Historische Studien, CVI (Berlin, 1913), pp. 11 ff.

28. Jesus Bergna Canon, "Fueros de Aragon de 1265 a 1381," *Anuario de derecho aragonès*, V, 455: "Que todos los judios . . . sean . . . en especial guarda del senyor rey," cited by Shneidman in *Historia Judaica*, XIX. p. 66 n. 72.

29. Ferdinand the Catholic's letter to the prior of the cathedral of Saragossa on August 17, 1481: "Mandamiento de cessar y sobresseer en

ellos, y ninguno no deve tener audacia tan temeraria de fazer nin proveer tales actos sino con consentimiento nuestro expresso, specialmente que proveer y ordenar sobre los judios, que son cofres nuestros y de nuestro patrimonio, no pertenesce a ninguno sino a nos e a nuestra propria persona." Baer, *Die Juden*, I, 898 no. 554. It is noteworthy that in this connection the Catholic monarchs did not use the traditional term "serfs" but the more modern circumlocutions of "chests" and "patrimony," essentially meaning the same thing.

30. Ferñao Lopes, *Chronica d'el rey D. Fernando*, in the *Collecçao de livros inéditos de historia portuguesa*, IV, 121–525, esp. pp. 502 ff.; quoted here in the English trans. by E. Prestage in the *Chronicles of Fernão Lopes and Gomes Eannes de Zurara*, pp. 41 f.; and, more generally, Meyer Kayserling, *Geschichte der Juden in Portugal* (Leipzig, 1867), pp. 23 ff. On the general evolution of Portuguese nationalism, see Albin Eduard Beau, *Die Entwicklung des portugiesischen National-bewusstseins* (Hamburg, 1944); and the more recent Portuguese essays collected in his *Estudos*, Vol. I (Coimbra, 1959).

31. See especially the York Anonymus' fourth tractate *De Conservatione Pontificum et Regum* in *Libelle de Lite*, in the excerpt trans. into English by Ewart Lewis in *Medieval Political Ideas*, II, 562 ff. See also Albert Brackmann, "Die Ursachen der geistigen und politischen Wandlung Europas im 11. und 12. Jahrhundert," *Historische Zeitschrift*, CXLIX (1934), pp. 229–39; and *idem*, "Der mittelalterliche Ursprung der Nationalstaaten," *Sitzungsberichte* der Preussischen Akademie der Wissenschaften, Phil.-hist. Klasse, 1936, pp. 128–42, esp. pp. 131 f.

32. Pseudo-Edward the Confessor's *Leges Ecclesiasticae e saecularibus suis depromptae*, xxi, in *PL*, CLI, 1193 f.: "Sciendum quoque quod omnes Judaei, ubicunque in regno sunt, sub tutela et defensione regis debent esse nec quilibet eorum alicui diviti se potest subdere sine regis licentia. Judaei enim, et omnia sua, regis sunt." Cited in the text from Joseph Jacobs's English trans. in *The Jews of Angevin England*, p. 68. It has long been recognized that this passage was not enacted by Edward himself nor by any of his contemporaries, but rather dated from the period of Roger Howden's *Chronica*, where it was first reported (ca. 1180). It was entirely in line with Henry II's declaration at the Diet of Clarendon of 1161 about the Crown's supremacy over the English Church. See Brackmann in the aforementioned *Sitzungsberichte*, p. 136.

33. John I's Charter of 1201, art. iii, in *The Rotuli chartarum*, ed. for The Record Commission by T. D. Hardy (London, 1837), I, p. 93 (in Jacobs's English translation, p. 212). Of course, in theory, the king, as the Jews' overlord, could freely inherit all their property. Under exceptional circumstances he did expropriate an entire estate, such as that of Aaron of Lincoln, the incomplete liquidation of which took the royal bureaucracy sixteen years. But, as a rule, the Treasury was satisfied with a moderate estate tax. In essence, this also held true of the estates of

practically the entire baronage of England, where an estate tax in practice substituted for the exercise by the king of his theoretical right of eminent domain. See my *SRH*, IV, 79, 278 n. 103.

34. John's decree (see preceding note). The king's purported deposition by Innocent III, which might have spelled a temporary end to England's national independence, has rightly been denied by C. R. Chenney in "The Alleged Deposition of King John," *Studies in Medieval History Presented to F. M. Powicke* (London, 1948), pp. 100–16. In fact, John's submission and following excommunication, as well as his subsequent enactment of the Magna Carta and its futile denunciation by the Pope— all highlighted the growth of national sovereignty of the English monarchy. See also Marcel David, *La Souveraineté et les limites juridiques du pouvoir monarchique du XI*ᵉ *au XV*ᵉ *siècle,* Annales de la Faculté de droit et des sciences politiques de Strasbourg, I (Paris, 1954), esp. pp. 212 ff.

35. Matthew Paris, *Chronica majora,* ed. by Henry Richard Luard, 7 vols. (London, 1872–73), esp. V, 487 f.; in the partial English trans. by J. A. Giles entitled *English History from the Year 1235 to 1273,* 3 vols. (London, 1852–54), III, 114. Modern scholars have compiled a number of lists of Jewish taxes during Henry III's regime. Some of the fullest are those presented by Peter Elman in "The Economic Causes of the Expulsion of the Jews in 1290," *Economic History Review,* VII (1936–37), 145–54, esp. pp. 153 f.; and by Cecil Roth in *A History of the Jews in England* (Oxford, 1941), pp. 270 f. These lists require a "drastic reduction," however, according to Frederick M. Powicke in his *King Henry III and the Lord Edward,* 2 vols. (London, 1947), I, 311.

36. Henry's grants to Peter de Rivaux are reproduced in the *Calendar of the Charter Rolls,* I, pp. 163, 166 f.

37. Henry III's *Mandatum* of 1253 began by stating: "Quod nullus Judeus maneat in Anglia nisi servicium Regis faciat; et quam cito aliquis Judeus natus fuerit, sive sit masculus sive femina, serviat Nobis in aliquo." This *Mandatum* is reproduced in Latin and in English translation in J. M. Rigg, ed., *Select Pleas, Starrs, and Other Records from the Rolls of the Exchequer of the Jews A.D. 1220–1284* (London, 1902), pp. xlviii f.

38. Henry de Bracton, *De legibus et consuetudinibus Angliae,* v. 6, 6, ed. by Travers Twiss, VI, 50 f.: "Judaeus vero nihil proprium habere potest, quia quicquid acquirit non sibi acquirit sed regi, quia non vivunt sibi ipsis sed aliis, et sic aliis acquirunt et non sibi ipsis." This statement by the famous English jurist, made in connection with the law of warranty, and comparing the Jew to a landless Christian—since neither of them owned land subject to foreclosure—has often been quoted in Jewish historical literature, but without reference to Bracton's very complicated juridical and historical theories. As a student of the Italian glossators of Roman law, Bracton tried to assimilate the status of the English king to

that of the ancient Roman emperor, as reflected in the Roman law codes. Hence, his theory of kingship, including the king's power over Jews, resembled in many ways the imperial doctrine of Jewish serfdom as defined in the contemporary German law books; of course, without the latter's direct reference to the Holy Roman emperors' succession to the ancient caesars and their mastery over the descendants of "captives" vanquished by Titus. It must also be borne in mind that the extant texts of Bracton's treatises leave much to be desired and that, generally, "Bracton's doctrine is a web artificially woven with threads of various kinds and various provenance." See Schulz's "Conclusion," in *English Historical Review*, LX, 175; Charles H. McIlwain, "The Present Status of the Problem of the Bracton Text," *Harvard Law Review*, LVII (1943), 220–40; and, more generally, his *Constitutionalism, Ancient and Modern*, 2d ed. (Ithaca, 1947); and the searching chapter devoted to Bracton by Ernst H. Kantorowicz in *The King's Two Bodies: A Study in Mediaeval Political Theology* (Princeton, 1957), pp. 143 ff. In contrast to his namesake H. Kantorowicz, this author accepts the more widely held assumption that Bracton's *De Legibus* was completed around 1259. *Ibid.*, p. 145 n. 173. See also above, n. 7.

39. Frederick Pollock and Frederick William Maitland, *The History of English Law Before the Time of Edward I*, 2d ed. (Cambridge, 1903–23), I, 471 ff. This view of the distinguished historians of English law still represents the regnant opinion among Jewish historians as well. Frank I. Schechter, especially, went all out in trying to prove "The Rightlessness of Medieval English Jewry," *JQR*, n.s. IV (1913–14), 121–51. Scholars were too prone to overlook the very serious reservations against this view expressed by Cyril M. Picciotto in his stimulating analysis of "The Legal Position of the Jews in Pre-Expulsion England, as Shown by the Plea Rolls of the Jewish Exchequer," *Transactions of the Jewish Historical Society of England*, IX (1922), 67–84. In all these discussions, however, there is no reference to the incipient nationalism and, connected with it, the growing secularization of English life. On the latter, see esp. J. R. Strayer, "The Laicization of French and English Society in the Thirteenth Century," *Speculum*, XV (1940), 76–86; and Georges de Lagarde, *La Naissance de l'esprit laïque au déclin du moyen âge*, I: Bilan du XIIIᵉ siècle, 3d ed. (Louvain, 1956).

40. While refraining from specifically naming the king, the barons clearly had him in mind when they spoke of the "powerful personages" who had conspired with the Jews in expropriating some of the large estates for the benefit of the Crown. See the data cited by Rigg in his *Select Pleas*, pp. xxxvii f.; and, more generally, R. F. Treharne, *The Baronial Plan of Reform, 1258–1263*, Publications of the University of Manchester, Historical Series, LXII (Manchester, 1932). On the expulsion of the Jews from England, by virtue of which the king gave up a

substantial, if declining, revenue from his Jewish "serfs" in return for a financial contribution voted by Parliament, see the older, but still highly informative, study by B. L. Abrahams, "The Expulsion of the Jews from England in 1290," *JQR*, VII (1894–95), 75–100, 236–58, 428–58.

41. See above, Essay 10.

42. Charles V. Langlois, "Formulaires et lettres du XII° du XIII° et du XIV° siècle," *Notices et extraits des manuscrits de la Bibliothèque Nationale et autres bibliothèques*, XXXIV, Part 1 (1891), pp. 19 f. n. 14; Robert Anchel, *Les Juifs de France* (Paris, 1946), pp. 116 f. These measures contrasted sharply with the judicial principle enunciated by the Paris Parlement, as late as 1319, in its order to the bailiff of Meaux. Here the royal official was told to remove certain Jewish defendants from the jurisdiction of the episcopal court, unless their crimes *talia sint, quod fidem catholicam tangent*. See the *Actes du Parlement de Paris*, ed. by Edgar Boutaric, 1st ser. II (Paris, 1867), 291 no. 5848. This decision was more in keeping with the general order issued by Philip the Fair and reproduced by Langlois. See also *SRH*, IX, 66 f., 271 n. 14.

43. J. L. A. Huillard-Bréholles, *Historia diplomatica Friderici Secundi sive constitutiones, privilegia, mandata, instrumenta quae supersunt istius imperatoris et filiorum ejus*, 7 vols. (Paris, 1851–61), Vol. II, Part 1, pp. 473 ff. (this is Frederick II's confirmation, in 1225, of Frederick I's earlier privilege).

44. Ottokar von Horneck, *Österreichische Reimchronik*, vv. 91239–778, especially 91276–78, ed. by Joseph Saemüller, 2 parts (Hanover, 1893) (*MGH*, Deutsche Chroniken, V), II, 1186 ff. This tale by the Austrian chronicler need not be taken at its face value. Yet it is symptomatic of what contemporaries considered probable. Otherwise, Philip IV's France was reaching a stage of national consciousness which far exceeded anything known in the earlier generations. See Laetita Boehm, "Gedanken zum Frankreich-Bewusstsein im frühen 12. Jahrhundert," *Historisches Jahrbuch*, LXXIV (1954), pp. 681–87; Mario delle Piane, "Saggio sull'ideologia nazionale nella Francia di Filippo il Bello," *Studi senesi*, LXVI–LXVII (1954–55), 65–96. In the light of these newly understood nationalist trends, the expulsions of the Jews from France in 1306 and thereafter, will likewise have to be reevaluated. See, for the time being, Isidore Loeb, "Les Expulsions des Juifs de France au XIV° siècle," *Jubelschrift . . . H. Grätz* (Breslau, 1887), pp. 39–56; and my *SRH*, XI, 211 ff., 389 ff.

45. E. J. de Laurière, *et al.*, eds., *Ordonnances des roys de France de la troisième race*, 21 vols. (Paris, 1723–1849), I, 47, 53; III, 475 art. 3. Of course, there remained many equivocal situations. Typical of the medieval ambiguity was, for example, the complaint of the bishop of Nîmes to Philip the Fair about the seizure of his Jews. Philip recognized in 1295 the bishop's mastery over the Jews, but simultaneously insisted

that these Jews were also the king's. He ordered their recapture from various barons. See the text reproduced by Léon Ménard in his *Histoire civile, ecclésiastique et littéraire de la ville de Nismes,* 7 vols. (Paris, 1750–55), I, 125 f. no. xciii (Preuves). On the earlier agreements, see my *SRH,* IV, 62 f., 269 f. n. 81.

46. Ulysse Robert, "Catalogue d'actes relatifs aux Juifs pendant le moyen âge," *REJ,* III (1881), 211–24, esp. 212 f.; and Israel Lévi, "Louis VIII et les Juifs," *ibid.,* XXX (1895), 284–88. Not surprisingly, French courts had frequent occasions to decide in controversies concerning the mastery over Jews. For instance, in 1260 a soldier, Philippe de Chauvry, secured a decision in his favor after proving that a particular Jew had been *cubans et levans* on his property, but he had to promise *quod non tractaret turpiter ipsum judeum.* Courts were called upon to decide even in a major conflict over the possession of a single Jew, Abraham, between the king of France and the duke of Burgundy. They finally decided in favor of the royal claim (1270). See Beugnot, *Les Olim,* I, 122 no. xiii, 364 f.

47. Baer, *Die Juden,* I, 487 ff. no. 330, 565 ff. no. 371.

48. See, for instance, the decree of John I of Castile dated September 3, 1380. Here the king threatened the Jews circumcizing Moorish slaves in the Jewish way: "qual quier o quales quier judios que lo fizieren, que ellos mesmos seyan nuestros cativos. E eso mesmo aquellas personas, a quien asi fizieren tornar de otra ley a la suya, para que mandemos fazer dellos lo que la nuestra merced fuere." See Baer, *ibid.,* II, 222 no. 227. Similarly, in the sharp decree of January 2, 1412, John II of Castile put the same sanction on the unauthorized Jewish emigration from Castile: "e ellos sean mis cativos para syenpre." *Ibid.,* p. 270 no. 275 art. 23. It may be noted that this entire law was repeated with some important modifications by Ferdinand I of Aragon. See the excerpts in Catalan cited by Baer, *ibid.,* I, 790 f. no. 485.

49. William's Goslar privilege of April 3, 1252, is conveniently excerpted from the Goslar statutes by Julius Aronius, *et al.,* in *Regesten zur Geschichte der Juden im Fränkischen und Deutschen Reiche bis zum Jahre* 1273 (Berlin, 1902), p. 249 no. 585. The crucial statement: "Ad hec nullam indebitam molestiam sive captivitatem Iudei civitatis sustinebunt a nobis, et defendemus ipsos amicabiliter et benigne tamquam speciales camerae servos: sed sicut debitum est servient nobis tamquam domino suo et Romanorum regi," is cited here, notwithstanding our main concern with West-European, rather than German, conditions, because it sheds light on the contrast between serfdom and slavery even in Germany, the center of the *servitus camerae.*

50. Martin Didaci d'Aux, *Observantiae consuetudinesque scriptae regni Aragonum in usum communiter habitae,* fol. xxix r., cited by Baer in his *Studien,* p. 14 n. 12, where one may find additional illustrations.

51. C. M. Picciotto in *Transactions of the Jewish Historical Society of England*, IX, 82.

52. Isaac b. Samuel of Dampierre cited in *Tosafot* on B.Ķ. 58a, s. v. אי נמי; later quoted with approval also by the Spaniard Moses b. Naḥman in his *Responsa*, no. 46, ed. by Simḥah Assaf in his ספרן של ראשונים, Publications of the Mekize Nirdamim (Jerusalem, 1935), p. 88. A similar position was taken by a number of later Spanish scholars in connection with an *affaire célèbre* concerning a controversy affecting the Jewish community of Perpignan after 1346. One of the scholars replying to the pertinent inquiry of Cresques Elias asserted bluntly: ומוסכם הוא מקדם בחצרות המלכים ומרגלא בפומיהו . . . שהיהודים בני חורין ואין ביד המלכים למחות בידם להעתיק דירתם אל אשר יהיה שמה הרוח ללכת. Another rabbi quoted R. Isaac's statement verbatim: כי דין היהודים כדין הפרשים להיות חפשים ללכת בכל מקום. See these answers, excerpted from a Bodleian MS by Baer in *Die Juden*, I, 315 no. 224a Replies 2–3. These rabbinic statements can give us merely an inkling of the Jews' interpretation of the nature of the "serfdom" of their community, but we cannot expatiate here on this aspect.

53. *Briefsammlungen der Zeit Heinrichs IV.*, ed. by Carl Erdmann and Norbert Fickermann, *MGH*, Die Briefe der deutschen Kaiserzeit, V (Weimar, 1950), pp. 31 f. no. 13. On the various uses of the term *servitus* in the Middle Ages, see also Charles de Fresne du Cange, *Glossarium mediae et infimae latinitatis*, new ed. by Léopold Favre, 10 vols. (Graz, 1954–55), VI, 454–58. It is noteworthy that we hardly ever find the designation of an individual Jew as *servus*, a designation which incidentally disappears also in many documents relating to villeins. See, for instance, the careful examination of that terminology in two French districts by George Duby in his "Géographie ou chronologie du servage? Note sur les 'servi' en Forez et en Mâconnais du Xᵉ au XIIᵉ siècle," *Hommage à Lucien Febvre* (Paris, 1953), I, 147–49.

54. Otto Stobbe, *Die Juden in Deutschland während des Mittelalters in politischer, socialer und rechtlicher Beziehung*, 3d ed. (Berlin, 1923), pp. 13 f.; Karl Bosl, *Die Reichsministerialität der Salier und Staufer*, 2 parts, Schriften der *MGH*, X (Stuttgart, 1950–51). In this careful examination of the numerous documents, extant particularly in Oppenheim, the author shows the gradual transition from a purely mercenary to a vassal-noble relationship between the *Ministeriales* and their kingly overlords.

55. Adolf Waas, *Die alte deutsche Freiheit, ihr Wesen und ihre Geschichte* (Munich, 1939), p. 29; A. Nitschke, "Die Wirksamkeit Gottes in der Welt Gregors VII.," *Studi Gregoriani*, V (1956), 115–219, esp. pp. 169 ff.

56. Eberhard Otto, *Adel und Freiheit im deutschen Staat des frühen Mittelalters: Studien über Nobiles und Ministerialen*, Neue deutsche Forschungen, CCCXXX (Berlin, 1937), p. 37. In many of these writings, to be sure, one senses the impact of the Nazi ideology and its disparagement

of liberty which dominated German thinking in the 1930s. But they do furnish some new insights into the medieval concepts of liberty which differed so greatly from those of our modern libertarian democracy. For a more balanced judgment see Herbert Grundmann's recent analysis of "Freiheit als religiöses, politisches und persönliches Postulat im Mittel-alter," *Historische Zeitschrift,* CLXXXIII (1957), 23–53. This vast sub-ject, too, and its impact on medieval Jewish status, will have to be discussed more fully in another context. For the time being see the analysis of the Jewish status in medieval West-Central Europe in *SRH,* esp. Vol XI, *passim.*

ESSAY 12

1. Ernst Walter Zeeden, "Grundlagen und Wege der Konfessionsbild-ung in Deutschland im Zeitalter der Reformationskämpfe," *Historische Zeitschrift,* CLXXXV (1958), 249–99.

2. V. H. H. Green, *Luther and the Reformation* (New York, 1964), p. 9.

3. Martin Luther, *Tischgespräche,* in his *Werke,* Weimar ed., IV, 338; LI, 195; and other passages in William Hazlitt's English trans. entitled *The Table Talk,* with a Memoir by Alexander Chalmers (London, 1883), pp. 346 ff. Luther actually believed that some Jews had tried to poison him. See Reinhold Lewin, *Luthers Stellung zu den Juden, Ein Beitrag zur Geschichte der Juden in Deutschland während des Reformations-zeitalters,* Neue Studien zur Geschichte der Theologie und der Kirche, I (Berlin, 1911), pp. 39 ff. and, on the medieval background of these apprehensions, my *SRH,* XI, 158 f., 364 f. n. 47.

4. Vadian (Joachim von Watt), *Deutsche historische Schriften,* ed. by E. Götzinger, I, 348, 390, 447; II, 243, 346, cited by Ludwig Geiger in his "Die Juden und die deutsche Literatur," *ZGJD,* II (1888), 517 ff.; *Andreas Osianders Schrift über die Blutbeschuldigung,* ed. by Moritz Stern (Kiel, 1893).

5. Albert A. Sicroff, *Les Controverses des statuts de "pureté de sang" en Espagne du XVᵉ au XVIIᵉ siècle,* in *Etudes de littérature étrangère et comparée* (Paris, 1960); H. Vuilleumier, "Les Hébraïsants vaudois au seizième siècle," *Recueil inaugural* of the University of Lausanne (Lau-sanne, 1892), p. 64; Wilhelm Becker, *Immanuel Tremellius: Ein Prosely-tenleben im Zeitalter der Reformation,* Schriften des Institutum Judaicum, VIII, 2d ed. (Leipzig, 1891).

6. Wolfgang Capito's Latin letter of April 26, 1537, in Luther's *Brief-wechsel,* in his *Werke,* Weimar ed., VIII, 76 ff. No. 3152; in Harry Bresslau's German trans. in his "Aus Strassburger Judenakten, II: Zur Geschichte Josels von Rosheim," *ZGJD,* V (1892), 326 f. It may be noted that two years earlier Capito had severely scolded Jacques Schor for ad-vocating general liberty of conscience. See his essay, cited by P. Dollinger

in "La Tolérance à Strasbourg au XVIᵉ siècle," *Hommage à Lucien Febvre*, 2 vols. (Paris, 1953), II, 241–49.

7. Martin Bucer, "Ratschlag, ob die Christliche Oberkait gebüren müge, dass sye die Juden undter den Christen zu wonen gedulden, und wa sye zu gedulden welche gestalt und mass," reproduced in his *Deutsche Schriften* (*Opera omnia*, Ser. I), Vols. I–VII (Gütersloh, 1960–64), VII, 319–94 (includes nine items in the documentary appendix and the editor's introductions); Hasting Eells, "Bucer's Plan for the Jews," *Church History*, VI (1937), 127–35; and, more generally, William Jesse Nottingham's 1962 Columbia University dissertation, *The Social Ethics of Martin Bucer* (typescript), esp. pp. 235 ff. See also the essay "John Calvin and the Jews," below; and my *SRH*, XIII, 239 ff.

8. Pastor Ehrhardt's statement, cited in Hartmann Grisar's well-known biography of *Luther*, 6 vols. (London, 1913–17), VI, 78; Ulrich Grotefend, *Geschichte und rechtliche Stellung der Juden in Pommern*, Diss. Marburg, 1931 (reprinted from *Baltische Studien*, n.s. XXXII), pp. 138 f.

9. Johann Christian Freiherr von Aretin, *Geschichte der Juden in Baiern* (Landshut, 1803), pp. 44 ff.; L. Löwenstein, *Beiträge zur Geschichte der Juden in Deutschland*, I: Geschichte der Juden in der Kurpfalz (Frankfort, 1895), pp. 29 ff.

10. See Umberto Cassuto, *I manoscritti palatini ebraici della Biblioteca Apostolica Vaticana e la loro storia*, Studi e testi, LXVI (Vatican City, 1935).

11. John Calvin, *Ad quaestiones et obiecta Judaei cuiusdam Responsio*, in his *Opera quae supersunt omnia*, ed. by Wilhelm Baum et al., 59 vols. (Brunswick, 1863–Berlin, 1900), IX, 653–74; and my analysis of this debate and of other aspects of Calvin's Judophobia in "John Calvin and the Jews," below. Further information might be forthcoming from the publication of more of Calvin's sermons, preserved in manuscript. Unfortunately, this project, begun in 1936, made insufficient headway in the subsequent two decades. See Hanns Rückert's ed. of *Johannes Calvin's Predigten*, resumed by the World Presbyterian Alliance with the publication of *Supplementa Calviniana Sermons Inédits*, ed. by Ervin Mühlhaupt et al. (Neukirchen, 1961–). On the abysmal state of preservation of that valuable source of information on the Genevan reformer, see Bernard Gagnebin, "L'incroyable histoire des Sermons de Calvin," *Bulletin* of the Société d'histoire et d'archéologie de Genève, X (1956).

12. Miguel (Michael) Servetus, *Biblia Sacra ex Sanctis Pagnini translatione . . . recognita et scholiis illustrata* (Lyons, 1542); Articles of accusation against Servetus and Servetus' letters to Calvin, reproduced in the latter's *Opera*, VIII, esp. cols. 555 f., 675, 703 ff., 764, 767; Aegidius Hunnius, *Calvinus Judaizans, hoc est Judaicae Glossae et corruptelae, quibus Johannes Calvinus illustrissima Scripturae Sacrae loca et testimonia de gloriosa Trinitate . . . corrumpere non exhorruit* (Wittenberg,

1595). On Servetus see also Jakob Guttmann, "Michael Servet in seinen Beziehungen zum Judentum," *MGWJ*, LI (1907), 77–94; and Louis I. Newman, *Jewish Influence on Christian Reform Movements* (New York, 1925), pp. 511 ff.

13. See the illustrations given in my *SRH*, 2d ed., esp. III, 5 ff. nn. 1 and 4. Not surprisingly, Catholic leaders, too, were prone to accuse the protagonists of Reform of being Judaizers or even descendants of Jews. For one example, in his letter of 1556 to the Orders of Calatrava and Alcantara, King Philip II of Spain sweepingly asserted that "all the heresies which have arisen in Germany and in France have been disseminated by descendants of Jews as has been and is being witnessed every day in Spain." Cited from a Madrid MS by Albert A. Sicroff in *Les Controverses*, p. 138 n. 184.

14. Hans Baron, *Calvin's Staatsanschauung und das konfessionelle Zeitalter*, Historische Zeitschrift, Suppl. I (Munich, 1924), pp. 48 ff. Even in Holland the victory of Calvinism was due to a variety of political and religious factors, among which Dutch nationalism, still in its early, formative stages, played a decidedly minor role. See the recent debates summarized by Peter de Jong in his "Can Political Factors Account for the Fact that Calvinism rather than Anabaptism Came to Dominate the Dutch Reformation?" *Church History*, XXXIII (1964), 392–417.

15. See Harold S. Bender, "The Anabaptists and Religious Liberty in the 16th Century," *Archiv für Reformationsgeschichte*, XLIV (1953), 32–51. Evidently, not all Anabaptists were of one mind. One of their leaders, Balthasar Hubmeier (Hubmaier), had already played a fateful role in the expulsion of Jews from Ratisbon in 1519. In general, he was an Anabaptist only with respect to the question of baptism, but otherwise remained a rather hide-bound protagonist of the status quo. See Wilhelm A. Schulze, "Neue Forschungen über Balthasar Hubmeier von Waldshut," *Allemannisches Jahrbuch*, 1957, pp. 224–74. Even he, however, spoke up against the burning of heretics, declaring that "the slayers of heretics were themselves guilty of the worst heresy." See his short pamphlet, *Von Ketzern und ihrer Verbrennern* (Nikolsburg, 1524); and some of his other writings collected in his *Schriften*, ed. by Gunnar Westin and Torsten Bergsten, Quellen und Forschungen zur Reformationsgeschichte, XXIX (Gütersloh, 1962).

16. Elisabeth Feist Hirsch, "Portuguese Humanists and the Inquisition in the Sixteenth Century," *Archiv für Reformationsgeschichte*, XLVI (1955), 47–68; Luther, *The Table Talk*, ed. by W. Hazlitt.

17. Marcin Bielski, *Kronika polska* (Polish Chronicle), Cracow, 1597 ed., p. 580; Majer Balaban, *Dzieje Żydów w Krakowie i na Kazimierzu* (A History of the Jews in Cracow and Kazimierz), 2d ed., 2 vols. (Cracow, 1931–36), I, 77 f. n. 4. These exaggerations by Bielski and other contemporaries concerning the extent of Jewish proselytism have been

reduced to their proper proportions by E. Zivier in his "Jüdische Bekehrungsversuche im 16. Jahrhundert," in *Beiträge zur Geschichte der deutschen Juden. Festschrift . . . Martin Philippson* (Leipzig, 1916), pp. 96–113.

18. William E. H. Lecky, *Democracy and Liberty*, 2 vols. (New York, 1896); Samuel Langdon, "Election Sermon of 1775" in John Wingate Thornton's *Pulpit of the American Revolution* (Boston, 1860), p. 239; John Cotton, *Moses, His Judicials*, published in England under the title, *An Abstract of the Lawes of New England* (London, 1641), more readily available in Peter Force's *Tracts and Other Papers Relating Principally to . . . the Colonies in North America*, new impression (New York, 1947), Vol. III, Part 9. See also other data in my address, "From Colonial Mansion to Skyscraper: An Emerging Pattern of Hebraic Studies," reprinted from *Rutgers Hebraic Studies*, I (1964) in my *Steeled by Adversity: Essays on American Jewish Life*, ed. by Jeannette M. Baron, Philadelphia, 1971, pp. 106–26, 598–602.

19. Elijah Levita, *Masoreth ha-Masoreth* (The Tradition of the Masorah: a Philological Treatise), ed. by Christian David Ginsburg (London, 1867), Introd., p. 96, with reference to Ps. 147:20. See also Gerard E. Weil, "L'Archétype de Massoret ha-Massoret d'Élie Lévita," *Revue d'histoire et de philosophie religieuse*, XLI (1961), 147–58; and, on the Protestant side, *idem*, "Une leçon de l'humaniste hébreu Elias Lévita à son élève Sébastien Münster," *Revue d'Alsace*, XCV (1956), 31–40.

20. Heinrich Bornkamm, *Luther und das Alte Testament* (Tübingen, 1948); Emanuel Hirsch, *Die Theologie des Andreas Osiander und ihre geschichtlichen Voraussetzungen* (Göttingen, 1919); Ezra Stiles, *The Literary Diary*, ed. with notes by Franklin Bowdich Dexter, 3 vols. (New York, 1901), especially in the passages analyzed by George Alexander Kohut in his *Ezra Stiles and the Jews* (New York, 1902); Jeremiah Mason, "Autobiography," in his *Memoirs and Correspondence* (Cambridge, Mass., 1873), p. 11.

21. B. B. Edwards, "Reasons for the Study of the Hebrew Language," *American Biblical Repository*, XII (1838), 113 ff., with the comments thereon by Joseph L. Blau and myself, eds., *The Jews of the United States, 1790–1840: a Documentary History*, 3 vols. (New York, 1963), II, 419 ff.; Cotton Mather, *Diary*, ed. by Worthington Chauncey Ford in the *Collections* of the Massachusetts Historical Society, 7th ser. VII, 200. See also Lee M. Friedman, "Cotton Mather's Ambition" in his *Jewish Pioneers and Patriots* (Philadelphia, 1943), p. 99.

22. Roland H. Bainton, "The Struggle for Religious Liberty," reprinted in his *Studies in the Reformation* (Boston, 1963), p. 212.

23. See S. N. Eisenstadt, "The Protestant Ethic Thesis in Analytical and Comparative Context," in *Diogenes*, No. 59 (Fall, 1967), 25–46.

24. See the early (1909–10) debate between Max Weber, Felix Rach-

fahl, and Eugen Troeltsch, cited in my essay on "John Calvin and the Jews" below. Despite the intervening accumulation of an enormous literature on this and the related subject of the relations between Jews and modern capitalism, the issue is still open to debate today.

25. Reinhold Lewin, *Luthers Stellung zu den Juden,* pp. 104 f.; Werner Sombart, *The Jews and Modern Capitalism,* English trans. by M. Epstein, with an introd. to the American edition by Bert F. Hoselitz (Glencoe, Ill., 1951), p. 49.

26. Hugo Grotius (De Groot), *Remonstrantie nopende de ordre dije in de Landen van Hollandt ende Westvrieslandt dijent gestelt op de Joden,* ed. from a Montezinos MS by Jacob Meijer (Amsterdam, 1949); and Meijer's analysis thereof in his "Hugo Grotius' *Remonstrantie,*" *Jewish Social Studies,* XVII (1955), 91–104. On the eminent jurist's theological orientation, see Arthur Löwenstamm's "Hugo Grotius Stellung zum Judentum," *Festschrift . . . des Jüdisch-Theologischen Seminars Fraenckelscher Stiftung* (Breslau, 1929), II, 295–302; and, more generally, Joachim Schlütter's review of *Die Theologie des Hugo Grotius* (Göttingen, 1919), esp. pp. 3 ff.

27. Lucien Wolf, "The First Stage of Anglo-Jewish Emancipation" (1903), reprinted in his *Essays in Jewish History,* ed. by Cecil Roth (London, 1934), pp. 115–43.

28. See my "Newer Approaches to Jewish Emancipation," *Diogenes,* No. 29 (1960), 56–81.

ESSAY 13

1. J. A. Galiffe, *Matériaux pour l'histoire de Genève,* 2 vols. (Geneva, 1829 [1830]), I, 167; Achille Nordmann, "Histoire des Juifs à Genève de 1281 à 1780," *REJ,* LXXX (1925), 1–41, esp. pp. 38 f. See also Emile Doumergue, *Jean Calvin, les hommes et les choses de son temps,* 7 vols. (Lausanne, 1899–1927), III, 252 f. (also offering interesting data on the Jewish quarter in Geneva). It is possible, however, that in his numerous sermons Calvin referred to Jews and Judaism more frequently than is now known. Perhaps further progress of H. Rückert's ed. of *Johannes Calvins Predigten* (which, begun in 1936, was resumed in 1958 in the so-called *Supplementa Calviniana,* sponsored by the World Presbyterian Alliance) will yield some new data on the Jewish question, too, from the hundreds of still unpublished homilies of the reformer. See the example from his sermon on II Sam. 22, cited below, n. 20. However, many sermons doubtless are irretrievably lost. The Geneva Library, which in the early eighteenth century still owned forty-four volumes of Calvin's homilies in MS, now possesses only twelve. See the latest review of the extant MSS in Georges A. Barrois's introd. to his ed. of Calvin's *Sermons sur le livre*

d'Isaïe Chapitres 13–29 (Neukirchen, 1961) [Vol. II of the series], pp. xx ff. See also above, Essay 12, n. 11.

2. Calvin's *De usuris*, reproduced among his "Consilia" in his *Opera quae supersunt omnia*, ed. by Wilhelm Baum *et al.*, 59 vols., Corpus reformatorum, XXIX–LXXXVII (Brunswick, 1863—Berlin, 1900), Vol. X, Part 1, cols. 245 ff.; his comments on Deut. 15:7–10, 23:19–20, *ibid.*, XXIV, 679 ff.; XXVII, 325 ff.; XXVIII, 111 ff.; and the controversial interpretations thereof, cited below, nn. 4 and 21. See also Théodore Reinach, "Mutuum date nihil inde sperantes," *Revue des études grecques*, VII (1894), 52–58, suggesting a relatively slight emendation of the text in Luke.

3. *Opera*, XXVIII, 117; XXXVII, 358. The editors were quite justified in including the Genevan ordinance of 1547 among Calvin's works, *ibid.*, X, Part 1, cols. 56 f.

4. This issue has preoccupied many leading students of both economics and Protestant theology. See esp. Karl Holl, "Zur Frage des Zinsnehmens und des Wuchers in der reformierten Kirche" (1922), reprinted in his *Gesammelte Aufsätze zur Kirchengeschichte*, 4 vols. (Tübingen, 1928), III, 385–403; Henri Hauser, "A propos des idées économiques de Calvin," *Mélanges d'histoire offerts à Henri Pirenne*, 2 vols. (Brussels, 1926), I, 211–24; and, particularly, André Bieler's recent comprehensive analysis of *La Pensée économique et sociale de Calvin*, with a Foreword by Anthony Babel (Geneva, 1959). See also Ernst Ramp's comparative study of *Die Stellung von Luther, Zwingli und Calvin zur Zinsfrage* (Diss. Zurich, 1949), esp. pp. 81 ff., 106 ff.; and Charles H. George, "English Calvinist Opinions on Usury, 1600–1640," *Journal of the History of Ideas*, XVIII (1957), 455–74.

5. See Wilhelm Niesel, "Verstand Calvin deutsch?" *Zeitschrift für Kirchengeschichte*, XLIX (1930), 343–46.

6. See the data assembled by Klaus Rudolphi in *Calvins Urteil über das politische Vorgehen der deutschen Protestanten nach seinem Briefwechsel* (Marburg, 1930); Philippe Dollinger, "La Tolérance à Strasbourg au XVIᵉ siècle," *Hommage à Lucien Febvre*, 2 vols. (Paris, 1953), II, 241–49.

7. Martin Bucer, *Der CXXX Psalm* (Strasbourg, 1546), p. 2; *idem*, *Von den Juden, ob und wie die unter den Christen zu halten sind* (Strasbourg, 1539) (reproducing the respective memoranda); Max Lenz, ed., *Briefwechsel Philipp's des Grossmüthigen von Hessen mit Bucer*, 3 vols. (Leipzig, 1880–91), I, 55 ff. These data are analyzed by Siegmund Salfeld in *Die Judenpolitik Philipps des Grossmütigen* (Frankfort, 1904); and by Hastings Eells in his "Bucer's Plan for the Jews," *Church History*, VI (1937), 127–35. On Bucer's utterances on the Jewish question and his likely encounter in Frankfort, in 1539, with Josel of Rosheim, see Harry Bresslau, "Aus Strassburger Judenakten," *ZGJD*, V (1892), 307–

44; and Selma Stern, *Josel von Rosheim: Befehlshaber der Judenschaft im Heiligen Römischen Reich Deutscher Nation* (Stuttgart, 1959), esp. pp. 125 ff. See also below, n. 24; and the fuller study by J. V. Pollet, *Martin Bucer: Étude sur la correspondance avec des nombreux textes inédits,* Vol. I (Paris, 1958), which includes an interesting correspondence of 1542 between Conrad Pellikan, Boniface Aberbach, and Bucer about the need for a translation of the Qur'an for missionary purposes similar to the use made of Hebrew studies to combat Jewish interpretations (pp. 181 ff.). See also the rich *Bibliographia Bucerana* assembled by Robert Stupperich and appended to Heinrich Bornkamm's succinct analysis of *Martin Bucers Bedeutung für die europäische Reformationsgeschichte* (Gütersloh, 1952).

8. Much has been written about Bucer's influence on Calvin's theological and economic thinking and also the impact of the Strasbourg environment upon the Geneva reformer. See esp. Georg Klingenburg's Bonn theological dissertation, *Das Verhältnis Calvins zu Butzer, untersucht auf Grund der wirtschafts-ethischen Bedeutung der beiden Reformatoren* (Bonn, 1912); Wilhelm Pauck, "Calvin and Butzer," *Journal of Religion,* IX (1929), 237–56; and Jean Daniel Benoit *et al., Calvin à Strasbourg, 1539–1541* (Strasbourg, 1938).

9. See the early examples cited in my *SRH,* 2d ed., III, 5 ff., 229 f. nn. 1 and 4.

10. *Clarissimis syndicis, et amplissimo Senatui Genevensis Reipublicae dominis nostris colendissimis* . . . in Calvin's *Opera,* VIII, 555 f. See above, Essay 12: "Medieval Heritage"; and *SRH,* XIII, 281 ff., 457 ff.

11. See the data assembled by Jakob Guttmann in his "Michael Servet in seinen Beziehungen zum Judentum," *MGWJ,* LI (1907), 77–94; and Louis I. Newman in his *Jewish Influence on Christian Reform Movements* (New York, 1925), pp. 511 ff. Nor did Calvin hesitate, in his meeting with Melanchthon in Frankfort in 1539, to criticize the Lutheran liturgy as too "Jewish." See his letter to his closest friend, Guillaume Farel, of April, 1539, in his *Opera,* X, Part 2, col. 340.

12. The relations between the two reformers, illumined in particular by their extant correspondence and by the final trial and death of Servetus, have intrigued many scholars. Of the large literature on the subject, we need but mention R. Willis's older, but still useful, *Servetus and Calvin: A Study of an Important Epoch in the Early History of the Reformation* (London, 1877); and Roland H. Bainton, *Hunted Heretic: The Life and Death of Servetus, 1511–1553* (Boston, 1953). See also the noteworthy eloquent, though somewhat exaggerating, description of the conditions in Geneva under Calvin's dictatorship by Stefan Zweig in *The Right to Heresy: Castellio against Calvin,* English trans. by Eden and Cedar Paul (New York, 1936). It may be noted that even some of those who were horrified by Servetus' execution were far from embracing the doctrine of

religious toleration. The clergy of the Vaud district across Lake Geneva may have condemned the proceedings as illegal and irreligious, and yet in 1554, when the Academy of Lausanne contemplated inviting the distinguished scholar, Immanuel Tremellius, a baptized Jew of Ferrara, to serve as its professor of Hebrew, the Berne authorities rejected him solely because of his Jewish descent. See H. Vuilleumier, "Les hébraïsants vaudois au seizième siècle," *Recueil inaugural* of the University of Lausanne (1892), p. 64; Achille Nordmann, "Les Juifs dans les pays de Vaud, 1278–1875," *REJ*, LXXXI (1925), 163.

13. Servetus' thirty letters to Calvin in the latter's *Opera*, VIII, esp. Letter xxv, cols. 703 ff. (at the end citing Maimonides); also Letter xiv, col. 675; Newman, *Jewish Influence*, pp. 588 ff.

14. Calvin's *Institutes of the Christian Religion*, i.8, 9–10, English trans. by Ford Lewis Battles, ed. by John T. McNeill, 2 vols., The Library of Christian Classics, XX–XXI (Philadelphia, 1960), I, 88 f., with reference to I Macc. 1:56–57; his *Commentary* on Ps. 22:17 in his *Opera*, XXXI, 228 f.

15. *Commentary* on Dan. 7:27 in his *Opera*, XLI, 82.

16. See the fragment reprinted by Hans Volz in his "Beiträge zu Melanchthons und Calvins Auslegung des Propheten Daniel," *Zeitschrift für Kirchengeschichte*, LXVII (1955–56), 116 ff.

17. Calvin's *Commentary* on Dan. 2:39, 44–45; 4:10–16; 7:27; 9:24–26, in his *Opera*, XL, 597 f., 603 ff., 658; XLI, 81 ff., 167 ff., 172 ff., 184 ff. See Abraham ibn Daud, *Sefer ha-Kabbalah* (Book of Tradition) in *Mediaeval Jewish Chronicles*, ed. by Adolph Neubauer, I, 60 ff.; *idem, Zikhron dibre malkhe Yisrael ba-bayit ha-sheni* (Memoir on the History of the Jewish Kings during the Second Temple [Mantua, 1513]), and my remarks thereon in *SRH*, VI, 207 f., 210, 428 ff. nn. 70 and 73. See also Gerson D. Cohen's remarks in his ed. of Ibn Daud's *Book of Tradition*, pp. xxxii f., 20 f., 114 f. (English), 15 f. (Hebrew).

18. Calvin's Sermon xliii on Dan. 12:1 in his *Opera*, XLII, 113 f. In general, Calvin was not very articulate in depicting the messianic expectations allegedly held by the ancient prophets, nor did he describe in any detail his own view of the final end of days after the second coming of Christ. See Heinrich Berger, *Calvins Geschichtsauffassung* (Zurich, 1955), esp. pp. 239 f.

19. *Commentary* on Isa. 38:8, 48:21; Obad. vv. 19–20; Mic. 5:1–2; Hab. 2:45; Hag. 1:1; Matt. 1:22–23, etc., in his *Opera*, XXXVI, 653; XLIII, 197 f.; XL, 66; XLVIII, 198 ff., 368 f., 551; XLIV, 80 f.

20. See his *Institutes*, iv.16, 14, in the English trans. by F. L. Battles, II, 1336 f.; his Sermon xiv on Evangelical Harmony, and his *Commentaries* on Acts 17:4; Rom. 7:4–5, 9:30, 11:28–32; I Cor. 1:23–24 in *Opera*, XLVI, 167 f.; XLVIII, 395; XLIX, 172 ff., 192 f., 228 f., 327 f. Time and again Calvin reverts to this theme of the election and repudia-

tion of Israel. In his sermon of Jan. 9, 1563, he launched an attack on both Jews and papists and declared, with something of a sigh, that "the Church will thus always have enemies which she will be unable to chase out." See his *Predigten,* ed. by H. Rückert, I, 679. It also was more than a mere archaic reference when Calvin, discussing the sale of Joseph by his brothers, declared that the Jews could not place the responsibility for that act on a few individuals, but that in fact this crime brought infamy to the whole people. In the context of a commentary on Acts (7:9; *Opera,* XLVIII, 135), such an observation doubtless called to the minds of most Christian readers the idea of the responsibility of the whole Jewish people for the crucifixion of Jesus. This connection appeared, indeed, in such contemporary Passion plays as that of Augsburg, a predecessor of the later famous Passion play of Oberammergau. Here the Jews, trying to persuade Judas to betray Jesus, are made to assert that they saved up the thirty pence from the time when Joseph was sold by his brethren. See the text ed. by A. Hartmann in *Das Oberammergauer Passionsspiel in seiner ältesten Gestalt* (Leipzig, 1880), vv. 213–20; and Hans Carl Holdschmidt, *Der Jude auf dem Theater des deutschen Mittelalters,* Die Schaubühne Quellen und Forschungen zur Theatergeschichte, XII (Emsdetten, 1935), p. 106. Incidentally, Bucer, too, had found the disparagement of Paul's Jewish contemporaries useful for his own purposes, such as the defense of his high appreciation of the Graeco-Roman pagan writers. See H. Strohl, *Bucer, humaniste chrétien,* Cahiers of the Revue d'histoire et de philosophie religieuses, XXIX (Paris, 1939), pp. 17 ff.

21. Calvin's second sermon on Deut. 15:7–10 in his *Opera,* XXVII, 325 ff. Other passages relating to usury have led Benjamin N. Nelson to find in them the opening to "the road to universal otherhood"; that is, the permissibility of interest among members of the same faith. See his *The Idea of Usury: From Tribal Brotherhood to Universal Otherhood* (Princeton, 1949), pp. 73 ff., 141 ff.; and the critique of this interpretation by Charles H. George in his aforementioned essay in the *Journal of the History of Ideas,* XVIII, 456 ff. See also above, n. 4.

22. *Opera,* IX, 653–74. This tract seems to be identical with a letter by Calvin to which J. F. A. de le Roi refers in *Die evangelische Christenheit und die Juden,* 3 vols. (Karlsruhe, 1884), I, 44. See also Jacques Courvoisier's observations thereon in his "Calvin et les Juifs," *Judaica,* II (1946–47), 203–8; and particularly my more recent remarks in *SRH,* XIII, 461 f. n. 97.

23. See H. H. Wolf's dissertation, *Die Einheit des Bundes: Das Verhältnis von Altem und Neuem Testament bei Calvin* (Halle, 1941 [typescript, *non vidi*]).

24. Josel of Rosheim's *Diary,* published by Isidor Kracauer in his "Rabbi Joselmann de Rosheim," *REJ,* XVI (1888), 92; *idem, Trostschrift an seine Brüder wider Buceri Büchlein,* published by Ludwig Feilchenfeld

in his *Rabbi Josel von Rosheim: Ein Beitrag zur Geschichte der Juden in Deutschland im Reformationszeitalter* (Strasbourg, 1898), pp. 180 ff. App. xvi. The fact that the Jewish controversialist fails to mention Calvin by name is the less astonishing as the Genevan reformer lived at that time as a fairly obscure French refugee and Genevan exile in Bucer's entourage in Strasbourg. When Josel published his *Letter of Consolation* (the Hebrew original of which is regrettably lost) in reply to Bucer's aforementioned pamphlet in the Hessian controversy, no one could have foreseen that shortly thereafter the Genevan population would change its mind and reinvite the reformer to its leading pulpit, thus giving him the opportunity to play his stellar role in the history of the Reformation. In fact, Calvin's name occurs but rarely in the contemporary German sources relating to the conferences of 1539–41. If the frequent use of New Testament sources by Calvin's Jewish spokesman militates against his identification with Josel, who, in his other recorded disputations, seems to have relied exclusively upon the words of the Hebrew Bible, we must remember that both Josel's *Diary* and his *Letter of Consolation* were written in Hebrew for Jewish audiences. Josel may have here omitted arguments from the New Testament which were unfamiliar to Jews and might have been resented by the unsophisticated masses. On Calvin's role in the German assemblies and his participation in the religious disputations, see F. W. Kampschulte, *Johann Calvin, seine Kirche und sein Staat in Genf*, 2 vols. (Leipzig, 1869–99), esp. I, 328 ff., 333 n. 1, 338 f.; and E. Doumergue's uncritical observations in his *Jean Calvin*, II. See also Selma Stern, *Josel von Rosheim*, esp. pp. 138 ff.; and above, nn. 7–8.

25. A. Diez Macho, "Cesarà la 'Tora' en la edad mesianica?" *Estudios biblicos*, XII (1953), 115–58; and other data cited in my *SRH*, 2d ed., II, 73 f., 161 f., 298 f., 360 f. n. 25; V, 124, 193 f., 347 n. 54, 380 ff. n. 58.

26. Query viii in *Opera*, IX, 663. This problem, too, had often engaged Jewish and Christian controversialists in their mutual recriminations. See my *SRH*, V, 118.

27. Query xxii in *Opera*, IX, 674. The problem of the Exile had likewise engaged the attention of controversialists of both faiths since ancient times.

28. One must bear in mind, of course, that in Poland Calvinism was but one of many rival Protestant factions, which, under the existing conditions of relative religious freedom, fought one another as vigorously as they combated Catholicism. Even Servetus, particularly after his martyr's death, gained a wide following there. In 1557, Simon Zacius, the superintendent of the Calvinist community of Vilna, bitterly complained of the spread of all kinds of heresies, such as those of the Anabaptists, the Libertines, the Schwenkfeldians, and the New Arians of the school of Servetus and his Polish follower De Goniądz. Cited by Stanislaw Kot in "L'influence de Michel Servet sur le mouvement antitrinitarien en Pologne

et en Transylvanie" in the collection of essays, *Autour de Michel Servet et de Sebastien Castillon*, ed. by B. Becker (Haarlem, 1953), pp. 72–129, esp. p. 78. See also Gottfried Schramm's review of the literature relating to the "Antitrinitarier in Polen, 1556–1658" in *Bibliothèque d'humanisme et renaissance*, XXI (1959), 473–511. This certainly was not the time for the Polish Calvinists to antagonize the ever-growing, but strictly neutralist, Jewish population in the country. See *also* the forthcoming Vol. XVII, Chap. LXVII, in *SRH*.

29. Calvin's letter to Farel of October, 1539, in his *Opera*, X, Part 2, col. 398. See also Fritz Büsser, *Calvins Urteil über sich selbst* (Zurich, 1950), p. 54.

30. Roland H. Bainton, ed., *Concerning Heretics. Whether They are to be Persecuted and How They are to Be Treated. A Collection of the Opinions of Learned Men both Ancient and Modern. An Anonymous Work attributed to Sebastian Castellio. Now First Done into English, Together with Excerpts from Other Works of Sebastian Castellio and David Joris on Religious Liberty*, Records of Civilization, XXII (New York, 1935). See also the aforementioned confrontation of Castellio and Calvin by Stefan Zweig in *The Right to Heresy*.

31. Calvin's *Institutes*, ii.8, 6; iii.19, 2 in Battles's English trans. I, 372, 835; the comments thereon by Marc-Edouard Chenevière in his Geneva dissertation, *La pensée politique de Calvin* (Paris, 1937), pp. 61 ff., 99 ff.; and by Fritz Büsser in *Calvins Urteil*, pp. 36 f. See also J. V. Bredt, "Calvinismus und Judentum," *Der Morgen*, III (1927), 243–50.

32. Calvin's *Commentaries* on Ps. 22:17; Dan. 4:10–16, in his *Opera*, XXXI, 228 f.; XL, 858.

33. It may be of interest to recall here the initial debates on the Weber thesis by Felix Rachfahl, Eugen Troeltsch, and Weber himself. See Felix Rachfahl's "Calvinismus und Kapitalismus," *Internationale Wochenschrift*, III (1909); Troeltsch, "Die Kulturbedeutung des Calvinismus" (1910), reproduced in his *Gesammelte Schriften*, IV, 783–801; Weber, "Antikritisches zum 'Geist' des Kapitalismus," *Archiv für Sozialwissenschaft und Sozialpolitik*, XXX (1910), 176–202. The subsequent literature on the Weberian and Sombartian theses is enormous and need not be repeated here.

34. See esp. Hans Baron's twin essays, *Calvins Staatsanschauung und das konfessionelle Zeitalter*, Historische Zeitschrift, Beihefte I (Munich, 1924), esp. pp. 48 ff., 115 ff.; and "Calvinist Republicanism and Its Historical Roots," *Church History*, VIII (1939), 30–42; as well as Josef Bohatec's more detailed analysis of *Calvins Lehre von Staat und Kirche, mit besonderer Berücksichtung des Organismusgedankens* (Breslau, 1937).

35. See my *Modern Nationalism and Religion* (New York, 1947; paperback ed., 1960), esp. the chapter on "Protestant Individualism," pp. 117 ff.

ESSAY 14

1. Diego Laynez' address reproduced in *Concilii Tridentini Acta*, VI, ed. by Stefan Ehses (in the collection of the conciliar documents, ed. by Sebastian Merkle *et al.*, Vol. IX), 94 ff.; and, more generally, H. Grisar, ed., *Iacobi Lainez Disputationes Tridentinae*, 2 vols. (Innsbruck, 1886), esp. I, 399 ff. App.; and M. Roca Cabanellas, "Diego Laynez en la última etapa del Concilio," *Il Concilio di Trento e la riforma tridentina* (Rome, 1965), I, 85–114. On the role of Laynez and other New Christians in the nascent Jesuit Order, see my remarks in *SRH*, XIV, 10 ff.

2. The literature on the Tridentine Council is enormous. The more recent publications, including various bibliographical compilations, are listed in *SRH*, XIV, 309 ff. nn. 17 ff.

3. Karl Stürmer, *Konzilien und ökumenische Kirchenversammlungen. Abriss ihrer Geschichte*, Kirche und Konfession, III (Göttingen, 1962), pp. 302 f.

4. Friedrich Nausea (Gran), *Miscellanearum libri VIII*, v. 15: "Qualis est et hic abusus, quod Judeos perfidissimos christianique nominis hostes ecclesie coniuratissimos non citra christiane religionis decrementum et contumeliam et exitium, questus dumtaxat vilissimi causa, commorari quasi judaizantes permittunt inter christianos suos subditos, quos utcumque iudeorum usuris excoriatos et ipsi quoque nihilominus excoriant, hocque pacto suo duplici conficiunt incommodo et ad inopiam nolentes volentesque detrahunt. Qualis est hic abusus, quod ipse Judeis baptismo ad fidem nostram conversis ac confirmatis christianisque fieri coeptis omnia eorum temporalia bona, quoniam per usuram sint iniquiter acquisita, spoliant et diripiunt, que certe deberent illis deinde penitentibus nomine Jesu Christi misericorditer ad vite necessitatem reddi, ne alioquin, quod sepenumero fieri comperimus, egestate compulsi, et despectui ab omnibus habiti, apostatent et christianos impietatis arguant, quemadmodum suo fortasse loco fusius hac de re docturus sum." Reproduced by Vinzenz Schweitzer, in his ed. of *Concilii Tridentini Tractatuum pars prior completens tractatus a Leonis X temporibus usque ad translationem Concilii conscriptos*, I (in S. Merkle's compilation, Vol XII), 119 ff., 364 ff., 412. See also H. Gollob's biography, *Bischof Friedrich Nausea (1496–1552). Probleme der Gegenreformation*, 2d ed. enlarged (Nieuwkoop, 1967).

5. Girolamo Aleandro, *De convocando concilio sententia*, in Schweitzer's ed. of the *Tractatus*, pp. 119 ff.; and other literature cited in *SRH*, XIV, 309 n. 17.

6. *Decretum de justificatione*, Introd. arts. 1–2 and canons 1–2 in H. J. D. Denzinger, comp., *Enchiridion symbolorum, definitionum, et declarationum de rebus fidei et morum*, 21st–23d ed., rev. by C. Bannwart and J. B. Umberg (Freiburg i. B., 1932), pp. 284 f., 295; in the

English trans. by R. S. Defarrari, entitled *The Sources of Catholic Dogma* (St. Louis, 1957), pp. 248 f., 259; and H. J. Schroeder, ed., *Canons and Decrees of the Council of Trent. Original Text with English Translation* (St. Louis, 1960), pp. 29 ff. (English), 308 ff. (Latin). On the significant formulation of the doctrine concerning responsibility for the crucifixion which finally found its way into the catechism published by the unfriendly Pope Pius V in 1556, see *SRH*, XIV, 23 f., 313 n. 22. In the papers of Cardinal Marcello Cervini (later Pope Marcellus II), one of the three papal legates to the Council's first assembly and an assiduous collector of its records, there is this brief reference to a discussion: "Utrum expediens sit abolere commentarios Hebraeorum. Defensio librorum Judaeorum" and then again: "Accusatio librorum Judaeorum." See Gottfried Buschbell, ed., *Concilii Tridentini Epistolae*, I (in S. Merkle's compilation, Vol. X), xxiii. But we have no further information about any discussion of this subject, or even about its being placed on the official agenda, before the Council's third period in 1562–63.

7. See the text of the Valdés Index in Heinrich Reusch's *Die Indices librorum prohibitorum des sechzehnten Jahrhunderts gesammelt und herausgegeben* (Tübingen, 1886; Photochemical offset, Nieuwkoop, 1961), pp. 209 ff.; and the comments thereon by that author in *Der Index der verbotenen Bücher. Ein Beitrag zur Kirchen- und Literaturgeschichte,* 2 vols. (Bonn, 1883–85), I, 300, where the differences between Valdés' Index and that issued by Paul IV are lucidly analyzed. See also the facsimile reproductions of the Valdés *Catalogus librorum,* issued by A. M. Huntington (New York, n.d.), pp. 5, 29, 63; and by the Real Academia Española under the title *Tres Indices Expurgatorios de la Inquisición Española en el siglo XVI* (Madrid, 1952), pp. 5, 23, 49.

8. *Ibid.;* I. S. Révah, "Un Index espagnol inconnu, celui édicté par l'Inquisition de Séville en novembre 1551," *Studia philologica. Homenaje . . . a Dámaso Alonso,* 3 vols. (Madrid, 1960–1963), III, 131–46, esp. pp. 132, 136, 140 f., and 145 f.

9. Heinrich Reusch, *Die Indices,* pp. 154 ff., 203, 205 f., 209 ff.; *idem, Der Index,* I, 258 ff., 294. The immediate impression of Paul's extremism is well illustrated in a letter by Latinus Latinius to his fellow-humanist Andreas Masius, dated Rome, January 19, 1559. With deep anguish the Roman student of Graeco-Roman letters stated: "I believe that for many years to come none of us will dare write anything but epistles." *Ibid.,* pp. 295 f.

10. See the text of the *moderatio* in Reusch's *Die Indices,* p. 208; and his comments thereon in *Der Index,* I, 299 f. As Reusch points out, the Spanish Inquisition felt so independent of even the Papacy's enactments that, apart from failing to mention Paul IV's Index in his own compilation, Valdés in 1561 forbade the circulation of Pius IV's *moderatio* before it received royal approval.

11. See Hubert Jedin, *Papal Legate at the Council of Trent, Cardinal Seripando*, trans. from the German by Frederic C. Eckhoff (St. Louis, 1947), p. 552; and other literature listed in *SRH*, XIV, 317 f. n. 30, 320 n. 41.

12. See above Essay, No. 10: "'Plenitude of Apostolic Powers' and Medieval 'Jewish Serfdom.'"

13. See *SRH*, Vols. IX and XIV, *passim*.

14. See François Secret, "Études sur une histoire du Pugio Fidei à la Renaissance," *Sefarad*, XX (1960), 401–7; Giovanni Domenico Mansi, ed., *Sacrorum conciliorum . . . collectio*, XXXIV, 912 f.; and *SRH*, IX, 282 f. n. 40; 288 ff. n. 4 item 1, 293 n. 6 item 7, 298 f. n. 9. See also below, n. 17.

15. See Joseph Hilgers, *Der Index der verbotenen Bücher. In seiner neuen Fassung bearbeitet und rechtlich-historisch gewürdigt* (Freiburg i. B., 1904), pp. 199 ff. As viewed by the Commission chairman Archbishop Brus, and two other colleagues representing Ferdinand—the layman Count Siegmund von Thun and Bishop Georg Drascovič of Fünfkirchen-Pecs (the spokesman for Ferdinand as king of Hungary)—in their report to the emperor on February 17, 1562, Brus' task was to prevent outright condemnation of all works of the Augsburg Confession. See Theodor Sickel, ed., *Zur Geschichte des Concils von Trient. Actenstücke aus österreichischen Archiven* (Vienna, 1870), p. 269. We shall see that Brus and his colleagues knew in advance that this was a very touchy subject and approached it rather gingerly.

16. Bernardo Navagero's report of 1540, reproduced in Eugenio Albèri's ed. of *Relazioni degli ambasciatori veneti al Senato*, 1st ser. (Florence, 1839–63), II, Part 2, p. 16; Giovanni Drei, ed., "La corrispondenza del card. Ercole Gonzaga, presidente del Concilio di Trento (1562–1563)," *Archivio storico per le provincie parmense*, XVII (1917), 201 ff. Nos. viii–ix; and other sources listed by Hubert Jedin in his biographical sketch of "Kardinal Ercole Gonzaga, der Sohn der Isabella d'Este" in his *Kirche des Glaubens, Kirche der Geschichte. Ausgewählte Aufsätze und Vorträge*, 2 vols. (Freiburg i. B., 1966), I, 195–205. To this essay, originally published in an Italian translation in 1946, add the literature cited in *SRH*, XIV, 310 n. 18. See also, more generally, Selwyn Brinton, *The Gonzaga—Lords of Mantua* (New York, 1927), esp. p. 173. Ercole's friendly relations with Jewish authors and his humanistic interests are illustrated by the Venetian rabbi Jacob Mantino's dedication to him of a Latin translation of Averroës' *Epitome Metaphisicae*. See the text of that dedication reproduced by David Kaufmann in his "Jacob Mantino: Une page de l'histoire de la Renaissance," *REJ*, XXVII (1893), 221 ff. It stands to reason that in trying to bring order to his duchy's chaotic fiscal administration and reduce its public debt, the cardinal-regent must have been in frequent personal contact with the leading

Jewish bankers of Mantua, who formed a distinct group in the Jewish community. See esp. Shlomo Simonsohn, *Toledot ha-Yehudim be-dukhsut Mantovah* (A History of the Jews in the Duchy of Mantua), 2 vols. (Jerusalem, 1963–65), *passim*.

17. Girolamo (Hieronymus) Seripando, *De Tridentino Concilio Diaria*, reproduced in Sebastian Merkle's compilation, II, 405; François Secret, "Girolamo Seripando et la Kabbale," *Rinascimento*, XIV (1963), 251–68; and Hubert Jedin, *Papal Legate at the Council of Trent, Cardinal Seripando*, esp. pp. 587 ff. On Hosius' attitude to the Council, see his letters ed. by Ernst Manfred Wermter in *Kardinal Stanislaus Hosius Bischof von Ermland und Herzog Albrecht von Preussen. Ihr Briefwechsel über das Konzil von Trient (1560–62)*, Reformationsgeschichtliche Studien und Texte, LXXXII (Münster, 1957); and, more generally, Joseph Lortz, *Kardinal Stanislaus Hosius. Beiträge zur Erkenntnis der Persönlichkeit und des Werkes* (Braunsberg, 1931), esp. pp. 75 ff.; and Henry Damien Wojtyska, *Cardinal Hosius, Legate to the Council of Trent*, Studia ecclesiastica, III (Rome, 1967).

18. See Samuel Steinherz, ed., *Briefe des Prager Erzbishofs Anton Brus von Müglitz 1562–1563* (Prague, 1907), *passim*. To the older biographical literature on Brus listed *ibid.*, p. 5 n. 1, add especially the recent sketch by Rudolf Till, "Antonius Brus von Müglitz, 1558–1563, Bischof von Wien," *Wiener Geschichtsblätter*, XIX [LXXIX] (1964), 258–69. On the confiscation of rabbinic books in Frankfort, the initial episode in the famous Reuchlin-Pfefferkorn controversy, and the pro-Jewish intervention of Archbishop Uriel von Gemmingen, see Isidor Kracauer, "Die Konfiskation der hebräischen Schriften in Frankfurt a. M. in den Jahren 1509 und 1510," *ZGJD*, [o.s.] I (1887), 160–76, 230–48; Max Freudenthal, "Dokumente zur Schriftenverfolgung durch Pfefferkorn," *ibid.*, n.s. III (1931), 227–32; and other data discussed in *SRH*, XIII, 182 ff. It is small wonder that in one of his directives to Brus (on February 23, 1562) Ferdinand insisted that the Index Commission "proceed with less severity than Paul IV, who generally wished to outlaw books of all infidels, even such which have no bearing on theology or any other now controversial matter, and do no harm to the Catholics." See Franz Bernhard von Bucholtz's *Geschichte der Regierung Ferdinand des Ersten. Aus gedruckten und ungedruckten Quellen*, 9 vols. (Vienna, 1831–38), VIII, 418 f.

19. See Francisco de Vargas' memorandum submitted between March 4 and April 29, 1551, to Cardinal Granvella, and published by Constancio Gutiérrez in his "Nueva documentación tridentina, 1551–1552," *Archivium historiae pontificiae*, I (1963), 179–240; II (1964), 211–50, esp. II, 225 ff., 246; Jacques Quétif and Jacques Echard, *Scriptores ordinis praedicatorum*, 2 vols. (Paris, 1719–23; new impression, New York, n.d.), II, 261–63; and other literature listed by E. Filthaut in a brief article on "Foreiro" in the *Lexikon für Theologie und Kirche*, 2d ed. rev.

(Freiburg i. B., 1960), p. 201. In his *Portugal no Concilio di Trento*, 6 vols. (Lisbon, 1944–46), esp. V, 224; VI, 122 f., José de Castro tends to exaggerate Foreiro's role in the preparation of the Index. Foreiro was but one of several nonvoting theologians attached to the Index Commission. These theologians were understandably recruited largely from among the Dominican friars, who had had generations of experience with the censorship of "heretical" books, but they included two Jesuits, Diego (Jacobus) Laynez and Alphonso Salmerón, who held far more tempered views. Because of the high prestige Laynez soon enjoyed in conciliar circles, his influence must have outweighed that of the other theologians. See Angelo Walz, *I Domenicani al Concilio di Trento* (Rome, 1961); above, n. 15; and below, nn. 20, 22, and 29.

20. See Brus' report to the emperor of February 3, 1563, reproduced by F. B. von Bucholtz in his voluminous *Geschichte der Regierung Ferdinands I.*, IX, 685 f. As late as January 24, 1563, Brus himself had complained that, except for the suffragan bishop of Eichstädt, no German prelate was present in Trent and that the archbishop of Salzburg had actually recalled his representatives. See S. Steinherz's ed. of *Briefe des Prager Erzbishofs*, pp. 88 f. No. 58; and, more generally, Hubert Jedin, "Die deutschen Teilnehmer am Trienter Konzil," *Tübinger Theologische Quartalschrift*, CXXII (1941), 238–61; CXXIII (1943), 21–37. On the exclusion of Laynez and Salmerón from the Commission's meeting see Laynez' letters to Francisco Borgia and Antonio Araoz (Loyola's nephew and Jesuit provincial of Spain) of May 17, and June 7, 1563, respectively, in his *Epistolae et acta* (in *Monumenta Historica Societatis Jesu*, Lainii Monumenta, VII), pp. 91 f. No. 1832, 124 ff. No. 1846; and, more generally, F. Cereseda, "Lainez y Salmerón en el Proceso del Catecismo di Carranza," *Razón y fé*, C (1932), 212–26; above, n. 1; and below, n. 22. The restraints imposed upon the archbishop by the sharp denominational divisions which he was trying to overcome at home are well illustrated by his memorandum published by Samuel Steinherz in "Eine Denkschrift des Prager Erzbischofs Anton Brus über die Herstellung der Glaubenseinheit in Böhmen (1563)," *Mittheilungen des Vereines für Geschichte der Deutschen in Böhmen*, XLV (1907), 162–77. In their first report to the emperor of February, 1562, Brus and his associates clearly expressed doubts about the efficacy of their work, doubts in which they were reinforced by some secret communications by Hosius, who had shortly before left Vienna, where he served as papal nuncio, to assume the duties of legate to the Council. See above, n. 17.

21. Theodor Sickel, ed., *Zur Geschichte des Concils von Trient*, pp. 268 f.; Samuel Steinherz, ed., *Briefe des Prager Erzbischofs Anton Brus von Müglitz, 1562–1563* (Prague, 1907), pp. 55 f., 109 ff., 120 f. n. The great change in the Spanish attitude to the Dutch humanist is fully described in Marcel Bataillon's *Erasme et l'Espagne, recherches sur*

l'histoire spirituelle du XVI⁰ siècle (Paris, 1937); with additional notes in the Spanish translation by Antonio Alatorre, 2 vols. (Madrid, 1950). The Jewish implications of this significant work have been analyzed by I. S. Révah in "Les Juifs et les courants spirituels espagnols au XVI⁰ siècle. A propos d'un livre recent," *REJ*, CIII (1938), 97–101. Brus was more successful in removing from the Index the works by Joannes Campensis, Georgius Agricola, Henricus Glareanus, and Ulrich (Udalricus) Zasius. See his letter to Maximilian II in Steinherz, pp. 109 ff. Ironically, Zasius' works were saved from inclusion in the Index only after a personal intervention by his sons. Otherwise, it appears, even his *Quaestiones de parvulis Iudeorum baptisandis* (Strasbourg, 1508), defending the extreme Scottist position of the Church's right to baptize Jewish children against their parents' will, might have been placed on the Tridentine Index. Though running counter to the majority opinion of canon jurists, this work certainly could not be classified as "heretical" in the technical sense. See Vinzenz Schweitzer and Hubert Jedin, eds., *Concilii Tridentini Tractatus*, II (in S. Merkle's compilation, Vol. XIII), 587 n. 4.

22. Francisco Sancho's letter of June 8, 1563, reproduced by J. Ignacio Tellechea Idígoras in his "Cartas y documentos tridentinos inéditos," *Hispania sacra*, XVI (1963), 191–248, esp. p. 204 No. 11. This particularly valuable documentation of discussions by the Index Commission and the Council as a whole owes its preservation mainly to its subsequent inclusion in the acts pertaining to Carranza's trial. The discussions deal, therefore, largely with the efforts of the Spanish members and inquisitorial agents to keep Carranza's Catechism in the Index. This general inflexibility did not appeal even to such native Spaniards as Laynez and Salmerón, who, evidently for this reason, were not invited to attend one of the pertinent meetings of the Commission. Even Archbishop Gaspar Cervantes of Messina, at that time under Spanish domination, wrote in his letter to Guzmán of August 23, 1563, about "the great hatred in which that Holy Office [of Spain] is held in Italy." *Ibid.*, pp. 216 No. 24 (citing a copy of the Index Commission's resolution of July 26, 1563), 230 ff. No. 38; above, n. 20. Certainly, Carranza's opponents could not even submit any evidence that he had ever owned or studied heretical works. A recent analysis of his library has shown that he possessed only perfectly orthodox writings, including some biblical books *ad hebraicam versionem castigati*. See J. Ignazio Tellechea Idígoras, "La Biblioteca del Arzobispo Carranza," *Hispania sacra*, XVI (1963), 459–99.

23. See Igino Rogger's Gregorian University dissertation, *Le Nazioni al Concilio di Trento durante la sua epoca imperiale 1545–1552*, Collana di monografie of the Società per gli studi trentini, XI (Rome, 1952). What is said here about the Council's two earlier assemblies, essentially held true during the meetings of 1562–63 as well.

24. Jacob Bonaventura's petition is not dated. It is reproduced from a

Vatican manuscript by Moritz Stern in his *Urkundliche Beiträge über die Stellung der Päpste zu den Juden. Mit Benutzung des päpstlichen Geheimarchivs zu Rom* (Kiel, 1893), pp. 135 f. No. 128 (in Latin); and by Josef Šušta, ed., in *Die Römische Kurie und das Konzil von Trient unter Pius IV. Aktenstücke zur Geschichte des Konzils von Trient*, 4 vols. (Vienna, 1904–14), III, 236 f. No. 65 (in Italian). The salient points in this petition are the description of the Talmud as "liber plurium voluminum confectus, qui inscribitur Talmud, eximius quidam interpres legis Hebraicae ac eorum vitae politicae vera norma et regula singularis"; and the request "ut de illarum mera benignitate et gratia speciali librum illum denuo cum illius censura diligenter inspici et examinari mandent necque illum ita absolute abolendum velint, quem tanquam illis necessarium multi summi pontifices pro illorum regimine signanter et expresse pluries permiserunt. Si qua vero in illo inveniuntur, quae Christianae religioni obstare videantur, deleri penitus poterunt et liber ab illis expurgatus imprimendus concedi, ita ut ab omnibus sine scandalo et haberi et perlegi possit."

25. Brus' report to Ferdinand of February 3, 1563, is excerpted in Stern's *Urkundliche Beiträge*, pp. 136 f. No. 129. It was first cited in a German translation (together with Ferdinand's reply) by Bucholtz; see above, n. 20. The memoranda by Christophorus Patavinus and an anonymous writer are reproduced in Vinzenz Schweitzer's and Hubert Jedin's ed. of *Concilii Tridentini Tractatus*, II (in S. Merkle's compilation, Vol. XIII), new ed., pp. 595 ff. No. VII, 599 ff. No. VIII.

26. Pedro Gonzalez de Mendoza's complaint about Duchess Eleanora in his *Lo Sucedido en el concilio de Trento*, published by J. von Döllinger in his *Ungedruckte Berichte und Tagebücher zur Geschichte des Concils von Trent*, 2 parts (Nördlingen, 1876), II, 64 ff., 154, is also reproduced in S. Merkle's ed. of *Concilii Tridentini Diaria*, II, 706. The bishop merely expressed the pious wish "que me empleara en otra cosa que fuera mas honesta, que en defender la cosa mas perniciosa que ellos tienen para si y mas injuriosa a nuestra religion." Coming as it did on October 26–27, 1563, but a short time before the final adoption of the conciliar resolutions, this intervention undoubtedly reflected redoubled efforts by the Jewish delegation to prevent the inclusion in the Index of Paul IV's unqualified outlawry of the Talmud. See M. Stern, *Urkundliche Beiträge*, I, 137 f. Nos. 131–32; S. Simonsohn, *Toledot*, I, 303 f.

27. The "Ten Rules Concerning Forbidden Books" and the anonymous *Adnotationes* thereon are reproduced by V. Schweitzer and H. Jedin in their ed. of *Concilii Tridentini Tractatus*, II (in S. Merkle's compilation, Vol. XIII), pp. 603 ff. No. 94 Docs. xii–xiii. The "Rules" became part and parcel of the new Index in its various editions. See *SRH*, XIV, 312 f. n. 21. On the minor changes in the formulation of the Ten Rules before they reached their final form, see Stefan Ehses, "Zur Vorgeschichte des Trien-

ter Index verbotener Bücher," *Erste Vereinsschrift* of the Görresgesellschaft (Cologne, 1921), pp. 74 f. Although included in the *Bullarium
romanum*, VII, 281 f., Pius IV's decree, *Dominici gregis*, of March 24,
1564, was merely a papal breve. See Joseph Hilgers's *Die Bücherverbote
in Papstbriefen. Kanonistisch-bibliographische Studie* (Freiburg i. B.,
1907), p. 18; and, more broadly, his *Der Index der verbotenen Bücher*,
pp. 8 ff. The new Index appeared in various editions and was widely
distributed. See *ibid.*, pp. 497 ff. Apps. iii and iv; and H. Reusch, *Der
Index*, pp. 342 ff.

28. See *SRH*, XIV, 160 f., 364 n. 12. The two crucial passages in the
"Tridentine Index" of 1564 read: "Regula I.: Libri omnes, quos ante
annum MDXV aut summi pontifices, aut concilia oecumenica damnaver-
unt, et in hoc indice non sunt, eodem modo damnati esse censeantur, sicut
olim damnati fuerunt"; and, in the section relating to anonymous works:
"Thalmud Hebraeorum ejusque glossae, annotationes, interpretationes et
expositiones omnes; si tamen prodierint sine nomine Thalmud et sine
injuriis et calumniis in religionem Christianan, tolerabuntur." See H.
Reusch, *Die Indices*, pp. 247, 279 f.; and the comments thereon in his *Der
Index*, I, 48 f., 321 ff., 330 ff. Neither the Jews nor enterprising publishers
hesitated very long to take advantage of the new permissiveness. In
1578–80 the whole Talmud appeared in Basel under the title, *Shas*—a
Hebrew abbreviation for the "Six Orders" of the Mishnah and Talmud—;
they omitted only the tractate 'Abodah zarah and expurgated some
passages from other tractates. Some of these alterations are listed, along
with other examples of the "Pontifical Expurgation of Some Rabbinic
Writings," in Christian Schoettgen's *Horae hebraicae et talmudicae*, 2
vols. (Dresden, 1733–42), II, 824 ff., esp. pp. 860 f.

29. J. Hilgers, *Der Index der verbotenen Bücher*, pp. 499 ff. Apps. iv
and v. Foreiro signed his Foreword as "Professor of Sacred Theology and
Secretary of the [Index] Commission" and emphasized that it was prepared by "Fathers chosen from almost all nations." Because of this public
statement José de Castro claimed that the Tridentine Index was "the fruit
of much work principally by our friar, Francisco Foreiro." See Castro's
Portugal no Concilio de Trento, VI, 122 f. This is undoubtedly an overstatement, although with his previous experience as a censor Foreiro may,
indeed, have quietly injected his opinion into the debates. He must also
have taken a hand in formulating the resolutions to be submitted by the
Commission to the plenary session. See above, n. 19.

30. The important passage in the Jews' letter of thanks to Brus reads:
"Ex eo, quod amplitudo tua, sicut accepimus, omnibus viribus pro restitu-
endo Talmud alioque correctissimo pluries pugnavit atque contenderit,
perfecte novimus, quem habueris animum nempe ad beneficentiam pro-
pensissimum. Quam ob rem tantae curae immemores effici nequeuntes,
ne nobis crimini detur, si non quas debemus, saltem eas, quas possumus,

tam nostro quam totius universitatis nomine tibi Reverendissimo immortales agimus gratias." This letter, first published by Gerson Wolf in *Das Tridentinische Concil und der Talmud* (Vienna, 1885), pp. 11 f., was republished by M. Stern in his *Urkundliche Beiträge*, I, 137 No. 130; and, again, by Gottlieb Bondy and Franz Dworský, eds., in their *Zur Geschichte der Juden in Böhmen, Mähren und Schlesien*, 2 vols. (Prague, 1906), I, 481 f. no. 655. In all these publications the date of the letter is given as February 16, 1563. But, for reasons which need not be elaborated here, I have suggested that this epistle really was submitted to the archbishop on February 16, 1564, after his return from Trent. See *SRH*, XIV, 310 f. n. 19, where the problem of who may have aided the communal elders in preparing this Latin epistle is likewise briefly discussed.

31. T. Sickel, ed., *Zur Geschichte des Concils von Trient*, p. 648; S. Steinherz, *Briefe des Prager Erzbishofs Anton Brus von Müglitz*, pp. 46 No. 17, 137 f. True, we have no evidence of any contacts between Italian Jews and the archbishop of Prague; but, apart from the entourage of Cardinal Gonzaga, the local host of the Council, Cardinal Cristoforo Madruzzo of Trent-Brixen, may have been helpful in introducing Bonaventura and other Jewish elders to the chairman of the Index Commission. Madruzzo's specific interest in Hebrew books and his help in the printing of Hebrew works in Riva di Trento in his archdiocese is discussed by David Werner Amram in *The Makers of Hebrew Books in Italy. Being Chapters in the History of the Hebrew Printing Press* (Philadelphia, 1909), pp. 298 ff., and other writers cited in *SRH*, XIV, 311 n. 19.

32. See Foreiro's aforementioned Foreword to the Tridentine Index; Cardinal Gaspar de Quiroga's Index of 1583, in H. Reusch's *Die Indices*, pp. 245 f., 429; Miguel de la Pinta Llorente, "Aportaciones para la historia de los Indices expurgatorios españoles," *Hispania*, XII (1952), 253–300, esp. pp. 269 ff. The slowness of the implementation of the Tridentine resolutions even in Italy is well illustrated by Giuseppe Alberigo in his "Studi e problemi relativi all'applicazione del Concilio di Trento in Italia (1945–1958)," *Rivista storica italiana*, LXX (1958), 239–98; and Alberto Monticone in "L'Applicazione a Roma del Concilio di Trento: I. Le visite del 1564–1566; II. I 'riformatori' e l'Oratorio (1566–1572)," *Rivista di storia della Chiesa in Italia*, VII (1953), 225–50; VIII (1954), 23–48. See also the documents reproduced by Edvige Aleandri Barletta in *Aspetti della Riforma cattolica e del Concilio di Trento. Mostra documentaria* (Rome, 1964), pp. 143 ff. In the long run, however, the impact of the Council was pervasive and enduring. See Hubert Jedin's general observations in his *Krisis und Abschluss des Trienter Konzils, 1562–63; ein Rückblick nach vier Jahrhunderten*, Herder-Bucherei, 17 (Freiburg i. B., 1964) and in his 1964 lecture, "Das Konzil von Trient in der Schau des 20. Jahrhunderts," reproduced in his *Kirche des Glaubens*, II, 565–76.

33. J. Hilgers, *Der Index der verbotenen Bücher*, pp. 197 ff., 506; François Dainville, "Pour l'histoire de l'Index. L'ordinance du Père Mercurian S. J. sur l'usage des livres prohibés (1575) et son interprétation lyonnaise en 1597,' 'Recherches de science religieuse*, XLII (1964), 86–98.

Index

ABOUT THE AUTHOR AND EDITOR

Dr. Salo Wittmayer Baron is Professor Emeritus of Jewish History, Literature, and Institutions on the Miller Foundation, and Director Emeritus of the Center of Israeli and Jewish Studies of Columbia University. He also served as Janet and Philip J. Levin Visiting Professor of Hebraic Studies at Rutgers University, The State University of New Jersey.

Dr. Leon A. Feldman is Professor of Hebraic Studies at Rutgers. He has also taught at Yeshiva University, University of Oxford (Linacre College), Hebrew University, and Bar ilan University. He has been the author and editor of numerous articles, book reviews, and books.

The text of this book was set in Caledonia Linotype. Composed, printed and bound by Quinn & Boden Company, Inc., Rahway, N.J.